The Home Repair Book

JAMES L. BRIGHT

J. G. FERGUSON PUBLISHING COMPANY/CHICAGO

Library of Congress Cataloging in Publication Data

Bright, James L.
    The home repair book.

    Includes index.
    1. Dwellings—Maintenance and repair—Amateurs' manuals.   I. Title.
TH4817.3.B74   1982   643'.7
ISBN: 0-89434-030-1
Library of Congress Catalog Card Number: 82-15423

                            J-10

Foreword

This book is constructed to be used as a practical tool for making home repairs and alterations. It tells what each type of repair is all about and describes, step-by-step, how to do it. Most of the chapters cover the many common types of repairs, such as repairs to interior walls and floors, plumbing and electrical repairs, heating and air conditioning repairs, and the maintenance of the exterior of the house. The remainder of the book explains how remodeling projects should be planned and how to design kitchens, bathrooms, attics, basements, and new storage areas.

Home repair tools, materials, and attitudes about what people can and should do for themselves have changed substantially in recent years. High-quality tools and new materials have been specifically designed for nonprofessional use. With changing attitudes about self-sufficiency, many individuals who were previously hesitant have found that they can make many repairs as satisfactorily as the proverbial handyman. This is especially true of women who have discovered that practice and acquired skill are needed, not innate know-how and strength. Carpentry and electrical and plumbing work are being demystified for more children, too. Many communities now enroll girls in shop and woodworking courses at the junior-high-school level.

At the beginning of this book, readers have an opportunity to acquaint themselves with the wide variety of standard tools used in making repairs and in remodeling. By concentrating on the particular tools that they expect to use, readers can avoid becoming bogged down in unnecessary details.

The wealth of information on materials is well organized and presented early so that readers can survey what is available and zero in on what they need. Again, this information is most effectively used in conjunction with the specific repair that is being undertaken.

To make instructions about repairs as clear and useful as possible, I have tried to be consistent in each area by telling what each repair is all about, by describing the range of choices available, by pointing out which approaches are the most practical, and by describing how to carry out spe-

cific repairs. Since pictures often explain better than words, illustrations have been used extensively to supplement the text.

The material on painting and wallpapering provides the know-how for simpler repairs and remodeling. It covers painting tools, types of paint, the preparation of surfaces, and paint application by different methods. Readers are guided through the major pitfalls of wallpapering from selecting wallcoverings to keeping strips straight while papering around corners and windows. Paneling and tiling walls are somewhat more complicated, but again, readers are carefully guided through the basics until they gain sufficient experience to figure things out on their own.

Repairing floors and stairs, refinishing wooden furniture, maintaining heating and cooling systems, saving energy, and fixing windows and doors are covered in the next series of chapters. You need to know a little about how floors and stairs are built before you can repair or alter them. Their structures are briefly described, followed by instructions for making repairs and installing new materials over old surfaces. Repairing and refinishing wooden furniture is summarized in one short chapter.

Keeping living spaces warm in the winter and cool in the summer has taken on a new importance since the energy crisis of the early 1970s. Although most home owners can do only a limited amount of technical maintenance and repair to their systems, almost everyone can learn to install insulation, weatherstrip, employ wood or coal stoves, and install fans, air-conditioning units, and humidity control devices. The chapter on heating, cooling, and saving energy provides a trouble-shooting chart and most of the background information necessary to perform these tasks.

Repairing and replacing windows and doors includes both the simple task of replacing glass and the fussy job of hanging a new door. Readers are introduced to the different types of windows that are available, told how to select and repair them, advised on door and window locks, and instructed in the installation of window and door units.

Plumbing and electrical repairs are several degrees

more difficult than an activity such as painting. As with other kinds of repairs, less-experienced individuals should start with simple projects to acquire a feel for the materials and how they are used. These chapters include a brief explanation of how each component works, with just enough information to clarify without overburdening. Trouble-shooting charts will help identify the causes of plumbing and electrical problems and determine how to overcome them. In step with the times, information is also provided for installing alarm systems for fire, smoke, and intruders.

Repairing roofs, chimneys, foundations, and exterior walls is not technically difficult, but it often requires specialized tools and more than average experience. Each aspect of exterior repair is described so that readers can knowledgeably decide which jobs they can do and which should be done professionally.

Remodeling, as treated in the second section of this book, stresses how to plan alterations, how to develop floor layouts, how to hire contractors and architects, and how to figure out costs and arrange financing. Cross references are provided to earlier chapters where specific types of repairs and improvements apply to the remodeling process. Chapters on kitchens, bathrooms, attics, and basements describe the basic elements of remodeling that are unique to each space. The chapter on kitchen design, for example, describes work centers, the selection of a floor layout, expanding storage, and selecting and installing cabinets, countertops, and appliances. A separate chapter on storage focuses on solving storage problems wherever they occur throughout the apartment or house.

Apartments, subdivision houses, and old houses have some remodeling problems that cannot be met in the usual ways. For apartments, a variety of methods are described to freshen appearances, reduce noise, and increase storage without making any structural alterations. Subdivision houses can be made more distinctive with the addition of dormers, new windows and doors, and new siding. There are many ways in which privacy can be improved with well-placed fencing, additions, or gardens. These features will also increase the resale value of a house. Well-constructed older houses are often a good investment and can be made comfortable and livable while preserving their more desirable architectural or historical qualities.

Individuals using this book who are inexperienced in home repairs would do well to start by selecting projects that are straightforward and fun. There is nothing like doing something successfully the first time to build confidence. Interior painting, wallpapering, minor repairs to lamps, and, perhaps, replacing worn washers, all are reasonably simple. With a modicum of trial and error, readers will soon be making many alterations and repairs without outside help. Good luck!

J. L. B.

Contents

vi   **Contents**

1 Tools

HAND TOOLS FOR AROUND THE HOUSE OR APARTMENT

Everyone is aware of tools, but few are aware of the differences among tools of the same kind. When you plunge deeper into repairs around the house, the jobs become more interesting as you discover that there are several kinds of screwdrivers with different blade length and tips, and innumerable variations among other familiar tools. You can get along with just a few tools, or you can acquire a whole collection which you may enjoy having and using.

We could parade a whole panorama of tools here, but it will be more efficient to describe only those that are used most often in a home workshop. Differences among them will be shown by relating them to repair jobs and generally describing how they are used.

Enjoy your tools. Spend some time in a hardware store comparing the differences between tools of the same kind. Pick them up and handle them. Think about them. Eventually, you can choose those you like and think you will need.

Once you've got them, learn how to take good care of them! A rust-pitted tool that breaks down in the middle of a job is worse than no tool at all.

HAMMERS: HOW TO CHOOSE THE RIGHT ONE FOR THE JOB

A *medium-weight, curved-claw hammer* (12- to 16-oz.) is good for jobs such as building bookshelves, nailing on clapboards, and installing flooring. A *lightweight, curved-claw hammer* (8-oz.) is better for hanging pictures and for other light jobs that require tacks, brads, or small nails. *Special-purpose hammers* are shaped for their particular uses: *Straight-claw hammers* for ripping boards apart; *upholstery* or *tack hammers* with magnetic heads for holding tacks; *ball-peen hammers* for metal work; *(wooden) mallets* for pounding chisels, or tamping bricks.

The curved-claw hammer has: a curved claw for pulling nails; a handle of wood, fiberglass, or steel; and a head with a slightly curved and beveled face for hammering.

Choose a hammer by picking up several hammers with handles of different shapes, weights, sizes, and materials. After taking a few practice swings, you will be able to select one with a weight and balance which is comfortable for you. By choosing a medium-priced or more expensive hammer, you can be sure that it has a hardened head made of forged steel (Fig. 1–1).

USING A HAMMER

Hammering and Pulling Nails

To hammer a nail in straight, hold the handle of the hammer near its end and swing it with short, light strokes. Concentrate on accuracy, not power. Hold the nail in place with your other hand until the first light strokes set it in place. Keep the hammer lined up in a straight line with your arm, and increase the distance and force of your swing as long as it remains accurate. A small nail for attaching paneling will require just a few light taps, while an 8d (8 penny nail) in a floorboard or a 10d nail in a 2-by-4 would require a number of firm, accurate blows. If a nail leans, straighten it with a few taps to its side before driving it in further. If it bends because of a knot in the wood or an angled blow, pull it out and use a new nail.

The curved claw provides a grasping tool with rocking leverage to pull nails. The V-shaped slot in the claw is placed underneath the nailhead. The grip between the nail and the wood is loosened by rocking the hammer back and forth. Once the nailhead is a little above the wood, a block of wood can be slipped underneath the front of the hammer for easier leverage and to protect the surface of the wood from being dented. If the head of the nail is sunk into or is

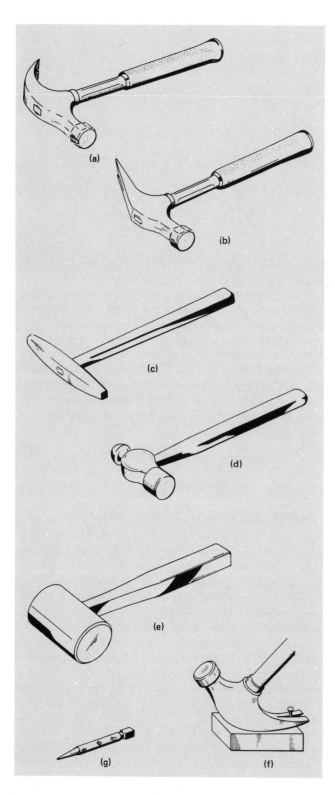

Fig. 1–1 Types of hammers: a) curved-claw, b) straight-claw, c) upholstery or tack, d) ball-peen, e) mallet. f) Pulling nail with wooden block. g) Nail set.

flush with the surface, you will have to find some way to raise it or remove enough wood around it to get the claw underneath it. Two boards can often be knocked apart far enough to raise a nailhead. As a last resort, dig around the nailhead with a sharp tool, such as a knife or an old screwdriver.

Setting Nails

In some kinds of work, nails must be driven in far enough so that the holes can be filled in. This is customary with flooring, paneling, and cabinetwork. To do this, use a *nail set* with a driving end no larger than the head of the nail. The nail set will force the nail into the wood without damaging the surrounding surface. Before this final step, the nail should be driven into the wood in the usual way until the head is just above the surface. The nail set is placed on top of the nail so that it is in a straight line with the nail and then both are driven with the hammer. Nail sets have either square or rounded heads and are made with diameters from 1/32 in. to over 4/32 in. (Fig. 1–1(g)). Since they are driven straight down (over the center of gravity of the nail), it doesn't matter if their diameter is a little less than that of the nailhead.

SCREWDRIVERS
Selecting Screwdrivers

It is useful to have several screwdrivers (Fig. 1–2), since the tip of a screwdriver must fit the slot of the screwhead evenly (if it does not, there is the risk of damaging the screwhead, wood, and screwdriver). Screwdriver sizes are described in terms of their blade *lengths* and tip *widths*. Longer blades give greater leverage.

A *medium-sized, standard screwdriver* (blade length, 4 to 6 in., tip width 1/4 or 5/16 in.) will fit screws used for attaching shelves, fastening hinges, or mounting electrical boxes.

A *small, standard screwdriver* (blade length 3 in., tip width 1/8 in.) will be necessary for the small screws of a towel-rack rod after the brackets are mounted on the wall with Phillips screws.

A *Phillips screwdriver* (blade length 4 in., No. 1 or 2 tip) is the only screwdriver that will fit the cross-slotted heads of Phillips screws (found in furniture, storm windows, and stoves).* There is some leeway in matching the width of the screwdriver tip to the slot in the screwhead. If the difference causes the screwdriver tip to slip around in the slot, borrow or buy a screwdriver of the right size.

*The "slot" in a Phillips screw is a cross, two slots intersecting at right angles.

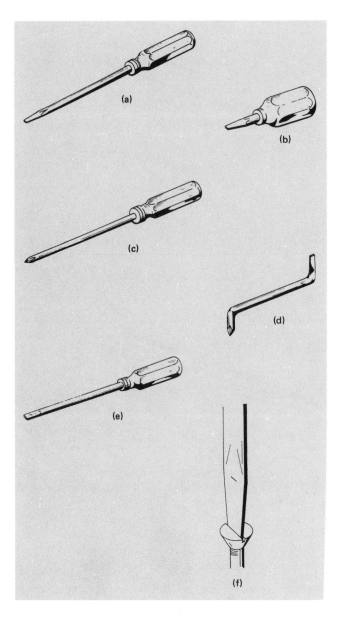

Fig. 1–2 Types of screwdrivers: a) standard 6-in., b) stubby, c) Phillips 6-in., d) offset, e) cabinet blade, f) Blade tip in slot.

Specialized screwdrivers will reach into tight places, sink screws into narrow holes, and place and remove screws rapidly. A short *stubby screwdriver* (blade length 1 1/2 to 2 in.), or an *offset screwdriver,* will reach screws where there is not enough room to manipulate for a standard-sized screwdriver. When the job requires a great many screws to be put in or removed, use a *spiral ratchet screwdriver.* (Its blade rotates several times as you push down on the handle.)

A screwdriver with a *cabinet blade* has a narrow tip which does not flare out. It will follow screws right into their holes where they are recessed in furniture or electrical fixtures.

Although screwdrivers seem to be ideal for prying things apart, their tips are easily damaged. During the process that hardens them for greater strength, they become brittle and will chip easily if misused. Tips that are chipped, chewed up, or twisted tend to slip out of the screwhead slots, and may mar the adjacent surface or chew up the screwhead itself. You may be able to salvage a screwdriver by locking it in a vise and filing it back into shape.

Using Screwdrivers

Using a screwdriver goes beyond just holding it and turning a screw. If there is no hole where the screw is to go, make one with a sharply pointed tool, such as an *awl* (or a drill). A small screw will quickly take hold in a small hole. A few clockwise twists of the screwdriver will drive the screw in. A medium-sized or large screw must have a larger, drilled hole. If two boards are to be screwed together, drill through both of them to at least three-quarters the length of the screw. The diameter of the hole and the drill should be about the same as that of the root of the screw (without its threads). With hardwoods, a larger hole must be drilled in the top board to match the diameter of the screw's shank between its head and the beginning of the threads. Unless the hole is large enough, the force of turning the screw may split the wood. If the screw is flatheaded and is to be flush with the surface, a *countersink bit* will drill out a cupped hole in the surface.

Removing screws may be as simple as inserting a screwdriver and turning it counterclockwise. (See Fig. 1–2(f).) It may be as complicated as having to heat the screwhead with a small torch to loosen it. Most situations are either simple or something only slightly more difficult. Often a screw can be worked back and forth, once it is loosened just a little. Eventually, it can be worked all the way out. It is important, in these cases, to have a screwdriver blade which evenly matches the slot in the screwhead. Extra leverage can be brought to bear on large screws that are too tight to turn by hand, by using a screwdriver with a square-shaped shank. A wrench is placed around the shank and pulled to increase the turning force. Problems with tight (or "frozen") screws can be avoided if a little wax is rubbed onto their threads before they are put in.

MEASURING TOOLS
Different Measuring Needs

"A good carpenter measures every cut three times"—according to an old maxim. To measure and mark lengths, depths, angles, and true verticals and horizontals, several

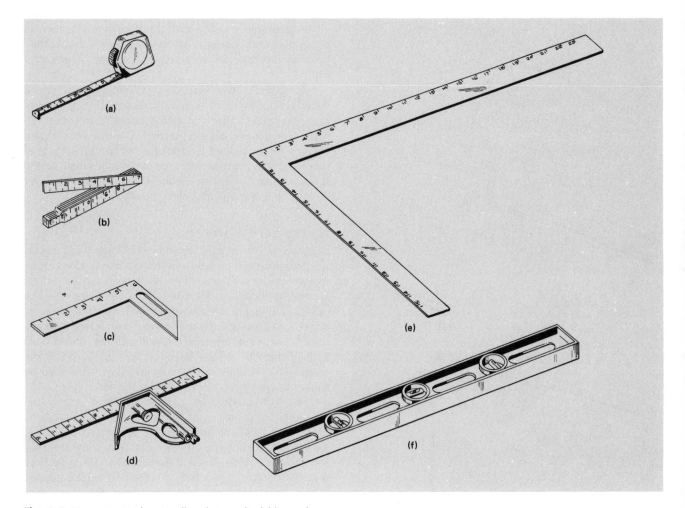

Fig. 1–3 Measuring tools: a) pull-push tape, b) folding rule, c) tri-square, d) combination square, e) framing square, f) carpenter's level.

measuring tools are needed. It is easier to measure the inside of a drawer with a *flexible rule* rather than with one that is rigid. But if you are measuring the length of a door or window by yourself, a *rigid rule* is easier to use.

To mark a board for cutting, use a *square* to be sure that the angle is true. To position a fence-post vertically, to stand a (2 X 4) stud true and plumb, or to mark a horizontal line for a lowered ceiling, use a *carpenter's level.* For putting down a tile floor, a long, straight guideline can be made by snapping a *chalk line* against the floor. (The same procedure provides a level line for shingling a house.)

Using Measuring Tools

A *steel tape* is one of the most versatile and accurate measuring tools. Steel *pull–push tapes* (8- or 10-ft. lengths are most convenient) are enclosed in a 2-in. deep case which automatically rewinds the tape when a button on its side is pushed. Because of their physical flexibility, they are handy for measuring around corners, around varied shapes, and inside enclosures such as cabinets and windows. A steel tape should be stretched taut from the lip on its end to the case. To make inside measurements, place the back of the case against an object such as a wall and pull the tape out to the desired length; the 2-in. depth of the case is added to the tape measurement.

Folding rules, wooden or nylon, are useful when making measurements that are not critical in accuracy. A typical folding rule will collapse into a little over 6 in. long (by about 5/8 inches wide). It will have a 6-in. sliding metal extension in one end, which can be extended to measure depths and make inside measurements.

There are several kinds of *squares:*

The *try-square* has a 6-in. blade fixed at a right angle to its handle for checking and marking right angles on corners and boards.

The *combination square* has a handle (with a level vial) angled at 45° and 90° which slides along a 12-in. blade. When the handle is tightened in place, the combination square can be used as an inside or outside try-square, a miter square for marking 45° angles, a depth gauge, a marking gauge, or a small level. The blade also can be used alone as a straightedge or as a 12-in. ruler.

The *steel framing square* has two long arms (for example, a 24-in. body and 16-in. tongue) at right angles to each other; this makes it an accurate tool for marking angles on large pieces of material, such as gypsum board, plywood, and rafters. Measurement scales are marked on the arms to calculate angles of all sizes for cutting. See Fig. 1–3.

Carpenter's levels (18 to 48 in.) commonly are made of aluminum with I-beam construction, and have two plumb vials and one level vial. By centering the bubble in the center vial, a horizontal line can be established for a shelf, floor, or other surface. The bubbles in the end vials will be centered when the level is held against a wall or other vertical surface (showing whether such "vertical" planes are "plumb"). Longer and shorter levels are available for masonry work, fitting into tight places, and leveling a taut guideline for a fence or wall.

Chalk lines are simply lengths of heavy string coated with chalk and pulled taut between two nails a few inches above the surface to be marked. By pulling back on the line at one end and letting it snap, you can make a long straight guideline of chalk on a large surface.

Wooden rods can be used by one person to measure the distance between two walls. Hold the rods (or any long, rigid sticks of lumber) together in a straight line and move them apart until the outer ends touch the walls. Grip them firmly where they overlap and lower them to the floor. Without letting the rods move lengthwise, use a push-pull steel tape to measure the distance from one end to the other. Since the distance between walls often varies from baseboard to ceiling and from one corner to another, this method can be used where an accurate measurement is needed for a specific point, such as in measuring rails for a suspended ceiling.

PLIERS
Pliers for Different Jobs

Pliers of different kinds and sizes are necessary for different jobs. Specialized pliers are available for gripping a rod, stripping or cutting wire, cutting metal, or reaching into a small opening. For simpler gripping, cutting, and bending, use the

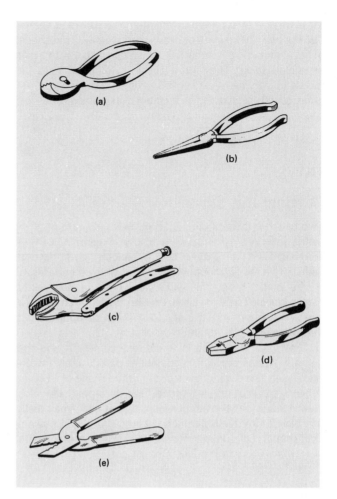

Fig. 1–4 Types of pliers: a) slip-joint, b) long-nosed, c) adjustable plier wrench, d) linesman's pliers, e) wire strippers.

all-purpose *slip-joint pliers* (7- or 8-in. lengths). They can be opened from their normal position to a wider gripping position by sliding the connection pivot from one channel position to another. They are available with curved handles, regular noses, angled noses, long noses, and "needle" noses, and other distinct shapes. See Fig. 1–4.

For electrical work, *linesmen's pliers* or *electrician's pliers* will cut and bend the heavy electrical wires in household circuits while a small pair of *long-nosed pliers* will grip, bend, and cut light wires in radios, stereos, and the like. To grip nuts, bolts, and other heavy fittings without damaging them, use an *adjustable plier wrench*. Large fittings, such as plumbing flanges, will require *engineer's pliers,* which open to several positions with the jaws parallel. When insulation is to be removed from a wire, use a pair of *wire strippers,* adjusted so that they will cut through the insulation but not the wire. For extensive cutting of electrical wires, it will be worthwhile to get a pair of *diagonal cutting pliers.* They will cut easily and cleanly. Thin sheets of tin, aluminum, and other soft metals can be cut with a pair of (metal) *snips.* They are available in different sizes for metals of varying thickness and strength. (They are sometimes called "shears.") For medium-duty cutting, *end-cutting nippers* will cut nails and heavy wire with relative ease.

SAWS

Cutting and Saws

Two or three saws of different types will take care of most cutting jobs. A *crosscut saw* (26 in. long, 8 teeth/in.) will cut across and with the grain of boards, paneling, and plywood with a moderately smooth edge. A *keyhole* or *compass saw* (12 in. long, 12 teeth/in.) will enlarge holes bored in solid panels to install light switches, copper tubing, or an exhaust fan. A *hacksaw* (12 in. long, 18 or 24 teeth/in.) will cut through pipes, plastic, and old bolts.

Saws are described in terms of their length and the number of teeth per inch, in addition to particular characteristics, such as a coping saw's *depth* or the shape of a blade. When a crosscut saw is referred to as an 8-point saw, this means that it has 8 teeth per inch. A saw with small teeth will have many teeth per inch (12 to 32) and will make a fine, smooth cut. On the other hand, a saw with large teeth (4 to 7 per in.) will produce a rough cut.

Crosscut Saw

A *crosscut saw* is an all-purpose saw for cutting wood. Its blade and teeth are designed to cut across the grain. For long cutting strokes, it has a long blade (24 to 26 in.) which may have a taper-ground back and tip to minimize binding. It may also have a back edge which is either straight or skewed for flexibility. The teeth cut wood by acting as a long line of small, rapidly-moving knife points which are sharpened with a bevel and alternately set (or tilted) at an angle to the blade so that the cut (or *kerf*) is wider than the blade (Fig. 1–5 (a) and (b)).

Before cutting a board, mark a guideline with a sharp pencil. Decide whether to cut down the center or on either side of the line. Use a square or a long straightedge for accurate angles and straight lines. Brace the board so that it won't move, and start the cut by pulling the saw toward you at a 45° angle to the board. Once the cut is started, the saw will move smoothly if you keep it lined up with your forearm and shoulder. By holding the saw lightly and using your entire arm, rather than just the wrist, you will be able to make a long, even stroke. Push downward slightly as the saw moves away from you on the forward stroke,

since the crosscut saw cuts on both its forward and back strokes. If the saw binds, you may be bending it or using too much force. Long, even strokes will cut through wood faster than short forceful strokes.

Ripsaw

A *ripsaw* has the same general shape and is about the same size (26 in.) as a crosscut saw, but its teeth are larger, fewer (5 1/2 teeth/in., on the average), and shaped differently to cut rapidly with the grain. When a board is too wide for its intended use, it must be cut lengthwise (or "ripped"), whether with a hand ripsaw or a power saw. If you are patient, you can use an 8-point crosscut saw, but it is slow work. Finer-toothed crosscut saws are even slower. Since there is less resistance to cutting along the grain than across it, ripsaw teeth are chisel-shaped—one side is vertical, the other sloped—to act as a long line of sharp, rapidly moving chisels. They are set just slightly to each side, not as much as those on a crosscut saw, to make the cut wide enough for the blade.

As you cut, hold the ripsaw lightly and in line with your forearm and shoulder (like the crosscut saw) but at a steeper (60°) angle to the board. Start the cut with the teeth near the tip of the saw. They are 1 point finer than the rest of the teeth. Because the teeth are sloped only on their forward side, the ripsaw cuts only on its forward stroke. If you are making a long cut which must be straight, clamp a long guide board along the cutting line for the saw to ride against. Once the cut is started, spread the two cut ends apart with a piece of wood or a nail; this will prevent binding. When you finish, you will find that the cut was fast but the edges are rough. They can be smoothed with a plane or sandpaper.

Hacksaw

A *hacksaw* will cut through almost anything that a wood-cutting saw can't handle (Fig. 1–5(d)). Use it to cut obstinate screws, bolts, old armored electrical cable, pipes, tubing, and breakable plastics. The elongated U-shaped frame (10 to 12 in.) holds removable blades, which vary in their metallic composition and the number of teeth, for cutting different materials. A 12-in. saw with 18 teeth/in. will take care of most jobs. The blade must be attached so that the vertical side of the teeth face forward. Use a blade which has enough teeth so that two or three are in contact with the object being cut. This will prevent the blade from breaking because of excess pressure on too few teeth. The cutting motion varies from that of a wood saw: Press down on the forward stroke with one or both hands to cut through hard materials. A long, smooth stroke is best. In tight spots, such as where a pipe is close to the ceiling, put the blade in *upside down,* so that the frame hangs downward and pressure can be applied more easily.

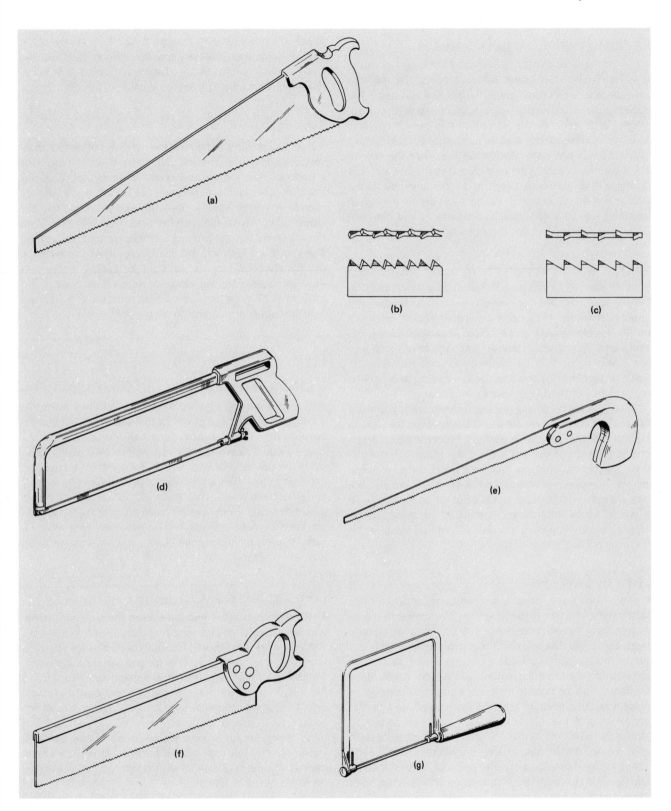

Fig. 1–5 Saws and saw teeth: a) crosscut saw b) cross crosscut teeth, c) ripsaw teeth, d) hacksaw, e) keyhole and compass saw, f) backsaw and miter saw g) coping saw.

Keyhole and Compass Saws

A *keyhole saw,* or the similarly shaped but longer *compass saw* (Fig. 1–5(e)), has a long, narrow blade projecting from a handle, that can fit into and enlarge small openings. The blade is narrow and flexible enough to cut a straight, curved, or circular pattern. Before starting to saw out an opening, draw an outline of the area to be removed and bore a 1/2-in. hole in one corner inside the line. Place the nose of the saw in the corner of the hole closest to the line and start sawing with short strokes. Keep the saw perpendicular to the surface and on the line until you have cut deeply enough to angle the saw to a 45° angle to the surface. You can then follow the line and cut out the opening.

Backsaw and Miter Saw

A *miter saw* is an elongated version of a *backsaw* (Fig. 1–5(f)). Both have medium-length, rectangular blades with a rigid steel reinforcing support along their backs. Their teeth are fine for the smooth cuts required in cabinetmaking, mitering, and cutting small lumber. Since the reinforcing support along the back of the blade is too wide to follow the blade through the slot as it cuts, the saw can cut only as deep as the depth of the blade, usually 4 or 5 in.

Start cutting by pulling the saw lightly toward you along the marked edge. If you are using a miter box, the slots in the box will hold the saw in position. Hold the board firmly against the side of the box so that the blade will not slip along the board. The saw can be leveled out after a few strokes. Wooden miter boxes have slots for 45° and 90°, but they are only wide enough to hold boards up to 4 in. or so in width. Metal miter boxes with attached saws may be adjusted to any angle but are similarly limited in the width of the board and depth of the cut.

Coping Saw

A *coping saw* has a deep, U-shaped frame attached to its handle to hold a thin blade which may be turned to follow an irregularly shaped pattern (Fig. 1–5(g)). A saw with a 6-in. depth and a 6-in. blade with 15 teeth/in. can be used to cut out decorative patterns inside a piece of wood, and to cut curved and other irregular patterns along outer edges. Since the frame must be outside the cutting area, its depth determines how far in from the edge the saw can be used. Skillful maneuvering of the thin, flexible blade is the key to using a coping saw. The blade must be mounted so that its teeth point toward the handle, making the backward stroke the cutting stroke. For edge work, the wood or metal should be held tightly in place and the blade placed at the starting point and pulled back until it cuts into the edge. The desired line can then be followed by twisting the blade on its pivots. To work inside a piece of material, drill a hole within the area to be removed so that an unattached blade can fit through it. The frame will straddle the edge so that the blade may be

attached while extending through the hole. Again the blade can be twisted as necessary to follow the marked pattern. Keep in mind that the distance between the blade and frame determines how far in from the edge you can cut.

Special Saws

It is usually possible to find just the right kind of saw for most special sawing jobs. To cut a bolt where there isn't room for a hacksaw, use a *utility hacksaw.* Its blade extends just a few inches beyond its handle and can be adjusted to slightly shorter or longer lengths. *Bowsaws* and *pruning saws* are shaped to cut rapidly through tree branches. Both have large ripping teeth, but the pruning saw can be attached to long poles to reach high into trees. *Dovetail saws* are essential in cabinetwork. They are just right for cutting tenons and dovetail joints. *Flooring saws* are different from all of the other saws because they are made to solve the special problems in cutting and laying flooring.

FILES

Cutting, Smoothing, and Sharpening

Files and rasps can be used to remove small quantities of wood, to smooth rough edges, or to sharpen tools. If you are beveling the edge of a shelf, use a *half-round, 12 in. wood rasp* to cut it down quickly. Then smooth it with a *flat, 10-in. wood file* or a *cabinet file,* followed by sandpapering. Soft cutting files and wood rasps are made for cutting and smoothing wood. Their teeth will dull rapidly if they are used on metals. Hard, metal-cutting files are made for various kinds of metals. A *mill file* is a useful file for sharpening metal blades; to sharpen the blades of a lawnmower or an axe, use a smooth, *flat, 10-in. mill file.*

Length, Shape, Cut, and Coarseness

The *length* of a file is measured from the base of its tang, which is tapered for attaching a handle, to its opposite end. A home workshop should include 10-in. files for standard work and 6-in. and 12-in. files for smaller and larger jobs.

A file's *shape* depends on its general uses. To select a file, first look at the shape of the cut that must be made. Select the right-shaped file for the job: *flat* for filing flat surfaces; *half-round* for curved surfaces and rounded corners; *triangular* for sharpening saws and cutting notches; *round* (*rattail*) for small circular patterns; *square* for square corners. A file may also be either tapered, or of uniform thickness along its length.

Cut refers to the pattern of a file's teeth. A *single-cut file* has a single series of sharp diagonal ridges along its surface. This cut produces the smoothest work. A *double-cut file* has two series of ridges crossing each other diagonally to form individual, sharp teeth. (This will produce a

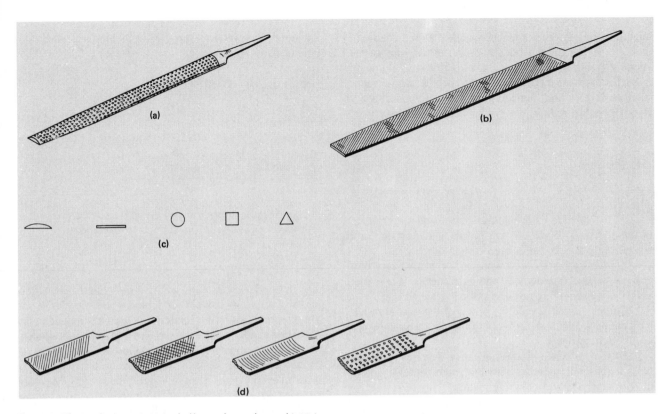

Fig. 1–6 Files and rasps: a) 12-in. half-round wood rasp, b) 10-in. flat wood file. c) Cross sections (l. to r.): flat, half-round, round, square, triangular. d) File cuts (l. to r.): single, double, curved-tooth, rasp.

rougher but faster cut than the single-cut file.) A *curved-tooth cut file* has a single series of sharp curved ridges for hard metal. A *rasp-cut file* consists of separate, sharply pointed teeth that are far enough apart for the rapid removal of wood. All of these ridges and teeth slant toward the front of the file or rasp, so that the forward stroke is the cutting stroke.

Degrees of *coarseness* increase from *smooth* to *second-cut* to *bastard* and to *coarse* (and sometimes to *rough*, beyond that). The size of the teeth actually increase with the length of the file even though the grade of coarseness remains the same. Because of this a 6-in. smooth file produces a smoother finish than a 10-in. smooth file.

If a standard file is not quite right for a filing job, there is probably a special file which will do it better. There are hundreds of files made for particular jobs: auger-bit files for sharpening auger bits; aluminum files for soft aluminum alloys; bandsaw files for sharpening the teeth on a bandsaw; foundry files for rough work. See Fig. 1–6.

Using Files

A file or rasp is easiest to use with an attachable handle slipped onto its tapered end, the tang. The surface to be filed must be steadied in a vise, or with clamps. For *straight filing*, grasp the file by both ends, point it away from you at a slight angle to the surface being filed, and push it forward over the surface. Lift the file as you bring it back, since it cuts only while moving forward. If you are making a rough cut, press down heavily; if a fine cut, press lightly. You can feel how much a file is cutting and also can judge its effectiveness by the size of the *filings*. To speed up cutting, start with a coarse double-cut file and finish with a smooth single-cut file. For very smooth or *draw filing*, turn the file so that it is perpendicular to the surface and draw it back and forth lightly.

Metal particles should be cleaned often from between a file's teeth. A file card will do this nicely.

SANDPAPER

Surfaces

To select the right kind of sandpaper, first consider the surface to be sanded. If it is painted wood, use an inexpensive, medium flint paper, which can be discarded as it becomes clogged with paint. For unpainted wood, use garnet or aluminum-oxide papers. Some hardwoods may require aluminum oxide, but other woods can be sanded with garnet. When working with metal, glass, or plastic, use aluminum oxide for the hard metals and silicon carbide for the softer, such as copper and aluminum, and also for plastics and glass. To polish metals, use crocus cloth or emery paper.

Abrasives

Sandpapers vary in hardness, coarseness, types of backing, and openness.

Silicon carbide has a blackish surface and is the hardest of the abrasives. It will cut soft metals, glass, plastics, and wood, but is too brittle to use on steel or iron.

Aluminum oxide, a brownish color, is also very hard and cuts well on hardwoods and hard metals. It is a good abrasive for removing rust and polishing metals.

Garnet, which is reddish, is one of the best abrasives for sanding wood. Cabinet work will require a quantity of it in different grades.

Emery cloth is a blackish abrasive which is tough but lacks a good cutting edge. Like aluminum oxide, it is good at removing rust and polishing metals.

Flint paper is a whitish quartz abrasive. Since it is not as hard as other abrasives, it is used mainly on softwoods and to remove finishes.

Crocus cloth contains a reddish abrasive which will polish metals and wood to a fine luster.

Some abrasives are made with both cloth and paper backings which are classified according to their weights. Lightweight *paper backings* are marked "A;" heavier backings are marked "C" or "D." Cloth backings are marked "J," "H," or "X," in order of increasing weight. *Cloth-backed abrasives* are best for power sanders and for working with water on metal.

Abrasive surfaces may be *"open"* or *"closed."* Closed surfaces have tightly packed grains of abrasive which cut rapidly but tend to clog up. Open surfaces, especially in coarse grades, may have as much as 50% of their surfaces clear of abrasive particles, to avoid clogging.

Grades

Sandpaper grades are classified according to grit sizes. Grades of flint paper are often described in words, instead of numbers, such as "coarse" or "medium." Emery paper may be marked according to an old system of measurement which uses No. 3 for coarse and No. 2/0 or 3/0 for fine paper. Grades between these are indicated with intermediate numbers. The newest numerical system of grading uses the lowest numbers for coarse grades, such as 30 or 40, and the highest for fine or very fine, such as 120 or 320. This

new numbering system is used with silicon-carbide and aluminum-oxide abrasives.

Sandpaper Grades By Mesh Size	
Very fine	220–600
Fine	120–180
Medium	60–100
Coarse	36–50
Very coarse	12–30

As a practical matter, you will be able to select the grades you need according to the surface to be sanded.

Using Sandpaper

Sand in the direction of the grain, and use increasingly finer grades of abrasive to avoid scratching wood surfaces. If you skip a grade or two, the scratches will be visible even after a final fine sanding. For a flat surface, fold a sheet of sandpaper tightly around a wooden block and keep it flat against the surface as you sand. A flat block can also be used to make an evenly beveled edge. For rounded edges, however, it is best to wrap a sheet of sandpaper around a rubber sanding block or pad, which will leave a curve rather than flattening out an edge. End and edge grain can be sanded if boards are clamped on either side and flush with the surface to be sanded. The sanding block will ride along the entire surface. See Fig. 1–7.

Fig. 1–7 Sanding block.

HAND DRILLS AND TWIST BITS

A well-made *hand drill* will cut small holes in wood, plastic, and thin metal. Its chuck holds twist drills with 1/4-in. shanks, though the drills themselves vary in diameter. They range from diameters of 1/32 in. to 1/4 in., increasing in jumps of 1/32 in. or, more commonly, 1/16 in. Although drill bits are made of different alloys, the cheaper carbon-steel bits can be used with the low speeds of hand drills since they will not overheat. High-speed drills can be used with either hand drills or power drills (Fig. 1–8).

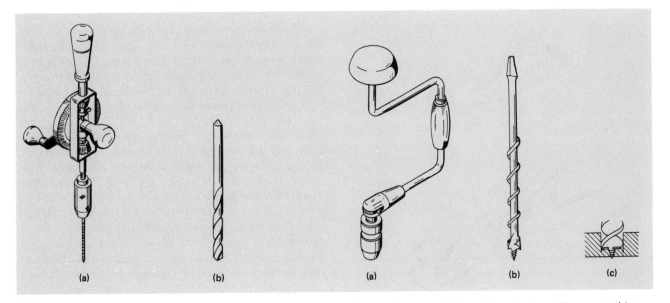

Fig. 1–8 Hand drill. b) Twist bit.

Fig. 1–9 a) Brace. b) Auger bit. c) Boring with an auger bit.

Using a Hand Drill

Before drilling into a hard surface, make an indentation as a starting point. (Use an awl for woods and plastic, and a center punch for metals.) This will keep the drill from slipping and damaging the surface. Hold the drill perpendicular to the surface, and apply a downward pressure on both the downward and upward strokes of the drive wheel. Avoid side pressure at the top or bottom of the turns, for this can bend or break smaller drill bits.

BRACES AND AUGER BITS

The crank shape of a *brace* gives it greater leverage than a hand drill. The greater the offset or "sweep" of the handle from the center, the greater the leverage of the brace. For most drilling, it is possible to use a brace with a 10-in. sweep and jaws which will grip auger bits with either tapered or rounded shanks. The jaws will hold bits from 1/4 to 1 in. in diameter and accessories, such as expansion bits, screwdriver tips, and countersinks. Expansion bits will cut 1-1/2 or 3-in. holes, depending on the bit. A brace with a screwdriver tip can exert enough pressure to loosen a frozen screw. And when a space is too small to rotate the brace in a *complete* circle, its ratchet mechanism will rotate the chuck as the handle is moved in a back-and-forth motion. This does the same job as the full rotation, but more slowly.

Auger bits are spiral-shaped but their shanks may be tapered or round. They range from 6 to 10 in. in length, though 6 in. is more common. (Even longer bits are available for special purposes.) Bit diameters range from 1/4 to 1 in., in increments of 1/16 in. To tell their diameters, look at the numbers stamped on their shanks. The numbers indicate the number of sixteenths; for example, "4" indicates that the diameter is 4/16 or 1/4 in. In addition to auger bits, several cutting and drilling tools can be used with a brace, such as twist drills for drilling metal, expansion bits for cutting larger holes, screwdriver tips, and countersink bits (Fig. 1–9).

Using a Brace and Bit

The screw tip of the auger bit should be placed in the indentation marking the center of the hole to be drilled. As you rotate the brace perpendicular to the surface and press down on its head, the bit's cutters will remove the wood, which then rides up the spiral and out to the surface. When the bit goes through the board, it will splinter the edges of the hole. To avoid this, clamp a block to the bottom of the board or drill halfway through from each side, until the holes meet in the middle.

PLANES

Choosing a Plane

Planes are designed to remove thin layers of wood with a chiseling action. Both *jack planes* (12 to 15 in. long) and *smooth planes* (7 to 10 in. long) will cut thin layers from the edge of a sticking door, smooth a rough or wavy edge of a long board, or cut an even bevel. *Block planes* (6 or 7 in. long) will loosen a tight drawer by smoothing its end, level the edges of short boards, or smooth cross-grain woods. *Surform planes* will cut down and smooth plastics and soft metals, in addition to smoothing wood.

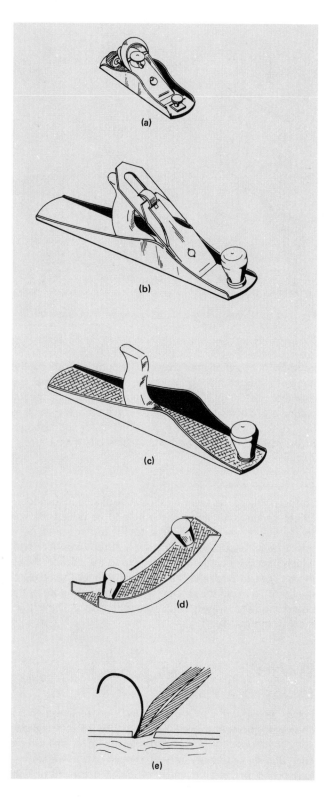

Fig. 1–10 Types of planes: a) block, b) jack, c) straight surform, d) curved surform. e) Planing.

Planes are constructed to provide highly controlled cutting of different depths and shapes. The blade is adjusted to project through the mouth, where it shaves a thin layer of wood that curls up and is broken off by the plane's iron cap. *Jack planes* are long enough to smooth out edges with wavy surfaces. *Smooth planes* shave in the same way, except that they cannot handle boards with long waves along their edges. *Block planes* are designed with the blade's bevel down and at a low angle, so that it can cut across the grain without splintering the wood. Some have adjustable blades just like the larger planes; some are fixed. The block plane is extremely versatile: It will cut with the grain, or across the grain; it will bevel, round corners, and camfer. The blades of *surform planes* are replaceable and have many small, sharp teeth to remove small shavings. They will cut wood, plastics, and soft metals, such as copper and aluminum. They are especially good for cutting end-grain and rounding corners, since their small teeth won't splinter edges as easily as standard planes do.

There are a number of specialized planes. A *rabbet plane* will cut a rabbet (or step) into the edge of a board, while a *grooving plane* will cut a long slot. A *spokeshave* * is a small plane with handles on its sides for smoothing convex or concave surfaces. A *jointer plane* (18 to 24 in. long) is used to smooth the edges of long boards (Fig. 1–10).

Using a Plane

Since the blade of a plane acts as a chisel which can be adjusted to remove thin layers of wood, the plane must be held flat against the surface of the wood, in order to maintain control of the cutting action. The blade should project evenly from side to side about 1/16 in. or less. If the plane is held slightly diagonally to the direction of the stroke, the blade will slice through the wood more easily. The stroke should be long and in the uphill direction of the grain for the greatest smoothness. Pressure should be applied evenly to the knob and handle. Take care to let up with the end of the plane as it approaches the end of the board. When planing end-grain or cross-grain with a block plane, cut from each edge toward the center, to avoid splintering the edges. The center can be smoothed off last. (When a plane is not being used, protect the blade's cutting edge by retracting it or by laying the plane on its side.)

CHISELS
Kinds of Chisels

Chisels are used to cut relatively small mortise recesses rather than long strips of wood. To cut a recess or mortise

*Formerly used by wheelwrights in shaping spokes for wagon wheels, and by furniture makers (for rungs of chairs, etc.).

for a hinge in the side of a door, use a *wood chisel* with a broad blade and a metal cap. Since this blade is sturdy and is attached to the cap, the chisel can be pounded with a hammer without damaging it. For light paring work by hand, a long, thin wood chisel (called a *paring chisel*) is best. To cut through old belts and chains, or to make a recess in masonry, use a *flat cold chisel.*

Butt chisels are wood chisels with short blades (2-1/2 to 3 in.) and are useful for working in cramped places. *Pocket chisels* are medium-length wood chisels (4- to 5-in. blade) and are used for most chiseling work. Both types are made in widths from 1/4 to 1-1/4 in. The *mill chisel,* which is the longest wood chisel, has a blade 8 to 10 in. long and an overall length of up to 18 in.

Chisels with thick blades to withstand pounding are called *firmer chisels.* If they are short, they are butt chisels; if long, pocket chisels. Modern chisels have a core of steel extending through the handle into a metal cap, or simply into a sturdy plastic handle. (Older chisels with wooden handles could be pounded only with a mallet.)

Gouges are hollow-bladed chisels curved to make concave cuts. As with other chisels, they are available in many shapes and sizes.

Cold chisels may have flat, rounded, or diamond-shaped ends, and vary in width from 1/4 to 5/8 in. The shape and width should be chosen for the kind of cutting you need. To cut holes in masonry, slice through narrow segments of metal, and for other general heavy work, use a flat cold chisel. You will also need a sledge for pounding, and goggles to protect your eyes from flying chips (Fig. 1–11(a through d)).

Using a Chisel

Before starting to cut with a chisel, draw an outline on the section of wood to be removed. In preparing a shallow recess which is to extend to the edge of the wood, use the chisel to cut straight down along the boundaries which run across the grain. Use a utility knife to cut the boundaries in the direction of the grain. The chisel then can be placed across the grain and pounded to cut a ladder-like series of segments. These are removed with the chisel blade flat and the bevel up, by cutting in from the edge and by wedging segments out from the boundaries. The surface can be smoothed by placing the bevel down and lightly cutting in the direction of the grain as it runs in an uphill direction (Fig. 1–11(e), (f)).

When cutting a recess enclosed on all sides, first remove some of the wood by drilling a series of overlapping holes with an auger bit along the full length of the section. The end boundaries should be cut first and the wood remaining around the holes removed by cutting with the chisel in the direction of the grain. The sides along the

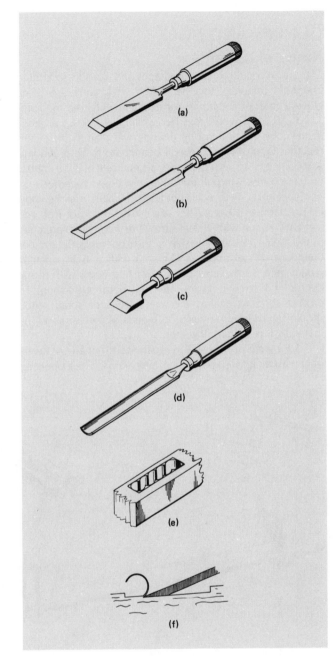

Fig. 1–11 Kinds of chisels: a) firmer, b) paring, c) butt, d) gouge. e) Cutting mortice with an auger. f) Smoothing a recess.

direction of the grain can be straightened with the chisel in the same manner. To smooth the bottom of the recess, place the chisel with the bevel side down, and remove thin slices of wood in the direction of the grain as it runs in an uphill direction.

CLAMPS AND VISES
Kinds of Clamps

Clamps are made in various shapes and sizes to fit around and hold materials together, often while they are being glued. A pair of *C-clamps,* for example, will hold medium-sized pieces of wood together while glue dries. For small gluing jobs, several *spring clamps* will clamp the pieces together tightly. When several boards are to be glued into a wide unit, such as a table top, several sets of *pipe clamps* or *bar clamps* will pull the outermost edges together.

C-clamps (3 to 6 in. openings) in pairs are the most useful clamps to have. They are usually made of iron and form a C-shape with a steel screw (for tightening) attached to the lower section. The size of their openings determines their size; for example, a C-clamp with a 6-in. opening would be a 6-in. clamp. Sizes from 1 to 8 in., with throat depths of 1 to 3 in., are useful in a home workshop. To protect surfaces against damage, pieces of scrap wood should be inserted between both ends of a clamp and the materials it is holding together.

Spring clamps (2- to 3-in. openings) are made of heavy steel with a clothespin-like clamping action. Their openings usually range from 1 to 3 in., and their lengths from 4 to 9 in. Several spring clamps will hold small pieces in place while they are being glued.

Pipe clamps and *bar clamps* are fixed to long, 1/2- or 3/4-in. diameter pipes or to bars, so that they may be extended to clamp wide pieces together. A set of pipe clamps consists of a fixed jaw attached to a pipe threaded on one end and a movable jaw which tightens up against the work. With some pipe clamps, both jaws are movable. Bar clamps work the same way but are attached to a 1- or 2-ft. bar rather than to a pipe. In both cases, scrap wood must be inserted between the jaws and the wood being glued to avoid damaging the surfaces. At least two sets of clamps must be clamped across the boards being glued to apply even pressure. Several sets of clamps and pipes may be used, with the pipes alternately above and below the pieces being glued, to create uniform pressure along their entire length.

There are other kinds of clamps for unusual gluing jobs. Pairs of *corner clamps* and *miter-box clamps* will hold the corners of narrow stock, such as picture frames, together while they are cut and glued. *Hand screws* or *wood-gluing clamps* are used in cabinet work; these consist of two paral-

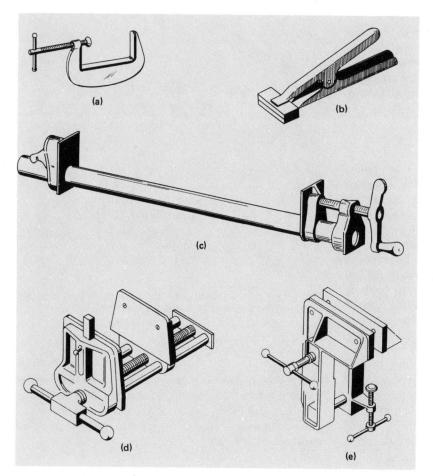

Fig. 1–12 Types of clamps: a) C-clamp, b) spring, c) pipe. Types of vises: d) woodworking, e) clamp-on bench vice.

lel wooden jaws connected by two threaded steel rods. The jaws open to 8 to 10 in., and are tightened at varying angles around the pieces being worked on, by tightening the adjustable steel rods.

Woodworking and Bench Vises

Vises differ from clamps in that they are attached to a firm base, such as a bench, and hold the material while it is being cut, drilled, nailed, or worked on in some other way.

Woodworking vises have large jaws covered with protective wooden pads. They are screwed or clamped onto the side of a workbench flush with its top. *Bench vises* have pipe jaws for working with metal, and clamp or screw onto the edge of a bench. They may be fixed in position, like small *clamp-on* vises, or they may *swivel* and lock at an angle to the base. When a workbench is available, both woodworking and bench vises are useful to have (Fig. 1–12(d and e)).

TOOLS FOR WALLPAPERING, WALL REPAIR, AND PAINTING

WALLPAPERING TOOLS

Wallpapering requires just a handful of inexpensive tools and a place to lay out and paste the paper. Tools are needed for measuring, cutting and trimming, pasting, marking vertical lines, and smoothing out the wallpaper.

Although you can get along with just a pair of scissors and a few sharp, single-edge razor blades, special cutting tools, such as wheel knives and utility knives, have their advantages in cutting and trimming. A pair of *12-in. scissors* makes long, straight cuts, which are very important in trimming. *Razor blades, utility knives,* and *wheel knives* not only will cut but will slice wallpaper where it abuts a baseboard or molding.

For measuring, there is a choice among *folding rules, steel tapes,* or *yardsticks.* A long *carpenter's level* or a *plumb bob* will mark a vertical line on the wall to align the edge of the first strip of wallpaper. The plumb bob has the advantage of making one long chalk line, while a line drawn along a carpenter's level must be extended to reach from the ceiling to the baseboard. When wallpaper has to be cut into vertical strips, a long carpenter's level will also serve as a straightedge.

An *8-in. pasting brush* and a *container* such as a plastic pail are all that you need to apply paste. A wide *smoothing brush* and a *seam roller* will smooth out and press the wallpaper snugly against the wall. The smoothing brush sweeps over the large areas, while the seam roller presses down the edges and squeezes out excess paste (Fig. 1–13).

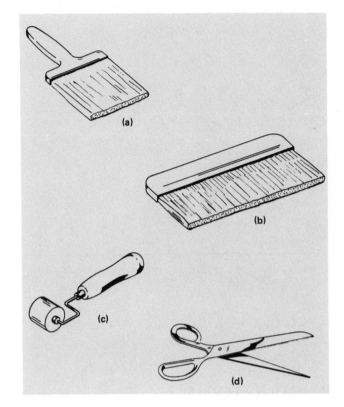

Fig. 1–13 Wallpapering tools: a) paste brush, b) smoothing brush, c) seam roller, d) scissors.

A *table* which measures at least 3 X 6 ft will serve as a place for unrolling, cutting, and pasting wallpaper. A smaller table will do if it is covered with a larger thick piece of plywood.

Stepladders, sturdy chairs, or *benches* will allow you to reach high enough to trim the wallpaper at the edge of the ceiling. By using a 6-ft. stepladder, you can get a close look at the line to be cut where the wall meets the ceiling.

WALL REPAIR TOOLS

Minor wall repairs require very few tools (Fig. 1–14). A pointed *can opener,* an old *screwdriver,* or similar narrow-pointed tool will clean broken plaster out of a crack or hole. Before patching, the edges of the old plaster must be wet with water by using an old paint brush, a sponge, or a spraying device. To apply spackling compound or patching plaster, use a flexible *1-1/2-in. putty knife.* A broader *4-in. plastering knife* will smooth the patched area. For final sanding, sandpaper can be wrapped around a *wooden sanding block.* (Sanding, of course, must not be attempted before the plaster patch is dry.)

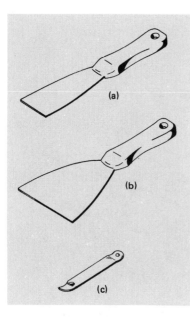

Fig. 1–14 Tools for wall repair: a) putty knife, b) plastering knife, c) can opener.

PAINTING TOOLS

A *1 1/2-in. sash brush* does a fine job on a window, but is too small and too slow for woodwork. Several sizes and kinds of brushes are necessary for most painting jobs. Woodwork requires a *2-* or *3-in. flat brush;* wall areas and ceilings, at least a *4-in. flat brush.*

Paint brushes have either natural or nylon bristles. With *natural bristles,* oil-base enamels flow more smoothly onto a surface. Natural bristles also produce the smoothest finish with varnish and polyurethane. Some substances, such as lacquer and paint remover, eat away at nylon bristles but not at natural bristles. *Nylon bristles* are ideal for latex paints since they don't soak up water. With oil-base paints and alkyds, they hold and release paint adequately but not as evenly as natural-bristle brushes do.

Brush quality depends on the length of the bristles, how well their ends are split (or *flagged*), the elasticity of the brushes as a whole, and the construction of the brush. Good-quality brushes, especially those with natural bristles, have long, well-flagged bristles for holding and releasing paint more smoothly. When pushed against a surface, the mass of bristles should have plenty of body and elasticity. Although a few individual bristles may fall out when the brush is spread out, most of them should stay tightly in place.

Brushes are shaped for different kinds of painting. *Angular sash brushes* lie more smoothly on a surface at right angles to the painter, as when painting the inside of a window sash. Small *round brushes* do a better job on rounded

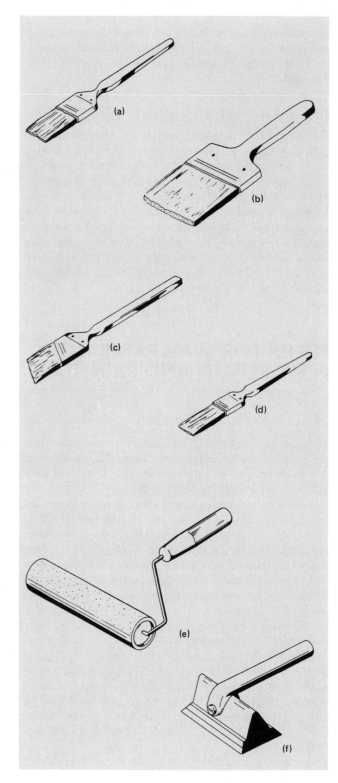

Fig. 1–15 Types of paint brushes: 1) sash, b) 4-in. flat, c) angular-cut, d) varnish. e) 9-in. roller. f) Paint pad.

surfaces. For painting outside walls, brushes should have a broad tip and plenty of body to hold paint and lay it down rapidly, if not evenly. Brushes for inside walls, especially those for woodwork, taper to a thinner tip so that a thin, smooth layer of paint can be put down. *Varnish brushes* are designed to release a thin, smooth coat. Their narrow shape, fine bristles, and taper make them ideal for applying thin coats of varnish, shellac, polyurethane, and lacquer. See Fig. 1–15(a through d).

To paint a wall rapidly, use a *9-in. roller* rather than a 4-in. brush. Pan-type rollers are made in different lengths, with several kinds and lengths of nap, and of different core materials. For walls, 7- and 9-in. lengths are common. Short, *3-in. angular rollers* work well for painting small, vertical areas. The rougher the painting surface, the longer the nap that should be used. For masonry, 1- or 1-1/4-in. nap is necessary to reach into crevices. For flat walls, a 1/4-in. nap provides a smooth finish. Nap made of *artificial fibers* can be used with latex, oil-based, and alkyd paints and also with stains. *Mohair nap* is the best choice for enamel. Like a bristle brush, it holds the enamel and releases it slowly in a thin, even layer. *Lamb's wool,* sometimes mixed with artificial fibers, works well with oil-base and alkyd paints but tends to mat with latex paints. Plastic cores will stay in good condition longer than cardboard cores, though the quality and durability of treated cardboard cores varies.

Pans, handles, and *extensions* are necessary with rollers. A good pan is rust-resistant and holds several quarts of paint. Extensions attach to roller handles so that they can reach high or awkward areas, such as ceilings and walls above one's reach from a ladder.

There are a number of special tools that may be useful in a particular painting situation. Look them over in the store and decide whether you need any of the following: paint pads, sash-painting tools, masking tape, trim guides, spray guns, sanding blocks, and brush combs.

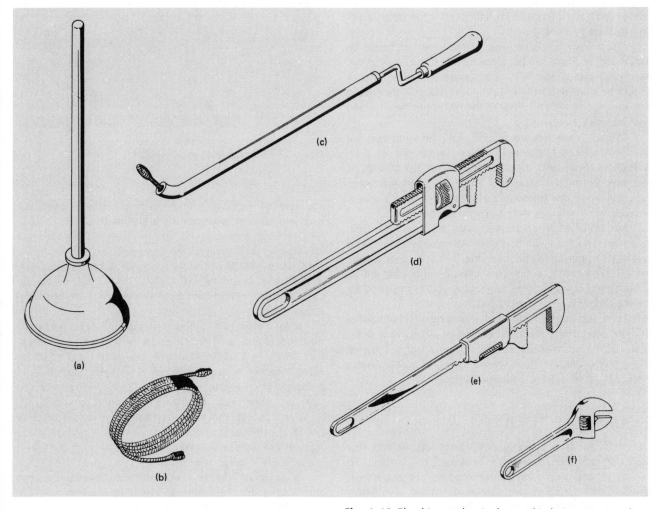

Fig. 1–16 Plumbing tools: a) plunger, b) drain auger, c) closet auger. Types of wrenches: d) Stillson, e) pipe, f) crescent.

PLUMBING AND ELECTRICAL TOOLS

PLUMBING TOOLS

In addition to other tools which you have on hand, four or five plumbing tools will take care of everyday repair problems with faucets, drains, and other plumbing fixtures. See Fig. 1–16. A 5- or 6-in. *"plumber's friend"* or *plunger* will open basin and bathtub drains that are not too badly clogged. For balky drains, wind a 12- or 15-ft. *drain auger* or *plumber's auger* into the drain to remove obstructions. If a toilet is clogged, use a shorter 3-ft. *closet auger.* Both augers are made of flexible, coiled-steel spring, and have handles for gripping and turning.

One or two *adjustable wrenches* (crescent, pipe, or Stillson) will grip most square, hexagonal, or round fittings.

Crescent wrenches grip both square and hexagonal fittings and have adjustable jaws lined up in the same direction as their handles.

Pipe wrenches have jaws that are perpendicular to their handles. Their grip becomes tighter as you pull on the handle. Because the jaws are toothed, pipe wrenches should be used only where it does not matter if their teeth mar the pipe or fitting, or where the fitting can be wrapped with a protective covering.

Stillson wrenches are shaped like pipe wrenches but their jaws operate like those of crescent wrenches. An 8-in. wrench is about right for pipes and fittings up to 1 in. in diameter. For fittings between 1 and 2 in., 14-in. wrenches have the larger jaw openings and greater leverage needed. Heavier work requires even larger wrenches.

Additional tools will be necessary to install and make extensive repairs on plumbing units. A simple *propane torch* will heat copper tubing for soldering. To cut copper tubing, use a *tubing cutter,* which cuts without the burring left by a hacksaw. For plastic pipe, use tubing cutters designed for cutting different sizes of plastic pipe.

There are special tools for plumbing repairs. Look some of them over in the plumbing section of a hardware store. A few of the more useful are: chain pipe wrenches, flaring tools, box wrenches, Allen wrenches for set screws, basin wrenches, cold chisels, and pipe threaders.

ELECTRICAL TOOLS

Electrical repairs and simple installations require very few tools. Pliers and screwdrivers may already be on hand. To cut, bend, and strip wire, you need pliers. Although most pliers have cutting edges, *linesman's pliers* are heavy enough to bend the heaviest household wire and also have strong cutting edges. *Long-nosed pliers* will hold small nuts

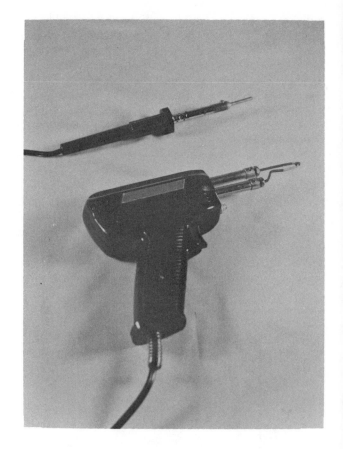

Fig. 1–17 Soldering iron; soldering gun.

and wires for working in small openings. *Wire strippers* cut wire and strip its insulation by adjusting to different sizes.

Although a medium-size *screwdriver* will be adequate for most work, an *electrician's screwdriver* with its untapered, narrow blade will allow you to get at recessed screws. A Phillips screwdriver with a No. 1 or 2 tip will fit the cross-slotted heads of Phillips screws used in many electrical appliances.

Most connections in the electrical wiring of a house are mechanical and need only pliers, wire strippers, and insulation. Once in a while, however, you may need to solder wires together or to a terminal. A light or medium-duty *soldering iron* of 40 to 100 watts, or a *soldering gun* of 150 watts will solder most electrical connections. See Fig. 1–17.

Even though the electricity has been turned off in a circuit, it's still safest to double check with a small *neon test light.* It will light up if current is flowing through the wires. (Be sure it's in good working order!)

A variety of other tools are necessary to install switches and fixtures, cut old cables, and hook up appliances. Common tools include a hacksaw, utility knife, keyhole saw, brace and bit, hammer, or other nonelectrical tools.

COMMON POWER TOOLS

ELECTRIC DRILLS
Drill Sizes and Accessories

Electric drills are among the simplest and the most versatile of the power tools. They are made in many sizes from the popular 1/4-in. drill to the larger 1/2- and 3/4-in. professional drills. Smaller electric drills are popular because of their relatively low cost and their suitability for many tasks with the help of accessories. A 1/4-in. *electric drill* will drill holes up to 1/2 in. across in wood much more easily and quickly than a hand drill will. See Fig. 1-18. With a *sabre-saw attachment,* the same drill will saw through wood, such as the siding of a house, to make a hole for a vent. When rough wood needs to be sanded, a *disc-sander attachment* can be attached to the drill. Different bits are used for drilling through wood, hard and soft metals, plastics, and masonry. Special bits are shaped to leave holes just right for countersinking screws and other fasteners. With so many kinds of drills and accessories available the best choice depends on the work to be done.

If you are not doing heavy professional-style construction, requiring sustained drilling of many good-sized holes, you can rule out the 3/4- and 1/2-in. drills. The 1/4- or 3/8-in. drills will take care of most nonprofessional work. The 1/4- and 3/8-in. sizes refer to the largest-diameter drill shank that will fit the drill. For drilling holes in wood, the cutting part of the drill and the hole can be up to twice the size of the shank, 1/2 in. for a 1/4-in. shank. For metals, the maximum size of the drill bit cannot be any larger than the shank. The main advantage of the 3/8-in. drill over the 1/4-in. drill is that it can drill larger holes.

Larger drills have more powerful electric motors for heavier drilling. The speed of the drill depends on size, too. Larger drills work slower. Their turning force becomes greater, however. A 1/4-in. drill may have a motor with 1/6- or 1/5-h.p., while a 3/8-in. drill may have a 1/5- or 1/4-h.p. motor. Professional drills have motors that range from 3/4- h.p. to over 1-h.p. Many smaller drills have fixed speeds. Others, and the larger professional drills, have variable speeds, which allow them to slow down and increase their turning force when cutting through heavy materials. Some drills are reversible so that they can be backed out of the material after the hole is cut.

To protect the user against electrical shock, an electric drill has either a shell grounded with a three-wire plug or a double-insulated, plastic shell which isolates the electrical wiring. This is particularly important when you are working around water pipes or grounded utilities, which you may touch while holding the drill.

Accessories available individually and in kits will fit most drills. One of the first accessories developed was the

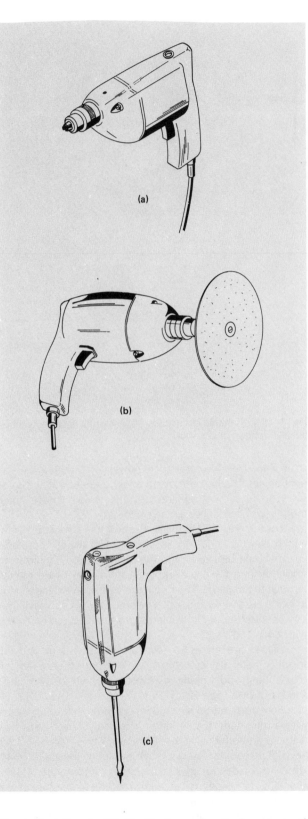

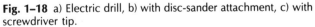

Fig. 1–18 a) Electric drill, b) with disc-sander attachment, c) with screwdriver tip.

disc sander. It fits into the chuck and rotates to smooth down a rough finish. A *polisher* can be attached in a similar manner. Saw attachments are available for light cutting. A *sabre-saw attachment* cuts like a compass or keyhole saw, where a reciprocating motion is needed. A small *circular-saw attachment* (up to 6 in.) will cut through standard 1-in.-thick boards, but not as fast as a standard circular saw. *Rotary grinders* can be attached to sharpen tools. *Paint-mixer attachments* will stir paint quickly and easily. A *screwdriver attachment* is handy when there are many good-sized screws to be driven. For drilling through hard materials such as steel or masonry, a *speed reducer* can be attached, which will reduce the speed of the drill and increase its turning power. If you need a drill-press arrangement, a *drill-press frame* can be purchased to hold the drill steady and perpendicular to the working surface.

Using a Drill

Large professional drills have handles for both hands, to give greater control and steadiness to the drill. Smaller drills, such as 1/4- and 3/8-in. drills, can be used with one hand on the handle but are much steadier and more easily kept from slipping when the second hand grasps the body of the drill. By holding the body, you can tell if the motor is becoming hot from overworking. If it is, cool it down by letting it rest for a while. If it is overheating because the material is too hard for the drill, use a speed-reducer or a larger drill.

High-speed drill bits have to be used with electric drills to withstand the effects of the heat and to maintain sharp cutting edges. This isn't as much of a problem with wood as with metal. When drilling into metal, light oil should be squirted onto the drill bit and the hole every few minutes, to ease the cutting process and cool the bit.

Repairs are infrequent with modern drills. The accompanying instruction manuals describe maintenance procedures. They usually involve little more than oiling the chuck, and sometimes replacing the motor brushes through access caps.

PORTABLE CIRCULAR SAWS

Saws and Blades

Portable circular saws are more flexible than fixed power saws and cut faster than handsaws. With accessories, they also will perform many nonsawing operations. They are made up of a powerful 1 1/2- to over 2-h.p. electric motor mounted in a housing which has a speed-controlling trigger, a blade guard, and adjustments for blade depth and angle. A variety of blades can be attached to cut wood, plywood, paneling, metal, plastic, and masonry. The smallest saws have 4-in. blades and are designed to cut through paneling, veneer, and plywood without splintering. Light, standard-

(a)

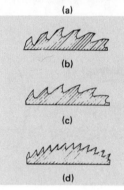

(b)

(c)

(d)

Fig. 1–19 a) Portable circular saw. Types of blades: b) combination, c) ripping, d) crosscut.

sized 7-in. saws have adequate power for cutting 2 X 4's at right angles, but lack the depth to cut them at 45°. Heavier saws use the same size blades as lighter saws but have larger motors and can cut to greater depths.

For the greatest flexibility, the best tool is a circular saw which can cut 1 1/2-in. stock at a 45° angle. The blade guard should be sturdy and the lower section should slide smoothly into the fixed upper guard as the blade moves through the material. The ripping guide has an extended arm to guide the saw in a rip cut. For protection from shock, the saw should be double-insulated or grounded with a three-wire cord and plug.

Blades are made for several types of cutting and for specific materials. *Combination blades* can be used for crosscutting and ripping hardwood, softwood, plywood, and hardboard. See Fig. 1-19.

Plywood and *veneer* blades cut through layered wood with a minimum of splintering. *Crosscut blades* have fine teeth for smooth cuts across the grain, while *ripping blades* have large teeth for fast but rough cuts along the grain. There are other blades for plastics, masonry, and metals. When attaching the blade, make certain that the teeth point in the right direction by mounting the blade so that the arrow on the blade's side points in the same direction that the blade rotates.

A portable saw can be attached to a *table* designed to convert it into a fixed table saw. The saw is bolted underneath the table so that its blade projects up through a slot, to cut boards placed on the table's surface.

Cutting with a Portable Saw

Before starting to cut, mark the guide line, adjust the blade depth so that the teeth will just break through the bottom of the board, and check to see that the blade's angle is correct. Where it is important that the angle be perfectly perpendicular, check it with a square and test it on scrap wood.

When a board is to be cut only partially through, as in cutting a groove or dado, set the depth adjustment so that the blade is at the right depth and test it.

With the front of the saw in position so that the guide is on the line, start the motor before the blade touches the wood. The saw should be moved ahead at an even pace without veering. If the blade binds, turn off the saw at once, back it up, and straighten the direction of the blade. For long, straight cuts, as in ripping, clamp a guide board to the stock against which to ride the saw. If the saw is close to the edge, the saw's own ripping guide can be adjusted to ride along the edge. As you approach the end of the cut, hold the saw so that it will stay under control as it moves off the end of the board. If the cut isn't intended to go to the end of the board, stop before the final mark so that a handsaw can be used to make the end of the cut perpendicular.

Maintenance of a portable circular saw requires occasional replacement of the motor brushes through access caps, light oiling at several points, and periodic regreasing of the gears.

SABRE SAWS
Kinds of Cuts

Sabre saws, with their reciprocating blades, cut curves with greater control and accuracy than either fixed or manual saws. Because they are portable, they can cut complicated curves or straight lines, and make their own holes for cutting into the center of panels. In the same way, they can cut small rectangles in baseboards for new electrical outlets, or make circular holes in the ceiling for electrical fixtures.

Lightweight sabre saws have 1/5-h.p. motors, 1/2-in. blade strokes, and one or two speeds. Heavier models have motors with up to 1-h.p. or more, blade strokes of 1 in. or more, and variable speed control. They will cut 1-in. wood stock with ease, and with the proper blades will cut thicker stock, plywood, pipe, sheet metal, linoleum, tiles, plastic, leather, rubber, and other materials. For cutting scroll work, some blades rotate 360°. For cutting bevels, the saw's shoe tilts to allow the blade to be set at angles up to 45°. As on most portable electrical tools, double insulation or a three-

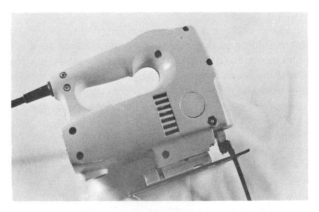

(a)

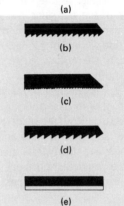

Fig. 1–20 a) Sabre saw. Types of blades: b) general-purpose, c) metal-cutting d) coarse-tooth, e) knife-edged.

wire cord and plug protect the operator against electrical shock.

Saw blades are held in a slot at the end of a reciprocating rod. Many blade holders have a setscrew, which tightens to hold the blank end of the saw blade. When this type of blade breaks near the upper end, it can be salvaged by filing the sides of the teeth near that end so that the blade can be inserted into the slot again. Saber saw blades are specifically designed for cutting different materials and for various degrees of smoothness. *General-purpose blades* will crosscut and rip all kinds of wood, soft metals, and steel. Blades for cutting wood may be *hollow-ground* with fine teeth for smooth edges or they may have large ripping teeth for fast cutting. *Metal-cutting blades* will cut brass, aluminum, and copper, but only *heat-treated blades* can be used on iron and steel. *Plywood* and *veneer blades* are designed for laminated materials. For rubber, leather, tile, cardboard, and wallboard, there are *knife-edged blades.* And for extensive scroll work, there are narrow *scroll blades.* See Fig. 1–20.

Accessories can assist in control and accuracy. A mounting table allows a saber saw to be bolted on so that it acts as a fixed jigsaw. Guides, such as a circle-cutting guide, control cutting for very accurate shapes.

Using a Sabre Saw

Before starting to cut, clamp down the material so that it won't move. Hold the saw with both hands. Start the motor so that the blade is in motion before it begins the cut. The saw should be rested on its base and its guide used to keep the blade exactly on the cutting line. By gripping the saw with two hands, you will be able to move it evenly to avoid heating up the motor and to control it when the blade hits gaps or knots.

The saw should be turned off before it is removed from the material being cut so that it won't accidentally jab the surface and break the blade as it leaves the slot.

There may be a slight but fine splintering in the wood along the top edge of the cut since the blade cuts on its upward stroke. To avoid this, clamp the material into position with the good side down. For a long straight cut, use the saw's ripping guide or clamp on a guide board so that the base of the saw can ride against it.

A pocket cut is easy with a sabre saw. Tip the saw forward onto the front of its base and start the motor. (You may need a guide board.) With the blade moving, gradually work the tip of the blade into the material at a flat angle. Keep the pressure light and slowly straighten up the saw until it is in the normal perpendicular position. There is no need to start by drilling a hole (as with a compass or keyhole saw).

SANDERS

Finishing

Power sanders can produce a fine finish or eat away with the speed of a wood rasp. Those that are used for finishing are called *finishing sanders.* The *orbital sander* (Fig. 1–21) is a motor-operated finishing sander which usually can be operated in an orbital or a straight-line motion. The orbital motion cuts faster but has a slight cross-grain motion which scratches the surface. The scratches are hardly visible, though, because the sanding pad moves with such rapid and short strokes. Whatever scratches there are can be removed by switching the sander to a straight-line motion which moves back and forth in the direction of the grain. Instead of a motor, some lightweight finishing sanders have a *vibrator* unit. This can produce a rapid but light back-and-forth motion which is adequate for very fine sanding.

Rough Sanding

Heavier power sanders are used to remove wood and paint, shape wood, and do intermediate rough sanding. *Disc sand-*

Fig. 1–21 Orbital sander.

ers with 4- to 7-in. rotating discs can cut through old paint and wood quickly with a circular pattern. (A *power drill* can be converted to a disc sander by adding a sanding disc attachment.) *Belt sanders* can be used for rough or finish sanding. When held at an angle to the grain, they will cut rapidly through a surface, leaving a rough pattern. This can be smoothed out by attaching fine sandpaper to the belt sander and operating it parallel to the grain.

ROUTERS
Router Bits and Adjustments

A router with a selection of bits can be used to make a professional-looking decorative edge for the top of a table, cut dados, rabbets and other joints, and hollow out areas for door hinges. The depth of the cut is adjusted by raising or lowering the router's collar so that the bit extends the proper distance below the base. The bit is attached with a nut to the collet chuck on the end of a shaft which rotates at speeds as high as 25,000 to 30,000 r.p.m.

There are a number of bits for different-shaped cuts. Most of them are under an inch wide and are available in at least two widths. Some of the bits are: rabbet, bead and quarter-round, cove, camfer, V-groove, dovetail, straight-face, ogee, combination, and veining. Choose a bit shaped to match the cut from which you want the wood removed. The bit should be either as wide (or narrow) as the cut in order to do the job in one pass. When you are ready to cut, insert the bit in the chuck and tighten the collet nut. The collar can then be adjusted so that the bit extends to the proper depth. Lock the collar in place and test the depth of the cut on scrap wood (Fig 1–22).

Cutting with a Router

The router's base should ride smoothly along the surface of the piece being cut. Grip the two handles on the sides to control the motion so that the router doesn't jump or move off the guideline. Start the motor and move the router from left to right. As it cuts, the bit will rotate clockwise into the wood. Move the router at a pace so that the bit removes the wood at an even and constant rate without overheating

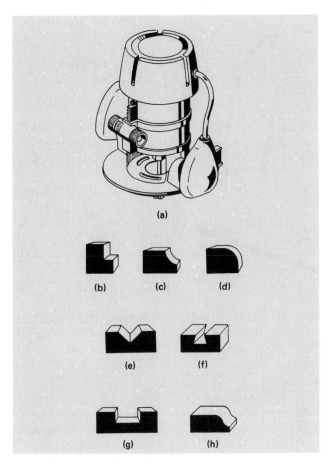

Fig. 1–22 a) Router. Types of cuts: b) rabbet, c) cove, d) camfer, e) V–groove, f) dovetail, g) straight-face, h) ogee.

(moving it too fast) or burning the wood (moving it too slowly). An edge guide, or other accessory guides, can be attached to the router's base for straight cuts, circular patterns, and to use with templates.

FIXED POWER TOOLS FOR HOME WORKSHOPS

Although relatively few people have workshops with large power tools, it can be helpful to know something about them.

Large power tools, long boards, and 4 X 8 sheets of plywood require plenty of space for storage and moving around while working. Such power tools are usually mounted on stands with rollers which allow them to be moved out of the way when not in use. A workbench can be built against a wall or in the middle of the room for access on all four sides. Tool racks, shelves, drawers, storage cabinets, and racks for lumber all require space. Heavy electrical wiring outlets, capable of supplying 20 to 30 amps, may be needed for tools with large motors.

A number of home-workshop power tools are available that are lighter and less expensive than the professional versions: table saws, radial arm saws, drill presses, jointers, wood lathes, jigsaws, bandsaws, and multipurpose tools.

TABLE SAWS

An 8- or 10-in. *table saw* is excellent for long, straight cuts. A board is placed on the table against the ripping fence and pushed through the spinning saw, which extends up through a slot in the table. For bevels or angle cuts, the table or the saw arbor usually can be tilted. Blades are the same as those used by portable circular saws. Special blades can be attached for dadoing and routing. Table saws are usually posi-

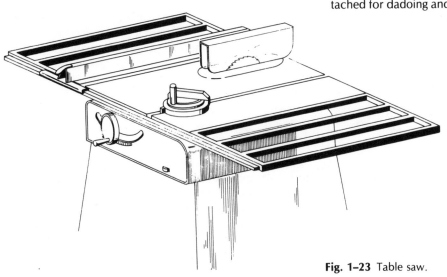

Fig. 1–23 Table saw.

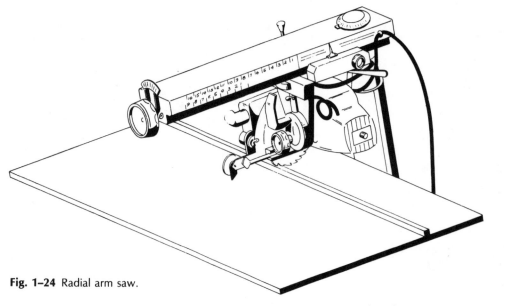

Fig. 1–24 Radial arm saw.

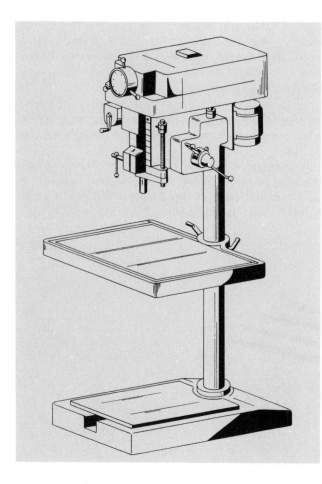

Fig. 1–25 Drill press.

tioned in the center of the work space so that long boards and large sheets of material can be maneuvered for cutting (Fig. 1–23).

RADIAL-ARM SAWS

An 8- or 10-in. *radial-arm saw* has more adjustable controls than a table saw, but it is limited in the board widths that it can handle. The motor, saw, and controls are mounted on a horizontal arm which swivels and rides up and down on a vertical column attached to the stand's base. By swiveling the arm, raising and lowering the saw, and tilting the saw and motor, the saw can be positioned to cut angles, bevels, and different depths. The width of the material that can be cut is limited by the distance between the saw's outermost position and the fence pushed back against the supporting column. There is no problem with ripping; the saw is turned 90°. Crosscuts are quick and accurate since the stock is placed on the table and against the fence as the saw is pulled through it. To convert the radial-arm saw for multipurpose work, there are attachments, such as dado and molding heads, disc sanders, planers, and grinders (Fig. 1–24).

DRILL PRESSES

A 15-in. *drill press* will drill holes in metal, wood, and other materials, and it will also cut dovetail and mortise joints and circular patterns, rout, grind and sand, plane, and shape. The drill press consists of a motor mounted in a head which is supported by a vertical steel column mounted on a heavy base. A metal table, also attached to the vertical column but below the drill head, holds the material being worked on. The drill bit itself is mounted in a chuck attached to the drill's spindle. A feed handle lowers the drill to a preadjusted

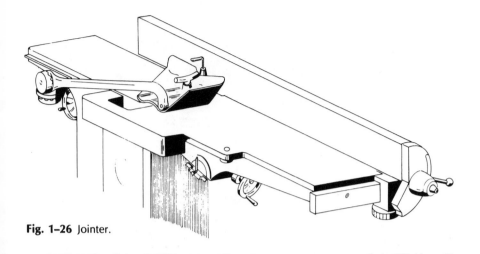

Fig. 1–26 Jointer.

depth into the stock being cut. For cutting different materials, the drill must be set at the right speed by attaching the belt which drives the saw to the proper step pulley.

The size of the drill press is equal to the diameter of a circle centered on its spindle and extended to its supporting column.

JOINTERS

A 6-in. *jointer* will make a straight edge on a board, plane it down to make it thinner or tapered, or cut bevels and rabbets. The cutting tool is made up of three cutter blades attached to a rapidly rotating steel cylinder. The blades extend up through a slot which separates the front and rear tables. To vary the amount of cut, the front table is raised or lowered so that, when the stock is pushed

along the front table, the rotating blades bite into it by the desired amount. Along the rear of the table is a fence to guide the stock. The width of a planing cut is determined by the width of the blades. A 6-in. width is common.

WOOD LATHES

A *wood lathe* is a device which rotates a piece of wood rapidly so that it can be rounded with wood turning tools. The piece is held between rotating spindles while gouges and wood-turning chisels are seated on a tool rest and moved up against the revolving wood to make a rough first cut. Skews, spear points, round noses, parting tools, and various-shaped gouges are used for several cuts, each increasingly finer. Finally, the piece is finished with sandpaper.

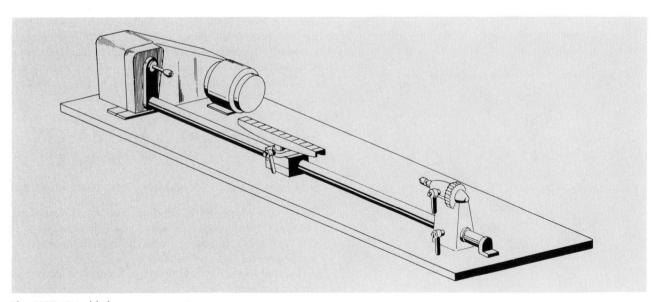

Fig. 1–27 Wood lathe.

The *size* of a lathe is in terms of the diameter of the circle centered on the spindle and extending to the base of the lathe. This is the limit of the thickness of a piece that can fit into the lathe. The maximum length that can be inserted between the spindles is called the *distance between centers.* The diameter of a typical wood lathe might be 12 in. and the distance between centers 36 to 40 in.

JIGSAWS

A *jigsaw* can cut scrolls, curves, and straight lines in wood, plastic, metal, and other materials. Its thin vertical reciprocating blade acts as a fixed sabre saw. Small jigsaws will cut 1-in. stock but heavier models are necessary for stock 2 in. thick and greater. For cutting sharp, short-diameter curves, there is a fine jeweler's blade 1/64-in. wide. Wider curves and straight-line cuts can be made with wider blades. Many jigsaw tables can be tilted for cutting bevels. Some can be converted to sabre saws by removing the structures over the table which interfere with the free movement of large pieces of stock (Fig. 1-28).

BANDSAWS

A *bandsaw* will cut scrolls, curves, and straight lines in thick stock. A blade in the form of a continuous steel belt revolves so as to cut in a downward direction. For fast cutting, such as ripping, there are 1/2- and 3/4-in. skip-tooth blades. For cutting curves, there are fine 3/16-in. wide blades and intermediate sizes of 1/4, 3/8, and 1/2 in. Most bandsaw tables can be tilted to 45° for cutting bevels (Fig 1–29).

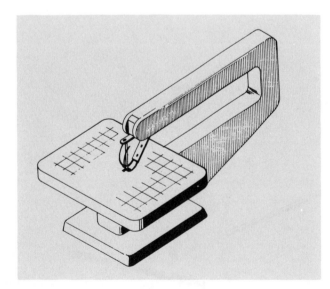

Fig. 1–28 Jigsaw.

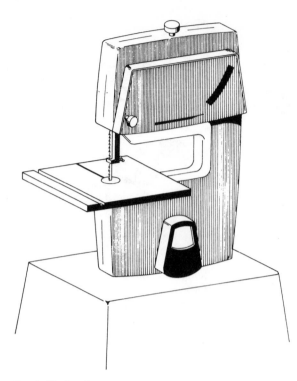

Fig. 1–29 Band saw.

MULTIPURPOSE TOOLS

Most of the large units described above can be converted for several operations with attachments. A drill press can also saw, cut joints, plane, shape, and sand. A radial-arm saw can cut dados and moldings, sand, drill, plane, and grind, in addition to sawing. There are also single power-tool units which have several types of tools operated by one motor. A wood lathe may be combined with a saw which has attachments for several other operations. By having attachments to convert a single power tool to other jobs or by obtaining a single multipurpose unit with one motor, you can increase the capabilities of your collection of tools.

STORAGE, CARE, AND SAFETY

STORAGE

To preserve your peace of mind, keep your tools where you can find them. Storage facilities can be built into spaces as small as the back of a door, or you can use a kitchen cabinet, part of an attic, or a corner of the basement. At a minimum, you will need shelves and hooks or hangers. Build or buy wooden or metal shelves. For hooks, nails can be pounded into the wall or perforated hardboard can be spaced out

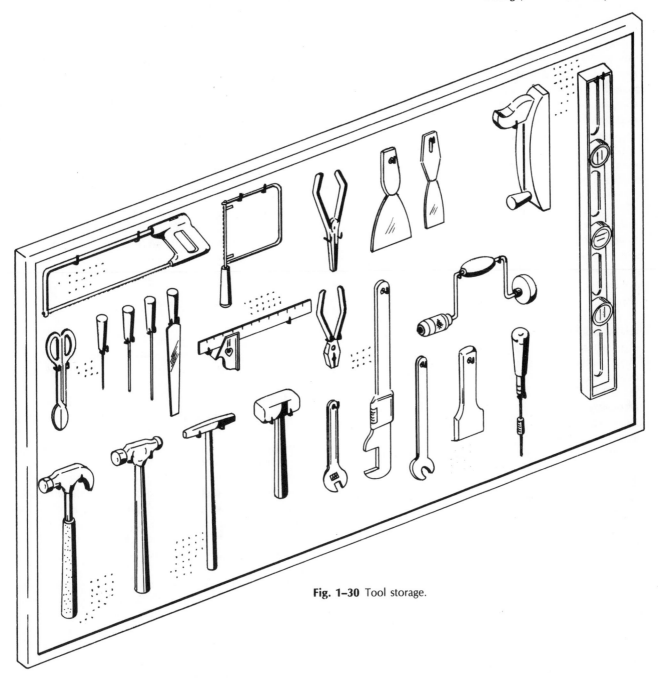

Fig. 1–30 Tool storage.

from the wall to hold commercial hangers. If you have room for it, build (or buy) a cabinet to store power tools.

Small tools, especially tools of different sizes and shapes like screwdrivers, should be visible and accessible. They can be mounted on wall brackets or hangers attached to 1/8-in. perforated hardboard. Long tools, such as squares and levels, can either hang on a wall or fit on a shelf. Saws should be hung vertically in a dry place, such as the end of a work bench. Large flat tools, like planes, portable power tools, and files, will need wide shelves. Shelves are necessary also for containers of nails, screws, and paint cans. Tools like

chisels, auger bits, and planes pose a storage problem: They have to be stored so that their sharp cutting edges are protected from other tools. Wrap them in cloth and keep them away from other tools.

CARE

Taking care of tools means keeping metal dry and rust-free, cutting edges sharp, wooden handles dry and tight, and power tools clean and properly maintained.

Store tools in a *dry place*. The amount of moisture in a basement workshop won't harm wooden handles, but it may cause metal to rust. Try to keep *rust* from forming by coating metal surfaces with a light film of oil, wax, or petroleum jelly. In order for these coatings to stick, the metal must be wiped off and cleaned first.

Once rust has a good start, it's hard to remove. Light rust can be removed with a kitchen scouring pad, steel wool, emery cloth, or a commercial jelly-type rust remover. If the surface is pitted with rust, it will be very difficult to remove the rust completely.

Several tools are necessary to *sharpen* edges. An aluminum-oxide grinding wheel can be attached to a rotary power tool for rough or fine grinding. A mill file is good for removing burrs and sharpening certain kinds of blades. Oil stones with coarse and smooth surfaces are used for final sharpening, with light oil, kerosene, or water as a cooling lubricant.

Thin knife blades can be sharpened with either a flat or hollow-ground edge on a grinding wheel. For the sharpest edge, where cutting doesn't require great force, use a hollow-ground cut. To sharpen a knife on a stone, slide its blade forward diagonally while holding the knife at the angle of the bevel. A kitchen knife should have a bevel of 15 to 20° while the bevel of a utility knife should be 20 to 30°. Pull the blade backward at an angle slightly greater than its bevel, to make an even sharper edge.

Burrs should be removed from chisel and plane blades by placing them flat side down on a stone and moving them in a circular direction. When the flat edge is smooth, turn it over and place the beveled edge against the stone for sharpening with a rotary motion. The length of the bevel should be about twice the blade's thickness at the inner edge of the bevel (Fig. 1–31 (a), (b)).

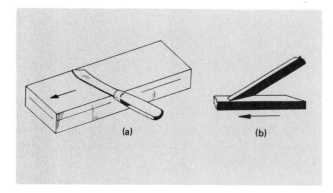

Fig. 1–31 Sharpening a) a knife, b) a chisel.

Some cutting edges require smooth bevels but not sharp edges. A file should be stroked diagonally forward along the bevels of wire cutters, paint scrapers, and grass clippers. Scissors are sharpened on an oilstone by sliding each blade diagonally along its bevel

Unless they need heavy grinding, lawnmower and axe blades are easily sharpened with files and handstones. Remove burrs and chips with the file and then use a rotary motion with the handstone for the final sharpening. Be sure to sharpen the axe blade with a convex curve for greater strength.

On auger bits, use a small mill file or special bit file to touch up the edges of the spurs and cutters. The spurs should be filed only on the beveled edge facing the screw tip. The cutters should be filed only on the edges away from the screw tip.

SAFETY

Each tool or group of tools has its dangerous elements. For hand tools, it's mainly bruises and cuts from sharp edges; for power tools, it's electrical shock and fire, flying debris, and even more dangerous cuts and bruises.

If you have the right tools available and keep them sharp and in good condition, you are off to a good start. Hand tools, such as chisels and drills, should be held so that they are under good control. With a handsaw, keep your fingers clear of the blade so that they won't be cut even if the saw slips. Hammers should be used only to pound in and remove nails. Protect your fingers from misdirected blows by holding the nail near its tip while tapping lightly to hold it in place. If you assume that tools will slip occasionally and allow for it by keeping your body clear, you will be able to avoid spearing yourself with a screwdriver or pinching yourself with pliers.

Power tools add to the force and speed of injuries. Loose clothing (and long hair) shouldn't be worn around any power tool. When you are using a drill press, lathe, or other tool which can throw fragments, be sure to wear goggles.

When using a power saw, keep the guard in place, use a notched stick to push narrow stock into place, hold boards firmly, and stand to the side of the saw.

GENERAL MAINTENANCE

Any tool with moving parts should be cleaned properly and oiled occasionally. The manufacturer provides instructions for care and maintenance and you should read these thoroughly and follow them.

2 Materials

METAL FASTENERS

NAILS

Wood can be fastened together in many ways but nailing is the fastest and most common. Nails are used for wall framing, floors, fences, and some furniture and toys. There are special kinds of nails for roofing, concrete, gypsum board, etc., but only four kinds of wire nails are used for the bulk of nailed fastenings: common, box, finish, and casing nails.

Common nails have a flat head and thick round body for strength in construction and other heavy work. *Box nails* are shaped like common nails but are thinner for easier driving in lighter construction, especially where splitting is a problem. *Finishing nails* have small heads for setting into the wood where the nailheads are to be covered over. *Casing nails* are similar to finishing nails but have tapered heads for driving into the surface to hold boards in place, as in blind nailing. *Special nails* are made for upholstery, shingles, gypsum board, flooring, and other materials. See Fig. 2–1.

Nail surfaces may be smooth or ridged with annular rings or helical threads for gripping. Although steel is the most common metal used in making nails, they are also made from aluminum, copper, brass, and stainless steel.

Finishes may be plain, cement-coated, galvanized, or blued. For work exposed to the weather, galvanized, aluminum, or copper nails can be used without rusting. *Nail points* are shaped to cut in several ways. The standard diamond point drives quickly but will split hardwood and the ends of lengths of softwood. A blunt point is better in these cases. For fast driving, a thin point is best but it does split wood easily.

Nail lengths are referred to by penny numbers (d) rather than in inches (see Table 2–1 and Fig. 2-2). The smallest nails, 1 in. long, are 2d nails, while the largest, 6 in. long, are 60d nails. With practice, it is not hard to remember the corresponding sizes: 6d nails are 2 in. long, 10d nails are 3 in. long, and 20d nails are 4 in. long. Nails less than 1 in. long are called *brads* and are measured in inches instead of by penny numbers. They are thinner, like finishing nails, and have smaller heads for setting. *Spikes,* on the other hand,

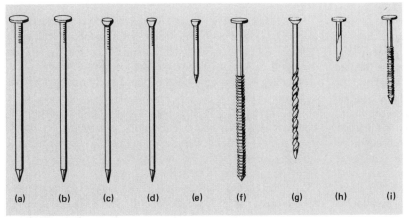

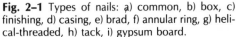

Fig. 2–1 Types of nails: a) common, b) box, c) finishing, d) casing, e) brad, f) annular ring, g) helical-threaded, h) tack, i) gypsum board.

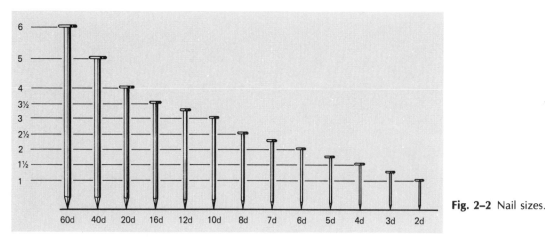

Fig. 2–2 Nail sizes.

Table 2–1   Nail Sizes and Weights

Penny (d) Size	Length (in.)	Approximate Number of Nails per Pound*	
		Common	Finishing
2	1	850	—
3	1 1/4	545	875
4	1 1/2	295	600
6	2	170	300
8	2 1/2	100	200
10	3	65	125
12	3 1/4	60	—
16	3 1/2	45	—
20	4	30	—
30	4 1/2	20	—

*The number of nails per pound varies somewhat with the manufacturer.

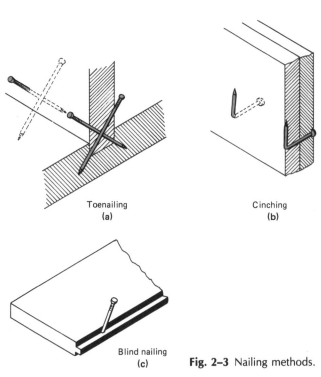

Fig. 2–3 Nailing methods.

look like large common nails, but they are thicker than nails relative to their length, and are used only for very heavy work.

Fastening With Nails

Common nails must be long enough to penetrate all the way through the top board and about two thirds of the way into an anchoring board. If there is danger of splitting, use thinner box nails or finishing nails or drill holes slightly smaller than the nail. The nails should be driven across the grain rather than with it. Driven across the grain, they force the fibers apart and are gripped tightly in place. Driven with the grain they remain loose and may pull out easily. The direction of the load on nails may make a joint strong or weak. The force of the load will not shear them off at right angles but it will pull them out if they run in the same direction as the load. To make a very tight joint, angle the nails slightly away from the perpendicular with each nail at a different angle so that it pulls against the others.

Toenailing (Fig. 2–3(a)) is used to attach a thick board such as a 2 X 4 perpendicular to another board to form a T joint. Nails are crisscrossed from opposite sides at the base of the 2 X 4 so that they extend into the bottom board. Toenailing prevents the vertical board from moving in either direction.

Cinching (Fig. 2–3(b)) makes a tight joint by extending the nail through a board and out its back where the nail is bent over. The pointed end can be bent flat or into a staple shape and bent back into the board, while the head is held tightly against the front surface.

Blind nailing (Fig. 2–3(c)) is essential in nailing tongue-and-groove paneling or floorboards. The nails are driven at an angle and their heads are set into the edges and covered with the next board that is laid.

SCREWS

Screws make stronger joints than nails and should be used where the load pulls in the direction of the length of the screw; where two pieces of wood must be pulled tightly together; where the structure is to be knocked down and taken apart later; or where overall strength greater than with nailing is required.

Several types of screws and accessories are available: wood screws, washers, and screw hooks for wood; sheet-metal screws for thin sheet metal; machine screws for both wood and metal; masonry screws for concrete slabs and blocks; and lag screws for heavy wood construction. Although most screws are made of steel or brass, some are made from aluminum, zinc, chrome plate or other alloys.

Wood screws are classified by their head shape, screw length, and gauge. A *flatheaded screw* is used when the head is to be flush with the surface. *Round-headed* and *oval-headed screws* are more decorative and are allowed to protrude above the surface. (They also are easier to remove than flat-headed screws.) See Fig. 2–4.

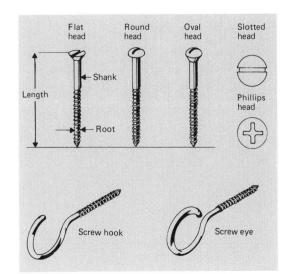

Fig. 2–4 Wood screws.

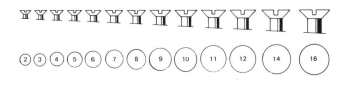

Fig. 2–5 Screw gauges.

Table 2–2   Wood Screw Sizes and Lengths

Gauge No.	Shank Diameter (in.)	Range of Lengths Available (in.)*
0	1/16	1/4–3/8
1	1/16	1/4–1/2
2	5/64	1/4–3/4
3	3/32	1/4–1
4	7/64	1/4–1 1/2
5	1/8	3/8–1 1/2
6	9/64	3/8–2 1/2
7	5/32	3/8–2 1/2
8	11/64	3/8–3
9	3/16	3/8–3
10	3/64	1/2–3 1/2
12	7/32	1/2–4
14	1/4	5/8–5
16	9/32	1–5
18	5/16	1 1/4–5 1/2
20	21/64	1 1/4–5 1/2
24	3/8	2–6

*The range of lengths available varies with the manufacturer.

The length of a screw is measured in inches but the diameter is given as the *gauge* of the screw (Fig. 2–5). For example, a No. 10, 3-in. screw has a diameter of 3/16 in. Screw diameters range from 1/16 to 3/8 in. (gauges No. 0 to 24), and lengths range from 1/4 to 6 in. Screws are selected by first deciding whether a flat, round, or oval head is needed. The necessary length can be determined by measuring the thicknesses of the wood to be joined. The screws should extend from the surface of the top board through into the bottom piece so that two thirds of the thread length is embedded in the bottom board.

Heavier-gauge screws provide greater strength, but for hardwoods, smaller-gauge screws are often strong enough and there is less risk of splitting the wood.

Fastening With Wood Screws

Splitting can be prevented and driving screws made easier by drilling pilot holes. An awl will make a big enough hole to start a small screw but holes must be drilled for larger screws in softwood. In hardwoods, holes must be drilled for all screws. The screw shank requires a larger hole in the top board than the narrower threaded section requires in the under piece. The hole for the threaded section should be slightly smaller than the diameter of the threads. In softwoods, the prepared hole should be about half the length of the embedded portion of the screw. In hardwoods, it should be extended the full length of the screw. When flat-headed screws are used a hole must be counter-bored so that the heads are flush with the surface. All screws are easier to drive and to remove if a little wax is put on the threads before they are driven into the wood.

Occasionally, the top piece of stock is too thick for the length of the screw. A hole can be counterbored so that a

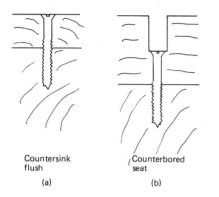

Countersink flush
(a)

Counterbored seat
(b)

Fig. 2–6 Seating screws.

flat-headed screw can be sunk and covered with a section of dowel. See Fig. 2–6.

Other Kinds of Screws and Accessories

Sheet-metal screws (Fig. 2–7) cut their own threads through sheet metal as they are turned since they are self-tapping screws. Most of them are short and small gauge. Their sizes are determined as for wood screws. Beside the standard wood screwhead shapes, metal screws also have a flat pan-shaped head which tightens flush against the surface.

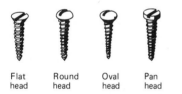

Flat head   Round head   Oval head   Pan head

Fig. 2–7 Sheet metal screws.

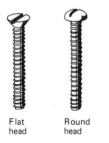

Flat head   Round head

Fig. 2–8 Machine screws.

Machine screws (Fig. 2–8) have blunt ends and are fastened with washers and nuts. Their sizes are measured by gauge and the number of threads per inch, such as a No. 8–32 machine screw.

Masonry screws may be either wood or machine screws which are held fast in a metal or fiber plug embedded in concrete or brick.

Lag screws serve to support heavy loads where a bolt cannot be used. They are heavier than standard screws and have a square or hexagonal head, which can be turned with a wrench with considerable force.

Screw-type hooks include semicircular screw hooks, circular screw eyes, square hooks, and other shapes. They are used to provide strong anchors for gates, curtain rods, tools, etc.

Washers spread the pressure from the head of a screw over a large area and protect the surface against being gouged by the screwhead. Flat and finishing washers fit flat, oval, and round screwheads, respectively.

BOLTS

Bolts are not used for work around the house as often as nails and screws are, but when they are needed, it is important to know what types, shapes, and sizes to get. Stove, machine, and carriage bolts are the most common, though there are many other types for special purposes. Heads may be square or hexagonal, so they can be turned with wrenches, or they may be dome-shaped. Sizes are determined by the length, diameter, and number of threads per inch. The threads spiral around the bolt at a flatter angle than on screws. They may extend all the way to the head, as on stove bolts, or just far enough for a nut to be screwed on. See Fig. 2–9.

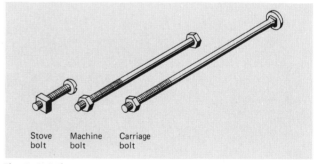

Stove bolt   Machine bolt   Carriage bolt

Fig. 2–9 Bolts.

Stove bolts are the small, slot-headed bolts found in metal casings of washing machines, stoves, and smaller pieces of sheet metal. Their heads may be flat, round, or oval, but the nuts are usually square. They may be as short as 1/2 in. or as long as 6 in., with correspondingly small or large diameters. Screwdrivers, rather than wrenches, are used to tighten them.

Machine bolts are medium-size bolts (1 to 6 in. long) for metal and wood construction. Their heads and nuts may be either square or hexagonal. When they are used with wood, washers are used to protect the surfaces under the head and nut.

Carriage-bolt heads are dome-shaped over a small square section which bites into the wood and prevents the bolt from turning as a nut is tightened on the other end. Carriage bolts range from about 1/2 in. to 10 in. in length. As with machine bolts, washers are placed under the nuts to prevent them from digging into the wood.

Nuts and *washers* vary in shape and size according to their special uses. The standard shapes are square and hexagonal. Wing nuts can be removed easily and may be used where the tightening pressures are not too great. Cap nuts will cover exposed bolt ends where they are otherwise visible. The end of the bolt, however, must not extend beyond the depth of the cap nut. Lock nuts are useful because they stay in place once they are threaded onto bolts. Flat or lock washers ensure that nuts and bolts stay tightly in place and also protect surfaces. Toothed washers help make a firmer grip by biting into wooden surfaces.

WALL ANCHORS

It is obvious that hanging things on brick and concrete walls presents difficulties. What is not as evident is that hollow walls can pose problems, too. Walls of plaster and lath may be strong enough to hold heavy cabinets if they are anchored at several points; but gypsum-board walls are weaker and may not be able to support cabinets of the same weight. Anchors made for use on hollow walls are very strong, usually surpassing the weight-carrying ability of the walls themselves; but with solid walls, the anchoring device is the weak link.

Nails and screws are adequate for hanging some things on hollow walls. Brads or picture hooks tapped into a 1/2-in. plaster or gypsum-board wall will support decorative objects that are not too heavy. For heavier objects, the nails must be long enough to penetrate into the supporting studs. Similarly, screws will hold up moderate weights such as cabinets, but only if they extend through the walls and into

the studs. When you cannot locate a stud at the point where you want to insert a screw, a connecting cross-piece can be attached to the wall by nailing or screwing it into the studs. The cross-piece will be able to support large objects regardless of where the studs are. See Fig. 2–10.

For hollow walls, there are several kinds of anchors, which work on one of two principles: expanding within a drilled hole, or expanding behind the wall. The wall itself must be strong and in good condition.

Molly bolts are hollow-wall anchors with sleeves which flare out behind the wall to pull the bolthead tightly into the front of the wall. The bolt must be just long enough so that it can flare out at the correct point behind the wall. To select the right size Molly bolt, it is necessary to know the weight of the load and the thickness of the wall. Bolt length, wall thickness, and weight information are provided in instructions furnished by the manufacturer of the Molly bolts. Molly bolts have one considerable advantage: the sleeve remains tightly in place even though the screw is removed.

Toggle bolts grip from behind the wall like Molly bolts, but cannot be removed without the gripping wings falling off. A fairly large hole (3/8 in. or larger) must be drilled through the wall so that the wings attached to the end of the bolt can pass through. When free of the hole, a spring spreads the wings, which pull against the back of the wall as the toggle bolt is tightened. The bolt must be inserted through the object to be hung before the wings are attached, since the bolt cannot be removed from its hole later.

Lead and *plastic anchors* and *fiber plugs* are sleeves which expand within hollow or solid walls, rather than gripping from behind. Plastic anchors and fiber plugs will support medium-weight objects when inserted in a good plaster or gypsum-board wall. They must fit snugly so that they make a tight grip as soon as they start to expand. Ordinary wood or machine screws can be used with these anchors.

In solid walls, lead and other split metal anchors are used. Holes for these anchors are drilled with either a heavy power drill and carbide-tipped bit or a hand-held star drill and small sledge. The power drill should be capable of

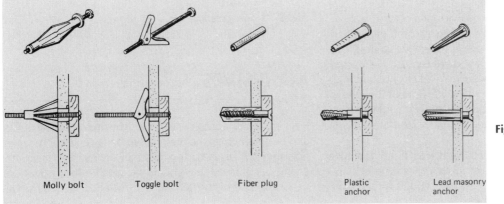

| Molly bolt | Toggle bolt | Fiber plug | Plastic anchor | Lead masonry anchor |

Fig. 2–10 Wall anchors.

working at lower drilling speeds such as are required when boring into masonry. The holes should be bored so that the anchors fit snugly. After they are tapped into place, they are expanded by tightening a screw or bolt. In some cases, the sides of the sleeve are forced out, while in others, a machine bolt with a tapered nut on the end pulls back against the sleeve to spread it apart.

RIVETS

Rivets make effective small fasteners for canvas, leather, and thin sheets of metal and wood. Several kinds of light rivets of different alloys are available for indoor and outdoor use. Only a ball-peen hammer and a metal block for backing are necessary to install them, though a rivet set (somewhat similar to a nail set) makes the job easier. The *rivet set* can be placed over the head of a rivet to help flatten and round it. When there is a lot of light riveting to do, it is worthwhile to get a small *pop riveter,* which works somewhat like a heavy-duty stapling gun. See Fig. 2–11.

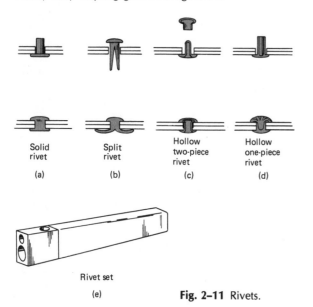

| Solid rivet | Split rivet | Hollow two-piece rivet | Hollow one-piece rivet |
| (a) | (b) | (c) | (d) |

Rivet set

(e)

Fig. 2–11 Rivets.

Solid rivets are used for heavier pieces of metal, or metal and wood. A hole is drilled through both pieces and burrs are removed so that the pieces fit tightly together. The rivets should be long enough to extend through the back a little more than the width of their own diameters before they are pounded down. To flatten them, the base of the rivet is placed against a solid block and its head is pounded with a hammer or rivet set. It is rounded off with a ball-peen hammer.

Split rivets are held in place with a small holding tool while they are pounded through leather or other materials. After they are all the way through, the work is turned over

so that the rivet's split legs can be flattened back against the surface.

Hollow two-piece rivets are made up of a solid, tapered section and a larger, hollow head. The tapered section is inserted into the hole from underneath and the hollow head placed over it. When the head is pounded, it flattens and grips the bottom section.

A *hollow one-piece rivet* is placed in the hole from beneath, so that its hollow end can be spread with a center punch and hammered back against the surface.

DOWELS

As fasteners, dowels are generally used with adhesives to strengthen joints. They may have spiral grooves cut into their sides to allow excess adhesive to squeeze out; their ends are camfered for easier driving. Diameters range between 1/8 and 1 in. (Pieces larger than this are called "rounds" instead of dowels.) Homemade dowels can be cut from standard 3-ft lengths of smooth-sided dowel, but each piece has to be camfered and grooved.

To use the dowels to strengthen a joint such as edge-glued boards in a table top, line up the edges to be drilled and mark them accurately. Then drill holes of the same diameter as the dowels, and slightly deeper than half their length. For greater control and accuracy, bore a small hole first to make the center and then bore the larger hole. Coat the dowels with a thin layer of adhesive and let it start to set before the dowels are tapped into place. As an aid in positioning, a doweling jig will hold the bit right on the mark. See Fig. 2–12.

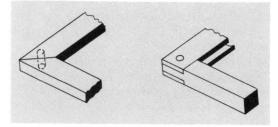

Fig. 2–12 Strengthening joints with dowels.

ADHESIVES

It is very important to choose the right kind of adhesive. The choice depends on the materials to be fastened or repaired, how they will be used, and how they are put together. Some of the possibilities that should be taken into account are: exposure to moisture or water; resistance to heat; drying time and temperature; flexibility; whether clamps can be used; whether the surfaces are large or small; whether joints are tight or loose; whether the materials are porous or not.

The many kinds of adhesives fall into categories according to whether they are made from natural or synthetic substances, what types of materials they must bind, and the conditions under which they work best.

There are several standard adhesives for wood joints and general workshop use. *White glue,* a *polyvinyl resin,* makes strong joints in wooden furniture for indoor use where it is dry. *Resorcinol* makes an even stronger joint in wood and withstands outdoor moisture, rain, and heat. *Casein* is a familiar workshop adhesive that has been in use for years. It is strong enough for many jobs, but will not withstand much moisture.

For small jobs, *cellulose, rubber-based,* and *plastic* or *model cements* all work well with both porous and nonporous materials.

Sheets of finishing materials can be fastened to large wooden surfaces, (such as laminated plastic and linoleum on countertops) with *contact cements.*

Ceiling and wall tiles, ceramics, and paneling are fastened with *mastics* with either a caulking tube or a toothed trowel.

For fastening metal to metal, glass, or almost anything else, *epoxies* create an extremely strong bond. They are especially effective with nonporous materials.

Special *plastic cements* are available to repair plastics, such as *vinyl, acrylic, styrene,* and *polystyrene.* Some of these cements are good for general household repairs with wood, glass, ceramics, and materials where waterproof adhesive is necessary.

Fiberglass requires a *polyester resin. Latex-based adhesives* are used for fabrics, carpeting, and clothbacked wallcoverings. For simply pasting paper and cardboard, inexpensive *natural pastes* and *rubber cements* will do. To seal kitchen, bathroom and other moisture prone areas against water, *silicone rubber sealants* are used, while *silicone glues* will fasten fixtures to walls in these same areas.

Kinds of Adhesives

White Glue (Polyvinyl Resin) White glue is a standard workshop adhesive for wood joints, but it is limited to materials to be used indoors since heavy moisture or high temperatures weaken it. It is effective for binding wood, and it can be used for other porous materials like fabrics, leather, and cardboard.

With metals, white glue causes corrosion. When it is used with wood surfaces that are to be stained, it should be wiped clear of the joints immediately since the stain will not penetrate areas where the glue has dried. White glue dries quickly and the joint can be handled in an hour or so, though it takes several hours to set and reach its full strength. The

temperature during the drying period should be 70°F or higher.

Resorcinol Resorcinol is the preferred adhesive for joints in wooden furniture, boats, and other porous materials that will be subjected to outdoor conditions of moisture and heat. It is a very strong synthetic adhesive packaged as a powdered catalyst and a wine-colored resinous liquid which must be mixed together. Where joints are loose, it serves as a gap-filler. Where they are tight, it bonds equally well. As with white glue, the drying temperature must be 70°F or more, and clamps should be used until the adhesive sets (about 8 hrs.). Its strength increases for several weeks after it dries.

Casein Glue With interior furniture, woods, and other porous materials, casein glue makes strong joints. Whether they are tight or loose and require a filler, it doesn't matter. The use of casein glue, made from milk curds, has stood the test of time, but it cannot withstand heavy moisture. Used in the proper applications, it is inexpensive and strong enough. It has one advantage over many of the synthetic adhesives: it can be applied, at low temperatures.

Cellulose Cements These clear household cements make strong, fast-drying joints in both porous and some nonporous materials.They are available under a number of labels and are intended for small jobs, such as repairing toys, making models, gluing small wood joints, and joining the broken pieces of decorative items. Cellulose cements, however, are not good for holding metal to metal because the solvents must be free to evaporate quickly. Joints made with cellulose cement suffer some shrinkage since it dries so quickly.

Rubber-Based Cements These are general-purpose cements for porous and nonporous materials, such as woods, fabrics, metal, glass, rubber gaskets, and porcelain. This type of cement is impervious to water and can be used to make small repairs on underwater objects. Although rubber-based cements are reasonably strong, they are not the first choice for wood-to-wood joints since there are other, stronger wood adhesives.

Plastic Cement There are many varieties of plastic cement for particular plastics or for general household use. These can be used for repairing shower curtains, glasses frames, ceramics, plastic swimming pools, and small household items, as well as for constructing plastic models. They are highly resistant to moisture but are limited in their ability to withstand heat. With large joints, they require clamping.

Mastics Rubber resin and latex-base mastics are the best adhesives for attaching paneling, ceramic tiles, vinyl floor tiles, linoleum, and wall and ceiling tiles. Mastics are applied with a notched trowel over large surfaces, or with a caulking-gun tube on narrower strips (e.g., on furring).

Contact Cements Contact cements are instant-bonding adhesives for attaching plastic laminates, linoleum, leather, tiles, and other nonwooden materials to large wooden surfaces. Their overall strength results from their large areas of contact. Both surfaces are coated and allowed to set slightly; they then bond as soon as they touch each other. The bond dries quickly at temperatures above 65°F and sets in a day or so. While it is being applied, it is highly flammable.

Epoxies Epoxies make the strongest adhesive bonds between any materials, whether porous or not. They are unaffected by heat or moisture. They are the only adhesives that make good metal-to-metal joints. They also work well with glass, plastics, porcelain, brick, and most other materials. The hardener and resin in epoxies interact chemically so that the adhesive hardens quickly and makes an exceedingly strong waterproof joint that does not shrink. The two ingredients should be mixed together in a ventilated area following the manufacturer's instructions taking care to avoid splattering the epoxy on the skin. Since the mixture hardens quickly, it should be used at once. The pieces being fastened must be exactly in position. For drying, the temperature should be 70°F or more. Epoxies set in a few hours.

Polyester Resin Cement This is the cement for repairing fiberglass. It also makes strong joints with wood and polished stones. It comes into frequent use in repairing fiberglass boats, camping equipment, and the like.

Silicone Rubber Sealants and Glues As a caulking compound, silicone rubber makes a flexible, waterproof seal for bathtubs, tiles, basins, metal, and fiberglass. As a glue, it will fasten fiberglass, metal, and ceramic fixtures to walls that may be exposed to heavy moisture.

COMMON HARDWARE

REINFORCING HARDWARE

Reinforcing hardware can help strengthen almost any kind of wooden joint. Metal plates come in a variety of shapes for use in strengthening chair legs, tabletops, cabinet sides, and heavier wooden structures. They vary in length, width, and weight, as well as in types of metal and finishes. There are four basic shapes, three of which are flat (See Fig. 2–13).

Mending plates are straight, flat metal plates that can be screwed flush or mortised into end-to-end or edge-to-edge joints. Where their appearance detracts from a piece of furniture, they can be recessed into a mortise and covered over. *Flat corner plates* are flat, L-shaped metal strips used in connecting the flat, flush surfaces of an L joint (such as corners on a wooden frame for a screen). *T-plates* are also flat, but they are shaped like crosses to connect the flush sides in a T joint. *Inside corner braces* are narrow strips of metal bent at right angles, with legs of equal or different lengths, for reinforcing inside corners. When they are to be used decoratively where they can be seen on chairs and tables, they can be purchased in attractive metals and finishes.

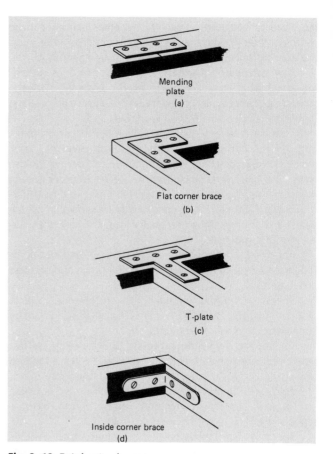

Mending plate
(a)

Flat corner brace
(b)

T-plate
(c)

Inside corner brace
(d)

Fig. 2–13 Reinforcing braces.

Wood that has been joined with nails, screws, or adhesives is more likely to need strengthening hardware than if dado or lap joints have been used. Screw holes should be drilled for reinforcing hardware to ensure that it is pulled tightly against the joint. One or two plates may be adequate for a single joint, but several plates or braces are often needed to balance stresses when the work involves large surfaces, such as tabletops.

SHELF HARDWARE

There are several types of shelf hardware for fixed shelves (Fig. 2–14), adjustable cabinet shelves, and adjustable wall shelves. A pair of *steel shelf brackets,* ribbed for strength, can be attached with screws to support heavily loaded shelves in a permanent position. These brackets are available in different lengths and weights according to the loads they are expected to bear. Screws for these must be anchored in solid materials such as studs or masonry. Where more modest loads are expected, adjustable brackets may be used. *Wall shelf hardware* consists of long, thin uprights with vertical slots which support flattened shelf brackets.

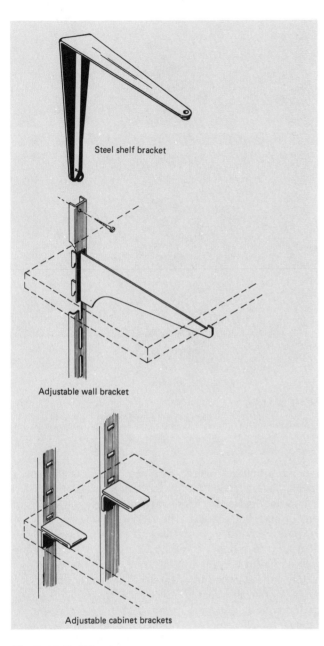

Fig. 2–14 Shelf hardware.

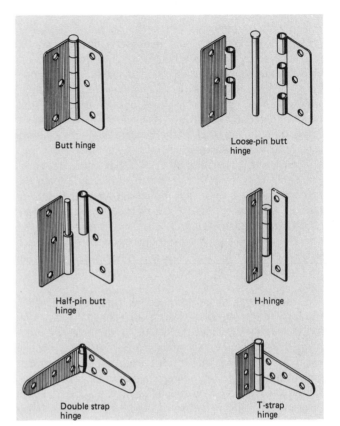

Fig. 2–15 Types of hinges.

brackets or clips. Two uprights are attached on each side of the cabinet, one toward the back corner and one toward the front. They may be screwed onto the surface or recessed. Short, doubled-over clips are inserted into each of the four slotted strips and the shelves may be moved up or down by repositioning the clips. With both fixed and adjustable shelf hardware, care must be taken in positioning them on the wall so that the supporting brackets and shelves will be level.

DOOR HARDWARE

Hinges

Most door hinges are butt hinges of some form. Cabinet doors, light folding doors, interior and exterior doors, and furniture doors all use different kinds of butt hinges (Fig. 2–15). Cabinet hinges are usually *tight-pin butt hinges* with leaves which are permanently attached to each other. To remove a cabinet door, one leaf of the hinge must be unscrewed. Since cabinet doors may be flush or may have an overlapping lip, their hinges vary considerably in shape. Doors which must fold or swing in both directions use *double-acting hinges*. Interior and exterior doors usually have either *loose-pin hinges* or *half-pin hinges* which can be re-

These movable brackets permit the shelves to be moved up or down. The tips of the brackets are designed to dig into the bottoms of the shelves to hold them in place. Therefore, the shelves should be slightly wider than the brackets. The strength of the brackets and shelves requires that the uprights be attached to a solid wall, such as plaster and lath or studs, and that they be properly spaced for the load. Cabinet shelves require supports at all four corners. *Adjustable cabinet hardware* consists of strips of uprights which have either horizontal slots or pairs of holes for inserting supporting

moved without removing the screws. The pin in the loose-pin type is worked loose and removed to free the leaves from each other. Doors attached with half-pin hinges can be lifted off the supporting half that is attached to the door jamb. Consoles for electronic equipment often use *continuous* or *piano hinges* to hold their doors or tops exactly in place. Ornamental hinges may be elaborately patterned or simple rustic hinges, such as the H hinge or H-L hinge used in colonial style cabinetry.

Some butt hinges and other door hardware are made specifically to fit either right or lefthand doors. Before buying the hardware, it is necessary to find out whether a door is right- or lefthand. As observed from the outside of a door, if a door is hinged on its right side and opens away from you it takes righthand hardware. If it opens toward you, it must be hinged on the left side to take righthand hardware. If it opens in the opposite manner, it will require lefthand hardware.

Strap hinges make up a second category of hinges. Although they were once widely used for many types of doors, in current practice double-leaf strap hinges are used mainly for heavy doors on garages or for gates. Each hinge leaf forms an elongated triangle which is fastened to the door or supporting wall. *T hinges* are strap hinges with one rectangular shaped leaf to attach to a narrow support. Strap hinges are available in lengths of a few inches to over a foot and are proportionately lighter or heavier to carry different loads.

There are also many special hinges: pivot hinges which fasten to the top of lightweight swinging and folding doors, spring-loaded hinges for some cabinet and screen doors, invisible knife hinges for consoles.

Locks

Door locks fall into three basic categories: mortise locks installed vertically within the door, auxiliary rim-type locks attached to the inside face of the door, and cylindrical locks inserted through the door. See Fig. 2-16.

Mortise locks consist of a thin rectangular case which holds the latch and dead-bolt mechanisms. A deep mortise must be cut in the edge of the door so that the lock will fit snuggly. Mortise locks are designed with their latches facing in different directions for right- and lefthanded doors. Because of the width of the mortise, doors must also have a minimal thickness of 1 3/8 in. Heavier mortise locks, which offer greater security, require even thicker doors. Holes are drilled through both faces of the door to attach the knob shaft and knob and also to insert the key.

Auxiliary rim-type locks mount on the inside face of the door and the adjacent door jamb. Their latches and dead-bolts are opened by a key from the outside and by a latch or key from the inside. The nightlatch rim locks are not nearly as secure as the vertical-bolt types. The vertical-bolt

Fig. 2–16 Door locks.

lock has a bolt mechanism that interlocks vertically with a mating plate attached to the door jamb.

Cylindrical locks include the key-in-the-knob locks and interior push-button locks. The locking mechanism is inside a cylindrical housing, which fits into a hole in the door. The latch and dead-bolt are released by a key inserted in the hollow shaft within the outside knob. From the inside, the handle can be turned to release the latch after the locking button has been released. Cylindrical locks may be purchased with high-security cylinders to make entering more difficult. A high-security cylinder combined with an auxiliary vertical bolt lock on a solid door will make it difficult for anyone without a key to open the door.

Tubular locks are a light form of cylindrical lock used for interior doors which are locked from one side, such as in bathrooms and bedrooms. Instead of being locked by keys, they have push buttons or small turning latches.

Other types of special hardware for locking doors include heavy bars, hasps and staples, sliding bolts, and fastening chains.

Accessory Hardware

Among other *accessory hardware* for doors, there are stops and catches which protect walls and hold doors closed. Where there are convenient baseboards, *standard stops* may be screwed horizontally into the wood. Where doors are stopped some distance from walls, floor stops can be attached directly to the floor. Both types of stops have plastic or rubber-cushioned heads to prevent damage to the doors. Another type of stop can be attached directly to the door and dropped into position to wedge against the floor. Only certain types of doors require catches. Gates and wooden screen doors may be held closed from the inside with simple hook and eye catches. Spring-loaded snap catches attach to the outside to hold screen doors tightly closed.

Cabinets employ several kinds of catches. Magnetic catches hold by the magnetic attraction between the unit attached to the door and the unit on the inside of the cabinet. Roller-type catches engage a fixed strike plate attached to the inside of the cabinet. Friction catches are shaped so that the projecting unit mounted on the door interlocks with the adjustable unit inside the cabinet.

OTHER HARDWARE

Windows, drawers, cabinet doors, and furniture use a variety of small hardware accessories. Windows require some form of sash lock. There are simple interlocking sash locks for double-hung windows, latch locks for sliding or hinged windows, and key locks for all kinds of windows. Windows also may have attachments such as metal stops to hold them up after opening. Pulls for drawers and doors may be almost any shape from knobs and rings to elongated handles. They may be made from wood, ceramics, plastic, or metal, finished to fit different decorative styles.

PAINTS AND CLEAR FINISHES

Among the many paints and finishes, only a few types may be formulated to protect a particular material from moisture and marring. A little knowledge of the major types of finishes and their uses, a little advice from a paint dealer, and information from the labels on the containers will be enough to select the right kind of finish for the job. Masonry, for example, requires special paints because the alkali in portland cement is destructive to most standard paints. Woods may require one type of paint in a moist bathroom and other types when used in dry interior areas, on floors, or for exterior siding. Some clear finishes are made to protect wood from outdoor moisture and weather, while others are made for wood which is kept dry and handled carefully.

Paints protect surfaces from moisture and a certain amount of wear by forming a thin, hard layer of film. This consists of colored pigment and binders left after the carrying vehicle has evaporated. Paints are classified according to the composition of their vehicles. The largest categories are latex (emulsion paints), alkyd, oil-base, and catalytic paints. Each type is made in many different mixtures for interior and woods, masonry, metals, floors and decks, gypsum board, and other materials. Each paint vehicle has its own individual characteristics that set it apart from other paints and make it the best choice for certain applications.

KINDS OF PAINT

Latex paint is popular not only because its finish is durable and attractive but because latex is easier to apply and clean up than are other types of paint. It is easier to use because its base or vehicle is water. As a result, spilled or spattered paint that has not dried can be cleaned up with a wet rag. Brushes, painting pads, rollers and pans, and other equipment used with latex paint can be washed clean in warm, soapy water. If necessary, latex paint may be thinned with water. Because water evaporates quickly, two or three coats of latex can be applied during the same day—each coat dries in an hour or so. Fresh plaster walls, which normally cannot be painted for some time because of their active alkalis, can be painted with latex as soon as they are hard. Dampness is no problem. When the outside of a house is too damp to paint with other paints, latex can be applied just as if the surface were dry. A little rain in the middle of the latex painting job will not hurt it.

Latex paints formulated for particular materials, such as exterior siding or masonry, are often just as effective as other paints made especially for these materials. There are latex paints for exterior wood siding and trim, asphalt siding, brick, concrete, asbestos cement, gypsum board, plaster, interior wood trim, plywood paneling, and certain kinds of metals. But other types of paint are better for some surfaces, such as floors and decks, some metals, and interior walls and woods exposed to very heavy moisture or frequent scrubbing.

Alkyd paint, composed of alkyd resins, forms one of the toughest, longest lasting films of any of the paints. It holds tightly in moist areas whether on exterior siding and trim or in kitchens, bathrooms, or basements. For the interior areas, the gloss and semigloss paints will retain their luster on window sills, doors, and other surfaces that need frequent scrubbing. Mineral spirits or turpentine can be used as a thinner, but for inside work, mineral spirits have the advantage of having little odor. Finally, alkyd paint dries quickly, within a number of hours.

Oil-base paints were once widely used but have been pretty much replaced by latex and alkyd except for use on exterior siding. For older houses which have been painted many times, oil-base house paints may adhere better than the newer types of paint. They can be used on masonry and metals in addition to wood, but there are better paints for these materials.

Enamels dry to leave a very hard, smooth gloss or semigloss surface. This hard, resistant coating is used on decks, floors, exterior trim, and even in interior areas where a glossy, hard surface is required to stand up to heavy use or scrubbing. Alkyd enamels are generally used for exterior trim. Both alkyd and latex enamels are used for interior woodwork.

Epoxy or *catalytic paints* interact chemically to produce a hard impervious coating, which will adhere to nonporous surfaces that other paints cannot grip. They are expensive but may be the only paint that will hold on areas of ceramic tiles, plastic panels, mirror surfaces, and metal fixtures.

Portland cement paint is the paint to use on previously unfinished concrete and brick surfaces. Damp walls are no problem. In fact, masonry walls have to be sprayed before and after cement paint is applied so that it will adhere and dry properly.

Special paints are made for use where standard paints fail. *Stain-killing paint* has a shellac base and is saturated with white pigment to cover surfaces previously finished with dark stains. It obliterates stains and serves as a base for standard paints. *Sand paint* consists of latex paint and a commercially prepared, fine sand which forms a rough, textured coating. It is used on ceilings to hide taped joints between sheets of gypsum board and to create a swirled, textured effect. There are also paints for rusty metals, areas that may be subject to mildew, boat bottoms, and other problem surfaces.

Paints are manufactured to be used under a range of conditions. They are basically divided into *exterior* and *interior paints*. For houses in hot, dry areas, exterior paint would be formulated to withstand high temperatures and intense sunshine. Other exterior paints may be made to withstand heavy moisture or mildew. They may also be self-cleaning, in that they chalk so as to remove surface dirt. Interior paints do not have to withstand exposure to severe weather, but they may have to withstand scrubbing, marring, mildew, and other injurious indoor conditions.

Varnish is a clear protective finish that allows the grain of the wood to show through on floors, furniture, and other wooden surfaces. There are several types and shades. Floor varnish is mixed for floors, interior varnish for furniture, and exterior or spar varnish for outside trim. Clear, light shades of varnish will darken wood surfaces only slightly, while darker shades will produce correspondingly darker finishes. Modern urethane varnishes are very hard and highly resistant to moisture and heat. Varnish can be used only on unpainted surfaces, though it can be applied to stained wood. Varnish dries slowly, in about 24 hours. During this time, dust tends to get into it unless the drying area is virtually dust-free.

Shellac produces a clear finish but lacks the heat and moisture resistance of varnish. It is a natural resin dissolved in denatured alcohol, and can be used as an undercoating for varnish, as a sealer for stains, or by itself. There are two types, white and orange shellac, which produce light or dark tones. Since it is organic, it breaks down if it is not used within several months after it is made. A date indicating its life expectancy is usually stamped on the container. The proportions of shellac resin to alcohol are described as a certain "cut." For example, shellac may be purchased in a 4- or 5-lb. cut (4 or 5 lbs/gal) and diluted to a 1½-lb. cut for finishing furniture. Shellac dries within an hour under normal conditions.

Lacquer in several thin layers can be used to create a clear finish for small, unpainted pieces of wooden furniture or ornaments. There are several types, some for brushing and others for spraying. There are also lacquers for glossy or satin finishes. Lacquer dries quickly so brush strokes must be smooth and accurate to cover the entire surface. Flow the lacquer on rapidly without brushing over any area already covered. Since it is difficult to see clear lacquer, be sure that each brush stroke is adjacent to the previous stroke or skip spots will appear when the lacquer dries.

WOOD

To select the right kind of wood for construction or furniture making, it is necessary to know about the different kinds of wood, what they are used for, how they differ, and how to order the correct sizes and amounts. Finished lumber, the form sold in lumber yards, is made by kiln drying and planing rough-sawn lumber. Both hardwood lumber (from broad-leafed trees) and softwood lumber (from needle-bearing trees) is sawn, dried, and milled in similar ways. Plywood is made by bonding together thin sheets of wood peeled from logs. Where and how plywood can be used is determined by types of the wood and adhesives, their grades and resistance to water, and the way the sheet is constructed.

Lumber and plywood are both used to make furniture and cabinets. Where surfaces are large and flat, veneered plywood can be attractive and cheaper than lumber. In house construction, lumber is used for the overall framing while plywood may be used as an underlayment for floors, roofs, and exterior walls. Other forms of wood such as shingles, moldings, and strips are also used in house construction.

As their names suggest, hardwoods tend to be harder and denser and have more attractive grains than softwoods. Hardwoods, such as maple, cherry, walnut, oak, birch, and exotic imports like mahogany are used in furniture, cabinets, high-quality veneer paneling, handles, and flooring. They are seldom used in construction, except for boat building, where their strength is important. Softwoods such as pines, fir, spruce, redwood, and cedar are primary woods for house construction and are also used for interior trim, shelves and furniture. Cedar's resistance to decay and its ability to repel some insects makes it useful for fence posts, shingles, and protective chests and closets. Pine is used for informal furniture, moldings, and strips because of its attractive surface and easy workability. The resistance of redwood to decay and its attractive coloring make it popular and practical for siding and outdoor furniture.

LUMBER

Finished lumber stocked by lumberyards has gone through a number of steps to make it usable. Logs have been sawed to produce lumber with the grain running in the desired direction. Plain sawing produces the maximum amount of good lumber from a log and results in lumber with either flat or edge grain. Quarter sawing produces lumber with an edge grain, which is less likely to warp than flat grain. See Fig. 2–17.

Before rough-sawn lumber is machine-planed to smooth its sides and surfaces, it has its full "nominal" dimensions: a rough-sawn 1 X 8 is 1 in. thick and 8 in. wide. Planing and kiln drying reduce these dimensions substantially. For example, the finished dimensions of a nominal 1 X 8 are 3/4 X 7 1/4 in. Similarly, boards of other sizes are actually smaller than the nominal dimensions used to describe them.

The cost of lumber is calculated by multiplying the cost per square foot times the number of square feet purchased. A square foot is simply a 1-ft length of board which is 1 in.

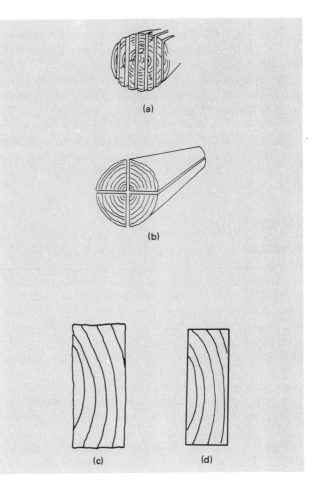

Fig. 2–17 Types of boards: a) plain-sawed, b) quarter-sawed, c) rough-sawn, d) finished.

thick and 12 in. wide (all nominal dimensions). The quantity of lumber for a job may be expressed in terms of the number of square feet required. Thinner pieces of finished wood such as strips and moldings are priced by the linear or running foot rather than by the square foot.

Lumber is graded and sold according to the number and kind of defects like knots, checks, and decay. *Select lumber,* which is the highest quality, is divided into several categories according to quality:

No. 1, or *2 Select,* or *B* and *Better,* is clear face material with a few minor imperfections that will not detract from appearance when covered with paint. Select grades are used in furniture, panel veneer, and where the surface appearance is important.

Common lumber, which is used in construction where knots and other defects are acceptable, is divided into five categories: *No. 1 Common* has a few sound and tight knots; *No. 2 Common* has more and larger knots and other defects; *No. 3 Common* has loose knots and knotholes; *No. 4* and *No. 5 Common* have major defects, which may weaken them. The first three grades of Common are used

Table 2-3 Lumber Sizes

Nominal size (in.)	Actual size (in.)
1 x 2	3/4 x 1 1/2
1 x 3	3/4 x 2 1/2
1 x 4	3/4 x 3 1/2
1 x 6	3/4 x 5 1/2
1 x 8	3/4 x 7 1/4
1 x 10	3/4 x 9 1/4
1 x 12	3/4 x 11 1/4
2 x 3	1 1/2 x 2 1/2
2 x 4	1 1/2 x 3 1/2
2 x 6	1 1/2 x 5 1/2
2 x 8	1 1/2 x 7 1/4
2 x 10	1 1/2 x 9 1/4
2 x 12	1 1/2 x 11 1/4
4 x 4	3 1/2 x 3 1/2
4 x 6	3 1/2 x 5 1/2

for siding, framing, shelves, sheathing, and solid wood paneling where they are clear enough of defects. The last two grades are used where strength is not important.

In ordering lumber, the grade, kind of wood, quantity, and dimensions of the stock must all be given, for example, No. 1 Common pine, 10 lengths of 8 ft., 1 X 6's. The sequence of information may vary but all of the information is necessary. Softwood is stocked in even lengths, such as 6 ft., 8 ft., 10 ft., etc., with the result that some short ends may be wasted. Hardwood can be purchased in both odd- and even-foot lengths.

PLYWOOD

Plywood can be used in rough construction, as a fine veneer paneling, or as finished siding. Basically, veneer plywood is constructed of thin layers, or plies, of wood bonded together, with their grains at right angles to each other for strength and to prevent warping or splitting. For outdoor use, waterproof adhesives are used to make exterior grades of plywood that will withstand the weather. Interior grades are resistant to the normal moisture in a house and may be used in all but very damp inside areas such as wet basements. Exterior plywoods use softwoods for both inner and outer layers. Interior plywoods may have hardwood or softwood veneers over inner layers of softwood. A variety of plywood called lumber-core plywood has a central core of wooden strips edge-glued together to balance stresses in the sheet. This solid central core allows screws and nails to hold firmly along the edge of the sheet, something they cannot do in standard laminated plywood. See Fig. 2–18.

Grades of plywood are more complicated than those of lumber because each side may be of a different grade. The grades of the face and back are designated by letters: A - clear, smooth, and paintable; B - solid surface veneer with tight knots; C - knotholes and small splits; Plugged C - like C but knotholes patched; D - large knotholes and other defects. The letters are combined to designate the grades of both the face and back of the sheet; for example, A-A (face–

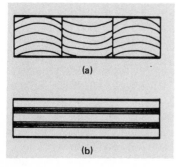

Fig. 2–18 Plywood: a) veneer-core, b) lumber-core.

back) for two smooth sides; A-B for a smooth face but lower-grade back; C-C for knotholes in both sides. The inner layers are usually C or D grades. If the plywood is to be used indoors where only one side shows, an interior A-B grade may be adequate. B-C or B-D grades are utility grades which will provide one smooth solid side as an underlay for flooring or as cabinet backing. Natural finished interior plywood of cabinet quality is indicated by the letter N.

Softwood plywoods are also classified in one of five groups according to the degree of stiffness of the woods used in their manufacture. Those of the highest level of stiffness (Group 1), for example, may contain wood from Douglas fir, Western larch or southern pines. The group number, face grades, interior or exterior classifications and other data are stamped on the back of each sheet of softwood plywood.

COVERINGS

FLOOR

Vinyl, linoleum, vinyl asbestos, cork, and asphalt are the major types of *resilient flooring*. They are called resilient because they tend to recover their normal shape after loads from heavy pieces of furniture have been removed. Unfortunately, they also tend to conform to the shapes of bumps, hollows, and projecting nails in the underlying floor, and so must be laid on a very smooth surface.

Most types of resilient flooring are available in either sheets or tiles. Sheets, cut from rolls of 6, 9, or 12-ft. widths, are difficult to lay because they must be cut in large, single strips to fit the exact shape of the room. In kitchen areas, these large pieces have the advantage of having fewer seams, in which to collect dirt, than smaller tiles. Tiles of vinyl, vinyl asbestos, asphalt, and cork are available in 12 X 12 in. squares, with thicknesses ranging from 1/16 to 1/8 in. Some patterns are still available in 9 X 9-in. squares. They are made in a great variety of colors, patterns, textures, and embossings and may have either self-stick or plain backs. Since they are small they can be replaced more easily than sheet flooring if they are damaged.

Among floor coverings *vinyl sheets* and *tiles* offer the greatest variety of designs, strong colors, and types of surfaces. They can be installed loose (under baseboard moldings) or held in place with adhesives. Many vinyls are cushioned with foam backing or a layer of foam between the vinyl and backing. These vinyls give the feeling of walking on carpeting. Vinyls have high resistance to stains from both acids and bases and can take hard wear and abrasion with little effect. Furthermore, they do not have to be protected with wax as do most other floor coverings.

Linoleum is noted for its durability and low cost; however, it scratches easily and must be waxed to protect its appearance. Since it is laid in sheets instead of tiles, it is difficult for the average person to install. Linoleum should not be installed on or below grade (ground level) or in areas of heavy moisture because it will soften and lose its resiliency and resistance to abrasion. Strongly alkaline cleaning agents will also injure it.

Vinyl asbestos tiles are often used in place of vinyl because of their lower costs and excellent wearing characteristics. They consist of a mixture of vinyl resins binding asbestos fibers together. These resins are tough and resist abrasion and chemical stains almost as well as pure vinyl. The wearing surface, which is uniform through the thickness of the tile, is semiporous and should be polished with a water-based emulsion to reduce absorption. Like vinyl tiles, it can be used on or below grade and on concrete. Vinyl asbestos colors are more subtle than those in pure vinyl tiles and can withstand strong cleaning solutions without being changed in appearance.

Asphalt tiles are cheaper than the other resilient flooring tiles, but they can easily be ruined by grease, oil stains, strong cleaners, paint, uneven subflooring, high and low temperatures, and heavy abrasion. They have been largely replaced by vinyl asbestos tiles because of the excellent wearing characteristics and relatively low cost of vinyl asbestos.

Cork tiles are ideal where it is important that the flooring be comfortable to walk on, quiet, resilient, and an effective insulator. Although cork is the most resilient of the resilient flooring materials, it is also the most porous. It stains, absorbs moisture, and wears easily. *Vinyl cork tiles* have a thin layer of vinyl bonded to the surface which withstands abrasion, stains, and moisture almost as well as vinyl and vinyl asbestos tiles. Cork tiles cannot be installed below grade because they absorb moisture and become loose.

Ceramic tiles can be used for a highly decorative floor covering that is scratch and stain resistant and washable. Among the several kinds of ceramic tiles, dark red unglazed quarry tiles in 6 X 6 in. squares were standard floor tiles for many years. Although they are still used, they are now made in many different sizes, colors, and shapes. Ceramic mosaics composed of 1 X 2 in. or 2 X 2 in. units are available in many patterns and colors for floors. They are held together by a detachable layer of paper, which is peeled off once the tiles are in place in the adhesive. Heavy-duty glazed 8 X 8 in. tiles also can be used as a floor covering. This is a standard size, but other sizes and shapes are also available. All ceramic tiles require a smooth and level floor as a base. Wooden floors are preferable because they are usually smoother than concrete or brick floors. Where the existing floor is extremely uneven, it may be simplest to install a layer of hardboard or plywood as a base.

Slate tiles, made from natural blocks of slate, will form very durable floor surfaces suitable for entryways and other heavily traveled areas. Slate is washable and easy to maintain, though it becomes slippery if it is constantly wet. Tiles are available in several natural colors of grey, red, green, blue, and black, and their shapes range from 6 X 6 in. squares to flagstone contours. They can be laid over concrete, brick, wood or any other solid and level floor by using mastic and grouting.

Wooden flooring may be either the common tongue-and-groove, endmatched strips or parquet squares. Both are generally made from hardwoods such as oak or maple. Their surfaces may be prefinished or, more often, unfinished. Tongue-and-groove strips are blind-nailed to plywood subflooring, while parquet squares are interlocked and attached with a mastic adhesive. Parquet tiles, usually 9 X 9 in., can stand hard wear since they are made of small strips of wood bonded tightly together. Both strip and parquet flooring require dry subsurfaces in order to remain smooth and unwarped. However, parquet may be used over a concrete floor that is below grade if the concrete is covered with a protective sheet of plastic.

Carpeting offers several advantages over other floor coverings; it offers softness and the ability to insulate and reduce noise. It is available for wall-to-wall installation in widths of 9, 12, and 15 ft. or as carpet tiles or room-size rugs. Wall-to-wall carpeting may be cushion-backed or it may be placed over pads of latex, vinyl foam, sponge rubber, or jute, which will provide a resilient surface to prolong the life of the carpet, and make a soft, insulated underlayer. Wall-to-wall carpeting may be tacked in place, bonded with an adhesive, or stretched and held by wooden strips with sharp protruding pins along the edge of the floor. Cushioned backing has a layer of sponge rubber or latex which maintains the shape of the carpet and holds it in place on the floor. If the carpeting does start to slip, double-face tape can be used around its edge to hold it down. Indoor-outdoor carpeting with a moisture-proof backing, rather than standard carpeting, should be used over concrete or tiles of vinyl and vinyl asbestos since the moisture that accumulates on these tile surfaces will cause mildew in unprotected carpeting. Carpet tiles have a foam-rubber backing and are available in 12 X 12 in. and 18 X 18 in. squares. Some are adhesive-backed while others have plain backs for installation over double-faced tape.

CEILING

Ceilings can be covered with tiles, gypsum board, plaster, or other materials. Tiles are the easiest to use, but gypsum board and plaster can make a ceiling look as if it were new. Of the two, gypsum board is easier for the nonprofessional to work with. Although ceilings can be covered with wallpaper, plywood paneling, and other materials, only the more common tiles and gypsum board will be described here.

Ceiling tiles may be of the acoustical type with a perforated or textured surface to reduce sound, or they may be plain tiles with a nonacoustical surface. Most of them are made of compressed fibers of wood, though some are made of mineral or fiberglass for greater resistance to fire and greater durability. Some surfaces are coated with vinyl so that they can be wiped clean of dirt and grease.

There are two general methods of making a tiled ceiling. Tiles may be attached with staples or adhesives directly to the ceiling or to furring strips attached to the ceiling, or they may be supported by a metal grid framework several inches below the original ceiling. To attach them directly to the ceiling requires that the ceiling be reasonably solid. If chunks of plaster are missing or if there are only joists (as in basement ceilings), furring strips of narrow boards can be attached around the edges of the walls and at intervals across the ceiling to serve as a base for the tiles. In some situations, there are advantages to lowering the ceiling. Tiles fit loosely into the grids and can be removed for access to pipes, wiring, or other fittings on the original ceiling.

Tiles that are to be attached to the ceiling or to furring strips are usually 1 X 1 ft., 1 X 2 ft., or 2 ft. square. Tiles or panels used in a lowered or dropped ceiling are larger; 2 X 2 ft. and 2 X 4 ft. panels are standard sizes.

Gypsum board can be attached to a damaged plaster or gypsum-board ceiling to make it look as though it were new. The old ceiling must be furred with narrow strips of wood so that the gypsum board can be nailed to a firm base. The furring strips are placed so that they back up all of the edges of the gypsum board sheets and provide support for the interior areas also. Since these sheets are heavy and awkward to handle, the thinner 3/8-in. thickness should be used. After the sheets are nailed in place, their edges must be taped with wallboard tape and covered with taping or joint compound. Each coating of compound is sanded smooth until the joint surface is flush with the rest of the ceiling. The entire ceiling can then be painted. To cover up rough areas, sand paint is sometimes used.

WALL

Wallcoverings include both materials specifically made for walls and materials usually found on other surfaces. They are in such diverse forms as liquid-based finishes (paints and stains), flexible coverings (fabrics and wallpapers), tiles (ceramic and vinyl), panels (plywood veneers, plastic laminates), and masonry (stone and brick). Each is noted for certain features. For moisture and mildew resistance, plastic panels, laminated plastics, and vinyl wallcoverings should

be chosen. Acoustical tiles, carpeting, and cork will quiet a noisy room. If ease of installation and care, together with permanence, are important, factory-finished plywood paneling can be used. Where decorative effects are the primary concern, everything goes: fabrics, wallpapers, rich woods, and tiles of all kinds.

Before deciding on a covering, it is eye-opening to look over the possibilities. A number of coverings suitable for walls are described briefly to give an idea of what they are like, where they are used, and what is good or bad about them.

Wallpaper is a printed, plain-paper stock which may be coated or uncoated. Coated stock has a thin coating of protective plastic over its surface and can be washed. Wallpapers are printed in a multitude of colors, patterns, textures, and designs for different rooms and a variety of decorative effects. A standard single roll contains 36 sq. ft., regardless of its width and length. Since widths vary from approximately 18 to 28 in., lengths differ but each roll is usually long enough to contain enough for two full strips. There is less waste when wallpaper is ordered in double or triple rolls. Some papers are prepasted, but unpasted papers require a coat of wet paste after they are cut. Because they are made of light paper stock, wallpapers are easily damaged by moisture and abrasion and may mildew and peel in very moist laundry, bathroom, and basement areas.

Vinyl wallcovering are noted for their bright, strong colors, tough surfaces, and heavy backings. Their colors and patterns are printed in vinyl inks on vinyl-impregnated materials laminated to fabrics or strong paper backings, and coated with protective surfaces of vinyl. This makes them a good choice for walls that receive hard use. In hallways, vinyls can take rubbing, occasional gouging, dirty hands, and heavy scrubbing. They can withstand clouds of moisture in heavily used bathrooms and laundries. Their inks also stay fresh and bright without fading on walls flooded with sunlight.

Vinyls may be printed in colors and patterns similar to wallpapers or they may be textured, shaded, or embossed to resemble such materials as woods, fabrics, or grass cloths. Some are even coated to achieve the "wet look."

Rolls of vinyl wallcoverings are wider than those of wallpaper; 27 in. is a common width, but a single roll contains the standard 36 sq. ft. Their heavy backings make hanging and stripping easier and faster than with wallpaper.

Metal foils, whether plain, patterned, or textured, make striking wallcoverings. Thin layers of aluminim foil on one wall can be combined with different materials on the other walls to create a strong focus in a room. Their major disadvantage is their fragility. They are easily punctured and torn and should be used only in protected areas.

Grass cloth is hand or machine woven from jute or other natural materials, which are attached to nonwoven backings. For strength, they are hung over a layer of lining paper. (Lining paper is a base layer of porous paper that provides the necessary adhesion and backing for grass cloth, fabrics, and several other wallcoverings.) The appeal of these natural materials, and also their weakness, is their lack of uniformity. Variations in shading and fiber width, and changes as they mellow and fade over time, are all part of their individual beauty. In fact, one grass-cloth manufacturer makes it a point to say, "If the customer expects the above materials never to variate in weave and color, then she or he is no customer for this manmade cloth decoration." Since grass cloth will not withstand abrasion and is quite expensive, it is usually used only where it can be protected. In areas of hard use, synthetic grass cloths may be an acceptable compromise. Vinyl grass cloths are fabric backed and come in multiples of single rolls.

Burlap makes an inexpensive, informal wallcovering. Although it can be used as it comes from the bolt, it is also manufactured with colorful patterns in backed rolls. When it is unbacked, it has to be hung over lining paper. Wallcovering rolls are plain or prepasted and come in widths of 36 and 45 in. and in single and multiple rolls. All burlaps suffer the disadvantages of fading, staining, and collecting dust and should be hung in relatively clean areas.

Fine fabrics such as silks, linens, antique satins, and velvets are used to cover walls where expense is not a problem. Many of the fabrics wear well in heavily used areas but others, such as silks and linens, must be protected and treated carefully. Either standard 54-in. wide bolts or fabrics backed and cut in 30 and 35-in. wide rolls as wallcoverings can be hung. Backed rolls are easiest to hang, but material from standard bolts can be attached over lining paper with adhesives, double-faced tape, or staples in a lattice framework.

Carpeting with a tightly woven, flat surface and strong backing is a good wallcovering for noisy, heavily used rooms such as children's rooms and family rooms. It comes in a great variety of colors, patterns, textures, and weaves, and can be vacuumed just as if it were on the floor. Hanging it on the wall is awkward. Usually it is hung horizontally with adhesives or carpet tacks.

Cork in thin layers is attached to a paper backing and cut into double and triple rolls of 30 and 36-in. widths. There are various shades which, like wood, have a warm, soft feel on a wall surface. The surfaces must be protected since the thin layers of cork are easily damaged by abrasion and stains. Solid cork panels and tiles can take more punishment.

Solid cork is a popular, decorative wallcovering that is also sound-deadening. It has the warmth of wood and is functional enough to serve as a bulletin board in its tight-grained forms. Solid cork is manufactured in 2-in. thick pan-

els that are 1 X 2 ft., 2 X 4 ft., and larger. Floor tiles of cork are intermediate between the thick panels and thin layers attached to wallcover backings. All of these can be attached to walls. Fading, straining, and abrasion are the major disadvantages of uncoated cork as a wallcovering.

Wood paneling of boards rather than plywood is the closest thing to old-fashioned wooden interior walls. Tongue-and-groove boards are cut for interior paneling in widths of a few inches to over a foot and in varied lengths up to 8 ft. Most solid paneling is softwood, though hardwood paneling is available. Surfaces are rough or smooth, wood color can be light or dark, and the wood itself can be clear or knotty. By planing and cutting, old barn siding or plain boards from a lumber yard can be cut into solid paneling that is less expensive than the precut tongue-and-groove boards. Whatever boards are used, they must be nailed to a firm backing of furring strips or a plaster wall. Once they are up, they make a good sound barrier between rooms.

Plywood paneling with a natural wood veneer is in the same price range as moderately expensive vinyl wallcovering. Plywood paneling that is printed to resemble the wood grain of a veneer surface, or paneling with a printed vinyl surface is cheaper than veneer paneling, but they are usually not as attractive. Both kinds of paneling consist of laminated layers of interior-grade plywood in standard sheets 1/4 in. thick and 4 ft. wide by 8 ft. long. Interior-grade plywood is moisture resistant but it is not waterproof and may warp if used in damp spaces. Natural wood veneers are made from beautiful hardwoods such as cherry, walnut, pecan, and oak, as well as from softwoods and expensive imported woods. These veneers are peeled in thin sheets from high-quality logs and laminated to a plywood base. Softwood veneers may be textured or smoothly finished. For an unfinished appearance, thicker exterior plywood paneling can be used on inside walls. And since it is waterproof, it can be used in damp basement areas also. Vertical grooves lengthwise on panel surfaces provide a place to nail the paneling to the wall. They also create the impression of random-width boards rather than a solid sheet of wood.

Since paneling is thin and flexible, it should be installed over a solid surface such as an existing wall, a layer of gypsum board, or furring. If it is attached directly to wall studs, it will not be as firm or as sound-deadening as when it is attached to a solid surface.

Panels can be attached in several ways, for example, with adhesives, clips, or brads of the same color as the paneling. When brads are used, they are nailed along the vertical grooves where they can be hidden by covering them with wood putty of the same color as the paneling.

Gypsum board (also called "drywall" and Sheet Rock, a trade name) can be used for new walls in place of plaster and lath, or it can be nailed over old walls or a ceiling for a solid, new surface. Since it is unfinished it serves as a base for paint or other wallcoverings. Gypsum board consists of a layer of gypsum (1/4 to 5/8 in.) sandwiched between front and back layers of treated paper. The standard size of panel is 4 X 8 ft., but there are others of different lengths and widths. For basement walls and other moist areas, there is a waterproof form that will not absorb moisture and crumble. This is especially good as a base for tile around a shower or bathtub. Another variety is factory treated to increase its resistance to heat and fire. Where a thicker sound barrier is needed, 5/8-in. gypsum board muffles sound better than the standard 1/2-in. sheet. Even the need for final finishing can be avoided by getting factory-finished vinyl-faced panels. These are available in several colors and patterns but are much more expensive than plain gypsum board.

Hardboard panels consist of wood fibers laminated into strong 3/16- or 1/4-in. panels, which bend but do not crack. They are often used in place of plywood panels even though they lack the real wooden surface. Their finished surfaces are printed onto the hardboard; these may be decorative colors and designs, or they may resemble wood grains, marble, or other natural materials. This printed surface is protected by a hard, baked-on plastic coating that resists stains and scratches. If the panel is unfinished, it can be painted or used as a base for other finished wallcoverings. Standard hardboard panels are attached with adhesive. Pegboard is a perforated form of hardboard with multiple holes for hanging kitchenware, tools, toys, and other small objects. To leave room for inserting the hangers through the perforations, pegboard must be spaced out from the wall.

Fiberboard is an old-fashioned, soft greyish board of compressed fibers, which is still available in panels and in thicker acoustical panels for soundproofing walls. It looks best when painted. Since fiberboard is soft, it cannot take much abuse. It is attached to furring or directly to walls with nails or staples.

Ceramic wall tiles are one of the few wall coverings that can withstand water, scrubbing, and sunshine. Patterns and shapes include decorative, Mexican, designer, Moorish, and plain tiles. The 4 1/4 X 4 1/4 in. square tile is standard, but there are other sizes of squares from 1 to 6 in. on a side. Ceramic mosaics are a variation in which small tiles (1 X 1 in., 1 X 2 in., or 2 X 2 in.) are attached to a facing sheet, which is removed once the mosaic is in place in the adhesive. Grout is then applied between the small tiles. Because they stand up under moisture and scrubbing, tiles are often the first choice for bathroom walls and areas around the kitchen sink. One of their few difficulties is the grout, which tends to stain and show dirt readily.

Metal and *plastic tiles* are basically decorative and will not withstand water or hard use as ceramic tiles do. Copper and aluminum tiles with natural finishes fit into contemporary wall design. Bright-colored aluminum tiles are also available with baked on enamel surfaces. These tiles are a

standard 4 1/4 X 4 1/4 in. square and are attached with adhesive or double-faced tape. Since moisture does not corrode aluminum or plastic tiles, these materials can be used for decorative areas in kitchens.

Ceramic and *plastic brick tiles* come as individual tiles or in prefabricated sheets. Plastic brick tiles resemble brick with its variations in color and shape. It may even be sandblasted to look weathered. Ceramic brick tiles are made of a layer of real brick attached to a tile backing. Since the ceramic layer can withstand heat, these tiles are often used as wall coverings behind stoves. Plastic brick tiles cannot withstand heat and should not be placed where the temperature might rise to 135°F. Neither kind of brick tile can be used in fireplaces. Adhesive is used to attach both kinds of tiles, though some have self-stick backs, and some ceramic brick tiles are designed to be nailed to a backing.

Mirrors, whether of plate glass, sheet glass, or acrylic, create optical space as wallcoverings, but only plate-glass mirrors reproduce reflected images without distortion. All are available as sheets or tiles. The tiles can be attached with double-faced tapes.

Vinyl and *vinyl-asbestos wall tiles* make durable wallcoverings with all the advantages of vinyls in floor coverings. There are also special tiles in 12 X 12 in. squares made especially for walls. Both kinds of tile can be attached with adhesives, though some are self-sticking.

Polyurethane foam wall tiles are molded into thick wood- or stonelike textures in 12 X 12 in. squares. Since they are combustible, they should not be exposed to temperatures over 135°F. Some have self-stick backs; others require adhesives.

Acoustical tiles designed for ceilings also deaden sound as wall coverings. They may be in 12 X 12 in. squares or larger. Some have sculptured surfaces; others are perforated to absorb sound. They can be painted but must be treated carefully since they are soft and are easily punctured. Cleaning acoustical tiles is difficult because dust settles in the perforations and on the textured surfaces.

Laminated plastics, which resist abrasion, stains, moisture, moderate heat, and mild impact, can be used to cover walls as well as countertops. They can be highly decorative, with surfaces in solid colors, wood grains, and patterns. Their finishes range from gloss to velvet and nonreflective. They are made in various widths and lengths. Particle board is usually bonded to the back of laminated sheets before they are attached to walls, though prefabricated sheets are available. Where there is a solid, smooth surface of hardboard or plaster, laminated plastic can be bounded directly to it. Molding may be used to cover joints, or they may be left as they are.

Bathroom panels may be made of fiberglass, laminated plastic, or plastic sheets. They may be form-fitted for tub enclosures in sizes such as 5 X 5 ft. or 2 1/2 X 5 ft.; they may be L-shaped for corners; or they may be flat 4 X 8 ft.

sheets. Some are made in solid colors, while others are patterned or designed to look like marble or stone. Their ability to withstand heavy moisture while remaining easy to clean makes them popular for bathroom and laundry areas. Manufacturers offer several systems for attaching bathroom panels. Most of them involve adhesives and molding to create tight, waterproof joints.

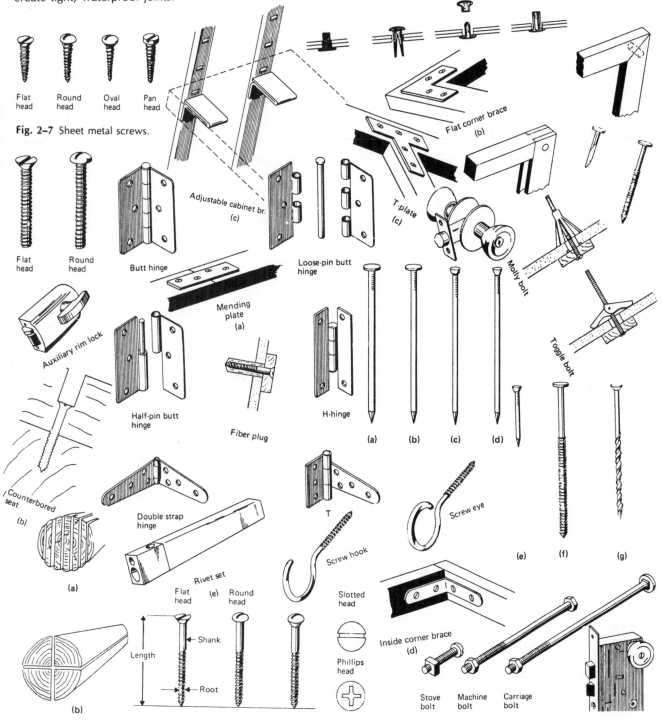

Flat head   Round head   Oval head   Pan head

Fig. 2–7 Sheet metal screws.

Flat head   Round head

Adjustable cabinet br. (c)

T-plate (c)

Butt hinge

Loose-pin butt hinge

Flat corner brace (b)

Molly bolt

Toggle bolt

Auxiliary rim lock

Mending plate (a)

Half-pin butt hinge

Fiber plug

H-hinge

(a)   (b)   (c)   (d)

Counterbored seat
(b)

Double strap hinge

T

Screw hook

Screw eye

(e)   (f)   (g)

Rivet set

Flat head   (e)   Round head

Slotted head

Inside corner brace (d)

Phillips head

Stove bolt   Machine bolt   Carriage bolt

(a)

(b)

Shank

Length

Root

3 Painting and Wallpapering

PAINTING

BRUSHES

The main tools used in painting are brushes, rollers, and spray equipment. Like any tools, they must be selected according to what needs to be done. In selecting a brush, the type and size depends on the type of paint or finish and the surface to be painted. Wall brushes must be wide for painting large, exterior walls. Sash brushes must be long and narrow with an angular cut for painting narrow window sashes. Regardless of their sizes and shapes, good quality brushes will release paint smoothly without losing their bristles in the paint and will last for years with good care.

Bristles

Whether a nylon or natural bristle brush should be used depends on the type of paint or finish. *Nylon bristles* can be used with almost any paint, including latex, alkyd, and exterior oil-base paints. They also can be used with enamels and varnishes, but the finish will not be as smooth as with natural bristles. Nylon bristles should not be used with solvents and finishes that attack nylon, such as paint remover, lacquer, epoxies, and some adhesives.

High-quality *natural bristles* have the ability to hold paint and release it in thin, smooth layers. (This is especially important with enamels and varnishes. The quality of their finish depends on laying down several thin layers.) Natural bristles are the best choice for oil-base paints, lacquer, shellac, varnish, and enamel. They should not be used with water-thinned paints like latex because natural bristles absorb water, swell, and eventually loosen.

You can judge the quality of a brush by its bristles. They should feel full to the hand. The greater their surface area, the greater their paint holding power. When pressed against a surface, bristles should be springy rather than rigid or flaccid. A brush with good bristles also will keep its shape. The mass of bristles should taper toward the center line of the brush instead of flaring out. The bristles in the better brushes are "flagged" (split at the tips) to hold more paint and to release it smoothly for an even finish. Less expensive brushes, especially those with nylon bristles, usually have plain tips. Bristles should be longer than the width of the brush. When a brush is worked back and forth in the hand, no more than a few loose bristles should fall out. A well constructed brush also has a strip running lengthwise through the center of the bristles at the wide metal ferrule.

Inexpensive brushes should be used where the paint or type of painting might damage a good brush, for example, in applying epoxy paints or contact cements. Use a worn old brush or a cheap new one.

Types and Sizes of Brushes

Choose as large a brush as feels comfortable for the type of surface being painted. Siding can be painted much faster with a 5-in. wall brush than with a 3-in. brush if it is comfortable to use. Similarly, a large pipe can be painted much faster with a large, round sash brush than with a smaller brush.

The four large classes of brushes are: wall brushes, trim brushes, sash brushes, and varnish brushes.

Wall brushes for interior and exterior walls are large (to hold plenty of paint) and blunt-tipped (to release paint rapidly). They range from 3 to 5 in. in width and have relatively short handles (see Fig. 3–1(a)). Because of their size, they are ideal for rapid coverage of large exterior and interior walls, floors and decks, and ceilings.

Trim brushes, which are long and narrow, are used in painting smaller surface areas, such as door trim, baseboards, and moldings (Fig. 3–1(b)).

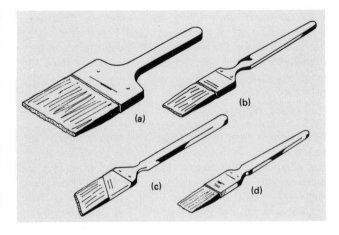

Fig. 3–1 Types of brushes: a) flat wall, b) trim, c) angular sash, d) varnish.

Sash brushes are designed especially to paint window sashes. They have unusually long handles and may be flat or round (Fig. 3–1(c)). The ends of some flat sash brushes are cut diagonally to make it easier to paint the inner surfaces of window sashes.

Varnish brushes are made from soft, fine bristles, which taper to a narrow chisel-like tip (Fig. 3–1(d)), that can release a thin layer of paint. This is important when painting with enamel, varnish, polyurethane, or lacquer. The best varnish brushes (also called enamel brushes) are made with well-flagged natural bristles to increase their paint-holding capacity and ability to release paint smoothly. Varnish brushes range from 1 to 3 in. in width and are longer than trim brushes. Their tapered tips make them particularly good at cutting in along narrow surfaces such as baseboards and moldings and for painting furniture and flat trim, which require very smooth finishes.

Round brushes rather than flat brushes should be used on rounded or irregularly shaped surfaces such as chair rungs, pipes, rails, etc. If wider flat brushes are used on these surfaces, the bristles will soon lump together with gaps between them. Flat brushes also can be ruined by using their narrow edges for painting.

Using a Brush

After pouring the paint into a clean container, dip the brush to one-half the length of its bristles (Fig. 3–2) and pat it on the side of the container to remove the excess paint. If there is too much paint on the brush, it may drip, work itself into the heel where it will cake, or flow too heavily onto the surface.

Brush with short strokes to apply paint, and with long strokes in the direction of the grain to smooth it out. Stroke from dry areas into wet areas to minimize brush marks. With enamel and varnish, the finish must be "flowed on" with short strokes so that it merges to leave a smooth, unbroken

PREPARING AND PAINTING SPECIAL SURFACES

Surface	Surface Preparation	Primer (If Any)	Finish Coat
Old Aluminum Siding	Scrub and wash thoroughly	None, unless recommended by manufacturer	Latex (acrylic) house paint designed for use on aluminum siding
Galvanized Metal	Allow metal to weather at least six months, then wash with paint thinner	Either latex metal primer or a solvent-thinned metal primer	Latex or solvent-thinned trim paint
Rusty Steel or Iron	Scrape loose or scaling rust or rub vigorously with a wire brush	Penetrating rust-resistant metal primer made for use on rusty surfaces	Either regular trim paint or top coat of metal paint made by the same company that makes the primer
Asbestos Shingles, Chalky Masonry	Rub vigorously with a wire brush and wash	Masonry surface conditioner	Latex house paint
Old Weathered Paint on Shingles	Rub vigorously with a wire brush and scrape where necessary	None, except when using a latex top coat, and then only if recommended by the manufacturer.	Heavy-bodied opaque shingle stain or latex house paint
Previously Stained Wood Shingles	Wash thoroughly if you plan to use a semitransparent stain. If you want to use a clear wood preservative, remove old stain first by wire-brushing or power washing.	None	Semitransparent stain or clear wood preservative
New Cedar Shingles	None	None	Weathering oils or weathering stains
Wood Decks	Wash and sand where necessary to remove dirt stains	None	Clear wood preservatives or semitransparent stain made specifically to be walked on (must specify decks on the label)
Painted Wood Porches, Decks	Scrape peeling and flaking paint	None	Alkyd-base porch and floor enamel
Plywood	Fill defects and sand	Latex wood primer	Latex trim or house paint
Wood with Knots and Sap Streaks	Prime knots and sap streaks	Pigmented, shellac-base stain killer and sealer or a latex-base stain killer	Any trim or house paint
Concrete Patios, Walks, Terraces	Clean thoroughly, scrape off peeling and flaking paint	None	Exterior-grade porch and floor enamel (will frequently need renewing in a year or two)

From *Mechanix Illustrated*, May, 1984.

surface. To hold more paint, a varnish brush should be dipped a little more than halfway into the paint. While the paint is still wet and not tacky, rough areas, or "skips," can be smoothed over with a wet brush. Next to the preparation

Fig. 3–2 Dipping a brush into paint.

Fig. 3–3 Washing paint from a brush.

Fig. 3–4 Combing the bristles out straight.

Fig. 3–5 Bristles caked with paint.

Fig. 3–6 Wrapping a brush in foil for storage.

of the surface before painting, the evenness of the strokes, and the uniformity of the paint have the greatest effect on the durability and life of the finish. Paint applied in thin, unbroken layers will adhere tightly to an undersurface and last a long time.

Care of Brushes

New brushes can be preconditioned to increase their performance. Brushes with natural bristles may be soaked in linseed oil, overnight or up to a full day (except when they are to be used for lacquer or shellac); they will then hold more paint and release it more smoothly. Before using these brushes, squeeze out the linseed oil and wash the bristles clean in mineral spirits or other thinner. Brushes with nylon bristles may be preconditioned by washing them with soap in warm water before they are used.

When painting is completed for the day, brushes should be cleaned, combed, shaped, and wrapped. They can be wiped on sheets of newspaper and then worked back and forth in a container of thinner or brush cleaner to remove excess paint (Fig. 3–3). Water should be used for latex paint; mineral spirits for alkyd paint; mineral spirits or turpentine for oil-base paint, varnish, enamel, and urethane; denatured alcohol for shellac and shellac-base paint; and lacquer thinner for lacquer. Brushes used in latex should be washed with soap and rinsed in warm water. Brushes used in other paints should be cleaned in a thinner before they are washed and rinsed in warm water.

Old brushes with paint caked on their bristles can often be salvaged by persistent soaking in a brush cleaner and by working the paint loose with a comb (Fig. 3–4) or other implement. (Use rubber gloves to protect hands from the cleaner.) Drilling a hole in the handle of the brush at a suitable height makes it possible, with a nail or length of wire, to support the brush in solvent or brush cleaner without letting it touch the bottom of the container (Fig. 3–5). Successive soakings and mechanical cleaning will bring most brushes back to a usable condition. They can then be shaped and wrapped in kraft paper (or foil) for storing (Fig. 3–6).

ROLLERS

Paint can be applied much faster with a roller than with a brush on walls, ceilings, wide trim boards, decks, clapboard and flush siding, and masonry. However, a brush is faster where there are awkward areas such as window sashes, crevices, and narrow strips.

Rollers perform best with latex and alkyd paints because these paints flow together without showing lap marks. Rollers do not work well with fast-drying paints such as shellac, shellac-base paint, varnish, fast-drying enamels, or lacquer. Brushes should be used with these finishes.

from *synthetics* (like nylon, Dynel and Orlon) work well with most types of paint but are at their best with latex because they don't absorb water. They are not as good as other roller materials for enamel and varnish; and they cannot be used with substances that chemically attack them, such as paint removers. *Lamb's-wool rollers*, either pure or mixed, are the best rollers to use with oil-base paints and oil stains. They can also be used with alkyd paints but not with latex, since they will absorb water and become matted. *Mohair rollers*, the most expensive of the three kinds, have a short nap, which will lay down a thin, smooth layer of paint or varnish. These are the best rollers to use with enamel, varnish, and oil-base paints but can also be used with alkyd and latex paints

The smoother the surface to be painted, the shorter the nap should be. Interior gypsum-board walls, plaster walls and ceilings, plywood, and similar surfaces should be painted with rollers having a nap 1/4 to 1/2 in. deep. Somewhat rougher surfaces, such as walls previously painted with sandpaint, exterior clapboards, and concrete, require a longer nap ranging from 1/2 in. to 1 in. Rough masonry, shakes, and heavily textured surfaces require a nap of 1 to 1 1/4 in., to reach into cracks and crevices. (For the smoothest finish, use a short-napped mohair roller; it serves the same purpose as a varnish brush.)

Types and Sizes

Standard rollers for flat wall surfaces and trim are cylindrical, and range in length from a few inches to well over a foot. In practice, 7- and 9-in. rollers (Fig. 3–7(a)) are usually used for walls and 3-in. rollers for trim. Short cone-shaped rollers (Fig. 3–7(b)) are designed to "cut in" the edges of ceilings and other corner surfaces without getting paint on the adjacent walls. There are rollers (Fig. 3–7(c)) shaped to fit the round and irregular contours of pipes, chair and table legs, or fences. There are even painter's mitts (Fig. 3–7(d)), which can be dipped in paint so that odd-shaped objects and hard-to-get-at spots can be painted by hand.

Rollers are made of a napped material bounded to a core. Paper and untreated cardboard cores are the least durable. Use plastic or plastic-impregnated cores which have a long working life.

Accessories

The best roller frame to buy is a thick wire frame with a wire cage mounted on ball bearings. This frame will hold the roller so that it will keep its cylindrical shape and rotate smoothly (Fig. 3–8(a)). When the roller equipment is ready to be cleaned, the roller can be slipped off the wire cage without the danger of sticking. (Some small special-purpose rollers have built-in frames.)

The short handle attached to the roller frame is threaded so that an *extension handle* can be screwed onto

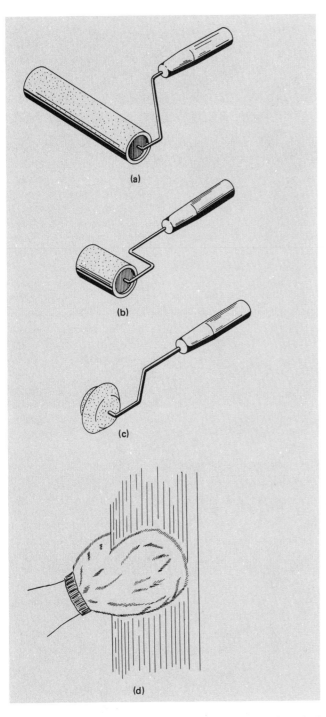

(a)

(b)

(c)

(d)

Fig. 3–7 Paint rollers: a) 9-in., b) edge, c) doughnut-shaped, d) painter's mitt.

Roller Materials

The type of paint determines which of the three types of roller materials should be used, while the texture of the surface determines the best length for the nap. Rollers made

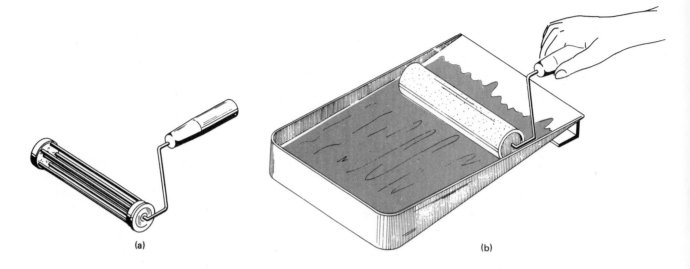

Fig. 3–8 a) Bird cage type frame. b) Paint tray and roller.

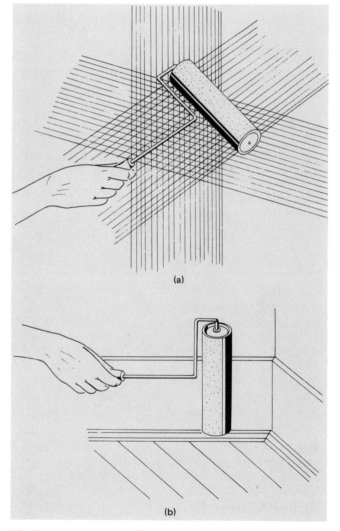

it, to reach ceilings and high wall areas. The extension should not be longer than 10 ft., or the roller will be difficult to control. For very high areas, use a ladder in conjunction with an extension handle.

A *roller pan* or *paint tray* is used to hold the paint (Fig. 3–8(b)). It has a ribbed upper section for removing excess paint, and a deep lower section for holding the paint. The tray should be rust-resistant, wide enough for the roller, and large enough to hold several pints of paint.

Using Rollers

A roller can be preconditioned by washing it in warm, soapy water followed by a thorough rinse. If it is to be used in latex paint, squeeze it out after rinsing and use it damp. With other paints, dry the roller first.

To prepare for painting, dip the roller into the paint until the nap is evenly saturated. Remove the excess paint by rubbing it on the ribbed section of the pan until the roller no longer drips. The initial stroke on a vertical surface should be upward so that the paint doesn't drip or spatter. Walls and other large flat surfaces may be painted with a series of W-shaped patterns first and then filling in by rolling cross-wise to the initial strokes (Fig. 3–9(a)). In doing this, paint should be rolled on from dry areas to wet areas. The edge of a painted area should still be wet when it is overlapped, to avoid lap marks. Finishing strokes should all run in the same direction.

Where the surface is irregular, as on clapboards and shingles, paint is rolled on in the direction of the clapboard edges and shingle crevices so that the nap will reach the more inaccessible spots. In addition to a standard roller, a

Fig. 3–9 a) Painting a wall with a roller. b) Painting trim with a roller.

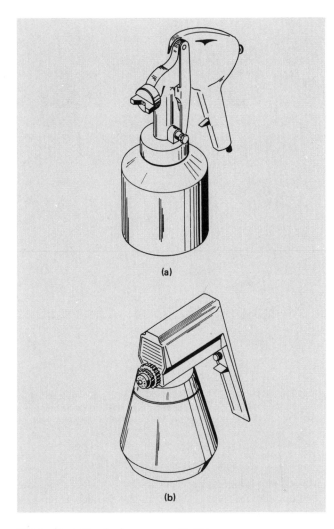

(a)

(b)

Fig. 3–10 a) Standard spray gun. b) Airless spray gun.

brush or small trim roller may be needed to paint irregular edges (Fig. 3–9(b)).

If a roller is pressed too hard or moved too rapidly, the paint will spatter on the floor and surrounding walls. Use slow strokes and "feather" the paint by lifting the roller slightly where wet paint overlaps.

Cleaning

Rollers should be cleaned as soon as the painting is finished. Like brushes, they must be cleaned in a thinner suited to the paint being used: water with latex, mineral spirits with enamel, alkyd, and oil-base paints.

Before removing the roller from its frame, roll out as much paint as possible on newspapers. Soak the roller in the thinner and work the nap back and forth with the fingers to speed up the process (rubber gloves will protect hands from

solvents). When the roller appears to be free of paint, wash it in warm, soapy water, dry it, and fluff it back into shape. Store rollers in a bag or foil to protect them from dust. Paint should also be cleaned from the tray, frame, and other equipment before it dries and hardens.

SPRAYERS

The great attraction of sprayers is that they can be used to paint large areas, or a series of small objects, much faster than with either a brush or roller, and will produce a durable, uniform finish. Since nothing touches the surface other than the paint spray, it is immaterial whether the surface is smooth, extremely rough, or creviced, or whether it is made of wood, glass, cloth, or masonry. Spraying is the ideal method for varnishing and lacquering since several thin, even layers can be easily applied.

To be able to take advantage of the capabilities of spray equipment requires more experience than to use a brush or roller. It takes practice to learn to set up and adjust the equipment, to diagnose operating problems, and to learn the techniques of painting all kinds of surfaces. Paints and other finishes must be properly thinned for spraying unless paints especially formulated for spraying are used. Spray vapor must be ventilated because it may be toxic and flammable.

Fortunately, there are some relatively simple paint sprayers that can be mastered with a little practice. Aerosol cans are expensive, but may be best for small jobs. Airless spray guns (Fig. 3–10(a)) are much easier to use than the traditional compressor sprayers because fewer things can go wrong. Since paint is sprayed without being mixed with air, there is no air-mixing system to fuss with and very little difficulty with overspray or spraying beyond the intended pattern.

Types

Standard paint sprayers (Fig. 3–10(b)) create a spray by using air pressure to force paint and air together. Their basic components include an air compressor (electric or gasoline, portable or stationary), air tank, hose, and spray gun, with an attached cup or separate paint tank to hold the paint. This equipment varies in horsepower, rate of paint flow, and maximum air pressure. Large stationary compressors have horsepower ratings from 1 to 4, while smaller compressors may have horsepower ratings of 1/2 or 3/4. Professional spray guns spray at rates of well over 10 cu. ft./min., with air pressure of 40 to 100 or more psi. Smaller spray guns are likely to work at rates of 3 to 10 cu. ft./min. at air pressures between 35 and 50 psi.

Spray guns actually control the mixing of paint and air. Paint is fed in from a container (usually a 1-qt. cup) attached to the base of the gun, or from a separate paint tank. Com-

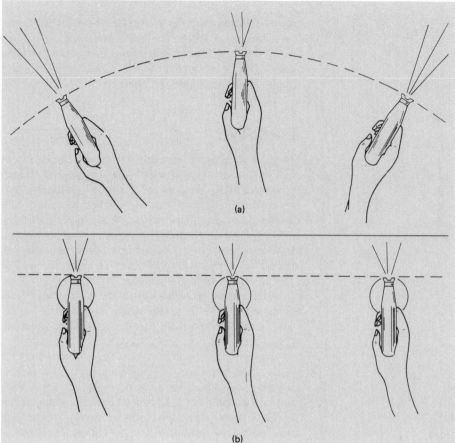

(a)

(b)

(d)

Fig. 3–11 a) Incorrect motion: spraying in an arc. b) Correct spraying motion; back and forth and parallel to the surface. c) Spraying in overlapped bands. d) Spraying corner.

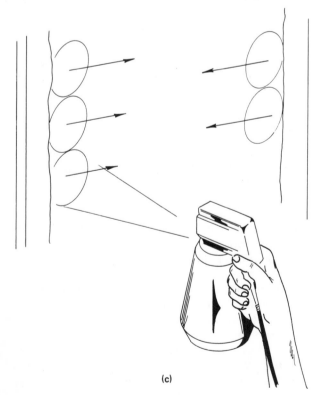

(c)

pressed air comes through a hose connected to an air tank. As the paint and air flow through the nozzles in the paint gun's head, they are mixed either within the head (internal mix) or just as they leave it (external mix). Internal-mix heads are used for heavier, slow-drying paints such as oil-base paints. External mix heads are used for other paints, particularly those that are fast-drying. Spray guns are further divided into pressure-operated and siphon-operated. Some are convertible from one type to the other.

The rate of paint flow and the air pressure of the compressor must be matched to the capacities of the spray gun. Controls on the gun adjust the spread of the spray pattern and the rate of the flow. Heads are available with different sizes of nozzles for different paints and finishes: the heavier the paint, the larger the nozzles.

Airless sprayers force paint through an orifice without mixing it with air. This produces a much more controllable spray pattern than do air–paint mixtures. Since paint can be applied more accurately with an airless sprayer, fewer areas have to be masked, or cleaned up after spraying. This is the easiest type of spray gun to use if the operator is inexperienced with spray painting.

Aerosol spray cans contain paint and a propellant under pressure which forces the paint out in a fine spray. Since

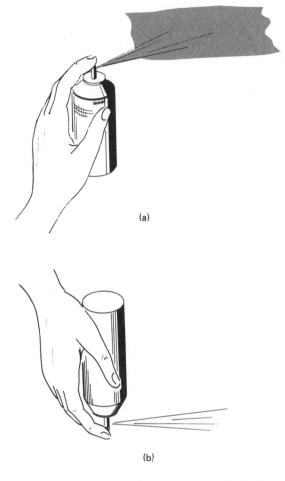

(a)

(b)

Fig. 3–12 a) Spraying with an aerosol can. b) Clearing paint from the valve.

they are self-contained and require only shaking before they are ready to be used, spray cans lend themselves to small jobs that do not require much paint such as radiators, toys, shelves, metalwork, etc. They are very effective in applying varnish and enamel in several thin layers, since each coat dries in a few minutes.

Spraying Techniques

Effective spraying comes with practice. The paint must be thinned for spraying according to the instructions on the paint can and the particular spray equipment. Hardware should be removed, and adjacent areas that are not to be painted masked to protect them from the overspray. Test the adjustment of the fluid-flow and paint-spread controls by spraying a band of paint on a practice surface. When the spray comes out at a workable rate and in the desired pattern (a large round spread or a smaller oval spread), practice painting horizontal strokes. Hold the gun perpendicular to the surface without tilting and 6 to 8 in. away. Start the

stroke before pressing the trigger, and move the gun parallel to the surface rather than in an arc (tilting or moving the gun in an arc (Fig. 3–11(a)) makes the paint layer thicker near the gun and thinner at a distance). Move the gun back and forth (Fig. 3–11(b)) to create a band overlapping the previous band by one-fourth to one-half of its depth (Fig. 3–11(c)). Since the paint is thinner at the edges of the bands, overlapping will make the overall thickness more even. Walls should be sprayed with vertical bands next to the corners to provide a painted surface where the horizontal strokes can be cut in.

A small oval spray pattern should be used for narrow objects and open work such as fences, radiators, pipes, etc. Direct the spray so that it hits the broadest expanse of surface at a right angle. Outside corners of buildings and individual boards (Fig. 3–11(d)) should be sprayed at their corners so that the pattern covers both faces, or a face and edge. Each side of an inside corner should be sprayed separately with a vertical band, so that the paint thickness will be uniform. Horizontal surfaces (such as a table top) that cannot be held at right angles to the spray gun are painted by tilting the gun and spraying back and forth from left to right moving toward the furthest edge. Because of the tilt, the paint cup should be only partially full.

After some experience, spots which are missed or painted too lightly can be spot-painted with a smooth, short burst of paint. If too much paint is applied to a small area, it will sag or run down. If this happens, wipe off the sagging paint and spray the spot again.

The principles of spraying that apply to larger paint sprayers also apply to aerosol spray cans. The paint has to be well mixed, in this case by shaking the can so that the mixer can stir the pigment into the vehicle.* Hold the can about 12 in. from the surface and move it across the area to be sprayed in a straight line (Fig. 3–12(a)). The bands of paint should be slightly overlapped. Do not use an arcing motion or tilt the can so that it is not perpendicular to the surface or the paint film will be uneven. The smoothest finish is made by applying several thin coats of paint, with a few minutes' drying time between each coat.

Aerosol spray should be used at temperatures close to 70°F for the best results. Because they contain flammable propellants and paint vapor, the spray cans must never be stored next to hot pipes, radiators or stoves, in the hot sun, near flame, or where the temperature may approach 120°F. Puncturing a can or throwing it into an incinerator is also hazardous. Since the spray mist and vapor may be toxic, the painting space must be ventilated.

After using a spray can, clean the tube (Fig. 3–12(b)) and valve by turning the can upside down and pressing the button on top until the propellant appears to be clear of paint.

*The vehicle is the solvent that carries the pigment.

Cleaning

The paint gun must be cleaned while the paint is still wet to avoid plugging up the nozzles. Loosen the gun from the cup to let the paint drain from the head. Then spray the proper thinner through the gun until it comes out clear. Finally, disassemble the gun and clean the paint from the internal parts with a rag or brush soaked in the appropriate thinner.

INTERIOR PAINTS

Interior paints must be more resistant than exterior paints to dust, stains, abrasion, and scrubbing. However, they don't have to withstand fading from the sun, extreme temperature changes, or weather. Therefore, they need less pigment and can be harder and smoother than exterior paints. Interior paints are chosen for their decorative effects, and for their ability to lighten dark rooms and to protect woodwork, walls, and ceilings. In kitchens, laundries, and bathrooms, they also help to keep surfaces cleaner and free of mildew and bacteria.

Flat and Gloss Paints

Interior paints for walls, ceiling, and woodwork are either flat paints or enamels.

Flat paints contain more pigment than enamels but less binder, and dry to a soft, flat flinish. They form a thinner, softer coat compared with enamels and may rub off if repeatedly washed.

Enamels are thick, hard, smooth, and glossier than flat paints because they contain more binder. There are three degrees of gloss: eggshell or satin, semigloss, and gloss. Eggshell enamel has the light sheen of a white egg shell. Semigloss enamel is smoother than eggshell and has a light, low shine. Gloss enamel is very smooth and has a high shine. Since semigloss and gloss enamels are smooth and slippery, there is little chance that dust, stain, mildew, or bacteria will adhere to them. When gloss enamels are washed and scrubbed, they don't wear down or become flat, but retain their gloss. Until recently, latex enamels were made only in eggshell and semigloss finishes and alkyds were relied on for durable gloss finishes. Now there are both alkyd and latex enamels in gloss, semigloss, and eggshell finishes.

Primers or undercoats are necessary with flat paints and enamels on bare wood. They assist in bonding the topcoat firmly to the surface being painted. A primer may also be used as a primer-sealer, to seal porous materials such as plaster, gypsum board, and softwoods, to avoid excess absorption. For wood previously finished with a dark wood stain, a shellac-base primer loaded with white pigment can be used to hide the stain so that it will not show through the topcoat. The primer and topcoat do not have to be of the same type of paint. Latex and alkyd primers may be used with either type of paint as a topcoat. Enamel, however, should have an enamel undercoat for the smoothest finish.

Walls and Ceilings

Most people like the soft finish of flat paints on their walls and ceilings. Flat paints can be used in livingrooms, bedrooms, dining areas, and other spaces that are not subject to grease stains or moisture, and will not need scrubbing. But they cannot take the battering from cooking, laundering, bathroom moisture, and periodic scrubbing in kitchens, laundries, bathrooms, children's rooms, and family rooms. Semigloss and gloss enamels are usually used in these spaces, since they stand up well to all of these conditions.

Ceiling paints have more hiding power than flat wall paints do because they contain more pigment. They are not as resistant to washing, but this is not of great importance since ceilings are dusted more often than washed. Latex primers should be used on gypsum board and new plaster, whether the topcoat is to be flat or enamel. If alkyd primers are used, they will roughen up the paper facing on gypsum board or will be spoiled by the alkalis in fresh plaster. Textured paints are used for walls and ceiling, sometimes for their decorative effect and sometimes to cover an unattractive undersurface (or both). Sand paints, such as latex sand paint, consist of flat latex paint and a fine grit or sand. It can be applied in swirls, long strokes, or with a strippled effect, with either a brush or roller.

Flat alkyd paints are noted for their durability, resistance to moisture, hiding power, and near odorlessness. Flat latex paints are the easiest to clean up since painting tools can be washed off in water. They also have the advantage of drying in an hour or so; thus a room can be painted with one or two topcoats in the same day.

Woodwork

Wood is usually painted with enamel because it needs a hard, smooth finish for protection. Flat paints do not protect it adequately from abrasion or scrubbing.

Gloss or semigloss enamels are used on woodwork in kitchens and bathroom spaces since they have the hardest finishes. Semigloss enamels may be preferred in some spaces because they have less glare than gloss enamels. They generally are used on doors, trim, baseboards, windows, shelves, and other wooden surfaces in livingrooms, bedrooms, and dining spaces.

Alkyd enamels can be washed shortly after they dry, while latex enamels cannot be washed for several days without being damaged. This is an important consideration in painting kitchens and bathrooms that must be back in operation as soon as possible after they are painted. Alkyd enamel keeps its color well and is particularly resistant to moisture.

Table 3–1   Table of Interior Paints and Surfaces

	Flat latex	Flat alkyd	Eggshell latex	Eggshell alkyd	Semigloss latex	Semigloss alkyd	Gloss latex	Gloss alkyd	Interior varnish	Polyurethane	Floor varnish	Floor enamel	Metal primer	Portland-cement paint	Rubber-base masonry paint	Aluminum paint	Epoxy	Wood stain	Latex masonry paint
Wood surfaces																			
Doors, windows, trim																			
Kitchen, bathroom			○	○	●	●	○	●	●	●								●	
Other living spaces	○	○	●	●	●	●	○	○	●	●								●	
Kitchen cabinets			○	○	●	●	○	●	●	●								●	
Wood paneling	○	○	●	●	●	●	○		●	●	●							●	
Shelves	○	○	○	○	●	●	○		●	●	●							●	
Floors										●	●	●						●	
Stairs										●	●	●						●	
Railings			○	○	●	●	○	●	●	●								○	
Hardboard	○	●	○	●	●	●	○	●	●	●									
Walls and ceilings of plaster and gypsum board																			
Kitchen, bathroom			○	○	●	●	○	●											
Other living spaces	●	●	●	●	○	○													
Radiators and pipes		●	○	○	●	●	○	●					●			●			
Heating ducts		●	○	○	●	●	○	●					●			●			
Metal doors and windows		○	○	○	●	●	○	○					●			●	●		
Masonry	●	○	○	○	●	○	●	○						●	●		●		●
Cinder block															●				
Concrete floors															●		●		●
Ceramic tile			○			○		○									●		

● Indicates preferred finish.
○ Indicates alternative finish.

Other Interior Surfaces

There are many objects and surfaces other than walls, ceilings, and woodwork, that may need painting. Flat paints and enamels can be used on some of them, but there are a number of special paints that often do a better job. Primers should be used in many cases. Aluminum and steel windows and doors, for example, need a metal primer when painted with latex but not with an alkyd paint. Rusty exterior metal must have a rust-resistant primer. Floors may be finished with wood stains, wax, floor varnish, or polyurethane, instead of being painted. Masonry and concrete floors can be painted with any of a number of special paints. Radiators can be painted with a flat wall paint, an enamel, or a metal primer, but not with metallic paints because they reduce heat radiation.

The accompanying table will assist the painter in choosing an acceptable type of paint for a number of different surfaces.

PLANNING AND PREPARING INTERIORS FOR PAINTING

Plans for painting interiors should be thought out ahead of time. Time must be allowed for repairing cracks and holes in the walls, removing peeling paint, sanding woodwork, and washing away dust and grease. Before buying the paint, colors have to be selected and the kind and amount of paint decided on. And since newly painted spaces need to be ventilated, the season should be conducive to opening windows.

Preparation

Furniture should be moved to protect it from paint and to clear it away from the walls and woodwork. Heavy pieces can be left in the center of the room and covered with a dropcloth, while lighter pieces are moved to other rooms.

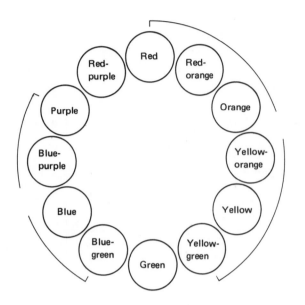

Fig. 3–13 Color wheel for planning decorative colors.

Curtains, rods, mirrors, pictures, and anything else removable should be taken down. There will be some fixtures in bathrooms and kitchens, such as mirrors and fans, which can be left in place and protected with masking tape. Radiators should be turned off, drained (if necessary), disconnected, and moved away from the walls. Plates covering electrical switches and outlets must be removed so that the walls can be painted around the electrical boxes. Ceiling lights should be loosened or masked. Doorknobs and other hardware should be removed or taped with masking tape. Sometimes it is simpler to remove window sashes and paint them separately to avoid the danger that paint may "freeze" them to the window stops.

Older houses may have calcimine (a cheap water-thinned paint) on the ceilings; this must be washed off since it will loosen and peel off if painted over. Wallpaper should be removed to give the paint a better base. If it is left on the walls, bubbles and seams should be repaired, to provide a smooth surface for the paint.

After the room has been emptied as much as possible and the remaining furniture and floor covered with dropcloths, the walls, ceiling, and woodwork must be prepared for painting. Small nail holes, cracks, and damaged or loose plaster or gypsum board must be repaired. Small holes and cracks can be cleaned out until their edges are firm, and then filled with spackling compound or patching plaster. Damaged or loose plaster or gypsum board should be replaced and smoothed over with a patching material. It may take several layers of spackling compound or patching plaster to build up the repaired area. The patch should be sanded down flush with the surrounding surfaces, cleaned off, and spot-primed before the wall or ceiling is painted. Loose trim such as baseboards and door and window trim should be

nailed down and the nail heads set and covered with spackling compound or wood dough (plastic wood). Like the wall repairs, they must be sanded flush and spot-primed also.

Preparation of woodwork depends on the condition of the paint. If it is tight and in relatively good condition, its gloss should be dulled to increase adhesion before it is painted. Wash it with ammonia , or sand it lightly. Where paint is peeling, scrape it and sand it smooth for spot priming. Thick, cracked paint or any paint that shows excessive peeling should be removed with paint remover or by scraping or burning. Rough areas and holes in woodwork must be filled with wood dough, spackling, or other filler, and sanded smooth.

When the repairs are complete, the room should be vacuumed to remove dust. The walls, ceiling, and woodwork should be washed and rinsed to clean off dirt marks and grease. Dirt can be removed with a household cleaning agent, but grease will require a wall cleaner such as trisodium phosphate.

Estimating

The amount of paint required can be estimated by measuring the walls and consulting the instructions for the type of paint to be used. Measure the wall height and length and multiply, to get the area in square feet. With most paints, a gallon will cover the walls of an average 12 X 15 room. Porous and rough-textured walls, however, require more paint. If ceilings are to be painted or a second coat applied, the additional amount of paint needed can be calculated by measuring the same way. Door and window areas can be measured and subtracted from the total area if they are extensive, or they can be ignored, to allow extra paint as a safety margin. Woodwork can be measured in the same way as wall and ceiling areas. The areas of doors and cabinets can be calculated. Window trim and baseboards should be measured in running feet and their total areas approximated. In a typical room without wall cabinets or wood paneling, the woodwork will require 20 to 30 percent as much paint as the walls, about a gallon of wall paint to a quart of trim paint.

Using Colors

One of the nicest things about using paint is that colors can be selected to create effects such as warmth, excitement, restfulness, and spaciousness. Bedrooms can be made more restful; family rooms warmer and friendly, and narrow rooms visually wider. The right colors must be chosen for the effect and then combined with other harmonious colors and applied in the proper proportions.

The *color wheel* (Fig. 3–13), which is an arrangement of colors in a circle according to how they are related to each other, can help in selecting harmonizing colors. The three primary colors (red, yellow, and blue), which are mixed to make all of the other colors, are equidistant from each other, with their mixtures in intermediate locations on the wheel. The secondary colors (green, purple, and orange), which result from mixing pairs of primary colors, are also equidistant from each other. The tertiary colors, for example, yellow-green, blue-green, blue-purple, red-purple, red-orange, and yellow-orange, fall between the primary and secondary colors which produce them.

Once an initial color is chosen for its effect, it can be combined with other colors in a number of ways. *Adjacent colors* on the color wheel, such as yellow, yellow-green, green, and blue-green, will go together without sharp contrasts. *Opposite* or *complimentary colors,* such as yellow and purple, create a strong contrast but still look well together. *Split complimentary colors,* yellow, red-purple, and blue-purple, for example, not only create a strong contrast but add life and variety to the color scheme. A combination of three colors can also be chosen by using *triads* of colors equidistant from each other like green, purple, and orange. With some experience, you may use the color wheel to combine four or more colors.

Colors containing some red or yellow in their mixtures convey a feeling of warmth, as they do in sunlight and firelight. These colors can be used to lend a cheerful feeling to a family room. Cool blues and greens, on the other hand, create a quiet restful atmosphere appropriate for a bedroom or den.

Dark colors absorb light and make walls seem closer and ceilings lower. A wide room can be made to seem narrower by painting its most distant walls darker than the others. In the same way, a high ceiling can be made to seem lower by painting it darker than the walls. Light colors not only reflect light for better illumination, but they can make rooms seem more spacious and low ceilings higher. By using dark and light colors according to the effects they cause, the apparent shape and size of a room can be visually changed and attractive features emphasized, such as windows, entrances, or a fireplace wall.

Working out color schemes, repairing walls, sanding woodwork, removing hardware, and washing off dirt and grease take considerable time. However, they all contribute to the final appearance of the room. If the woodwork is not cleaned and sanded, the paint will not adhere properly and will begin to check and peel long before it should. The time spent in preparing for painting is worthwhile.

PAINTING METHODS FOR INTERIORS

Paint has to be thoroughly mixed. Pigment tends to settle to the bottom of the can and the lighter vehicle and additives rise. Some of the paint should be poured into another container, so that there is room to stir the pigment thoroughly into the remaining vehicle. Once the pigment is dissolved, the paint that was poured out can be returned and mixed

with the rest of the paint. Sometimes paint is poured back and forth between containers several times to ensure that it is thoroughly mixed. If a separate container is used to carry the paint while painting, the top should be kept on the original can to keep the remaining paint fresh. Clean excess paint from around the rim and hammer the top on tightly with a hammer or your foot. A cloth can be placed over the top to catch paint that splatters.

If a can has been opened before, the paint may have a skim on it. This should be freed and carefully removed to avoid leaving fragments in the paint. Those pieces which escape should be strained out by pouring the paint through a fine mesh of cheesecloth or a screen.

When a shade of paint has to be mixed by the dealer instead of coming from stock, it's better to buy more paint than you need rather than just enough. If more paint has to be mixed, it may not be exactly the same shade as the first batch. (The two should not be used side by side on the same wall.)

It is important to read the instructions on the label since the paint manufacturer is the best source of information about the best manner of applying the paint. For example, instructions provide information about thinning, the type and percentage of thinner, and whether the paint includes a mildew preventative. (If it doesn't, a mildewcide can be added for surfaces prone to mildew.)

New surfaces, patches, and knots should be primed. The choice of primer depends on the material and the type of paint used for the topcoat. Enamel on new wood should have an enamel undercoat, though flat paint can be used as a primer. Alkyd and latex paints can be applied over either alkyd or latex primers. If new wood is to be varnished, white shellac should be used as a primer and sealer.

Old wood in good condition needs to be primed only when the color is to be changed or a dark stain covered over. The same primers can be used as on new wood. Dark wood stain is covered best with a white-pigmented shellac-base paint.

New gypsum board and plaster walls should be primed with a latex primer regardless of the type of paint used for the topcoat. Plaster walls that have cured for six months or more may be primed with alkyd, latex, or other primers. Old walls will not need priming, but they may need two coats of paint if the color is to be changed.

Woodwork should be spot-primed before and after being patched. When patches are dry and sanded, prime them with the same paint as the rest of the wood. Prime wall patches in the same way. Knots in wood must be sealed with a primer sealer such as shellac or a shellac-base stain killer, to prevent them from bleeding through the paint.

Ceiling and Walls

To avoid messing up surfaces already painted, the usual order is to paint the ceiling first, and then the walls, doors,

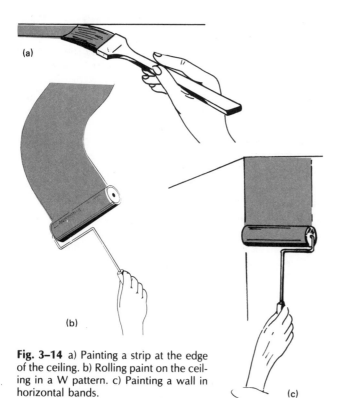

Fig. 3–14 a) Painting a strip at the edge of the ceiling. b) Rolling paint on the ceiling in a W pattern. c) Painting a wall in horizontal bands.

the end of the strokes will feather the wet edges together and form an even coat.

When a brush is used to paint a ceiling, a 2-in. thick plank can be supported between two stepladders to make it easier to reach the ceiling. A wall brush that is at least 4 in. wide should be used for the main part of the ceiling and also to cut in the edges. Since the brush is upside down much of the time, be sure to dip it lightly into the paint and remove the excess by slapping the brush against the side of the container.

Start at a corner of the ceiling and paint a 2- or 3-ft. strip across the narrowest part. The edge of the previous strip should still be wet when the next strip is painted. Each section of the strip should be painted crosswise to fill in the area thoroughly and then painted with finishing strokes in the direction of the strip for a uniform appearance. Sand paint and textured paints are often painted in swirls and in several directions for an attractive, rough finish.

Large wall areas can be painted faster also with a 9-in. roller than with a brush. Rollers leave a distinct stippled surface which may be less acceptable on walls than the smoother finish of a brush would be. Like the ceiling, walls are painted in strips so that the edges will still be wet when the adjacent area is painted. Paint a narrow horizontal strip next to the ceiling with a trim brush or edge-roller. Then start with a roller or brush in an upper corner and paint a vertical strip 2 or 3 ft. wide down to the baseboard. With a roller, an open vertical pattern can be painted on the upper third of the wall (Fig. 3–14(c)), filled in with horizontal strokes, and finished with vertical strokes for a uniform direction. A doughnut-shaped corner roller or a trim brush can be used in the corners. With a brush, follow the same vertical pattern in a wide band, filling in with horizontal strokes, and finishing with vertical strokes. A trim brush can be used to cut in the woodwork so that paint does not edge over onto door and window trim or baseboards.

Where paint is too heavy, it may drip or run down the wall. Go back and check the previous strips occasionally to smooth out drips and lap marks before they dry. Skips can also be painted in with a wet brush before the surrounding paint dries.

Doors

Woodwork, especially areas likely to be handled such as doors and windows, is usually painted with a semigloss or gloss enamel to protect the wood and for easier washing. Enamel, however, must be applied with care and quite rapidly so that the edges are kept wet. Sags and drips must be smoothed out quickly with a wet brush.

Doorknobs and surface lock hardware should be removed and the door sanded and washed (and primed, if new wood) before being painted. Flush doors are painted

windows, wood trim, and baseboards. However, if the walls and woodwork are to be painted with the same kind of paint (flat latex for example), walls and woodwork could be painted together without running into problems.

The easiest way to paint a ceiling is by using latex paint and a 9-in. roller with an extension handle. The roller will cover the ceiling much faster than a brush and can be used while standing on the floor. Since the standard roller cannot paint into corners without getting paint on the wall, an edge-roller or a 2-in. trim brush should be used first to paint a 2- or 3-in. strip along the edge of the ceiling adjacent to the wall (Fig. 3–14(a)).

The roller should not be too full or the paint will splatter; excess paint should be squeezed out by rubbing the roller on the grooves in the paint tray. Start the roller at one corner of the ceiling. Apply the paint in 2- or 3-ft. strips across the narrow dimension of the ceiling; the edge of the previous strip will still be wet when the next strip is painted. This will allow the paint to flow together so that there won't be lap marks between the strips. Latex paint flows together well anyway, but alkyds and other paints may show marks if the edges of the strips have dried. Each section of the strip should be rolled crossways or in a W-pattern first (Fig. 3–14(b)), and then lengthwise to fill it in. The final strokes should all be in the same direction, the lengthwise direction. Painting from dry to wet areas and lifting the roller lightly at

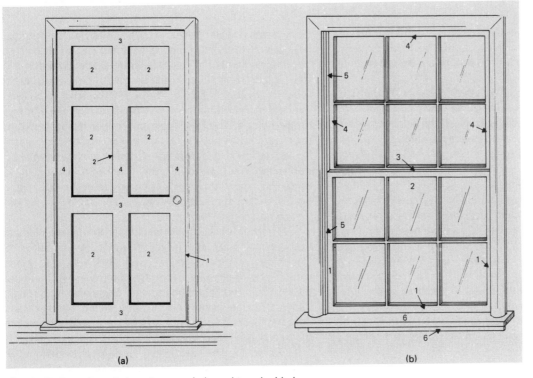

Fig. 3–15 Steps in painting a) a panel door, b) a double-hung window.

from top to bottom with the finishing strokes in the same vertical direction.

There is a prescribed sequence for painting panel doors which keeps runs and sags to a minumum, minimizes lap marks between areas, and ensures that finishing strokes are in the right direction. The door edge which opens into the room is painted *first.* (See Fig. 3–15(a).) Paint which overlaps from the edge onto the face of the door should be wiped off with a rag soaked in thinner. *Second,* the moldings around the panels and the panels themselves are painted. Later when painting the rest of the door, go back and smooth out the paint that may have run down from the moldings into the corners of the panels. *Third,* paint the horizontal crosspieces (rails) starting at the top of the door and ending at the bottom. *Fourth,* paint the vertical strips (stiles) on the sides and between the panels. On all surfaces, be careful to wipe off paint that runs into adjacent unpainted areas. When that section is painted later, paint can be brought up smoothly to the edge of the painted area. Hinges can be painted with the same paint as the door but paint must be kept clear at freely moving joints and screw-head slots.

Windows

Double-hung and casement windows are likely to require extensive scraping, sanding, and repair because they are exposed to moisture and handling. Alkyds and semigloss or gloss enamel will hold up better than most paints. Polyurethane or exterior varnish should be used where a clear finish is needed on unfinished or stained wood.

Metal windows are usually made of steel or aluminum. Steel windows must be sanded and primed if they are rusted and then painted with a metal paint. Aluminum windows do not have to be painted for protection, but enamel or lacquer can be used if desired. An angular sash brush will allow the inside edges to be painted with a minumum of paint on the glass even if the glass isn't taped to protect it.

The prescribed sequence for painting double-hung windows (Fig. 3–15(b)) is somewhat more complicated than with doors, since the sashes must be moved, and there are more types of wood pieces to paint. *First,* lower the top sash almost to the sill (and raise the bottom sash) so that the lower rail of the top sash and lower sections of the adjacent vertical stiles can be painted. *Second,* paint the horizontal and then the vertical dividers (mullions) between the panes of glass in the upper sash. *Third,* lower the bottom sash a little more than halfway and pull the top sash nearly to the top so you can paint the horizontal top rail and then the two vertical sides (stiles) of the upper sash.

Fourth, follow the same step-by-step procedure with the bottom sash (which is now in good position for painting). Both sashes should be left open until the paint is dry.

Fifth, the window jambs against which the sashes slide up and down can be painted, together with the narrow strip (parting strip) between the two sashes. (These areas may even be left unpainted, if it makes raising and lowering the sashes easier, though the finish casing should be painted.) *Sixth,* the window sill and apron under it are the last sections to be painted.

Casement windows are painted by following the standard sequence of painting horizontal and vertical dividers (mullions) between the panes of glass, the horizontal rails, vertical stiles, and the sill and casement frame.

Baseboards

These may take as much preparation as windows since they are likely to be gouged and dirty. Once they are repaired, they should be painted with a hard semigloss or gloss enamel. Use a trim brush to cut in the top of the baseboard next to the wall. (A shield of plastic or cardboard will help keep paint off the wall.) Use a wet rag to wipe up paint which finds its way past the shield. The bottom of the baseboard next to the floor should be cut in next. Finally, the space between the upper and lower painted strips can be filled in and the paint stroked on in a uniform horizontal direction.

EXTERIOR PAINTS

Exterior paints and finishes include house paints, trim enamels, wood stains, masonry paints, floor and deck enamels, primers, clear finishes, and special paints for metals and other materials. House paints, which are used to paint the sides of a house, have more pigment than interior paints. They form a thicker film, withstand fading better, and are sufficiently elastic to stretch as wood expands and contracts with temperature changes. They may also contain additives for special purposes such as preventing mildew and resisting damaging fumes.

House paints are oil-base or latex paints formulated for clapboards and other wooden siding. Their elasticity allows them to stretch and contract as the siding reacts to summer and winter temperature changes. *Oil-base* house paints have excellent adhesion and are often used over previously painted surfaces. They form a thicker film and cover better than latex paints when it is desired to change the color of the house. Oil-base paints dry to a glossy finish in from one to several days but they become dull in time. The white-pigmented oil-base paints are noted for their self-chalking ability. *Latex* house paints form a porous film that allows them to "breathe." This helps avoid blistering and peeling when they are used with a primer on new wood. (This characteristic is not particularly helpful when latex is used over old, nonlatex paints, because the old paint may peel and cause the latex topcoat to peel also.) Exterior latex paint keeps its color well and does not readily fade in the sun.

Since it has a water base, it can be used on damp siding, dries rapidly (usually within a day), and is easy to clean from painting equipment. One-coat house paints, whether oil-base or latex, contain more pigment than standard paints, in order to cover in one coat. They are formulated to be used over old paint that has been well prepared, or over a primer on new wood. The time they save will generally be worth their extra cost.

Alkyd trim enamels are exterior gloss enamels for doors, windows, and other trim. They form a hard, thick, protective coat, which holds its color well in strong sunlight. Since they are not elastic like house paints, they should not be used for large areas of siding.

Wood stains are stains (oil or latex) containing pigment that can penetrate and protect wood such as unfinished clapboards, wooden shingles, and other wooden siding, with a layer of pigment. Some stains have less pigment but provide color while letting the natural grain show through. Others (opaque stains) contain more pigment and obscure the grain. Because stain is absorbed more readily, more stain than paint is needed to cover a house.

Primers may be latex, alkyd, or oil-base, depending on the topcoat to be used. They are used on bare spots, new wood, and sometimes over old paint to increase the adhesion of the top coat. Latex primers don't dry as fast as exterior latex paints since they contain oil to help increase their adhesion. Rust-inhibiting primers are necessary for most metals.

Masonry paints include latex, Portland cement, rubber-base, oil-base, and catalytic paints. *Latex masonry paint* can be used on unfinished or new masonry without being damaged by alkali, but it requires a primer when used on previously finished masonry. Like other latex paints, latex masonry paint forms a coat that keeps moisture from penetrating from the outside, while letting moisture escape through its pores to prevent blistering and peeling. Either latex house paint or masonry paint can be used on asbestos shingles. Latex masonry paints for floors are formulated to withstand abrasion better than latex masonry paints for walls, but continued exposure to pools of water will damage both types. *Rubber-base masonry paints* are excellent for masonry floors, walls, and swimming pools, because they resist alkali, prevent water from penetrating, and withstand abrasion. The floor and deck mixture is thicker than the rubber-base paint for walls. *Portland-cement paint* will seal an unfinished masonry wall, but it tends to wear off when exposed to weather on exterior masonry and does not hold up well on floors. *Catalytic masonry paints* are very resistant to abrasion and form a strong bond with an unfinished masonry surface. However, they are the most expensive of the masonry paints.

Clear finishes do not stand up well on exterior walls because they lack pigment to protect them from sunlight. If an exterior varnish or polyurethane is used, it will have to be renewed every couple of years.

Wooden shingles and shakes can be painted with oil-base or alkyd *shingle paints,* with latex house paints, or with wood stains. Decks and porch floors should be finished with either a wood stain or *exterior deck and floor enamel.* Wood stains penetrate well and hold up to heavy use better than most deck enamels.

The table of exterior paints will assist in choosing paints for different surfaces.

EXTERIOR PREPARATION

House paint applied over a well prepared surface can be expected to stay in good condition for four or five years. Surface preparation involves repairing cracks, holes, loose boards, window sashes, etc., and getting the surfaces ready by scraping, sanding, and washing. As a first step, it's helpful to inspect the house and make a list of repairs that will be required. This also will provide a good idea of how much scraping, sanding, and priming needs to be done.

Minor Repairs

One of the biggest problems in making repairs is to keep moisture from getting behind the wood and paint, where it causes blistering and peeling. Siding, trim, door and window frames, shingles, and masonry should be watertight before they are painted. Attachments to the house that are not to be painted with the house should be removed, if possible. This might include exterior electric lights, hardware, window screens, screen doors, storm doors, and shutters.

Dry weather and moderate temperatures are required for painting. Manufacturers' instructions usually suggest temperatures no lower than 50°F and no higher than 90°F. Oil-base and alkyd paints also require dry surfaces.

Broken or badly cracked clapboards, shingles, floorboards, and other replaceable wood should be removed. Before new pieces are put in place, check to see that the subsurface is in good condition. Cracks are most likely to form around window and door casings and in other joints between the trim and siding. These should be cleaned out and caulked with a caulking gun (Fig. 3–16(a)). Small holes can be filled with putty and smoothed flush with the surface. Nailheads that protrude should be set below the surface and the holes filled. Loose clapboards, shingles, trim, and other boards should be nailed down tightly (Fig. 3–16(b)). These steps will help keep moisture from getting under the paint. Loose glazing compound in window sashes can be replaced and painted after the wood is cleaned and soaked with linseed oil. Cracks in masonry should be cleaned out and filled with a patching compound. Wooden gutters deteriorate quickly once their waterproofing wears off; they may

need to be cleaned out, repaired, caulked, and primed. Metal gutters and downspots will rust and stain the siding if they are made of galvanized steel. Rust should be cleaned off with a wire brush and a coat of rust-inhibiting primer applied.

Surface Preparation

After repairs have been made and the outer shell of the house is reasonably watertight, the old paint must be prepared so that it will bond to the primer and the new topcoat. If the paint is somewhat weathered but tight and smooth, it just needs to be brushed, washed with a detergent, and rinsed with a hose. But if the paint is blistered and peeling, it must be removed and the area sanded smooth. Loose paint, blisters, cracked and wrinkled paint, and other types of defective paint can be scraped off with a paint scraper, putty knife, wire brush (Fig. 3–16(c)), burned off, softened with a semi-paste paint remover, or sanded off with a disk sander. A paint scraper (Fig. 3–16(d)) is adequate for removing loose paint in small patches, but when paint must be removed over large areas, a disk sander will be much faster. Where thick paint must be completely removed, it can be heated and softened with an electric paint remover or a propane torch, and scraped off. A propane torch (Fig. 3–16(e)) is safer on a flat surface than on clapboards where it might ignite the wood in a crevice. An electric paint remover is the safest. Removing paint with paint remover is slow and the chemical is expensive, but it may be the best method for small areas such as on doors or window sashes. After the defective paint has been removed, the bare area should be sanded and the edges of the surrounding paint smoothed down. Apply a primer so that it covers the bare wood and the edge of the old paint to form a seal. Caulked cracks and joints, filled holes, new boards, glazing compound, and other new surfaces should be primed also. Knots should be sealed with shellac before they are primed.

The last steps before starting to paint are to dust and wash the surfaces, and cover shrubbery and other objects to keep them clean of paint. For ordinary dirt and dust, detergent in warm water will be enough. Rust stains and other stains may require a solution of trisodium phosphate. Mildew should be scrubbed thoroughly with a mixture composed of warm water (3 qts.), household bleach (1 qt.); trisodium phosphate or borax (2/3 cup), and detergent (1/3 cup), taking care to protect hands with rubber gloves and eyes with goggles. All of these solutions should be rinsed off and the surface dried before it is painted.

Three Stripping Techniques

A closer look at the three most common stripping tech-

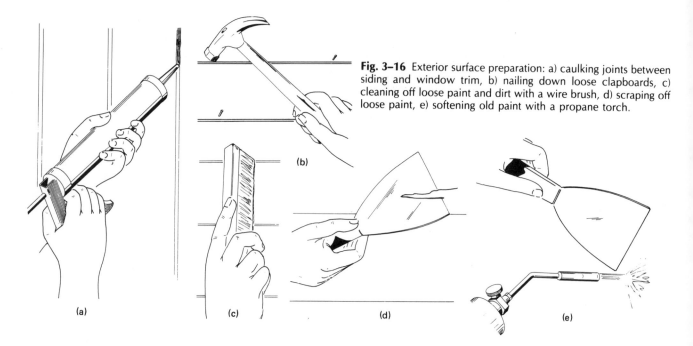

Fig. 3–16 Exterior surface preparation: a) caulking joints between siding and window trim, b) nailing down loose clapboards, c) cleaning off loose paint and dirt with a wire brush, d) scraping off loose paint, e) softening old paint with a propane torch.

(a)   (c)   (d)   (e)

niques will help to clarify the advantages and disadvantages of each. The three are: applying paint and varnish remover, sanding with hand scrapers or a portable belt sander, and stripping with heat.

The *chemical strippers,* or paint and varnish removers, come in liquid and semipaste forms. The former usually work best on horizontal woodwork, or on doors or other items, such as window sashes, that can be detached and laid horizontally. The semipaste strippers are most appropriate on vertical surfaces because the remover adheres to the area to be cleaned. For both liquid and semipaste removers you have a choice of solvent cleanup, water cleanup, or no cleanup. Water sprayed on the cleanup area as a jet is impractical indoors and is for that reason normally used on outside wood. The solvent cleaners are highly toxic and can be bought in both flammable and nonflammable form; the latter is safer and is to be preferred, but even with nonflammable solvent the home handyman should follow user instructions regarding respirator, gloves, goggles, long-sleeved shirts, and other protective equipment.

No-cleanup removers are often not quite what they purport to be. They may leave bits of residue that have to be cleaned off with a solvent. Otherwise, the no-cleanup removers are quite effective.

In stripping, work in one area at a time. Remover is applied liberally. After pouring, you can spread liquid remover with a brush or spatula. A wide-mouth can serves as a container/dispenser for semipaste remover, which is applied with a brush. In either case, brush as little as possible after applying. The remover should be allowed to soak in for 20 to 30 minutes. You can use a

putty knife to lift the softened paint off the surface. Use a knife with rounded corners to avoid gouging the wood. If the surface is uneven, brush the "sludge" off with 2/0 steel wool.

Using a Scraper or Sander: A hand scraper or portable, electrically-powered sander is usually the answer to stripping flat surfaces. The sander, expectably, is more efficient than the scraper for stripping broader areas—

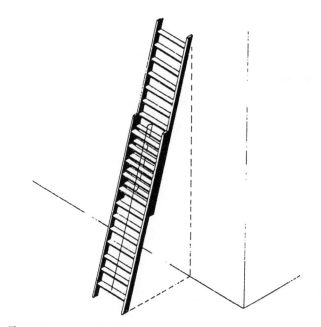

Fig. 3–17 Positioning a ladder.

and requires some advance practice. Unless you sharpen your sanding skills on scrap wood, making sure you "land" gently, keep the pressure even at both ends, and keep the device in motion constantly, you run the risk of digging into the wood. You'll want to work within an area determined by the comfortable reach of your arms.

Some other tips are pertinent. Remember, when stripping old, lead-based paint, to take all protective precautions: goggles, double-cartridge filter mask, long-sleeved shirt, long pants, ventilated but closed-off room, and so on. Allow two days of nonuse so that any lead dust in the room can settle and vacuum thoroughly before working there again. When stripping, an abrasive belt—50- to 80-grit—works best at first, followed by a 129-grit belt to smooth off the surface.

Stripping with Heat: An electric heat plate used in combination with a putty knife (as a scraper) works well, generally, on wide, flat surfaces. But the plate has to be handled with care. Held on wood surfaces for four to eight seconds, it can soften strips of paint about three inches wide. The knife is used to remove softened paint along one strip while the plate is applied to another.

The heat gun is probably the best solution where you are stripping narrow, contoured, or irregular surfaces such as moldings. After softening the paint by passing the gun over it slowly—at a range of several inches—you'll need steel wool or a scraper to do the removing part of the job. Remember that you have to keep your free hand clear of the air stream and that you need to protect yourself from toxic lead vapors.

PAINTING EXTERIORS

How much space a gallon of paint will cover depends on the surface material, the type of paint, and whether the paint is a primer or topcoat. Most house paints will cover 450 to 500 sq. ft./gal. on ordinary clapboard siding. Asbestos and wood shingles and rough surfaces such as stucco require 20 to 40 percent more paint for the same area. Bare wood requires more paint than prepainted surfaces; thus in estimating gallonage for primer, be sure you allow for the porosity of the unpainted surface (because it absorbs more liquid).

The number of gallons needed to cover a house can be found by dividing the total area to be painted by the number of square feet a gallon of paint will cover; for example, a 3,000-sq.-ft. area divided by 500 sq.-ft./gal. equals 6 gal. To find the total area to be painted, measure the distance around the house and multiply it by the average height of the house. (A house with an average height of 25 ft. and a perimeter distance of 100 ft. would have a total area of 2500 sq. ft. to be painted.) If the surface is rough or unusually absorbent, plan on using more paint. To find the amount of paint needed for the trim, allow for 20 to 30 percent of the amount of paint required for the sides of the house.

Paint and Tools

Before paint is used, it should be stirred until it is fully mixed. Lumps and pieces of paint skim should be filtered out. A full can should be partially poured into another container so that the pigment at the bottom can be mixed with the paint vehicle. When the paint is well mixed, the paint that was poured out can be returned and stirred until all of the paint is uniform. (It also is helpful to pour back and forth between containers to blend it.) Carry paint in half-filled cans or separate containers, so that brushes can be dipped and wiped on the inside to remove excess paint.

Brushes are old favorites for painting exteriors and are more effective than other painting tools for irregular surfaces where crevices and other hard-to-get-at recesses must be coated with paint. Several brushes may be required for the sides and trim: a wall brush (3 1/2 or 4 in.), trim brush (2 or 3 in.), and an angular sash brush (1 1/2 or 2 in.). Rollers are at their best with flat siding, but they can be used on clapboards also. Edge rollers and a trim brush will take care of edges and other areas inaccessible to the roller. Paint pads hold more paint than a brush and perform well on open, accessible surfaces such as clapboards and plywood siding. On shingles, they are not as effective because they cannot get paint into the crevices as well as brushes do. Paint-spraying equipment can be used to paint any type of surface. A simple, airless type of sprayer can be used for limited areas, but for painting an entire house, the large professional type of sprayer, with a compressor and separate paint tank, is much more efficient.

Extension ladders and scaffolding are used for areas above the reach of a stepladder. Wooden extension ladders are heavier than metal; this makes them awkward to carry, but they are more stable when placed against a wall. The foot of an extension ladder should be positioned at a distance from the wall equal to one-fourth of the ladder's height, for the safest angle. When in position (Fig. 3–17), the ladder should never be completely extended. Several rungs of the top section should line up with those on the bottom section for the greatest strength. Various attachments are available that make working on ladders safer or easier. Paint cans can be attached with S-hooks and paint trays with other hardware. A bow-shaped brace can be hooked onto the top of the ladder to hold it out from the wall, allowing the area immediately behind the ladder, such as a window, to be painted. Otherwise, ladders should never be positioned against windows or doors.

Scaffolding may be a better choice than an extension ladder where the area is large or there are several people working at once. It is usually erected so that it is braced

Table 3–2   Table of Exterior Paints and Surfaces

	Latex house paint	Oil-base house paint	Wood stains	Trim paint	Exterior varnish	Polyurethane	Deck varnish	Deck enamel	Metal primer	Latex masonry paint	Portland-cement paint	Rubber-base paint	Asphalt roof coating	Aluminum asphalt paint
Clapboards	●	●	●											
Wood shingles	●		●											
Other wood siding	●	●	●		○	○								
Asbestos siding	●													
Aluminum siding	●	○												
Masonry walls										●	●	●		
Wood trim	○	○	●	●										
Wood doors and windows	○	○	○	●	○	○								
Metal doors and windows	○	●		●										
Wooden floors			●				○	●						
Concrete floors										●		●		
Asphalt roofs													●	●
Wood shingle and shake roofs			●											
Galvanized drains iron and steel		●		●					●					

● Indicates preferred finish.
○ Indicates alternative finish.

against the house and supported by 4 X 4's or other heavy timbers. Once it is in place, scaffolding is easier to work from than an extension ladder. On a ladder it is not safe to hang out sideways to reach a wider area or to paint very much above the top of the ladder. Consequently, ladders have to be moved frequently. Ladders and scaffolding can be combined by placing planks between two ladders, or between a ladder and scaffolding or some other support.

Priming

Bare wood, whether new or old, must be primed and sometimes treated with a wood preservative. Pentachlorophenol or another preservative can be applied to unpainted wooden shingles, gutters, and other wood exposed to heavy moisture, to diminish wood rot. A primer should be compatible with the topcoat to create the maximum bond between the wood and paint. New wood may require one or sometimes two coats over a primer. A single topcoat may be enough if it contains adequate pigment. One-coat house paints contain additional pigment and are formulated to go over a primer or old paint in good condition.

New wood shingles are frequently stained with a shingle stain rather than being painted. But when they are painted, they must be primed to prevent bleeding. The primer should be covered with two coats of paint. Shingles that have been previously stained can be restained or painted. Once they have been painted, however, they cannot be stained again.

On previously painted wood, a primer is needed only to spot-prime bare wood where the paint has been removed. Old paint in very poor condition, however, also should be covered with a primer. One topcoat will usually be enough over old paint unless the color is being changed. In that case, use a one-coat house paint or a second coat of standard house paint.

Painting Sequence

Exterior areas are painted in a sequence from the top to the bottom of the house, to prevent paint from dripping and splattering on finished work. The highest parts of the house, the gables, dormers, and cornice and fascia boards of the eaves are painted first. Painting continues in bands down the sides. Trim around windows and doors and downspouts is painted next. Finally, decks, floors, and removable appendages such as screen doors, screen windows, and shutters are painted.

Painting Methods

Starting at the eaves, paint a 3- or 4-ft. band horizontally across the side of the house. On clapboards paint the edges of several boards first and then their flat sides (Fig. 3–18(a)).

Apply the paint liberally with short strokes, followed by long strokes back and forth to spread it evenly. Paint from dry areas into wet areas. The edges of the adjacent band should still be wet. By feathering these edges together with light strokes, lap marks will be avoided. When finishing for the day, try to complete a band at a window or other trim so that the dried vertical edge will not appear as a lap mark when painting is resumed.

Houses with wood or asbestos shingles should be stained or painted similarly in horizontal bands (Fig. 3–18(b)). The brushwork will differ, since a well loaded brush has to be used with vertical strokes to get paint into the openings between the shingles.

After the main body of the house has been painted, windows, doors, and other trim should be painted with trim enamel. Caulked seams and the joints between the siding and trim should be carefully covered with paint to prevent water from getting behind the boards and under the paint. Floors and decks are painted with deck enamel or stained after the doors and rails are painted.

Wood shingle or shake roofs usually are not painted, but sometimes they are stained. If they are to be stained, this should precede the painting of the rest of the house. Asphalt roof shingles may be painted to change their color or help the roof last longer. Asphalt roof coating or aluminum asphalt paint should be applied before the body of the house is painted.

Masonry that forms part of a house may be painted within the sequence of the house. It will have to be brushed and washed clean like the rest of the house before being covered with latex, rubber-base, or Portland-cement paint. Metal gutters and downspouts, flashings, iron railings, and other rust-prone metals must be cleaned of dirt and rust and painted with a primer, at the same time that the rest of the house is prepared. Some metals, such as aluminum and copper, do not need to be painted, but for decoration they can be finished with house or trim paints over a primer. Paint will prevent copper from staining the siding. Galvanized iron gutters and downspouts and other iron and steel will rust if not protected from moisture and air by a rust-inhibiting primer and topcoat. Most new metal, and metal which has been exposed to weather, must be cleaned or conditioned before being primed. Use mineral spirits to cut through a film of grease so that the primer can form a better bond. New metals should be conditioned with a metal conditioner, as required by the type of paint to be applied.

PAINT FAILURES

Paint may fail to maintain a tight, smooth film for several reasons. On improperly prepared surfaces, paint may crack either through the outer layer or all the way to the bare wood. It may peel off if the undercoat is dirty, greasy, or loose. Moisture under the paint causes blistering and peeling which cannot be corrected without eliminating the source of the moisture. Poor painting methods may cause several types of paint failure. If the paint is applied too thickly, it may sag and run or the surface paint may dry before the paint next to the wood dries, leaving a wrinkled effect. Too thin a coat of paint may result in excessive chalking. Paint over wet undercoat or paint applied during wet, cold weather may remain tacky for some time.

Most of these problems can be avoided in the normal course of painting by thorough preparation and cleaning of the surface, taking steps to eliminate the moisture problem, and careful observation of good painting methods. Of these, eliminating the source of moisture is probably the most difficult. Cracks and joints can be caulked, loose boards nailed down, leaks from gutters and downspouts stopped, and the exterior made watertight, but moisture from the inside of the house may still seep through the walls to condense and be absorbed into the wood siding under the paint. Exterior wall areas of bathrooms, kitchens, laundries, and children's rooms with vaporizers are inundated with escaping moisture and will be likely to blister and peel.

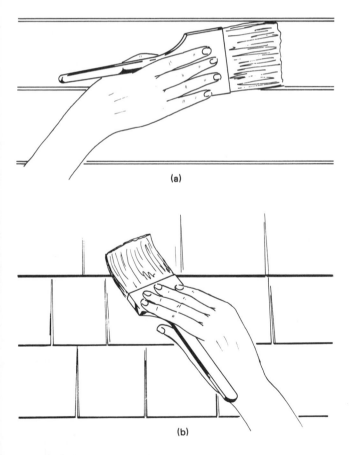

(a)

(b)

Fig. 3–18 a) Painting clapboard siding. b) Staining wood shingles.

The way to attack the problem is to reduce the moisture going through the walls and construct some form of moisture barrier in the walls. Vent fans in bathrooms and kitchens, vented clothes dryers, and a good airing with open windows will get rid of a lot of moisture. Attic louvers, crawl-space louvers, and small vents installed in the outside walls will help get rid of moisture already trapped in the house and between the walls. In new construction and remodeling, wall insulation is installed that has a vapor barrier facing the inside wall to keep moisture from passing through.

Before deciding what to do with paint that fails to hold, the type of failure and its possible causes must be determined. The types of failure usually can be separated by their distinct appearances.

Alligatoring consists of an alligator skin-like pattern or small cracks or checks over an area (Fig. 3–19(a)). It may be caused by painting over an undercoat which is not dry enough, using too much oil as a thinner, or painting over varnish or grease. The paint must be removed and the bare wood primed.

Bleeding causes paint to become discolored. Resin, creosote, and alkalis should be sealed with shellac, aluminum paint, or some other effective sealer. The discolored paint and staining substance should be scraped clean and the surface sealed before it is repainted.

Blistering consists of paint bubbles (Fig. 3–19(b)), which eventually break, exposing bare wood. They almost always indicate the presence of moisture in the wood under the paint. The blisters and loose paint must be scraped off so that the wood can dry out before it is primed and repainted. Unless the source of the moisture is found and eliminated, the paint is likely to blister again.

Chalking is excessive if a heavy coat of paint dust comes off when paint is rubbed with the hand or a piece of cloth. Normal chalking produces a much lighter layer of paint dust which helps to clean dirt and old paint from the walls. Excessive chalking may be caused by too thin a layer of paint, painting over a porous surface, painting with an oil-base paint during wet weather, or by a poor quality paint. The chalked surface must be brushed clean and washed with a strong detergent before it is repainted. To avoid having the new paint chalk, two coats of paint or a primer and top coat may be needed, especially over a porous surface.

Checking consists of small cracks in the surface of the paint, but it is not as extensive as the checks in alligatoring. It may be caused by not allowing sufficient time for the undercoat to dry or by a poor quality paint. Checked paint must be removed and the area primed before a finish coat is applied.

Cracking (Fig. 3–19(c)) is the actual cracking of all of the layers of paint down to the bare wood. Scaling occurs when the cracked paint scales off. Cracking may be caused by a poor quality paint, insufficient mixing of paint, inadequate brushing out of poorly mixed paint, or painting over a damp surface. When housepaint loses its elasticity, it can no longer expand and contract with the wood and will crack, especially where there are many layers of old paint. Cracked and scaling paint must be removed before the surface is painted again.

Crawling may occur shortly after paint is applied. The paint seems to form in drop-like bubbles. Instead of continuing to paint, stop and consider the following possible causes for the crawling and the proper steps to correct the problem: The surface may be too damp or cold, or it may be greasy or waxy; the paint may not be mixed enough, or it may be of poor quality. After trying to eliminate the cause, paint a test strip before going on with the painting. The bad paint should be removed and the surface repainted.

Fading occurs normally as the pigment in paint is broken down by exposure to the sun and atmosphere. It may be unusually rapid under some conditions: poor priming, too much thinner, poor quality paint with insufficient pigment, too thin a coat or too few coats, exposure to some kinds of fumes, and exposure to the sun. The house will have to be repainted with a well-pigmented paint to regain its color.

Mildew looks like blackish dirt (Fig. 3–19(d)) but it is a fungus, which grows on paint in damp, shaded areas. It can be avoided by using paint containing a mildewcide. Where it is already growing on the paint, mildew must be scrubbed off with a solution of household bleach (1 qt.), trisodium phosphate or borax (2/3 cup), detergent (1/3 cup) in warm

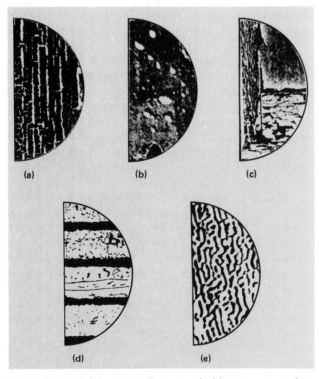

(a)   (b)   (c)

(d)   (e)

Fig. 3–19 Paint failures: a) alligatoring, b) blistering, c) cracking and scaling, d) mildew, e) wrinkling.

water (3 qt.). The surface should be rinsed and dried before repainting with a mildew-resistant paint. Mildewcide also can be bought separately and added to paint.

Sagging and *running* are caused by applying paint too thickly, not brushing paint out, or by a waxy, greasy, or very glossy undersurface. Whatever the cause, the sagging paint should be removed and the surface repainted.

Tackiness or *slow-drying* paint may be caused by painting in wet, cold weather, painting over a wet under-coat, applying too thick a coat, or using a poor quality paint. Good-quality paint will dry eventually, but old, poor-quality paint may remain tacky until it is cleaned off.

Wrinkling of the paint surface (Fig. 3–19(e)) is a surface phenomenon in which the outer paint film dries in a wrin-kled pattern leaving the paint beneath it still wet. It is caused by applying too thick a coat of paint. Wrinkled areas should be scraped clean before being repainted.

REPAIRING WALLS AND CEILINGS

Walls and ceilings are likely to develop cracks, dents, open joints, exposed nails, holes, bulges, and other injuries. Most of these are minor and can be repaired by cleaning and patching. Major problems, such as bulging plaster or water-damaged gypsum board, require removing and replacing sections of the wall or ceiling.

Most walls and ceilings are made of gypsum board, or plaster and lath. Gypsum board (also called drywall, Sheet Rock, and wallboard) is made in standard 4 X 8 ft. sheets (and other sizes) which can be nailed directly to wall studs or furring strips. The sheet consists of a layer of gypsum (1/4, 3/8, 1/2, or 5/8 in.) sandwiched between a facing and a backing of heavy paper. Since it is one of the cheapest coverings and is easy to install, gypsum board is widely used in constructing new houses and apartments and in remodel-ing. Plaster walls and ceilings are found in older houses and more expensive new construction. Plaster is backed by wooden, metal, or gypsum-board lath which, in turn, is nailed to the wall studs or furring strips. This backing makes a convenient support for patching plaster when repairing small holes.

There are several good patching compounds. The ready-mixed compounds are expensive, but for small re-pairs they are reliable and simpler to use than powders, which have to be mixed. *Spackle* can be purchased ready-mixed or in a powder form. It's good for small cracks and holes because it shrinks much less than most other patching materials. It also contains adhesive to help it bond to wood, gypsum board, plaster, and other porous materials. *Gyp-sum-board joint compound* also comes ready-mixed or in powdered form. The ready-mixed compound is relatively

cheap and can be used for filling cracks and smoothing irregular surfaces, as well as for taping joints. *Patching plas-ter* is cheaper than spackling compound and sets slowly enough to be used to fill cracks and holes. It is mixed with water until it is thick enough to stay in place in a crack. *Plaster of Paris* can be used for patching, but it has to be worked into place quickly since it sets rapidly. *Wood dough* or *wood putty* is useful for filling small cracks and crevices, but it is more expensive than most other patching materials. The easiest way to make *plaster* is to use a ready-mixed powder and water. Plaster should be used instead of patch-ing materials to repair large areas of plaster walls and ceil-ings.

REPAIRING CRACKS

Plaster cracks when the wooden frame of the house moves in any way. Normal drying of new wood, settling of a house, or even shrinking of the plaster itself will cause cracks in the ceilings and walls. The surface of gypsum board is unlikely to crack because of its heavy paper facing, but joints be-tween sheets of gypsum board may open up. There isn't much that can be done to prevent plaster from cracking, but it can be repaired once it has cracked.

Hairline cracks should be cleaned out to remove loose bits of plaster without disturbing the solid edges (Fig. 3-20(a)). Wet the crack with water, and rub in a patching paste of ready-mixed spackling compound. It's better to have the patch slightly higher than the surrounding surface rather than recessed. After it is dry, the patch should be sanded flush with a fine-grade abrasive and sealed with shellac or a primer-sealer before it is painted.

Small cracks larger than hairline cracks should be cleaned of loose and weak plaster with a sharp-pointed tool like a puncturing-type can opener. (Be careful not to turn a small crack into a large crack by overzealous scraping.) The dry plaster in a crack will absorb moisture from the patching compound, causing the patch to shrink, unless the dry plas-ter is first saturated with water from a sponge, spray gun, brush, or other device. After the crack is thoroughly wet, use a flexible putty knife to fill it with spackling compound or patching plaster (Fig. 3–20(b)). Smooth off the surface but not so much that it recedes. Before it becomes too hard, the patch should be sanded down with a fine-grade abrasive wrapped around a flat sanding block. Paint the patch with a primer-sealer to reduce absorption. (Fig. 3-20(a)(b)).

Large cracks are patched like small cracks except that the edges should be undercut and the layers of patching plaster built up gradually. Push the plaster deep into the crack so that it fills the widening gap. Be sure that it is forced tightly against the rough edges so that the two will bond together. Deep cracks may have to be filled with two layers of patching compound. A very thick single layer will sag. Build up the final layer so that it can be sanded flush with

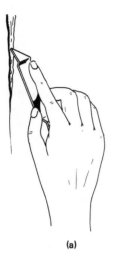

(a)

(b)

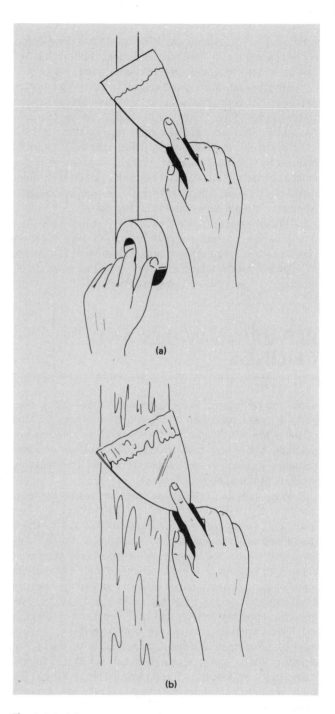

(a)

(b)

Fig. 3–20 a) Cleaning out a crack. b) Filling a crack.

the surface. Use a medium-grade abrasive to remove excess patching material, followed by a fine-grade abrasive for a smooth finish.

Small cracks between sheets of gypsum board can be filled with joint compound, smoothed over, and sanded when dry. Large cracks may require that the original layers of joint compound and the tape be removed with a putty knife and new tape and joint compound placed over the joint. Apply the compound in a 4-in. wide band along the joint (Fig. 3–21(a)), and press the tape down lightly to embed it without squeezing out the compound (Fig. 3–21(b)). Cover the tape with a thin coat of joint compound and let it dry overnight. Rough ridges should be smoothed by sanding or wiping with a wet sponge or rag. (Caution: Many brands of

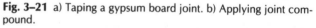

Fig. 3–21 a) Taping a gypsum board joint. b) Applying joint compound.

joint compound contain asbestos fibers which can be inhaled when the dried compound is sanded.) After the first layer is smoothed off, another layer of compound is applied over the tape, extending 2 in. on either side beyond the first layer. A third layer should be applied, wider than the previous layer, and feathered out smoothly against the surface of the gypsum board.

REPAIRING HOLES

Small holes in gypsum board are repaired by cleaning away loose pieces, wetting the edges with water, and filling the gap with spackling compound or patching plaster. After the patch has dried, it should be sanded smooth with a fine-grade abrasive. If the hole is too large, the patching compound will fall right through. Some form of backing must be inserted to support it. A piece of wire mesh or cardboard a little larger than the hole can be pushed through (Fig. 3–22(a)) and held over the back of the hole with a short length of string. Patching compound is pushed into the hole to bond the backing to the edges (Fig. 3–22(b)). When the first thin coat of compound dries, the backing will stay firmly in place and the rest of the hole can be filled.

For still *larger holes in gypsum board,* a patch will have to be cut from a piece of scrap gypsum board. Cut around the hole in a rectangular pattern with a utility knife. From the scrap gypsum board, cut a patch the same shape and size as the hole. The fit doesn't have to be exact since the edges can be cut down if the patch is a little too large, and taping compound can fill in to some extent if the patch is a little too small. Coat the edges of the hole and the patch with joint compound and place the gypsum-board patch in the hole, being careful that it doesn't go in too deeply. To provide a temporary handle to hold the patch, attach to the front of the patch an adhesive picture hanger, brad, or small screw. When the compound dries, the joint between the patch and the wall or ceiling should be covered with tape and joint compound. The entire gypsum-board patch can be covered with a final layer of compound to help make it flush with the rest of the wall. In cases where a large hole is backed by a stud or furring strip, the patch can be nailed directly to the wood and its edges taped and covered with joint compound.

Small holes in plaster should be cleaned of loose particles, the edges thoroughly wet with water, and the opening filled with spackling compound or patching plaster. Larger holes will require more than one layer of patching compound. The first layer of compound should be forced into the lath so that it is firmly anchored. Scratch grooves over its surface so that the next layer of patching plaster has something to grip. Fill in the final layer of patching plaster so that it is flush or just slightly recessed. If it is recessed, apply a surface layer of spackling compound. Each layer of patching compound should be wet down before the next layer is applied. The final layer should be sanded flush with the surface and sealed before it is painted or covered with a wallcovering.

Large holes in plaster that are a foot or more wide should be patched with ready-mixed plaster. Use a trowel to apply the plaster almost flush with the surface. When this layer is dry, finish with a coat of plaster or patching compound. Draw a wide straightedge across the hole so that it removes excess patching material. A wet trowel will help

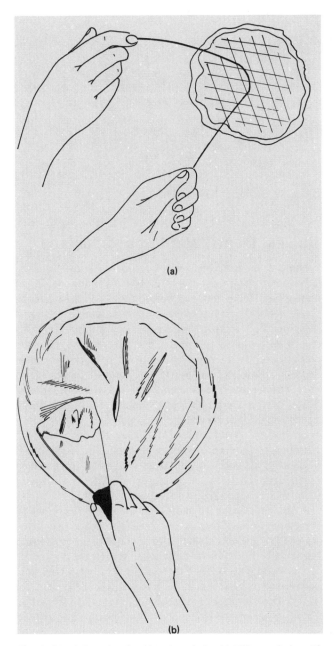

Fig. 3–22 a) Inserting backing in a hole. b) Filling a hole with patching plaster.

make a smoother finish. When the patch is dry, sand it flush and seal before painting.

Another way to fill a large hole in plaster is to cut a patch from gypsum board. Coat the back of the gypsum board with patching plaster and place it against the lath so that it fills most of the hole. Use patching plaster to cover the face of the gypsum board for the finishing coat. Smooth down the wet patch and sand it flush (when dry) in the usual manner.

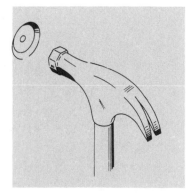

Fig. 3–23 Driving in a popped nail.

Bulges, Dents, and Popped Nails

When plaster gets wet it will often break loose from the lathing and bulge or start to crumble. All of the weakened plaster has to be removed before the area can be made sound. If only the surface layer of plaster crumbles, it should be scraped clean so the underlayers can dry out. The area can be repaired by applying a new finish coat of patching plaster over the dry sublayer. More often, all of the plaster is weak and loose and has to be removed. Broken laths should be replaced and the hole patched with ready-mixed plaster or with a large section of gypsum board capped with a finishing coat of patching compound.

Dents in gypsum board or plaster can be filled with spackling compound or joint compound. The dent should be cleaned out and wet with water first so that the patching compound will bond. If the patching material shrinks, a second layer will have to be applied.

Annular ring nails that are used to fasten gypsum board sometimes come loose and pop out. Their heads may bulge under the joint compound or they may break the surface. These nails should be driven back in if they are backed by sound wood (Fig. 3–23). If there appears to be nothing solid behind them, they should be pulled out and the hole repaired. In either case, a second annular ring nail should be placed a couple of inches away and pounded into solid wood to fasten the gypsum board at that point. A hammer with a beveled face should be used to hammer the nail and indent the gypsum-board facing. This indentation can be filled and finished like any small dent.

WALLPAPERING

Before hanging wallpaper, decisions have to be made about the type of wallcovering, pattern, number of rolls needed, preparation of the walls, refinishing the rest of the room, and how the covering is to be hung.

TYPES OF WALLCOVERINGS

Although wallcoverings include almost anything that can be used to cover and decorate a wall, wallpaper usually refers to either paper or vinyl wallcoverings. *Ordinary wallpaper* is made by printing patterns on long, wide rolls of plain paper. After they are printed, the rolls are cut to standard widths and lengths. When too much paste is used, the paper weakens (because it absorbs water) causing it to tear easily. This can be avoided by using wallpaper which has been coated with a thin layer of plastic. *Coated wallpapers* are resistant to moisture and can be wiped with a damp sponge, but they cannot withstand scrubbing or repeated exposure to water. Their greater resistance makes them preferable to uncoated papers for children's rooms and family rooms. *Vinyl wallcoverings* are made by printing with vinyl inks (which withstand fading) on vinyl-impregnated materials laminated to fabric or strong paper backings. A tough protective coating of vinyl on the surface of the wallcovering makes it impervious to water and very resistant to abrasion.

Most wallpaper is printed in large quantities on automatic printing machinery. Handprinted wallpaper, however, is created by an individual silk-screen process. Since the artist-craftsman produces his design on a limited number of rolls, the papers are quite expensive, but they have their place where wallpaper with a unique, artistic design is important to a room's decor.

Prepasted wallpaper is ordinarily wallpaper which has already been coated with adhesive for convenience in hanging. The adhesive won't stick until it is wet with water. Instructions with prepasted rolls recommend submerging each strip in a container of water before unrolling it for hanging. If this procedure is unduly messy, the strip can be cut and placed on a pasting table like any other wallpaper. The adhesive can be wet with a paste brush dipped in water or the adhesive can be ignored and paste applied with a brush in the usual manner.

NUMBER OF ROLLS

Wallpaper comes in rolls of different widths and lengths. Single rolls, by industry practice, contain 36 sq. ft. Consequently, if a roll is 18 in. wide it will be longer than a roll which is 27 in. wide, since the areas are the same. Most wallpaper widths are between 18 and 28 in. There are also double and triple rolls, which are uncut multiples of a single roll. A double roll contains 72 sq. ft., and a triple roll, 108 sq. ft. Often there is less waste if the wallpaper is purchased in multiple rolls. A single roll can be purchased separately if it is needed for the last few strips.

The number of rolls required to cover a room can be determined by measuring the distance around the room and referring to an estimating chart (Table 3–3), or by calculating the area to be covered and dividing by the number of square feet in a single roll. To use the chart, measure the distance

Table 3-3 Wallcovering Estimating Chart

Distance Around Room in Feet	Single Rolls for Wall Areas Height of Ceiling			Number Yards for Borders	Single Rolls for Ceilings
	8 Feet	9 Feet	10 Feet		
28	8	8	10	11	2
30	8	8	10	11	2
32	8	10	10	12	2
34	10	10	12	13	4
36	10	10	12	13	4
38	10	12	12	14	4
40	10	12	12	15	4
42	12	12	14	15	4
44	12	12	14	16	4
46	12	14	14	17	6
48	14	14	16	17	6
50	14	14	16	18	6
52	14	14	16	19	6
54	14	16	18	19	6
56	14	16	18	20	8
58	16	16	18	21	8
60	16	18	20	21	8
62	16	18	20	22	8
64	16	18	20	23	8
66	18	20	20	23	10
68	18	20	22	24	10
70	18	20	22	25	10
72	18	20	22	25	12
74	20	22	22	26	12
76	20	22	24	27	12
78	20	22	24	27	14
80	20	22	26	28	14
82	22	24	26	29	14
84	22	24	26	30	16
86	22	24	26	30	16
88	24	26	28	31	16
90	24	26	28	32	18

Deduct one single roll for every two average-size doors or windows.

around the room and the wall height between the ceiling and top of the baseboard. The chart shows the number of single rolls required for the combinations of distance around the room and wall height, but it doesn't allow for uncovered doors and windows. From the number of rolls indicated in the chart, subtract one single roll for every two normal-size doors, windows, or other areas that will not need to be covered.

To estimate the number of rolls needed by the area to be covered, find the area of each wall by measuring its width and height and multiplying them together. For example, one wall of a 15-ft.-wide room with an 8-ft. ceiling would have an area of 120 sq. ft. Add the areas of all of the walls together and divide by 30 sq. ft. (allowing the difference between 30 and 36 sq. ft. for waste in trimming) for a single roll. For example, if a total wall area of 480 sq. ft. were divided by 30 sq. ft., it would indicate that 16 single rolls were needed, without allowing for doors and windows.

Border paper is purchased by the running yard. Measure around the room and convert the total distance to yards. To determine the number of rolls required to cover a ceiling use the chart after measuring the distance around the room or find the area of the ceiling. The area is found in the same way as for the area of a wall, and divided by the usable 30 sq. ft. in a single roll, to determine the total number of rolls required.

Order all of the wallpaper at the same time to ensure that the shading and trim are uniform. Rolls in the same lot will be printed with identical inking mixtures and pressures. If rolls are from different lots, they may differ in the shade and intensity of color, and their edges may not match. When the wallpaper arrives, check to see that the pattern is correct. If you find wrinkles, stains, or other damage, return it for replacement.

PREPARATION FOR PAPERING

Before hanging wallpaper, walls must be repaired and cleaned, and woodwork, ceilings, and floors must be painted and finished. Open joints, cracks, and holes in walls and separations between walls and baseboards should be filled and sanded smooth. Hairline cracks can be left but spackling compound or patching plaster should be used to repair larger cracks.

Plaster walls should be sanded with a medium-grade abrasive until they feel smooth. Walls in older houses may be made of sand plaster, which contains large particles that will appear as small bumps under the wallpaper unless they are sealed and sanded. These hard-to-see bumps can be found by sliding your hand over the wall. After the wall is sanded, it should be washed to remove substances that might interfere with the paste or show up under the wallpaper. A solution of washing soda will remove most dirt but trisodium phosphate will be needed to remove grease and heavy stains. The walls should be rinsed and dried before the wallpaper is hung. Gypsum-board walls, which are covered with a heavy paper facing, do not have to be sanded but should be primed with a latex primer to seal the surface.

Old Wallpaper

Old wallpaper may be stripped or it may be covered with new wallpaper if it is in good condition. The easiest alternative is to cover it. To be sure the new wallpaper will hold and lie smoothly, check to see that there are no more than two previous layers. Rough seams must be sanded, glossy facings dulled with an abrasive, and loose paper pasted down. Even when these precautions have been taken, new wallpaper may pull loose or blister where excess paste saturates and loosens the old wallpaper underneath. The safest alternative is to remove all of the old wallpaper. In fact, vinyl coverings require a bare wall.

Wallpaper is removed by softening the paste with water and scraping and peeling the strips from the wall. The process is messy. Drop cloths or plastic sheets should be laid on the floor next to the wall to catch the debris and water. Rub a wet sponge over an area of paper to soak it and weaken the paste. Scrape the paper loose with a wallpaper scraper or a putty knife. The sponge and scraper can be used in unison by moving up and down each strip.

Coated wallpapers should be sanded to break the protective layer of plastic before they are soaked. Vinyls and other fabric-backed wallcoverings hold together as a strip. Loosen one corner first; the entire strip can then be peeled off. A wet sponge may have to be worked under the strip as it is peeled to weaken sections that won't pull loose.

A wallpaper steamer will help where there are several layers to strip. (Glossy or painted wallpaper surfaces may have to be roughed up with sandpaper so they will absorb moisture.) A steamer heats water to produce a steam, which flows through a hose to a flat perforated plate held against the wall. The steam quickly soaks through several layers of paper and loosens them sufficiently to be scraped or pulled off.

Old wallpaper on gypsum-board walls poses a problem. If the gypsum board was not primed and sealed before being papered, the paper facing on thy gypsum board may peel off when wallpaper is removed. In this case, the old wallpaper should be repaired so that it is smooth and painted over with a primer-sealer. It can then be covered with new wallpaper. If the gypsum board was primed first, the paper can be stripped in the usual manner; take care not to gouge the paper facing.

Painted Walls

Painted walls in good condition need the least preparation. Small nailholes and cracks should be filled and the wall washed and rinsed. If the paint is glossy, it can be dulled for better adhesion by washing with washing soda, or sanding lightly.

Unpainted Walls

New plaster walls shouldn't be papered until they have cured for several months or have been treated to neutralize the alkali. If they are papered earlier, the alkali in the plaster should be neutralized by washing with a zinc sulfate solution. New gypsum board can be papered after it has been primed with a latex primer. Grooves, nicks, and open joints in either plaster or gypsum board must be repaired and smoothed down before the wallpaper is hung.

Old plaster walls which have never been painted have usually been covered with wallpaper. They should be repaired and washed before they are papered. Old gypsum board walls which have never been painted are likely to be dented and scratched. They should be repaired and primed with a latex primer.

Sizing

Size, which is applied to walls with a paste brush, is used in conjunction with some pastes for better adhesion. It is commonly used on plaster and gypsum-board walls when it is necessary to use wheat paste or special adhesives for heavy wallcoverings. Size is dissolved in warm water and the entire wall is coated and allowed to dry before the wall is papered. Instructions with wallpaper and other coverings will indicate whether the walls should be sized.

TOOLS AND MATERIALS

Only a few steps in hanging wallpaper require special wallpapering tools. Most tools may be borrowed or adapted from other functions.

Pasting and sizing: An 8-in. paste brush (Fig. 3–24(a)) is used to size walls and apply paste to wallpaper. They can be mixed in plastic buckets or similar containers.

Cutting and trimming: Long wallpapering scissors (12-in. in length) are ideal for making fast straight cuts, but ordinary scissors will serve almost as well (Fig. 3–24(b)). Razors will cut as well as trim wheels and trimming knives, as long as they are new and sharp. A long straight edge (4-ft. level) is necessary for cutting folded strips vertically.

Keeping strips vertical: A carpenter's level (Fig. 3–24(c)) or a plumb bob (Fig. 3–24(d)) can be used to mark a vertical guideline on the wall.

Smoothing wallpaper: A wide smoothing brush (Fig. 3–24(e)) is essential to smooth out wrinkles and bubbles and press wallpaper tightly against the wall.

Fastening seams: A seam roller (Fig. 3–24(f)) is needed to flatten out seams so that each edge adheres to the wall.

Measuring: Either a folding wood rule or a steel tape (Fig. 3–24(g)) will be adequate for measuring.

Working surface: Any reasonably smooth surface that is at least 3 X 6 ft. can serve as a place to paste and cut wallpaper. A piece of plywood or several wide boards on top of a table will do.

Climbing and reaching: An old chair, stepladder, or other steady support is necessary to stand on in hanging wallpaper.

Removing old wallpaper: Sponges, a wallpaper stripper, putty knives, and drop cloths are essential. A steamer is optional.

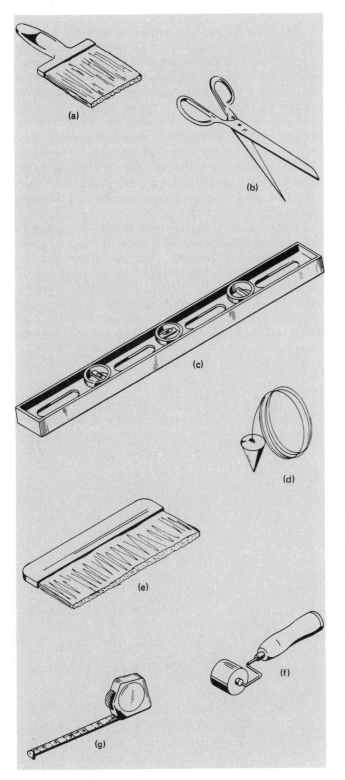

Fig. 3–24 Wallpapering tools: a) paste brush, b) scissors, c) carpenter's level, d) plumb line, e) smoothing brush, f) seam roller, g) push-pull tape.

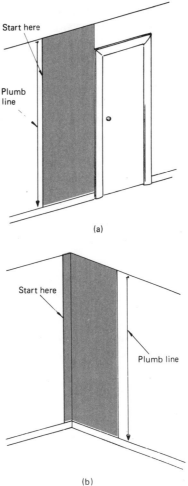

Fig. 3–25 Positioning the first strip a) starting adjacent to a door, b) starting in a corner.

Patching materials: Spackling compound, patching plaster, plaster of Paris, and wood dough are all useful in filling various sizes of cracks and holes.

PREPARING THE PAPER

The starting point for the first strip is important. If it is started in a corner or adjacent to a door or window, the poor match of the final strip will not be so obvious (Fig. 3–25(a)). Strips can be hung from left to right, for example, around the room so that the last short strip is placed over the door or window next to the first strip. Since the width for the last strip is unlikely to be the exact width of the wallpaper, this strip will have to be cut vertically to fit.

If the wallpaper is a solid color or has a simple pattern, the first strip can be started in any convenient place (Fig. 3–25(b)), since the contrast with the last strip will be inconspicuous. On the other hand, if the pattern is strong, it may be advisable to start the first strip in the center of a wall to emphasize the symmetry of the overall design. Full-length strips should be hung starting from the initial strip in the center in one direction to the left or right until encountering the first door, window, or other obstacle. Strips should then be hung on the other side of the center strip and continued around the room in the opposite direction. If the pattern is strong, the level of the ceiling should be checked with a carpenter's level. If the ceiling is not level, draw a level line around the walls as a guide for the wallpaper pattern so that it will not seem to rise inexplicably as the ceiling becomes higher. Place an attractive element in the pattern just below this line.

Cutting and Matching

Measure the distance between the ceiling and the top of the baseboard where the first strip will be hung, and add 4 to 6 in. to the measurement. Roll out the wallpaper on the pasting table, mark off this measurement, and cut the first strip. As long as it is sharp, you can use a long pair of scissors, a new razor blade, or a utility or trimming knife. Check the accuracy of the measurement by holding the strip where it is to be hung to see if it overlaps the ceiling and baseboard by a few inches. If the length is correct, several more strips can be cut after the patterns are matched at the edges.

To match the patterns, unroll another length from the roll, and place it uncut next to the first strip so that the patterns match at their edges. If the pattern is a straight pattern, similar on both edges of the paper, the pattern will match when the tops of the two strips are almost even with each other. If the pattern is a "drop" pattern, the second strip will extend beyond the top of the first strip by the distance of the drop. In either case, match the edges, and cut the roll so that the bottom of the second strip is even with the bottom of the first strip. Several strips can be cut and stacked for pasting before the first one is hung. However, no more should be cut than will cover the wall area that requires full-length strips.

Each subsequent strip in a drop pattern will sacrifice the excess at the top to waste if the strips are cut in sequence from the same roll. There is a way to avoid this. In a drop pattern, the pattern is identical at the same level around the room on every other strip. By cutting the odd strips from one roll and the even strips from a second roll, the patterns will match, and there will be little waste from either roll. Each group of strips should be marked to distinguish it from the other one.

Pasting and Hanging

The first strip of wallpaper must be hung vertically as a guide for the strips that follow. The easiest way to do this is to mark

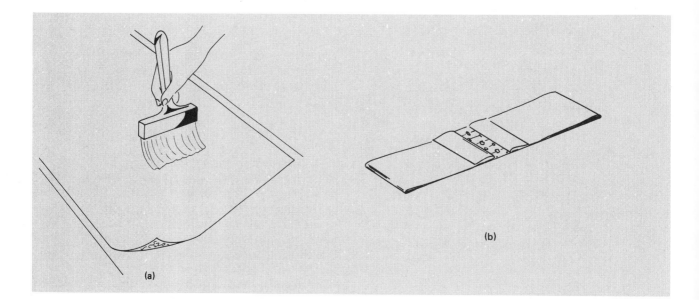

Fig. 3–26 a) Brushing on paste. b) Folding a pasted strip.

a vertical line on the wall and butt the edge of the strip to it. If the strip is to be started at the edge of a door, the line should be marked the width of the wallpaper from the door less an inch to allow for overlapping the door trim. For example, for 28-in.-wide wallpaper, measure horizontally 27 in. and make a pencil mark. A vertical line can be drawn from this point by using a carpenter's level or a plumb bob and string. Line up the carpenter's level at the marked point and draw a line along its edge. The level will have to be moved upward and downward to extend the line. A plumb bob can be hung from a nail held on the marked point high on the wall. When the plumb bob stops swinging, the string will indicate where the line is to be drawn. Draw several pencil marks directly behind the string and connect them with a straightedge. Alternatively, the string can be coated with colored chalk (such as blue carpenter's chalk), held tightly in place at both ends, and the middle pulled back and released, so that the length of the string snaps against the wall, leaving a vertical chalk line.

Ordinary light-weight wallpapers are hung with either a wheat or cellulose paste. Vinyl wallcoverings and other heavier materials require the special pastes described in their instructions. Mix the paste with water following the directions on the package. To avoid breathing in dust from the paste, wear a painter's mask.

Stack the strips of wallpaper face down with their edges lined up evenly, and apply paste liberally along the middle of the top strip. Brush it outward (Fig. 3–26(a)), and apply more paste until the backing is covered. The edges should be carefully coated but the last few inches at either end can be left unpasted, since they will be trimmed off. Skip spots can be found by looking at the pasted surface in the direction of a window or light so that light glares on the paste; the skips will show up as dull spots.

To make the pasted strip easier to handle, the ends are folded over so that the pasted backing is inside the fold (Fig. 3–26(b)). When about two thirds of the strip is covered with paste, fold the completed end so that it covers almost all of the pasted area. The sides should be evenly aligned. Pull the rest of the strip up on the table, paste it, and fold it over to meet the end folded previously. You may have to slide the folded sections to align their edges. In folding, loop the ends instead of creasing them to avoid a permanent crease.

The first strip can be hung as soon as it is pasted, or it can be put aside until several other strips are ready. If the wallpaper is light and absorbs moisture quickly, it should be hung as soon as it is pasted or it will weaken and be likely to tear. Some heavier wallcoverings take a while to absorb the paste to the point where they are ready for hanging.

When the first strip is ready to be hung, unfold the short fold toward the top, and hold the strip up on the wall so that it lines up with the vertical guide line. A few inches should overlap onto the ceiling (Fig. 3–27(a)). Press the pasted upper section against the wall with your hand, and use the smoothing brush to smooth the paper outward from the

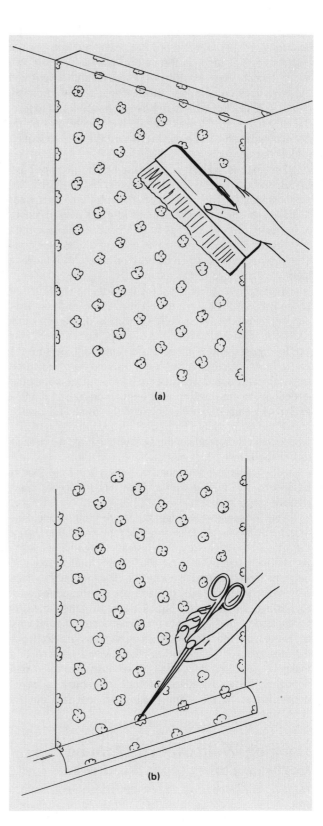

(a)

(b)

Fig. 3–27 Hanging the first strip: a) smoothing, b) trimming.

center so that the paste holds it in position. Next, unfold the lower part of the strip and brush it down and into position with its edge aligned on the vertical guideline. If the strip seems to slant, peel the lower part loose, and slide it until the edge lines up correctly. Brush the strip firmly from the center in both directions to remove air bubbles and to force the strip tightly to the wall. The ends of the bristles on the smoothing brush can be used to pound the strip to make a fold in the corner.

The excess wallpaper overlapping the ceiling, baseboard, and door casing can be trimmed (Fig. 3–27(b)) with a pair of long scissors or other sharp blade, such as a razor. With scissors, use the closed ends to make a sharp crease in the paper where it bends to overlap the ceiling and the baseboard. Pull the paper loose and cut along the crease. The trimmed end can then be brushed smoothly into place. With a razor, use a flat metal edge (a wide scraper or straightedge) as a guide. Hold the flat side of the guide flush to the wall, and cut along the edge. This will make an even cut and allow the strip to butt the ceiling or the top of the baseboard. The edge of the strip overlapping the door casing can be creased and trimmed in the same way. Be sure that the edge is not cut short or it will leave a narrow gap between the casing and wallpaper. It is better to err in the other direction—to cut the strip a little too wide so that it has to fold a sixteenth of an inch against the trim. The overlap above the door should be pasted flat against the wall after a horizontal slit is made in the strip where it passes over the top of the trim.

After the strip is smoothed out, wash it and the abutting baseboard and ceiling with a clean wet sponge or rag to remove paste and dirt.

The remaining full-length strips are hung in the same manner as the first strip except that they are butted against the edge of the preceding strip instead of a pencil guideline. As a strip is hung, it can be slid slightly to eliminate gaps between the edges and to correct vertical mismatches in the pattern. When it's exactly in place, use the smoothing brush to remove wrinkles and bubbles and to flatten the strip tightly against the wall. Trim the top and bottom, and wash the paste from the strip. After seams have had ten to twenty minutes to dry, go back and roll them with a seam roller to make sure that the edges stay down. Press the roller hard enough to flatten the edges but not hard enough to leave a depression along the seam. Paste often squeezes out and should be washed off.

Hanging Wallcoverings Around Corners, Doors, and Windows

Hanging wallpaper around corners is slow because most strips have to be cut vertically to fit (Fig. 3–28). If a full-width strip is hung around an inside corner without being cut vertically, it will soon pull loose. By cutting the strip so that

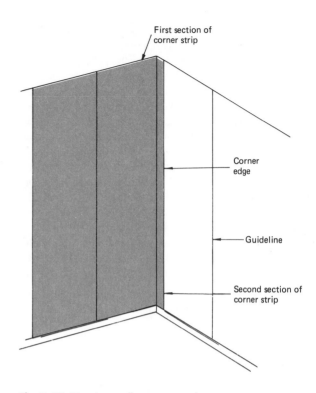

Fig. 3–28 Hanging wallpaper around a corner.

one section extends an inch or less around the corner and the remaining section butts the edge of the first strip, both sections will adhere tightly to the wall. When it is apparent that another full-width strip will extend around the corner by more than an inch, measure the distance between the edge of the last strip and the corner. If the walls and corner are not plumb, the measurement should be to the furthest part of the corner. Mark off this measurement plus one inch for rounding the corner on the next folded and pasted strip on the pasting table. Measure in from the edge which is to match the strip already hung. Mark this distance at the top and bottom of the folded strip so a long straightedge can be placed between the marks. Hold the straightedge down tightly and run a razor blade along its edge to cut the strip vertically. The razor has to be pressed down hard to cut through both layers. Keep the straightedge in place until the two sections of the strip are completely separated. When the first section of the strip is hung butting the previous strip, its other edge will extend around the corner by approximately an inch depending on how plumb the corner is. Use the bristles of the smoothing brush to pound the strip into the corner and to flatten the edge extending onto the next wall. Trim the top and bottom. The second half of the strip must be hung so that its leading edge is vertical. Measure the width of the strip and mark off that distance horizontally from the edge of the first section in the corner. Draw a vertical guideline on the wall at that point in the same way

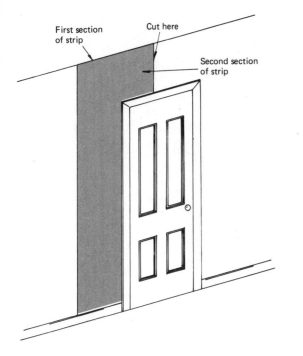

First section of strip

Cut here

Second section of strip

Fig. 3–29 Hanging wallpaper around a door.

as for the first strip. Align the strip on the vertical guideline and check to see if there are any gaps between the edges at the corner. If there are, slide the strip toward the corner until the gaps are covered. The small amount of overlap will not be noticeable. The leading edge of the strip establishes a vertical guide for the following strips. Smooth the strip, trim the top and bottom, and wash it before hanging the next strip. At intervals, go back and use the smoothing brush to press the strip into the corner until it adheres tightly. Wallpaper is hung around outside corners in a similar manner. The fold around the corner may be more difficult to paste down than on an inside corner.

Wallpapering around doors and windows (Fig. 3–29) also requires that strips be cut vertically. If a full-width strip is so wide that it would overlap the door or window trim by more than an inch, it should be cut. Measure the distance from the edge of the last strip to the edge of the trim. Mark off this distance plus one inch for trimming on the matching edge of the next folded and pasted strip. Use a straightedge and razor to cut the strip into two sections in the same way as a corner strip would be handled. Hang the first section so that it butts the edge of the previous strip and slightly overlaps the edge of the door or window trim. Brush it down until it is smooth and the overlap is folded against the trim. This edge can be trimmed with scissors or a razor. Crease the strip with the side of the scissors where it butts the trim. Pull the edge loose and trim along the crease with scissors, or place a straightedge flat against the wall flush to the trim

and trim the strip with a razor. The top of the strip over a door or window should be sliced horizontally where it meets the trim and smoothed down flat. Cut a short full-width strip to go between the trim and ceiling or baseboard, and hang it so that its edge butts the last strip. Short strips have to be hung above and below window trim so that they line up vertically. When a full-width strip extends beyond the door or window trim, it must be cut vertically so that the first short section will end at the edge of the door or window. Use a full-length pasted and folded sheet for this. Measure the distance from the edge of the last strip to the side of the casing and subtract one inch. Cut the strip and hang the first section. The second section should be matched to the short first section and butted to the edge of the trim. After it is smoothed down and trimmed, other full-length strips can be hung until the next corner or obstacle is encountered.

Removable fixtures such as plates on electrical outlets and switches should be removed before the wall is papered. The wallpaper can be hung over the electrical box and cut through around the sides of the box. Light fixtures and pipes that can't be moved can be papered around by holding the wallpaper strip in place next to the fitting and slitting it horizontally so the wallpaper can be worked around the fitting. Cut a hole at the end of the slit to go around the pipe or fixture.

Wall areas that can't be seen because they are behind fixtures such as washing machines or radiators can be covered or left uncovered, as you like. To cover the area, the fixture should be moved if possible. If it can't be moved, work from above and push the paper down into place with a small broom or short length of wood.

Wallpaper repairs should be inconspicuous. Small holes can be patched by tearing out a section of pattern similar to the piece to be replaced from a piece of scrap wallpaper. Tear the patch from the scrap so that the paper around the patch is torn away from the backing rather than toward the face of the patch. This will peel some of the paper from around the back edge of the patch and allow it to feather into the rest of the wallpaper. Heavy wallcoverings may have to be cut instead of torn. Blisters in wallpaper often flatten out by themselves. Those which don't can be cut with a razor in a cross pattern and pasted down. Seams may pull loose where there is too little paste or the paste dries before the strip is hung. Rub more paste under the edges, roll them down, and wash the surface.

Washable wallcoverings can be washed with warm water, but if they are greasy, they should be washed with a mild, nonabrasive detergent. Stains can be removed from wallpaper that is not washable with special soil removers designed for these wallpapers.

Wallcoverings similar to wallpaper are hung in the same general way. Some, like handprinted papers and grass cloth, have to be hung over lining paper. Lining paper is a heavy brownish paper that provides a smooth base and a good bonding surface for special wallcoverings. It is hung just as ordinary wallpaper is; since it will be covered, it doesn't have to be hung as carefully but lapped edges should be avoided. Murals are hung over lining paper also, and must be centered on a wall according to the directions with the rolls. Flocked paper must be hung very carefully, since the flock facing can be damaged easily. Paste must be kept off the flocking and the facing must be brushed and smoothed in such a way that it isn't injured.

PANELING

The grain and natural finish of wood paneling creates an attractive, warm surface, which requires very little care. Paneling can be installed over old walls with or without furring and over studs in basements and attics. Its prefinished surface is very durable and will generally outlast paint and wallpaper.

TYPES OF PANELING

The most common forms of wall paneling are plywood panels, individual boards, and hardboard panels. Standard-size panels are 4 X 8 ft., while boards may be of random width but of uniform length.

Plywood panels are constructed in several ways. Veneer plywood panels have a thin surface veneer of fine hardwood such as cherry, oak, or walnut, which is laminated to several layers of softwood backing. Printed plywood panels do not have a natural wood veneer but instead have a wooden surface printed to resemble a wood veneer or other material. Vinyl-surfaced plywood panels are covered with a thin layer of vinyl printed to resemble veneer or printed in colors and designs. Veneer paneling costs about the same as a vinyl wallcovering while the printed panels are cheaper.

Paneling composed of individual boards is two or three times as expensive as veneer-plywood paneling. The boards are usually made from good-quality softwoods such as pine or redwood. They are available in various lengths to reach from the ceiling to the floor. Their widths may be the same or they may vary to create a random pattern. The edges are cut to lock together with a tongue and groove or other fitting.

Hardboard panels are made of laminated wood fibers rather than thin layers of wood. Their surfaces may be unfinished or finished. Finished surfaces are printed to resemble wood veneer and other natural materials or they are printed in solid colors or multicolored patterns. A baked-on enamel coating protects the surface from scratches and moisture.

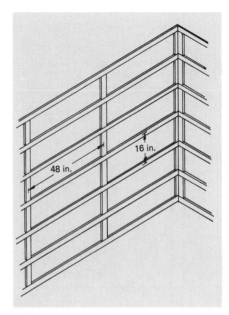

Fig. 3–30 Attaching furring to studs.

Preparing Walls

All types of panel must be backed by a solid supporting surface such as furring, studs, or a flat surface. Furring is the most common type of backing. This is made up of thin lengths of wood such as 1 X 2 in. strips, which are available in various lengths. Studs placed 16 in. on center will also form a good backing. For a very firm backing, gypsum board can be nailed to studs or furring and panels can be attached over the gypsum board. Another solid backing is an old wall that is reasonably level.

If panels are to be placed over an old wall, the wall must be smoothed by filling recesses and sanding the bumps. Anything that might be covered by the paneling, such as covers on electrical outlets and switches, should be removed. Baseboards and door and window casings can be left in place with plywood and hardboard paneling, since their 1/4-in. thickness will butt the trim without extending too close to its edge. When board paneling is placed over old walls, door and window casings and baseboards will have to be removed. After the new thickness is allowed for, the casings can be replaced or new casings can be installed.

When furring strips are nailed over an existing wall, they should be nailed through to the studs (Fig. 3–30)). Strips must be nailed horizontally along the wall flush to the ceiling and 1/2 in. above the floor. Other horizontal strips should be nailed 16 in. apart (between centers) in ladderlike fashion between the ceiling and floor strips. Vertical strips have to be nailed in each corner (before the horizontal strips) to support the edges of the panels. Other vertical strips must be placed every 48 in. on center where the edges of the

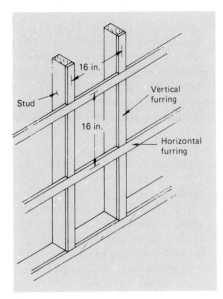

Fig. 3–31 Furring an old wall.

panels come together. Measure 48 in. from the corner and mark this as the center line for the first vertical strip. Continue to measure from each center line to the next and nail up a strip. Where panels must go around doors and windows, nail furring strips to provide support under the edges. The vertical strips, except for those in the corners, will have to be cut in short lengths to fit in between the horizontal strips. All of the furring strips should be in one plane so that the panels can lie flat against them (Fig. 3–31). Wherever a strip dips in, it can be wedged out with a piece of shingle until it is level with the other strips.

Masonry walls can be furred out in the same general way as an old plaster wall. It will be more difficult to attach the furring strips, however. Masonry nails, adhesive anchors, and other types of anchors can be used. Where stones or bricks jut out to form a very uneven surface, 2 X 2 in. or 2 X 3 in. studs can be erected against the wall to form a plumb backing. Exterior masonry walls should be covered with a heavy sheet of polyethylane before the paneling is installed to protect it from moisture.

Furring strips can also be attached directly to studs. Studs may be exposed where an old wall surface has been torn out. They may have been put up to form a new wall. The furring should be nailed horizontally across the studs, just as if it were a solid wall. Vertical strips are required in corners and on the studs at 16 in. intervals to support the edges and backs of the panels. If the studs are not placed to support the edges every 48 in., additional studs and furring may have to be nailed in. Whenever studs are exposed on an exterior wall, there is an opportunity to install wall insula-

tion to serve as a vapor and sound barrier in addition to retarding heat flow. Staple roll insulation between the studs before nailing on the furring.

If panels are to be attached directly to studs, furring will not be necessary. The studs must be placed 16 in. on center so they will be in position to support the edges of each panel. Supplementary lengths of 2 X 4 can be nailed flush with the studs wherever a panel edge needs support. The distance between studs is not as important with board paneling which can be run the entire width of the room or butted over studs wherever they happen to be.

Installing Plywood Paneling

Standard 4 X 8 ft. panels are long enough to reach from the floor to the ceiling in most rooms. Therefore, only the width of a wall needs to be measured to determine how many panels are required. For example, a 15-ft.-wide wall with no doors or windows will require four panels. When there are doors and windows, subtract their widths from the width of the wall but allow a partial panel for covering areas over and under their casings. For example, a 15-ft.-wide wall with a 3-ft.-wide window and a 3-ft.-wide door casing would require three panels instead of four. Horizontal sections of the third panel would have to be cut to fit over the door and over and under the window.

Panels should be placed in the room for a few days before they are installed. This allows the plywood to adjust to the room's temperature and humidity. Try to position them so that air can circulate around them freely.

Since the grain and shading of each panel is different, some look well side by side and some don't. Place the panels against the walls around the room so they can be compared. Exchange them until the combination is attractive. Number this sequence with chalk so the panels can be installed in order.

Either adhesive or nails can be used to fasten panels in place. Adhesive in a caulking cartridge is used to lay down a bead along the furring strips under the edges and behind the central part of the panel. When panels are attached to old walls, the adhesive is placed directly on the panel. Panels also can be fastened with small colored finishing nails or brads. These are nailed through the grooves, where the nailheads are inconspicuous and along the top and bottom of the panel, where they can be covered with molding. Long finishing nails are necessary to reach into studs when paneling is placed over an old plaster and lath wall.

First Panel. Start the first panel in a corner. Cut its height to fit from floor to ceiling with 1/4-in. gaps at the bottom and top. Butt the corner edge against the adjacent wall or furring strip (Fig. 3–32). The leading edge of the panel should be vertical. Check it with a carpenter's level or plumb bob. The edge of the panel in the corner may no longer be flush with the adjacent wall if the walls are not plumb. There are

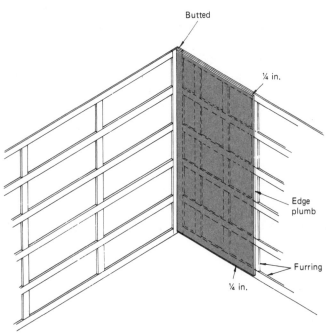

Fig. 3–32 Positioning the first panel.

two ways to take care of this. Corner molding will cover the gap if it is no wider than 1/4 in. or so. If the gap is large, or if corner molding is not to be used, the edge can be cut to fit the corner. With the panel held in place, mark a line on the edge of the panel parallel to the corner wall. Saw along this line to give the edge of the panel the proper contour.

Sections of the panel that cover electrical switches and outlets must be cut out. Measure to the electrical box from the points where the edge and bottom of the panel will be positioned on the wall. Transfer the measurements to the face of the panel and draw an outline of the box. Cut out the section by boring holes inside the corners and sawing along the lines with a keyhole saw.

Using Adhesive. If the panel is to be attached with adhesive, lay beads along the furring strips behind the panel (Fig. 3–33). If it is to be placed flush over an old wall, lay the beads on the back of the panel. A bead should be laid around the periphery just inside the edge and every 16 in. across the back. Place the panel in position against the wall with a 1/4-in. shim holding it off the floor. After checking to see that the leading edge is still vertical, nail a few brads partially into the top of the panel. These will hold it in place as the panel is pushed flat against the wall. This smears the adhesive on the wall and the back of the panel. Pull the bottom of the panel out 8 to 10 in. from the wall, and hold it clear with a block of wood so that the adhesive can become tacky on both surfaces. After 10 minutes or so the block should be removed and the panel pushed tightly

against the wall. The panel must be pounded along its edges and other areas directly over the furring and beads of adhesive. Hold a broad wooden block cushioned with several layers of soft cloth against these areas, and tap it soundly with a hammer so that the panel is pushed tightly against its backing. The nails can be removed when the adhesive is dry and the holes can be filled with a matching filler or covered with molding.

Using Nails. When a panel is to be nailed, it can be placed in position as soon as it has been cut to fit. Place it on 1/4-in. shims and check to see that the leading edge is vertical. Hold the top in place with a few nails along the edge. If the panel fits satisfactorily, the corner edge can be nailed with brads every 6 in. The next brads should be nailed along the top and bottom moving away from the corner. Place these so that they will be covered by the molding and baseboard (Fig. 3–34). Brads should be nailed through the grooves every 12 in. or so over the supports behind the middle of the panel, moving away from the corner edge. If a brad fails to enter the furring behind the panel, pull it out and fill the

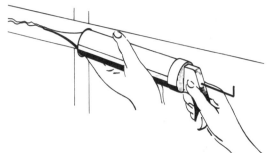

Fig. 3–33 Fastening panels with adhesive.

Fig. 3–34 Fastening panels with nails.

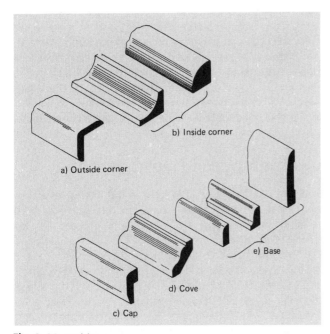

Fig. 3–35 Moldings.

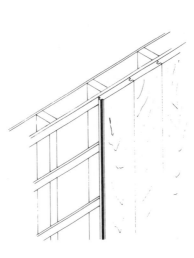

Fig. 3–36 Board paneling.

hole with a filler that matches the color of the panel. If the panel is nailed flush over an old wall, it should be installed with finishing nails long enough to go through into the studs. All of the exposed brads and nails should be set with a nail set and covered with a matching filler.

Remaining Panels. After the first panel is attached, the remaining panels are butted tightly and installed in the same way. Each should be checked to be sure that its edges are vertical. Full-length panels must be cut vertically to fit around doors and windows. Measure the width from the leading edge of the last panel to the edge of the door or window casing. Mark this off on the panel and cut it to fit. Short sections above a door are measured and cut in the same way.

The face of the panel can be easily damaged while it is being cut. Lay the panel face up across a broad supporting surface, such as several boards between two sawhorses. A type of saw should be used that will not splinter the face of the panel as it is cut. A crosscut saw with at least 10 teeth/in. will make a smooth cut. If a table saw is used, a fine-toothed blade such as a veneer blade should be used.

Moldings

Molding can be used to cover joints between panels on inside corners (Fig. 3-35(a)), ceiling and floor edges, and other rough edges or openings. Measure the lengths needed to cover these edges and buy the prefinished wood or vinyl molding to match the panels. Outside corner molding (Fig. 3-35(b)) will cover the exposed edge of a panel and protect the corner from damage. Ceiling molding will finish off the

top of the panel and cover the nails along the edge (Fig. 3-35(c)). Base molding or cove molding (Fig. 3-35(d) and (e)) can be used to cover the gap at the bottom of the panel and will make it easier to clean the floor along the wall. The molding should be nailed in place with brads and the holes filled.

INSTALLING BOARD PANELING

Individual boards can be fitted together and nailed into place much like plywood paneling (Fig. 3-36). When they are placed vertically, they need to be backed by horizontal strips of furring. There should be strips at the top and bottom of the wall and every 16 or 24 in. between centers. Vertical strips are required only in corners and around doors and windows. Boards also can be run horizontally and nailed directly to the studs. If they are not long enough to cover the full width of the wall, they must be cut so that their ends butt where they can be nailed over a stud. Unlike plywood paneling, boards do not fit well over old walls where thickness is a problem. They may extend out beyond door and window casings. If casings can be removed and thickness isn't a problem, solid boards will help deaden sound going through the wall.

Allow the board paneling to adjust to the room's temperature and humidity for a few days. If the boards are to extend from the ceiling to the floor without a ceiling molding or baseboard, they should be cut with only one-eighth inch leeway. If the ceiling and floor joints are to be covered, cut them so that there are 1/4-in. gaps at the ceiling and the floor.

The first board should be placed with its groove against the corner. Line up the leading edge so that it is vertical. If there is a large gap between the edge of the board and the corner, a line should be drawn or scribed on the edge parallel to the corner and the board cut to fit. When the board is in position, nail along the corner edge with 8d finishing nails every 6 to 8 in. Nail the top and bottom in the same way. Nails on the face of the board should be set with a nail set and the holes filled in. The leading edge of the board should be blind-nailed into the furring. Slant the finishing nails into the edge of the board above the tongue so that they will extend into the furring or stud underneath.

The remaining boards are fitted onto the tongues of the boards already in place and blind-nailed into the furring. Boards will have to be cut to fit around windows, doors, and other obstacles. The butt ends should always be supported by backing so they can be nailed down.

WALL TILES

Ceramic wall tiles can be used as a decorative and completely waterproof covering. Their resistance to moisture and heavy scrubbing is particularly important where they are used in bathrooms, laundries, and kitchens. Decorator tiles and metal tiles are more likely to be used for their aesthetic effects.

TYPES OF TILES

Wall tiles may be practical and functional, decorative, or both. Ceramic tiles and mosaics are both highly decorative and practical. They are made in a variety of bright colors and designs, and they are waterproof and resistant to scrubbing and fading. Plastic tiles are more functional than decorative. They don't have the durability or appearance of ceramic tiles, but they are waterproof and aren't easily marred by scratches. Metal tiles are noted for their decorative use. Aluminum, stainless steel, and copper tiles are used to make decorative backsplashes and for wall designs. They are available with natural surfaces or bright, baked-on-colors.

TILING TOOLS AND MATERIALS

A few special tools are needed to install ceramic tiles: notched trowel, tile cutter, tile nippers, and rubber squeegee. Other tools such as a carpenter's level, plumb line, file or stone, and sponge can be borrowed from a collection of standard tools. A professional type of tile cutter can be borrowed or rented from a tile dealer, or a simple glass cutter can be used. Wall-tile mastic is applied to walls to attach tiles. One gallon will cover about 50 sq. ft. Powdered grout is mixed with water to fill the gaps between the tiles. One pound of powder will cover about 20 sq. ft. of tile.

Plastic tiles are cut with a saw or special plastic tile cutter. An ordinary fine-toothed handsaw will cut straight lines and a coping saw will make irregular cuts. Metal tiles are cut with a hacksaw or tin snips. A hacksaw can be used to cut a tile in half, but tin snips are needed to cut contours.

PREPARATIONS FOR TILING

Standard-size field tiles (tiles used in the interior of a tiled area) are 4 1/4 X 4 1/4 in. square, but decorative tiles can be almost any size (Fig. 3-37(a)). Ceramic mosaic tiles, for example, are usually mounted on 1 X 1 ft. square sheets, and cap strips for finishing trim are long and narrow, usually 2 X 6 in. Whatever type of tile is used, if the area is a rectangle or a square, the number of tiles on one side of the area can be multiplied by the number of tiles across the bottom, to find the total number required. To count the number of tiles, mark off their 4 1/4 X 4 1/4 in. widths and heights along the two edges. For example, if there will be a column of fifteen tiles on one side and a row of ten tiles across the bottom, 150 tiles will be needed to fill the total area.

Trim tiles are used to cap the top row of field tiles and to form rounded edges and corners on outside verticle columns and corners. In estimating the number of tiles required, count the trim tiles separately. The main types of trim tiles are cap tiles (Fig. 3-37(b)) or strips, cove base tiles, and down corner tiles. *Cap tiles* are rounded on their top edges to form a finishing row over the last row of field tiles. *Cap strips* are rounded in the same way (Fig. 3-37(c)) but they are long and narrow and are used to form a thin border. *Cove base tiles* have an outward concave curve at their base (Fig. 3-37(d)) and are made to be used with floor tiles. *Corner cove tiles* also have a rounded edge for a right or left corner. *Down corner tiles* have two rounded edges (Fig. 3-37(e)) and a rounded shoulder to finish off the corners of a tiled area.

Almost any flat wall surface which is sufficiently rigid can be tiled. A wall without adequate support from studs or furring may flex and crack the grout. Cracks and holes in plaster and gypsum board walls should be repaired and bumps sanded down before tiling. Painted walls should be sanded to roughen their surfaces in order to hold the mastic. If a new gypsum board wall is installed for tiling around a bathtub or shower, the special moisture resistant type of board should be used. (The bottom edge of the gypsum board should be at least 1/4 in. above the edge of a tub rather than resting on it.) Plaster and gypsum board walls can be made more moisture resistant by coating them with a sealer or by applying a thin layer of mastic to form a waterproof film.

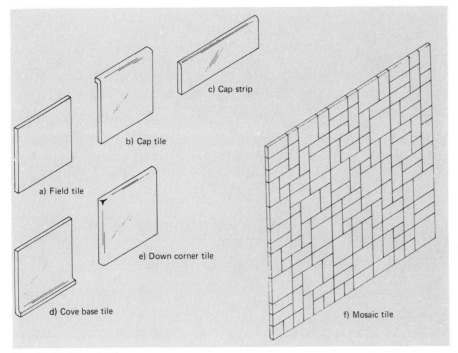

Fig. 3–37 Ceramic tiles.

INSTALLING CERAMIC TILE

Guidelines

The first step in installing tile is to establish horizontal and vertical guidelines (Fig. 3-38). Floors and tops of bathtubs are seldom horizontal and few walls are plumb. However, tiles must be placed in level rows and plumb columns or they will look slipshod. The patterns also should be symmetrical with the outer columns composed of partial tiles of equal widths.

The first horizontal row of full-size tiles will be placed a full tile height above the lowest point in the area to be tiled. To establish a horizontal guideline, use a carpenter's level to find the lowest point of the area to be tiled. Hold a full-size tile butted against the top of the bathtub or counter at this point. Draw a short line along the top of the tile and use a carpenter's level to extend it across the area of wall to be tiled. (If the bathtub or counter is level, there will be room for a row of full size tiles under this line. If it isn't level, other tiles under the line will have to be cut to fit before they are applied.

To establish vertical guidelines for the outermost full-width tiles, measure the maximum width of the total area to be tiled and draw a plumb line in the center. If the middle tile in the first horizontal row is centered on this line, the partial tiles in the outermost columns will be of equal width. They may butt an adjacent wall, an outside corner, or be finished with trim tiles. The outside guidelines can be

located by marking off full widths along the horizontal guideline starting next to the space for the centered tile. Use a plumb line or carpenter's level to mark these vertical lines on the wall. Tiles applied within the lines will be full size. Outside the lines, tiles must be cut to partial widths to form the edge of the tiled area before trim tile is applied.

Applying Tiles with Mastic

Wall-tile mastic is applied with a notched trowel. The notches leave thick beads of mastic separated by empty grooves. Since mastic is very sticky and hard to remove, the area under the wall should be protected with dropcloths or newspapers. Try to keep mastic off the face of the tiles. Spread it over a small section of the wall where the tiles are to be applied. It should form a uniform layer without excessively thick or thin spots. If the layer is right, the mastic will completely cover the back of a tile when it is pressed into place and won't squeeze out from around the edges.

The first tiles should be placed in a row with their bottom edges butting the horizontal guideline. Start the row by placing a full-size tile with its side edge against the inside of one of the outer vertical guidelines and its bottom edge on the horizontal guideline (Fig. 3-39). Press and slightly twist the tile as it is placed in position to spread the mastic evenly over its back. Be careful not to slide the tile, or mastic will ride up over its edge. (If this happens, remove the tile and clean off the mastic before using it again.) Continue the row by butting each tile against the tile already in place. The tiles

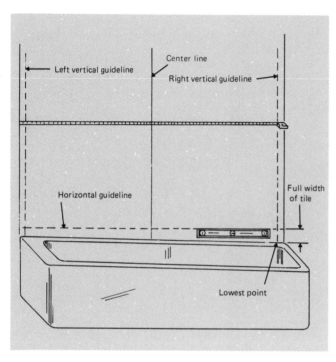

Fig. 3–38 Establishing guidelines.

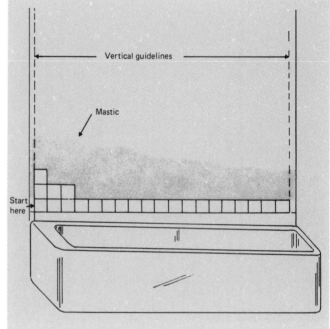

Fig. 3–39 Placement of tiles.

will be automatically separated by 1/16 in. or so by two small spacers on each edge. This leaves room for grout. When the first row is finished, check it with a carpenter's level. If any of the tiles are out of line or if the row is not level, straighten out the row.

After the first row of tiles is in place, continue applying tiles in horizontal rows directly over each other. Check the rows and columns with a carpenter's level and by standing back and looking to see if the lines formed by the gaps between the tiles are straight. A few tiles will probably have to be moved to get rid of jogs. Continue applying the full-size tiles until the area between the guidelines is covered. As new rows are formed, tiles in previous rows must be pounded with a block and hammer to anchor them in the mastic. Use a short length of board cushioned with several layers of cloth and cover several tiles at a time. Tap firmly with a hammer but not hard enough to crack the tiles.

Partial tiles should now be cut to cover the remainder of the area outside the guidelines. The first tile under the horizontal guideline will be full-size, since this is the tile initially used to establish the line. The other tiles in the row will probably have to be cut to fit between the edge of the tub and the guideline. Tiles are cut on a tile cutter by scratching a straight line across their faces with the cutter's wheel and then snapping them apart over a thin ridge on the cut-

ter's base. They can also be cut by scratching a straight line with a sharp glass-cutter and snapping them across a narrow ridge such as a long nail or sharp edge. The rough edges are smoothed with a course file or stone. Tiles to be butted outside the vertical guidelines are cut in the same way. At any given height on the wall, the partial-width tiles will be of equal width on both sides of the tiled area, creating a symmetrical pattern.

Tile nippers are used to cut tiles that are to go around pipes and other obstacles. Cut into the tile with small bites to avoid cracking it. If a pipe is to go through the center of a tile, cut the tile in half with a tile cutter and nip out the openings for the pipe in both halves. A pair of pliers can be used in a pinch, if tile nippers aren't available.

Trim tiles are installed last (except for cove base tiles, which make up the first row above a floor). Cap tiles or strips should be placed along the top row and down both sides. Down corner tiles are placed at corners with two exposed edges. Trim tiles don't have spacers. Their edges should be butted against the spacers of the field tiles.

If ceramic accessories such as soap-holders are to be installed, outline their location on the walls before tiling. Tile around this area. The accessory can be installed after the wall has been tiled. It should be fastened with mastic to the uncovered wall area. Holes may have to be cut in the wall for accessories that are recessed, such as toilet paper holders.

Grouting. The openings between the tiles must be filled with grout after the mastic has dried. Mix powdered grout with water until it forms a paste. Be sure that all of the openings between the tiles are filled. Excess grout on the tile faces can be wiped off with the squeegee after it has been cleaned. The grout will start to thicken at once and harden in 15 or 20 minutes. The grout between each tile should be smoothed down with the end of a round clothespin or other object of similar shape. In a short while, the grout in the joints will be hard enough so that grout can be wiped off the face of the tiles with a damp sponge or rag. If this isn't done in time, the grout will harden and will be difficult to remove. Allow the grout to cure for several days before getting it wet.

Ceramic Mosaics

The only difference in installing standard ceramic tiles and ceramic mosaics is in using the mosaic sheets. The individual mosaic tiles are attached to a 1 X 1 ft. facing sheet, which can be cut with scissors. Guidelines are established in the same way as with 4 1/4 X 4 1/4 in. tiles and the mosaic sheets are installed in the mastic. The facing sheet is removed after the mastic dries. The tiles are mounted in rows and pounded with a cushioned block and hammer to fix them in the mastic. Individual tiles should be aligned over the tiles in the row below. Where there are pipes or other obstacles, several tiles can be cut out of the facing sheet with scissors, and nippers can be used to shape those that remain. Mosaic tiles should be grouted so that the group is flush with the faces of the tiles. The edges are finished with standard ceramic strips.

Installing Plastic and Metal Tiles

Plastic and metal tiles are installed using the same principles used for ceramic tiles. The walls must be sound and smooth. Horizontal and vertical guidelines must be established. A special mastic for plastic tiles is applied. The tiles are pressed into place so that the mastic doesn't ride up over their edges. Since plastic tiles don't have spacers, mastic tends to squeeze up between them when they are butted together. This ridge of mastic must be removed before it dries. Use a pointed tool wrapped in a piece of cloth. A special solvent should be used to remove mastic from the faces of the tiles. To cut plastic tiles, use a fine-toothed handsaw for straight cuts and a coping saw for cutting openings for pipes, faucets, and accessories.

Metal tiles can be fastened with mastic, like other tiles, or with double-faced tape. However, they should not be installed in bathrooms where they are exposed to heavy moisture. They can be cut with tin snips for irregular openings and with a hacksaw when they have to be cut straight across.

4 Floors and Stairs

This chapter describes some of the most common ways in which floors and stairs can be improved. Chiefly, it describes the types of materials, preparations, and the processes of installing flooring that are within the capabilities of people without professional experience. The chapter also points out a few types of installations that usually require professional assistance.

STRUCTURE

FLOORS

Hardwood floors, carpeting, and resilient materials are generally laid over wooden subfloors. (Some tiles and carpeting, however, can be installed directly over concrete slabs.) Wooden subfloors consist of plywood or wide boards supported by 2 X 6-in. or 2 X 8-in. joists resting edgewise. Sheets of plywood are laid in a staggered pattern over supporting joists (Fig. 4-1). If boards are used, they may be laid either diagonally or at right angles to the joists. Joists are spaced 15 in. apart* and are supported by heavy sills and beams. The sills are fastened atop the foundation walls and support the ends of the joists, while beams (held up by thick posts) support the midsections. Bridging braces are usually used between joists to increase the rigidity of the entire framework.

Floors constructed of concrete slabs may be covered with subfloors supported by wooden screeds (levelling devices laid on freshly poured concrete). When the subfloors are made of plywood, most types of flooring can be installed without a special underlayment. Vinyl-type tiles, for example, can be installed on either a plywood subfloor or directly on a concrete slab.

*Some instructions would say "16 in. on centers" (for 2-in. joists).

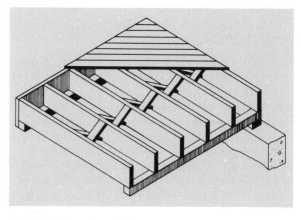

Fig. 4–1 Structure of a floor.

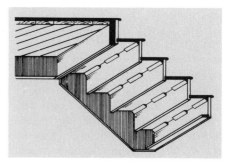

Fig. 4–2 Structure of stairs.

STAIRS

Stairs consist of horizontal treads backed by vertical risers and supported by stringers on both sides (Fig. 4-2). Stairs with treads and risers supported by the edges of notched stringers, called open stringers, are the easiest to repair.

Treads and risers can also be supported with dado joints if the stringer is of the unnotched or closed type. The treads and risers themselves may be fastened together with either butt joints or stronger dado joints. (A dado joint is formed by inserting the edge of a board in a supporting groove cut into the face of another board, such as when shelves are inserted in the dadoed sides of a bookcase.) Supporting blocks are sometimes fastened in the joints between the treads and risers under the stairs for additional strength.

Handrails may be supported by balusters that rest on the treads. The balusters may be toenailed to the top of the treads or they may fit into notches at the ends of the treads. When a tread is being replaced, the balusters should be removed, and replaced after the new tread is laid.

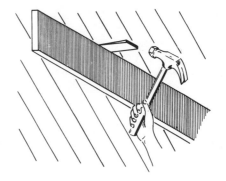

Fig. 4–3 Placing a wedge between a joist and subflooring.

REPAIR OF FLOORS AND STAIRS

FLOORS
Creaks and Squeaks

Floors that creak or squeak can usually be silenced if the subfloors and joists are accessible from underneath. The noises are caused by boards and nails rubbing together as someone walks over the floor. The subflooring may have pulled loose from the joists, the joists may have warped or shrunk, nails may have pulled loose, or the finish floor may have warped or pulled loose. The rubbing and noise can be stopped by tightening the joints between the joists and flooring.

If possible, locate the subfloor boards that are rubbing by having someone walk on the floor while you observe from underneath. If there is a gap between the subfloor and a joist, use a piece of shingle as a wedge to fill the gap (Fig. 4-3). A little adhesive on the shingle will hold it in place. Where there is a gap between a joist and several boards in the subflooring, place a short length of 1 X 4-in. board (a cleat) along the side of the joist, push it flush against the floor boards, and nail it into place (Fig. 4-4); this will keep the boards from moving. Warped or weak joists can be strengthened by adding bridging between them. Lengths of 2 X 6-in. board should be cut to fit crosswise between the joists and nailed into place. Where subflooring moves up and down between joists, a 2 X 6-in. bridge should be pushed up against the subflooring and nailed to the joists (Fig. 4-5).

Where the joists and subflooring are concealed by ceiling materials for the lower story, loose subflooring can be fastened down from above if the joists can be located. Use a small block of wood and a hammer to tap along the finish floor at right angles to the finish boards until the tapping sounds dulled (Fig. 4-6(a)). These spots are probably over the joists and should be about 16 in. apart. Drill a pair of

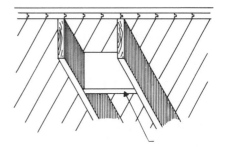

Fig. 4–4 Using a cleat to support subflooring.

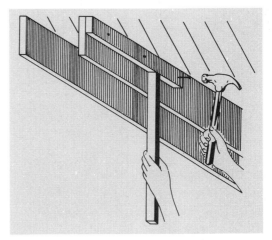

Fig. 4–5 Using a bridge to support subflooring.

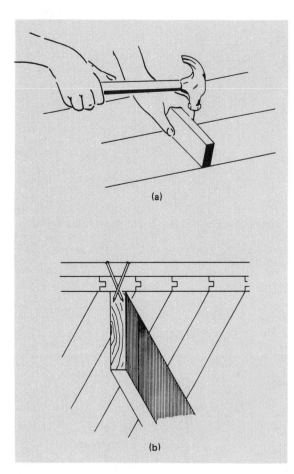

Fig. 4–6 Fastening loose subflooring from above: a) locating loose flooring by tapping, b) nailing from above.

small pilot holes slightly angled to each other in the finish board and drive annular-ringed nails through the flooring and into the joists (Fig. 4-6(b)). Sink the heads and fill the holes with wood putty.

Boards in the finish floor may have pulled loose from the subfloor. Use a hammer and a wooden block cushioned with a cloth to pound the boards down in the noisy area. If the cracks between the boards are wide enough, an adhesive such as white glue or resorcinol can be worked between the boards to hold them tightly together (Fig. 4-7(a)). Where the boards cannot be pounded down, they can sometimes be nailed down or pulled down from beneath. To nail the finish boards down, the joists have to be found and annular-ring nails driven through pilot holes into the joists. Wood screws slightly longer than the thickness of the subflooring can be used with washers to pull the finish flooring down to meet the subflooring. Drill shallow pilot holes through the subflooring (and slightly into the finish flooring, but not through it) from beneath and drive the screws into the finish flooring at every inch or so in the loosened area (Fig. 4-7(b)).

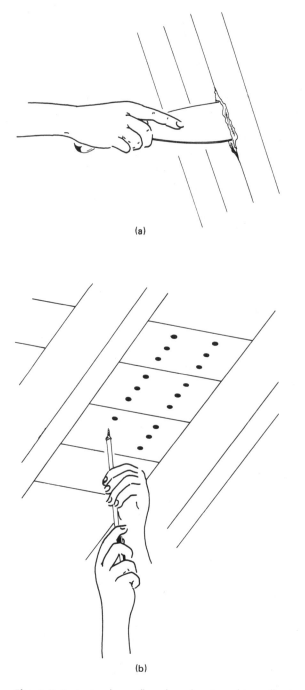

Fig. 4–7 Fastening loose floor boards: a) working adhesive into cracks, b) pulling down from below.

Cracks and Scratches

Deep scratches should be filled with wood putty or other filler and sanded flush with the surrounding surface. The area can then be rubbed with fine steel wool and refinished

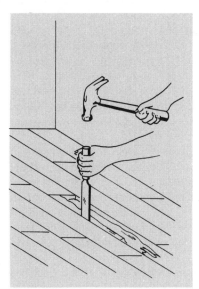

Fig. 4–8 Removing damaged floor boards.

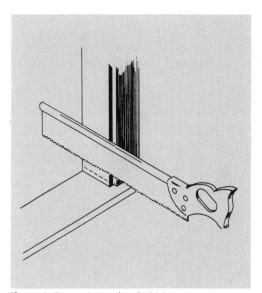

Fig. 4–9 Removing a threshold from under a door jamb

to match the rest of the floor. If the floor is stained darker than the wood, mix the stain with the filling material before it is applied.

Square-edged boards often shrink, creating cracks between them. Large cracks can be patched with thin strips of wood cut to fit. The strip should be pounded into place and its protruding edge planed and sanded down. Small cracks should be filled with some type of wood filler that matches the coloring of the finish boards. Wood putty, plastic wood, or sawdust mixed with white glue can be used. All fillers should be sanded and the areas refinished.

Replacing Floor Boards

Damaged tongue-and-groove floor boards are difficult to remove and replace. To remove the damaged parts, an individual board or several boards must be cut through lengthwise and across the width. Several tools can be used. A portable circular saw can be set for the depth of the finish flooring and used to cut along a line across several boards and lengthwise just inside the edge nails. A section of an individual board can be removed by boring holes next to the edges at the ends to be cut. A keyhole saw is then inserted in the holes to cut across the board. The damaged length can be split and removed with a chisel (Fig. 4-8).

Square-edged boards are easier to remove than tongue-and-groove boards. After the section is cut crosswise, the nails should be driven through the board and into the subflooring with a small nail set. This will allow the board to be pried free. Planks that are held in place by screws covered with plugs can be removed by drilling out the plugs and removing the screws. If the planks are also tongue-and-grooved, the tongued edge must be cut with a chisel or an electric saw. Blind-nailed planks will have to be removed by cutting them like other blind-nailed strips.

Replacement floor boards should be cut to fit with a slight leeway at the ends. Tongue-and-groove boards must have either the tongue or the lower part of the grooved edge cut off so that they can be fitted into place. The cut edge should be coated with an adhesive to bond it to the next floor board. For further strength, it can be face-nailed into the subflooring. Use a wood filler to patch cracks and any holes left by set nails.

Where the subfloor and finish flooring have been removed between joists, the ends of the replacement boards should be supported by 2 X 4-in. cleats nailed along the upper side of the joists. The cleats, in effect, extend the width of the joists.

Replacing Thresholds

Thresholds may have to be removed when new flooring is installed over an old floor, or when they are badly worn or damaged. If the threshold is placed within the door frame between the jambs, it can be removed without much trouble. The vertical strip (or door stop) that is fastened to the door jamb and butts the threshold must be pried loose and removed. The threshold can now be pried loose since it is fastened only with face nails. If the nails are angled so that the threshold won't come loose, it may have to be split with a chisel and removed in pieces. If the ends of the threshold are under the door jambs, they will have to be sawed off with a backsaw placed flush against the jambs (Fig. 4-9).

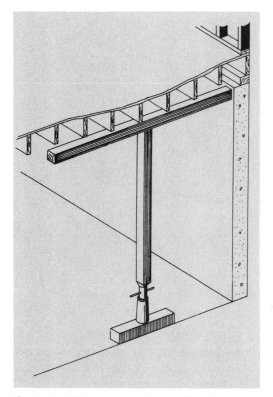

Fig. 4–10 Raising a sagging floor with a house jack.

The sagging section of a floor may be raised and straightened by using a house jack and a post to press a crossbeam upward against the joists. The jack should be placed on a 4 X 4-in. or 6 X 6-in. timber to spread the downward force over a broad area. A 6 X 6-in. beam should be braced under the joists in the sagging area with a 6 X 6-in. post placed on top of the house jack. Center the vertical post on the crossbeam. The post and beam will force the joist upward as the jack is cranked. When the timbers are in position, crank the jack until the slack is taken up and the first resistance of the flooring is felt (Fig. 4-10). From this point on, the house jack must be turned only a fraction of a turn each day so that the rise will be gradual enough for the framing, walls, and ceiling to adjust without cracking. Two full turns over a period of a week should be adequate for most situations.

When the jack has raised the joists so that the sag has been removed, permanent posts can be installed. Steel posts or wooden posts, either 4 X 4's or 6 X 6's, can be braced under both ends of the crossbeam and the jack backed off until the posts bear the weight of the floor. (Adjustable jack posts are also available. These permanent posts can be adjusted to raise the floor further if necessary.) Regardless of the type of posts used, they should be placed on heavy concrete footings. Concrete should be poured to form footings 18 to 24 in. deep and about 24 in. square.

Further repairs may be required if sagging is caused by foundations crumbling under the ends of the joists or beams. Once the joists have been raised and the load has been taken off the foundation walls, the crumbling concrete or bricks can be cleaned out and replaced by new bricks and mortar. The new supporting materials should be built up until the foundation walls again support the ends of the joists.

If the footings under supporting posts have crumbled, they should be replaced. A house jack, post, and beam are used to raise the floor, and the old posts are removed. New footings are poured and the sound old posts placed back in position on the new footings.

STAIRS
Stopping Squeaks

Squeaking stairs are usually caused by loose treads that are rubbing against nails, risers, or stringers. Once the source of the squeak is located, the two boards can be fastened together or wedged to prevent further movement.

Treads are either butted against the risers or interlocked in dado joints. The joints are fastened with nails and supporting blocks or with screws. When the front edge of a tread becomes loose, it can be nailed down against the riser with finishing nails set at slight angles to each other (Fig. 4-11(a)). To strengthen the joint, wooden blocks or short lengths of

A new threshold of oak or maple should be purchased that is longer than the door opening. A cardboard template can be drawn and cut to fit around the door jamb and against the casing on each side. From this, the new threshold should be cut to fit between the jambs and to butt the casing. Several thicknesses of roofing paper or heavy cardboard can be used under the threshold, if necessary, to raise it so that its lips match the level of the adjacent boards. Finish nails should be used in pilot holes along the shoulders to nail the threshold to the flooring.

Sagging Floors

Floors may sag for a number of reasons. If the structure is relatively new, a sagging floor may indicate that the joists or beams are too small or too far apart for the loads. In older houses, sagging floors may be caused by warped joists, settling posts, crumbling of the foundation under the ends of the beams or joists, or the settling of some parts of the foundation walls.

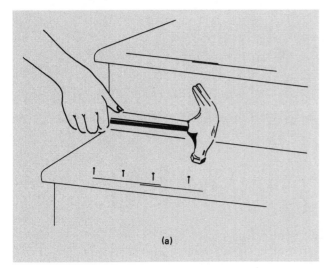

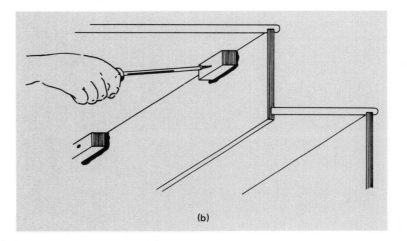

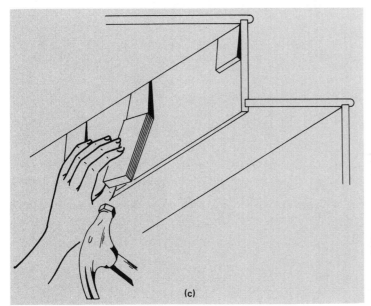

Fig. 4-11 Tightening loose treads: a) nailing down front edge, b) using supporting blocks, c) shimming loose joints.

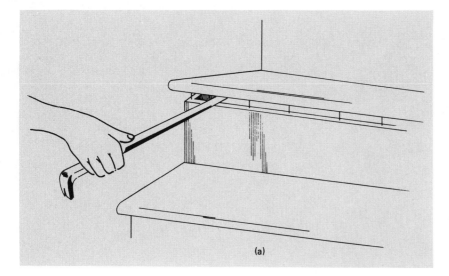

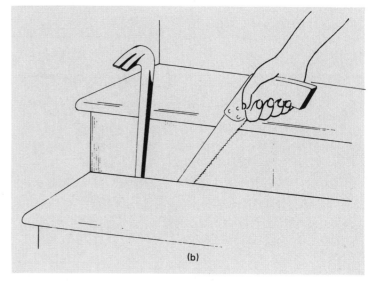

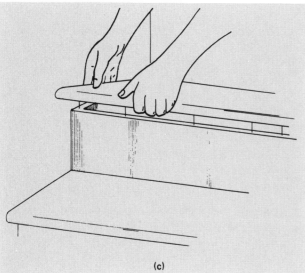

Fig. 4–12 Removing a stair tread: a) prying tread loose, b) cutting the nails, c) working the tread loose.

2 X 2 can be screwed into the joint formed by the back of the tread and the undersurface of the riser (Fig. 4-11(b)). When the rear edge of a tread becomes loose, the gap can be wedged to prevent further movement (Fig. 4-11(c)). Prepare small wedges and pound them into place, being careful not to enlarge the space any further.

If the stairs are exposed underneath, a better solution would be to work from under the stairs to knock the tread back into place and fasten it with nails or screws. Gaps between the treads and stringers can be wedged in a similar manner to stop movement and squeaking.

Replacing Treads and Risers

Worn or damaged treads and risers can be removed from the front of the staircase if at least one side is open. If the staircase is constructed with closed stringers, it will be necessary to have access to the back of the stairs.

Trim molding and balusters should be removed first. The molding in the joint between the riser and the nose of the tread should be pried free and removed. If balusters are toenailed into the treads, saw through the nails with a hacksaw flush with the tread. If the end of the baluster fits into a notch at the end of the tread, the outside trim should be removed and the baluster wedged out. If the baluster is nailed into the notch, it should be sawed off flush with the tread.

The front edge of the tread can be pried up slightly with a crowbar (Fig. 4-12(a)) so that a utility hacksaw blade can be used to cut the nails fastening the tread to the riser (Fig. 4-12(b)). When these are cut, the tread can be worked up and down until the rear edge starts to come loose from the riser behind it. If the tread and riser are butted, a hacksaw blade can be used to cut nails that are driven through from behind the riser and into the tread. If they are fastened with a dado joint, the tongue of the tread may have to be split off with a chisel. The end of the tread may also be nailed into a dado in the closed stringer. It should come loose as it is worked back and forth (Fig. 4-12(c)).

Where treads and risers are fitted into dados between closed stringers, they must be removed from the back of the stairs. The nails that fasten the treads to the risers must be cut and the pieces slid out from the dados. Loosen the risers with a small crowbar or wedge from the back. This will provide room to cut the nails holding the tread in place so that it can be pounded free. Trim and supporting wedges and blocks must be removed also. Where there is no access from the back of the stairs, removal is different and a carpenter's help will be needed.

Old treads which have not been damaged in the process of being removed can be turned over and installed upside down if there are no interfering notches. Otherwise, new treads and risers should be installed. The supporting edges of the stringers should be checked with a level and evened up by planing or wedging as necessary. Adjacent risers should be squared off in the same way. After the new risers and treads are cut and fitted into place, they should be fastened with finishing nails, screws, and 2 X 2-in. blocks. The front edge of the treads should be nailed into the supporting risers. Screws can then be driven from the rear of the back riser into the rear edge of the tread. Blocks can be glued into the joints formed by the tread and the supporting riser and fastened with screws. (Pilot holes should be drilled for all screws.) Where treads and risers are held by wedges, the wedges should be coated with adhesive, driven into place, and the projecting ends sawed off.

IMPROVING FLOORS AND STAIRS

Sooner or later floors have to be refinished or their coverings replaced. Finished hardwood floors wear down and become scratched or otherwise damaged. Old floor boards shrink, and cracks form between their edges. Carpeting and resilient flooring also wear down and become stained and marred with use.

There is a wide choice of ways to improve the appearance of floors and stairs. Good wooden floors can be sanded and refinished, or left as they are and covered with any of several floor materials. Floors that are already covered can have their coverings replaced. Sometimes new coverings can be installed over old coverings (such as tiles that are difficult to remove).

Battered floors in old houses may be patched and covered to minimize the refinishing problem. Even old tiled floors and concrete floors can be covered with carpeting backed with a moisture-proof layer of foam. Resilient flooring, such as vinyl, asbestos, and linoleum is among the most durable for hard-use areas, such as bathrooms and kitchens. Another possibility for these areas is ceramic floor tiles. The attractive designs of ceramic floor tiles and mosaics and their ability to repel water make them a practical alternative to resilient tiles. Where there are old wooden floors, the finish flooring can be torn out and replaced with new hardwood strip flooring, or the boards can be left and covered with a thin hardwood veneer.

Where the wood beneath several layers of paint (or some other old finish) is sound and attractive, the upper surface of old wood can be machine-sanded. The floor can then be refinished quite inexpensively, compared with the cost of covering it with carpeting or other types of flooring coverings.

Preparation. Some floors must be repaired before they are refinished or covered. Sagging floors are an extreme example of a condition that should be corrected. In most cases, a sagging floor can be completely repaired by someone without previous experience with floor problems. Sections of damaged floor boards have to be removed and replaced in floors which are to be refinished but not covered. Even well-finished floors and stairs develop squeaks and creaks from loose boards and nails. The boards have to be fastened down to quiet them. (See pp. 89 and 92–96 on repairing floors and stairs.)

COVERINGS

RESILIENT FLOORING

Resilient flooring is among the more durable coverings for areas where traffic is heavy and spills and stains may be frequent. Vinyl, vinyl asbestos, and linoleum are commonly used in kitchens, bathrooms, and family rooms. Asphalt tiles are inexpensive utility tiles that can withstand moisture and are used for areas above and below grade. Cork tiles make the softest flooring and are often used for their sound deadening effect. (See also pp. 42–43 in Chapter 2, "Materials.")

Types and Sizes

Resilient flooring materials are available in both *tiles* and *sheets*. Vinyl, vinyl asbestos, asphalt, and cork are available as tiles; vinyl and linoleum are available as sheets. Although the standard tile size is now 12 X 12-in., some patterns are still manufactured in the 9 X 9-in. size. Sheets of vinyl and linoleum are cut from rolls of 6-, and 9-, or 12-ft widths. The wider rolls allow a one-piece installation in small rooms, but strips from 6-ft rolls are easier to install.

Number of Tiles Required

The number of 12-in. tiles required to cover a rectangular floor can be found by multiplying the length of one wall by the length of the adjacent wall (in feet). For example, a 10 X 15-ft floor will require 150 tiles. (Another 5 percent should be added to allow for waste.) If the room is not rectangular, a large rectangle can be drawn in the main part of the room and smaller rectangles in the remaining areas, to determine the number of tiles required. When 9-in. tiles are used, the number of tiles along each of the two adjacent walls can be multiplied together to determine the total number required.

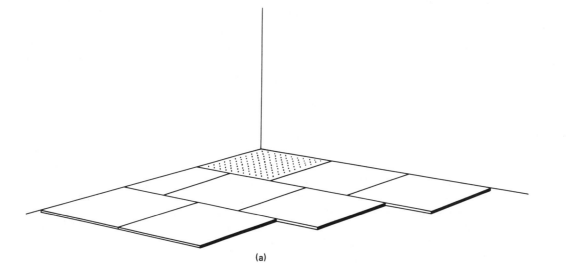

(a)

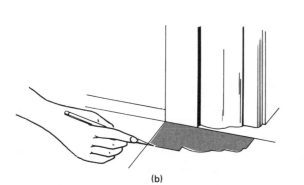

(b)

Fig. 4–13 Installing an underlayment: a) staggering the sheets, b) marking to fit around trim.

There will be four of these smaller 9-in. tiles for every 3 ft along the wall. For example, a 10 X 15-ft room will require 14 X 20 tiles or a total of 280 9-in. tiles. Another 18 or so tiles should be added to allow for poor trimming and other waste.

When more than one tile color or design is used, the number of each required can be found by drawing a sketch of the floor pattern and counting the tiles. If two different tiles are to be used in equal proportions, find the total in the usual way and divide it in half.

Preparing Floors

Resilient flooring must be installed over a smooth surface because it tends to conform to the shape of the floor beneath it. Wooden floors that are in good condition and are made up of boards 3 in. wide or less (narrow boards form a smoother surface) can be covered directly with tiles. Humps and splinters should first be sanded down, nails set, and gaps and nailholes filled. Paint should be roughened by

sanding, so that adhesive will have a better grip. Also remove dirt, wax, and grease.

An underlayment of hardboard, particle board, or plywood should be installed over wooden floors in poor condition, over single-layed subflooring, and over floors made from boards over 3 in. wide. Hardboard for underlayment is available in 4 X 4-ft and 4 X 8-ft sizes, with points marked every 4 in. for nailing.

Hardboard, particle board, or plywood underlayment should be left in the room for a few days to adjust to the temperature and humidity before it is installed. Prepare the floor by removing the shoe molding from along the baseboards. Stagger the sheets of hardboard so that there are no continuous lines of joints between sheets. If the sheets are positioned so that no four corners come together, they will be properly staggered (Fig. 4–13(a)). The sheets should be nailed rough side up with coated or annular-ring nails every 4 in. The nails are placed at the intersections of 4-in. squares. These points are marked on hardboard, but other types of underlayment can be marked with chalk or estimated. This

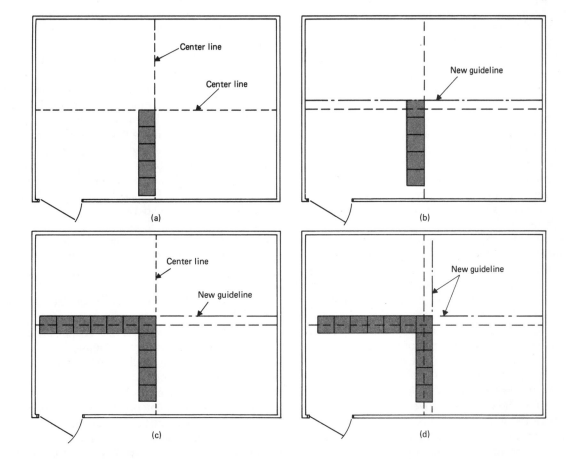

Fig. 4–14 Establishing guidelines for floor tiles: a) initial placement of tiles, b) adjusting the first row, c) placing a row at right angles, d) final placement and guidelines.

will also place nails every 4 in. along the edges of the sheets. (Such close spacing keeps the underlayment from buckling.) Butt them with 1/32-in. spacing between their edges to allow for expansion. Where a partial sheet is required, or a sheet has to be cut to fit wall or door trim (Fig. 4–13(b)), mark the cutting line on the sheet and cut it with a saw before nailing it in place.

Although most tiling materials can be installed on below-grade concrete with a special mastic, linoleum should be used only on dry, above-grade surfaces. Damp concrete can be covered with a moisture-proof sheet of polyethylene or a plywood subfloor laid over a framework of 2 X 4-in. screeds.

Installing Tiles

Tiles should be installed so that the rows next to the walls are one-half tile (or more) wide. Lines that connect the centers of the opposite walls should be marked on the floor with a chalk line (Fig. 4–14(a)). As a preliminary step, place a row of tiles along one line from the center of the room to one wall. Place the first tile inside the lines with its corner at the intersection. The distance of the last full tile in the row from the wall will determine how the row has to be moved so that the partial tile next to the wall will be wide enough. If the distance (for 12-in. tiles) is 6 in. or more, the placement is good. If the distance is less than 6 in., move the row 6 in. away from the wall. For example, if the distance is 4 in., by moving the row 6 in. away, the width of the last tile at both walls will be 10 in. (See Fig. 4–14(b)).

Another row of tiles must be laid at right angles to the first row to establish the tile width at the adjoining wall (Fig. 4–14(c)). Follow the same procedure as for the first row; both rows will then be positioned correctly (Fig. 4–13(d)). Mark the position of the tile in the center of the room and also the outside edges of the two intersecting rows before removing them.

Adhesive or *mastic* should be applied only in the immediate area to be tiled. Use either a brush-on adhesive or a mastic, which is applied with a notched trowel. The adhesive must have the proper degree of tackiness before the tiles are laid. Follow the directions for the particular adhesive being used. (See "Adhesives," pp. 34–36.)

Tiles are laid along one side of a guideline and built up in pyramid fashion to cover one half of the floor at a time (Fig. 4–15(a)). Start by butting the first two tiles in the center of the floor at the intersection of the guidelines. Extend the row and build the tiles in pyramid fashion toward the facing wall. As areas coated with adhesive are covered, apply more adhesive to the next section. Tiles should be placed down flat in the adhesive and butted to the adjacent tiles. Do not *slide* them into place, because this will cause the adhesive to ride up over their edges. Where tiles meet the threshold in a doorway, use a protective metal strip to cover their edges.

The row of partial-width tiles is cut and placed next to the wall after the full-size tiles are installed (Fig. 4–14, 15(b)). To measure a tile for this row, hold a full-size tile against the wall and over the area to be covered. Mark the tile at the edge of the preceding tile in the row and cut it with a utility knife or scissors. Where there are pipes or complicated trim, make a pattern with cardboard and pencil so the tile can be cut accurately. Asphalt tiles can be broken along a line scored by a sharp knife by snapping them over a straight edge.

Installing Sheet Flooring

Installing linoleum or standard vinyl sheet flooring with adhesive requires professional experience. However, most homeowners will be able to install standard vinyl loose-laid or use the new flexible vinyl sheet flooring. In either case, the first step is to install a smooth underlayment to prevent irregularities in the previous flooring from showing through.

The edge of standard sheet vinyl is trimmed to the approximate shape by using a pattern made of newspaper that has been cut to fit each wall (Fig. 4–16(a)). The vinyl can be rolled out with its edges along the walls so that the edges can be trimmed to fit more exactly (Fig 4–16(b)). With irregular wall contours or bulges, place the sheet next to the wall and draw, or scribe, the trim line on the flooring parallel to the contour of the baseboard. (A tool known as a "contour guide" can be used to make this easier.) There should be a gap of at least 1/8 in. between the edge of the vinyl and the baseboard (or cabinet bases) to allow for expansion. When the edges are trimmed and the sheet lies flat, the shoe molding along the wall can be nailed into the baseboard. There should be a little leeway between the vinyl and the bottom of the molding. When a large floor is covered, two strips of vinyl have to be installed. If there is a pattern, overlap the strips to match the pattern and cut a common seam. In this case, adhesive must be used under the seam to hold the strips in place.

Flexible vinyl sheet flooring can be folded like carpeting and is fastened down with staples or adhesive. Staples are used where they will penetrate floorboards, plywood, particleboard, linoleum, and uncushioned vinyl and vinyl-asbestos flooring. Otherwise, adhesive is used, such as over concrete or ceramic floor tiles. The vinyl flooring is laid flat on the floor with its edges folded up at the baseboards where they can be trimmed with a straightedge and utility knife. Trimmed edges are fastened down with a stapling gun or adhesive bottle. Because of its construction, the vinyl contracts and smooths out after it is installed. This characteristic also allows the material to be stretched a little, if necessary, to cover gaps at the baseboard molding (before it's stapled).

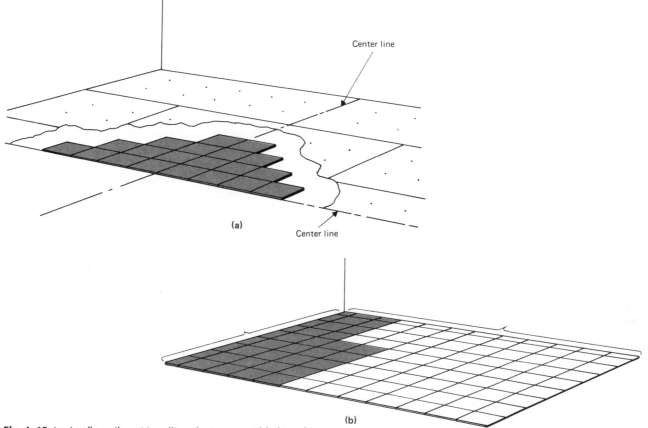

Fig. 4–15 Laying floor tiles: a) installing tiles in pyramid fashion, b) installing partial-width tiles.

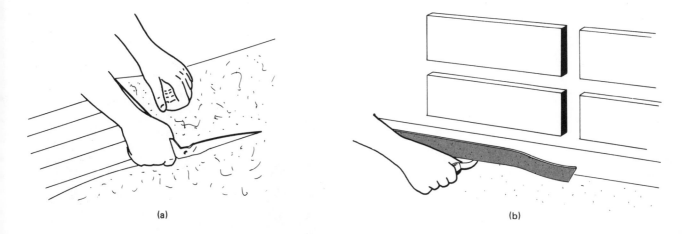

Fig. 4–16 Installing loose-laid sheet vinyl: a) trimming to approximate shape, b) trimming edges to fit around walls.

Repairing Tile Flooring

Damaged tiles can be removed by softening their adhesive and prying the pieces loose with a putty knife. Heat helps soften adhesive but it also can damage the tiles. An adhesive solvent is the safest thing to use. Since asphalt tiles are fairly resistant to heat, a propane torch, a hot iron and a protective cloth, or a heat lamp can be used to warm them (Fig. 4–17(a)(b)). The edges will loosen enough to allow for inserting a putty knife to pry the tile loose (Fig. 4–17(c)). Other tiles should be carefully cut through with a sharp utility or linoleum knife. Solvent can be worked under the edges of the cut with help from a putty knife. Repeated applications of solvent and prying will eventually loosen the pieces of the tile so they can be removed. The old mastic should be cleaned from the subfloor so that the base of the new tile will be flush with the other tiles (Fig. 4–17(d)). Spread the

mastic on the back of the tile and press it into place (Fig. 4–17(e)). Wipe off any excess mastic that squeezes out at the edges of the tile.

Repairing Sheet Flooring

Linoleum and sheet vinyl can be patched with similar material of the same thickness. Lay the new piece over the area to be replaced, match the pattern, and hold the piece in place with tape or a few thin nails partially driven in a few inches from the edges (Fig. 4–18(a)). Use a sharp knife such as a linoleum knife to cut through both the new and old pieces just an inch or so within the edge of the replacement piece (Fig. 4–18(b)). The old material can be removed with a putty knife and the subfloor cleaned of mastic. Fresh mastic should be spread over the exposed area and the replace-

(a)

(b)

(c)

Fig. 4–17 Repairing tile flooring: a) softening adhesive with a propane torch, b) softening adhesive with an iron, c) prying the tile loose, d) cleaning off the old mastic, e) laying the new tile.

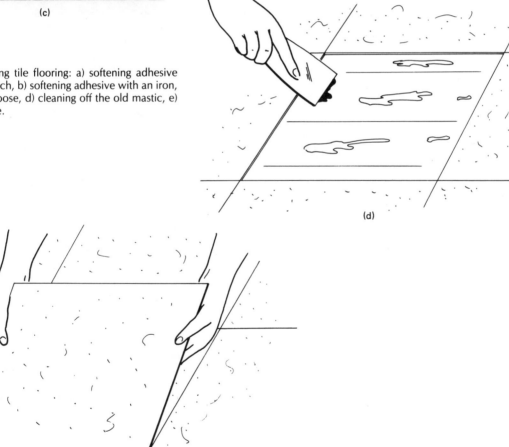

(d)

(e)

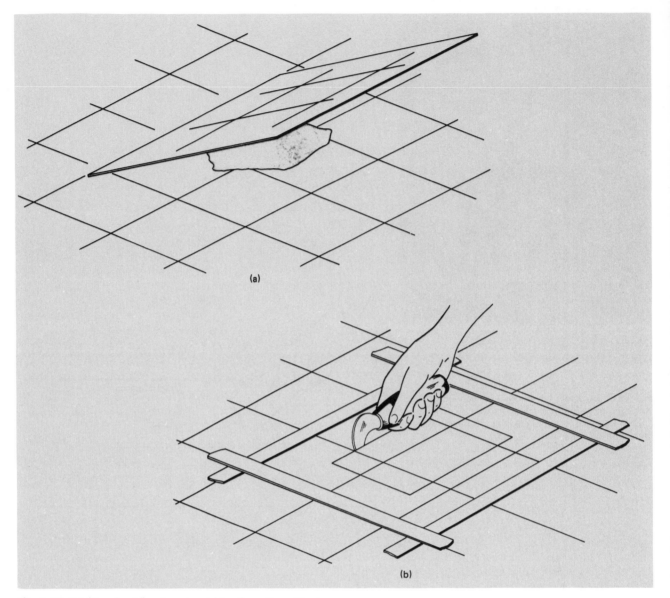

Fig. 4–18 Patching sheet flooring: a) matching the pattern, b) cutting through both pieces.

ment piece pressed into place. A layer of roofing paper can be used under the replacement piece if necessary to raise it flush with the surrounding surface.

CARPETING

Wall-to-wall carpeting requires only a smooth surface and can be installed over old wooden floors, resilient tiles and sheets, plywood, concrete, and other surfaces.

Rubber-backed carpeting, indoor–outdoor carpeting, and carpet tiles and strips can be installed without professional experience. Standard wall-to-wall carpeting, however, requires stitching, tacking or tackless strips, and stretching into position. These steps are difficult without professional experience or assistance.

Types of Carpeting and Padding

Most wall-to-wall carpeting is made of wool or synthetic fibers. Carpet manufacturers use a number of standard syn-

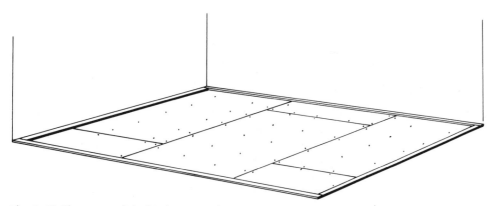

Fig. 4–19 Placement of double-face carpeting tape.

thetics produced by the chemical industry under various trade names, such as Orlon (an acrylic), Dynel (a modacrylic), Kodel (a polyester), and Herculon (a polypropylene olefin). These fibers vary in their abrasion resistance, resiliency, and soil resistance. A dealer in carpeting is a good source of information about which types of carpet material should be chosen for different uses. He can also advise as to whether a carpet should be woven, knitted, or tufted.

Rubber-backed carpeting and some types of indoor–outdoor carpeting are backed with a moisture-proof layer, such as foam rubber, which allows them to be used over vinyl tiles, concrete, and other potentially moist surfaces. Separate padding is used under standard carpeting to increase its life and make it softer underfoot. The most popular types of padding are latex foam, vinyl foams, sponge rubber, and jute. The widths of the strips of padding depend on whether they are cut from 4½-, 12-, or 15-ft wide rolls.

All types of carpeting are available in several widths, which vary with the manufacturer. Rolls are made in 6-, 9-, 12-, and 15-ft widths. Individual carpet tiles are made in standard 12 X 12-in. squares and larger sizes. Strips of carpet are available for installation in 3 X 5-ft pieces and other sizes. Remnants of various sizes may sometimes be available at lower cost.

Amount and Size of Carpeting

The number of square yards of carpeting required for a floor depends on the size of the room and how the strips of carpeting are laid. If the room is wide enough to require more than one strip, the strips should be laid to minimize waste. Regardless of whether the carpeting is laid as a single strip or as several strips, it should be wide enough to extend at least 3 in. beyond the widest points in the room and into the doorways. For example, a room 14 ft wide would require carpeting from a 15-ft roll. The length that would have to be cut (including the extra 3 in. at both ends of the room) from the roll should be multiplied by the width of the roll to

determine the area required. For example, a room 14-ft wide and 20-ft long would require a 15-ft roll; 15 ft X 20 ft 6 in. equals 307½ sq. ft, or a little more than 34 sq. yd.

The number of carpet tiles required can be determined in the same way as with resilient tiles. Multiply the lengths of two adjacent walls in a rectangular room to find the number of 12-in. carpet tiles needed. Allow a few extra for errors in cutting and waste. Larger tiles and strips of carpeting can be blocked out on a plan of the floor to find the number required.

Preparing Floors

Floors to be covered with carpeting must be free of bumps, projecting nails, loose boards, holes, large cracks, and other irregularities. Old wooden floors may have to be patched with wood strips or a concrete-like filler. Nails should be set and loose boards nailed down. Resilient tiles may be covered with carpeting if they form a reasonably smooth surface. Plywood or hardboard should be nailed so that the seams are flush and do not form ridges. Concrete should be patched and made as level as possible. (Only indoor–outdoor carpeting and rubber-backed carpeting should be used over resilient flooring or concrete because the backing is moisture- and mildew-resistant.)

Installing Wall-to-Wall Carpeting

Although standard wall-to-wall carpeting may be too difficult for the nonprofessional to install, rubber-backed carpeting, carpet tiles, and indoor–outdoor carpeting can be installed without professional experience. Double-face (adhesive) carpeting tape can be used to fasten the borders of rubber-backed carpeting and seaming tape used to hold edges of adjacent strips together. (Professionals are more likely to spread adhesive over the entire floor.) Place the tape along the edge of the floor around the room where the

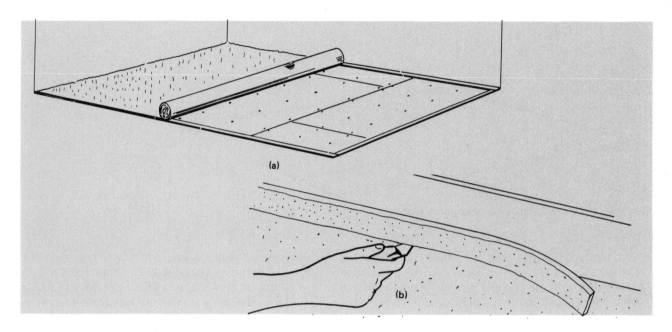

(a)

(b)

Fig. 4–20 Installing rubber-backed carpeting: a) unrolling the carpeting, b) trimming the carpeting along the wall.

edge of the carpeting will fall (Fig. 4–19). The protective paper on the upper side will prevent it from sticking prematurely. Unroll the rubber-backed carpeting so that it turns up a few inches on each wall. When the carpeting is in position, roll one end away from the wall and remove the protective paper over the face of the exposed tape. The carpet can be rolled back into position and pressed firmly against the tape (Fig. 4–20(a)). Use a sharp utility knife to trim the carpeting along the contour of the baseboard (Fig. 4–20(b)). Where two strips of rubber-backed carpeting are used, fasten them in the same way but use seaming tape on the floor under the edges where they form a seam. Follow the directions for applying the adhesive to the seaming tape and the bottom of the carpeting. The patterns and the lay of the piles in the two strips should be mated before they are cut and placed in position. Metal strips should be used to protect the carpeting where it enters a door opening.

Indoor–outdoor carpeting is installed in strips using seaming tape. The strips are rolled out and trimmed in a manner similar to that used in installing cushion-backed carpeting. Follow the directions for applying the adhesive to the tape and carpeting.

Carpet tiles may be purchased with self-sticking adhesive backs or with nonadhesive backs. Both types can be installed according to the guidelines for installing resilient tiles.

Minor Carpet Repairs

Extensive wear has created a tear or bald spot in your carpeting. Perhaps a closet door has scraped one small area, leaving what amounts to a hole at a given point.

You can fix it. Essentially, you cut out the damaged section, then replace it with a patch of identical size.

You'll need some leftover carpeting from the original installation. If you have no leftovers, cut a piece from beneath a radiator or from a carpeted closet. Your tools and supplies should include a utility knife—preferably with a sharp, heavy blade—masking tape, a steel ruler, and double-faced tape. Steps to follow are:

Cut a patch that will cover the hole, torn area, or worn spot. Make the cuts between rows of pile—if the rows are clearly visible.

Using a steel rule to guide your knife, with the patch as a guide, cut out the damaged part. Pushpins will help to keep the patch aligned while cutting out the piece of carpeting.

After cleaning the floor under the hole with a damp cloth and detergent, apply the adhesive side of double-faced tape to the floor.

Insert the patch and press it firmly into place. Two right-angle edges should fit tightly against corners of the opening in the carpeting.

WOOD FLOORING

Hardwood flooring is another attractive covering that can be installed over surfaces such as old floors, plywood subfloors, and concrete. The underlying floor doesn't have to be as smooth as for tiles or carpeting, but it should be level.

Usually wood flooring can be installed by someone without previous experience since it is manufactured to lock together easily and is available in prefinished forms.

Types of Wood Flooring

Hardwood strips are the most popular type of wood flooring. Plank flooring and parquet or block flooring, however, are also widely used. All are available prefinished or unfinished.

Hardwood floors are made from strips of maple, oak, birch, and other hardwoods manufactured in several qualities, from Clear and Select to No. 2 Common. These strips can be purchased in widths from 1½ to 2¼ in. and thicknesses from 3/8 to 25/32 in. The wider and thicker strips are used more frequently. Strips are locked together by the tongues and grooves on their edges and ends.

Plank flooring consists of wider strips (3 to 8 in.) of the same kinds of hardwood used for narrow strips. The thicknesses vary from 3/8 to 25/32 in. and the edges are tongue-and-grooved.

Parquet or *block flooring* is made up of 9 X 9-in. or 12 X 12-in. squares of narrow hardwood strips bonded together. Oak is used for these blocks more than other hardwoods. The surfaces may be prefinished or unfinished, and the back may be coated with a self-stick adhesive or may be plain. Some blocks are also backed with a layer of foam to protect the wood from moisture. Tongue-and-groove edges hold the blocks together.

Wide softwood boards with square edges also can be used for flooring, as they were in earlier years. However, denting and cracks between boards are serious problems. The boards gouge and dent relatively easily compared with hardwoods. They can be protected somewhat with a hard polyurethane finish. Without tongue-and-groove fittings, the boards will not butt smoothly, and they tend to pull apart as the wood ages and dries out.

Preparing the Subfloor

Rigid hardwood strips and planks can be nailed directly to almost any level subfloor except concrete. They can be nailed over an old wooden floor in poor condition, over plywood attached to floor joists, over damaged tiles, or over a framework of 2 X 4's covering a concrete floor. Subflooring should be nailed down tightly and protruding nails set. If the floor sags, it should be leveled as much as possible before installing the flooring.

Building paper or 15-lb. asphalt-saturated felt is often laid over the subfloor to provide a smooth, dry surface for flooring. The strips of felt should run in the same direction as the hardwood strips or planks. Position the felt so that the edges of the strips overlap a few inches. No adhesive is required since the felt will be held down by the flooring.

Baseboards can be removed or left in place, but shoe moldings should be removed. Similarly, thresholds and door casings can be removed, or the flooring can be cut to fit around them. If the flooring is thick, the threshold may have to be raised.

Parquet flooring tends to follow the contours of an uneven floor because of the small size of the blocks. Gaps and holes in the subfloor must be patched or filled. Bumps should be planed or sanded down. If the floor is too rough, a smooth plywood or hardboard underlayment should be installed. Concrete floors should be smoothed and covered with sheets of polyethylene attached with mastic unless foam-backed parquet is used.

Installing Hardwood Strip Flooring

Hardwood strips are laid either the long way in a rectangular room or at right angles to the joists over a board-type subfloor. The strips are positioned so that the joints between their ends are staggered several inches apart from row to row. It is helpful to lay out a few rows, or *courses,* before nailing them, to establish the desired pattern. Flooring material should be stored in the room for several days before it is used so that it will adjust to the room's moisture and temperature conditions.

A *guideline* should be drawn on the floor parallel to and about 10 in. from the wall where the first row of strips is to be installed. Place the *first strip* against a corner with its grooved edge toward the wall (Fig. 4–21(a)). Leave a 1/4- to 3/8-in. gap between the edge of the strip and the baseboard for expansion. Continue placing strips along the wall until the last piece in the row can be marked to be cut to fit. Maintain a constant distance between the edge of the strips and the guideline to keep the edges parallel to the wall. The last piece should be marked and cut on its tongue end to complete the course. Before nailing hardwood strips, drill pilot holes along the edge to be nailed. Being careful not to split the wood, face-nail (pound vertically) the strip next to the wall with finish nails every 8 to 10 in. along the edge to be covered by the shoe molding. Use cut flooring nails every 8 to 10 in. at a 45-degree angle just above the tongue to blind nail all of the strips into the subfloor. Set the nails with a nail set to avoid damaging the tongue and to allow the next strip to fit snugly (Fig. 4–21(b)).

The grooves of *succeeding strips* are fitted over the tongues of the strips already in place. Use a hammer or mallet and a scrap piece of flooring with its groove toward the new strip to pound the strip tightly into place. (Fig. 4–21(c)). Blind-nail each strip every 8 to 10 in. from above the tongue into the subflooring. If strips are bowed along their narrow edges, straighten them by nailing a block of wood to the subfloor next to the strip and driving a wedge between it and the block. The wedge will force the strip to straighten out and fit over the tongue of the previously laid strip. Nail the strip in place to keep it straight after the wedge

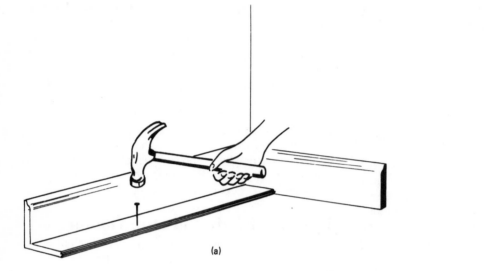

(a)

(b)

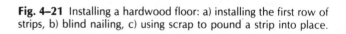

Fig. 4–21 Installing a hardwood floor: a) installing the first row of strips, b) blind nailing, c) using scrap to pound a strip into place.

(c)

and block are removed. To ensure that the end joints are staggered, lay out several courses before nailing the first strips in place.

The last few courses next to the wall opposite the starting point cannot be blind nailed because there isn't room to hammer. Fit them into place and use a narrow board or crowbar to force them tightly against the previous strips. Face-nail these strips with finishing nails so that the nails are covered by the shoe molding. The last course should be narrow enough to leave an expansion gap. If a full-width strip is too wide or too narrow, it should be rip-cut or cut lengthwise.

Strips must be cut to fit around door casings, thresholds, and other obstacles. Hold the strip next to the object and mark it to fit or draw a cutting pattern on a piece of paper and transfer it to the strip. Since there is no shoe molding to cover these joints, the flooring should be cut to fit flush.

When the flooring is completely installed, it should be machine-sanded with several grades of abrasive, from coarse to fine (unless it is prefinished), and protected with wax or another finish. (See "Refinishing," pp. 111–112.)

Installing Plank Flooring

Plank flooring that is fastened with nails is installed the same way as strip flooring. Some types of planks are designed to be fastened with adhesive or screws. Either a special adhesive or a mastic is spread on the subfloor and planks are fitted together like hardwood strips. Where planks are fastened with screws, the screws are countersunk and wooden plugs are placed in the holes.

Installing Parquet Flooring

Store parquet flooring for several days in the room where it is to be used so it can adjust to the temperature and humid

conditions. Parquet flooring can be installed following the same principles as those for installing resilient tiles. Guidelines are established by connecting the midpoints of opposite walls. The area in the middle of the floor on one side of a guideline should be covered with mastic. The blocks are built up in pyramid fashion over one half of the floor, starting at the center (Fig. 4–22). The tongues and grooves of the blocks should be fitted tightly into the adjacent blocks as they are placed in the mastic. A 1/4- to 3/8-in. expansion gap should be left between the baseboard and the edges of the blocks. Blocks in the rows next to the walls may have to be cut to fit. Blocks butting thresholds and door casings also will have to be trimmed to fit.

Installing Hardwood Flooring Over Concrete

On a concrete floor, hardwood strips can be installed over a framework of short lengths of 2 X 4's, called screeds. The floor is first covered with a moisture-proof layer of mastic. After the mastic is dry, full-length 2 X 4's or 2 X 6's are laid flat around the perimeter of the floor. Short lengths (2- to 4-ft) of 2 X 4's are laid at 12-in. intervals parallel to each other with their ends overlapping by at least 6 in. Flooring strips are installed across the screeds. They are nailed to the 2 X 4's wherever they cross and to both 2 X 4's where the screeds overlap. The strips are fitted together with tongue-and-groove joints and their end joints are staggered in the same manner as over a solid subfloor (Fig. 4–23).

CERAMIC FLOOR TILES

Ceramic floor tiles are one of the few flooring coverings that are waterproof. Consequently, they are mainly used in rooms where moisture is a problem, such as bathrooms and laundries. They also stand up well to abrasion, scratching,

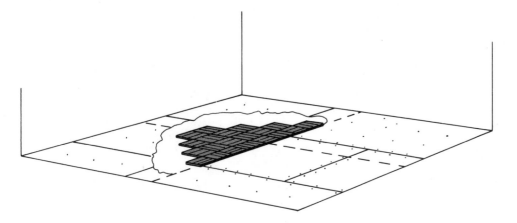

Fig. 4–22 Installing parquet flooring.

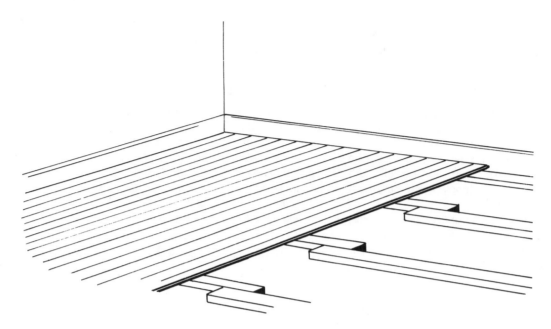

Fig. 4–23 Installing strip flooring over concrete.

and the heavy foot traffic found in entryways and patio areas.

Types of Tiles

Floor tiles are made from the same kinds of materials as ceramic wall tiles but they are thicker and more varied in shape and design. Square, 8 X 8-in. tiles are manufactured to be used individually or as a part of designs made up of four or more tiles. Hexagonal-sided tiles of approximately the same size are also used (Fig. 4-24(a)). Many floor tiles consist of smaller ceramic tiles of various shapes fitted together and attached to a backing of netting or other material. The spacing between tiles varies and depends on the design and type of tile. Mosaic tiles are made in different size sheets and have the closest spacing of the floor tiles (Fig. 4-24(b)). Most tiles are glazed for durability, appearance, and easier cleaning.

Preparing Floors for Tiling

Floors to be covered with tiles must be smooth and level or the tiles will be uneven and may crack where they are not fully supported. A smooth wooden floor makes the best base. Old floors should be patched and smoothed off or covered with an underlayment of hardboard or plywood.

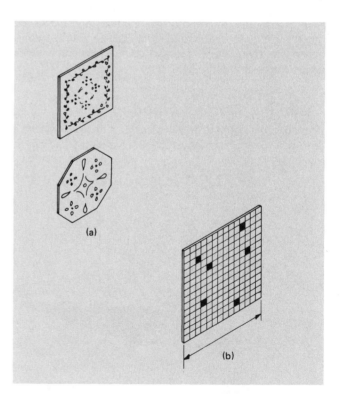

Fig. 4–24 Ceramic floor tiles: a) square and hexagonal tiles, b) mosaic tile.

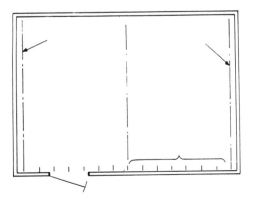

Fig. 4–25 Guidelines for tiling.

Establishing Guidelines

A finished floor of ceramic tile in a room with square corners should have its rows parallel to the walls. The borders should consist of rows of partial tiles of about the same widths. As you look through a doorway into the room, the columns of tile should appear to run perpendicularly away from the door to the opposite wall.

Since opposite walls in most rooms aren't parallel and corners are seldom square, guidelines for the tiles have to be marked on the floor. As with wall tiles, find the center of one wall (the wall with a doorway) and lay out the tiles from that point toward both side walls as a preliminary step. The edges of the last full-size tiles at both ends of the row should be marked so that two guidelines can be drawn perpendicular to the starting wall. (In laying out the tiles, toothpicks or cardboard must be used to space the tiles since they do not have built-in spacers like wall tiles). The starting wall and these two guidelines enclose the area to be covered with full-size tiles (Fig. 4-25).

Installing Tiles

Apply the flexible mastic used for ceramic floor tiles with a notched trowel over a small area where the first tiles are to be installed. (Fig. 4-26(a)). Tiles should be started in a squared corner where a perpendicular guideline meets the starting wall. Press the tile or sheet of mosaics into the mastic. The next tile should be spaced 1/16 in. or more away. Sheets of mosaic tiles should be placed so that the spaces between them are the same as those between the individual mosaics. Use spacers wherever the tiles butt the wall. After a small area has been covered, use a mallet and piece of wood cushioned with cloth to tap the tiles so that they are pressed firmly and evenly into the mastic. Apply more mastic to the next section to be covered and continue

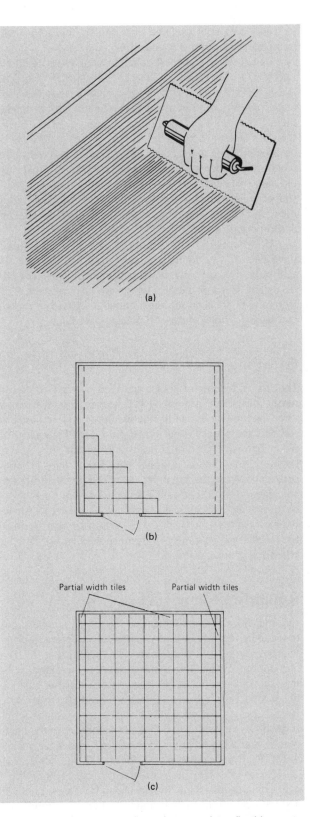

Fig. 4–26 Installing ceramic floor tiles: a) applying flexible mastic, b) installing full-size tiles, c) installing partial-width tiles.

installing tiles until the area enclosed by the guidelines is completely covered (Fig. 4-26(b)).

Partial-width tiles must be cut to form a row next to the wall (Fig. 4-26(c)). Hold the tiles over the spaces where they are to be laid and mark them for cutting (include the allowance for spacing). Ceramic tiles can be cut with a standard tile cutter or with a glass cutter. Use a straightedge to guide the glass cutter in scoring the surface of the tile. The tile can be broken along the scored line by placing it across a long nail or other ridge and snapping it. Tile nippers or pliers will nip out small pieces of tile when fitting them around irregular shapes such as pipes. Before the cut tile is laid, the rough edge should be smoothed with emery cloth, a file, or a carborundum stone.

Floors covered with ceramic mosaic tiles will appear to have tiles in a continuous pattern from wall to wall. The spaces between the last full sheets and the walls are filled by cutting strips of mosaics which are just the right width. Where very small spaces must be filled, individual mosaics can be cut from a sheet and placed in position.

Grouting

The spaces between the tiles are filled with grout after the mastic has dried at least 24 hrs. Mosaic tiles with sheets covering their faces can be uncovered when the mastic has set. Mix the special grout powder used for floor tiles with water until the mixture is paste-like. Remove the spacers between the tiles and apply the grout with a rubber squeegee. Work the grout into all of the joints and use the squeegee to smooth it off. Grout between floor tiles should be flush with the surface. As the grout begins to harden, wipe off excess grout with a wet cloth or sponge. A special tile cleaner should be used to remove the film from the tiles when the grout is hard.

Repairing Floor Tiles

Ceramic floor tiles may become loose or cracked. Loose tiles can be removed, cleaned of mastic and grout, replaced with new mastic, and the joints filled with grout. Cracked tiles are more difficult to remove. In older installations, tiles may be set in mortar rather than mastic. In either case, the tile has to be chipped out and replaced. For tiles set in mastic, use a hammer and a chipping tool such as an old screwdriver or cold chisel. Place the tool against the center of the tile and pound just hard enough to crack it further (Fig. 4-27). Pry the cracked pieces loose with the screwdriver being careful not to puncture the underlying floor if it is made of gypsum board. The grout can be cleaned out with a sharp-edged tool such as a glass cutter or pointed bottle opener. If the tile is set in mortar, the adjacent tiles may crack when the first tile is struck to chip it out. You may have

Fig. 4–27 Removing cracked tiles.

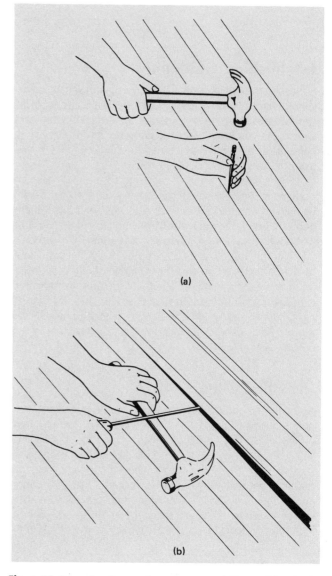

Fig. 4–28 Preparing for sanding: a) countersinking nail heads, b) removing shoe molding.

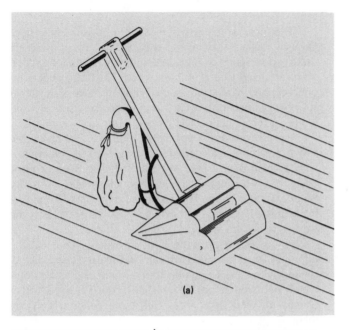

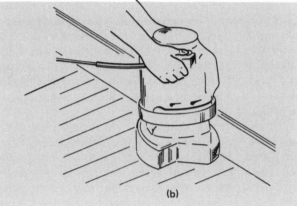

Fig. 4–29 Sanding a hardwood floor a) with a drum sander, b) using an edge sander along the wall.

to use a chipping hammer to remove it by making small, light chips. The mortar should be cleaned out beneath the tile, also.

It may be difficult to find new tiles to match old ones. However, a contrasting tile that goes well with the old tiles may create a desirable decorative effect. The surface under the old tiles should be patched with spackling compound or patching plaster, and smoothed off flush with the base of the other tiles. When the patch is dry, apply mastic and press the new tiles into place. Grout should be worked into the joints and smoothed off after the mastic is dry.

REFINISHING

Previously finished hardwood and softwood floors can be restored to their original appearance by sanding and refin-

ishing them. For the heavy sanding, sanding machines can be rented or professional floor refinishers employed. Paint remover, instead of sanding, may be used to remove old finishes where sanding is not desired. After the finish sanding is completed, several coats of floor finish are applied to the bare wood, followed by two coats of protective wax. New, unfinished floors require only a light, finish sanding before they are stained or covered with a finish.

PREPARATIONS FOR SANDING

Defects in floors should be repaired before the wood is sanded. Cracks should be patched or filled with wood putty. Damaged boards should be replaced and loose boards nailed down. Check the nails to see that they are sunk so that they cannot tear the sandpaper (Fig. 4-28(a)). Remove the shoe molding so the floor can be sanded right up to the baseboards (Fig. 4-28(b)).

SANDING

Drum Sander

A drum sander is used to remove the old finish and expose a smooth and clear layer of wood (Fig. 4-29(a)). For the first sanding, a coarse sheet of sandpaper is wrapped around the sander's drum and clamped in place. Sanding is started as close to the wall as possible with the drum raised above the floor. Lower the drum gradually and control the sander so that it moves slowly across the floor sanding in the direction of the grain and the wooden strips. Keep the sander moving evenly or it will cut valleys into the flooring. Sand the entire floor in slightly overlapping strips. When the coarse sanding is complete, vacuum the floor thoroughly, and sand it again with a medium grade of sandpaper. As the sandpaper wears down or tears, replace it with new sheets. The finish sanding should be done with a fine-grade sandpaper after the floor is vacuumed. With a parquet floor, use only a fine-grade sandpaper for the entire sanding, since coarser abrasives will damage the strips laminated at right angles.

Edge Sander and Sanding by Hand

Sections of the floor close to the walls and stairs, which cannot be sanded with a large drum sander, are sanded with an edge sander (Fig. 4-29(b)) or by hand with a sanding block. The edge sander uses a sanding disk to remove old finish and wood. Because the circular scratches from the rotating disk are hard to remove, a medium-grade abrasive should be used for the initial sanding. The fine-grade abrasive used for the finish sanding will remove the circular scratches from the earlier sanding.

Corners and areas behind pipes and other obstacles must be sanded by hand. A paint scraper may be needed where the old finish is thick and difficult to cut through with sandpaper. By wrapping a sheet of sandpaper around a wooden sanding block, the areas unreached with the drum and edge sanders can be smoothed down to merge with the rest of the floor.

APPLYING FINISHES

Freshly sanded or newly stained floors should be coated with a finish to enhance their appearance and protect them from scratches and moisture. Apply the finish as soon as possible to prevent sanded floors from absorbing moisture or from being marred. The dust from the finishing sanding should be removed with a brush attachment on a vacuum, being careful not to mar the floor with shoe marks.

The most widely used finishes are polyurethane, floor varnish, shellac, sealers, and wax. Before any of these are used, wood stains or fillers are sometimes applied. Wood stains are used to darken bare wood. Fillers are applied to open-grained hardwoods such as oak to make a smoother surface for the finish. Fillers should not be used on softwoods or close-grained hardwood strips such as maple.

Varnish protects floors from moisture and stains but shows scratches and darkens with age. It may be applied with a brush over a filler or coat of shellac. Two or three coats should be applied, and each should be allowed to dry for twenty-four hours. The varnished area should be as free from dust as possible, so that no dust will settle into the varnish while it is drying.

Polyurethane forms the hardest protective film of all the floor finishes. It is applied like varnish and each coat is lightly sanded with steel wool after it dries. Dust should be completely removed before the next finish coat is applied. Cover heavily traveled floor areas with three coats of polyurethane.

Shellac can be used for light protection where moisture is not a problem. Although shellac is not as resistant to stains and moisture as varnish, it does not darken with age. Two or three coats of a 3-lb. cut should be applied with a light sanding between the coats. Dust is not as much of a problem as with varnish since shellac dries in a few hours. Shellac also may be applied as a single-coat sealer before staining or before varnishing.

A sealer protects the floor by penetrating the wood, rather than by forming a surface film. Sealers generally contain a filler and are applied liberally with a brush, a roller, or a clean cloth. Let the sealer soak into the wood, and remove the excess with dry cloths after ten to fifteen minutes. After the first coat has dried overnight, rub it with steel wool and vacuum the dust before applying a second coat. The second coat will be thinner and should also dry overnight before it is waxed.

Two thin coats of wax, liquid or paste, should be applied over varnish, shellac, sealer, or polyurethane when they are thoroughly dry. Wax can also be used as the only protective coating where floors are to be left as natural as possible. Apply the first thin coat with a soft cloth according to the manufacturer's instructions. When it is dry, apply a second equally thin coat. Wax can be polished by hand, with a soft cloth, or with a machine polisher.

Floor finish can be touched up where spots are worn or where there are stains by rubbing with steel wool and using the same finish to cover and feather the edges of the area. Rub the refinished section with steel wool to match it to the older finish. Apply two thin coats of wax and dull or polish them as necessary.

5 Wooden Furniture

Pieces of furniture that are worth salvaging can be renovated by making minor repairs and refinishing the wood. A basically good finish can be restored by cleaning, repairing scratches, and waxing. Loose joints have to be glued and clamped, fractured pieces repaired with an adhesive or reinforcing hardware, and loose veneers fastened down.

Finishes in poor condition should be removed and the piece refinished. Varnish, shellac, lacquer, boiled linseed oil, and wax are clear finishes that allow the beauty of the wood grain to show. Enamels obliterate the grain and form a glossy, smooth coating. For an antiqued appearance, glazing is applied over an enamel and wiped to give a worn appearance.

Fig. 5—1 Touching up a small scratch.

REPAIRING WOODEN FURNITURE

SCRATCHES AND GOUGES

Scratches and gouges are repaired by filling them with filler colored to match the surrounding wood. When it is dry, the filler is sanded and the area refinished so that it blends in with the rest of the surface.

Small scratches can be touched up by using touchup sticks (Fig. 5–1) (if the right color is available); applying a little iodine on mahogany; dabbing on oil paint from artist's oil colors blended to match the finish; or rubbing a varnish finish with alcohol. The area then should be rubbed down and rewaxed to blend in the repair so it will not be apparent to the eye.

Larger scratches must be filled with more substantial fillers (Fig. 5–2(a)). Plastic wood and wood dough, which are available in many different wood tones, are easier to use than most fillers. The putty-like substance should be worked into the scratch and built up slightly above the surface (Fig. 5–2(b)). When it is hard, the filler should be sanded down and feathered into the surrounding area. Sticks of colored wax or shellac also can be used; the wax or shellac is melted and allowed to run into the scratch (Fig. 5–3). As it hardens, smooth it off with the flat side of a knife. Finally, rub it down with a fine abrasive powder or pad. Wax should be sealed with a thin coat of shellac if it is to be covered with varnish.

Deep scratches and cracks should be filled in several steps with thin layers of plastic wood or wood dough. If a different surface filler is to be used, the plastic wood can be built up to within 1/16 in. or so of the surface before the final layer is applied.

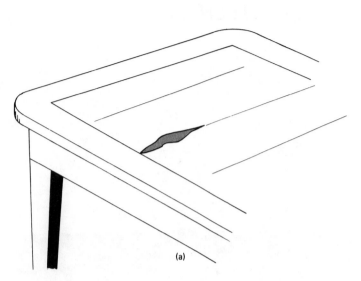

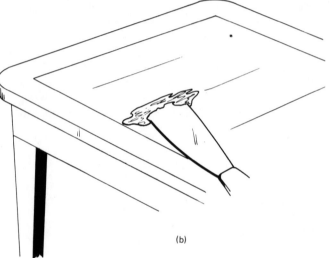

Fig. 5–2 Filling a crack with plastic wood: a) medium-size crack, b) applying the filler, c) finished patch.

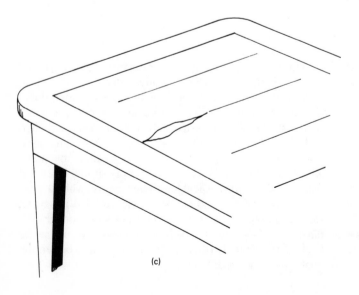

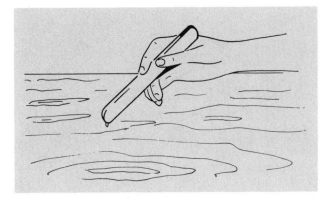

Fig. 5–3 Patching with a shellac stick.

STAINS AND BURNS

White and dark stains are caused by setting something wet or hot on a finish or spilling a staining liquid. Since the types of finishes vary, it may take some experimenting to find the best way to remove the stains. Both very fine abrasives and chemicals are used. Sometimes an abrasive pad or a fine powder such as pumice and a little oil will remove enough surface film from the finish to remove the stain also. More often a chemical has to be used. A commercial wood cleaner may do the job. If it doesn't, there are specific treatments for different stains.

White stains caused by moisture or hot objects can be treated with ammonia on a rag (Fig. 5–4(a)), a paste of cigar ashes and water (or cigar ashes and oil, Fig. 5–4(b)), or lighter fluid. One of these will probably remove (or cover) the stain, depending on the type of finish.

Dark stains in the wood under the surface can be treated with oxalic acid crystals dissolved in warm water. Follow the directions on the container for making oxalic acid. Use a rag to apply the solution to the darkened areas until they disappear. Clean the area with a damp cloth and let it dry. If the area is discolored, it can be touched up with artist's oils, with the same technique used for scratches.

LOOSE VENEERS

Sometimes the glue under thin veneers becomes moist and weak and the veneer peels loose. This can be repaired in one or two ways. Old glue can be heated and reset or the surfaces can be cleaned and a new adhesive applied.

To heat the old glue under a veneer, use an ordinary iron set on low heat, and protect the veneer's finish with a

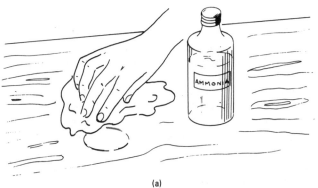

(a)

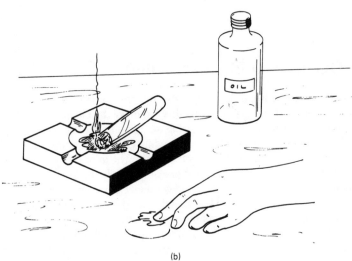

(b)

Fig. 5–4 Removing a white stain: a) using ammonia, b) applying cigar ashes and oil.

Fig. 5–5 Heating a veneer with an iron to soften the glue.

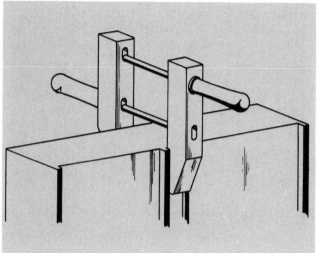

Fig. 5–6 Using clamps on glued pieces.

layer of kraft paper and a few layers of newspaper or a layer of cloth (Fig. 5–5). The iron will heat the wood and glue quickly. When the veneer feels hot, it should be pressed down and weighted with heavy objects, or clamped. Use pieces of cloth to protect the finish.

A new coat of adhesive can be applied once the old glue has been cleaned out. If the loose veneer is brittle, it can be made more flexible by moistening it with a wet cloth and heating it with an iron. Fresh adhesive should be applied to both surfaces and the veneer pressed down. Wipe off excess adhesive that squeezes out from the edges. Heavy weights or clamps should be used to hold the veneer in place until the adhesive dries.

LOOSE AND BROKEN JOINTS

Joints that are loose, or have separated but are not damaged, can be cleaned and clamped together. To make the cleaning easier, separate the pieces if possible, scrape off the old glue without cutting into the wood, apply white glue or a stronger adhesive, and put the pieces together again. The joint should be held together with some form of clamps while the adhesive is drying (Fig. 5–6). If woodworking clamps are not practical, a heavy cord can be wound around opposite ends of the jointed pieces and tightened by twisting.

Loose joints are sometimes caused by one of the pieces wearing down. In this case, an adhesive such as resorcinol should be used, which can also act as a filler; or the worn piece can be built up. To build up a worn dowel or tenon, wrap it with thread and coat it with adhesive.

Right-angled joints can be reinforced with small blocks of wood (Fig. 5–7(a)) or reinforcing hardware (Fig. 5–7(b)). Triangular-shaped reinforcing blocks can be glued inside joints between tabletops, legs, and sides where they are not visible. Reinforcing hardware, such as flat corner plates and inside corner braces, can be used in the same way, either where they are not visible or where their presence does not detract from the appearance of the furniture.

Broken joints that are not under pressure can be cleaned and fastened together again with white glue or a stronger adhesive. The pieces must be clamped tightly together until the adhesive has dried.

Broken joints that bear pressure require additional reinforcement. Depending on whether the point of repair is visible or not, a metal mending plate or a blind pin such as a dowel can be used. The mending plate can be screwed on the surface over the break after the pieces have been joined with adhesive; or a dowel can be inserted in holes bored into the two broken ends so that the pieces will match up and pull together. Apply adhesive to both edges of the broken joint and to the dowel before the joint is clamped together (Fig. 5–8).

DRAWERS

Many things can go wrong with drawers, especially in inexpensive softwood furniture and built-ins. Drawers may bind or become so loose that they won't stay shut. They may not ride evenly on their guides. The drawer itself may start to come apart.

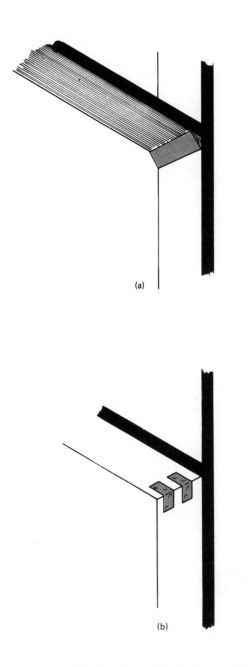

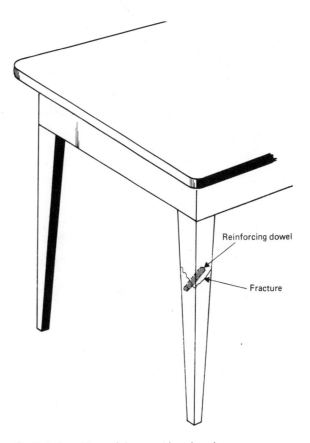

Fig. 5–8 Repairing a fracture with a dowel.

Fig. 5–7 Reinforcing joints with a) triangular block support, b) inside corner braces.

Drawers may fall apart under heavy loads or simply after sustained use, if they are not well built. The entire drawer should be removed and inspected. Loose joints, whether they are stapled or dovetailed, should be realigned and fastened together so that they are square. Wooden reinforcing blocks, guides, and stops should all be glued in place.

Guides that are loose or not lined up properly will cause jamming and must be repositioned (Fig. 5–9(a)(b)). Pry up the guides and position them perpendicular to the back of the cabinet so that they line up with the sides of the drawer (Fig. 5–9(c)). Glue them into position, sand down their bearing surfaces, and coat them lightly with wax.

The cause of binding can usually be located by a careful inspection of the drawer and the way it moves on its guides. A coat of wax on the guides may be enough to make the drawer slide smoothly. If not, a plane (or sandpaper) can be used to smooth down areas that are binding on the runners, the glides, or the face of the drawer. Where an edge absorbs moisture and swells so that the drawer will no longer fit the opening, the edge should be planed down.

DOORS

Cabinet doors may sag and fail to close after they have been in use for some time. Hinges may work loose, the joints may separate, or moisture may cause the wood to expand.

If tightening the hinge screws doesn't help, larger screws should be used. The hinges may have to be removed and the enlarged holes filled by pounding small wooden

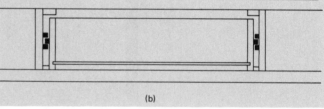

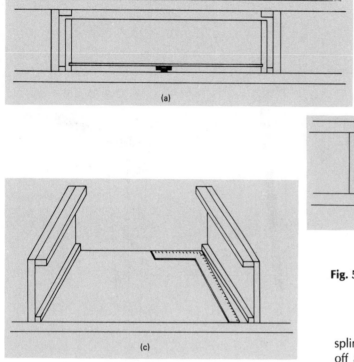

Fig. 5–9 Drawer guides: a) center, b) side. c) Aligning the guides.

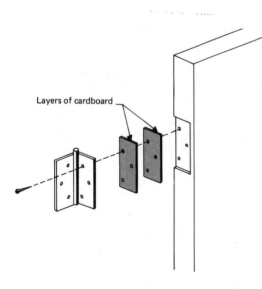

Fig. 5–10 Shimming a recessed hinge.

splinters into them. The ends of the splinters should be cut off and adhesive worked in to bond the pieces together. When the adhesive is dry, smaller holes can be drilled and the screws replaced for a tighter grip.

Where a door sags, a hinge recessed into the edge can be recessed further or moved closer to the surface. It's easiest to adjust a hinge set in too deeply on a sagging door. Remove the hinge and insert a layer or two of cardboard to hold it closer to the surface (Fig. 5–10). To set a hinge farther back into the edge, remove some of the underlying wood with a chisel.

Loose joints in doors can be reglued or fastened with reinforcing hardware. Use flat corner plates for corners and T-plates for T-joints in the middle of a door.

An edge that binds because it has absorbed moisture should be planed just enough so that it will still fit in damp weather. It can then be refinished and sealed with shellac or another sealer to prevent further absorption.

STAINING FURNITURE

Light-colored woods such as pine, maple, birch, and bass-wood usually look better when darkened with a stain. Stains allow the degree of darkening to be controlled while letting the natural grain of the wood show through. Several types are made in a variety of natural wood and bright nonwood colors.

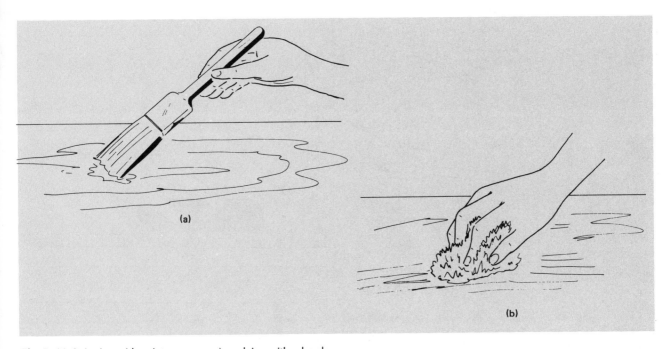

Fig. 5–11 Stripping with paint remover: a) applying with a brush, b) rubbing with steel wool.

PREPARING THE WOOD

Stain must be applied to smooth, bare wood. Previous finishes of paint, shellac, lacquer, or varnish should be removed. A paste-type paint remover and a scraper or putty knife are the most effective tools for stripping paint. In some cases heat is used to soften up paint or polyurethane, abrasives are used to reach into corners, or a bleach is required to remove deep stains. After the piece has been stripped, the chemicals are washed away and the surface rubbed with a fine grade of steel wool to pick up remnants. After the wood has dried, it should be lightly sanded with very fine inexpensive paper and steel wool to remove any remaining paint remover and to smooth the raised grain (Fig. 5–11(a),(b)).

The stripped wood should be sanded with a medium-grade abrasive, followed by finer grades, to provide a uniformly smooth surface for the stain. Since rough wood will absorb more stain and consequently will appear darker than smooth wood, the areas to be stained should be sanded with the same grade of abrasive. Mechanical sanders, such as vibrating or belt sanders (Fig. 5–12(a)), can be used on large flat areas. For sanding by hand, wrap a sheet of garnet paper around a sanding block (Fig. 5–12(b)). After the finish sand-

ing with the finest grade of sandpaper or steel wool (Fig. 5–12(c)), vacuum all of the dust from the surface and crevices.

TYPES OF STAINS

The most common wood stains are oil stains (wiping stains), NGR (or "non-grain-raising") stains, and water stains.

Oil stains (wiping stains) consist of pigment suspended in a penetrating vehicle that doesn't raise the grain of the wood. To maintain a consistent color, the stain has to be stirred frequently. These work best on softwoods such as pine and fir, since the pigment creates variation by lodging in the large, spring-wood pores. To control the variation, a thin wash-coat of shellac should be applied to soft wood before it is stained. A ratio of one part of shellac to two or three parts of alcohol is about right for pine.

Non-grain-raising (NGR) stains are mainly employed in commercial furniture manufacturing rather than for home use because they are difficult to control. Since they don't contain water, NGR stains don't raise the grain; therefore, no further sanding is required.

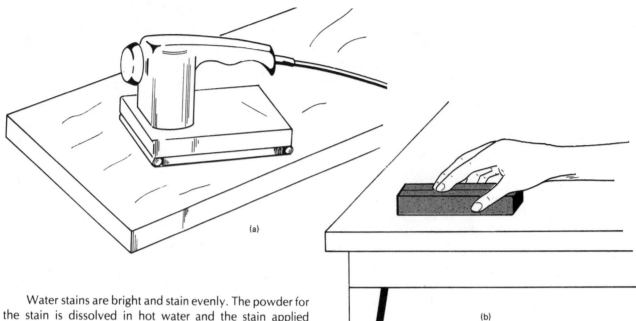

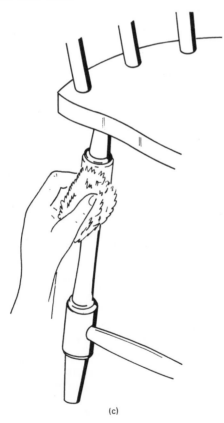

Water stains are bright and stain evenly. The powder for the stain is dissolved in hot water and the stain applied freely. Porous spring wood and less porous summer wood stain more uniformly with water stains than with wiping stains. The wood is actually dyed by the water stain. Since water raises the grain, the surface must be lightly sanded after the stain dries.

Fig. 5-12 Sanding stripped wood with: a) belt sander, b) sanding block, c) steel wool.

PAINTING

APPLYING STAINS

Oil stains (wiping stains) should be stirred thoroughly before they are used. If a softwood is to be stained, cover it with a thin wash of one part shellac and three or four parts alcohol, to seal the larger pores and to allow the stain to penetrate more evenly. Apply the stain with a cloth or brush and let it soak in (Fig. 5-13). The longer it soaks in, the darker the finish will be. The stain can be wiped off with a clean cloth from five to fifteen minutes after it is applied. If the surface looks too dark, some of the stain can be removed with a cloth soaked in paint thinner.

Water stains are particularly effective in giving some of the darker hardwoods such as walnut and cherry the proper hue. The powder must be dissolved in water that is close to boiling. When it has cooled, the stain is applied liberally with a sprayer or cloth and allowed to soak in. The excess should be wiped off. If the first application doesn't produce a dark enough finish, use a second or third coat. The stain must dry overnight and then be very lightly sanded with a fine-grade abrasive to smooth the raised grain.

ENAMELING

If color is preferred to wood tones, furniture can be painted with bright enamel paints. Semigloss and gloss enamels are used for tables, chairs, and other furniture likely to be handled frequently and thus require washing.

If the previous finish is in good condition, it can be lightly sanded and painted over. Use an enamel undercoat to increase the adhesion of the finish coat and make it last longer. Enamel should be applied with a good enamel brush. Dip the brush deeply into the paint and flow the paint on so that it runs together. Do not brush over an area after it is painted. A second coat can be applied if the first doesn't cover the old finish adequately.

ANTIQUING

A glaze used over a base coat of enamel gives furniture an antique (or "distressed") appearance. The surface should be lightly sanded and cleaned. A semigloss enamel in a light shade will show the glaze best. Apply the enamel and let it dry. Apply the darker glaze over the enamel and let it dry for a short time before wiping it. If an antiquing kit is used, follow the directions for drying and wiping. The glaze should

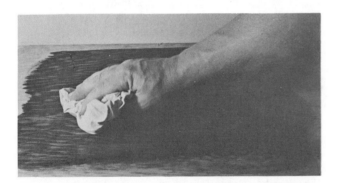

(a)

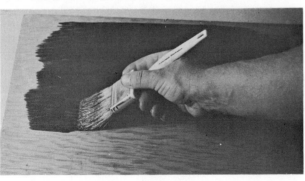

(b)

Fig. 5–13 Applying an oil stain: a) with a cloth, b) with a brush.

be wiped lightly to remove more from the center than the edges, in order to give the edges a darker, worn appearance. When the glaze has dried, wax the surface to protect it from wear.

Milk Paint: To achieve the look of early American primitive furniture, some do-it-yourself fans use what is called milk paint. Mixed by combining powder of various colors with water, usually in equal parts, the paint is extremely durable. You can create your own color shades by increasing or decreasing the amount of water in the mix. The paint should be stirred thoroughly, if possible with a drill-powered beater, and strained through painter's strainer-grade cheesecloth, or some similar material, to remove lumps.

Before painting for the worn, comfortable look of old Country furniture, the piece to be painted should be wiped with a water-dampened cloth. You may also want to stain the furniture a day in advance of your painting session; with the stain as a base, you can later create wear spots—with darker wood showing through—by rubbing the completely dry milk paint with 000 steel wool in selected areas. Some antique lovers apply a second coat of milk paint about four hours after applying the first. You can also, as a final step, coat the surface with a Danish or antique oil, imparting a sheen, then buff with steel wool. Painting with one color and allowing it to dry, then painting over that with a second color, you have the option of wiping off some of the second coat before it dries or "steel-wooling" after it dries. Your furniture then really shows its age!

PROTECTING FINISHED SURFACES

VARNISH

Varnish provides a clear, hard finish that allows the wood grain to show. There are several types of varnishes and sheens. Urethane varnishes are noted for their tough film and resistance to scratches and heat. Vinyl varnishes have the flexibility to expand and contract with a wooden surface without cracking. Alkyd varnishes are widely used where there are no unusual protective requirements. Like enamel paints, varnishes are made with satin, semigloss, and gloss sheens.

Dust and the need for a long drying time combine to make a perfect varnish finish very difficult to achieve. Varnish takes twenty-four hours to dry. Varnishing should be done in a dust-free room that is dry and heated to minimize dust particles in the finish.

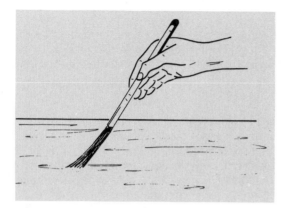

Fig. 5–14 Proper brush angle for applying varnish.

Bare or stained wood should be smooth and clean. A shellac wash (one part of shellac to four or five parts of alcohol) can be applied to seal the wood and raise the grain. When it is dry, sand the wood lightly to smooth the raised fibers and remove the remaining dust. Instead of sealing with shellac, the first coat of varnish can be thinned with one part of turpentine to four parts of varnish. After twenty-four hours, lightly sand the first coat with steel wool, clean off the dust, and apply a second coat of varnish.

An old varnished surface should be sanded lightly before new varnish is applied.

To apply varnish, dip the bristles of a varnish brush to one third of their length. Stroke the varnish on in the direction of the grain, without lapping the edges of the strips. (Fig. 5–14). When the surface is covered, brush crosswise to smooth the varnish. For the final strokes, dip the tips of the bristles in the varnish and lightly stroke or "tip off" the varnish in the direction of the grain.

Sand lightly with a sanding block after the varnish has dried from twenty-four to thirty-six hours. This will remove dust particles and smooth the surface for the next coat. Several thin coats can be applied in this manner. The final coat should be waxed when it is dry, a day or two after its application.

SHELLAC

Shellac is easier to apply than varnish since it dries faster and is less likely to collect dust. White shellac should be used where the finish is to be light. Orange shellac is more attractive with darker woods. Buy fresh shellac to avoid deterioration.

For finishing furniture, shellac should be dissolved in alcohol to make a one or one-and-one-half-pound cut. The "cut" refers to the number of pounds of shellac resin in a gallon of alcohol. Shellac is usually purchased in a four- or five-pound cut.

The first coat of shellac will seal the larger pores and raise the grain. After it dries, sand it lightly and clean off the dust. Several coats of shellac are necessary to build a smooth, clear finish. After the last coat has dried for twenty-four hours, apply at least two thin coats of wax to protect the finish.

LACQUER

Lacquer dries quickly. However, it requires experience to build a smooth finish. A brushing lacquer is manufactured for brushing and a spraying lacquer for spraying. Several coats of lacquer are applied over bare or stained wood that has been sanded smooth (lacquer acts as a paint remover on a painted surface) to create a hard, clear finish.

When brushing, apply lacquer with long strokes. Let the lacquer flow on without trying to retouch spots. When spraying, apply lacquer in very thin coats to avoid running and sagging. Drying times vary with the composition of the lacquer being used. Follow the directions on the can.

The final coat of lacquer can be polished to a high lustre or protected with a thin coat of wax.

OTHER FINISHES

Linseed oil and wax are also used separately to protect refinished wood. Boiled linseed oil gives darker woods (such as walnut) a natural finish and protects them against moisture and heat. The linseed oil is mixed with one-half to one part of turpentine to act as a drier, warmed if possible, and rubbed with a clean cloth on the wood. After it has penetrated, the surface should be rubbed hard with a soft cloth or the palm of the hand until the wood actually becomes warm from the friction. Several coats of boiled linseed oil should be applied a few days apart in this manner. From time to time, the oil should be replenished.

Thin coats of wax can be used to build a highly polished film to protect finishes from moisture and marring. A wax finish is especially valuable over shellac because of the moisture problem. It is used also over varnish, lacquer, and linseed oil. Build an even layer of wax by applying two or more thin coats. The final coat can be buffed for a smooth, glossy surface.

6 *Insulating, Caulking, Heating, and Cooling*

The efficiency of heating and cooling systems has become more important as gas, oil, and electricity have become more expensive. Anyone who lives in a house where he is paying for the heating or cooling, or anyone who is planning to build a new house, will find it worthwhile to know more about how heating and cooling systems operate. New houses can be built to make maximum use of their heating systems and air conditioners. Systems in existing houses can be operated more efficiently if they are kept in good repair. Many homeowners are capable of making such minor repairs and maintaining their own heating and air conditioning systems.

Heating, cooling, and humidity problems can be approached in various other ways, also. Insulating walls and attics will greatly reduce fuel costs. Wood-burning stoves and other old-fashioned heating methods can be used to supplement central heating. Houses without air conditioning can be kept cooler with devices such as awnings and attic fans, which use little energy.

This chapter illustrates how heating and cooling systems operate, what can be done to maintain their efficiency, and how to save energy.

Thermostat Setting. Thermostats should be relocated, if necessary, to an inside wall, where there is an "average" amount of heat (Fig. 6–1). They should not be close to heating units, fireplaces, cold drafts, or sun-warmed windows. A large amount of fuel can be saved by the single step of lowering the thermostat and house temperature by several degrees. For example, 22 per cent less fuel is needed to heat a house to 66°F than to heat it to 70°F. Furthermore, if the thermostat is set to 60°F for the night, more fuel will be saved during the night than is needed to heat the house to 66° or 68°F the following morning.

Storm Windows and Storm Doors. Heat escapes readily through a single thickness of glass. By adding storm windows, a dead air space is created which stops the direct transfer of heat to the outside air. Windows with a double thickness of glass (such as "Thermopanes") will have the same effect. Storm doors are equally important.

Periodic Maintenance of Heating Systems. A homeowner can keep the heating system operating at its highest efficiency by a little cleaning, oiling, and care of heating

USING LESS FUEL FOR HEATING

The increasing cost of fuels has brought a change in attitudes toward heating. New houses are being designed to conserve heat by lowering ceilings, decreasing window sizes, and fully insulating walls and ceilings. Homeowners with older houses are taking a variety of steps, from insulating to adding wood stoves. Fuel consumption can be cut substantially without taking radical steps by following a dozen or so time-proven techniques.

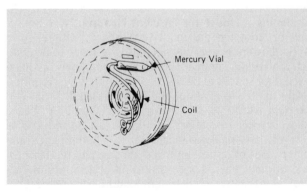

Fig. 6–1 Bimetallic-coil type thermostat.

units. Filters in warm-air systems should be cleaned or replaced to prevent them from retarding heat flow. Oil cups on oil burners and blowers should be oiled occasionally. Radiators must be bled (or vented) and registers vacuumed. Symptoms of more serious problems can often be observed during periodic inspections, and the serviceman can be called in time to prevent a breakdown.

Installing Humidifiers. If humidity is increased, air of a lower temperature can be made to feel warmer. Humidifiers can be installed in warm-air systems so that moisture is added to the heated air before it is delivered. They can also be installed independently in a central location to supply more moisture directly throughout the house.

Closing Off Rooms. During cold weather, rooms that are not used frequently should be closed off and the heating units turned off (and hot-water units should be drained). The downstairs in a two-story house can be sealed off from the upstairs by installing doors to close off the stairway. In this way, heat from the downstairs area will not be lost to bedrooms which are kept cooler by their own separately-controlled heating units.

Closing Fireplace Dampers. Fireplace dampers should be closed when there is no fire. Open dampers allow warm air from the room to flow continuously up the chimney. As much heat can be lost through an open vent as would be lost from an open window on a cold day.

Painting Radiators. Radiators painted with metallic paints such as aluminum lose about twenty percent of their heating capacity if the paint surface deteriorates. Wirebrush rust spots and apply a fresh coat of enamel or other paint formulated to cover metal, to regain the full heating capacity.

Adding Supplementary Heat. Wood stoves and electrical, gas, and oil space heaters can be used to supply heat to heavily used living areas or kitchens. The cost of their fuel should be more than offset by the fuel saved in the central heating system. The initial cost of a stove or heater may make supplementary heating uneconomical unless it is used long enough to spread the cost over several years.

Designing a House for Efficient Heating. New houses can be designed and built with heating efficiency in mind. Lower ceilings will decrease the space to be heated. Cathedral ceilings should be completely avoided except for spaces to be used only during warm weather. Walls and ceilings should be fully insulated. Walls can be built with 2 × 6-in. studs, rather than 2 × 4's, to allow thicker insulation. Windows can be reduced to one of the smaller standard sizes. Thermopanes and other types of double or triple glazing will reduce heat loss through glass. Zoned control of heat should be employed to allow greater temperature differences between living spaces, sleeping spaces, and other areas.

CONTROLLING AIR FLOW

Plugging the Leaks. The best home heating plant in the world will be wasted if air can infiltrate around doors, air conditioners, windows, and exterior trim. Caulking and weatherstripping offer the best means of stopping such infiltration.

The cost of caulking and weatherstripping is minimal, especially in comparison with the cost of the energy lost through air leakage. By one estimate, a one-eighth-inch crack around a standard exterior door means the home is losing heat through the equivalent of 29 square inches. That leak can cost the homeowner up to $30 and more annually, depending on where the door is located. The National Bureau of Standards adds that *every* square inch of open space, or crack opening to the outside, costs 50 cents in additional heat annually. The figures apply not only to homes that face typically bitter northern winters, but also in other heating zones, to a lesser degree.

An investment in the necessary caulking and weatherstripping materials seems minor in the face of such figures. Caulking adequate to plug the cracks and holes in the average home costs $20 to $30 depending on the type of caulking material purchased and how it is used. Weatherstripping may cost up to $125 or more.

Caulking may save $15 to $25 per year while weatherstripping may save you three or five times that sum.

In caulking and weatherstripping, the homeowner is actually trying to block the movement of warm air. According to principles of physics, only heat flows; it moves to cooler places from warmer ones. Where heat leaves, colder air rushes in, replacing the warmer.

Caulking and weatherstripping represent basic steps in any energy-conservation program. The Department of Energy lists six other basic elements of an energy conservation campaign:

1. Storm windows and storm doors
2. Attic insulation
3. Wall insulation
4. Underfloor insulation
5. Maintenance of mechanical systems
6. Maintenance of water heating system

All these subjects are covered in this volume.

BASIC PRINCIPLES

Infiltration differs from ventilation. Any air that enters a home without being controlled in any way is *infiltrated* air. That air can get into the home around windows or doors, vent fans, or fireplace dampers. It has infiltrated because it has entered without being controlled. If a window is opened deliberately, or if a fan is turned on, the air that enters or moves is *ventilated* air.

Caulking and weatherstripping reduce the flow of infiltrated air, but they also stop drafts. Can they become too efficient? Can they seal a home so tightly that there is insufficient circulation to maintain a healthy environment?

The experts say No.

The assessments have a solid basis in fact. In most houses, 70 to 100 per cent of all the interior air is exchanged with new outside air *every hour.* But for normal ventilation only a 20 per cent hourly turnover of air is required. Thus it appears to be virtually impossible to seal a home so completely that an unhealthy situation could arise.

Wind Action

Where a home needs caulking or weatherstripping, wind action multiplies the problems. Wind forces air against and into the home through cracks or crevices. The positive pressure of the wind can actually force air into a building through walls. In the construction phase, contractors today use sheathing, building paper, and vapor barriers to create resistance to wind pressure.

A wind blowing against a house has a double effect. First, it forces air directly against the structure, seeking out holes, cracks, and weak points. Second, as it passes beyond the building it draws air away, sucking it toward the downwind side of the house. The negative pressure created by the suction draws air from the house into the out-of-doors through any gaps that may exist.

The Chimney Effect

Another air phenomenon that increases infiltration has been termed the "chimney effect." Basically, the chim-

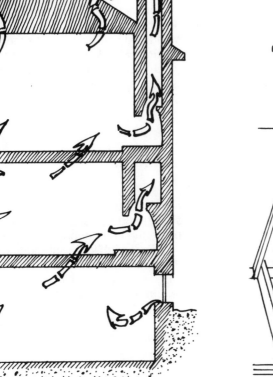

(a)

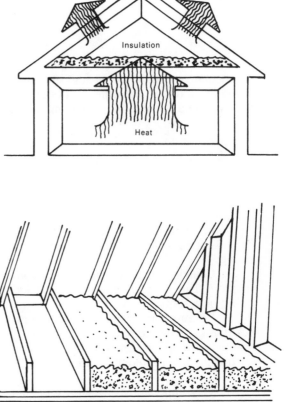

(b)

Fig. 6-2 a) The Chimney Effect, b) Insulating to reduce the Chimney Effect.

ney effect comes about because warm air rises.

The chimney effect can probably be observed in most older homes. Warm air rises up stairwells, escaping eventually through open doors or cracks into attics or the outside atmosphere. The cracks or gaps around windows downstairs and upstairs enhance the effect and contribute to the upward rush of air.

Among the primary direct causes of a chimney effect in any home is a fireplace. In use, the fireplace heats air that rises and causes an upward draft. The draft carries smoke and gases up the chimney and at the same time sucks warm air out of the living area of the house. When not in use, the fireplace creates a "mini-chimney effect." Warm air escapes up the open chimney, causing a continuous draft and removing heated air from the home.

Again the wind can augment the effect. A wind blowing across the top of the chimney creates a slight suction that draws warmth from the home with somewhat greater force. The same thing occurs when a draft passes through the furnace flue. Warm air rising through a room and escaping through a window, cracks in the ceiling, or a stairway can create the same effect.

CAULKING

Caulking may be differentiated from weatherstripping on one fundamental ground: while weatherstripping is applied to windows, doors, and other cracks or openings that will have to be opened later, caulking results in a permanent seal. Caulking is used, then, on windows, doors, and other places that can be permanently sealed.

Weatherstripping is used primarily where outside air penetrates or where two parts of the house meet, leaving a possible or actual gap. Caulking, by contrast, is applied:

- around door frames, along the lanes where they meet the walls;
- around window frames, where these meet the walls;
- where the house meets the foundation;
- where pipes or wires enter the house;
- at corners where two walls meet the siding;
- where chimneys or masonry meet siding or roofing;
- where aluminum storm windows touch window frames.

The Products

Caulking compounds come in two different forms: cartridge and knife grade. Where filler is needed in advance of caulking, such materials as oakum, caulking cotton, or glass fiber can be used. One of these would be appropriate before actual caulking where large cracks or gaps are encountered.

A standard half-barrel gun is the best tool for applying caulking. Standard cartridges fit into the gun. But remember the temperature: caulking should be done, for best results, when the temperature is 45°F or higher.

SOME TIPS FOR CAULKERS

Some things to remember when caulking parts of the typical home include the following:

1. Caulking cannot replace inferior construction. The joint or crack being sealed should be essentially sound.

2. Because the outside temperature affects the caulking compound, it is usually wise to warm up the compound in the oven when working on cool days in the 45° to 60° range.

3. Very importantly, the surface or surfaces to be caulked should be primed before application of any compound. Painting after the job is done will also extend the job's life expectancy.

4. Caulking compound should be pressed or pushed into larger gaps or cracks, not just laid on. That means a tool of proper size should be used. The net effect is to improve the compound's adhesive qualities.

5. If a job looks substantial, there is wisdom and economy in buying cartridges by the case. A complete job on the typical home will require that amount of caulk.

6. The caulk buyer will find better bargains at glass company outlets or larger hardware stores than in small "decorator" hardware stores.

7. Smoking is extremely unwise during caulking operations. Most caulking products give off flammable fumes.

8. Weatherstripping between surfaces that have to be moved, such as a window sash and window frame, is also not recommended.

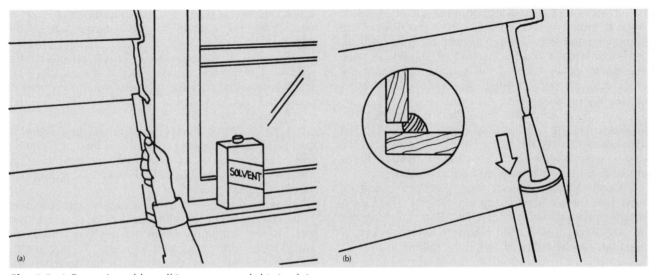

Fig. 6-3 a) Removing old caulking compound, b) Applying new caulking.

Three different kinds of caulk are commonly used today. These are the traditional or resin-based compounds, rubber-derived materials such as latex and butyl, and synthetic-based compounds. Each type has different characteristics. The kind that would be useful in any specific situation depends on the specific needs and the amounts required.

Caulk, like other materials, comes with descriptive data. Such information indicates how surfaces should be prepared before caulking, what kinds of surfaces the caulk will adhere to, and how long the caulk should be allowed to cure before it can be painted over. It is important to read these instructions before buying to make sure you have the right product.

The different kinds of caulk, from the least to the most expensive, may be described as follows:

Oil-base: This caulk bonds to most surfaces if they are dry and clean. But oil-base caulk is less durable than other types, and for that reason has fallen into disfavor. Additionally, oil-base caulk allows for little expansion or contraction.

Latex: Now regarded as a good all-purpose caulk, the latex compound dries rapidly. Moderate in cost, it can easily enjoy a life of five years or more. It is widely used to fill small cracks and joints, to patch plaster walls, and so on. It can be painted without difficulty.

Butyl: Another moderately priced caulk, butyl is widely used for sealing seams and gaps in gutters and joints where metal meets masonry. It also serves well where wide cracks have to be closed. Once cured, it remains flexible to a degree. It will also have a life of five years or more, and can be painted.

Vinyl: Because it is highly adhesive, waterproof, and weatherproof, vinyl is well adapted to special uses. These include application in or around wet areas such as bathtubs and showers. Vinyl is a somewhat more costly caulk, but has virtually an indefinite life once it has been properly applied.

Silicone: Also known more formally as elastomeric hypolon polysulfide silicon, this compound comes in colors but cannot be painted. It has exceptional adhesive qualities and long-lasting elasticity. Those qualities make silicone useful for caulking around tubs, showers, fixtures, and outdoor outlets. It is used in small quantities because it is expensive.

The Techniques

Applying caulking requires little skill beyond elementary coordination. But take some care to ensure that the surfaces to be caulked are clean. Dirt, peeling paint, and older, deteriorated caulking should be removed.

Most homeowners handle caulking jobs themselves. But in many cases a high ladder will be required if upper-story or roof caulking is needed. High-ladder work necessitates both precautionary measures and a high level of caution on the job.

After the surfaces to be caulked have been cleaned, the prepping operation begins. Cut the tip of the nozzle on the caulking cartridge at a 45° angle. The nozzle tapers to a dull point; it's wise to determine first how wide a bead will be needed, then to cut the nozzle appropriately at the point on the nozzle that will deliver the proper-sized bead.

In applying the caulking, hold the gun at an angle. Also, it should be moved away from the flow of the compound and along the gap or opening to be caulked.

How wide a bead is needed? It should be wide enough to cover both of the surfaces adjoining the crack, gap, or opening. The bead should, in fact, overlap slightly on both sides.

Skillful caulking takes some attention to detail. The trick is to get the bead to flow evenly and neatly. The foresighted caulker has a rag handy, especially in the early stages, to wipe up excess caulk or remove dirt or grease that may have escaped an earlier cleaning.

Caulking guns are not always needed. Caulking rope, for example, can be applied by hand. The rope is simply finger-pressed into crevices. Rope caulking has an advantage: it will often retain its flexibility and, if need be, can be removed simply by pulling it off.

WEATHERSTRIPPING

Weatherstripping presents some new, but for the most part, easily mastered challenges. Because windows and doors require both different techniques and different materials, they are properly discussed under separate headings. First, however, a word about materials.

Weatherstripping Materials

It has been suggested that there are as many different types of weatherstripping materials as there are hardware stores in the United States. While not quite true, that statement suggests accurately that the market does offer a wide variety of types. At least 100 different kinds of weatherstripping can be bought in many parts of the country.

Because of this confusing variety, choosing the right kind of weatherstripping is not always easy. Yet making the proper choice may determine how well or poorly the weatherstripping works: the degree to which it helps reduce air infiltration.

Cost does not always serve as the best index to quality. Weatherstripping may cost as little as 5 cents a foot or as much as 60 or 70 cents a foot and more. But the price of any specific kind of weatherstripping tells you little about quality.

The do-it-yourself weatherstripper can measure each window, door, or other space to be covered, then total up the amounts. About 10 per cent should be added to the total to account for waste. To buy exactly what is needed may necessitate some splicing and skimping. Where either becomes necessary, the effectiveness of the stripping may be reduced. Effective weatherstripping, expectably, depends on a tight fit.

As a rule, the best materials cost the most. Since that, as noted, is not true of weatherstripping, other guidelines must be used. The conscientious energy conserver still wants to use the best materials. Otherwise he may be wasting his time on a job that will not last. He should ask questions at the lumberyard, hardware store, or other point of sale. He should read the manufacturer's directions for use of the different types. Then, finally, he has to make his own judgment.

Kinds of Weatherstripping. Three broad categories of stripping have been found most useful for windows. The three are spring metal strips, rolled vinyl, and foam rub-

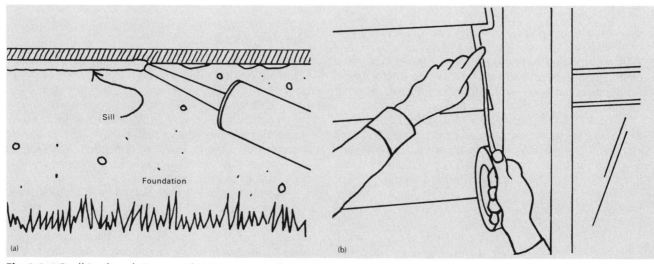

Fig. 6-4 a) Caulking foundation gaps, b) Using rope caulking to fill wide gaps.

Table 6-1 Three basic types of weatherstripping

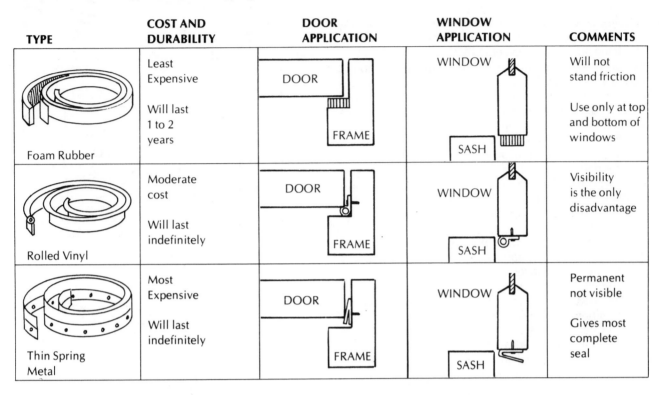

TYPE	COST AND DURABILITY	DOOR APPLICATION	WINDOW APPLICATION	COMMENTS
Foam Rubber	Least Expensive Will last 1 to 2 years	DOOR / FRAME	WINDOW / SASH	Will not stand friction Use only at top and bottom of windows
Rolled Vinyl	Moderate cost Will last indefinitely	DOOR / FRAME	WINDOW / SASH	Visibility is the only disadvantage
Thin Spring Metal	Most Expensive Will last indefinitely	DOOR / FRAME	WINDOW / SASH	Permanent not visible Gives most complete seal

ber strips. All three may also be used on doors. Table 6–1 shows graphically the three basic types and lists their characteristics.

Where doors are to be weatherstripped, the homeowner has a range of materials to choose from. In addition to the three types already listed, interlocking metal channels, insulated molding, and door thresholds may be used. The latter do not classify precisely as kinds of weatherstripping; rather, they include such door additions as the plain sweep, the pop-up sweep, and the door "shoe."

Installation: Windows

Different installation procedures may be followed with different kinds of weatherstripping. In part, this is because of the ways in which the different kinds are manufactured. Some materials can be glued in place; others must be attached with nails or screws.

The three types of stripping most commonly used on windows are installed as follows:
Spring Metal Strips. Each sash of the typical double-hung window should be open when spring metal strips are installed. The stripping is then cut to fit. In this process

the do-it-yourselfer should make sure that the pulleys in the upper channels remain uncovered.

The strips are then aligned in the appropriate channels. A small nail is driven into each of the holes in the stripping to hold the strip in place. With each section secured, use a long screwdriver or similar tool to pry up the spring metal leaf. Prying should be done with an eye to ensuring the best possible seal. When properly done, the leaf is held by tension against the window.

A strip of the spring metal is next fastened to the bottom surface of the lower sash's bottom rail. Another strip goes on the upper surface of the upper sash's top rail. Both strips should compress when the two parts of the window are shut, barring the passage of air. Both should also be long enough to reach from end to end of each rail. Also splicing should be avoided, if possible.

A final step involves installation of stripping where the sashes meet. Simply nail a single strip, cut to length, to the inside surface of the upper sash's bottom rail. This piece of stripping may have to be flattened to fit.

Casement windows present a simpler problem. Here, metal weatherstripping is tacked to the frame with the open side facing the inside. With stripping attached this way, the windows may still be opened and closed without difficulty.

Metal strips are particularly effective—and durable—where extensive abrasive action takes place, as in double-hung windows. Such stripping is all but invisible. Installation is, for that reason, somewhat challenging. If the amateur carpenter does not trust himself to do the job properly, he may want to call in a professional.

Rolled Vinyl. Rolled vinyl weatherstripping also provides an effective seal when used on windows. This type has a bulb edge. Installed correctly, the edge compresses slightly, giving the sealing effect.

Rolled vinyl comes in two basic shapes. One is the tubular gasket, a hollow or solid tube attached to a flat strip for nailing. The other is the reinforced tubular gasket. The latter has the same basic design, but also boasts a reinforcing strip of aluminum or other metal. The second strip is attached to the nailing strip for added strength.

The reinforced vinyl weatherstripping usually costs more than the nonreinforced. But the extra investment should pay off in longer life.

Double-hung windows can easily be weatherstripped with rolled vinyl. The stripping is simply attached along the outside of each window. Afterward, the joint between the sashes can be sealed by tacking more stripping to the lower edge of the upper sash.

Care should be taken in installing rolled vinyl to make sure the strip is lined up properly before it is nailed in place. In this way you make sure you have a snug seal. Take care also to ensure that the movement of the window is not hampered.

Awning or casement windows require a slightly different approach. Here, attach the rolled vinyl strips to the outside of the window frames.

Foam Rubber. Foam rubber comes in long rolls. It is easier to install than the other two kinds of window weatherstripping. But it has some limitations. It cannot, for example, be used where it may be subjected to rubbing or abrasive action. Such action quickly wears away the foam weatherstripping.

A second limitation may be noted. Foam rubber is attached with an adhesive that may not hold up well under weathering. Thus it may have a short life, a factor that may negate the advantage of initial low cost.

Whatever its limitations, foam rubber and similar weatherstripping materials can be unrolled and pressed into place in minutes. The protective tape is first peeled off to expose the adhesive side. Press the rubber stripping onto the tops of the upper rails of double-hung windows and onto the bottoms of the lower rails.

Foam rubber is still more practical on casement or tilt-out windows. It can be installed on all four sides of the window frame. When the window is closed, the foam provides a seal around the entire window.

Foam weatherstripping need not be made of rubber. Foam strips are also made of vinyl, neoprene sponge,

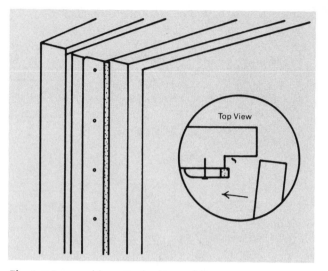

Fig. 6-5 Foam rubber attached to molding.

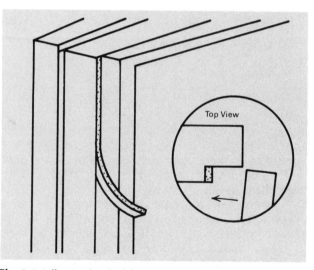

Fig. 6-6 Adhesive backed foam.

and foam polyurethane. The quality of the various materials varies widely.

Vinyl Channels. Some windows present special weatherstripping problems. An example is the *jalousie,* or slatted window. The weatherstripping devised for this window is actually a clear vinyl channel that slips over one slat. Each slat receives one channel. A similar kind of channel weatherstripping is sometimes used on casement windows. But most casements are factory weatherstripped and do not require further work.

Installation: Doors

Doors represent a key aspect of the typical home's thermal envelope. Outside or prime doors are major "infil-

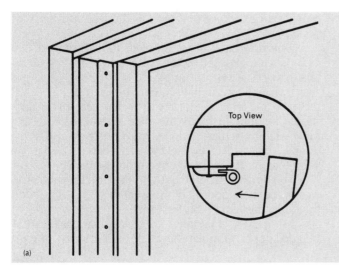

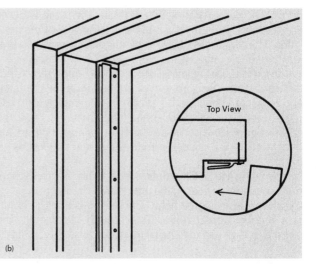

Fig. 6-7 a) Rolled vinyl with aluminum channel backing, b) Spring metal.

tration inlets'' unless they are carefully and properly weatherstripped. Even then, some discretion in the opening and closing of these doors may become necessary if excess cold is to be kept at bay in cold weather.

Even interior doors should be weatherstripped in some cases. Critical doors are those leading to unheated living spaces, attics, basements, and garages.

Outside doors should be inspected with a view to locating all possible gaps or cracks—not just those underneath the door. Often, a door will allow cold winter air, or hot summer air, to enter through a crack above the door proper. On a windy day, the air may blow in gustily.

A simple cure for air leaks high up around the door is molding plus foam rubber weatherstripping. Molding is added at the top and sides if it is not already there. Once this has been nailed down, tubular gasket weatherstripping can be tacked to the molding.

Other basic forms of weatherstripping are specifically designed to close gaps *under* doors. Some of these double as weatherstripping for the sides or tops of doors. The main types already mentioned, with installation suggestions, follow:

Foam Rubber. Because it is the easiest to install and the cheapest of all the various kinds of door weatherstripping, foam rubber has found wide favor. As with windows, it can be pressed onto the appropriate surface in minutes. It must, of course, first be cut to the right length. The backing has then to be peeled off before it is pressed into place on the insides of the stops.

Rolled Vinyl and Spring Metal. Both of these types may also be used to insulate around the sides and tops of

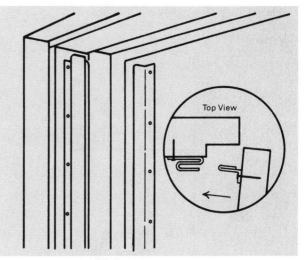

Fig. 6-8 Interlocking metal channels.

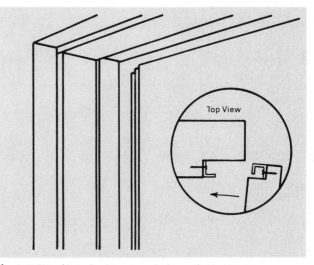

Fig. 6-9 Fitted interlocking metal channels (J-strips).

doors. They are installed in essentially the same ways as on windows. Rolled vinyl is tacked to the face of the door stops. The bulb edges have to be aligned carefully so that they fit snugly against the door when it is closed.

Nail the spring metal strips to the door jamb, not the door stops. Be sure to make allowance for the latch and lock; gaps have to be left for free operation of these parts. Once the strip has been nailed down, raise the outer edge with a screwdriver or other tool. When the door is closed, this edge provides the seal that keeps air out.

Interlocking Metal Channels. Once again, if interlocking metal channels are used the amateur carpenter may want to call for professional help. The reason is that the channels require a relatively skilled "touch" to install. The effort and expense may be worth it because the channels provide an excellent seal around the tops and sides of doors.

One drawback may be noted. Once installed, the channels are exposed to the weather and rusting could take place as a result.

Interlocking channels have to be aligned precisely if the male and female strips are to fit. The head of the door should be done first; nail the male strip to the door and the matching female strip to the door frame. On the door's hinge side, reverse the procedure. The female strip goes on the door, the male on the jamb.

The lock side of the door has to be done last. Again, the male portion of the weatherstripping goes on the door, the female on the jamb.

J-strips, a special kind of interlocking weatherstripping for doors, eliminate some of the problems of stan-

Table 6-2 Weatherstripping under doors.

TYPE		COST	DURABILITY	COMMENTS
Sweep		Least expensive	1 to 2 years	Visible, for use on flat thresholds May drag on rug
Door Shoe		Moderate cost	Indefinite Vinyl insert replaceable	Useful on wood, unworn threshold Note drip cap to shed rain
Vinyl Bulb Threshold		Moderate cost	Indefinite Vinyl insert replacement	Useful where there is no threshold With wear, vinyl bubble will flatten and tear Can be replaced
Interlocking Threshold		Most expensive	Permanent	Exceptionally good seal Should be recommended

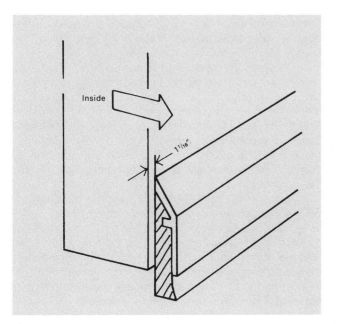

Fig. 6-10 Sweep.

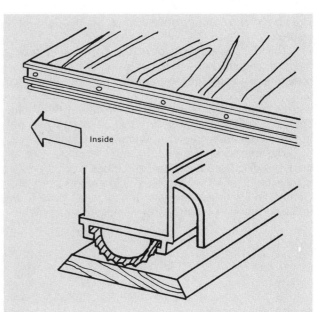

Fig. 6-11 Door Shoe.

dard channels. For example, the J-strips are not visible. Because they are hidden, they are not subject to rusting. J-strips have two essential parts: a door strip with a J-shaped protrusion and a matching channel in the door frame.

J-strips offer long life and effective sealing. But they require professional installation because of the difficulty involved in making the two parts fit exactly.

Installation of J-strips requires some special carpentry work. A rabbet has to be routed into the edge of the door and into the jamb as well. If the routing is done properly, the strips fit and the cold air is sealed out.

Insulated Molding. Yet another weatherstripping material for doors, insulated molding, was designed for use specifically on double doors. The molding is nailed to the face of one door—the one that is usually kept closed.

Door Thresholds. As indicated, some devices and materials have been developed for use in weatherstripping door thresholds exclusively. These include the sweep, the door shoe, the vinyl bulb threshold, and the interlocking threshold.

The *sweep* is simply attached to the bottom of the door where, as its name indicates, it serves as a sweep to ward off cold (or hot) air. Since there are inside sweeps and outside sweeps, care should be taken to attach the stripping in the appropriate place. Before installing, the sweep should be cut slightly shorter than the width of the door so that it will clear the door's edges.

Even earlier, of course, the door should be checked to determine whether a sweep would be more useful inside or outside. A door that opens in would normally have an inside sweep. But if the door opens over a rug or carpeting, an outside sweep may be more serviceable.

The door sweep's aluminum mount may have slots for the mounting screws. Thus it is easy to test and adjust the height of the stripping. Adjustments can be made to compensate for actual or expected wear.

The "pop-up" or *automatic sweep* is somewhat more complex than the simple type. The pop-up snaps up when the door is opened, in that process moving out of the way of obstructions or carpeting. The sweep lowers automatically when the door is closed.

The pop-up sweep is attached flush with the door bottom. It goes on the inside of the door, held in place by screws. The push-rod strike plate has to be positioned on the door frame so that it will trip the sweep and turn it up. A recess is chiseled for the plate, which is then attached flush with the door jamb.

To install a *shoe,* the door has to be removed. The shoe, which is most useful on a wooden threshold, has to be cut to fit the door opening exactly. The vinyl strip with which the shoe is equipped is removed, the shoe is screwed into place, and the vinyl is then snapped back into position. The vinyl has a special drip-cap that sheds rain.

For best results, the shoe has to be installed with care. The bottom of the door has to be cut so that it fits exactly with the shoe. For this work a portable circular saw is ideal. The saw-cut should be beveled slightly.

The door can be rehung once a snug, but not tight, fit is assured.

The *vinyl bulk threshold* and the *interlocking threshold* have become known, respectively, as a special-purpose threshold and the most durable of all weatherstripping thresholds. The moderately priced vinyl bulb type is used principally where there is no raised threshold. The vinyl bulb that provides the sealing effect wears out in time, but can be replaced without difficulty.

The interlocking threshold, most expensive of all the types discussed here, is also the best from a performance point of view. It closes below-doors gaps efficiently, and will last for years. It may never have to be replaced unless it is torn up or damaged accidentally.

INSULATION

Insulation has been called the most rewarding of all methods of saving energy and money. Once installed, insulation does its job forever. If properly installed in the first place, it requires no maintenance.

In terms of cost, insulation ranks among the most important parts in an energy-saving program. Estimates on how much energy can be saved through adequate insulation vary. But experts believe Americans could save between 20 and 30 per cent of the energy used to

heat their homes if they installed good insulation. Adequate insulation would save about 10 per cent of the energy used to cool American homes.

Conserving energy, saving money, and increasing comfort are the triple goals of insulating. But in a physical sense, insulation has a more immediate purpose. It blocks the flow of heat from an area of higher temperature to an area with a lower temperature. This heat transfer is a continuous process. Heat moves from living spaces in the home that are adjacent to unheated attics, garages, and basements as well as others that abut on the outdoors.

Heat transfer takes place *through* the building envelope (conduction) as well as through doorways, apertures, or other openings (infiltration). This means heat passes through walls, floors, ceilings, the roof. In colder weather, heat passes to the out-of-doors; in hot weather the warmth passes into the home from the outside.

Insulation is designed to reduce or eliminate that movement of warm air—in either direction.

INSULATING MATERIALS: COSTS AND KINDS

Costs

Some insulation may already be present in the attic and walls, reducing potential energy-conservation needs and dollar savings. Other parts of the house may re-

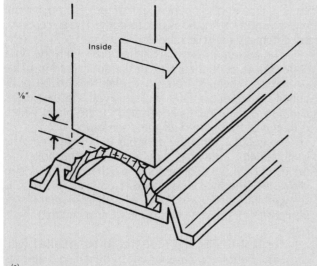
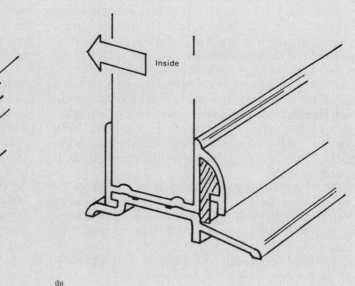

Fig. 6-12 a) Vinyl bulb threshold, b) Interlocking threshold.

Table 6-3 Types of insulation and basic characteristics.

Form	Method of Installation	Where Applicable	Advantages	Materials
Blankets or Batts	Fitted between wood-frame studs, joists, and beams	—All unfinished walls, floors, and ceilings	—Do-it-yourself —Best suited for standard stud and joist spacing, which is relatively free from obstructions —Blankets: Little waste because it's handcut —Batts: More waste, but easier to handle than large rolls	Rock wool Glass fiber
Loose Fill (poured in)	Poured between attic joists	—Unfinished attic floors and hard-to-reach places —Irregularly shaped areas and around obstructions	—Do-it-yourself —Easy to use for irregularly shaped areas and around obstructions	Rock wool Glass fiber Cellulose fiber Vermiculite Perlite
Blown Fill	Blown into place by special equipment	—Anywhere that frame is covered on both sides, such as side walls —Unfinished attic floors and hard-to-reach places	—The only insulation that can be used in finished areas —Easy to use for irregularly shaped areas and around obstructions	Rock wool Glass fiber Cellulose fiber
Rigid Insulation	Must be covered with ½-inch gypsum board or other finishing material for fire safety	—Basement masonry walls —Exterior walls under construction	—High insulating value for relatively little thickness	Poly-styrene board Poly-urethane board Iso-cyanurate board

quire additional insulation. Some parts may have none. Such factors help determine how much *could* be spent on insulating materials.

How much would it cost to insulate the typical frame house of perhaps 1,500 square feet? If the homeowner starts from scratch, in a house with no insulation, and does the work himself he can spend as little as $400 or as much as $800 to $1,000. If he hires an insulation contractor, he may spend 50 per cent more than that. Thus the amount of insulation purchased and the difficulty involved in installing it represent basic factors in the cost equation.

Reducing the overall costs of insulating depends in part on "getting a good deal" when purchasing the materials. Getting a good deal, in turn, hinges at least initially on an awareness of what is needed and what it does.

A mistake here will not be fatal. But it will definitely inflate costs unnecessarily. Rock wool or fiber blankets or batts were priced typically at 30 cents a square foot for six-inch widths and 20 cents for 3.5-inch widths in early 1980. Loose fill cost about $5.25 for three cubic feet, and blown fill carried a price tag of about 75 cents a square foot, contractor-installed. The blown fill would normally be used to insulate a standard 3.5-inch-thick wall. Rigid insulation of polystyrene or some other material could be purchased for 20 cents a square foot in the three-quarter-inch thick board size.

Inflation, of necessity, affects such prices. Beyond that, however, the homeowner faces the need to know something about the basic insulation materials.

Fig. 6-13 U.S. Heating Zones.

R-VALUE FOR:	ZONE 1	ZONE 2	ZONE 3	ZONE 4	ZONE 5
CEILINGS	R-26	R-26	R-30	R-33	R-38
WALLS	R-13	R-19	R-19	R-19	R-19
FLOORS	R-11	R-13	R-19	R-22	R-22

Kinds of Materials

Table 6–3 shows four commonly used insulating materials and their basic characteristics. The Department of Energy describes these four kinds of materials in thumbnail form as follows:

Blankets or batts: These are fibers that have been made into sheets for easy installation. Both blankets and batts come in widths that correspond to standard stud spacings. Blankets are actually continuous rolls. These can be cut to desired lengths. Batts, on the other hand, come in precut four- and eight-foot lengths.

Loose fill: A type of material that is designed to be poured into spaces requiring insulation, loose fill is just what the name indicates: loose material that can be poured into place.

Blown fill: Loose fibers or plastic foams that can be blown into finished areas with special pneumatic machinery.

Rigid insulation: Plastics or fibers that have been pressed into boards.

What Kind of Insulation? The question, What kind? can be answered with another question: Which areas of the house are to be insulated? The answer to that second question will help provide an answer to the first.

As one example, an overhead area needs insulating—the attic roof, perhaps. Since insulating material cannot be blown into such an area, the logical, and almost inevitable, alternative is fiber sheets, meaning batts or blankets. These can be attached between the beams of an unfinished ceiling.

Finished walls are another story. The only practical way to insulate such walls is to blow in fill. That process in turn, as noted, requires pneumatic machinery. Table 6–3 shows where the various kinds of insulating materials are normally used.

Different kinds of insulation can be used in combination. Batts or blankets, for example, are frequently installed in attic floors over loose fill and that pattern may just as readily be reversed. Batts may be used to "hold down" loose fill material.

Whatever the material, the homeowner should make sure the insulation materials purchased for use in the home meet federal standards or the specifications established by the American Society of Testing Materials (ASTM).

R-Values as Guideposts. The R-value of any element used in insulation represents its effectiveness: its resistance to heat flow.

Some examples of the R-values of common types of insulation may be noted. Widely used 3.5-inch fiberglass batts are rated at R-11. Standard 6-inch fiberglass or mineral wool blankets have a rating of about R-19 while 7 to 8 inches of rock wool fill, poured into a wall, have a value of about R-22. Four-and-one-half inches

Table 6–4   R-Values for Different Thicknesses of Insulation (in inches)

	Batts or Blankets		Loose and Blown Fill[a]				
R-Value	Glass Fiber	Rock Wool	Glass Fiber	Rock Wool	Cellulose Fiber	Vermiculite	Perlite
R-11	3.5	3	5	4	3	5	4
R-13	4	3.5	6	4.5	3.5	6	5
R-19	6	5	8.5	6.5	5	9	7
R-22	7	6	10	7.5	6	10.5	8
R-26	8	7	12	9	7	12.5	9.5
R-30	9.5	8	13.5	10	8	14	11
R-33	10.5	9	15	11	9	15.5	12
R-38	12	10.5	17	13	10	18	14

SOURCE: Department of Energy.
[a]The R-value for urea-formaldehyde foam is 4.2 per inch of thickness. However, a bulletin from the Department of Housing and Urban Development (HUD) indicates that the effective R-value of this type of fill is only 3.3 per inch when installed, due to a 6 percent average linear shrinkage. Therefore, urea-formaldehyde foam in a 3.5-inch wall cavity would have an R-value of 10.5.

of urea-formaldehyde foam have an R-value of 18. R-values assigned to the various kinds of insulating materials are shown in Table 6–4.

The R-values serve as guidance in making purchases of insulation materials. Blankets or batts come with the R-values clearly specified. But other materials may be unmarked. In consequence, it pays to know the ratings of the various materials.

The R-values table should be used in conjunction with Table 6–5, which shows the recommended R-values for different parts of the home in the various U.S. heating zones. As Table 6–5 indicates, the R-value target for Zone 5 attic floors is well above the same value for Zone 1 attic floors.

Assume that Roberta Bowen lives in an 1,800-square-foot frame house in Eau Claire, Wisconsin. Eau Claire, as the Heating Zones map shows, is in Heating Zone 4. To insulate her attic floor, Roberta would need insulation rated at R-33. Using batts of rock wool, Roberta would have to install nine inches of insulating material if she is to be adequately protected against Wisconsin's winters. Nine inches of rock wool in a quantity adequate to cover a 20 × 15-foot floor would cost about $393 (20′ × 15′ × 9″ × $1.75).

If you use both tables and the map in this way, it becomes a simple matter to figure out how much insulation should go where in the typical home. In general, only the amount recommended should be installed in any given area. Adding insulation indiscriminately beyond that point will not be worth either the expense or the effort. In this case *just enough* is all that is needed.

Other Considerations. Urea-formaldehyde foam, once viewed as, in many ways, the best insulating material available has been the subject of much study and controversy in recent years. Early in 1982, the Consumer Product Safety Commission ordered a ban on all future sales of insulation made of formaldehyde. It was chiefly the Commission's fear that formaldehyde might cause cancer in humans that led to the ban.

An estimated 500,000 homes have been insulated with urea-formaldehyde foam since the mid-1970s as part of a massive campaign by the federal government to persuade homeowners to conserve energy. Some users have complained of bad odors and health problems. Research has shown that formaldehyde causes cancer in laboratory animals and such adverse effects as nausea, headaches, dizziness, respiratory ailments, bloody noses, and eye and skin irritations in humans. The symptoms develop anywhere from a few days to more than six months after gas or fumes were released from the foam.

Table 6–5   Recommended R-Values, by Heating Zones

Heating Zone	Attic Floors	Exterior Walls	Ceilings over Unheated Crawl Space or Basement
1	R-26	R-value of full wall	R-11
2	R-26	insulation, which is	R-13
3	R-30	3-1/2″ thick, will	R-19
4	R-33	depend on material used.	R-22
5	R-38	Range is R-11 to R-13.	R-22

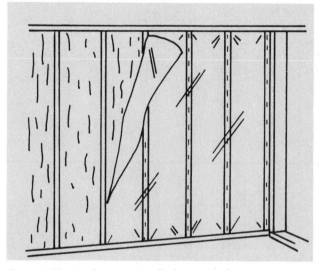

Fig. 6-14 Plastic sheeting installed over insulation serves as a vapor barrier.

The Consumer Product Safety Commission suggested that homeowners not remove any formaldehyde foam insulation that may be in their homes if they have not experienced health problems. The Commission estimated that removing the foam from an average home could cost $15,000. The ban provided no redress for homeowners who may have to remove the dangerous materials.

Other insulating materials have specific characteristics. Polystyrene foam, or styrofoam, lacks fire resistance. Yet it can be used effectively in finished areas of new construction—sometimes in combination with ordinary mineral wool. The polystyrene foam is used in tongue-and-groove board form, replacing standard wooden sheathing. With the mineral wool added, it provides about double the insulation value of the wool alone.

Partly because it is relatively cheap and partly because of its flexibility and ease of installation, mineral wool has become increasingly popular. It can be used in blankets or batts in many different situations. It can be installed between studs and joists or rafters by the homeowner himself. Batts involve more wastage than blankets, but are easier to handle. Both batts and blankets are fire resistant.

Extra-thick mineral wool batts or blankets are unusable in many situations. The materials may completely fill stud-wall cavities, or the spaces between rafters or joists, sometimes without providing the necessary R-value. In such cases insulating materials with lower k-values—materials that allow less heat to escape for a given thickness—must be used.

Among the loose-fill insulating materials, cellulose fiber, vermiculite, and perlite are widely used. Cellulose fiber is poured or blown into structural spaces. It spreads out better than loose mineral wool because of its smaller tuft size, but is not vermin- or fireproof. It may be chemically treated to resist fire; the long-term effectiveness of the treatment has, however, been questioned. No cellulose fiber should be used unless the bags in which it is sold indicate that it meets federal specifications.

Vermiculite and perlite are primarily useful in small, hard-to-reach spaces. Both can be poured easily, and both distribute well in tight places. For example, both vermiculite and perlite can be poured down into the spaces between wall studs because they filter around obstacles or obstructions such as pipes, electrical cables, and outlets better than other kinds of loose fill.

Moisture Control

You have undoubtedly noticed how moisture sometimes condenses on windows or other cold surfaces in your home. This moisture in warm interior air can condense just as easily in your walls, or under your roof. That tendency poses a problem associated with insulation.

Insulation in a wall or roof prevents heat from inside the home from reaching wall or roof sheathing. These layers remain almost as cold as the outside air. Moist air from the inside of the house may then touch the cold sheathing, producing condensation. The sheathing may become soaked. Rotting can take place. The insulation may become saturated, and its effectiveness reduced. Moisture that soaks into the building structure can also cause mold growth or peeling paint.

There are two main defenses against moisture problems: using vapor barriers with insulation and adequate ventilation.

Vapor Barriers. No insulation should be used without vapor barriers that keep humidity inside the house. The barriers go next to the interior walls, where it is warm in winter; they face the inside of the house.

Vapor barriers are special backing materials. They may be paper, foil, or plastic that keep the insulation material from becoming damp. The barriers also keep dampness from reaching structural wood.

A secondary advantage of vapor barriers may be noted. They help cut down on air infiltration. That means they reduce the amount of air entering the house from the outside.

Both batts and blankets are available with vapor barriers already attached. Where other insulating materials are used, various kinds of barriers can be improvised. Plastic sheeting that can be bought at any hardware store serves as a vapor barrier where loose-fill insulation is the selected material. Polyethylene sheeting also creates an adequate vapor barrier when used with batts or blankets that have no barrier material attached.

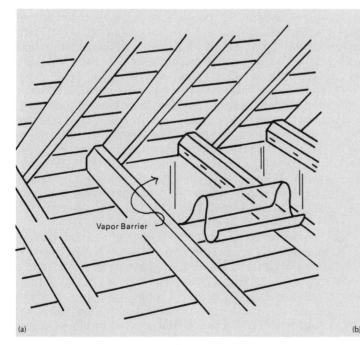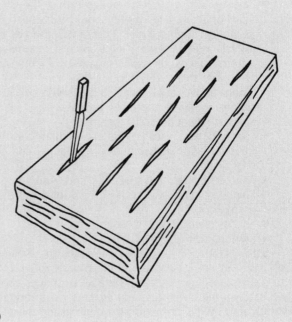

Fig. 6-15 a) Lay vapor barrier on attic flooring before installing insulation, b) Slash vapor barriers when laying new insulation atop old layers containing their own vapor retarder.

Where vapor barriers appear impractical, as in finished walls insulated with blown fill, two coats of oil-based paint or a layer of wallpaper that contains plastic will create an effective vapor barrier. In such cases the paint or wallpaper necessarily goes on the surface of the interior wall.

Vapor barriers may, under certain conditions, be placed against outer, rather than inner, walls. This can occur in regions that have hot, humid climates. The decision on where to place vapor barriers in these regions may have to be made in consultation with a contractor or other professional.

Obviously, the best vapor barriers are nonporous. This type of material resists the passage of moisture. The heavy kraft paper attached to batts and blankets offers convenience along with serviceability. The paper has flaps or flanges that make it possible to staple the batt or blanket to the studs or joists. Thus the flange helps to hold both the vapor barrier and the insulating material in place. The foil backing on some fiberglass insulation offers a similar advantage. The foil both keeps moisture inside and reflects heat.

Uniquely, rigid plastic foam boards require no separate vapor barriers. This kind of insulation serves as its own vapor barrier.

When insulating an attic floor, materials with their own self-contained vapor barriers go face down. The vapor barrier is then next to the ceiling, facing the inside of the house. The same rule applies when an attic roof or basement wall is being insulated. The attached vapor barrier faces the attic interior or the *inside* of the basement.

At times new insulation has to be applied where some insulation is already in place. Insulating materials with barriers attached should not simply be laid on top of the "old" insulation. Rather, the old should be removed and the new installed. Then the old can be placed on top of the new. If the old insulation already has a vapor barrier, it should remain in place and new insulation with *no* vapor barrier should be added. Applied this way, the materials will not trap moisture in the insulation between the vapor barrier and a wall or ceiling.

By accident or miscalculation the handyman may have purchased batts or blankets with vapor barriers attached, only to find existing insulation material in place with its own vapor retarder. The new insulation can be slashed in places with a knife and laid in place on top of the earlier layer. The insulation will then be able to dry out if moisture accumulates.

Where to Insulate?

In general, insulation can be installed in nine parts of the typical home:

● Ceilings under cold spaces.

- Exterior walls. Experts suggest that the short walls of a split-level home should be considered as well as higher walls. Where living areas adjoin garages, storage rooms, or other unheated interior spaces, the walls separating such spaces will more than likely require insulation as well.
- Floors above cold areas such as vented crawl spaces, garages, and open porches.
- Spaces between "collar beams."
- Spaces between sloping rafters, with air gaps left for ventilation between the insulation and the roof deck.
- Spaces between the studs of "knee walls."
- Spaces between the joists of the floor outside the living room.
- Spaces inside dormer walls.
- Dormer ceilings.

Some of these open spaces or areas are more important, from an energy-conservation point of view, than others. Because heat rises, the surfaces or spaces above the heat distribution points rank as the most important. That means ceilings primarily; the ceilings are the parts of the home that most need insulation.

Importantly, that also means walls and the common added features of walls, such as windows and doors.

It also means floors. Where floors have ceilings on their lower sides, the homeowner has a very important combination of needs. But floors over cold areas, as the above list indicates, should also receive attention.

Techniques

Some insulation techniques can be noted and learned without difficulty. These are most appropriately con-

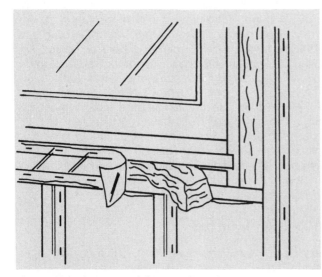

Fig. 6-16 Insulate around doors and windows.

sidered in terms of specific jobs that the handyman can do himself.

Insulating the attic stands first on the list of parts of the house that the do-it-yourselfer can easily insulate. The attics of many homes in the United States have never been finished. This is particularly true of older homes. In these structures the job of insulating can usually be completed in a day or two, given some advance figuring, minimal study of the alternative types of insulating materials, and adequate preparation.

Clothing should be practical. Loose-fitting, comfortable old clothes generally make the work as tolerable as possible. A long-sleeved shirt and gloves are appropriate, as are protective gloves, a dust mask, and goggles (particularly when installing fiberglass).

A number of tools and types of equipment may be needed. These include a sharp knife with a serrated edge if batts and blankets will have to be cut to size; a measuring tape and a rake that may be needed to push batts and blankets into tight corners or spaces in which headroom is lacking; a portable light with an extension cord if other sources of light are not available or are inadequate to light the more remote corners; a staple gun if roof insulation is part of the plan; and possibly some plywood boards to walk and kneel on in floorless areas. The rake may also be valuable if it becomes necessary to smooth out loose fill. Boards should be at least two feet wide by four feet long.

Safety and other considerations derive from common sense, from the nature of the area in which the handyman is going to work, and from the characteristics of the materials he will be using. The plywood boards ensure against falling through the ceiling under the floor. The threat of projecting nails in the slanting room suggests extreme caution when walking, working in tight places, or standing up. Smoking while working with most insulating materials should be avoided.

The Unfinished, Floorless Attic. Once prepared, the do-it-yourselfer can go to work. Presumably, he has bought the materials he needs, figuring his requirements as closely as possible and allowing for some wastage.

For the floorless attic, batts, blankets, or loose fill would normally be recommended. The batts or blankets would be placed beneath the joists; the fill would be spread between them. The vapor barrier, if separate from the insulating material, goes down before the insulation is placed or spread. If attached to the batts or blankets, the vapor barrier goes face down. Some batts come with protective paper on the side away from the vapor barrier. The paper should be stripped off after the batt has been laid in place. Batts or blankets used on attic floors need not be stapled in place.

If there is a trap door or hatch cover in the floor, it should have its own small segment of insulating material. But here the material should be stapled in place around

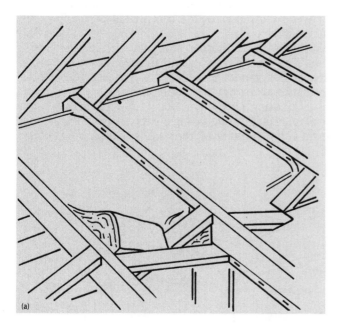

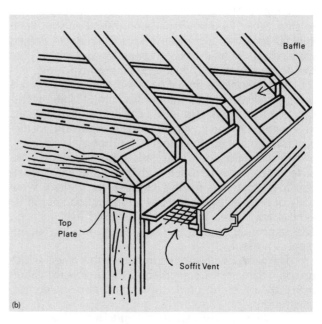

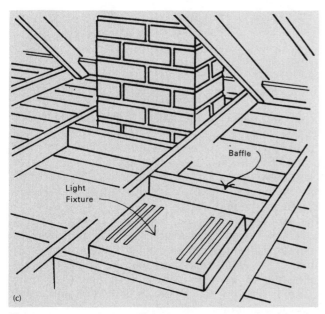

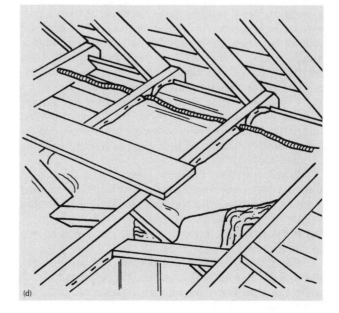

Fig. 6-17 a) Using batts and blankets to insulate attics, b) and c) Use baffles to keep insulation away from light fixtures and soffit vents, d) Pass insulation underneath wiring.

the edges of the door or hatch. Insulation should also be placed under attic walkways. If necessary, sideboards should be removed from the walkways, then insulation should be pushed into place.

Other parts of the unfinished attic should be insulated. Some kind of wraparound insulation should be applied to hot water pipes and hot air ducts. When working on ducts, it pays to check for air leaks. These should be sealed with duct tape before insulating.

A common rule should be noted: when insulation is being installed in attics without flooring, it is not necessary to stop at the ceiling joists. The insulation materials, in other words, can go higher than that level. But insulation materials should not touch the roof at the eaves.

Insulating material that cannot burn should be inserted into spaces between a chimney and wood framing. Ideal materials for this purpose are mineral wool batts or blankets. Newly installed insulation should be kept at least three inches from recessed light fixtures. The same rule applies if other heat-producing equipment is present.

The danger with such equipment is that a heat build-up could damage the equipment. If flammable insulation materials are being used, they could also, of course, catch fire.

Sometimes light fixtures protrude through the attic floor from the ceiling below. If loose-fill insulation is to be used, baffles should be nailed around the fixture projections to separate the insulating materials. Loose fill poured between joists should be smoothed with a board to make certain all gaps have been filled. As in the cases of overhead lights, batts or blankets would be cut off three inches from the fixtures.

If insulation appears to be needed over the fixture, at least 24 inches of clearance should be provided through construction of a wooden framework. Soffits and other vents should be kept clear as well through the use of baffles.

When installing blankets, they should be passed under wiring whenever possible. Pieces of blanket should be cut somewhat too long; then the ends should be placed firmly against top plates.

Floored Attics. Where the attic has a floor, you have a choice to make.

Alternative No. 1: If you do not plan to finish the attic within the foreseeable future, it is better to insulate under the attic floor. As with many such projects, the best material is probably blown fill. But the choice of material will depend on the R-value needed to make the floor optimally heat-resistant.

Alternative No. 2: If the attic will be finished in the near or moderately distant future, insulation of the roof may be called for. Another justification of such a project would be to save money that would otherwise be spent on a contractor. The method chosen depends on the

R-value needed; but blanket or foam insulation installed between the rafters of the roof would probably prove adequate.

Finished Attics. A finished attic presents a different problem. The attic has heat, and in most cases numerous spaces that cannot be reached with ease. Thus blown insulation offers the best solution.

Choosing alternative No. 2, it often makes sense also to insulate while taking a step toward finishing that extra room or suite of rooms. As a beginning, collar

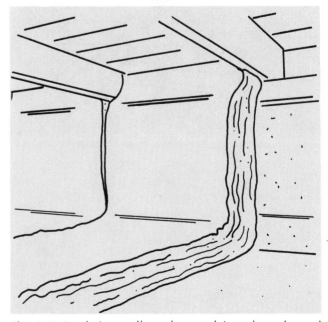

Fig. 6-18 Insulating walls and ground in unheated crawl spaces.

beams are nailed to the rafters at the planned ceiling height. Next, insulating blankets with vapor barriers are cut to length and placed between the rafters and collar beams. The blankets are stapled along the flanges. The joints between the flanges are taped to keep vapor from passing through. Blankets are also stapled to the studs to insulate the end walls.

The Attic-less House. The house that has no attic may nonetheless need upper-region insulation. But where the home typically has a mansard or flat roof, the choices are limited. Blown fill represents the best possible choice unless the homeowner plans to put a new roof on his house. In that process he could add rigid insulation and cover it with roofing material.

Again, cost may be a factor if blown fill is under consideration. But the homeowner can obtain prices and estimates of the amount of time and material that would be required. At least three or four estimates should normally be sought.

Lower Floors, Basements, Crawl Spaces. Methods of installing insulation in lower floors, basements, and crawl spaces have also become highly developed. But the lower portions of the house in general do not deserve quite the attention that the upper portions receive. An exception would be made if special problems arise in the lower areas. "Problems" might include places around the foundation through which air can leak. In this case, the solution might be to seal all gaps with caulking or weatherstripping. Little else may be needed.

Insofar as the lower parts of the house are concerned, at least five types of spaces can be identified. Each requires a slightly different insulating technique.

●*Unheated crawl spaces* with walls need to be insulated if they are not already protected. The simplest method involves enclosing the inside of the crawl space walls with blankets. Typically, the outer walls of the building, and of the crawl space, will be partly underground, partly over.

Blanket insulation offers a cheap way to insulate in such cases. But urethane foam may serve even better if the house's foundation is made of stone. Foam may also be superior if the building's masonry is cracked. The foam would be installed from the inside where possible —and from the outside if that proves impossible. If installed outside, the foam should be protected from the sun and weather by a protective coating of some kind.

Under any circumstances the crawl space should

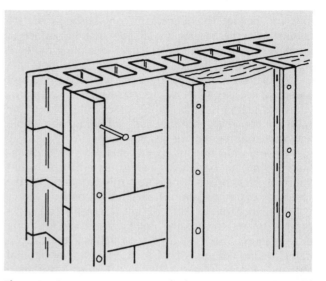

Fig. 6-20 Furring strips are attached to basement walls with masonry nails.

have two, three, or more vents. These are kept open in the warmer months to allow warm air to escape. In the colder months they should be sealed to prevent loss of heat.

If the floor of the crawl space is earth, a vapor barrier should be installed over this entire area.

●*Unheated basements* or garages that have a heated room or rooms on the floor above generally need insulation to separate their cooler air from the warmer air on the next floor. Otherwise, the cooler air seeps upward. Usually, batts can be placed between the joists of the basement ceiling. The batts are held in place with wire mesh. Alternatively, ceiling panels may be used to hold the batts in position.

In some cases the ceiling of the basement, unheated garage, or crawl space will be finished. The floor of the room above will also, of course, be finished. In this situation the best insulation is blown fill, which is mechanically blown into the spaces between the joists.

●*Full basements* represent a different challenge. Such areas should normally not be cut off from the heat of the house, since some heat is needed to keep pipes from freezing. Thus insulation along the basement walls will be useful since it will keep any available heat in the basement.

Before installing the insulation, check the walls of the basement carefully to make sure they are dry. Any dampness seeping into the insulation will reduce its efficiency. The dampness could even render the insulation completely useless.

Preparations should extend further to include a survey of the need for electrical outlets. Any outlets that might be needed after insulation should be installed be-

Fig. 6-19 Wire mesh holds batts between joists of basement ceiling.

fore work begins. The outlets must, obviously, project far enough from the basement walls to reach the surface of the new, insulated wall. If possible, insulating material should be packed behind wiring pipes and outlets.

Insulation is usually unnecessary when the full basement is entirely below ground level. The earth provides adequate insulation in this case. But if part of the walls are above ground level and part below, the whole wall can appropriately be insulated.

In very cold regions special measures may be required to protect basements against extreme frost penetration. Professional advice is normally required to make sure such extra insulation is installed properly.

Insulation of the walls of full basements can comprise a first step toward finishing the basement for living or recreational use. A favored approach is to construct a frame around the entire basement, including horizontal top and bottom plates and vertical studs. Insulation blankets are placed between the studs.

A second technique involves the use of furring strips to provide the framework to which the insulation can be attached. The furring strips can be hung on the basement walls with masonry nails or a construction adhesive made for the purpose.

Select furring strips and studs according to the thickness of the insulation to be used. One-inch-thick blankets would fit with two-by-two-inch furring strips; two-by-fours would be appropriate where 3.5-inch blankets are contemplated. In either case, staples are driven through the flanges of the blankets to secure them to the furring strips.

Once the full basement has been insulated, it can be finished quickly with paneling or drywall. This interior material is easily nailed to the furring strips or studs, whichever was used.

Rigid foam panels insulate full basements with much the same effect as blanket insulation. In fact, the foam panels provide greater R-value protection per inch of thickness. Remember that foam panels have to be covered with gypsum drywall that is at least one-half-inch thick. Some insulation boards or panels, such as polyisocyanurate, do not need to be so covered; the paneling or drywall can, of course, be applied anyway for appearance.

Again, the installation technique is relatively simple. Wooden nailing strips are attached horizontally along the tops and bottoms of the masonry walls. The strips make up the only framework the handyman will need. They should normally be two inches wide and as thick as the foam boards. An ideal combination of sizes is one-by-two-inch nailing strips and three-quarter-inch insulation board. But in colder climates one-inch-thick boards may be preferred. In this case, thicker nailing strips may be required.

Once all preparations have been made, the rigid foam panels go on one at a time. They have to be fitted around obstructions; they can be scored with a utility knife and broken to create apertures of the appropriate size. In the same way, openings for windows can be cut in the boards.

The boards are applied over mastic ribbons. Boards can be positioned either horizontally or vertically and simply pressed into place. Drywall can then be nailed over the insulation boards at top and bottom; if desired, add moldings and baseboards and paint the walls for greater attractiveness.

•*Concrete slabs* are difficult to insulate effectively. But the homeowner can at least check to find out whether infiltration is taking place around the slab. If infiltration is a problem, a carpet and pad may be added as insulation. Little else can be done without programming a relatively extensive reconstruction job.

•*Open crawl spaces* are sometimes found under homes that stand on piers. The task of insulating the open spaces may range from monumental to impossible. The alternative is to insulate between the floor joists of the heated rooms overhead—in other words, above the unheated (and open) crawl space. The same techniques used to insulate above unheated basements will again be useful.

•*Heated crawl spaces* can be insulated using basically the same method employed where the problem was

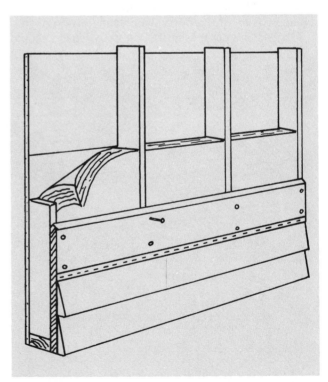

Fig. 6-21 Drywall nailed over styrofoam insulation boards.

an unheated crawl space with walls. That means blankets with attached vapor barriers. Again, the vapor barrier should face toward the interior side since it is warm in winter. Other steps follow a similar pattern:

Where the joists run at right angles to the walls of the foundation, place pieces of blanket insulation on the sill plate and against the header, then secure with strips of wood nailed to the sill plate. The blanket is cut in segments long enough so that, laid down the wall and out on the floor, it extends at least two feet inward into the crawl space.

Where the joists run parallel to the basement walls, tuck the blanket snugly against the header and floor, then attach. In this situation, make certain that no spaces are left between blanket segments. Cold air could seep in through such openings.

The floor of the crawl space should be covered with a vapor barrier over its entire area. Polyethylene sheeting can be used but it should be laid after the blankets are in place. Otherwise it may be torn and crumpled while work is under way. The sheeting goes *under* the trailing segments of blankets that reach down over the floor. In fact, the sheeting should reach up at least six inches on the foundation wall behind the blankets. As a further precaution, lay down the adjoining sheets of plastic film in such a way that each sheet overlaps its neighbor by at least six inches. Alternatively, securely tape the edges of adjoining sheets together to prevent leakage.

With all those steps completed, place weights on the trailing ends of the blankets. The weights can be rock or bricks, pieces of wood, or other heavy objects —one to each strip of blanket.

STORM WINDOWS AND STORM DOORS

The addition of storm windows will substantially reduce the loss of heat. A great deal of heat is lost through the glass and also through cracks around window sashes. A storm window fitted tightly to the window frame creates a space that keeps warm inside air separated from cold outside air, and reduces the flow of heat. If moisture forms on the inside window, it indicates that cold air is getting past the storm window and cooling the outside of the window sashes. But if the moisture forms on the inside of the storm window instead, the warm air is leaking from inside the house past the sashes and con-

SOME DO'S AND DON'TS OF HOME INSULATION

When insulating, DO treat electrical wiring with care. DON'T pull it or twist it out of the way.

DO wash carefully after applying insulation.

DO work in attics from the outside toward the center so that you are continually moving toward the area offering the most headroom.

DO patch a torn vapor barrier, using a strip of barrier from a scrap section of blanket or using polyethylene sheeting and tape.

DON'T leave gaps along vapor barrier edges when insulating walls.

DO keep the flanges tight against the studs.

If it appears impossible to undertake a general insulation of your home, DO start somewhere —preferably in the attic.

DO seek information on costs of materials and other facts about insulation from governmental agencies, local public utilities, contractors, lumberyards, and others who might be able to help.

When hiring a contractor, DO check on cost and quality of materials to be used in insulating your home.

When insulating over attic rafters, DO leave a ventilation space between the rafters and the roof.

DO check the labels describing the mastic you plan to use when attaching foam insulating boards to basement walls. Some mastics will melt the plastic and you want to have the right kind.

DO insulate common walls and floors separating apartments or townhouse units if the units are separately heated.

DO work toward insulation with a specified R-value even when dealing with a contractor. Not all brands of insulation have the same value and you want to make sure you have what you need.

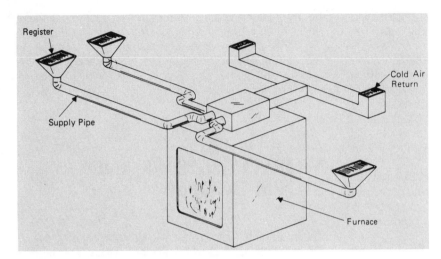

Register

Cold Air Return

Supply Pipe

Furnace

Fig. 6–22 Warm-air heating system.

densing on the storm window. A leaking storm window can often be sealed by caulking the joint between the edge of the window and the outside casing.

Since storm doors are constantly opened and closed, they must be aligned to fit tightly in order to retain their effectiveness. The latch should hold the door firmly against the stops, and the gap between the door and the threshold should be sealed with a vinyl flap of some kind. If there are any openings between the door's metal frame and the house, they should be filled with caulking.

COMPARING HEATING METHODS

Heat can be delivered in several ways. Traditional distribution systems use air ducts and pipes. Warm air flows upward to the registers and the cooled air returns to the furnace through ducts. Hot-water and steam systems use pipes that deliver hot water or steam to radiators and other heating units. Older systems relied on the expansion of warm air or hot water to assist in circulation, but modern forced warm-air and forced hot-water systems use blowers and pumps. Newer electrical heating systems deliver heat by using resistance-type heating units located in each room. Since power is supplied to these units by heavy wiring, they require no furnace or chimney.

The type of heat source used in a heating system is usually determined by the cost and availability of fuel, in addition to personal preference. Oil, gas, coal, and electricity are widely used in central heating systems and have heating efficiencies of up to 85 per cent. Any of them can be used with the several distribution systems. Electricity can be used to heat air or hot water in standard heat distribution systems, as well as to heat electrical

units installed in individual rooms.

Some of the major distribution systems and methods of generating heat will be described to provide a basic understanding of the units involved and how the systems operate. With this background, the homeowner will be able to perform minor maintenance and anticipate more serious problems.

WARM-AIR HEATING

Spaces heated by warm-air systems receive their heat through registers fed by ducts from the furnace. The heated air may rise by expansion, as in a *gravity hot-air system;* or it may be forced through the ducts by a blower, as in a *forced warm-air system.* Furnaces in gravity systems must be lower than the spaces to be heated. Because of the heat loss in ducts, gravity systems use short supply ducts, which requires that the registers be located along the inside walls. This results in uneven heating because the heat will not move naturally toward the colder outside walls. The flow through the cold air in the return ducts is also likely to be slow.

The blower in the forced warm-air system allows the use of longer ducts, which can supply registers located along the outside walls of a room. By drawing in the cold air and forcing out the heated air, the blower can produce more heat than a gravity system with the same furnace. The force of the blower also allows an air filter to be used to clean the air going through the supply ducts. Heating is more uniform with a forced warm-air system and can be controlled better since the blower can be regulated (Fig. 6–22).

Forced warm-air furnaces are shaped differently for use in different locations. Some are designed for large basements; others are used in crawl spaces or on the same level as the spaces to be heated. The *highboy furnace* is used in large basements where the supply

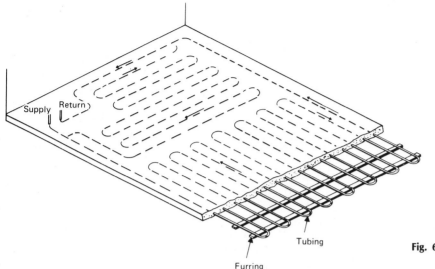

Fig. 6–23 Hot-water radiant heating system in a floor.

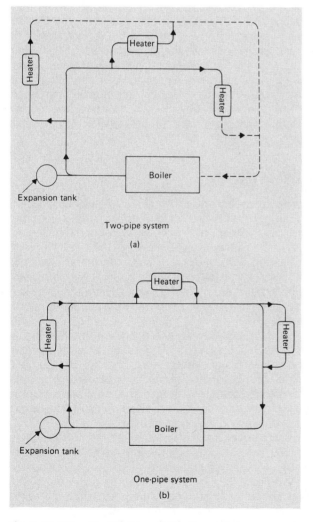

Fig. 6–24 Hot-water and steam distribution systems.

ducts are attached to the top of the furnace (the plenum). For smaller or partial basements, a *lowboy furnace* is used, which has both its supply and return ducts located on the top. Where the furnace is to be located on the same level as the space being heated, a *counterflow* version of the highboy furnace is used which supplies heat through ducts on the bottom and receives the return air through ducts on the top. The *horizontal furnace* is designed for areas such as crawl spaces where the furnace must lie on its side. Heated air is supplied from a duct on one end and cool air is returned to the other end.

There are two types of duct systems for delivering warm air to the registers. *Radial system* designs all have ducts that run directly from the furnace to the registers along the outside walls. This is the cheapest system to install and usually uses round ducts. *Extended-plenum systems* consist of large rectangular ducts that run horizontally from the plenum on the furnace and feed the registers by individually branching ducts. Similarly-shaped return ducts collect the cooled air and return it to the furnace. These larger ducts improve the efficiency of the heating system by reducing the resistance to the forced air flow and can be used for central air conditioning also.

HOT-WATER HEATING

Hot water can be used to operate several types of heating units. Radiators, baseboard units, and wall units transfer heat from hot water to the surrounding air through either cast iron tubes or multiple fins. Because of their greater overall area, the finned-tube type of heater is much more efficient and, therefore, cheaper than the cast-iron elements. The most even heat is produced by baseboard units, because their heat rises uniformly from the lowest point in the room around the outside walls. In radiant

Fig. 6–25 Setting the aquastat.

hot-water systems, water flows through panels of tubing embedded in concrete floor slabs, in ceiling plaster, or in interior walls (Fig. 6–23). Heat is transferred from the tubing to the concrete or plaster, which in turn heats the surrounding air.

There are two types of hot-water systems: gravity systems and forced hot-water systems. *Gravity systems* rely on natural convection currents to carry the heated water from the boiler through the supply pipes to the heating units. When the water passes through the heating unit, it cools and flows back to the boiler through a second set of pipes. The rate of flow is relatively slow and the maximum temperature of the water does not exceed 180°F. Gravity systems, which have an open expansion tank, often in an attic, are called open systems while those using a closed expansion tank adjacent to the boiler are called closed gravity systems.

Forced hot-water systems (hydronic systems) use a circulating pump to increase the rate of water flow in a system under pressure. Since these are closed systems, the water can be placed under greater pressure and the temperature raised to almost boiling. This results in greater efficiency and allows the furnace, distribution system, and heating units to be smaller than those with a gravity system. Hot water for faucets can also be generated by sending the water through a coil immersed in the hot water within the boiler. This keeps the water hot when the boiler water is not being distributed by the pump. When the boiler water is circulating in winter, the faucet water will be cooler.

Several piping systems are used to distribute hot water and return cooled water to the boiler. Gravity hot-water systems use two separate pipes, one to deliver the hot water to the heating unit and one to return the cooled water to the boiler. Forced hot-water systems, on the other hand, may use one of several systems.

The *two-pipe system* provides hot water at approximately the same temperature to all of the radiators in the system (Fig. 6–24(a)). More uniform heating throughout the house is achieved at the expense of installing two sets of pipes. The *one-pipe system* employs one continuous pipe, which delivers hot water to the heating units and collects the return water (Fig. 6–24(b)). Each heating unit is connected to the pipe by its supply and return pipes, so that it can be shut off from the system. The *one-pipe loop system* also uses one pipe but the flow runs directly through each heating unit so that when one of them is turned off the entire system is blocked. *Zone-heating systems* may use any of the standard distribution systems to supply different sections, or zones, of the house. Independent thermostats in each zone control the flow of hot water through the supply pipes.

The water temperature and level in a hot-water system are automatically controlled by a limit control and automatic feed valve. The desired temperature is set on an aquastat (Fig. 6–25), which regulates the water temperature and prevents overheating. Although the water level is automatically controlled by a feed valve, an altitude gauge indicates the desired level and the actual level. A red needle is set to mark the desired level, while a black needle moves to indicate the actual level of water in the system. If the black needle falls below the red needle, the automatic feed valve may not be operating properly or the tankless heater may be leaking.

STEAM HEATING

Steam-heat systems use the same types of heating units and piping as hot-water systems (though hot-water pipes are smaller). Steam rises from the water in the boiler and flows under its own pressure through the supply pipes to the heating units, where it heats the metal elements, condenses, and runs back to the boiler. One-pipe distribution systems are normally used, though two-pipe systems can be installed to carry away the condensed water separately.

As the steam flows into the radiator, it forces the air out through an air vent. If the air vent is blocked or closed, the steam cannot enter and the radiator will remain cold. Normally, radiators or other heating units in a steam system heat up (and cool) much more quickly than in a hot-water system because steam can be generated and supplied rapidly.

Since boiler water is lost to steam, it must be replenished every few days when the furnace is operating constantly. A water gauge between two try-cocks attached to the side of the boiler indicates the water level. The boiler should be kept filled to the point where the water rises half-way in the gauge. If there is insufficient water, a furnace with a low-water cutoff will automatically cut

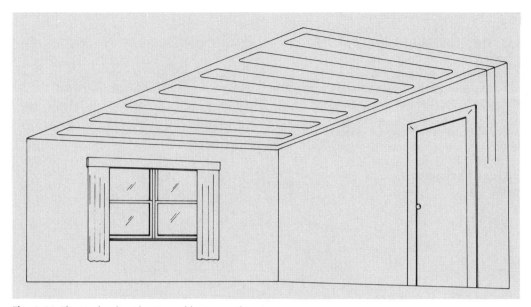

Fig. 6–26 Electrical radiant heating cables in a ceiling.

off. On top of the boiler, a gauge indicates the steam pressure. If the pressure rises to 3 to 5 lbs., the pressure control will turn off the burner. As an additional safety measure, the safety valve will open at approximately 15 lbs./sq./in.

ELECTRICAL HEATING

Electrical heating systems are simpler to install than other systems, because the heating units are supplied by wiring, rather than by pipes or ducts, and require no furnace or chimney. Baseboard units, for example, are attached along outside walls in place of baseboards and heat the surrounding air, which rises to provide even heating. Heavy resistance-type heating elements in the unit generate energy, which heats the fins in contact with the air. Wiring for electrical heating can also be installed in the ceilings (Fig. 6–26) or walls while a house is being constructed. Heating panels are used for ceilings and walls that are already finished.

Electrical heating employs zone heating for individual rooms. Separate thermostats in each room control the heating elements. Since it takes longer for electrical heaters than for other systems to heat the surrounding air, the walls and ceilings or attic must be fully insulated. This means a 6-in. thickness of fiberglass in the attic, 4-in. or equivalent in the walls, and 2-in. in floors over cold spaces. In the event of brief power failures, this insulation will keep the house from cooling off rapidly.

BURNERS AND FURNACES

Almost any type of burner or furnace can be used to supply heat to warm-air, hot-water, or steam heating systems. Coal furnaces have been replaced in most of the United States by oil or gas burners for supplying central heating systems. Electrical furnaces and boilers, though fewer in number, are also used. The type of furnace chosen depends on the local cost of fuel, the cost of the furnace and installation, and on personal preference. A general knowledge of the operation and major components of these burners and furnaces will help in detecting problems and in trouble shooting.

Oil Burners

The function of an oil burner is to mix oil and air in the proper proportions for burning and to provide heat to a boiler or warm-air system. This requires units for storing oil, delivering it to the burner, blowing in air, and a combustion chamber and controls.

Oil is pumped from the oil tank to the burner by a pump powered by an electric motor. There are two types of burners.

Gun-type burners are more widely used than pot burners (Fig. 6–27). The gun and nozzle convert the oil flow to a fine spray, which is mixed in the combustion chamber with air forced in by the blower. Electrical sparks generated by a transformer ignite the oil-air mixture. This ignition process is intermittent and stops after the burner is operating.

In a *pot burner,* the oil is pumped into the base of the pot where it is vaporized, mixed with air in controlled proportions, and burned. This method of burning requires a constant pilot flame.

Oil burners are controlled by several automatic and manual switches. An emergency cutoff switch near the burner, or at the entrance to the furnace area, can cut off electricity to the entire system. Without electricity, the oil pump, blower, and transformer cannot operate. An automatic control in the chimney, a stack switch, will turn off the electricity to the burner if the oil-air mixture doesn't ignite within a few seconds after the burner starts operating.

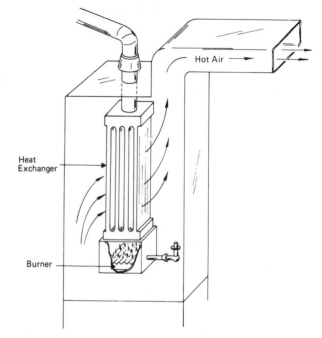

Fig. 6–28 Operation of gas burner.

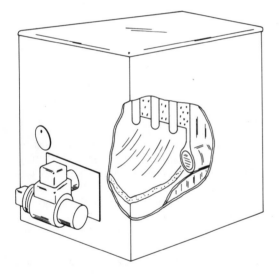

Fig. 6–27 Gun-type oil burner and furnace.

The amount of gas delivered to the burner is controlled by a gas-control valve. Since the pressure can vary, an automatic pressure-regulator sets the delivery pressure. In the vent, a draft diverter, resembling an inverted funnel, prevents downdrafts from blowing out the pilot light and allows gases to escape only up the vent. There may also be a heat-sensitive safety shutoff on the vent that shuts off the furnace when a clogged chimney causes gas to reverse.

Gas Burners

Gas burners are simpler than oil burners. There is no pump, or storage tank. Gas is piped into the house to either a single or multijet burner head, where it mixes with air and is ignited by a pilot light. A flame spreader spreads the flame so that it heats the plenum (Fig. 6–28).

To prevent gas from flowing when the pilot light is out, heat from the pilot light controls an electrical valve in the gas line. When the pilot light goes out, the valve closes and shuts off the gas. There is also a manual control, called the main shutoff, which will shut off the gas.

Gas burners have several other controls. A thermostat turns the burner on and off, just as with an oil burner.

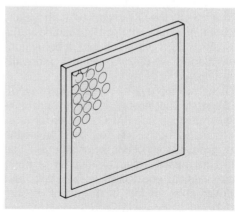

Fig. 6–29 Filter for warm-air system.

Electric Furnaces and Boilers

Electricity can be used as a source of heat in warm-air and hot-water systems. In an electric furnace, a blower forces air past electrical heating elements and through ducts to registers. Cool air returns through another system of ducts and the cycle is repeated. In an electric boiler, the electric heating elements are located inside the boiler where they heat the surrounding water. Hot water is pumped in the conventional manner through pipes in the distribution system.

MAINTENANCE AND REPAIR

Most serious repairs to heating systems require the services of a serviceman. However, there are a number of steps the homeowner can take to keep the system operating effectively without expensive help. Cleaning filters and registers in warm-air systems is simple but important to the flow of clean, warm air. The homeowner can adjust cold or noisy radiators by bleeding trapped air and draining trapped water. He can also drain and flush rusty water from a boiler without professional assistance. By watching for wear on moving parts, leaks, and other signs of more serious problems, a homeowner can seek aid in time to prevent unexpected breakdowns.

DISTRIBUTION SYSTEMS

WARM-AIR SYSTEMS

Dirt and dust are a continuing problem for warm-air systems since they clog *filters* and *registers*. Filters should

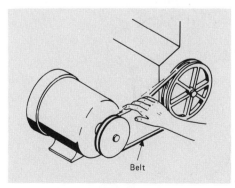

Fig. 6–30 Adjusting belt on blower.

be checked every month or so during the heating season. If they are visibly dirty, clean them by washing or vacuuming (depending on the type of filter), or replace them if they already have been cleaned several times (Fig 6–29). In any case, filters should be replaced at least once a year, preferably just before the heating season starts. Registers should be removed and vacuumed to remove wads of dust. When they are replaced, there should be no air leaks around their bases. If you feel warm air escaping around the edges, use a strip of felt to seal the leak.

Dampers, which control the flow of warm air through the ducts, must be balanced for even distribution to the registers. Dampers in ducts that supply the more distant registers must be opened wider than those supplying registers closer to the furnace.

The *belt* that operates the blower is likely to become worn or frayed in time. Look at it periodically and replace it before it breaks. Loosen the bolts that hold the belt tight, remove and replace the belt, and hold the new belt taut while the bolts are retightened. There should be no more than ½ to 6 in. leeway in the center of the belt (Fig. 6–30).

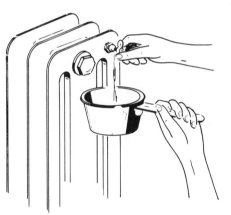

Fig. 6–31 Bleeding radiator valve.

HOT-WATER AND STEAM SYSTEMS

Hot-water *radiators* will not heat well if air is trapped in them. Before the heating season starts, bleed each radiator until all of the air is forced out and hot water begins to escape. Open the air vent and be prepared to catch a cupful of hot water (Fig. 6–31). As soon as the water begins to escape, close the valve. As the radiators are vented, more water will automatically be added to the

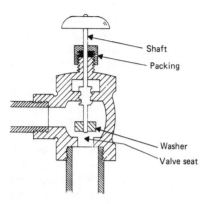

Fig. 6–32 Radiator shutoff valve.

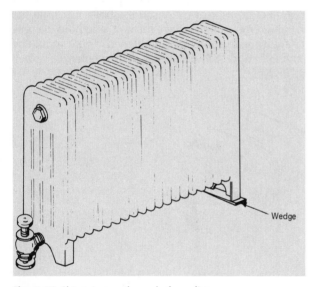

Fig. 6–33 Shimming up the end of a radiator.

boiler to keep the system full. The air valve in steam radiators automatically releases air as steam flows into the radiator. (Plugged valves can be boiled in hot water with a little baking soda.) Adjustable air valves can be varied to allow air to escape more easily in radiators that heat slowly because of their distance from the boiler. Adjust the valve on each radiator so that steam is evenly distributed to all of the radiators in the system.

Shutoff valves at the base of the radiators may leak if the packing fails (Fig. 6–32). Leaks can sometimes be stopped by tightening the packing nut just below the knob. If water or steam continues to leak, the packing nut should be removed and fresh packing installed. When making the repair in a steam-heating system, the valve should be closed and the thermostat turned down to delay the generation of steam. In a hot-water system,

sufficient water must be drained from the system so that the valve is above the water level. When the repair is completed, water is added to fill the system again.

Cold radiators and hammering in a steam system are caused by trapped water. If the radiator is not at an angle to drain condensed water back into the supply pipe, water will collect in the bottom and obstruct the flow of steam. This can be fixed by raising the vented end of the radiator with small wedges until hammering stops and the radiator heats up (Fig. 6–33).

FURNACES

Boilers, whether used in steam or hot-water systems, should be drained and flushed annually and occasionally cleaned with a boiler-cleaning compound. In hot-water systems, close the shutoff valve between the boiler and expansion tank. Turn off the burner, and open the drain faucet near the base of the furnace. Drain off the dirty water (Fig. 6–34) and flush the boiler with fresh water by opening the water-feed valve. When the drain water becomes clear, close the drain faucet and continue filling the boiler until the gauge (water gauge on a steam system, altitude gauge on a hot-water system) indicates that the system is replenished. The burner can then be turned on. (The expansion tank shutoff valve should be re-opened in a hot-water system before the burner is turned on.) During the heating season, the low-water cutoff control on the boiler can be kept clear of sludge by draining a few quarts of water through the cutoff valve every week or two.

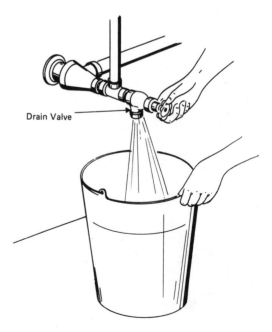

Fig. 6–34 Draining a boiler.

When *water gauges* become filled with rust, the water level is obscured (Fig. 6–35). They should be removed and cleaned or replaced. To remove a gauge, close the shutoff valves above and below and drain the water from the gauge through the drain cock below the lower shutoff valve. The large nuts and washers that attach the glass to the valves can be loosened and the gauge removed. If washing and scrubbing with a stiff brush fail to clean the inside of the gauge, it should be replaced.

Oil and *gas burners* and *electrical-heating elements* require the attention of professional servicemen. The non-professional should not do much more than add a few drops of SAE 30 oil to oil cups on oil burners (Fig. 6–36) and blowers, or relight pilot lights in gas burners, following the directions for the particular unit. He or she can safely push the reset button once (and only once) on an oil burner to restart it after the stack switch has shut it off. If the burner fails to restart or shuts off again, professional assistance will be needed.

TROUBLE SHOOTING HEATING SYSTEMS

Some heating-system problems develop slowly, others suddenly. By knowing how the system operates and what to look for when problems occur, a homeowner can distinguish between those problems he can take care of by himself and those that should be left to a serviceman. Simple problems such as hammering radiators, clogged filters, and loose blower belts can be handled without expensive professional help. More technical problems may be solved less expensively in the long run if a serviceman is called as soon as they are recognized.

The problems described here have both simple and complex causes. The more difficult it is to determine the cause, the more likely it is that a serviceman will be needed, even if the cause is found. Remedies for some of the simpler causes are described in the section on maintenance and repair.

USING OLD-FASHIONED HEATING METHODS

When wood and coal were the main sources of heat, people knew a lot about building fires and heating. Fireplaces were inefficient, but ingenious methods were used to coax all of the heat possible from them. Wood-

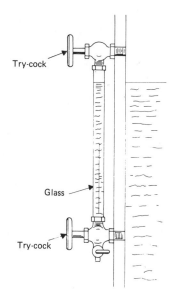

Fig. 6–35 Steam boiler water gauge.

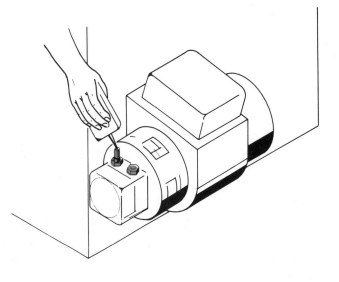

Fig. 6–36 Lubricating burner oil cups.

burning and coal-burning stoves made better use of fuel and were used to heat living spaces and for cooking.

Stove design has improved so that more heat can be extracted from wood and coal today. When wood alone burns, the solid matter releases no more than half of the heat energy in the wood. The remaining energy leaves the heated wood in the form of combustible gases, which usually rise up the chimney without being heated to a

INSULATING YOUR HOME

HEAT LOSS BY INFILTRATION

All buildings exchange air with the outside environment. Some of this exchange is necessary for ventilation. However, most homes have too high an exchange rate, more than one complete change of air per hour. Sealing the openings and cracks will reduce this rate substantially.

Houses also have a chimney effect which causes the warm air to rise and dissipate through the roof and chimney areas. As the warm air rises and leaks out, cooler air at the lower levels is pulled in through cracks in the foundation, between door and window joints to the siding, and through unprotected doors and windows.

HEAT LOSS BY CONDUCTION

Conduction is the heat lost through the exteri
surfaces of a building.

The rate at which heat dissipates from t
warm side to the cold side of walls and roof
determined by the type of materials used.
materials will reduce this transfer from heat
cold, but some materials are more effective th
others.

Three types of insulation will dramatically
duce the conduction rate. They are loose fill, su
as rockwool, cellulose and wood fibres, a
glass batt or blanket rolls rigid board, li
fiberboard and foamed plastics.

Sealing Exterior Cracks and Openings

Heat loss through cracks and unprotected or loose fitting doors and windows is estimated to run as high as 55 per cent on windy days. Sealing these openings is the most effective and least expensive change a homeowner can make to reduce fuel costs.

1. Caulk the joints between window and door frames and house siding. Also around the chimney and foundation where they join the siding.

2. Protect each door and window with storm doors and windows. Seal doors not used.

3. Weatherstrip around all doors and where the windows contact the sills.

4. Replace or repair loose, missing, or torn shingles.

5. Check flashing around the chimney to be sure it is in good condition and fitting snugly to chimney and under the shingles.

6. Foam insulation blown in between the studs will reduce the second greatest area of heat loss.

Sealing Exterior Cracks and Openings

Heat loss through cracks and unprotected or loose fitting doors and windows is estimated to run as high as 55 per cent on windy days. Sealing these openings is the most effective and least expensive change a homeowner can make to reduce fuel costs.

1. Caulk the joints between window and door frames and house siding. Also around the chimney and foundation where they join the siding.

2. Protect each door and window with storm doors and windows. Seal doors not used.

3. Weatherstrip around all doors and where the windows contact the sills.

4. Replace or repair loose, missing, or torn shingles.

5. Check flashing around the chimney to be sure it is in good condition and fitting snugly to chimney and under the shingles.

6. Foam insulation blown in between the studs will reduce the second greatest area of heat loss.

Interior Insulation and Ventilation Will Reduce Heat Loss

1. Insulate interior walls, if exposed, with batting between the studs before applying interior panelling. Be sure a vapor barrier is facing inside, toward the living area.

2. Apply attic floor insulation between the joists.

3. The vapor barrier side of the insulation should be down, facing the living area below the attic floor.

4. Ventilation is important to control moisture in an insulated attic. Insulation on attic walls must not cover roof and eaves vents as air passage must not be restricted. Vents should be covered with screens.

Interior Insulation and Ventilation Will Reduce Heat Loss
1. Insulate interior walls, if exposed, with batting between the studs before applying interior panelling. Be sure a vapor barrier is facing inside, toward the living area.
2. Apply attic floor insulation between the joists.
3. The vapor barrier side of the insulation should be down, facing the living area below the attic floor.
4. Ventilation is important to control moisture in an insulated attic. Insulation on attic walls must not cover roof and eaves vents as air passage must not be restricted. Vents should be covered with screens.

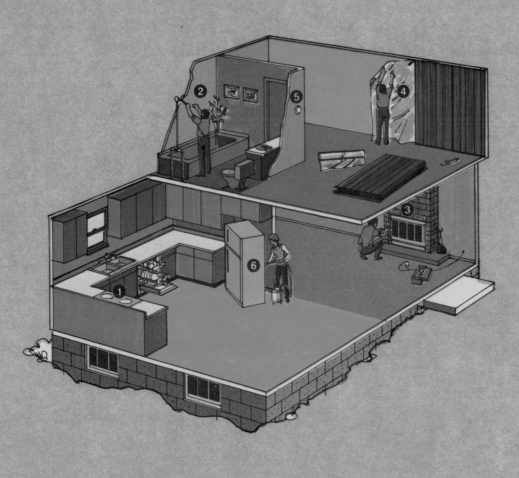

Interior Energy Saving Opportunities

1. Select appliances that are energy efficient such as electric igniters on gas stoves to eliminate the waste of a steadily burning pilot light. Run dishwasher with only full loads.

2. Flow restrictor valves placed inside shower heads will reduce normal water flow of seven to ten gallons per minute to three gallons per minute without loss of water pressure. Replace washers to eliminate leaky water faucets.

3. Glass doors on the fireplace opening and moving the damper to a closed position when not in use will reduce heat loss up the chimney.

4. When remodeling a room in the basement or upper floors place a vapor barrier, like styrofoam or polyethylene, between the old wall and panelling.

5. Reducing the thermostat setting five degrees at night when combined with a clock or set-back device will reduce fuel costs by 10 to 12 per cent.

6. Vacuum the coils on back of the refrigerator periodically to eliminate dust which causes heat build-up and consequently consumes more electricity.

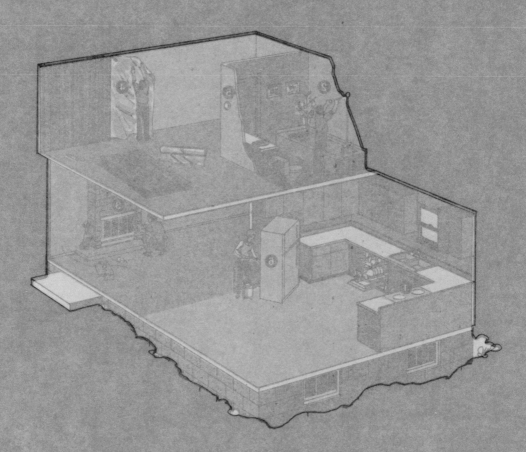

Interior Energy Saving Opportunities

1. Select appliances that are energy efficient such as electric igniters on gas stoves to eliminate the waste of a steadily burning pilot light. Run dishwasher with only full loads.

2. Flow restrictor valves placed inside shower heads will reduce normal water flow of seven to ten gallons per minute to three gallons per minute without loss of water pressure. Replace washers to eliminate leaky water faucets.

3. Glass doors on the fireplace opening and moving the damper to a closed position when not in use will reduce heat loss up the chimney.

4. When remodeling a room in the basement or upper floors place a vapor barrier, like styrofoam or polyethylene, between the old wall and paneling.

5. Reducing the thermostat setting five degrees at night when combined with a clock or set-back device will reduce fuel costs by 10 to 12 per cent.

6. Vacuum the coils on back of the refrigerator periodically to eliminate dust which causes heat build-up and consequently consumes more electricity.

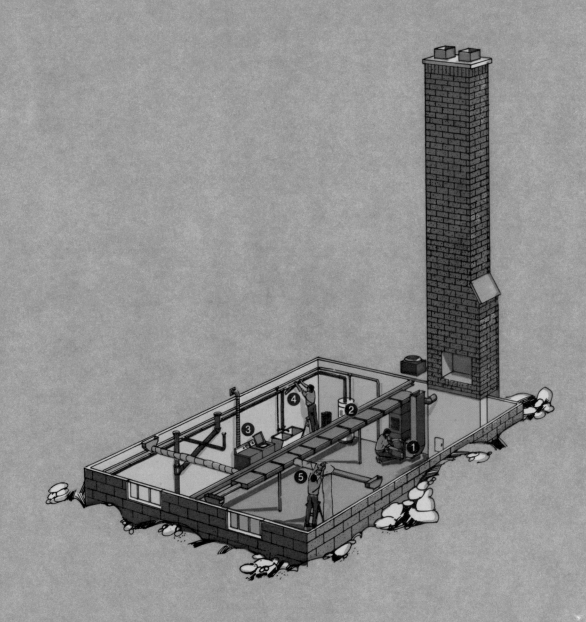

Conserve Heat and Energy in the Basement

1. Furnace and air conditioners should be kept clean, the air filters replaced periodically. The spray nozzle on oil fired furnaces should be replaced yearly and soot should be vacuumed from the boiler at the same time. One-quarter-inch of soot can reduce furnace efficiency by 25 per cent.

2. Hot water heaters should be checked for water temperature and the thermostat dropped to 120 degrees or 140 degrees if a dishwasher is used. Drain the heater occasionally to eliminate sediment build-up which causes efficiency loss.

3. Washer should be used with full loads to conserve hot water. Dryer vent should be insulated and flutter valve outside checked to be sure it closes properly.

4. Insulate hot water pipes to reduce heat loss. Older water heaters should be insulated.

5. Air duct joints should be taped and ducts insulated wherever they pass through unheated (or uncooled) areas.

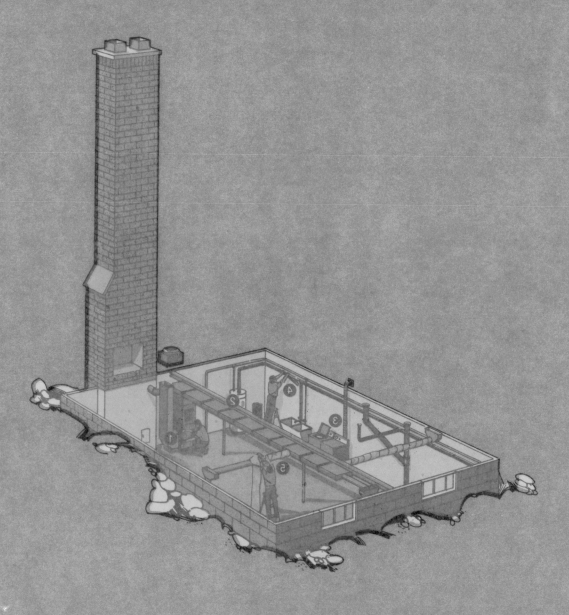

Conserve Heat and Energy in the Basement

1. Furnace and air conditioners should be kept clean, the air filters replaced periodically. The spray nozzle on oil fired furnaces should be replaced yearly and soot should be vacuumed from the boiler at the same time. One-quarter-inch of soot can reduce furnace efficiency by 25 per cent.

2. Hot water heaters should be checked for water temperature and the thermostat dropped to 120 degrees or 140 degrees if a dishwasher is used. Drain the heater occasionally to eliminate sediment build-up which causes efficiency loss.

3. Washer should be used with full loads to conserve hot water. Dryer vent should be insulated and flutter valve outside checked to be sure it closes properly.

4. Insulate hot water pipes to reduce heat loss. Older water heaters should be insulated.

5. Air duct joints should be taped and ducts insulated wherever they pass through unheated (or uncooled) areas.

high enough temperature to burn and release their energy. By directing these volatiles over the coals and supplying additional oxygen, modern stoves have increased their efficiency by more than fifty per cent.

STOVES

Since they were not airtight, old wood-burning and coal-burning stoves lost most of their volatiles and heated up the chimney through uncontrolled updrafts. Modern airtight stoves are well sealed to avoid this and to allow greater control of the rate of combustion.

Norwegian stoves are noted for their tight joints, tightly fitting doors, and heating efficiency (Fig. 6–37(a)). The primary draft from the door on the front of the stove can be controlled to burn logs evenly from one end to the other in the same manner that a cigarette burns. A secondary draft, also from the front, provides oxygen to burn the combustible gases (Fig. 6–37(b)).

Large wood-burning stoves designed to heat entire houses also use a secondary draft to burn volatiles. Air in the primary draft is also preheated in some models to create a higher temperature in the firebox. Some of these stoves can burn almost any type of wood; and their size allows them to heat a house with only two or three full loads a day.

Non-airtight stoves, such as the *Franklin stove,* are also useful sources of heat (Fig. 6–38). The Franklin stove has an open front like a fireplace, but it is much more efficient. The air around the stove is heated and circulates through the room. The rate of combustion can be controlled for more even burning by closing the doors over the front opening.

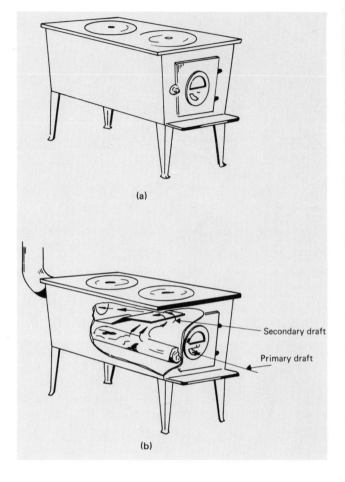

Fig. 6–37 Norwegian stove: a) airtight structure, b) air flow through stove.

MALFUNCTION	CAUSE
Oil burner won't start	Emergency switch turned off. Thermostat defective or set too low. Blown fuses in switch box. Circuit-breaker open. Oil tank empty. Fuel line blocked. Low boiler water. Stack switch dirty or defective.
Gas burner won't start	Pilot light out. Electricity shut off at switch or main box. Gas supply shut off. Main gas valve closed. Thermostat set too low or not operating properly. Low boiler water.
Electrical heating unit won't heat	Electricity shut off. Thermostat set too low or not operating properly. Defective heating unit.

Insufficient heat in warm-air system	Dirty filter or registers. Loose or broken belt on blower. Burners not operating properly. Dampers not set to balance heat delivery through ducts. Burner operates too infrequently. Thermostat not operating properly. Units in heating system too small for space to be heated. Inadequate air return to furnace. Electrical malfunctions.
Thermostat not operating properly	Dust obstructing points or other elements within the thermostat. Mercury bulb not level, or magnetic switch corroded or dirty.
Radiators or convectors cold	Burners not operating. Air trapped in hot-water radiator. Radiator valve shut off. Low boiler water. Expansion-tank valve shut off. System not balanced for heat delivery. Air valve defective.
Hammering steam pipes and radiators	Water trapped in steam radiator.
Noisy warm-air systems	Ducts loose. Electric motor loose and vibrating. Blower belt too tight. Blower not operating properly, vibrating.
Low boiler water	Water evaporated in steam heating system; needs to be replaced through manual feed valve. Automatic feed valve in hot-water system not operating properly. Boiler or return lines leaking.
Pilot light out	Gas supply shut off. Main gas valve closed. Extinguished by downdraft. Orifice clogged.
Air trapped in hot-water radiators	Air released from fresh water in system. Water drained from system. Automatic air vents not functioning.
Water trapped in steam radiators	Condensed steam unable to return through supply pipe. Radiator not tilted enough toward supply pipe.
Air valve not releasing air	Clogged with dirt or corrosion. Valve-release element defective.
Smell of gas in gas-heated system	Gas leak or defective valve.
Blower won't start	Electrical switches shut off. Loose or broken belt. Burned out motor.
Radiator valve leaking	Packing nut loose. Packing needs to be replaced.
Smoky vent in chimney	Poor oil-air mixture. Too much oil being used.
Using too much oil	Nozzles worn. Filters dirty. Blower dirty. Burner unit too large for system. Excessive heat loss in house.
Not enough heat delivered by heating system	Thermostat located in space warmed by sun or fireplace, or placed too close to heating unit. Thermostat defective. In steam systems, radiators or convectors blocked by trapped water or by trapped air in hot-water systems. Limit control set too low. Boiler not operating properly. Distribution system not balanced.
Too much heat delivered by heating system	Thermostat located in unusually cold space. Thermostat defective. Burner unit too large for space being heated.
Heating not even in all spaces	Delivery system not balanced. Dampers in ducts not balanced for even delivery. Air vents and air valves not operating properly. Radiators blocked by air or water. Heating units not located for best distribution of heat. Some ducts or supply pipes too long for system. Heated spaces not equally insulated.

Parlor stoves, cooking stoves, and other loosely built stoves were often used for burning coal rather than wood. Their fireboxes and doors were smaller than those on wood-burning stoves. Firebricks instead of cast iron lined the fireboxes allowing only small logs to be burned. These stoves can be modified to burn wood by replacing the firebricks with cast iron to make their fireboxes larger.

Wood and coal stoves require chimneys for venting. Brick chimneys, especially if they are in the center of the house, absorb heat from the vented gases and help heat the house by warming the adjacent walls. A good updraft requires a long stretch of chimney between the stove and air outside. Therefore, stoves located on the first floor burn better than those on higher floors, which have less chimney above them.

FIREPLACES

An open fire in a fireplace offers more visual enjoyment than heat. The fire radiates heat to whatever is immediately in front of it, but it doesn't create warm circulating air to heat the room. The heating efficiency of a fireplace is less than twenty percent, unless it is fitted with auxiliary heating devices. Combustible gases are not burned to release their heat. Air that is heated by the burning wood rises directly up the chimney without being drawn into the room. In fact, air in the room is drawn into the fireplace opening and passes up the chimney without being heated. When the fire dies down, an open damper will allow a constant flow of warm air from the room to escape to the outside.

Devices have been added to fireplaces to take advantage of the heat that is normally lost. Heat-o-lators consist of ducts lining the sides of the fireplace, which conduct heat from inside the fireplace to registers in adjacent spaces. These generally have to be installed when the fireplace and walls are being built. Coiled tubing is another device used in fireplaces to heat water, which rises to a hot-water storage tank. These systems are common in Europe where small coal-burning fireplaces are used daily in cold weather.

COOLING BY TRADITIONAL METHODS

There are a number of traditional methods to keep living spaces cool during hot weather without using air-conditioning. Some methods reduce the effect of the sun in heating up a house, or they keep hot air from entering. Others cool by ventilating and replacing hot inside air with cooler night air from the outside.

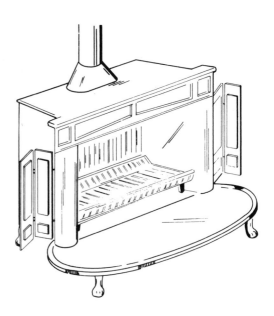

Fig. 6–38 Franklin stove.

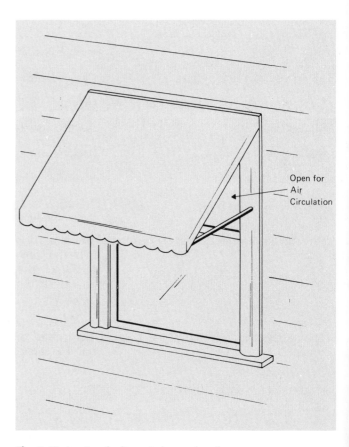

Open for Air Circulation

Fig. 6–39 Awning shading window and wall area.

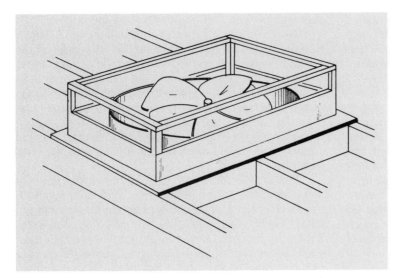

Fig. 6–40 Fan installation in attic.

KEEPING THE HEAT OUT

The effect of the direct rays of the sun can be minimized by shading windows and walls and using light-colored exterior paint and roofing to minimize the absorption of heat. Light-colored awnings are effective in preventing the sun from passing through windows by shading the glass and nearby walls (Fig. 6–39). Shades can be used to block the sun also, though they are not as effective as awnings. Trees are one of the best sources of shade. Houses that are fortunate enough to have large shade trees close to their southern or western exposures are protected by shade and by a cool curtain of air. If the exterior walls are painted a light color, they will reflect much of the heat from the sun and take longer to heat up. Light-colored roofing materials act in the same manner. Hot air also can be kept out by closing windows on the sunny side of the house when the morning air is still cool and slightly opening a few windows on the shaded side for ventilation.

Insulation is as important in keeping a house cool in hot weather as it is in keeping it warm during winter. Attics should have 6 in. of insulation and walls 3 in. to prevent heat from being transferred to the cooler inside air. Windows and doors should be kept closed, except for ventilation on the shaded side, and their joints should be weatherstripped to prevent leaks.

REMOVING HOT AIR

Attic fans cool by removing hot air so that it can be replaced by a natural flow of cooler air from the outside. Cooler air will flow in at ground level as hot air moves out through attic louvres. Smaller room-size fans perform the same function on a lesser scale.

Fans are placed either in a gable at one end of the attic or directly over an opening in the attic floor (Fig. 6–40). When the fan is mounted in a gable, an opening is cut through the attic floor and covered with a register so hot air can be drawn into the attic. When the fan is mounted horizontally over an opening in the attic floor, it is installed over a shutter, which automatically opens and closes with the operation of the fan. In this position, the fan must have an unobstructed space above it in which to discharge the hot air so that the air can leave the attic through louvres in the gables or eaves.

Fans are rated by their size and the number of cubic feet of air that they remove in one minute (CFM). To find the number of cubic feet of air in the rooms, halls, and stairways to be ventilated, multiply the length times width times height of each space, and add them together. Do not include spaces that won't be ventilated, such as storage rooms and closets. An attic fan should be able to change the total volume of air in the house once every minute in the warmer parts of the country and once every minute and a half in the cooler sections. For example, if the spaces to be ventilated have a total of 10,000 cu. ft., a 36-in. fan might be adequate for one change every minute. If the air has to be changed only every minute and a half, 6666 cu. ft. would have to be changed in one minute and a smaller, 30-in. fan would be sufficient.

Installing attic fans requires some skill in carpentry to prepare the ceiling opening and to install louvres in the attic. The fan must be mounted so as not to cause the ceiling or gable wall to vibrate. Assistance may be necessary to supply electricity through a separate circuit from the main service box. Follow the instructions for mounting the fan, which accompany the model purchased.

Kitchen and bathroom ventilating fans are installed in the walls or ceiling and ducted to the outside. (Range hoods may be either ductless or ducted.) Window fans are installed by simply mounting them in the window.

Ceiling Fans

The "Casablanca fan," or ceiling fan, has come increasingly into its own for at least two reasons. First, present generations of these fans are both more efficient and more affordable than ever before. Second, ceiling fans have proved their worth as energy savers. They perform the latter task in cold weather by driving down toward the floor a room's warmer air. Uncirculated, this air simply hugs the ceiling, where it does no one much good. In summer the ceiling fan brings cooler floor-level air upward and moves it around.

The good fan has reversing switches that give you six different choices of speeds—three for each direction. No matter where in your home you want to install a fan, you should be able to find an appropriate type. But remember that you normally have to have seven feet of clearance from floor to blades and 18 inches of clearance from the tip of any blade to any wall. You'll want to avoid installing a fan over the arc of a hinged door.

Choosing a fan should not be difficult. You can select from any number of sizes and styles, but should consider warranties and services along with operating features and designs. For very little extra you can get a fan with a light. The types of control used with modern fans are, basically, four in number: rheostat wall switches; unit-mounted pull chains; electronic wall switches that do the entire control job, from setting fan speed and direction to adjustment of light intensity if you have a fan with a light; and remote control switches that can both select fan speeds and turn the fan on and off from any point in the room.

The type of control you select will obviously depend on your needs and tastes. You can even install a double rheostat, an arrangement that enables you to control the fan speed and light—if any—from a wall switch. Computerized wall controls are sold with some units; they give you the ultimate in control, providing random light patterns for home security, automatic light shutoff, and full control over direction and speed.

Installing the ceiling fan starts when you switch off the power at the breaker panel or remove the appropriate fuse. Assuming that you are replacing an existing light fixture, once you've made sure with a tester that the power is really off you remove the wall switch and the overhead light. It's a good idea to follow instructions regarding another test: if your owner's manual says you should hang a 50-pound test weight from the ceiling junction box to see how firmly it's anchored, use whatever weights you can find to conduct the test.

Now you can go ahead and install the fan's hanger system. Take care not to damage the insulation on the "pigtail" wires that come down from the ceiling. These should be threaded through the holes in the fan's mounting bracket, the bracket should be attached to the outlet, with the canopy in place the fan should be hung from the canopy, and the optional light fixture—again, if you have one—should be attached to the fan. The fan control unit should then be set in place in the wall switchbox.

With a little additional work, you can install your fan in a ceiling that has no light fixture. With the power off, you have only to locate the spot where the fan will go, cut a hole between two joists, and nail a fitted piece of 2 × 4 into the space between the joists. Now you have your fan support—about 1½ inches above the surface of the ceiling so that the outlet box will come down flush with the ceiling. With the outlet box screwed in place, you should carefully pry a section of baseboard from the wall below the point where the new wall switch will be located. A hole drilled through the bottom wall plate serves as an entry for new cable. Trace the outline of a new switchbox on the wall, remove a piece large enough to receive the wall switch, and feed cable upward from the lower cable hole and through the gap for the wall switch.

A licensed electrician should do the final honors. The cable has to be installed—connected to the breaker or fuse box and run out for the other connections. The local building codes will tell you what gauge wire is required for such installations.

AIR CONDITIONING

Types of Air Conditioners

Air conditioners are manufactured in various models and sizes to cool individual rooms, several rooms, or an entire house. *Room units* fit into window openings or into frames mounted through the wall to the outside. Most window-mounted units can be installed without any special preparations other than providing a separate electric circuit. Wall-mounted units require an opening to be cut in the wall and a frame mounted to hold the unit. Many large room-type units have the capacity to cool several adjoining rooms and require a separate 230-V circuit.

Central Air-Conditioning Systems, like central heating systems, supply the entire house from a central source. Units can be installed with their own ducts for distributing cool air, or they can be set up to use the distribution ducts and blower in a warm-air heating system. When all

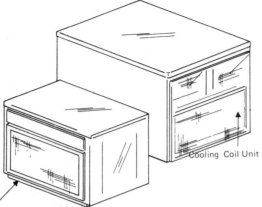

Condenser and Compressor

Fig. 6–41 Air-conditioning units for split system.

of the components of a central air-conditioning system are installed in one place, it is called a *single-unit system.* The cooling coils, condenser, and compressor are usually mounted adjacent to the central-heating system and installed as an integrated unit. When the condenser and compressor, the noisier components, are installed separately outside and the cooling coils and a drain system are installed inside, the system is called a *split system* (Fig. 6–41). This arrangement is quieter but more expensive to install.

Cooling Capacity

Air-conditioning units are rated by their capacities to cool air in terms of BTUs. Since a BTU is a unit of heat (the amount of heat needed to increase the temperature of one pound of water one degree Fahrenheit), the rating in BTUs indicates how much heat a unit can remove from the air. A small room-size unit, for example, might be rated at 6,000 BTUs. Cooling capacities are also referred to in tons, which can be easily translated into BTUs. A unit with a cooling capacity of 1 ton has a capacity of 12,000 BTUs. Central air-conditioning units might have capacities of 30,000 to 60,000 BTUs, or 2½ to 5 tons.

Determining the capacity needed to cool one or more rooms or an entire house is very complicated. Air-conditioning dealers use lengthy forms and tables, which take into account the type of construction, insulation, windows, roofing, use of the room, and the size of the spaces to be cooled, among other things. The rule of thumb used for average conditions is 12,000 BTUs of cooling capacity for every 500 sq. ft. of floor space. For example, a 20 × 25-ft. room would require a unit with a capacity of at least 12,000 BTUs. A room twice as large would require 24,000 BTUs.

Installing Room Units

Room units should be mounted in a central location

away from outside doors in order to distribute cool air evenly throughout a room. To circulate the cooled air, the cooling coils and fan are located in the section of the unit opening into the room. Inside air is cooled as it is blown over the cooling coils. Heat transferred to the liquid refrigerant in the coils is expelled to the outside air through the compressor and condenser.

The operation of the unit is controlled by several devices to maintain the desired room temperature. Modern units are turned on and off by a thermostat to keep the room cooled to the proper degree. Fans of two or more speeds can be manually or automatically set to maintain the desired rate of cooling. There are also elements for processing the air, such as removable filters that clean the air. In many models, outside air can be blown in to replace stale inside air whether the cooling system is operating or not.

Window-type units are designed for both double-hung windows and casement windows (Fig. 6–42). Installation kits include a mounting frame, rubber gaskets to close the gaps over and under the unit, and side panels for the gaps on the sides. Windows should be weather-stripped to stop air leaks around the units. Wall-type units require that frames be built in the wall a foot or more above the floor so that the casing will fit snugly without vibration. The exterior joints should be caulked to prevent water and air from leaking in. Separate electric circuits are desirable for both types of units to protect the motors. Those with cooling capacities of 12,000 BTUs or more usually require a 230-V circuit.

Installing Central Air-Conditioning Systems

Central air-conditioning units and their ducts can be installed easiest when a building is under construction. The large ducts can be installed without having to tear

Fig. 6–42 Room air-conditioning unit installed in double-hung window.

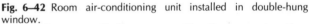

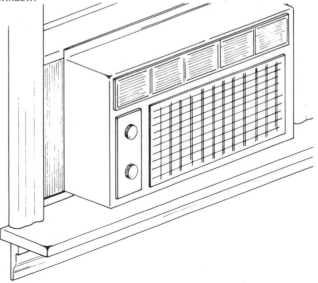

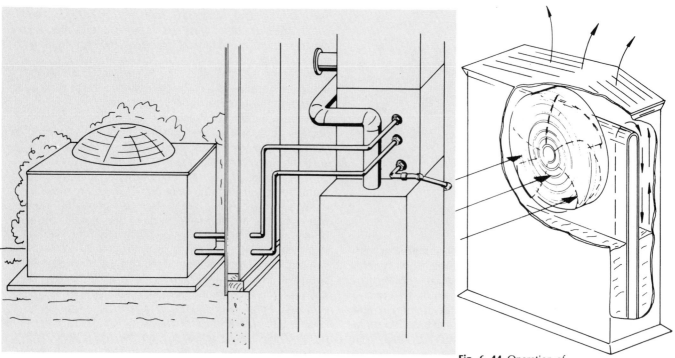

Fig. 6–43 Split air-conditioning system.

Fig. 6–44 Operation of evaporating-type humidifier.

open walls and ceilings. Installing central air conditioning in older houses is difficult and expensive unless there is a system of large ducts for a warm-air heating system, or the house is on one level. Units can be installed that use the ducts and blower of an existing warm-air system, or an independent blower can be added. Dampers are used to close off the section of the duct system not being used, the heating section or the cooling section. Single-level houses with accessible basements or attics can have central air-conditioning systems installed with relatively short supply ducts. Compact units are available that will fit into either partial basements or small attic spaces.

Like room units, central cooling units cool inside air with refrigerated coils. The air is also cleaned and its moisture content reduced before it is sent through the ducts. In a split unit, liquid refrigerant vaporized by heat from the inside air flows through tubing to the outside compressor and condenser, where the heat is transferred to the outside air and the refrigerant is condensed (Fig. 6–43). Locating the compressor and condenser outside the house reduces noise from the system and provides an unobstructed space for the transfer of heat outside.

Maintenance and Repair

Air-conditioning units will require less professional maintenance if filters and grilles are kept clean and the voltage in the supply circuit is kept close to the specifications. Variations in voltage, from the load of other utilities on the same circuit, or from local voltage variations, will damage the motors. Instructions for maintenance that accompany each particular unit should be followed to obtain maximum efficiency from the system.

CONTROLLING HUMIDITY

Too much or too little moisture in the air creates a host of problems. During winter, the heating system may dry inside air to a relative humidity of less than thirty percent. This causes rapid evaporation, which can dry the nose, throat, and eyes to the point of discomfort. Dry air also makes the temperature seem lower than it actually is. It causes wooden furniture to dry out and sometimes crack at joints and weak points. The air itself reacts by allowing static electricity to build up.

During hot, humid periods, inside air may carry enough moisture to reach a relative humidity of eighty percent or more. This reduces evaporation from the skin, making the air seem sticky and temperature higher than it actually is. The moisture encourages mildew and mold to grow in unventilated spaces, and causes wooden doors and windows to swell and stick. Moisture condenses on cold-water pipes and toilets, and may cause water stains.

Humidifiers

Humidifiers can add moisture to the air either through existing ducts or directly to the surrounding space. Furnace-mounted humidifiers attached to the plenum add moisture to forced warm air. An automatic humidity control maintains the relative humidity of the air in the warm-air supply ducts at the desired percentage. Independent humidifiers supply moisture directly to the surrounding air. Permanent units with automatic water supplies can be installed to provide enough moisture to raise the humidity in large spaces. For smaller areas, movable units can be set up in a central location in the house during winter to counter the drying effect of the heating system.

Humidifiers operate by either evaporating or atomizing water so that it can be absorbed and carried in the air. In the evaporation type of humidifiers, a fan flows dry air through a water-saturated pad or belt (Fig. 6–44). The moisture evaporates and is carried away by the moving air.

The capacity of a humidifier is expressed as the number of gallons of water it can add to the air in 24 hrs. (at 75°F and 30 per cent relative humidity). A medium-sized humidifier can add 10 gal. or more a day. The humidifier should be large enough to keep the relative humidity over 30 per cent during the winter. Controls on the humidifer automatically govern the amount of water transferred. A *humidistat* measures the relative humidity and turns the fan on and off to maintain the desired humidity. Most fans have two or more speeds to vary the rate of moisture flow into the air.

Units that combine a humidifier and an electronic air cleaner are quite expensive. The air cleaner removes pollen, smoke particles, dust, and other pollutants unaffected by filters in warm-air systems. Electrostatic filters, which are much more effective than mechanical filters, remove 85 to 95 per cent of the pollutants in the air.

Dehumidifiers

By removing moisture from warm, humid air, dehumidifiers reduce condensation problems and make the air feel more comfortable. Moisture is removed from the air by a fan, which blows across refrigerated coils (Fig. 6–45). Water dripping from the coils is collected in a pan, which can be drained automatically or by hand.

Dehumidifiers are rated by the number of pints of water they remove from the air in 24 hr. (at 80°F and 60 percent relative humidity). A medium-size, portable dehumidifier can remove 20 to 30 pints of water a day. This can reduce the relative humidity into the winter range of 30 to 50 percent. The air temperature must be at least 65 to 70°F for the humidifier to operate.

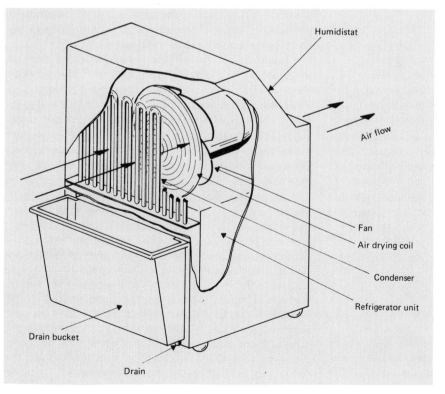

Humidistat

Air flow

Fan

Air drying coil

Condenser

Refrigerator unit

Drain bucket

Drain

Fig. 6–45 Operation of a dehumidifier.

7 Windows and Doors

Repairs to windows and doors require more willingness to diagnose problems and employ common sense than skill in carpentry. Broken sash cords are awkward to replace, for example, but it isn't difficult to figure out how to do it. Although sticking windows and doors might call for sandpapering or planing, they can often be repaired by cutting a paint seal or tightening hinges.

Those with more ambition can take on more complicated tasks such as installing new windows and doors. You will need advice from a supplier, a little information from the following pages, and a great deal of persistence (especially the first time).

TYPES OF WINDOWS

Windows differ principally in the methods of fastening and opening. *Double-hung windows* are held in place by wooden strips so that they can slide up and down. *Casement windows* are fastened to window frames by hinges and are cranked open by a sliding arm or an arm attached to a worm gear. *Sliding windows* slide horizontally in tracks built into the frames. These are the main types of windows used in both older and modern houses and in apartment buildings. Most specialized types of windows such as jalousie and awning windows operate in a similar manner. In colder regions, storm windows (as described later in this chapter) are often fastened over the window frames to insulate the inner sashes.

DOUBLE-HUNG WINDOWS

A double-hung window consists of an upper sash and a lower sash, and a frame in which the sashes slide vertically (Fig. 7–1). The sashes themselves consist of horizontal *top* and *bottom rails* and vertical slide pieces called *stiles*. If there is more than one pane of glass, they are separated by narrow strips called *mullions* or *muntin bars*. Both sashes are held in their channels by vertical strips of wood. The lower sash is held on the inside of the window by a flat piece of molding called an *inside stop*. The thin vertical strip that separates the lower and upper sashes is called a *parting strip*. The strip that holds the upper sash from the outside is called the *blind stop*.

The window frame is made up of side jambs on the sides, a head jamb at the top, and a sill and stool at the bottom, together with the stops and sash mechanisms. The side jambs, when fitted with stops and parting strips, form vertical channels for the sashes. The horizontal piece at the bottom of the frame which extends into the room is called the *stool*. It is fastened to the *sill* which slops downward to the outside. Together, the stool and sill form a ledge that encloses the bottom rail of the lower sash.

Double-hung windows can be opened from either the top or bottom by sliding the appropriate sash. The sashes are kept open by either sash weights or a spring balance. With a sash-weight balance, a sash cord or chain attached to the side of the stiles extends upward along the channel, over a pulley, and into an enclosed box-like compartment where it is attached to the sash weight. With a spring balance, metal tubes enclosing a spring and twist rod extend vertically along the channels.

Remember that windows in particular are undergoing revolutionary changes. Among the developments that make window buying a challenging experience is low-emission—"Low-E"—glass, a generic term that indicates the presence of an atom-thin layer of metal oxide that blocks the emission of radiant heat.

In cooler or cold climates at least half the heat loss through windows from a warmer interior to a colder exterior is due to a radiant effect. Low-E glass prevents the escape of costly heat in this way, approximately doubling the insular value of a window. The metal oxide layer cannot stop convection and conduction, two other sources of heat loss, but it does make a big difference where radiant loss is concerned.

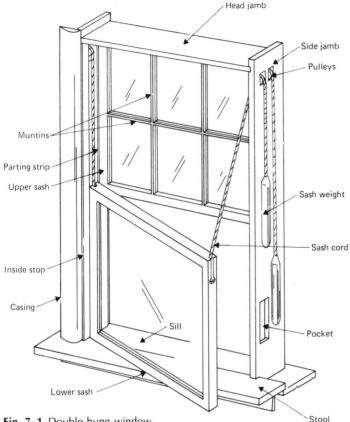

Fig. 7–1 Double-hung window.

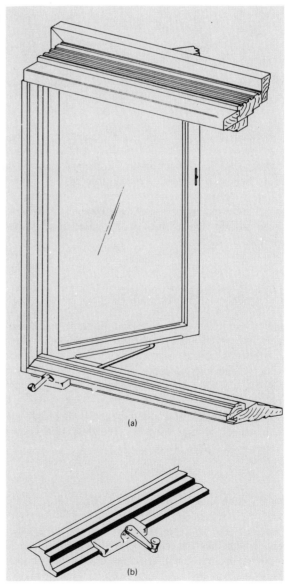

Fig. 7–2 Casement window: a) sash and frame, b) worm gear.

Various companies have begun to produce Low-E glass for use in the Sunbelt. Unlike the greyish cast of the Low-E glass sold in cooler regions, the warm-climate glass has a bronze tint. It ensures maximum savings on air-conditioning bills when used in conjunction with shutters, awnings, or landscaping.

A cold-weather Low-E window lets in almost as much light as ordinary double-pane glass. Also, because it blocks interior heat that is trying to escape, the area close to the window remains warmer than it would otherwise be. On cold nights less condensation forms on the Low-E window, meaning fewer puddles on the sills in the morning.

CASEMENT WINDOWS

Casement windows consist of one or more sashes that are hinged on one side and mounted in a frame (Fig. 7–2). The sashes are opened outward by an arm, which either slides or is cranked by a gear mounting on the frame. Like other windows, each sash may have one large pane of glass or several smaller panes separated by muntin bars. In wooden casements, glazier's points hold the glass in place and are covered with the glazing compound that seals in the glass.

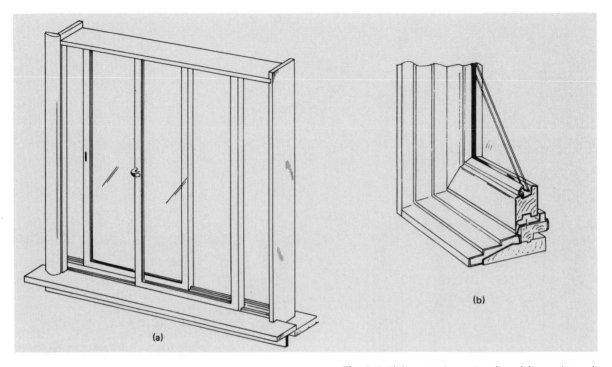

Fig. 7–3 Sliding window: a) sash and frame, b) track.

Metal casements use spring clips instead of glazier's points. Some types, however, are constructed with the glass clamped between metal strips and protected by rubber seals. Good-quality casement windows are made with precision so that the sash will fit the frame snugly when the window is closed.

SLIDING WINDOWS

Sliding windows work somewhat the same as double-hung windows would if they were installed sideways. The main difference is that sashes in sliding windows ride on horizontal tracks built into the upper and lower sections of the frame (Fig. 7–3). Some sashes have rollers built into the frame so that they can ride more smoothly. Although some sliding windows are made of wood, most are made of lighter aluminum, especially large windows. The glass is held in place in sashes by a tightly fitting rubber gasket.

SPECIALIZED WINDOWS

Jalousie windows consist of a series of horizontal glass louvers, which overlap when closed (Fig. 7–4). They are mounted in a frame so that a single cranking mechanism will cause each unit to pivot and open to a flat position. Since

they cannot be made airtight, they are more practical in moderate climates or in spaces that do not have to be heated or cooled. *Picture windows* are permanently fixed in their frames and must be supplemented by some other type of window, such as an awning window, for ventilation. *Awning windows* have sashes that are hinged on the top so that they can swing out from the bottom to permit ventilation even during rainy weather (Fig. 7–5). They are often mounted under picture windows as part of the unit.

COMMON REPAIRS

REPLACING GLASS

Glazed Windows

Repairing broken glass involves removing old glass and putty, preparing a new bedding, and installing the new glass. Small panes can be replaced with the sash in place but large panes are easier to handle if the sash is removed and placed on a table or workbench. The remaining pieces of glass should be removed (with gloved hands) starting at the top of the sash. If the pieces are difficult to pull out, wiggle them, and pry under the putty with a putty knife until the glass

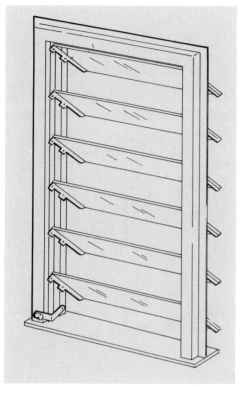

Fig. 7–4 Jalousie window.

Fig. 7–5 Awning window.

comes loose. Where the putty is too hard to pry loose, it can be softened with heat from a soldering iron or propane torch. All of the old putty and glazier's points (spring clips on metal windows) should be removed and the wood scraped and sanded, if necessary (Fig. 7–6(a)). Coat the cleaned surfaces with linseed oil or a primer to prevent them from absorbing oil from the new putty or *glazing compound*. (Glazing compound will remain more elastic than putty, though either can be used.) Before installing the new glass, line the groove with a bedding of glazing compound about ⅛ in. thick, to act as a seat for the new glass (Fig. 7–6(b)). The pane should be cut ⅛ in. smaller than the size of the opening and pressed lightly into the bedding. Insert glazier's points every 4 in. along the edges of large panes, and use at least two on each side for small panes of glass. (Spring clips should be placed in the holes in metal sashes.) Push or tap the points about halfway into the wood so they can hold the glass tightly against the sash. To seal the outside, a thick bead of glazing compound or putty should be run around the edge of the glass and pressed into place with the fingers (Fig. 7–6(c)). Use a putty knife to press the compound into a triangular shape by sliding the knife forcefully along the bead (Fig. 7–6(d)). The outer edge of the glazing compound should be flush with the outer edge of the sash. The inner edge should be the same height as the sash on the inside of the glass. When the glazing has dried for a few

days, paint it, to seal out moisture and to keep it from cracking. The paint should extend 1/16 in. or so beyond the glazing onto the glass in order to prevent water from getting between them. Normally, broken windows are replaced with ordinary, single-strength window glass. However, if a window is located where it is likely to be broken frequently or where broken glass would be especially dangerous (as in a stormdoor or in a childrens' play area), the broken glass should be replaced with a transparent acrylic panel or tempered glass.

Rubber Seals and Gaskets in Metal Windows

Some types of metal casement windows use metal strips rather than glazing to hold glass in place. The strips can usually be removed by unscrewing the machine screws that hold them. If the gasket is intact, the new glass (⅛ in. smaller than the opening) can be pressed into position and the strips replaced.

Sliding windows and a few other types of metal windows may use a rubber gasket to hold the glass and to seal the fitting. The sash on a sliding window must be taken apart to remove broken glass. In some cases, the sash may be constructed in such a way that it will have to be repaired by a professional who has the necessary tools and knowledge.

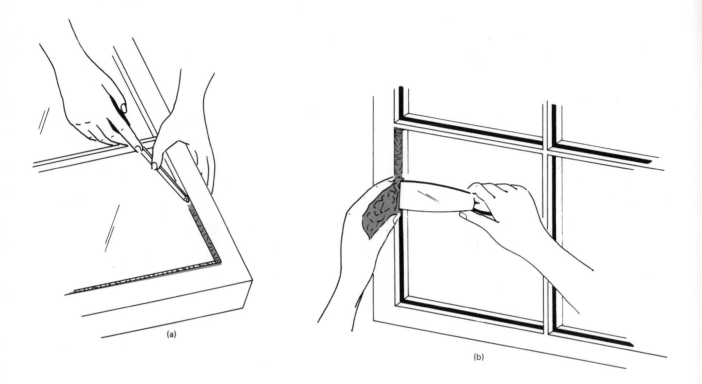

(a)

(b)

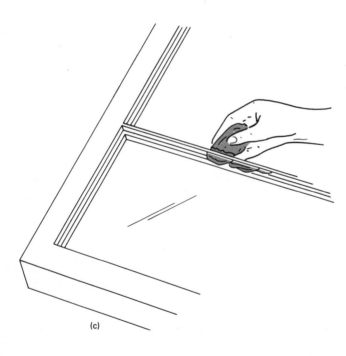

(c)

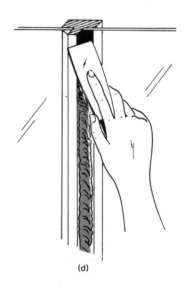

(d)

Fig. 7–6 Replacing broken glass: a) removing old putty, b) applying a bed of glazing compound, c) applying a seal of glazing compound, d) beveling the compound.

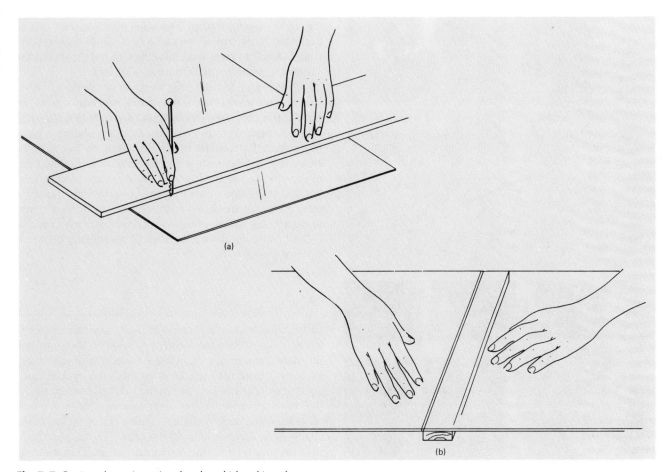

Fig. 7–7 Cutting glass: a) scoring the glass, b) breaking glass over a straightedge.

Cutting Glass

Cutting glass accurately and cleanly comes with practice and requires a sharp glass cutter. Place the glass on a padded, flat surface where there is adequate room to work. To reduce chipping, wipe the area to be cut with turpentine or a light oil. Using a wide straightedge as a guide, draw the glass cutter along the glass with a single, even stroke (Fig. 7–7(a)). If the stroke is too light, it won't score the glass. If it is too heavy, it will chip the glass. Don't go over the scored line a second time. A sharp cutter that is properly used will make a uniform line without skips on the first stroke.

The edges must be bent away from the scored side of the glass in order to break it. One method is to extend the scored section beyond the edge of a table and tap the underside with the knob end of the glass cutter. The glass should break along the scored line. Glass can be broken in various other ways, such as placing the scored line just over the edge of a straightedge (Fig. 7–7(b)) or dowel pressing down carefully.

DOUBLE-HUNG WINDOWS

Stuck Sashes

Sashes frequently become stuck when paint dries between them and the stops or parts of the frame. Moisture also causes binding. Occasionally, the sashes or stops will absorb enough moisture to expand and bind so that neither sash can be moved. Both of these conditions can be remedied with a few tools and patience.

Recently painted windows can often be freed by using a wide tool, such as a hatchet, to pry under the lower sash on the outside of the window (Fig. 7–8(a)). Slide the edge of the blade into the widest part of the crack under the sash and work it back and forth. If the paint is still fresh and elastic, it will give way at the joints and the sash will slide upward. If there is paint in the channels above the lower sash, the channels should be cleaned out with a chisel or other sharp tool and sanded lightly and waxed before the sash is pried up.

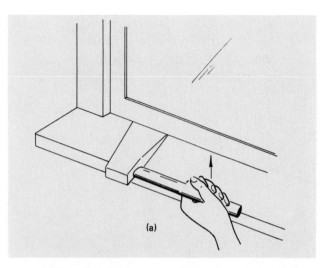

(a)

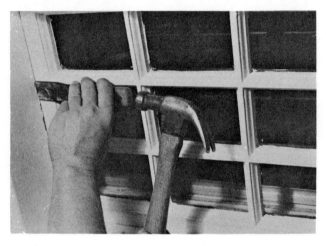

(b)

Fig. 7–8 Freeing a paint-stuck sash: a) prying the sash from the outside, b) cutting a paint seal.

Old paint must be cut with a sharp tool such as a chisel or knife to avoid chipping. Run the chisel along the joint between the sash and the inside stop, stool, parting strip, blind stop, or sill, to cut the paint whereever it binds (Fig. 7–8(b)). This should free the sash so that it can be moved. If it continues to stick, use a small block of wood and a hammer to tap against the inside face of the stiles. This may loosen the part that is sticking. The lower sash can also be pried up from the outside if necessary.

If the sashes remain stuck, the stops and parting strips may have to be removed (Fig. 7–9(a)). Inside stops are fastened with either screws or nails. Remove the inside stops so that the lower sash can be lifted out. If the upper sash is stuck, the parting strip will have to be removed also. With

the sashes out, the stops and sides of the sashes can be inspected to determine the cause of binding. If paint is the culprit, sand it down until the edges of the stops and the sashes are smooth, and rub them with wax.

Swollen sashes or *stops* must be removed to be repaired. If the inside stop or the parting strip bind against the sides of the sash, they should be sanded or lightly planed to create more clearance. When the stop is replaced, a piece of cardboard should be used as a spacer to maintain the clearance. Swollen sashes may bind against either the stops or the channels of the frame. If the stops are at fault, sand the side of the stop rather than the sash. If it's the frame, try using a wooden block and hammer to tap along the channel to expand the frame enough to accommodate the sash (Fig. 7–9(b)). Another alternative is to sand or lightly plane the sides of the sash (Fig. 7–9(c)).

Loose Sashes

Sashes may fit loosely because of poor carpentry or shrinking with age. When the loose fit is between the stops and the sashes, the stops can be repositioned closer to the sash by using a cardboard spacer to establish the desired clearance. If the poor fit is between the sides of the sashes and the channels, however, the repair is more difficult. A length of spring-type copper weatherstripping can be tacked to the channels on either side to fill the gaps. A more permanent solution would be to add a thin strip of wood to one side of the sash and finish it so that it becomes part of the sash. This would extend the sash to fit snugly between the two channels.

Replacing Sash Cords

When the problem is a broken sash cord, frozen pulley, or tangled cords or chains, the sashes have to be removed (Fig. 7–10). The process of lifting a sash out and balancing it while removing a broken cord is awkward but necessary, and becomes easier with experience. Remove the inside stops first. This may be difficult if they are fastened with nails instead of screws. Once the stops are out of the way, the lower sash can be lifted out and the knotted or nailed sash cords pulled free from the sides of the sash. If a cord is intact, hold onto it and feed it toward the pulley so that the weight lowers slowly. The box-like channel or pocket in which the weights ride up and down may be accessible through a removable wooden cover at the lower end of the frame (which was covered by the inside stop). This cover may be screwed or nailed in place. Work it loose and remove it so the weights inside the pocket are accessible. In some windows, there may be no pocket cover and the entire outer casing may have to be removed.

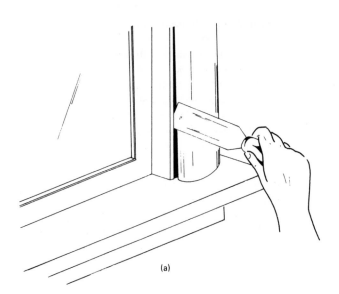

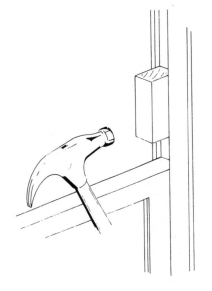

(a)

(b)

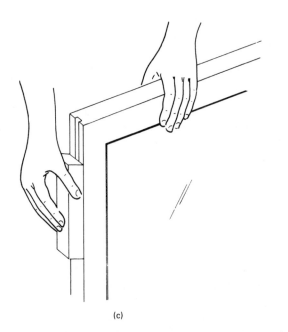

(c)

Fig. 7–9 Repairing swollen sashes and stops: a) removing the inside stop, b) using a block to expand the frame, c) sanding the side of a sash.

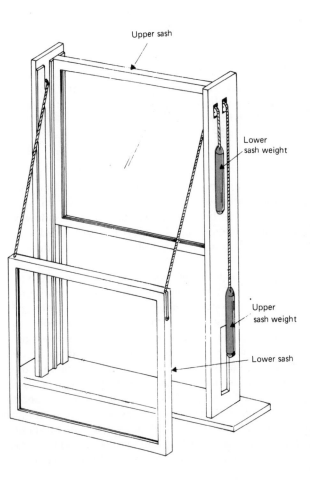

Upper sash

Lower sash weight

Upper sash weight

Lower sash

Fig. 7–10 Operation of sash cords and chains.

A new sash cord can be installed by feeding it through the pulley (use a piece of string weighted on one end to pull the cord if necessary), tying it to the sash weight, and cutting the other end so that it can be knotted and attached to the side of the sash. The cord should be cut long enough so that the weight is just below the pulley when the lower sash is closed. For the upper sash, the weight should be just above the base of the pocket when the sash is raised all the way. The upper sash can be removed only after the lower sash has been taken out and the parting strip removed.

A long-lasting sash chain can be used to replace a broken sash cord. It is fastened to the weight by winding a short piece of wire around the chain after it has been run through the hole in the top of the sash weight.

Tangled sash cords can be straightened out when the weights are accessible. Tangling may be caused by cords that are cut too long or obstructed inside the pocket.

Frozen pulleys often can be loosened with penetrating oil. If they are too badly rusted or if they are broken, the pulleys should be removed by taking out the screws holding them in place and prying them free. The sash has to be removed in order to thread the cord or chain through the new pulley.

CASEMENT WINDOWS

Like double-hung windows, casement windows may become stuck with paint, swollen in their frames, or warped. They may also have the additional problems of loose hinges and jammed operating mechanisms.

Sashes

A new coat of paint may seep into the joints between the sash and window frame. If the paint is fresh, the seal can sometimes be broken by pushing on the window while cranking it open. If this doesn't work, the painted joint can be broken by using a sharp knife or chisel to cut through the paint.

When unprotected wooden sashes are exposed to rain or heavy moisture, they tend to absorb the moisture and swell. If a sash swells enough, it will no longer fit the frame. Before anything is done, the wood must be dried out. A closed sash will dry out in time if the air is warm and not too moist. A sash that is swollen so that it cannot be closed should be covered with plastic on the outside to protect it from rain while it has a chance to dry. If the sash binds when dry, locate the section that is causing the trouble and sand it with a sanding block. If more wood has to be removed, take the sash out and use a plane. A wooden sash should be coated with a finish to protect it against moisture. Use a wood preservative, sealer, varnish, polyurethane, paint, or

whatever finish fits in with the rest of the interior, provided only that it is waterproof.

When sashes become warped, they won't seat properly in their frames. If this occurs when the sash is wet, try closing the window, nailing a block to the frame, and using a wedge to force the warped part back against the frame. As the sash dries, it may resume its proper shape. If it remains permanently warped, the best solution is to replace it.

Hinges

As windows are opened and closed over a period of time, the screws holding the hinges tend to loosen. The hinges pull away from the frame or sash, and the sash sags and fails to fit. If the screw holes are still sound, tightening the screws will pull the sash back into position. If the wood around the holes has been chewed up, the holes can be refilled, or longer screws can be used. Try longer screws first. If they won't take a firm grip, the old screw holes should be filled with short slivers of wood, match sticks, or toothpicks coated with adhesive so that they will pack tightly. Pound them in, let the adhesive dry, and cut off the protruding ends with a sharp chisel. Longer screws can now be used in the same location. The new wood will hold the screws.

Where a hinge is recessed too much, it can be shimmed out. Remove the hinge and place a few thin layers of cardboard or thin sheet metal directly under it. When the hinge is replaced, it will force the adjacent section of the sash out far enough to correct for a slight sag. This method will work only if there is adequate space between the frame and sash for the window to close.

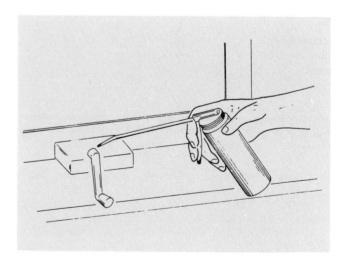

Fig. 7–11 Lubricating the crank mechanism on a casement window.

Opening Mechanisms

Opening mechanisms suffer from dirt, rust, and wear like any other moving, metal parts. Dirt or paint that obstructs any of the external parts should be scraped out. For example, channels in a sliding type of opening device clogged with caked dirt should be cleaned out. Metal surfaces that slide against each other should be coated with wax or petroleum jelly. Gear mechanisms may need only a little light lubricating oil or graphite to make them operate smoothly (Fig. 7–11). If this isn't enough, the mechanism can be removed for inspection so that the gears are visible. Use a wire and brush to clean away caked grease or rust, and apply fresh grease or petroleum jelly to the gears. If the gears or other critical parts are badly worn or damaged, the unit should be replaced with a unit that has the same arm reach and other dimensions.

SLIDING WINDOWS

The most serious cause of jamming in sliding windows is damaged tracks or rollers. To inspect the sliding mechanism, lift the sash off its track and remove it from the frame. When the sides of a metal track are bent, the sash will bind or slide with difficulty. This can be corrected, by straightening the sides. Use a wooden block a little smaller than the width of the track as a backing, and tap the bent section with a wooden mallet or hammer until the side is reasonably straight (Fig. 7–12). It's more difficult to hammer outward from the inside of the track, but a small wooden block can be used to make it easier. Broken sections of wooden tracks can sometimes be repaired with adhesive and sanded back to shape. Tracks that jam because of paint or caked dirt and grease should be scraped, cleaned, or sanded as necessary and lubricated with wax.

Rollers may fail to turn smoothly because of dirt and accumulated grease. Clean off the offending substance and lubricate the rollers with graphite. Occasionally a roller will break. Since the rollers are built into the sash, the repair should be turned over to a window repair shop.

If paint causes the window to jam, it should be cut with a sharp tool along the joints between the sash and the frame. Don't try to force the window by prying, or the frame, track, or sash may be damaged.

STORM WINDOWS

Besides insulating against heat and cold, storm windows protect sashes from the weather, prevent condensation on the inside glass, and reduce the volume of noise entering from the outside. Without storm windows, rain and snow

Fig. 7–12 Straightening bent metal track.

eventually break down the paint on the sashes, enter the joints and cracks, and start rotting the wood. Joints become loose and the sashes start to come apart. The sun contributes by drying out the wood, which cracks as it shrinks. Without storm windows, condensation occurs when warm, moist inside air flows against the glass cooled by cold outside air. The condensate collects on the bottom rails, where it causes the paint to peel and the wood to rot. Outside noise passes readily through single thickness of glass but is substantially reduced by storm windows enclosing a dead-air space.

WOODEN SASHES

Wooden sashes need to be kept in good repair or they will deteriorate rapidly and provide little insulation. Joints that start to come apart should be pulled together and mended with flat corner braces and adhesive. A more permanent repair can be made by drilling pilot holes and inserting long wood screws to hold the joint together. If there is loose putty, it should be removed and replaced with fresh glazing compound to keep the glass air and water tight. Broken or damaged fasteners and hangers should be straightened or replaced. If a wooden storm window doesn't fit tightly on the casing, the edges should be weatherstripped or caulked for the season.

ALUMINUM WINDOWS

Aluminum storm windows have the advantage of having frames that can be caulked since they remain permanently in place. If the frame fits the opening and is properly caulked under the edges when it is installed, no water or air can pass between the house and the aluminum.

Although aluminum storm windows are more permanent than wooden storm windows, they need to be repaired

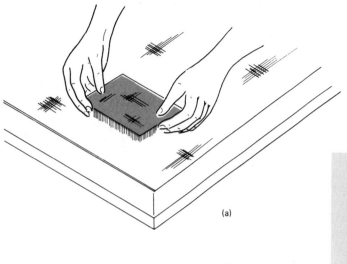

(a)

(b)

Fig. 7–13 Patching screens: a) repairing a large hole, b) darning a patch over a small hole.

from time to time, especially if they were not installed squarely. If the sides of the frame are too wide or too close together when the frame is installed, the sashes will be either too loose or too tight. Sides that are only a little tight can be widened slightly by tapping them apart with a wooden block and a hammer. Otherwise, the frame should be removed and repositioned for the proper fit. Caulking between the aluminum frame and window casing may dry out or loosen after a while. Old caulking should be cleaned out and a bead of fresh caulking applied along the edge of the frame. Screws holding the corner joints sometimes become loose and should be checked and tightened periodically. Damaged latches are difficult to remove and should be repaired by a window repair shop.

SCREENS

Screening, rather than the frame, is usually the first part of a screen that has to be repaired. Small holes can be repaired or patched but the screening should be replaced if there are rips or large holes. New screening is available in plastic, fiber glass, aluminum, copper, bronze, and steel. Of these, plastic, fiber glass, and aluminum require the least care.

PATCHING AND REPAIRING SCREENS

Strands that are not broken but just pushed apart can be realigned with any sharp-pointed instrument. Even if a few strands are broken, they can be pushed back and held in place with a coat of shellac, varnish, or clear nail polish.

Plastic screening can be repaired by using plastic adhesive to attach a small piece of plastic mesh over the hole.

Metal screening should be repaired with patches made of the same type of wire as the screen. These can be cut from scrap screening or purchased ready-cut in packages. One method of attaching a patch is to bend the wires around the edges and insert them through the mesh around the hole. First, remove a few strands of cross wires on each side of the patch and bend the remaining tips perpendicular. Place the patch over the hold and push the tips through the mesh (Fig. 7–13(a)). To hold it in place, bend the tips back over the patch and trim them if they are too long. When the

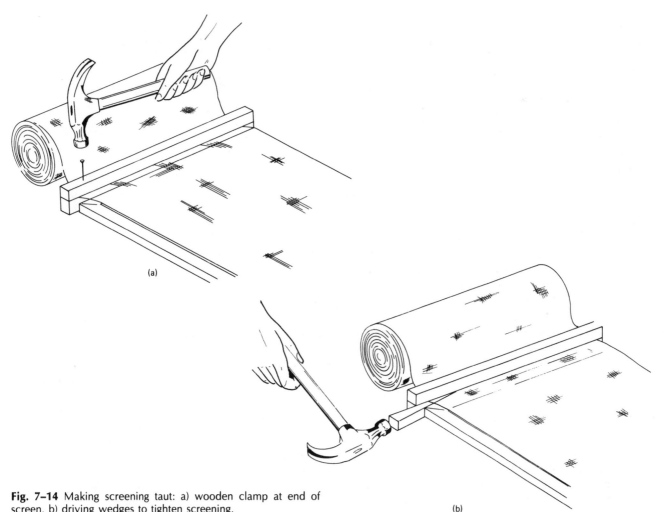

(a)

(b)

Fig. 7–14 Making screening taut: a) wooden clamp at end of screen, b) driving wedges to tighten screening.

patch has weathered a little, it will tend to blend into the screening.

Patches from plastic or metal screening can be fastened by weaving several strands of wire along the edges. The patch should be large enough to extend an inch or two beyond the hold on each side. With the patch flush over the hole, weave the strands through the patch and screening (Fig. 7–13(b)). The tighter the weave, the tighter the patch will be.

REPLACING SCREENING

The most difficult part of replacing screening is keeping the screening square and taut. Aluminum frames are simpler to work with than wooden frames because the screening is held in a channel around the perimeter by a plastic or metal spline. Screening in wooden frames must be stretched as it is installed and tacked or stapled so that the stresses are even.

Wooden Frames

Old molding must be removed carefully so it can be used to hold the new screening. Before prying the molding loose, use a sharp knife to cut the layer of paint where the molding joins the frame. A flat tool, such as a putty knife, can be worked under the center of each section of molding to pry it up, beginning at the center and moving toward the ends. Pry next to each brad in order not to split the molding. Remove the brads or staples holding the screening to the frame.

The replacement screening should be large enough to extend an inch beyond the edge of the molding. Draw a chalk line along one side of the frame parallel to the edge to serve as a guideline. With the edge of the screening on the line, tack the screening to the frame along one end only. The screening must be stretched taut before it can be attached anywhere else. There are several ways to do this. One way is to construct a clamp. To do this, place the frame on a workbench and nail a 1 X 2-in. strip of wood to the bench close to the end of the frame. Pull the screening evenly over this strip and nail a second strip over the first, clamping the screening between them (Fig. 7–14(a)). The screening is stretched by driving narrow wedges between the wooden strips and the top of the frame (Fig. 7–14(b)).

As the frame is forced away from the wooden strips, the screening pulls taut, and can be tacked or stapled to the end of the frame next to the wooden strips. Once the ends of the screening are fastened tightly to the frame, the wedges can be removed and the wooden strips dismantled. The sides of the screening should be pulled taut by hand and tacked along the sides of the frame. When the sides are completely fastened, tack the screening to the center rail. Cut off the excess along the edges with a utility knife or tin snips, and tack the old molding back in place. After filling the brad holes with plastic wood, paint the entire frame and molding, to keep moisture from entering the joints and causing the wood to swell.

Aluminum Frames

Screening is held in place in aluminum frames by a flexible plastic or metal spline, which forces the edge of the screening into a narrow channel. Damaged screening can be removed by prying the spline loose. Special tools designed to force screening and spline into the channel should be used to repair screens with aluminum frames. The replacement piece should be large enough to extend to the edges of the frame. Align the new screening so that it fits squarely. Fasten one side by inserting the spline while keeping the screening carefully aligned (Fig. 7–15). At the end of the channel, bend the spline around the corner and continue fastening the screening while holding it taut and square. The excess screening that extends beyond the spline can be trimmed either before or after the spline is forced into the channel.

CARE OF SCREENING

Plastic, aluminum, and fiberglass screening need little care other than vacuuming or washing when it becomes dirty. Copper and bronze won't rust, but they will tarnish unless they are protected with a thin coat of exterior varnish. Galvanized-steel screening should be protected with a coat of screen paint to keep it looking new. Vacuum and wipe screens with a dry cloth after they are taken down, so they will be clean and ready to be installed in the spring.

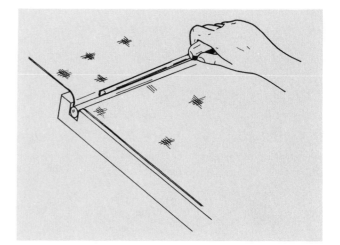

Fig. 7–15 Pressing spline into channel on aluminum frame.

REPAIRING FRAMES

Wooden frames on screens suffer the same types of damage as frames on wooden storm windows. Since screens are less rigid than storm windows, the corner joints are more likely to become loose with handling and should be reinforced. Either inside corner braces or flat corner braces can be used to strengthen corner joints after an adhesive has been worked into the opening. Screws inserted through the edge of the side piece and into the end of the rail will form an even stronger joint. Cracks along the direction of the rails or sides can be repaired in the same manner with reinforcing hardware or screws. To keep moisture out of the wood and to prevent it from swelling, all sides and edges of the frame should be painted with exterior paint. Damaged fasteners, catches, and other hardware should be straightened or replaced and screwed tightly to the frame.

INSTALLING WINDOWS

In a frame house, new windows can be installed and old windows replaced with larger windows by opening the wall and building a supporting framework of 2 X 4's (Fig. 7–16). (In a house with exterior walls of masonry, the job should be left to a professional.) Before starting, some thought should be given to the window's location, its size, and type. From the outside, the window will look best if it fits in with the style and pattern of the other windows. Either the tops or the bottoms of the windows should be aligned with each other. From the inside, the window should be located where it fits in with the other windows and doors in the room and where there are no utilities in the wall that can't be easily moved.

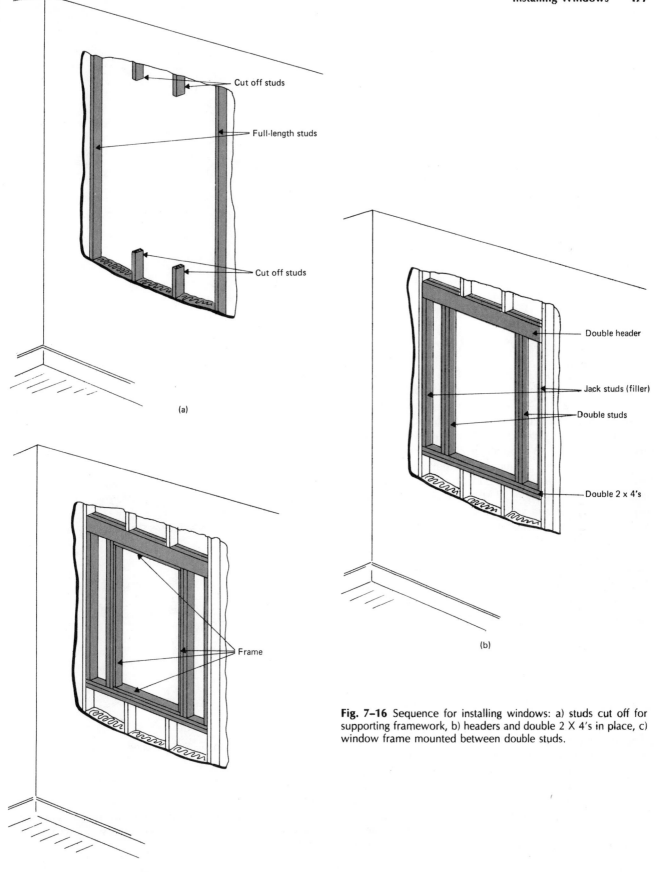

Cut off studs

Full-length studs

Cut off studs

(a)

Double header

Jack studs (filler)

Double studs

Double 2 x 4's

(b)

Frame

(c)

Fig. 7–16 Sequence for installing windows: a) studs cut off for supporting framework, b) headers and double 2 X 4's in place, c) window frame mounted between double studs.

OPENING THE WALL

The inside wall can be opened and the outside wall left intact until framing is completed, or they can both be opened at the same time. Outline the shape of the new frame on the inside wall and use a chisel, keyhole saw, saber saw, or other cutting tool to remove the gypsum board or other wall material several inches back from the outline. On the outside, bore a hole in a corner of the section to be removed and use a saber saw or reciprocating saw to cut through the siding and sheathing.

The size of the new frame determines where the studs are to be cut. Allow space for a double header, double sill plate, and shims. Cut the studs at the bottom first and then at the top.

BUILDING THE FRAMEWORK

Cut and nail in place a header made from a pair of 2 X 4's between the full-length studs on either side of the opening (Fig. 7–17). The 2 X 4's should be on edge with shims between them so that their sides are flush with the sides of the studs. (Openings wider than 48 in. require thicker headers, 2 X 6's or 2 X 8's). Similarly, cut and install a pair of 2 X 4's over the cut-off studs on the bottom so that they extend to the full-length studs on both sides of the opening (Fig. 7–18). Short sections of studs should be placed between the header and supporting 2 X 4's on the bottom and nailed to the full-length studs on both sides.

Side supports of double 2 X 4's are installed, extending from the header to the lower support, if the full-length studs are not in proper position next to the sides of the new frame. Place the side supports so that the frame will fit between them with ½ in. or so to spare for shimming. Toe-nail these side studs to the header and to the double 2 X 4's under the frame so that they are plumb.

INSTALLING THE WINDOW

Slide the window frame into the supporting framework and check it with a carpenter's level to see whether it is square. Use shims to square the frame and hold it in position temporarily. If possible, open the sash to see if the frame binds. If the window operates smoothly, nail the frame to the supporting framework on all four sides (Fig. 7–19). Gaps between the frame and supports and between studs should be filled with insulation before they are covered. The openings

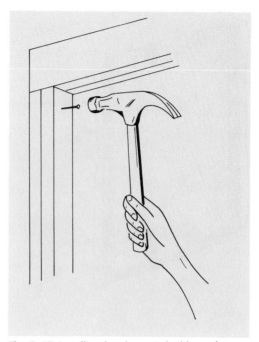

Fig. 7–17 Installing header and double studs.

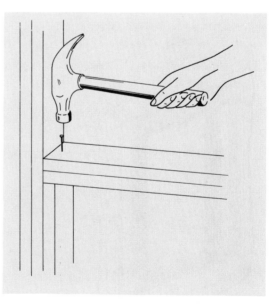

Fig. 7–18 Installing double 2 X 4's under the frame.

on the inside and outside should be covered with gypsum board, sheathing, and siding before the trim is installed. Follow the style of the trim on the other windows for uniformity.

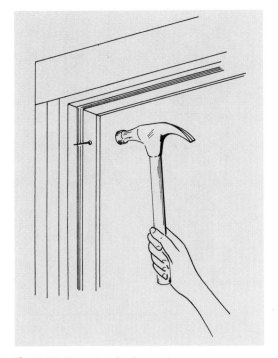

Fig. 7–19 Fastening the frame to the supports.

REPAIRING DOORS

Because they are frequently opened and closed, doors take more of a battering than windows do. Their hinges, tracks, and latching and locking mechanisms wear and break down, and have to be repaired. Exterior doors stick and won't latch properly.

Most doors are either hinged or slide on tracks. Exterior doors are generally made of solid wood or are constructed with panels. Interior doors are more likely to have hollow cores, though some styles have panels. These, as well as folding doors, swinging doors, and other kinds of doors, move on hinges. Closet doors, sliding glass doors, overhead garage doors, and some types of specialized doors use tracks as supports and guides for opening and closing.

The homeowner can repair many of the more common problems afflicting doors. With persistence, he will also be able to install new doors, or at least replace lock hardware on old doors.

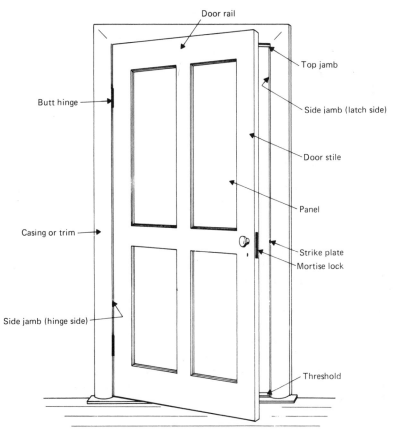

Fig. 7–20 Typical interior door, frame, and casing.

CAUSES OF STICKING

Hinged doors will bind and stick if the hinges aren't attached correctly, or if the doors or frames have changed in size or shape since they were installed. A door that is improperly hung in the first place may have a hinge set too deeply in its mortise, or not deeply enough, causing the door to sag. Even if a door has been hung correctly, it may sag if the screws in one of its hinges become loose. The entire side or end of a door may bind if it absorbs enough moisture through an unpainted area, such as an unfinished top or bottom edge. Moisture causes doors to swell until they are too large to fit the original openings. Frames that were once plumb and square are forced out of shape as floors and walls settle.

The first steps in repairing a sticking door are checks to determine where it binds and why. Look at the hinges to see if any of the screws are loose. With the door closed, check the opening between its edges and the jambs. Mark the area that binds with a pencil on the edge of the door. With the door open, use a carpenter's level to see if any sections of the frame or door are out of square (Fig. 7–20).

Binding along a short section is usually caused by loose or improperly installed hinges. Binding along long sections or an entire side results from wood swollen with moisture or from a misshapen frame. Whatever the cause, it is the door that must be adjusted to fit the frame, not the other way around.

ADJUSTING HINGES

Sagging From the Top

A top hinge that is loose or insufficiently recessed will allow a door to sag and bind against the upper section of the side jam on the latch side. (A bottom hinge that is recessed too deeply has the same effect.) Correct this by tightening the screws (Fig. 7–21) cutting a deeper mortise for the hinge (Fig. 7–22). If the screws won't grip because the screw holes are too large, fill the holes with match sticks or splinters of wood coated with adhesive, and trim the ends flush when the adhesive is dry. Drill pilot holes and install screws slightly longer than the originals. Alternatively, fill the holes with dowels by boring out the screw holes to the proper size and pounding adhesive-coated lengths of dowel in place. Trim off the dowel when the adhesive dries, and drill the pilot holes.

To cut a deeper mortise, the door has to be removed. Loose-pin hinges can be taken apart by tapping the pin with a light hammer. Put a wedge under the bottom of the door for support and remove the bottom pin first. As the pin in the top hinge is removed, the door will come loose and can be carried to the working area. Doors fastened with half-pin

Fig. 7–21 Tightening hinge screws.

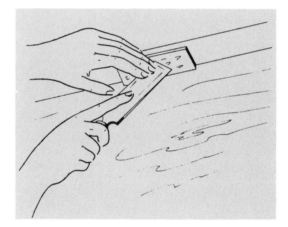

Fig. 7–22 Cutting a mortise deeper.

hinges must be lifted so that the leaves separate. Deepen the mortise by removing a thin layer of wood from the bottom with the flat side of a wood chisel. Ideally, the hinge should be flush with the edge of the door.

Sagging From the Bottom

A door will sag away from a bottom hinge that is loose or insufficiently recessed and bind against the lower part of the side jamb. Correct this condition as you would a loose top hinge. Tighten the screws, refill the screw holes and replace the screws, or deepen the mortise as required.

Sometimes sagging and binding at the bottom is caused by a top hinge that is recessed too deeply. When this appears to be the case, remove the hinge and place a hard

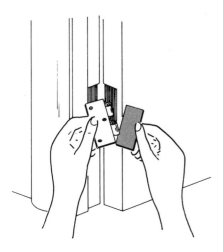

Fig. 7–23 Shimming out a hinge.

Fig. 7–24 Planing the edge of a door.

piece of cardboard cut to fill the mortise to shim out the hinge (Fig. 7–23). Two or three layers of thin cardboard or sheet metal may be necessary to shim the hinge out far enough to correct the sag.

Planing

A door that binds along an entire side or on the top or bottom is probably the victim of too much moisture or a sagging frame. Mark the edges of the door to indicate how much it has to be sanded or planed. If the top binds, the door can be left on its hinges while the top is sanded or planed. If the bottom or either side binds, the door should be removed and placed where it can be worked on. Regardless of whether it is the latch or the hinge side that binds, only the hinge side should be planed.

Use a good sized plane (such as a jack plane or a smooth plane) to keep the edge of the door straight and smooth (Fig. 7–24). When planing the top or bottom, cut from the edges toward the center to avoid splitting the ends of the side rails. When planing the sides, cut from one end to the other in the direction of the grain to prevent splitting. Sand the planed edge with a finishing-grade abrasive, and paint or seal the bare wood to prevent moisture from being absorbed.

Adjusting Latches

Mortise locks must be precisely aligned in order for the latch bolt to seat in the opening in the strike plate. If a door sags or is warped, the latch bolt will become misaligned or fail to reach the strike plate. The latch bolt won't seat if it isn't

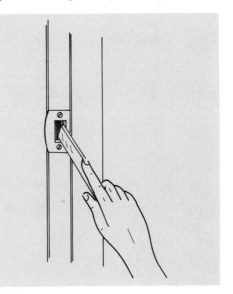

Fig. 7–25 Enlarging the opening in a strike plate.

lined up with the strike plate or if it fails to reach the opening in the plate. Misalignment is corrected by filing a larger opening in the plate (Fig. 7–25) or by elongating the mortise in the desired direction and moving the strike plate (Fig. 7–26). The gap remaining above or below the plate can be filled in with plastic wood. If the gap between the plate and latch is so wide that the bolt doesn't reach, the plate can be shimmed out with cardboard or thin sheet metal (Fig. 7–27). Sometimes the stop prevents the door from closing far enough for the bolt to seat in the strike plate. In this case, move the strike plate slightly away from the stop, or remove the stop and reposition it back farther from the strike plate.

Fig. 7–26 Moving a strike plate.

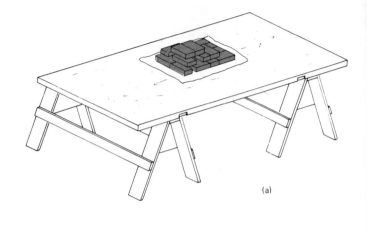

(a)

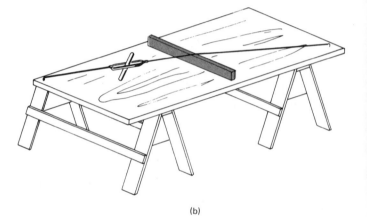

(b)

Fig. 7–28 Straightening a warped door: a) weighting a door with bricks, b) using a turnbuckle.

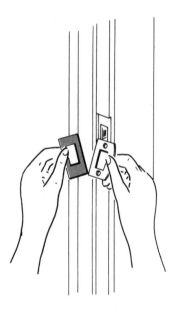

Fig. 7–27 Shimming out a strike plate.

Straightening Warped Doors

The most common cause of warping is uneven stresses in the wood and joints due to moisture. Exterior doors are particularly susceptible to warping from moisture that enters through cracked or peeling paint on the door's outside face or through an unpainted top or bottom edge. If the warp is slight, the gap between the door and stop can be covered by adjusting the weatherstripping, or sometimes by moving the stop. If the warp is severe, the door will probably have to be replaced. Moderate warps, however, can sometimes be straightened out by creating new stresses opposite to those that caused the door to warp in the first place.

A door that is warped from bottom to top as viewed from the side should be placed across end supports and weighted in the middle (Fig. 7–28(a)). Place two sawhorses, or other side supports, under each end of the door, with the convex side of the warp facing upward. Thirty to forty pounds of bricks piled on a protective cloth or paper in the center of the door will help to straighten it out. If this doesn't work, try wetting the door and weighting it rather than

Fig. 7–29 Misaligned guide for sliding door.

throwing it away. Sand the paint on both sides so the moisture can penetrate the wood, wet the door, and weigh it down over end supports.

Another method of straightening a warp is to attach a wire and turnbuckle across the warp (Fig. 7–28(b)). Attach screw eyes diagonally opposite each other at a corner on the outer limit of the warp and at a corner on the hinge side. Fasten a wire with a turnbuckle between the eyes, and slide a block of wood under the wire in the center of the warp. As the turnbuckle is tightened gradually from day to day, the wire will pull the sides of the door back toward uniform plane.

Adjusting Sliding Doors

Sliding doors must be adjusted occasionally to keep them from jamming or jumping off their tracks. Lighter doors (such as sliding closet doors) will jump off their top tracks if the guides move out of alignment or break, if screws pull loose, or the rollers break. Most of the track can be inspected without removing the doors. Align the guides if they aren't lined up parallel to the track. (Fig. 7–29) Tighten loose screws. Remove anything that obstructs the rollers. If the rollers or track appear to be broken, the door should be removed and the broken units taken to a hardware store to find a replacement.

Heavy sliding doors usually are supported by floor tracks, which can become bent or dirty from traffic through the door. The result is a sliding door that binds or jams completely. Dirt can be removed with a brush or solvent, but a bent track has to be bent back into shape or replaced. If the metal isn't too thick, a wood block and hammer can be used to pound the side of the track until it straightens out. Broken rollers are more serious and often require the attention of a shop that sells and repairs sliding doors.

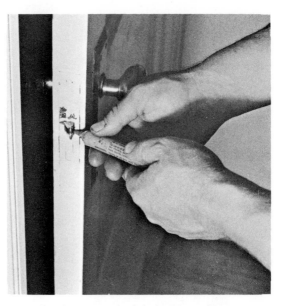

Fig. 7–30 Lubricating a latch bolt with graphite.

Lubricating Doors

Door hardware and wooden surfaces that rub against each other should be lubricated occasionally to keep a door operating smoothly. A variety of lubricants can be used: powdered graphite, silicon spray, light lubricating oil, petroleum jelly, wax or paraffin, grease sticks, and heavy grease. They each have their particular application and can cause difficulty if used in the wrong places. Oil and grease, for example, attract dust and dirt and should not be used in cylindrical lock mechanisms.

Hinges can be lubricated with graphite, silicone, or light lubricating oil. The lubricant should be applied to the pin to quiet the squeaking as the door is opened or closed. If there is rust or obstructing paint, it should be removed with a wire brush, steel wool, or paint remover, and the hinge thoroughly cleaned before it is lubricated.

Latches should be lubricated with a light oil around the edge of the latch bolt and dead bolt (Fig. 7–30). Use only graphite or silicone spray in a cylinder case and key mechanism.

Door edges that fit a little tightly against the jambs can be rubbed with paraffin to prevent them from sticking. A little paraffin or lubricant from a grease stick on the strike plate will smooth the latching process.

Spring mechanisms and pneumatic closers can be lubricated with graphite or a light oil (Fig. 7–31). Give any moving parts, including the spring, a light coat of lubricant, and wipe off the excess after working the door back and forth.

Garage door tracks should be lubricated with heavy grease. Clean out old grease that has collected grit, and

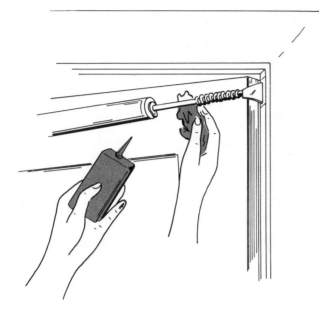

Fig. 7–31 Lubricating a pneumatic closer.

apply fresh grease to the sections next to the wheels or ballbearings. Wheels will need a squirt of light oil where they are mounted on their axles.

Door handles will turn more smoothly if a little graphite is applied to the joint where the knob rotates against the rose.

Other Types of Doors

More specialized types of doors share much of the standard hardware used on hinged and sliding doors and can be repaired in a similar manner. *Swinging doors* and *folding doors* use hinges and either spring mechanisms or tracks and rollers. Their hinges have to be adjusted, guides aligned, springs lubricated, and tracks and rollers repaired. *Storm doors* suffer the same problems as storm windows and ordinary hinged doors and can be repaired in the same ways.

Garage doors differ considerably from the other types of doors. Their overhead tracks can become loose or misaligned and must be screwed down tightly and greased. The wheels or ballbearings that ride in the tracks may start to bind if they are not lubricated with light oil. Latches and locks should be lubricated with graphite to keep them from freezing. A one-piece wooden door may absorb moisture and warp if it isn't kept painted. It may even sag in the center from its own weight. A reinforcing rod placed across the

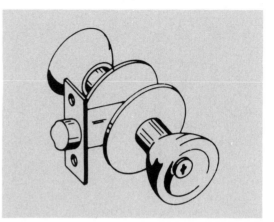

Fig. 7–32 Cylindrical lock.

door and tightened with a turnbuckle against a block wedged between the rod and door will pull the sides back to normal.

INSTALLING AND REPAIRING LOCKS

Locks have to be installed when new doors are hung or when older locks are replaced. Templates are provided with new locksets to mark the location and size of the holes and mortises that must be cut. Detailed instructions are also provided to describe how to install the lock. A brief description is given below of the steps required to install the most common types of locks: cylindrical locks, mortise locks, and auxiliary rim-type locks.

Cylindrical Locks

A cylindrical lock fits into a large hole in the face of the door and operates by either a key in the outside knob or a push button (Fig. 7–32). To install the lock, place the template at the desired height (about 36 in.) and fold it around the edge of the door. The center of the hole to be cut for the cylinder will have a standard setback of 2 ⅜ in. Mark the centers of the cylinder and latch bolt holes. Use a hole saw or brace and expansion bit to cut a 2 ⅛-in. diameter hole for cylinder (Fig. 7–33(a)). Bore a 15/16-in. diameter hole for the latchbolt as indicated by the template on the edge of the door (Fig. 7–33(b)). Slide the latchbolt into the hole so that a line can be traced around the edge of the latch plate for the mortise on the door. Use a wood chisel to remove wood to the depth of the latch plate, and smooth the bottom of the mortise so that the plate is flush with the door (Fig. 7–33(c)).

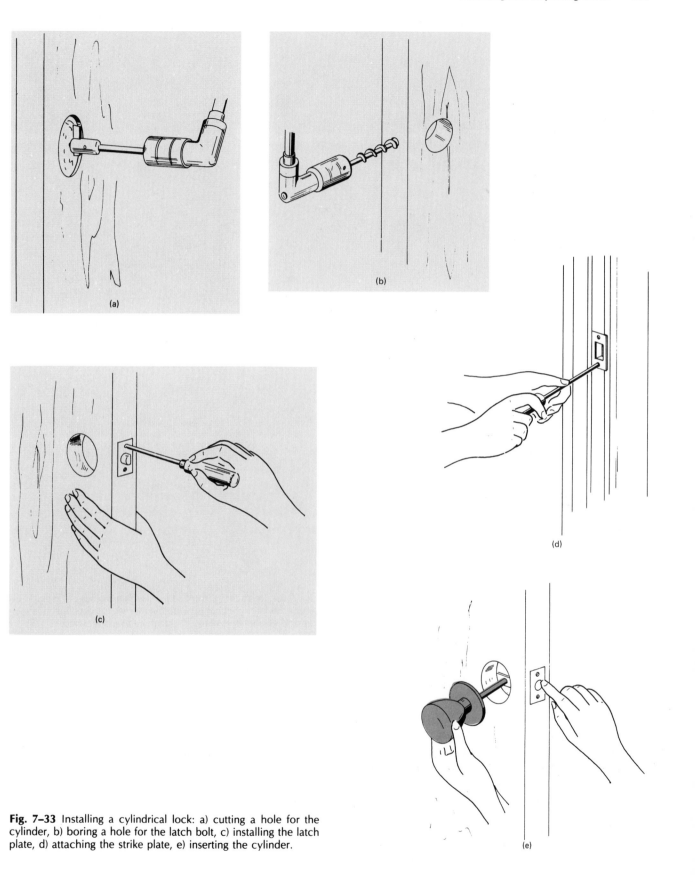

Fig. 7–33 Installing a cylindrical lock: a) cutting a hole for the cylinder, b) boring a hole for the latch bolt, c) installing the latch plate, d) attaching the strike plate, e) inserting the cylinder.

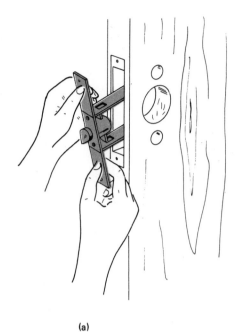

(a)

(c)

(b)

Fig. 7–34 Replacing a mortise lock with a cylindrical lock: a) inserting the latch mechanism into the mortise, b) installing the cylinder and escutcheon plate, c) attaching the strike plate.

With the latch bolt in place, mark its center on the jamb and use the template to cut a mortise for the strike plate. Drill pilot holes and attach the strike plate with screws (Fig. 7–33(d)). Insert the cylinder and knob from the outside and fit the end of the latch bolt mechanism into the cylinder (Fig. 7–33(e)). Turn the outside rose to fit the width of the door, attach the inside ring (or rose) to the door with screws, and slide the rose and inner knob into place.

Cylindrical lock kits are available with hardware to replace mortise locks and to cover the old holes. A template is used to mark and cut out the hole for the cylinder. The deep edge mortise is covered with a new latch plate (Fig. 7–34(a)), while an escutcheon plate covers the holes next to the knob. (Fig. 7–34(b)). The long strike-plate mortise is covered with a new strike plate (Fig 7–34(c)), which fits the bolt on the cylindrical lock.

Fig. 7–35 Mortise lock.

Mortise Locks

Modern mortise locks can be installed in new doors to harmonize with the style of the house (Fig. 7–35). Without professional equipment, the deep mortise has to be cut by boring a line of holes with a brace and bit (Fig. 7–36(a)). The mortise is shaped with wood chisels until the lock housing fits flush with the edge of the door. Holes must also be bored for the cylinder and the spindle (Fig. 7–36(b)). Mark the outline of the mortise for the strike plate by using a template, and remove the wood so that the plate can be installed. Once the housing, spindle, and knobs are installed (Fig. 7–36(c)) the latch should seat against the strike plate and the installation is complete.

Auxiliary Rim-Type Locks

Auxiliary or secondary locks may be used for additional security. Nightlatches and vertical-bolt locks are the most common types used. Of these, vertical-bolt locks are the strongest and most secure. Both types are mounted on the rim of the door so that their deadbolts interlock with strike plates fastened to the door jambs.

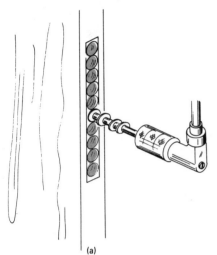

(a)

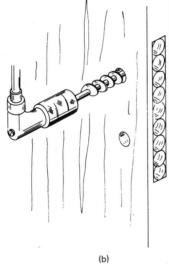

(b)

(c)

Fig. 7–36 Installing a mortise lock: a) boring out a deep mortise for the lock housing, b) boring holes for the cylinder and spindle, c) installing the lock housing.

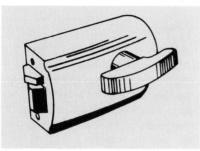

Fig. 7–37 Rim-type lock.

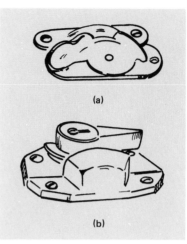

Fig. 7–38 Window locks: a) spring-held snap bolt, b) key-operated sash lock.

Nightlatches are mounted on the inside of the door with a cylinder projecting through a hole in the door from an outside plate (Fig. 7–37). Use the template to mark the location of the cylinder hole and the connecting screws. Bore the hole and attach the outer plate, the cylinder, the connecting screws, and the inside lock housing. The template will indicate where to mount the strike plate on the door jamb.

Vertical-bolt locks are installed in much the same way as nightlatches. A hole must be cut for the cylinder and strike plate, as indicated by the template. The major difference between the locks is in their operation. A vertical bolt interlocks with the unit attached to the jamb, instead of a horizontal latch or dead bolt seating within a strike plate.

WINDOWS

Sash locks can be installed to make windows secure against intruders. Most sash locks are mounted on the lower sash so that they can be locked into hardware on the upper sash

TROUBLE SHOOTING CYLINDRICAL LOCKS

MALFUNCTION	CAUSES AND REPAIRS
Key won't turn in cylinder.	• Cylinder doesn't interlock with bolt. Remove rose and rotate cylinder until it interlocks. • Tumblers may have been damaged. Replace cylinder. • Key may be a poorly ground duplicate. Use the original key.
Key turns but bolt won't move or fails to seat in strike plate.	• Bolt jammed with rust, dirt, or paint. Clean and lubricate. • Bolt not lined up with strike plate. Move strike plate as required. • Warped door causes misalignment between bolt and strike plate. Straighten door.
Key won't go into cylinder.	• Keyway blocked by dirt, ice, or other obstacle. Lubricate with graphite or silicone spray. If ice is suspected, heat key and insert to melt ice. • Key bent. Straighten key in vise, or have key duplicated.
Bolt fails to reach strike.	• Gap between jamb and edge of door too wide. If caused by door sagging, adjust hinges. If strike plate is recessed too far, shim it out.
Bolt doesn't move when key turned.	• Cylindrical lock broken or loose. Remove lock and consult locksmith.
Key broken in lock.	• Remove cylinder and force key out by inserting thin wire between cams and into keyway. If it fails to come out, consult locksmith.

or window frame. Sash locks include both spring-held snap bolts and key-operated locks. Spring-held snap bolts (Fig. 7–38(a)) are fastened to the stiles on the lower sash to hold it in position against the inside stop. The bolt slides into holes drilled in the stop to hold the sash closed or a few inches open. Key-operated sash locks (Fig. 7–38(b)) are mounted on the lower sash to prevent intruders from unfastening the lock by breaking the glass and reaching inside. Templates usually accompany these sash locks to show the homeowner how the locks should be mounted.

HANGING DOORS

Hanging a new door in an existing doorway is more complicated than it might appear. The old frame is likely to be out of square, making it necessary to trim the door odd amounts in odd places. If the hinge jamb isn't almost plumb, the door won't swing on its hinges properly. Check the side and head jambs to see how far out of square they are. If they aren't too far off, you should be able to install the door yourself; otherwise, the wisest decision is to call a carpenter.

MEASURING AND TRIMMING

Measure the vertical distances on both sides of the door frame between the threshold and head jamb and the horizontal distances between the jambs at the top, middle, and bottom of the frame. Since most frames are unlikely to be rectangular, these measurements will help in selecting a door of approximately the right size. New doors and frames are made in several standard sizes. If a door can't be purchased to fit exactly, get one a little larger than the opening so it can be trimmed to fit. In an older house, it may be possible to find a used door that matches the other doors. (Investigate local "salvage" companies.) Examine used doors carefully to see if they are warped or cracked. Hanging a door is difficult enough without having to work with a warped door.

Mark the door for trimming after it has been held up against the door frame to see where and how much it has to be trimmed. If it fits into the frame without trimming, there will be less planing and sanding (unless it's too small for the doorway). Move the door to the work area and mark it for trimming. Draw guidelines on the hingeside (if the holes are already cut for the latch) and on the top or bottom. Allow clearances between the door and the frame and threshold as follows:

Sides and top   1/16 to ⅛ in.,
Bottom   ½ to ⅞ in.,

depending whether the door opens over an uncarpeted or carpeted floor. Trimming is done with a saw, plane, or sandpaper. If the side or top has to be trimmed by more than ¼ in., tack a straight length of wood along the guideline and cut a strip off the door with a crosscut saw. If less than ¼ in. is to be trimmed, use a jackplane or sandpaper, depending on the amount of wood that has to be removed.

Fit the door into the frame for the first trial. If it is an unexpectedly good fit, use small wedges to establish the desired clearances between the frame and the door (Fig. 7–39). Usually, a door will have to be removed several times and trimmed or sanded a little more on an edge or corner before it will fit. When the clearances finally appear to be correct, remove the door and plane a bevel of about ⅛ in. along the latch edge of the door slanting toward the stop bead. This will help the door to open and close without binding on the jamb.

INSTALLING HINGES

When the door has been trimmed to fit satisfactorily, mortises can be cut and the hinges installed. If the frame doesn't already have mortises, mark the location of the hinges on the side jamb. The standard mounting is 7 in. below the top of the door and 11 in. above the floor. Modify these distances as necessary to match the hinges on the other doors in the house. Trace the hinge on the jamb so that there is a clearance of at least 3/16 in. between the side of the hinge and the stop bead.

Cut the mortises in the jamb with a wood chisel after going around the outline with the chisel or a sharp knife to prevent the wood from splitting beyond the boundary. Make a ladderlike series of cuts diagonally to the surface with the chisel. Remove these segments from the side by holding the flat side of the chisel downward and cutting along the bottom of the mortise (Fig. 7–40). Square the sides of the mortise so the hinge will fit in flush with the edge of the door. Mount the hinges by drilling pilot holes and fastening them with screws.

Mortises in the door are cut after the hinges are mounted on the frame so that their exact locations can be marked on the door. Wedge the door into position, and mark the door at the top and bottom of both hinges (Fig. 7–41). Remove the door and use a combination square and single butt to outline the boundaries of the mortise (Fig. 7–42). There should be a clearance of about 3/16 in. between the side of the hinge and the side of the door facing the stop bead (Fig. 7–43). For general guidance, look at the way the hinges are installed on the other doors. Use a chisel to cut the mortises in the door in the same manner as the mortises were cut in the jambs (Fig. 7–44).

Fasten the hinges to the door so that they are flush with the surface. The door is now ready for hanging.

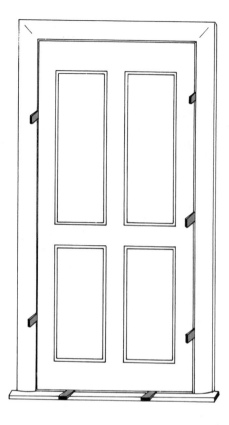

Fig. 7–39 Wedging a door into position.

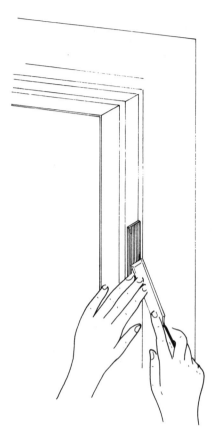

Fig. 7–40 Cutting a mortise in the side jamb.

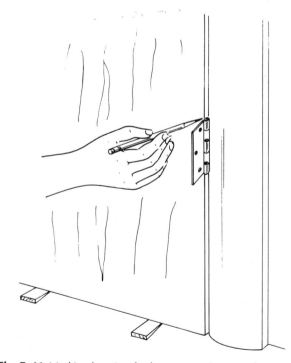

Fig. 7–41 Marking location for bottom mortise on a door.

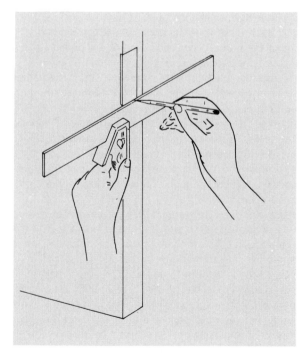

Fig. 7–42 Outlining the mortise.

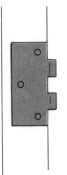

Fig. 7–43 Location of butt for proper clearance.

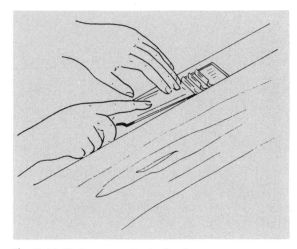

Fig. 7–44 Cutting a mortise in the door.

HANGING

A door with loose-pin hinges is easier to hang than one with half-pin hinges. With *loose-pin hinges,* the door can be fitted into the frame and positioned (with the help of wedges underneath it) so that the butts interlock. Slip the pin in the top hinge first and wiggle the door and tap the pin to work it into place. Insert the pin in the lower hinge in the same way.

Doors with *half-pin hinges* are hung by raising the door high enough for the pin in one butt to enter the other. Both the top and bottom hinges have to be aligned at the same time for the pins to slide into place.

If something has gone awry and the butts won't line up with each other, the butts on either the jamb or door will have to be moved. Mark the amount the butts have to be moved and remove the door and hinges. Extend the mortise and fill in the unused section with plastic wood. Reattach the butts so they will line up with their counterparts.

Adjust the fit of the door in the frame by marking any points that bind when the door is opened and closed. Areas on the top and latch side can be sanded without removing the door. If the hinge edge binds or there isn't enough clearance above the threshold, remove the door and plane or sand it a little more. Don't remove any appreciable amount of wood from the latch side if the holes for the latch are already cut. Trim the hinge side of the door instead.

Finishing Touches

Once the door is definitely in position and swings on its hinges without binding, the holes and mortises for the lock can be cut. Follow the instructions accompanying the lock and the steps described earlier to install the unit. Other accessories, such as mail slots and viewing tubes in exterior doors, can also be installed at this time.

The door can be primed and painted either before or after the lock mechanism and accessories are installed. Both the top and bottom edges should be painted or sealed to prevent the wood from absorbing moisture and swelling.

INSTALLING DOORS

A new door can be installed in a wall by cutting an opening for the frame and nailing in additional supporting studs and a header to frame the doorway. Before starting, check to see if there are electric wires, pipes, tubing, or other utilities in the wall where the door is to be placed. Walls below or next to bathrooms, laundries, or kitchens are likely to contain pipes and tubing. Electrical outlets, switches, and lights are good clues as to the location of electrical wiring. Wires can be relocated without much trouble but pipes and tubing are expensive to move and often can be avoided by moving the door 16 in. to another stud.

OPENING THE WALL

Draw an outline around the wall area that is to be removed. Allow room for the new frame plus space for the header to extend between studs. *Cut plaster* or gypsum board and lath with a cold chisel, hammer, and saws. *Cut studs* at the top first and then a few inches above the bottom to avoid the nails. The top cut should be high enough to allow for the height of the frame, spacing with wedges, and a double header of 2 X 4's or 2 X 6's. Make the top cuts square so the remaining section of stud can be toenailed into the top of the header (Fig. 7–45(a)).

BUILDING THE FRAMEWORK

The framework of 2 X 4's that holds the new frame consists of double studs on both sides and a double header across

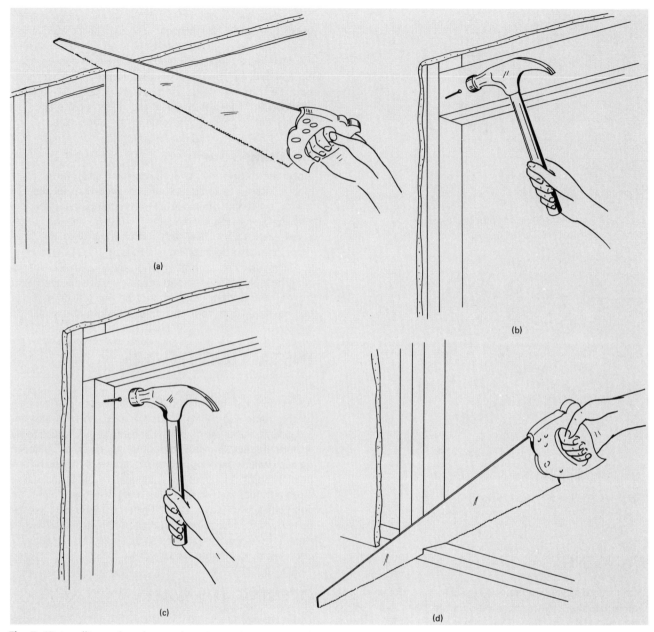

Fig. 7–45 Installing a door frame: a) cutting studs at the top, b) installing a double header, c) nailing a supporting stud under the header, d) sawing the sole plate.

the top. If there is already a stud at one side of the opening it can be used as a framing stud. If no studs are in position to support the sides of the frame, additional studs will have to be installed on both sides.

Nail a double header set on edge between the full-length studs on either side of the opening (Fig. 7–45(b)). Use a level to keep the header horizontal. Use wedges between the headers to shim them out flush with the sides of the studs. Place supporting studs under the header and flush against the full-length studs on both sides (Fig. 7–45(c)).

Install double studs on one or both sides of the opening for the frame (depending on whether an existing full-length stud can be used) between the header and sole plate. Toe-nail them to the header and plate. Use a level to make the studs as plumb as possible.

Saw the sole plate on both sides of the opening flush to the double studs and pry it free from the subflooring (Fig. 7–45(d)).

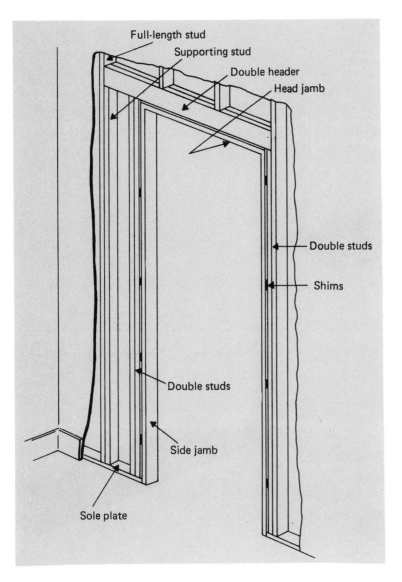

Full-length stud
Supporting stud
Double header
Head jamb
Double studs
Shims
Double studs
Side jamb
Sole plate

Fig. 7–46 Door frame, double studs, and header.

INSTALLING THE FRAME

Assemble the precut frame accompanying the new door and place it within the double studs if it fits. The lower ends of the jambs may have to be trimmed before it can be placed in the opening.

Shim the frame until the side jambs are plumb and the head jamb is horizontal. Measure the inside dimensions and compare these with the matching door. The door should either just fit, with ⅛-in. clearances at the sides and top and ½-in. clearance at the bottom (allowing for the flooring), or it should be slightly larger than the opening.

Nail the frame to the double studs and header with 10 d casing or finishing nails placed every 10 to 14 in. just inside the edges of the jambs (Fig. 7–46). Check the jambs with a carpenter's level from time to time and adjust the shims to keep them square.

Reinforcing blocks can be nailed behind the sections of the jamb where the strike plate and hinges are to be installed. Insulation should be stuffed between the frame, studs, and double header, and replaced in the openings between the studs next to the doorway. The walls can be recovered with gypsum board or lath and plaster after the threshold is installed. Trim is nailed around the outside of the frame after the wall material has been attached.

INSTALLING THRESHOLDS

Thresholds are placed between the jambs so that they extend from the far side of the stop bead to slightly beyond the edges of the jambs. Oak and other hardwood thresholds are more durable than pine and are available in several sizes. Buy a length that will cover the gap left where the sole plate

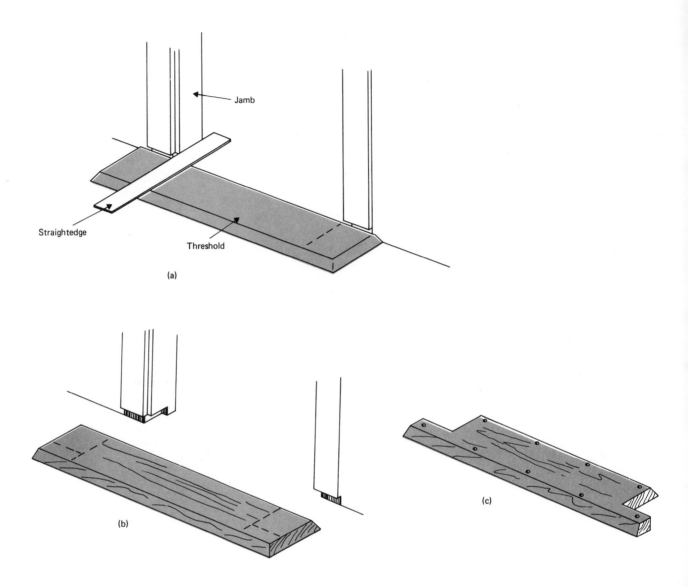

Fig. 7–47 Installing a threshold: a) measuring and marking the width of the threshold, b) marking rectangular area to be cut, c) threshold with pilot holes.

was removed and will extend over the edges of the finish flooring.

Measure the threshold by placing it flat and centered on the floor next to the opening between the jambs. Extend a line across the face of each jamb continuing across the threshold (Fig. 7–47(a)). This serves as a guide for the width of the threshold between the jambs. If the jambs aren't square, adjust to these dimensions as necessary. The depth of the threshold within the jambs should be equal to the distance between the far side where the stop bead will be attached and the inner edge of the jamb. Measure this and

mark it off perpendicular to the lines already marked on the threshold. The two lines will form rectangles on both sides of the threshold, which should be cut out with a crosscut saw (Fig. 7–46(b)). The remaining ears will extend around the edge of the jamb flush against the wall or casing.

Nail the threshold in place by drilling pilot holes every few inches along the upper edge of the bevels on both sides (Fig. 7–47(c)). The threshold can be shimmed up on one or both sides to keep it level. Use at least 8d casing or finishing nails, countersink them, and fill the holes with plastic wood.

8 Plumbing

PLUMBING SYSTEMS

The plumbing system supplies water and carries away waste. Cold water is supplied by the town system or by a well and pump and carried to the fixtures and hot-water heaters by the supply pipes (Fig. 8–1(a)). Drain pipes carry waste water from the fixtures to a main drain system that empties into the sewer or septic tank (Fig. 8–1(b)). Gases are removed and atmospheric pressure maintained in the drainage system by vent pipes leading to the roof.

WATER-SUPPLY LINES

Cold water enters the house through a water meter and main cutoff valve. Leaks or flooding from any fixtures or pipes in the house can be stopped by closing this main shutoff. Cold water is carried to the fixtures and hot-water heater by pipes that decrease in size from ¾ in. for a main line to ⅜ in. for flexible tubing connecting lavatory faucets. Since the water is under 50-psi pressure in most supply systems, shutoff valves are installed in the lines at each fixture to shut off the water when the fixture is being repaired or in an emergency.

DRAIN–WASTE–VENT SYSTEM

Because it drains water, carries away solid waste, and vents gases to the outside, the drainage system is referred to as the drain–waste–vent system (or DWV system). At each fixture, there are P-traps or drum traps containing water that prevent sewer gases from entering the house through the fixture. The trap is connected to a 1½- or 2-in. drain pipe that should slope downward approximately ¼ in./ft. Waste from toilets is discharged into a 3- or 4-in. soil pipe connected to the main drain.

Vents from the drainage system at each trap carry away the gases. The vent at the toilet is an extension of the soil pipe called a soil stack. Gases from drains at other fixtures are vented either by a secondary, 1½-in. vent (called a revent) to the main vent or by main vents directly to the roof.

Venting allows air to enter the system to prevent a vacuum from forming that would pull water from the traps into the drainpipes. Older plumbing installations are likely to have only one main vent, but modern installations may have more than one vent that extends through the roof and re-vents at each fixture. Local plumbing codes specify minimum requirements for venting.

EMERGENCIES AND TROUBLE SHOOTING

EMERGENCIES

Plumbing emergencies raise visions of flooding from burst pipes or overflowing toilets. Some would also consider it an emergency if an important fixture, such as a garbage disposer, dishwasher, or hot-water heater, failed to operate.

Fortunately, flooding can be brought under control by closing the proper shutoff valves. Besides the main shutoff valve (Fig. 8–2) at the entrance of the water service into the house, there are shutoff valves at each fixture (Fig. 8–3), and at the connection to the water main at the street. Flooding from a disconnected supply hose to a washing machine, for example, can be stopped by closing the shutoff valve where the hoses are connected to the water-supply lines. Similarly, water can be turned off below the toilet tank, under a lavatory in the bathroom, or where a dishwasher supply line connects under the kitchen sink. In the case of a leak in a main supply pipe in the wall or cellar, turn off the main

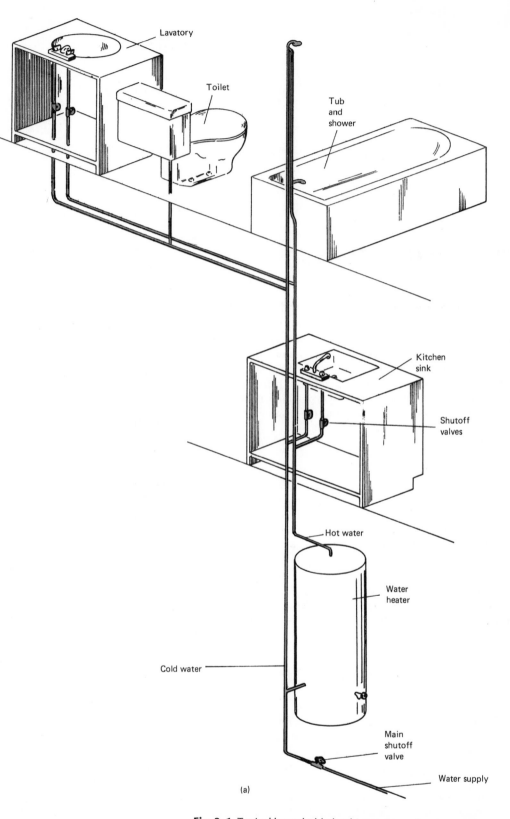

Fig. 8–1 Typical household plumbing system; a) water-supply system, b) drain–waste–vent (DWV) system.

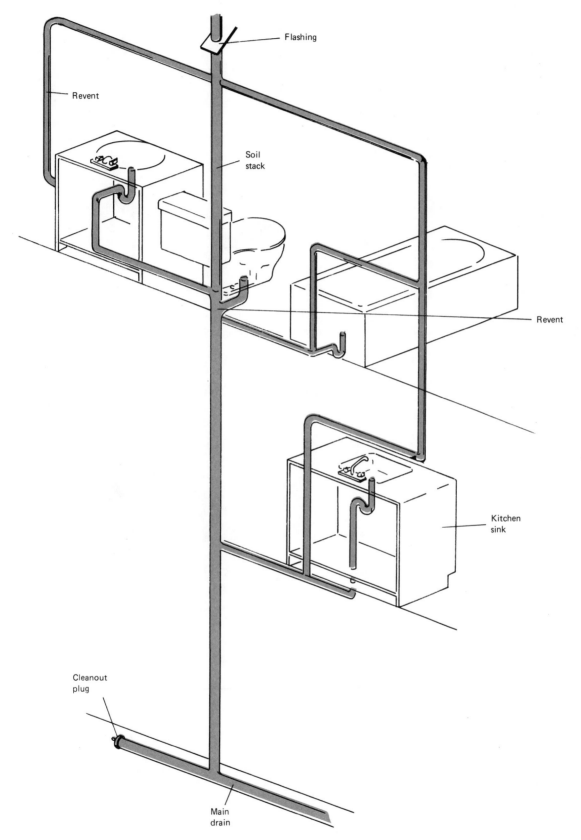

Flashing

Revent

Soil
stack

Revent

Kitchen
sink

Cleanout
plug

Main
drain

(b)

Fig. 8–2 Main shutoff valve.

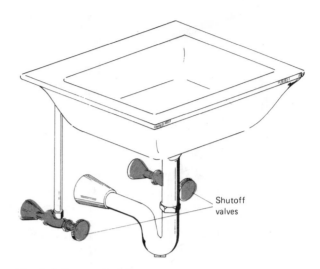

Fig. 8–3 Fixture shutoff valves.

shutoff valve at the water meter. This will stop the flow of water in the main supply pipe and the hot-water system.

Leaks at hot-water heaters, toilets, and other accesso-ries can be stopped by closing the shutoff valve at the unit. For other plumbing problems at these fixtures, refer to the troubleshooting chart and the text.

TROUBLE SHOOTING CHART

FAUCETS*

Fig. 8–4 Lavatory faucet.

Spout leaks	• Washer (washer-type faucet) or rubber diaphragm (washerless-type faucet) worn. Replace.
	• Washerless assembly faulty. Remove and have worn parts replaced.
	• Internal assembly on single-handled faucet defective. Repair with kit for the particular type of faucet.
	• Valve seat scored or worn. Grind with reseating tool or replace valve seat.
Water leaks around handle	• Packing nut loose. Tighten.
	• Packing defective. Replace with graphite or asbestos packing.
	• O-ring defective. Replace.
Swing spout leaks at base	• O-ring worn. Replace.
Handle binds and squeals	• Stem binds. Lubricate threads with petroleum jelly.

*See section on Leaking Faucets under Common Repairs

TOILETS*

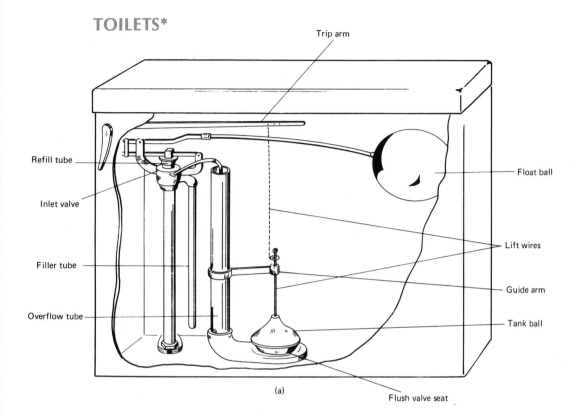

Trip arm

Refill tube

Inlet valve

Filler tube

Overflow tube

Float ball

Lift wires

Guide arm

Tank ball

(a)

Flush valve seat

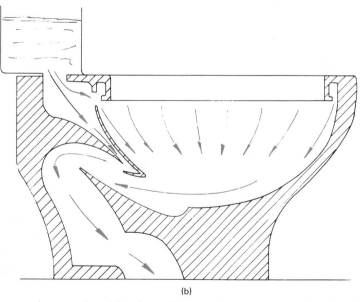

(b)

Fig. 8–5 Toilet operating mechanisms: a) tank, b) bowl.

Continuously running water, whistling, or singing

• Float not rising far enough to fully close inlet valve. Replace leaking float. Bend arm downward or away from side of tank.
• Tank ball not seating in flush valve. Replace worn tank ball. Clean or replace valve seat. Bend or replace crooked guide wires.

*See section on Toilets under Common Repairs.

• Inlet-valve washers worn. Replace washers.
• Ballcock assembly worn out. Replace with flapper flush valve, Fluidmaster-type unit, or diaphragm-type assembly.

Partial flushing

• Guide arm holds tank ball too low. Slide arm higher on overflow pipe.
• Shutoff valve partially closed. Open fully.
• Inlet valve defective. Replace.
• Adjust water height in tank.

Tank leaks

• Inlet coupling nut loose. Tighten.
• Washer at inlet worn. Replace.
• Flush-valve gaskets or washers worn. Replace.

Toilet bowl leaks

• Gasket or sealing ring at floor flange faulty. Remove bowl and replace seal.

Toilet bowl overflows

• Drain clogged. Raise float to close inlet valve. Push tank ball down to close flush valve. Close shutoff valve. Clear obstruction with bulb-type plunger or closet auger.

DRAINS*

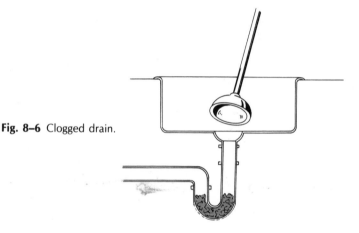

Fig. 8–6 Clogged drain.

Clogged drain in sink, lavatory, or bathtub

• Grease, soap, hair or other obstruction in drainpipe. Dissolve with boiling water or caustic cleaner. Try plunger or drain auger. Clean sludge from cleanout plug in P-trap or drum trap. Remove entire P-trap, if necessary.

Clogged drainpipe, soil pipe, or sewer pipe

• Obstruction in main drain lines. Open cleanout plug and use drain auger, hose, sewer rod, or power auger to clear line.

PIPES†

Small leaks in pipes or fittings

• Pinhole leak from corrosion. Seal with rubber patch and pipe clamp, self-stick tape, or epoxy sealant.
• Poor seal at fitting. Disassemble and rejoin or replace fitting.

Large leaks

• Pipe corroded or damaged. Turn off water at shutoff valve. Replace pipe or fitting, or call plumber.

Noisy pipes

• Pipe loose and banging. Tighten or shim pipe-hangers and clamps. Add reinforcing supports.
• Water hammer. Install air chambers where needed.
• Excessive water pressure. Install reducer.

*See section on Clogged Drains under Common Repairs.
†See section on Pipes under Common Repairs.

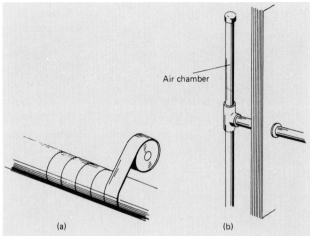

Fig. 8–7 Pipes: a) sealing a small leak, b) air chamber.

Frozen pipes

- Pipe blocked by ice. Open faucet and heat pipe moving away from faucet for drainage. Use: hot water on cloth-wrapped pipes; hot water in hose inserted into faucet; hair dryer; heat lamp; propane torch.

WASHING MACHINES*

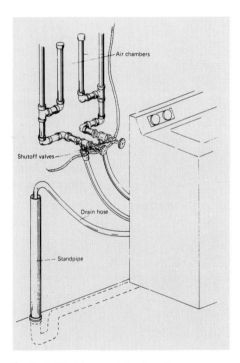

Fig. 8–8 Washing machine installation.

Tub fails to fill with water

- Shutoff valves closed. Open valves.
- Hoses kinked or blocked at strainers. Straighten hoses and clean strainers.
- Inlet-valve assembly defective. Call serviceman.

Drain hose floods floor

- Hose empties on floor instead of in standpipe. Push hose 6 in. into standpipe and wedge in place.

*See section on Washing Machines under Major Plumbing Fixtures.

Washer leaks on floor

• Fittings or connections in machine defective. Repair connections or have serviceman replace fittings.

Washer tub overflows

• Water-level control or inlet valves defective. Close shutoff valve and call serviceman.

DISHWASHERS*

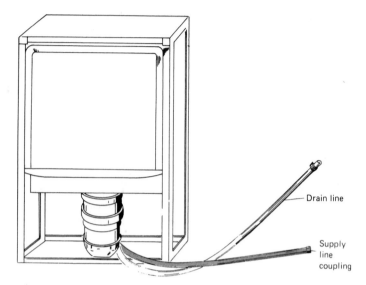

Fig. 8-9 Dishwasher and plumbing.

Fail to fill

• Shutoff valve closed. Open valve.
• Supply tubing crimped. Replace tubing.
• Inlet strainer blocked. Remove and clean.
• Inlet valve assembly faulty. Call serviceman to replace.

Water leaks onto floor

• Supply or drain fittings loose or defective. Tighten loose fittings. Replace defective fittings.
• Door gasket worn and leaking. Replace gasket.

Wash or rinse water fails to stop running

• Faulty inlet-valve mechanism or timer. Turn off machine and close shutoff valve. Call serviceman.

GARBAGE DISPOSER†

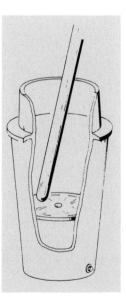

Fig. 8-10 Freeing jammed garbage disposer.

*See section on Dishwasher under Major Plumbing Fixtures
†See section on Garbage Disposers under Major Plumbing Fixtures

Disposer won't operate

- Blades jammed. Turn off switch. Push blades with stick or broom handle until freed from debris; manually crank blades in reverse, or use automatic reverse switch. When blades are free, push reset button.

HOT-WATER HEATERS*

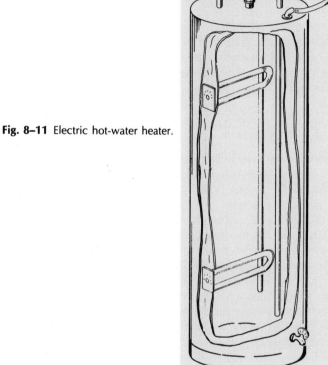

Fig. 8–11 Electric hot-water heater.

Fails to heat water

- Circuit breaker open or fuse blown. Close breaker or replace fuse.
- Pilot light out in gas unit. Relight.
- Gas shutoff closed. Open and relight pilot light.
- Oil burner fails to operate. Call serviceman.
- Thermostat defective. Clean or replace.
- High-limit cutoff has turned off unit. Reset.

Water supply fails

- Cold-water shutoff valve closed.

Water not hot enough

- Thermostat set too low or defective. Set higher, clean, or replace.
- Heater too small or recovery rate too slow for needs. Replace with larger unit.
- Heater element burned out. Replace.

Tank or pipes leak

- Hole in tank from corrosion. Replace tank.
- Faulty connections between tank, pipes, or fittings. Disassemble and connect properly.

Unit overheats

- Thermostat mechanism defective. Replace.

*See section on Hot-water Heater under Major Plumbing Fixtures

COMMON REPAIRS

LEAKING FAUCETS

Two-handle faucets have separate handles for the hot and cold water and may employ washers or rubber diaphragms and metal disks to control the flow. Washer-type faucets control the flow by a washer-type valve at the base of the faucet's stem. Washerless-type faucets use metal disks with holes.

Single-handle faucets control the mixture of hot and cold water with one handle. The operating mechanisms may use cams, disks, cartridges, or other units, depending on the type of faucet. These units can be repaired by using kits provided by the manufacturers for their particular types of units.

Washer-Type Faucets

Leaks from the spout indicate that either the washer or valve seat needs to be repaired. When water leaks from the base of the handle, it's likely that the packing under the packing nut isn't doing its job.

The faucet should be disassembled with a screwdriver and wrench and the washer, valve seat, and packing inspected. Keep track of each step in the sequence in order to be able to reassemble the faucet (Fig. 8–12).

Start by *turning off the water* at a shutoff valve. Remove the decorative cap that covers the screw on top of the faucet. (Use a fingernail file to pry it loose). Unscrew the brass screw to detach the handle from the stem. When the handle is lifted off, either a nut holding a decorative bonnet or a packing nut will be visible. If there is a bonnet, use a wrench to remove the nut and lift off the bonnet. With the bonnet out of the way, loosen the packing nut (turn the wrench counterclockwise) and turn the stem until it lifts out of the valve.

Inspect the washer attached to the end of the stem. If it is old or worn, the washer will be ragged, or compressed, or the rubber may have hardened or cracked. Remove the brass screw that holds the washer, and replace the washer with a flat or beveled washer of the same size (Fig. 8–13). Before reassembling the faucet, coat the threads of the stem and packing nut with a little petroleum jelly to ease the wear. If the stem appears to be damaged, replace it with a new stem from a plumbing supply house.

Valve seats that are worn or burred prevent washers from seating tightly and allow water to leak through the valve. The leak can be repaired by smoothing the valve seat with a grinding or reseating tool or by replacing it. To grind the valve seat, insert the tool into the valve, using the packing nut as a guide. Turn the tool gently clockwise a few times to smooth the soft metal (Fig. 8–14). This will create bits of

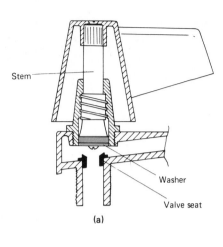

(a)

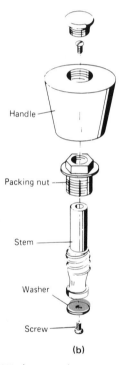

(b)

Fig. 8–12 Washer-type faucet: a) cross-sectional view, of faucet, b) disassembled components.

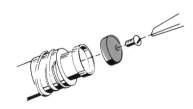

Fig. 8–13 Replacing a washer.

Fig. 8–14 Grinding a valve seat.

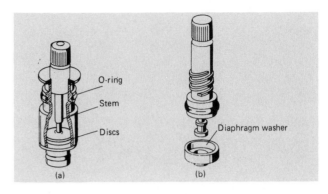

Fig. 8–16 Disk-type washerless faucet: a) stem and internal parts, b) stem and rubber diaphragm.

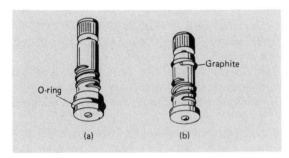

Fig. 8–15 Faucet packings: a) O ring, b) graphite.

metal that can be blown or cleaned out of the valve. When the seat is free of burrs and feels smooth, the faucet can be reassembled. If a valve seat has to be removed, use a valve-seat wrench and rotate it counterclockwise. An identical seat valve can be installed by turning it clockwise after applying pipe joint compound to the threads.

The *packing nut,* not the washer or seat valve, is supposed to prevent leaks around the stem by holding the packing to the stem. Leaks at the base of the stem indicate that either the packing nut is loose or that the packing or O-ring on the stem is worn (Fig. 8–15). With the faucet disassembled, slip the O-ring or old string-type packing off the stem. With O-ring-type packing, use a new ring that is identical to the old ring. With string-type packing, wrap a short length of graphite packing around the stem above the threads, where it will seal when the packing nut is tightened. Coat the threads of the packing nut with a little petroleum jelly before reassembling the faucet.

Reassemble the faucet by reversing the steps followed in taking it apart. Twist the stem back into the valve, replace the packing nut, and attach the bonnet and handle.

Washerless-Type Faucets

Washerless faucets are disassembled in the same manner as washer-type faucets and can be recognized by the rubber diaphragm or metal-to-metal fitting at the end of the stem instead of a washer and brass screw (Fig. 8–16). Disks contained in the body of the stem rotate to control the flow of water by aligning their openings. A stem nut is used, rather than a packing nut, because of the different channels of flow. Some types will have an O-ring just below the positioning lug at the upper end of the stem. Other types lack the O-ring completely.

Worn parts must be replaced with identical units. Take the entire stem assembly to a plumbing supplier to obtain the correct-size rubber diaphragm or other parts. If there is extensive wear, the entire stem unit should be replaced.

Single-Handle Faucets

Since there are several types of single-handle faucets, a repair kit designed for the particular type and model must be used to replace worn parts (Fig. 8–17). Instructions in the kit describe how the faucet should be disassembled and worn parts replaced. In general, spouts and faucet handles are removed first, followed by strain plugs and valve seat in tipping-valve-type faucets, by the disk unit in disk-type faucets, and by the valve cartridge in cartridge-type faucets. Follow directions for lubricating the moving parts before reassembling the unit.

Swinging Spouts

Swinging spouts on kitchen sinks leak at their base when their O-rings or washers become worn (Fig. 8–18). Loosen the nut at the base of the spout and remove it to expose the O-ring or washer. Replace the O-ring or washers with new units of the same size, and replace the nut.

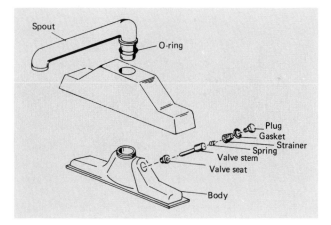

Fig. 8–17 Single-handle faucet.

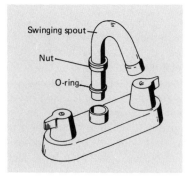

Fig. 8–18 Swinging-spout faucet.

TOILETS

Most toilet problems involve the flushing mechanism or a clogged drain pipe. Occasionally, a toilet tank or bowl will leak, but the flushing mechanism causes most toilet problems. Flushing mechanisms look complicated, but their operation is fairly simple. To understand descriptions of the process of repairing toilets it is necessary to know the names of the parts and what they do (Fig. 8–19).

Operation of a Toilet

The main components of a toilet are the tank that holds the flush water, the bowl, and the flushing mechanism (located in the tank).

The *toilet flushes* when water enters the bowl through the flush valve in the bottom of the tank. This valve is opened when the tank ball, which serves as a stopper, is lifted by a lift wire attached to the flush arm.

The tank *refills* through a float valve (inlet valve) assembly and refill tube. Water flows from the refill tube into the

tank and also into an overflow pipe to seal the trap. Water is prevented from flowing out by the tank ball that closes the flush valve. As the water rises in the tank, it carries the float ball on its surface. When the water is about ¾ in. below the top of the overflow pipe, the float arm reaches an angle at which it closes the inlet valve, and the water stops flowing into the tank.

Continuously Running Water

The sound of continuously running water, whistling, or singing indicates that there is a small flow of water through the tank and into the bowl. There are several situations in which the water may run in this manner. The float ball may not rise far enough to close the inlet valve. In this situation, water running through the inlet valve may make a whistling or singing sound. Or the tank ball may not seat tightly in the flush valve, so that water leaks around the edges and flows into the bowl. Another possibility is poor seating caused by a worn tank ball, rough valve seat, or bent lift wires. Finally, the inlet valve may leak if the washers in the ballcock assembly are worn. Water will flow into the tank and out through the overflow pipe.

Float Ball. To see whether the float ball is rising high enough, remove the top of the tank and lift the float. If the sound of running water water stops, the float isn't rising high enough by itself to close the inlet valve. This may be due either to the float rubbing against the back of the tank or to the way the float arm is bent. If the float is rubbing, bend the arm slightly away from the back of the tank. If the float is too low in the water, bend the arm downward to make the inlet valve close earlier (Fig. 8–20). If the float is filled with water or damaged, it should be unscrewed and replaced with a plastic float.

Tank Ball and Valve Seat. Anything that prevents the tank ball from seating tightly will allow water to drain out of the tank and into the toilet. Turn off the water at the shutoff beneath where the inlet pipe enters the wall. Flush the toilet to remove most of the water from the tank, and inspect the tank ball. If it is old and worn or if the edges are worn, replace it with a new ball. Check the valve seat for anything that might prevent the tank ball from seating tightly. Caked residue should be removed with a rag and wet-or-dry abrasive paper or cloth. If the seat is obviously old and decayed, it should also be removed and replaced.

The tank ball is guided into the seat valve by guide wires and a guide arm. If these are bent or misaligned, the ball won't seat properly (Fig. 8–21). With the tank full of water, flush the toilet and watch how the tank ball descends. It will drop smoothly into the valve seat if the wires and guide are correctly aligned. If the guide wires are bent out of shape, bend them back or replace them if they won't stay in place. If the guide is misaligned, loosen it and readjust it to its proper position.

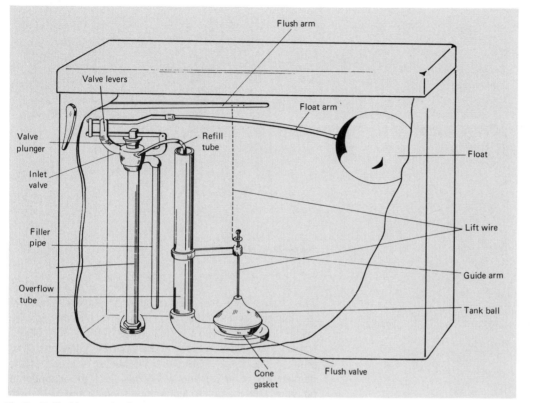

Fig. 8—19 Flushing mechanism.

Fig. 8—21 Improperly seated tank ball.

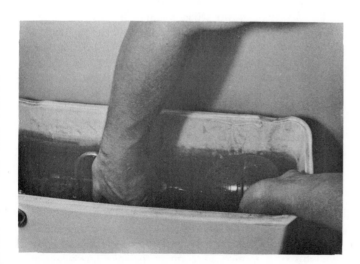

Fig. 8—20 Bending the float arm.

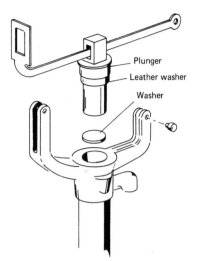

Fig. 8—22 Inlet valve.

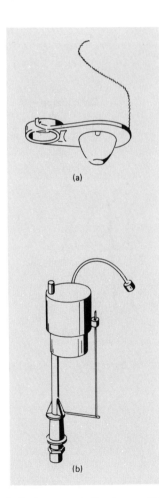

Fig. 8—23 Replacement ballcock assemblies: a) flapper flush valve, b) fluidmaster-type.

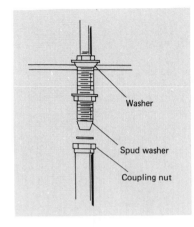

Fig. 8—24 Inlet pipe fittings.

Inlet Valve. Worn washers or other parts in the inlet-valve mechanism will let water run continuously into the tank. To inspect the washers in the float valve, remove the thumb-screws that hold it in place and lift out the valve lever and plunger (Fig. 8–22). The valve washer on the end of the plunger and other washers will be visible. If these appear to be worn, take the unit to a plumbing supplier and have them replaced.

Replacing Ballcock Assembly

Troublesome ballcock assemblies should be replaced with new units or, better yet, more reliable types of flushing mechanisms. One of the most widely used replacements is the *flapper flush valve.* (Fig. 8–23(a)). It consists of a rubber flapper with an extension that slides down around the over-flow pipe and covers the valve seat (like a large, hinged stopper). The flapper is raised and lowered to flush the toilet by a chain or lever attached to the flushing arm. A *Fluidmas-ter-type* unit allows the water to flow into the tank at a rapid and continuous rate until the inverted float cup shuts the inlet valve (Fig. 8–23(b)). A *diaphragm-type flush valve* that senses the depth of the water above it can be installed at the flush valve opening in the bottom of the tank. Regulator screws are used to adjust the valve to respond to different depths of water.

To *remove the ballcock assembly,* close the shutoff valve to stop the inflow of water, and flush the toilet to empty the tank. The float arm should be unscrewed and the water remaining in the bottom of the tank soaked up with cloths or a sponge. Disconnect the inlet line where it is attached beneath the tank, by loosening the coupling nut (Fig. 8–24). The inlet pipe can be removed by turning the locknut beneath the tank counterclockwise. Lift the inlet pipe and the rest of the ballcock mechanism out of the tank. A new flushing unit can now be installed in the same openings.

Partial Flushing

The bowl will not flush completely unless all of the water in the tank flows out. If the handle on the toilet tank has to be held down during the entire flushing process, remove the tank top to see what is happening. If the tank ball seats and closes the flush valve before all of the water has flowed out, the guide arm is probably attached too low on the overflow pipe. The tank ball is forced to close too early by suction from the rushing water. Loosen the screws and raise the guide arm slightly. Flush the toilet again while observing the tank ball. Readjust the guide arm if necessary, until the tank ball stays up.

If the tank fails to fill with water in the first place, the flushing will also be incomplete. Check to see whether the shutoff valve is closed or only partially open. When it is open all the way, water should flow into the tank. If the flushing mechanism is operating correctly but the float is too low, the inlet valve will close before the tank is filled. In this case, the float should be repaired or replaced as described earlier.

Leaking Tanks

Water on the bottom of a toilet tank or on the floor beneath it may come either from a leak or from condensation. In warm weather, moisture from the air condenses on the outside of the tank and drips on the floor. Condensation can be distinguished from a leak because moisture condenses over the entire surface of the tank. Although a leak could occur at the same time as condensation, water leaking from the inlet or flush valve will be found closer to the source of the leak.

The inlet line is coupled to the inlet pipe at the bottom of the tank. If water appears to be leaking from the joint, the coupling nut may be loose or the threads or washers damaged. Try tightening the nut first. If the water continues to leak from the joint, close the water shutoff and remove the inlet coupling. The unit should be inspected for damage and taken to a plumbing supplier to replace the coupling, if necessary.

Leaks at the fittings on the inlet pipe or the flush valve are caused by worn washers and gaskets. Detach the tank from the bowl, or from the separate pipe in a wall-mounted installation, and inspect the fittings. With a bowl-mounted tank, loosen the nuts at the rear and beneath the bowl that hold the tank down (Fig. 8–25(a)). Use the wrench with care to avoid a slip that might crack the porcelain. When the nuts and washers are removed, the tank can be lifted off the bowl (Fig. 8–25(b)). With a wall-mounted tank, the locknut that

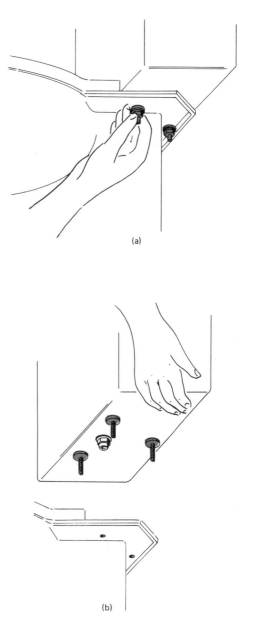

Fig. 8–25 Removing the tank: a) loosening the nuts, b) lifting off the tank.

attaches the pipe or spud to the tank will have to be loosened with a wide spud wrench before it can be detached.

The gaskets and washers at the flush valve should be inspected for wear or damage that might account for the leak. On a bowl-mounted tank, the locknut that holds the flush valve in place must be removed before the valve and washers can be removed (Fig. 8–26). Install replacement gaskets, valves, and washers by following the steps in reverse for disassembling the tank attachments.

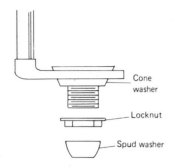

Fig. 8–26 Flush valve fittings.

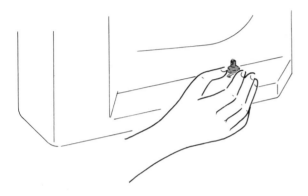

Fig. 8–27 Loosening nut on hold-down bolt.

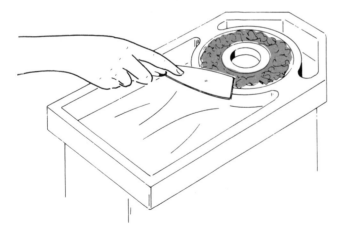

Fig. 8–28 Scraping off old sealing material.

LEAKING BOWLS

When the seal between the toilet bowl and the floor flange fails, water may leak down through to the ceiling below or out around the base of the bowl. In such a case, the bowl has to be removed and a new sealing ring or gasket installed.

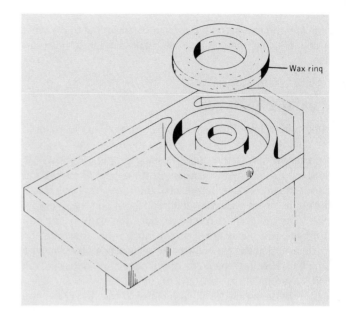

Fig. 8–29 Installing a new wax bowl ring.

After emptying and removing the tank, bail the water out of the bowl. Loosen the nuts on the hold-down bolts under the caps on both sides at the base of the bowl (Fig. 8–27). (Penetrating oil will help if the nuts are frozen.) Rock the bowl to free it from the seal and lift it off the flange. With the bowl on its side, the old sealing material can be scraped from around the toilet outlet (Fig. 8–28). Scrape the old wax from the flange also. A new rubber gasket or wax bowl ring should be installed (Fig. 8–29). Rubber gaskets attach to the bottom of the bowl around the outlet. Wax rings may attach to the bowl or to the flange, depending on the type of fitting. When the new ring is in place, the bowl should be replaced on the flange and aligned for a permanent seal. Replace the hold-down bolts and replace the nuts and bolts with new ones to minimize corrosion. The bowl and tank can be reassembled by following in reverse order the several steps taken in detaching them.

Clogged Toilet Drains

When the narrow drain in a toilet bowl becomes clogged, water entering the bowl from the tank is unable to flow out and will rise and overflow the sides. At the first indication that the water in the bowl is rising unusually high as the toilet is flushed, remove the top of the tank and lift the float while pushing the tank ball down to close the flush valve. The shutoff valve should be closed to prevent more water from entering the tank. Of the several ways to clear the blockage, try the simplest first.

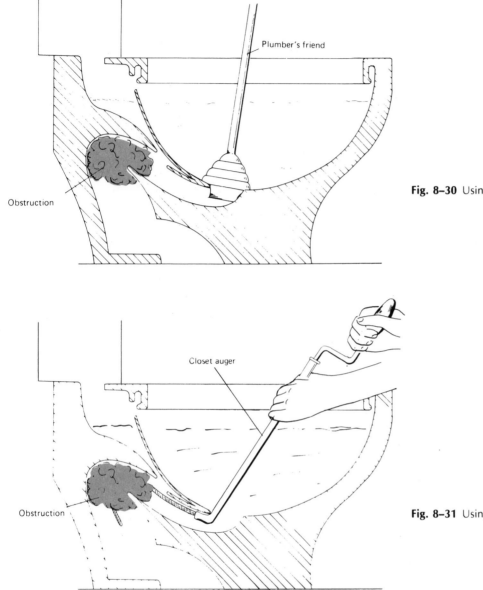

Obstruction

Plumber's friend

Fig. 8–30 Using a plumber's friend.

Closet auger

Obstruction

Fig. 8–31 Using a closet auger.

A *bulb-type plunger* or *two-way force cup* with an extended rim for toilets should be pressed down over the drain opening and worked up and down to loosen the blocking material. This may be enough to free the material and allow it to pass down the drain (Fig. 8–30). (The tool is called a "plumber's friend.")

A *closet-auger* (toilet auger) is shaped to fit into a toilet drain. Insert the coiled wire at the end of the hollow tube into the drain and turn the auger handle to rotate the wire as it is pushed farther into the drain. The end of the coiled wire will snag the blockage so it can be pulled out (Fig. 8–31).

A plumber's *Drain auger* or *bent wire* can also be used to free the blockage, though they are more awkward to use. You will have to reach into the bowl to guide them into the drain and around the curves. Use a plastic garbage bag to protect your arm. The drain auger should be twisted (like the closet auger) to snag the blocking refuse.

Do not use a caustic drain cleaner to clear a clogged toilet drain. Not only will it not clear the material, it will damage the vitreous china bowl.

CLOGGED DRAINS

Causes

Drains are clogged by substances, such as grease, soap, and hair that tend to stick and build up inside the drain pipes. There are also other culprits such as tree roots that obstruct sewer pipes between the house and street, and types of garbage that cake the inside of the drain. These can be attacked with solvents, plungers, drain augers, water hoses, sewer rods, power augers, and other ingenious devices.

Clearing Drains

Solvents. Grease-caked drains in kitchen sinks can often be cleared with boiling water or a caustic cleaner. The hot water causes the grease to melt and run down the pipe, while the caustic cleaner dissolves the grease. In tub and shower drains, a caustic cleaner may be necessary to dissolve the soap or hair that blocks the drain. Drain stoppers can be removed by turning, unscrewing, or just lifting them out. Pour in caustic cleaner with care, add a small amount of cold water according to the directions, and rinse with cold water after the cleaner has worked for fifteen minutes or so. Rinse thoroughly, since caustic cleaners are harmful to the skin and lungs.

Plungers. A plunger can be used to force an obstruction loose by the pressure of surging water. For the most effective seal, coat the rim of the plunger with petroleum jelly. With several inches of water in the basin or tub, tip the plunger to release any trapped air as it is placed in the water and over the drain. Cover the overflow drain and any other drain opening, such as a double-sink drain. Work the plunger up and down several times, preferably in step with the surge of the water in the drain (Fig. 8–32). Every few minutes, remove the plunger to see whether the drain has been cleared. If this fails to work, a drain auger should be used.

Drain augers. To physically force the blockage free or to snag and remove it, use a drain auger. The coiled wire is pushed down the drain with a rotating motion until it meets an obstacle and won't go any farther. Slide the tubular handle along the auger and lock it against the auger next to the drain opening. In this position, handle can be turned to work the end of the coil into the obstruction (Fig. 8–33). Every so often, pull the auger out to remove whatever it has snagged. When the drain seems to be cleared, rinse it with hot water.

Traps. Sink traps usually have a cleanout plug. If the plunger and auger haven't been able to open the drain, place a pail under the trap and remove the cleanout plug (Fig. 8–34). Sludge in the trap can be worked loose with a wire inserted through the open plug. If the wire can't reach the obstruction or if the blockage is particularly stubborn, the entire trap can be removed by loosening the coupling nuts (Fig. 8–35). Once free, the trap can be cleaned from both ends. *Drum traps* are sometimes used in older plumb-

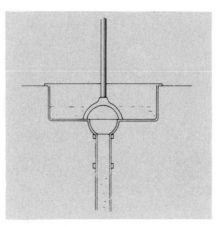

Fig. 8–32 Using a plunger to open a drain

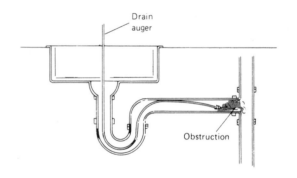

Fig. 8–33 Using a drain auger to open a drain.

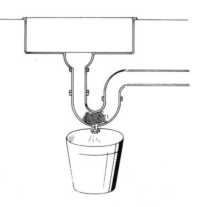

Fig. 8–34 Opening a cleanout plug in a trap.

Fig. 8–35 Removing a sink trap.

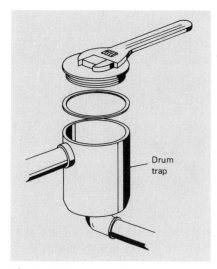

Fig. 8–36 Opening a drum trap.

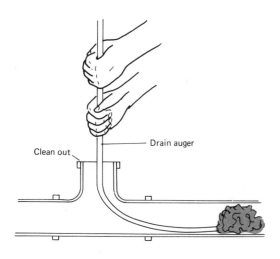

Fig. 8–37 Auger in a main drain pipe.

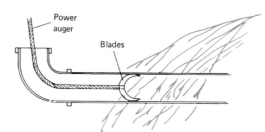

Fig. 8–38 Power auger in sewer pipe.

ing systems and in tub drain lines. Sludge and debris that collect in the trap should be removed from time to time to keep the drain functioning smoothly. Use a wrench to loosen the cleanout plug on the bottom or top of the tap (Fig. 8–36). The sludge and water should be drained into a pail and the inside of the trap wiped out with a rag. If the gasket is worn, it should be replaced by making or buying a new one. Use an elastic-type pipe compound to seal the fitting.

Main Drain Pipes and Soil Lines

An obstruction in a main drain line or soil pipe will block several drains at the same time. If only a couple of drains are blocked, the blocked drains provide a clue to the location of the blockage. Look for the cleanout fitting in the main drain pipe closest to the two drains. Open the cleanout (use a pipe wrench and mallet) to drain the water, and run a drain auger into the pipe (Fig. 8–37). If the blockage is within reach of the auger, it can be snared. Otherwise, use a longer auger or open another cleanout closer to the obstruction.

The sewer pipe that runs from the house to a sewer line along the street or to a septic tank may be blocked by roots entering between the pipe joints or by other obstructions. To get a cleaning device into the line, open the most convenient cleanout to work from, and run an auger or sewer rod into the pipe. Work through the pipe to snag the obstruction. Roots must be cut with a power auger with sharp blades powered by an electric motor (Fig. 8–38).

PIPES
Stopping Leaks

Small, pinhole-type leaks in sections of pipe between joints can be easily sealed with a *piece of rubber and a clamp.* Wrap a large patch of inner-tube rubber around the pipe and hold it in place with a pipe clamp (Fig. 3–39(a)) or a hose clamp (Fig. 8–39(b)). Clamps for sealing pipe leaks are also available commercially in various sizes for different size pipes and tubing. For a temporary repair, electrician's tape

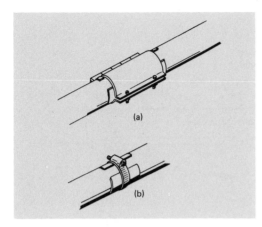

Fig. 8–39 Sealing a pinhole leak with a) pipe clamp, b) hose clamp.

Fig. 8–40 Using electrical tape to seal a leak.

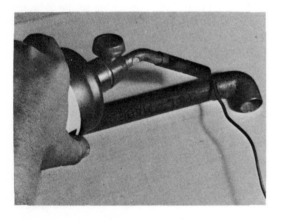

Fig. 8–41 Sealing a leak with solder.

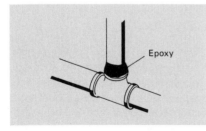

Fig. 8–42 Sealing a leak with epoxy sealant.

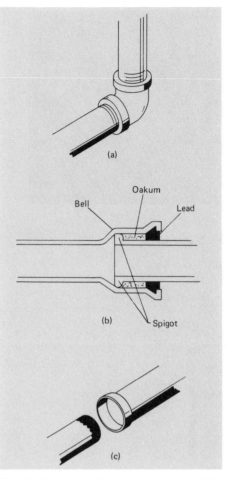

Fig. 8–43 Types of pipe joints: a) threaded joints in steel pipe, b) lead and oakum joint in cast-iron pipe, c) solvent-cement joint in plastic pipe.

can be used. Wrap the tape around the pipe so that it extends a few inches on both sides of the leak (Fig. 8–40). Electrician's tape is very effective on drain pipes where there is little water pressure.

Leaks at joints in copper tubing can be permanently repaired by *resweating the joint* (Fig. 8–41). Drain the water from the tubing, clean the joint with steel wool until it is bright, and heat it with a propane torch until it is hot enough to melt solder. Let the solder flow into the joint between the tubing and the fitting until the joint is sealed.

Epoxy sealant can also be used to seal a small leak in either a straight section or around a joint (Fig. 8–42). The area around the hole must be cleaned and dried thoroughly before the epoxy is applied.

Leaks in joints in other types of pipes are more difficult to repair because of the way they are joined. Steel pipes are threaded (Fig. 8–43(a)), cast-iron pipes are leaded (Fig. 8–43(b)) or sealed with a gasket, and plastic pipes are ce-

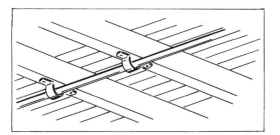

Fig. 8–44 Loose pipe hangers.

mented (Fig. 8–43(c)). Although electrical tape may provide a temporary repair, permanent repairs require equipment for cutting pipe, rethreading, or heating lead. For the average homeowner, these repairs are best left to a plumber.

Noisy Pipes

Loud noises in pipes are caused either by the pipes moving and banging or by *water hammer.*

Loose pipe supports, such as pipe hangers and clamps, allow the force of moving water to force a pipe into an adjacent pipe or against joists or studs (Fig. 8–44). Track down the source of the noise and look at the hangers and clamps to find the cause of the movement. Supports can be tightened by using wedges made of rubber between the pipe and support. If this doesn't work, install additional supports, especially if there is a long run of unsupported pipe or tubing. If the noise and banging is located in an inaccessible wall, try adding supports where the pipe enters the wall.

Water hammer is a phenomenon caused by the sudden stoppage of flow when running water is turned off at a faucet or other valve. The force of the water striking the inside of the pipe causes vibrations and a loud hammering sound. In a good plumbing installation, water hammer is avoided by installing air chambers behind and above each faucet to cushion the force of the water (Fig. 8–45). These air chambers or cushions are usually attached behind the wall.

To eliminate water hammer, where there are insufficient air cushions in the plumbing system, additional air chambers must be installed. Chambers can be purchased that attach behind the faucet. Chambers consisting of coiled copper tubing (Fig. 8–46) can be attached behind the faucets to avoid opening up the wall to get at the plumbing. Where the plumbing is exposed, as in a laundry area, a capped length of tubing can be added above the pipe leading to the faucet. If the hammering problem is general throughout the plumbing system, a large air chamber (Fig. 8–47) can be installed next to the main water inlet, to eliminate the problem for the entire system.

Ineffective air chambers may have become partially filled with water, or they may be clogged with sediment. To clear the water, close the main water shutoff, and the toilet

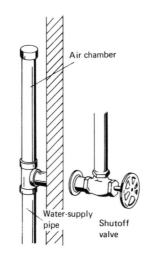

Fig. 8–45 Air chamber.

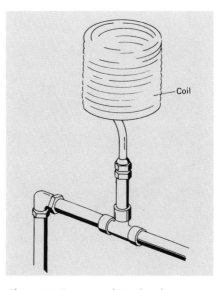

Fig. 8–46 Copper coil air chamber.

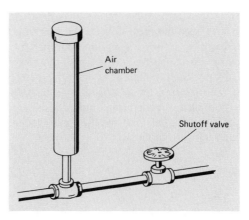

Fig. 8–47 Large air chamber at main shutoff.

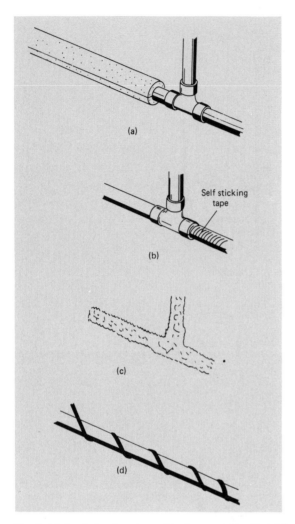

Fig. 8–48 Insulation for pipes: a) jacket-type, b) self-sticking tape, c) liquid base, d) electrical heating cables.

tank shutoff, and open all of the faucets. This will drain all of the water from the system. When all water is drained, close the faucets and open the main shutoff. The air chambers will be filled with air. If a particular air chamber still hammers, it may be caked with sediment. Close the valve on that section of pipe, open the faucet to drain the water, and remove the cap on top of the air chamber by heating copper tubing or turning a threaded joint. Caked sediment should be cleaned out with a stiff wire and the cap replaced with solder or pipe joint compound.

Freezing

Water and drain pipes in unheated or underheated areas, such as outdoors, in crawl spaces, or between uninsulated

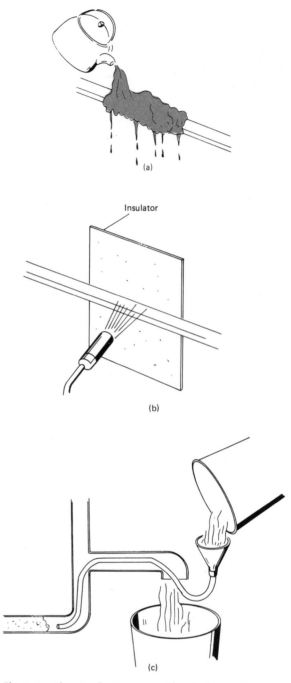

Fig. 8–49 Thawing frozen pipes with a) boiling water on wrapped pipes, b) propane torch, c) hose and hot water.

walls, may be ruptured by expanding ice when the water freezes. The best way to avoid this is by insulating or draining the pipes.

Insulation for pipes is available in several forms. Jacket-type insulation is commonly used to insulate hot water and

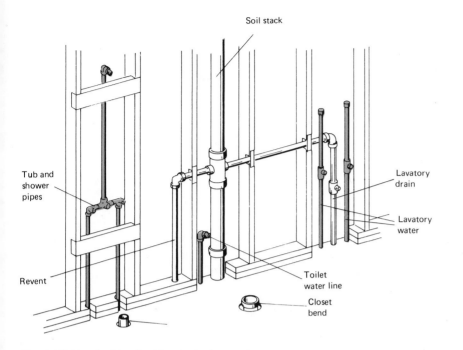

Soil stack

Tub and
shower
pipes

Lavatory
drain

Lavatory
water

Revent

Toilet
water line

Closet
bend

Fig. 8–50 Roughed-in plumbing for bathroom fixtures.

steam pipes (Fig. 8–48(a)). Asbestos tape, self-stick insulating tape (Fig. 8–48(b)), and liquid-base insulators (Fig. 8–48(c)) also can be applied to protect pipe to several degrees below freezing. For greater reliability and protection, where a pipe is constantly exposed, electrical heating cable can be wrapped around the pipe (Fig. 4–48(d)) and covered with a layer of insulation. Besides protecting the pipe from freezing, insulation reduces the loss of heat from heating pipes and prevents condensation from cold water pipes in warm weather.

Thaw frozen pipes carefully to avoid rupturing them. If the pipe is heated to too high a temperature, the ice may turn to steam and rupture the pipe or a joint with explosive force. Start by opening a faucet in the frozen pipe and applying heat by working from the faucet along the pipe toward the frozen sections. As the ice melts the water will be able to flow out of the faucet. If the pipe is exposed, a number of heat sources can be used. One of the safest is to wrap the pipe with cloths and to pour very hot or boiling water over them (Fig. 8–49(a)). They will absorb the heat and pass it on to the pipe to melt the ice. This is somewhat messy and may be impossible with pipes next to the ceiling. A heat lamp, portable hair drier, or propane torch (Fig. 8–49(b)) can also be used. Be careful (especially with a propane torch) to heat the pipe only to the point where it can still be safely touched by the hand. If the pipe becomes hotter than this, steam may form. Where the pipe is in the wall and inaccessible, hot water can be poured into the system to melt the ice. Work a length of hose into a cleanout

or through a faucet and hold it above the level of the pipe while pouring hot water into the hose through a funnel (Fig. 8–49(c)). The water will gradually melt the ice and cool. Remove the hose occasionally to drain the water into the sink or a pail.

WORKING WITH PIPES AND TUBING

Supply and DWV lines are made up of lengths of pipe or tubing connected by fittings. In new construction or remodeling, the pipes are roughed in to the point where the fixtures are to be installed (Fig. 8–50). Later, the fixtures are connected to the main lines by smaller-diameter pipe or tubing.

TYPES OF PIPE AND TUBING

Some types of pipe can be used for both the supply and DWV system. Copper pipe can be used for either, but it is very expensive in the large sizes required for the DWV system. Plastic pipe is used for cold-water supply pipes and DWV systems, but it is not yet fully acceptable for carrying hot water. Galvanized steel pipe has been a standard material for water-supply lines for years. Cast-iron pipe is used only for DWV systems.

Fig. 8–51 Copper pipe.

Fig. 8–52 Galvanized steel pipe and fittings.

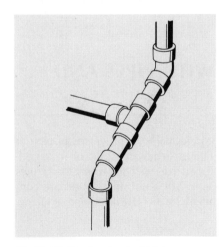

Fig. 8–53 Plastic pipe in DWV system.

Copper Pipe and Tubing

Copper is used as either rigid copper pipe (Fig. 8–51) or smaller flexible tubing. Rigid ½-in. pipe is frequently used in roughing in to connect a fixture to the main supply pipe. Smaller ⅜-in. flexible tubing is used to connect fixtures to

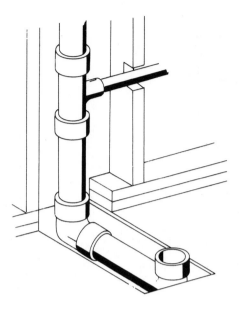

Fig. 8–54 Cast-iron pipe in soil stack.

the ½-in. pipe. Although copper pipe and tubing is one of the easiest materials to work with, it is more expensive but not as strong as some other types of pipe. Copper pipe is joined by heating fittings with a propane torch and flowing solder into the joint.

Galvanized Steel Pipe

Galvanized pipe (Fig. 8–52) is stronger and cheaper than copper, but it corrodes and can become caked with calcium deposits. It is commonly used for water-supply systems in older installations. Threaded fittings are used to join the pipes.

Plastic Pipe

Plastic pipe (Fig. 8–53) is widely accepted for DWV systems and for accessible cold-water supply systems. It is not considered as acceptable as copper or galvanized steel for cold-water supply lines between walls or for hot water. *PVC* (polyvinyl chloride) pipe and *ABS* acrylo-nitrile-butadiene-styrene) are used in DWV systems and cold-water supply systems. CP VC (chlorinated polyvinyl chloride) pipe is the only type usable with hot water. *Polyethylene tubing* is a flexible hose-like tubing used for outdoor installations, such as well-pumping and irrigating systems. Plastic pipe and tubing is easy to work with, cheap, and it doesn't corrode or sweat. However, it cannot withstand excessive water pressure and must be well protected by air chambers. The pipe is jointed by solvent welding, while tubing is connected with fittings and clamps.

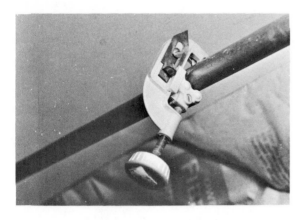

Fig. 8–55 Cutting copper pipe with a pipe cutter.

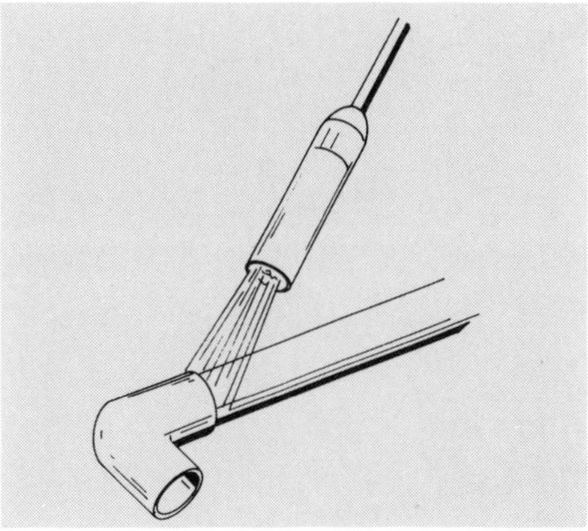

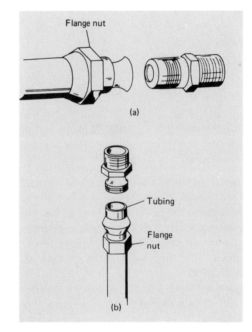

Fig. 8–56 Sweating copper pipe.

Cast-iron Pipe

Cast-iron pipe (Fig. 8–54) is used only in DWV systems. It will not corrode and is strong, but heavy and awkward to work with. Cast-iron pipe is jointed by bell-and-spigot joints, compression joints, or by no-hub connections. In the older system, the spigot end of a pipe is fitted into the enlarged bell end of another section of pipe. The joint is sealed with molten lead over an oakum caulking. Compression joints use a neoprene gasket in the spigot. No-hub pipes are joined by a neoprene gasket fitted over the ends of pipes butted flush together. The gasket is held in place by a screw-tightened metal clamp.

CUTTING AND JOINING PIPE AND TUBING

Pipe and tubing are cut in similar ways with a hacksaw or special pipe cutter, but the methods used for joining them are quite different.

Copper Pipe and Tubing

Copper pipe and tubing is relatively thin-walled and easily crimped and damaged. The thickness of the walls is designated by one of three letters: type K, thick wall; type L, medium wall; type M, thin wall. The medium-wall pipe, type L, is usually used in domestic installations, though some plumbing codes allow type M. Copper tubing is made in types K (thick walled) and L (medium-thick walled). Most household installations use Type L tubing.

Hacksaws or *pipe cutters* are used to cut copper pipe and tubing (Fig. 8–55). Whenever cutting with a hacksaw, use a miterbox to make a square cut, and remove burrs with a rattail file.

Fig. 8–57 Joining copper tubing: a) flared fitting, b) compression fitting.

Rigid pipe is joined by soldering, but tubing can be joined by solder, flare fittings (Fig. 8–56), or compression fittings (Fig. 8–57(a)). Flare and compression fitting (Fig. 8–57(b)) allow the tubing to be easily disconnected by unscrewing the threaded fittings from the fixture.

Before soldering, the pipe and fitting must be dry, clean, and free of burrs. Clean the end of the pipe and the inside of the fitting with steel wool until they shine. Apply soldering flux to the two areas. As the pipe is joined to the fitting, turn it a little to spread the flux. Heat the fitting but not the pipe

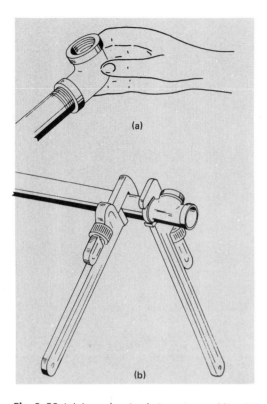

Fig. 8–58 Joining galvanized pipe: a) assembling fittings and pipe, b) tightening joints with wrenches.

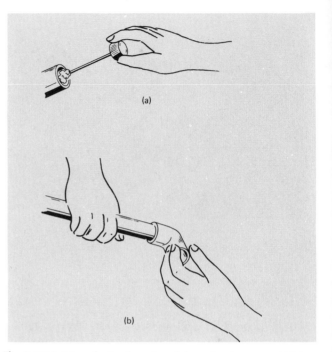

Fig. 8–59 Joining plastic pipe: a) applying solvent cement, b) joining the pieces.

with the propane torch. Heat from the fitting will be passed on to the pipe and solder. When the fitting is hot enough, hold wire solder against the lip of the fitting at the joint. Solder will flow into the gap by capillary action, even though it may have to rise vertically. When the solder forms a complete ring around the fitting, wipe off the excess with a cloth for a smooth bead.

When two or three pipes are to be sweated to the same fitting, they should all be soldered at the same time. If one end is already soldered, it can be wrapped with a wet cloth to protect it from heat while the other end is being sweated.

Galvanized Pipe

Galvanized pipe is joined by threaded fittings. Since the fittings at each end of the pipe are threaded in opposite directions, a length of pipe can't be unscrewed once it is installed. It has to be cut with a hacksaw or pipe cutter.

The pipe should be cut squarely and the burrs removed with a pipe reamer or rattail file. A special threading die is used to cut threads on the ends. Coat the threads with pipe-joint compound and turn the pipe by hand as far as it will go (Fig. 8–58(a)). Two pipe wrenches are used to tighten the joint; one turns the fitting one way while the other turns

Fig. 8–60 Joining plastic tubing.

the pipe in the opposite direction (Fig. 8–58(b)). Where a length of galvanized pipe may have to be disconnected, it should be joined by a union—a small fitting threaded on both ends—that can be easily disconnected.

Plastic Pipe

Plastic pipe can be cut with a special pipe cutter or any fine-toothed saw (e.g., hacksaw, handsaw, power saw). When cutting with a saw, use a miter box to make a square cut. Burrs left by the saw or pipe cutter can be removed with a sharp knife or a pipe reamer.

Since the pipe must fit smoothly into the fitting, it should be tested before solvent cement is applied. Rough spots that impede the pipe can be removed with sandpaper. When ready to join the pieces, coat the end of the pipe and the inside of the fitting with the special solvent cement made for the plastic pipe being used (Fig. 8–59(a)). PVC and ABS plastics use a one-can type of cement, but CPVC plastics require applications from two different cans. Slide the pipe into the fitting and turn it to spread the cement over the joining surfaces. Since solvent cement sets quickly, the pieces must be joined immediately after the cement is applied and held together for a minute or so (Fig. 8–59(b)). Although the solvent cement welds quickly, water shouldn't be run through the pipe right away. Wait a few hours (longer if the temperatures approach freezing).

Flexible polyethylene tubing can be cut with a sharp knife or fine-toothed saw. Lengths are joined by rigid connectors that are inserted in the ends of the tubing and held by hose clamps (Fig. 8–60).

Cast-iron Pipe

Cast-iron pipe for DWV systems can be cut by either a hacksaw or cold chisel. The lighter service-weight pipe used in domestic installations is cut by scoring the circumference of the pipe with a hacksaw. The pipe should be scored to a depth of 1/16 in. or more. To break it, extend the scored section of pipe over a ledge of some kind and hit it with a hammer until it breaks along the line. Extra-heavy cast-iron pipe is cut by scoring with a cold chisel until it separates.

Cast-iron pipes may be joined in one of several ways. With a bell and spigot joint, the spigot end of a pipe is inserted into the enlarged bell of another section and caulked with rope-like oakum. The oakum is tamped down and the joint sealed with molten lead poured around the bell (Fig. 8–61(a)). The bell faces upward in vertical joints to receive the lead and to minimize internal obstructions to the flow of waste. In horizontal joints, a joint runner must be attached around the joint to contain the molten lead until it cools.

No-hub cast-iron pipes are connected with a gasket and clamp. A neoprene gasket is slipped over the end of one pipe and the two ends brought flush together. The gasket is worked along until it is centered over the joint. A large screw-tightened clamp is placed around the gasket where it presses firmly to form a seal (Fig. 8–61(b)). This type of joint allows more flexibility in aligning the pipes than a bell and spigot joint does.

Two other types of fittings are used: compression fittings and the Durham system. *Compression joints* (Fig. 8–61(c)) are made by using a neoprene-rubber gasket in the bell end of a cast-iron pipe. The gasket is lubricated and the hubless end of the next pipe slid into place. The force of the pipes compresses and seals the gasket. The *Durham system* uses threaded galvanized pipe and threaded cast-iron fittings to form a DWV system.

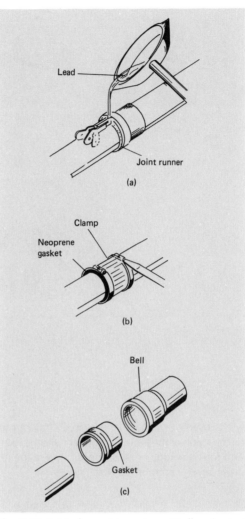

Fig. 8–61 Joints for cast-iron pipe: a) bell and spigot, b) no-hub, c) compression.

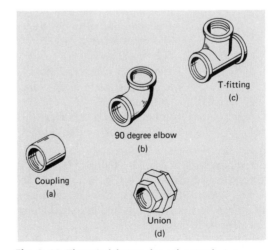

Fig. 8–62 Threaded fittings for galvanized pipe.

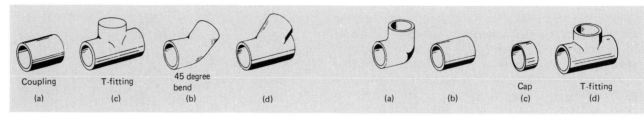

Fig. 8–63 Fittings for copper pipe.

Fig. 8–64 Fittings for plastic pipe.

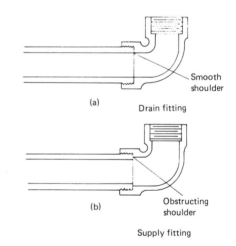

Fig. 8–65 Fittings for flared copper tubing.

FITTINGS

Fittings are the short connecting links that join piping or tubing. They are used to connect lengths in a straight run, to change the direction of the pipes, to connect another pipe into a line, and for numerous other purposes. The following are some of the more common fittings:

Coupling	Joins two pipes in a straight run
Elbow or *Bend*	Changes the direction of the run
T-fitting	Joins another pipe to a run
Union	Threaded on both ends to join pipes for easy disconnection
Reducer	Joins larger to smaller pipes
Adapter	Joins pipes made of different materials
Cap	Covers the end of a pipe
Closet bend	Connects soil pipe to a toilet

Galvanized pipe requires threaded fittings (Fig. 8–62(a)-(d)), but fittings for rigid copper pipe (Fig. 8–63(a)-(d)) and plastic pipe are smooth (Fig. 8–64(a)-(d)). Copper tubing uses smooth fittings for sweated joints and threaded fittings for flare joints (Fig. 8–65(a)-(d)).

Fitting employed in drainage systems differ from those in supply systems since drainage fittings must not offer any internal obstructions to the flow of waste (Fig. 8–66). Cast-

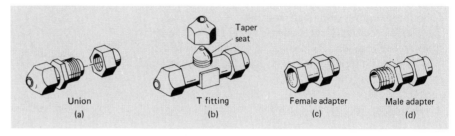

Fig. 8–66 Fittings for: a) drainage, b) supply.

iron fittings are all drainage-type fittings. Both types of fittings are made for copper, plastic, and galvanized pipe. Drainage fittings are, of course, generally larger than the supply fittings.

VALVES

Globe valves and gate valves are the most common types of valves used in household plumbing systems. A *globe valve* controls the flow of water by seating a washer at the end of the valve stem against a valve seat to block the passageway through the valve. An ordinary faucet works in this manner. *Gate valves* control the flow of water by blocking the entire width of the pipe. A tapered extension at the end of the valve stem moves downward across the diameter of the pipe when the valve handle is turned clockwise. This type of valve allows the water to flow without restriction when the valve is all the way open. Shutoff valves are constructed in this manner.

INSTALLING PLUMBING

To install new fixtures, supply and DWV pipes often have to be extended and roughed in. Plumbing is roughed in by running branches from supply and DWV lines to the points where they connect to the fixtures. Lavatory, bathtub and shower, sink, toilet and other fixtures have their own prescribed requirements for roughing in. The local plumbing code lists the types and sizes of pipe, locations, and other plumbing specifications, in addition to telling you what plumbing work you can do and what work requires a licensed plumber.

The *main water-supply system* is usually made up of ¾-in. pipe. The size of pipe and tubing is designated by its nominal diameter instead of its actual diameter. A ¾-in. pipe is actually somewhat larger than ¾ in. Branches of ½-in. pipe are used to connect fixtures, such as kitchen sinks, bathtubs, and washing machines, to the hot- and cold-water pipes. Lavatories and toilets are generally connected with ⅜-in. tubing.

The *DWV system* uses 3- or 4-in. pipe for the soil pipe, soil stack, and main drainpipe. Fixtures are connected to the main drain pipe by smaller-size pipes that vary from 1¼ to 2 in. in diameter, depending on the volume of water to be carried away. A bathtub, for example, would use a 2-in. drainpipe, while a lavatory would need only a 1¼-in. pipe. Vent pipes also vary in size. The soil stack, an extension of the soil pipe, is the largest vent, usually 4 in. in diameter. Secondary vents or revents use 1½-in. pipe to connect fixture drains to the main vent.

PLANNING

New fixtures should be located close to existing supply and DWV lines to minimize the cost and complexity of the installation. If the fixture is quite close to the main soil stack, for example, it may be wet-vented. When a fixture is close enough to a main vent to vent through its own drainpipe, it is said to be wet-vented. The local plumbing code will specify maximum distances for wet-venting.

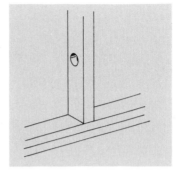

Fig. 8–67 Hole in a stud.

Once the location of the new fixture has been established, determine where the branches to the supply and DWV lines should go. Run the pipe between studs and joists with as little cutting as possible. In first-floor installations, pipe can be attached with strapping under the joists in the cellar. Measure the lengths of pipe needed and allow for the overlap of pipe and fittings and for the spacing between pipe ends in the fittings. Decide on the size, type, and amount of pipe and the kinds and number of fittings that will be required.

CUTTING AND NOTCHING

Where pipes have to be run through studs and joists, the following rules of thumb for cutting and notching should be observed, to minimize the loss of strength in the wooden members.

Holes can be bored in the center of studs (Fig. 8–67) and joists anywhere along their lengths, but the holes should not exceed one-half the depth of a stud or one-fourth the depth of a joist.

Notches can be cut to two-thirds the depth of a stud in the upper half and to one-third the depth in the lower half, without additional reinforcing. In a joist, notches should be cut only within the sections extending one-fourth the way in from the ends. To prevent undue weakening, the notch should be cut no deeper than one-fourth the depth of the joist.

Notched studs and joists can be *reinforced* by metal plates or short lengths of 2 X 2 (Fig. 8–68). Nail the plate or board over the face of a notch in a stud or in the bottom of a joist. When a notch is cut in the top of a joist, nail the supports on both sides of the joist and under the notch.

ROUGHING IN

Extensions from the DWV system to the fixture should be installed first. Each type of fixture has its own size require-

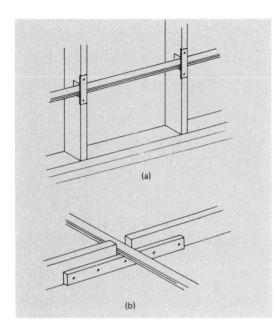

Fig. 8–68 Reinforced notch: a) in a stud, b) in a joist.

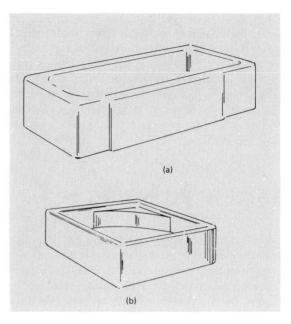

Fig. 8–69 Modern bathtubs: a) standard, b) square.

ments for drainage and venting. The drainpipe should slope downward ¼ in. per foot toward the main drain line. Branch pipes for hot and cold water can be connected into the main lines with T-fittings and run parallel a few inches apart to where they are capped at the wall or floor next to the fixture. Use strapping to hold the pipes so they won't vibrate or bang. Supply lines will require T-fittings and air chambers in the walls where they are connected to the fixtures. Supply pipes roughed in at a wall should extend an inch beyond the wall. Install the cold-water pipe on the right and the hot-water pipe on the left side.

MAJOR PLUMBING FIXTURES

BATHTUBS AND SHOWERS

To install a new bathtub or shower, the old unit must be disconnected and removed, the plumbing extended, the walls framed (for a built-in unit), and the tub or shower installed and connected. The surrounding walls must be protected with a waterproof covering.

Types of Units Available

The standard bathtub is 60 in. long and approximately 30 in. wide, although square tubs and other shapes are available

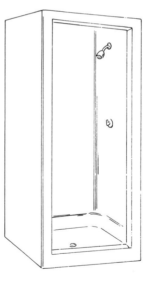

Fig. 8–70 Fiberglass shower enclosure.

for irregular-shaped spaces (Fig. 8–69). Built-in fiberglass or plastic shower units are approximately 32 to 48 in. wide and 78 to 84 in. high (Fig. 8–70).

Tubs are made of procelain-covered steel, cast iron, and fiberglass. Cast-iron tubs are by far the heaviest, while the fiberglass are the lightest. Modern prefabricated shower units are made of either fiberglass or laminated plastic.

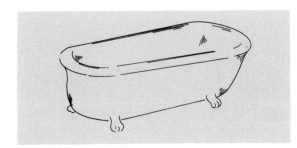

Fig. 8–71 Four-footed cast-iron tub.

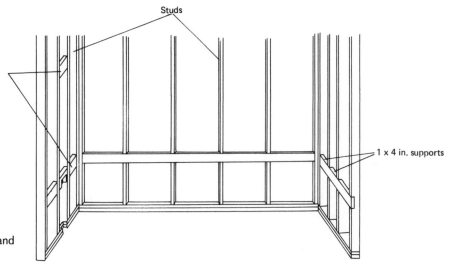

Fig. 8–72 Supporting framework for tub and pipes.

Removing Old Tubs

Pipe fittings in old tubs are often corroded and difficult to disconnect. A propane torch or penetrating oil may help loosen them. If the tub is an old-fashioned, four-footed cast-iron tub (Fig. 8–71), the fittings will be accessible at the faucet end of the tub. If the fittings are in a wall or under the floor, look for an access panel. Otherwise, the wall or floor must be opened up. Disconnect the water-supply lines and drain pipe at the couplings close to the floor from where they will be extended for the new plumbing.

Building the Frame and Extending the Plumbing

Built-in steel and fiberglass tubs must be supported on their three wall sides (Fig. 8–72). (Cast iron tubs don't need side support.) After the tub is selected, nail 1 X 4-in. wooded strips to the studs along the walls where the edges of the tub are to be butted. The plaster should be removed so that the

strips can be nailed directly to the studs at the height necessary to support the flanges of the tub. Use a carpenter's level to keep them horizontal. A framework of 2 X 4's should be built at the head of the tub to support the water-supply lines for the faucet and shower head. Crosspieces between the studs will allow the lines to be aligned correctly. Install an access panel on the other side of the wall at the head of the tub for future repairs.

When the new framework is constructed, a plumber or an experienced homeowner can extend the old drain and water-supply lines with adapters and tubing to rough in the new plumbing for the tub and shower (Fig. 8–73).

Installing the Tub and Shower

Once the supporting framework is built and the pipes roughed in, the tub or shower unit can be moved into position. Place the tub so that its end and side flanges rest on the strips nailed to the wall. Some flanges have openings for nailing to the strips. Cast-iron tubs are sufficiently heavy and stable to stay in position without the wooden strips. Finally,

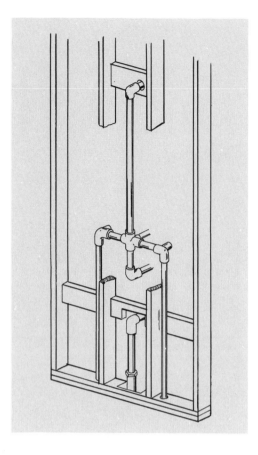

Fig. 8–73 Roughed-in plumbing for tub and shower.

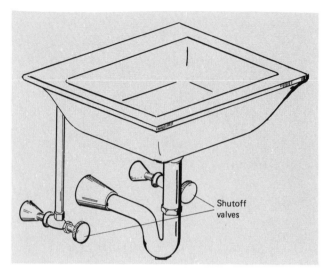

Fig. 8–74 Lavatory installation.

the roughed-in plumbing is connected to the drain and water-supply pipes with couplings and connecting pipe.

Waterproof walls must be installed around built-in tubs and the seams caulked or grouted. Waterproof gypsum board should be used under ceramic tiles and grout used to fill the gap between the tiles and the edge of the tub. Fiberglass and laminated plastic panels can be purchased prefabricated to fit around standard-size tubs. They are made in flat sheets and L-shaped panels for walls and corners; moldings are used to seal the seams. Single-unit prefabricated fiberglass tubs and wall panels can be used to minimize the problem of waterproofing seams.

After the walls are finished, attach the faucet handles, shower head, tub spout, and accompanying plates and bonnets, to make the installation complete.

Beyond making a simple extension, roughing in plumbing can be quite complicated. Each type of installation has specific requirements for fittings and pipes. The homeowner without much plumbing experience who plans to do his own work should seek detailed advice from someone who is experienced, from instructions accompanying the fixture, and from literature that deals at length with the subject.

SINKS AND LAVATORIES

Kitchen sinks and bathroom lavatories are hooked up in much the same way. Both are connected to water-supply lines by rigid tubing or flexible tubing and coupling nuts. P-traps are used to connect both fixtures to the drain system. Drain pipes for kitchen sinks, however, have a diameter of 1½ in., while lavatory drains are 1¼ in. Sinks and lavatories are attached to the cabinet or wall in different ways, depending on the type of unit. Stainless-steel sinks have a lip that rests on the edge of a countertop and is clamped from beneath. Other types of countertop sinks require a supporting metal rim and clamps. Wall-mounted lavatories are supported by a wall bracket, which is sometimes assisted by chrome legs.

Sinks, lavatories, and faucets can be replaced with new units without major changes in the plumbing (Fig. 8–74). The drain and water-supply lines and faucets must be detached before the unit can be lifted out. New sinks and faucets can be purchased that will fit or adapt to the existing fittings. Often the most difficult part of the procedure is loosening corroded or frozen coupling and flange nuts on the old fixtures. Persistence, penetrating oil, and the proper tools will eventually do the job.

Removing a Sink or Lavatory

After closing the shutoff valve, disconnect the flexible tubing that connects the valves to the faucets. Loosen the coupling nuts just above the shutoff valves with a wrench (Fig. 8–75). The coupling nuts at the upper end of the flexible tubing are difficult to get at, since they are under the basin. Use a basin wrench to reach into this inaccessible space. If the entire sink or lavatory is to be removed, these coupling nuts will

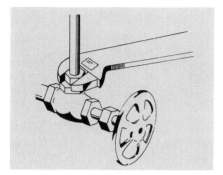

Fig. 8–75 Disconnecting flexible tubing at shutoff valve.

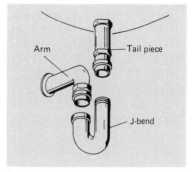

Fig. 8–78 Installing the drain and trap.

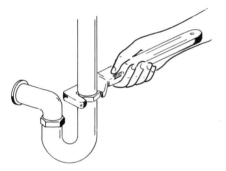

Fig. 8–76 Disconnecting the drain pipe.

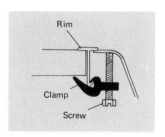

Fig. 8–77 Rim and clamps.

be easier to get to once the basin is lifted out.

The *faucets* are fastened beneath the sink by nuts and washers. Loosen and remove these in order to lift the faucets out. The lever mechanism that operates the pop-up drain mechanism should also be disconnected.

The drain pipe is disconnected at the coupling where it is attached to the trap (Fig. 8–76). The trap's J-bend can be removed completely by loosening the coupling at the other end also, where it is attached to the drainpipe leading into the wall.

Unfasten the clamps that hold the rim or lip and lift the sink out of the countertop (Fig. 8–77). Stainless steel sinks

are relatively light, but porcelain-covered cast-iron sinks or lavatories are heavy and may require bracing or additional help in lifting. Wall-mounted lavatories are removed by lifting them free of their wall brackets after their drain and supply pipes have been disconnected.

Installing New Units

Measure the size of the sink opening, the diameter of the drain pipe, and the lengths of the old flexible tubing and drain pipe. If he knows these dimensions, your supplier will be able to provide the right size of hardware and any necessary adapters. Outline the edge of the countertop opening with a thin bead of plumber's putty to seal the lip or rim. Lower the sink into the opening (after installing a rim if necessary) and fasten the clamps that hold the sink to the counter.

Install the faucets after laying a bead of plumber's putty to seal the base. Slide the faucet assembly into its holes and slip the washers and nuts on the threaded sections and tighten them. If the unit already has flexible tubing attached, the ends should be connected to the coupling nuts at the shutoff valves. Otherwise, install the flexible tubing separately.

Connect the drain by sliding coupling nuts and washers onto the drain pipes extending from the sink and the wall (Fig. 8–78) so that the couplings can be slipped over the ends of the J-bend when it is installed. If the new fittings won't align, use elbows, adapters, or couplings to connect the drain. Once the problem of connecting the drain is clear, a supplier will be able to provide the necessary fittings.

To *install a new drain* in a sink, line the edge of the drain opening with a bead of plumber's putty and press the drain down against it. Slide a rubber washer over the threaded section beneath the sink and screw on and tighten the flange nut with a spud wrench. A coupling is used to fasten the drain tailpiece to the threads on the drain.

Leaky drains are repaired by loosening the coupling to the J-bend and using a spud wrench to remove the flange nut that holds the drain to the sink. The drain can be lifted out, cleaned, and replaced with a fresh bead of plumber's putty.

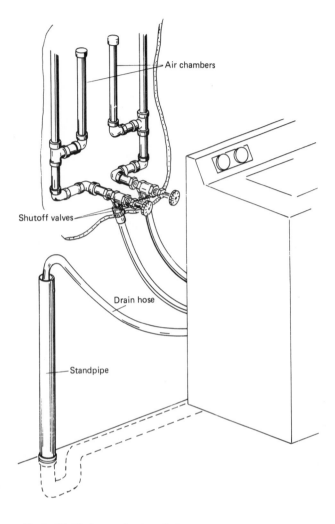

Fig. 8—79 Clothes washer installation.

WASHING MACHINES

A washing machine requires hot and cold-water lines and a standpipe-type drain connection. If a machine is being installed for the first time, the supply lines will have to be extended from the closest hot- and cold-water lines and the standpipe tied in with the drain system (Fig. 8–79). Depending on the local plumbing code and the homeowner's experience, the homeowner may be able to install these connections himself. If a washing machine is being replaced, the new machine can be hooked up to the lines and drain used previously.

Water-supply lines for washing machines require extra-long air chambers and individual shutoff valves (Fig. 8–80(a)). The air chambers should be ¾ in., (that is, larger than the supply line), and from 18 to 24 in. long. This extra length will prevent water hammer when the intake valves in the

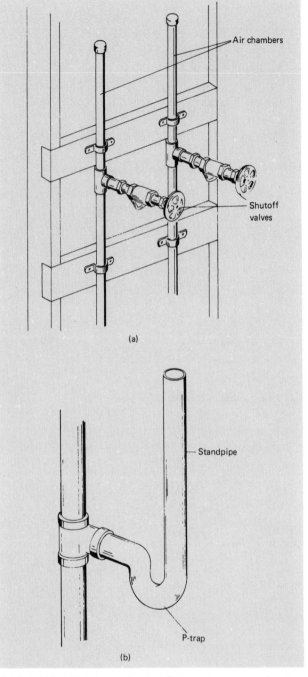

Fig. 8—80 Plumbing for washer installation: a) water-supply pipes, b) standpipe and P-trap.

washing machine are suddenly closed. The faucets or shutoff valves have threaded fittings for the couplings on the hoses connecting to the washing machine. Besides allowing the mixture of hot and cold water to be controlled, the valves can be closed when the machine isn't being used, to reduce the water pressure on the machine's valves.

The *drain hose* from the washing machine is inserted into the open top of a 1½ in. standpipe-type drain (Fig. 8–80(b)) that extends above the water level in the machine. The specific height depends on the machine and local plumbing code. A P-trap is installed at the base of the standpipe to seal the drain.

After the washing machine has been connected, run it through several wash, rinse, and spin cycles. Check the supply couplings for leaks and tighten them if necessary. The drain hose should be inserted well into the standpipe and wedged if necessary to prevent it from working free and flooding the floor.

DISHWASHERS

Dishwashers require only two plumbing connections, a hot-water supply and a drain. To take advantage of existing plumbing, dishwashers are usually installed close to kitchen sinks (Fig. 8–81).

The *hot-water line* is connected by a special coupling at the dishwasher inlet and by a T-fitting under the sink. To connect the flexible tubing at the sink, either the hot-water line must be cut and a T-fitting sweated in place, or a saddle-T and shutoff valve must be installed. T-fittings should be located above the sink shutoff valve so that the same valve can also be used for the dishwasher.

The *drain hose* or *tubing* from the dishwasher should be connected to a fitting on the sink drain above the trap. The drain pipe should be disconnected and an adapter inserted to allow the smaller drain line from the dishwasher to connect to the 1½-in. sink drain (Fig. 8–82(a)). If a garbage disposer is installed in the sink, the dishwasher drain can be attached to the fitting provided on the disposer after the knockout plug has been removed (Fig. 8–82(b)).

GARBAGE DISPOSER

If a garbage disposer (Fig. 8–83) is being installed in a sink for the first time, the drain unit and the drain pipe immediately under the sink will have to be removed. The garbage disposer has its own sink-drain unit and a fitting for connection to the trap. Instructions accompanying the garbage disposer will provide instructions about installing the unit.

Remove the drain from the sink by loosening the coupling nut that connects the drain tailpiece to the trap. With the trap detached, use a spud wrench to remove the flange nut on the bottom of the drain. Slip off the washer and ring and lift the drain out of the sink. Before installing the new unit, clean the old putty from the edge of the drain hole.

Install the new drain unit by applying a thin bead of plumber's putty around the drain opening and pressing the sink flange into the putty to seal the joint. From beneath the sink, slide the gaskets, ring, and mounting ring over the

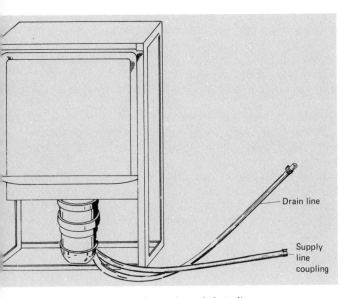
Fig. 8–81 Dishwasher with supply and drain lines.

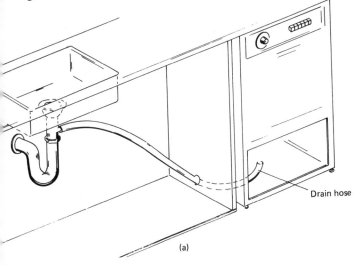
(a)

Fig. 8–82 Types of drain connections: a) to sink drain, b) to garbage disposer.

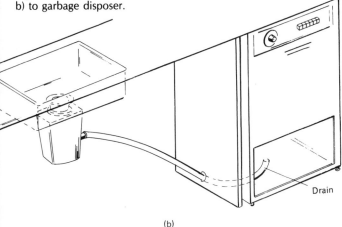
(b)

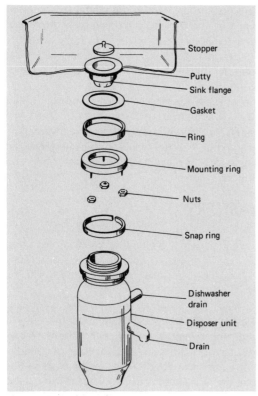

Fig. 8–83 Garbage disposer.

Stopper
Putty
Sink flange
Gasket
Ring
Mounting ring
Nuts
Snap ring
Dishwasher drain
Disposer unit
Drain

flange and hold them in place with the snap ring. Tighten the small threaded bolts in the mounting ring to pull the assembly tightly together.

The *disposer* is slipped over the ends of the small bolts on the bottom of the mounting plate and secured with nuts. Position the disposer so the drain and dishwasher connections face the connecting lines before tightening the nuts. The last step is to connect the drain outlet to the drain pipe above the trap.

HOT-WATER HEATERS

Hot-water heaters are self-contained in that they use a source of heat separate from the furnace to heat water for the hot-water system. The water may be heated by an oil or gas burner (Fig. 8–84(a)(b)) attached at the bottom of the tank or by an internal electrical heating element (Fig. 8–84(c)). Hot-water storage tanks resemble hot-water heaters but have no heater and only store water fed from a coil heated by boiler water in the furnace.

Kinds of Hot-Water Heaters

Electric, gas, and oil water heaters are the standard types today as they have been for years. But within those categories there are various subtypes. Solar heat may

also be used to heat water for home use. The main types of heaters available include the following:

Electric Hot-Water Heaters. The standard electric heater is usually somewhat more efficient than the gas water heater. But the electric appliance takes longer to heat the water in a tank once the hot water is used up. As a further disadvantage, electric resistance heaters generally have higher operating costs.

The heat-pump water heater represents a significant advance over the standard electric heater. The heat-pump takes heat—heat that would otherwise be wasted—from the air in the house and transfers it into the water tank. Typically about 50 percent more efficient than the conventional electric water heater, the heat-pump comes in two models: integral, which has a tank, and the remote, which has no tank. Both systems utilize a condensate near the refrigerant coils. But the condensate has to be piped or drained out of the house.

Gas Water Heaters. The burner below the water storage tank identifies the standard gas-fired water heater. A thermostatic control signals the burner unit to maintain a supply of hot water. Later models have submerged heating chambers inside the water tank; such construction eliminates most of the heat loss that takes place around the open flame.

Obviating the normal need to vent the gas-fired heater through the roof, other newer models can be vented through walls. The convenience of wall venting makes these models especially attractive to owners of multifamily buildings. Each apartment or living unit can have its own direct-vented gas water heater, making possible separate metering. Some top-of-the-line gas-fired systems combine house- and water-heating functions

Oil Water Heaters. Designed primarily for homeowners who already heat with oil, oil-fired water heaters may cost more than comparable units using another fuel. But the oil water heater is particularly useful in the home that has a central boiler supplying hot water for heat and for household use in sinks, tubs, and the dishwasher. Oil also reheats water rapidly.

Two other kinds of water heaters have special characteristics and advantages:

Solar Heaters. Taking heat directly from the sun, solar water heaters operate on a simple principle. They employ a collector to capture solar heat and a heat transfer fluid that becomes heated in the collector and then flows through pipes into a special storage tank or the home's hot-water tank. The fluid may be water or an antifreeze mixture. The collector is usually a network of pipes that are exposed to the sun's rays.

Solar water heaters range widely as regards complexity and price. One system may be as simple as a roof-mounted water tank called a *thermosiphon*. Another system may have collectors that move throughout

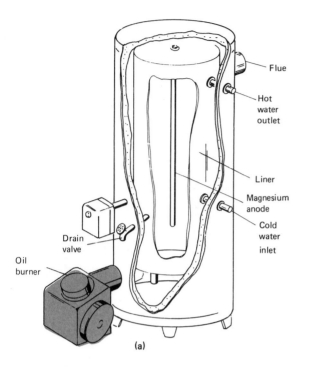

Fig. 8–84 Types of hot-water heaters: a) oil, b) gas, c) electrical.

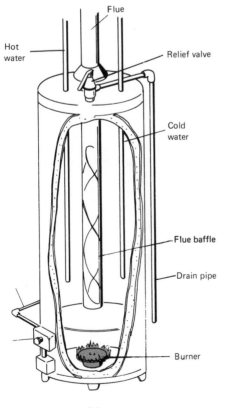

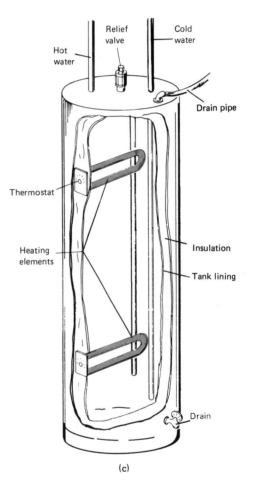

the day to track the sun's movements. An efficient system supplies 50 to 75 percent of the average home's hot water needs. The amount of heat delivered by any particular system depends, primarily, on a household's water consumption, the amount of sunlight a home is exposed to in the course of a day, and other factors.

Instantaneous Hot-Water Heaters. A twist of a hot-water faucet activates an instantaneous heater. Using electricity or gas, this heater has little or no water storage capacity; it does, however, have a high-temperature

burner that can heat water as it is being used. The instantaneous heater wastes very little heat, and can often supply all the needs of a family with low hot-water requirements. In such a family the average individual would use about 20 gallons of water per day.

In the standard water heating system, cold water enters the lower end of the lined tank and rises as it is heated by the burner under the tank or by the electrical heating element. At the top of the tank, hot water is drawn into the hot-water system, and then replaced by fresh cold water.

Operation of Hot-water Heaters

Cold water enters the lower end of the lined tank and rises as it is heated by the burner under the tank or by the electrical heating element. At the top of the tank, hot water is drawn off into the hot-water system, and then replaced by fresh cold water.

A *thermostat* mounted on the tank determines the temperature of the water by controlling the burner or electrical element. Most thermostats are adjustable for water temperatures from 110°F to 180°F (depending on the type of unit). To prevent overheating, the *high-limit cutoff* will turn the burner or electrical element off in the event the thermostat doesn't work. As a safeguard against damage from excessive temperature or pressure, a *temperature-pressure relief valve* mounted on top of the tank opens to lower the pressure in the unit if the other controls fail. On gas-heated units, an automatic switch shuts off the gas supply if the pilot light fails.

The tank is protected from sedimentation by one or more *rods.* Magnesium anodes are commonly used. *Fiberglass insulation* reduces the heat loss between the tank and casing. At the bottom of the tank, a *drain valve* allows water containing sediment to be drawn off periodically.

Removing an Old Hot-Water Heater

Before it can be removed, a heater must be disconnected from the heat source, inlet and outlet pipes, and flue. Turn off the electricity to an electrical or oil-heated unit, or the gas to a gas-heated unit. Close the shutoff valve in the cold-water inlet line, and disconnect the flue, if the unit is heated by oil or gas. The water remaining in the tank should be drained with a hose from the drain valve.

Remove an oil or *gas burner* by unbolting it from the opening at the bottom of the tank's casing. If it is an electric heater, open the circuit-breaker and disconnect the electrical line at the tank.

Disconnect inlet and *outlet pipes* at their couplings to the water-supply lines. Flexible connectors can be loosened with a wrench but pipes without couplings or unions must be separated by heating sweated joints or by cutting with a hacksaw.

Installing Hot-water Heaters

Standard-size, hot-water heaters contain from 30 to 80 gal of water. If the new heater is approximately the same size as the old one, it can be connected to the same fittings with a minimum of change. Otherwise, the inlet and outlet pipes will have to be extended or modified to reach the fittings on the new tank.

Install the burner at the base of the tank, following the directions accompanying the new unit. Or, if it is an electric heater, reconnect the supply cable. Attach the flue to the outlet on the heater.

Connect the inlet and outlet fittings to the supply lines. If the connections to the old tank had to be cut, use flexible connectors to join the tank fittings and the supply lines. These are threaded onto steel pipes or sweated onto copper pipes.

Fill the tank with water by opening both the shutoff valve and a hot-water faucet. When water runs out of the faucet, the tank is full and the faucet can be turned off. The burner or electrical-heating element can be turned on when the tank is full and the flue is attached. Set the thermostat to the desired temperature and check the unit to see that it operates properly during its trial run. If the inlet or outlet couplings leak, tighten them with a wrench. After the heater is in operation, drain water from the bottom of the tank every few weeks to remove sediment.

PUMPS

Pumps are sometimes used to provide the supply system with water or to remove unwanted water. Submersible pumps and jet pumps are used to provide water under pressure from wells and other sources (Fig. 8–85(a)(b)). These pumps can raise water from 200- or 300-ft wells with ½- to 1½-hp electric motors.

Sump pumps are used to remove unwanted water from basements and other low areas (Fig. 8–85(c)). When installed in a basement that is below the water table, the pump will turn on automatically when actuated by a float-type switch. A remote-control switch also allows the pump to be turned on at water levels too low for the float switch. Debris is filtered out by a strainer in the pump's intake.

Either plastic pipe or a length of hose can be used for the suction and discharge lines, but well pumps are more likely to be installed with plastic pipe.

CONDENSATION

Pipes and fixtures sweat when moisture from warm, humid air condenses on their cold surfaces. This can produce enough water to stain celings or form a pool around a toilet. Sweating can be stopped by removing the moisture from the air, insulating the pipes or fixtures, or warming the water. Dehumidifiers are often used in moist basements during the summer to remove moisture from the air.

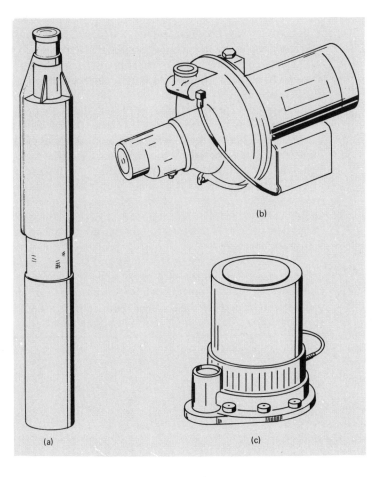

Fig. 8–85 Types of pumps: a) submersible, b) jet, c) sump.

INSULATING

Insulation around pipes creates a nonconducting barrier between the cold metal and moist air. The same types of insulation are used to prevent sweating that are used to prevent pipes from freezing. Wrap on self-sticking insulating tape or asbestos tape; paint on a liquid-base insulation; or fit asbestos or foam jackets around the pipes and fittings (Fig. 8–86).

Toilet tanks can be insulated with foam. Drain the tank, wipe out the remaining water, and glue the fitted foam sections to the inside walls. Plumbing suppliers can provide kits for different types of tanks. The layer of foam prevents the cold water from cooling the sides of the tank to the point where condensation forms.

WARMING THE WATER

Pipes and fixtures containing warm water aren't cold enough to sweat. Although it's not feasible to warm the

Fig. 8–86 Installing pipe insulation.

water in the entire cold-water system, it's possible to warm the water in the toilet tank. To do this, a line has to be extended from the nearest hot-water pipe to a mixer valve where the hot and cold water are combined. Warm water from the mixer flows through the inlet valve and into the toilet. The warm water will prevent the tank from sweating. Another method of warming the water in the tank is to use a water heater designed for a fish tank. Whenever any electrical device is used near plumbing, care should be taken to avoid an electric shock.

WATER TREATMENT

A water supply may contain minerals, gases, sediment or other substances that make it undesirable for household use. Most of these impurities can be removed by filters or replaced by less objectionable substitutes. Hard water that contains calcium and magnesium ions can be softened by substituting softer sodium ions. Dirt, sediment, and iron can be removed by filters. Objectionable odors and tastes can be absorbed by using charcoal filters.

SOFTENING HARD WATER

Well water and other hard water can be softened by installing a water softener in the main water line (Fig. 8–87). The softener exchanges sodium ions for the suspended calcium and magnesium ions to make the water softer.

The hardness is measured by the number of grains of calcium carbonate per gallon. Soft water, for example, contains less than 1 grain per gallon, while extremely hard well water may contain 10 to 50 or more grains per gallon. These suspended minerals prevent soap from being effective in wash water and combine with dirt to leave scum spots and rings on clothes and fixtures. Suspended minerals are also deposited inside galvanized pipes and fittings, restricting the flow of water.

Water softeners have different softening capacities. A small softener can handle water with 30 grains per gallon, while a large softener might handle hardness up to 70 or more grains per gallon. The hard ions are exchanged for sodium ions as the water is run through resin containing sodium. The resin is "regenerated" periodically by washing away the calcium and magnesium ions with salt water. Most softeners regenerate automatically.

To provide soft water to the entire system, the softener should be installed in the main line after the meter and cutoff valve. Where soft water is needed only for certain uses, such as washing and drinking, the softener can be installed so that the other cold-water lines bypass it. Sometimes only the hot water needs to be softened. In this case, the softener should be connected in the supply line leading to the hot-water heater.

REMOVING SEDIMENT, MINERALS, GASES, AND OTHER SUBSTANCES

Several types of filters are used to remove foreign matter, gases, and other substances. Cartridge filters (Fig. 8–88(a)) are generally disposable, while most tank-type filters (Fig. 8–88(b)) can be cleaned and used again. Filter units are often used in combination with a water softener to provide clean, soft water. Water softeners also remove small amounts of iron, but a filter is required to remove any appreciable amount.

Sediment such as dirt, clay, sand, silt, and other nonsoluble materials can be removed either by a disposable, cartridge-type filter or by a permanent tank filter mounted in the cold-water line before the water softener. The tank-type unit automatically backwashes to clean the filter.

Gases and odors such as sulfur and chlorine are removed by charcoal filters. The filter absorbs the impurities and must be replaced or regenerated periodically. The cartridge-type of filter is designed to be installed just ahead of a cold water faucet.

Iron compounds cause rust spots and stains on porcelain and other materials. If a water softener doesn't remove enough iron, an iron filter can be installed to treat the water before it reaches the softener. Both automatic backwashing and poisonous potassium permanganate are used

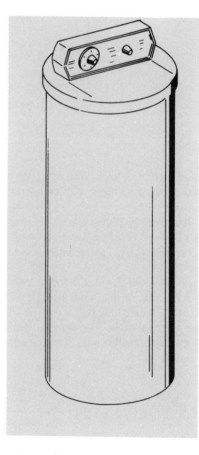

Fig. 8–87 Water softener.

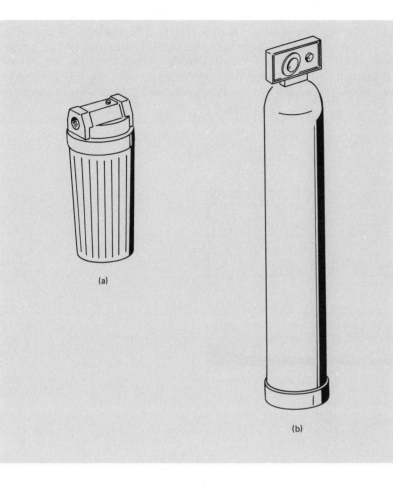

Fig. 8–88 Water filters: a) cartridge type, b) tank-type.

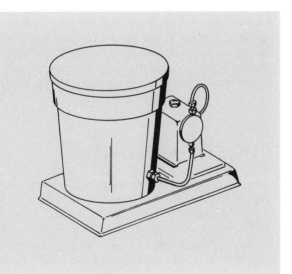

Fig. 8–89 Chemical feed pump.

to regenerate the filter periodically. The potassium permanganate replaces used-up oxygen and must be flushed away thoroughly.

Acids in water eat away at the inside of pipes and joints and etch glassware and dishes. A neutralizing filter will reduce the acidity of the water to a normal range.

A *chemical feed pump* can be used with private water supplies to purify water by injecting chlorine (Fig. 8–89). It can also be used to inject a neutralizing compound into highly acid water. This process reduces odors and disagreeable tastes.

SEPTIC DISPOSAL SYSTEMS

Where town sewerage lines are unavailable, waste may be disposed of by using a septic tank and a seepage field. The solid waste carried to the septic tank is decomposed by bacteria into liquid, gaseous, and sludge wastes. The liquid effluent is piped to the seepage field where it is absorbed into the soil, but the sludge must be periodically pumped out. Local health and building codes specify how septic systems should be built and where they can be located. Seepage fields, for example, should be placed downslope from houses and wells and are usually required to be at least

Liquid waste or effluent is carried from the outlet of the septic tank to the *seepage field* by a network of pipes (Fig. 8–91). A watertight pipe connects the septic tank to a *distribution box* from which open *distribution pipes* extend into the seepage field. These pipes allow the liquid waste to escape into the surrounding soil. Several types of pipes are used. Perforated, 4-in. plastic or fiber pipes are inexpensive

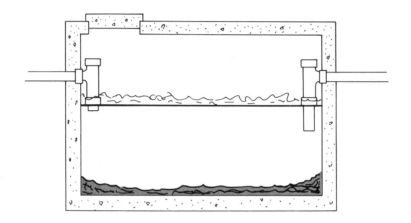

Fig. 8–90 Cross-section of septic tank.

100 feet away from water supplies. In some cases, the characteristics of the soil are such that local codes will not permit septic systems to be installed, at all.

STRUCTURE

A watertight *sewer line* connects the DWV system in the house to the septic tank. This line may be constructed from plastic, concrete, cast-iron, cement-asbestos, fiber, or vitrified-tile pipe. The first length of pipe from the house is generally made of cast iron because of code requirements. From the foundation of the house to the septic tank, the line should slope downward about ¼ inch per foot.

The size of the *septic tank* depends on the amount of waste that has to be processed. Health and building codes generally require a 900-gal tank for a three-bedroom house and a 1000-gal tank for a four-bedroom house. The tank may be constructed from precast concrete, concrete block, steel, brick, and, in some localities, redwood. The septic tank should be placed where it will be accessible for pumping out and buried so that its top is a foot or two below the surface (Fig. 8–90).

and easy to work with because of their light weight. Concrete or clay tiles may also be used by spacing them apart so that the waste escapes between them. The distribution pipes are placed in a trench lined with gravel to improve the drainage. Once they are in position, they are covered with a few more inches of gravel and finally protected from infiltrating soil by a layer of asphalt-saturated roofing paper. When the septic tank and the pipes are covered with soil, grass and small plants may be planted over the surface.

SEPTIC SYSTEM PROBLEMS

For a septic system to operate properly, the septic tank and the pipes must be of the right size and they must be correctly installed. If the tank is too small for the amount of waste that is discharged, it will probably overflow. This is likely to occur where new appliances, such as washing machines, garbage disposers, and dishwashers, are connected to an old septic system. Although the amount of waste water can be decreased by curtailing use of the appliances, the best solution is to install a larger septic tank and to extend the distribution or seepage field, if necessary.

Detergents often cause a septic system to break down. Many types of detergents retard the action of bacteria in the septic tank and also coat the pipes and tank with a slippery, grease-like, layer. This tends to prevent the solid wastes from breaking down and blocks up the system. To minimize

water can be piped directly to a seepage field or discharged into a simple seepage pit. Local health and building codes should be consulted to see what alternatives are available.

If sludge isn't pumped out of the septic tank before it reaches the bottom of the outlet, the system will become clogged, waste will back up into the house, and the effluent will overflow. Check the depth of the sludge with a long pole

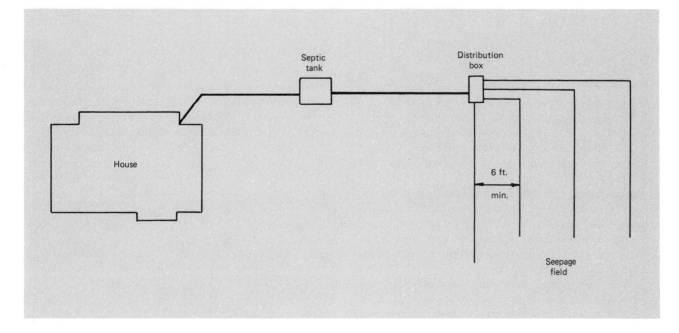

Fig. 8–91 Septic system and seepage field layout.

the effects of detergents, use those that are specially formulated for septic systems. Grease from sinks and dishwashers can also block up the system just as it can clog any drainage system. Perhaps the best solution is to install a separate grease trap and disposal system, similar to the septic system. Grease traps are designed so that they can be cleaned periodically of grease.

Where the amount of waste discharged is too great for a septic tank to handle, some local codes allow all but the waste from the toilet to be disposed of in some other manner. Sink, dishwasher, washing machine, and tub or shower

or stick. The depth at which the sludge should be pumped out depends on the capacity of the tank and the depth of the liquid between the tank outlet and the bottom of the tank compared with the depth of the liquid above the sludge. A 1000-gal septic tank, for example, with a 4-ft depth to the bottom of the tank should be pumped out if the distance between the top of the sludge and the tank outlet is 6 in. or less. (Many homeowners will prefer to have the tank pumped out before the sludge reaches this depth.) A septic tank cleaning service should be employed to do the job.

9 Electrical Systems

Electricity enters the house through a 2- or 3-wire hookup from the main power lines (Fig. 9–1). Modern installations with three-wire hookups provide 120 and 240 volts of alternating current. Older installations with two wires provide only 120 volts. These wires are connected to the main service panel where circuit breakers or fuses control electricity to individual circuits.

Circuit wiring branches out from the service entrance to provide electricity throughout the house. There are usually several general-purpose 15- or 20-amp circuits that provide power for lights, wall receptacles, and small appliances. Kitchen-type circuits require heavier wiring with circuit breakers or fuses capable of handling a minimum of 20 amps for toasters, refrigerators, dishwashers, and other large appliances. Many appliances have their own separate circuits because of their heavy current requirements. For example, refrigerator motors require a heavier current to start, and electric ranges require a continuous heavy current at 240 volts.

Each circuit consists of two or more wires sheathed in heavy plastic, fiber or thermoplastic insulation, armored cable, or a combination of plastic insulation and pipelike *conduit*. The cables and their wires are protected by metallic or nonmetallic boxes where they are connected to receptacles, lights, switches, and to secondary branches. The boxes provide mechanical strength for the unions and decrease the danger of electrical fire between the walls.

EMERGENCIES AND TROUBLE SHOOTING

EMERGENCIES

Electrical emergencies involve either the failure of electrical power or the danger of electrical damage or injury. There is little the homeowner can do when the power fails outside the house, except call the power company, unless the house has its own generator. If power fails at the service panel or in one of the house circuits, the homeowner can take steps to restore service. The dangers of fire from overloaded circuits or electrical shock can be met by turning off the electricity.

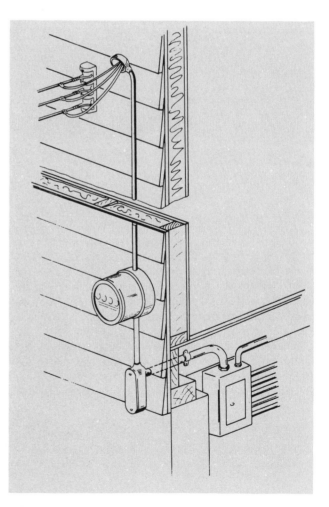

Fig. 9–1 Service entry.

When an appliance, fixture, or circuit loses power, the service panel should be checked for a blown fuse or tripped circuit breaker. If the fuse was blown because too many appliances overloaded the circuit, some of the appliances should be connected to another circuit. If the problem was caused by a short circuit, the fixtures, appliances, and other components in the circuit must be checked for a shorted connection.

When an emergency is in the making (such as wires smoking or sparking), the electricity should be turned off immediately. Electricity for a fixture or appliance can usually be turned off at a wall switch. The circuit breaker should be tripped, or the fuse removed, to cut off electricity to an entire circuit. If the emergency has progressed to the point of fire or electrical shock, the fire department or ambulance should also be called. A person touching a hot wire may be unable to free himself to turn off the electricity. Someone else will have to turn it off before the injured person can be removed.

Proper wiring and prompt repairs will avert most electrical emergencies. Use the following trouble-shooting chart and information in the text to make minor repairs.

TROUBLE SHOOTING

Electrical circuits

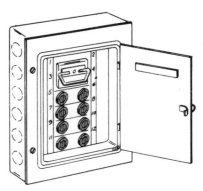

Fig. 9–2 Fuse-type service panel.

Fuse blows or circuit breaker trips.

• Overloaded circuit. Reduce the number of appliances or fixtures on the circuit.
• Hot wire short-circuited. Turn off electricity. Locate short in appliance, fixture, or circuit wiring, and insulate hot wire or repair connection.

No current in circuit.

• Fuse blown or circuit breaker tripped. Find cause, repair, and replace fuse or reset circuit breaker.
• Main switch or disconnect in service panel open. Reconnect current.

Outlets

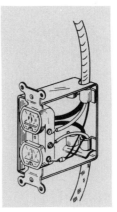

Fig. 9–3 Duplex receptacle.

No current at outlet.

• Circuit open at service panel. Replace fuse or reset circuit breaker.
• Wiring connections faulty. Turn off current, locate the fault, and repair connections.
• Receptacle defective. Turn off current. Remove faulty receptacle and replace with a new one.

Switches

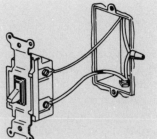

Fig. 9–4 Single-pole wall switch.

Fails to turn on current.

- Circuit open at service panel. Reset circuit breaker or replace fuse.
- Switch wired incorrectly. Turn off current. Inspect wiring connections in switch box and rewire.
- Switch internally defective. Turn off current. Replace switch.
- Wiring between switch and service panel faulty. Check other connections in circuit with test lamp to isolate defective faulty wiring. Turn off current and replace faulty section of cable.

Lamps and other light fixtures

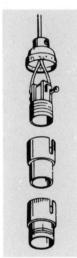

Fig. 9–5 Lamp socket components.

Fails to light.

- Bulb not screwed tightly into socket. Twist bulb tight.
- Bulb burned out. Replace.
- Lamp cord not plugged in. Connect to outlet.
- No current in circuit. Turn on wall switch or restore current at service panel.
- Wires loose at socket terminals. Turn off current, disassemble socket, and fasten wires to terminals.
- Socket unit or switch defective. Disassemble and replace.

Light blinks on and off.

- Bulb loose. Twist tight.
- Wires loose. Unplug and tighten connections.
- Socket or switch defective. Turn off and replace units.

Causes fuse to blow or circuit breaker to trip

- Overload circuit. Connect fixture to another circuit.
- Fixture is causing short circuit. Turn off current and look for bare wire that causes short. Insulate wire or correct connection.

Fluorescent lights

Fails to light

- No current in circuit. Turn on switch, reset circuit breaker, or replace fuse.
- Tube not making contact in socket. Straighten pins, remove dirt or corrosion, twist ¼ turn in socket.

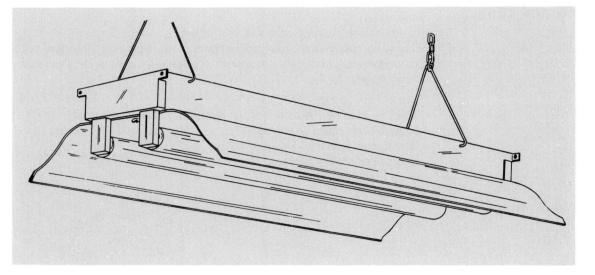

Fig. 9–6 Fluorescent light.

	• Socket unit defective. Replace and rewire. • Tube worn or defective. Replace with tube of same wattage. • Starter worn out or defective. Replace with starter of same wattage. • Wires loose. Reconnect. • Wiring between components incorrect. Compare with wiring diagram on ballast and rewire. • Tube, starter, ballast not of same wattage. Replace with components of matching capacities. • Ballast defective. Replace.
Light dim	• Old tube wearing out. Replace. • Air temperature too low for fixture. Raise temperature or use low-temperature fixture.
Light blinks on and off.	• Old tube wearing out. Replace. • Connections at socket or terminals poor. Reconnect wires. • Starter defective. Replace. • Air temperature too low for fixture. Raise temperature or use low-temperature fixture.
Light in tube swirls	• New tube breaking in. Swirling will stop when tube is broken in. • Turn tube end for end in socket.
Ends of tube black.	• Tube wearing out. Replace. • Starter wearing out or defective. Replace.
Humming sound in fixture.	• Inexpensive ballasts hum. Replace with sound rated ballast. • Components improperly matched. Replace mismatched components.
New tube burns out quickly.	• Tube has wrong wattage rating for other components. Replace with matching rating. • Ballast or wiring imposing high voltage on lamp. Replace ballast.

Doorbells and chimes

Rings continuously.

- Pushbutton stuck. Pry button free and repair.
- Bare wire causing short circuit. Inspect pushbutton, wiring at pushbutton, bell, and in between, for bare wires touching. Separate wires and insulate them with electrical tape.

Fails to operate.

- Push-button contacts corroded. Clean off.
- Wires loose at push button, bell, or transformer. Reconnect.
- Wires broken. Splice together.
- Transformer defective. Replace.
- Doorbell or chimes defective. Replace.

Small motors

Fig. 9–7 Split-phase motor.

Universal motor won't start or runs erratically.

- Brushes worn or spring tension weak.
- Replace brushes or temporarily increase spring pressure.
- Commutator dirty. Clean with fine-grade sandpaper.

Split-phase motor won't start.

- Centrifugal switch dirty or corroded. Clean switch.

Shaded-pole motor won't start.

- Switches or terminals dirty or corroded. Clean with solvent or rub with sandpaper.
- Wires loose at terminal. Tighten connection.

WORKING WITH ELECTRICITY

Local codes prescribe the types and sizes of wires and other specifications for electrical installations. They also indicate which repairs and installations a homeowner can perform himself and which require a licensed electrician. By starting with minor electrical repairs, the homeowner may gain enough experience to install new circuits and fixtures, with the permission of the electrical inspector, to the extent allowed by his local code. This brief description of wiring, circuits and fixtures, tools, and safety provides a general background for later instructions for electrical repairs and installations.

SERVICE ENTRANCE PANEL

Modern three-wire electrical services are capable of delivering a total of 100 or more amps of current to household circuits (Fig. 9–8). Larger-capacity 150- or 200-amp services are required for installations with electrical heating systems and central air conditioning. Old services may consist of no

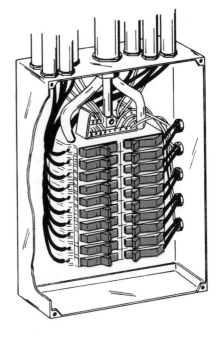

Fig. 9–8 Circuit-breaker type service panel.

more than two 15- or 20-amp circuits—a total capacity of 30 or 40 amps.

The current in the service entrance cables passes through either cartridge fuses or a main circuit breaker. In a fuse-type service, pulling the main pullout disconnects and removes the cartridge fuses and cuts off power to the entire system. In a circuit-breaker panel, tripping the main circuit breaker cuts off the power.

Electrical cables from the house circuits enter the service panel through knockouts and are connected through individual fuses or circuit breakers to power from the entrance wires. The neutral wire (white or natural grey insulation) is connected directly to the neutral bar in the center of the service panel that joins the neutral wires from the entrance line and the circuits to a cold-waterpipe or other type of ground. The hot wire (black or red insulation) in each circuit is connected to the load side of a fuse or circuit breaker. When everything in the system is operating normally, current flows from the hot service-entrance wires through the fuses or circuit breakers to the individual circuits.

The amount of current in a circuit is limited by the amperage capacity of the circuit's fuse or circuit breaker. If a short circuit or overload occurs, the fuse will blow or the circuit breaker will trip and cut off the power. This prevents fires from wiring overheated by excessively heavy current. A 15-amp circuit breaker, for example, will trip if an electric frying pan and toaster are inadvertently operated from the circuit at the same time.

WIRES

Several different types and sizes of electrical cables are required in a typical household installation. The type depends on how the cable is to be used, while the size depends on the amount of current to be carried. The insulated wires are made of either copper or aluminum, though copper is the most common. Of the many types of cable available, the following are most widely used domestically.

Types

Type-NM electrical cable (Fig. 9–9(a)) is sheathed in heavy protective plastic, fiber, or thermoplastic for dry, indoor use. Within the cable are two to four insulated wires and one bare or green wire. Two-wire cable actually consists of two insulated wires (white for neutral, black for hot) and a bare or green wire for grounding. (A ground wire is required by the 1975 Code.) Three-wire cable contains three insulated wires (white for neutral, black and red for hot wires) and a bare or green wire for grounding. The wire with green insulation is used only as a ground wire. Romex is a popular brand of type-NM cable.

Armored cable (Fig. 9–9(b)) consists of a flexible, spiral-wound steel casing enclosing two or three insulated

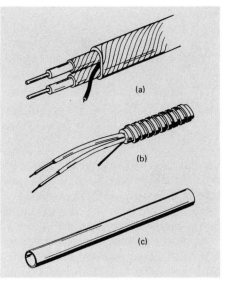

Fig. 9–9 Types of electrical cable: a) type-NM cable, 14-2 with ground, b) armored cable, 14-2 with ground, c) thin-wall conduit.

wires and a bare, thin, tape-like bond wire. Some local codes may require that armored cable be used in certain installations instead of type-NM cable. The steel casing protects the wires against mechanical injury better than the nonmetallic sheathing on NM cable. Armored cable can corrode and should be used only in dry, indoor areas. It is often referred to as BX or BX armored cable; BX is a trade name.

Conduit (Fig. 9–9(c)) is a third type of cable installation. It consists of pipelike tubing containing an electrical cable, for locations where an unprotected cable might be damaged, or where it is required by the local code. After the conduit is in place, the electrical cable is run through the tubing and connected. Since it is waterproof, when installed properly, conduit can be used for both indoor and outdoor wiring.

Type-UF electrical cable is used for outdoor and underground installations. An impervious plastic jacket protects the insulated wires from moisture and rot. The cable can be buried in the soil without any other protection.

A few other types of electrical cables and wires are also used in household installations. Heavy, well-insulated, three-wire cables are used for service entrance wiring and 240-volt appliances, such as ranges and electrical clothes dryers. Ground wires connecting service entrance panels to cold-water pipes are often encased in an armored jacket or conduit.

Cables are designated as to their type and the size and number of wires that they contain. A type-NM cable with three insulated No. 12 wires, for instance, is designated as type-NM, 12–3 cable with ground wire.

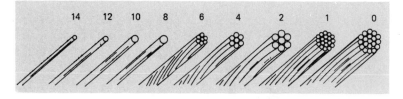

Fig. 9–10 Wire sizes.

Size

The larger the diameter of a wire, the greater amount of current it can carry without overheating (Fig. 9–10). Consequently, the largest-size wires are used for kitchen-type circuits with heavy appliances. The larger the wire, the smaller its gauge number. For example, either No. 14 or No. 12 wires can be used for general-purpose circuits, but kitchen-type circuits with heavier current requirements require either No. 12 or No. 10 wires. Since large-diameter solid wires are hard to bend, No. 6 and larger wires are made up of heavy strands. Light-duty cords use stranded No. 18 or No. 16 wire. For the same current-carrying capacity, aluminum wires must be one size larger than copper wires. For the same amperage, for example, either No. 14 copper wire or No. 12 aluminum wire could be used.

CIRCUITS

Electrical fixtures and appliances in a typical household installation require at least three different types of circuits.

General purpose circuits for lights and small appliances have 15- or 20-amp capacities. The wiring requires 15-amp fuses or circuit breakers and at least No. 14 wire. However, the trend is toward general-purpose circuits capable of carrying 20 amp.

Kitchen, dining, and laundry circuits are installed for appliances with heavy current requirements such as toasters, clothes washers, and hot-plates. These are 20-amp circuits that use No. 12 or 10 wires.

Special circuits are installed for individual appliances with high current requirements. A clothes dryer, for example, might draw between 20 and 30 amp at 240 volts (20 amp X 240 V equals 4800 watts). Refrigerators, dishwashers, furnaces, water heaters, and similar units require separate circuits that meet their current requirements.

Number of Circuits

The number of circuits of each type depends on the size of the house and the electrical appliances to be used. Although local codes vary, the National Electrical Code makes recommendations for a minimum number of circuits in relation to the size of the house based on a watts per sq ft formula.

For *general-purpose circuits,* the Code recommends a minimum of one 15-amp circuit for every 375 sq ft of floor space, or one 20-amp circuit for every 500 sq ft. Receptacles are recommended every 12 ft along the wall for convenience in plugging in lights and appliances.

For *kitchen-type circuits,* a minimum of two, 20-amp circuits are recommended with kitchen-counter outlets every four feet. Additional circuits should be added for more than the average number of appliances.

The number of *special circuits* depends on the number of appliances that require their own circuits. A typical house may require six or more separate circuits for such appliances.

Circuit Capacity

The capacity of a circuit to handle several appliances at the same time depends on the size of the wire and capacity of the fuse or circuit breaker. The ratings of the appliances (in watts) can be added to determine the overall load on the circuit. A 1000-watt toaster and a 1000-watt electric frying pan would require a circuit capable of supplying more than 2000 watts. A 15-amp circuit can safely supply only 1650 watts (15 amp X 110 V equals 1650 watts) without causing the fuse to blow. A 20-amp circuit can safely supply 2200 watts (20 amp X 110 V equals 2200 watts), enough for the toaster and frying pan to be used at the same time.

Special circuits must be matched to the ratings of the units they serve. For example, a kitchen range with a rating of 11,000 watts will require a 240-V circuit capable of carrying 50 amps. Motor-operated units, such as dishwashers and refrigerators, draw a larger amount of current when starting than when running continuously. Their circuits must have the capacity to handle the starting surge of current without tripping the circuit breakers. Special fuses and circuit breakers are made to withstand momentary overloads in this type of circuit.

BOXES, SWITCHES, AND OUTLETS
Electrical Boxes

Electrical boxes are required wherever wires are joined to each other or to electrical terminals. The box provides support for the junction, protects the installation from mechanical damage, and allows access to the wires. Although most

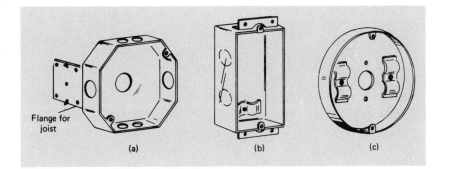

Fig. 9–11 Types of electrical boxes: a) octagonal junction, b) outlet and switch, c) shallow ceiling.

electrical boxes are made of steel, other materials are also used, such as plastic or Bakelite.

Junction boxes (Fig. 9–11(a)) are a standard type of box for joining wires. The cables enter through knockout holes in the side or back of the box where they are clamped in connectors to prevent chafing. The octagonal, 4-in. junction box, a convenient size to work with, has a cover plate that can be removed for access.

Outlet boxes and *switch boxes* (Fig. 9–11(b)) are rectangular and may be joined to gang several units together. In new work boxes are nailed to the studs so that their front edges are flush with the finished wall. If they are being installed in existing walls, old work boxes are used that can be held in place with metal supports inserted behind the lath or with screws. After the receptacle or switch is installed, the box is covered with a faceplate.

Ceiling boxes (Fig. 9–11(c)) are nailed to a joist or header, or attached to a crosspiece or hanger where a ceiling fixture is to be installed. The fixture canopy covers the box and transfers the weight of the fixture to the box and joist.

Switches

Switches (Fig. 9–12) are installed in the circuit's hot wire (black), and the neutral wires (white) are connected directly to each other with wire connectors. (A two-wire switch loop is the only exception to this rule.) Single-pole switches are used to turn a fixture on or off from one location, while a pair of three-way switches will allow a fixture to be controlled from two different locations. Several switches or outlets may be ganged together. A wall plate is used to cover the face of the box.

Outlets

Modern installations use duplex receptacles (Fig. 9–13) with a grounded terminal for three-wire circuits. The bare ground wire in the cable is attached to a green terminal on

Fig 9–12 Wall switch.

Fig. 9–13 Receptacle.

the side of the receptacle and to the box. This connects the ground prong on three-prong plugs to the grounded house circuit. Adapters have to be used to plug three-prong appliance plugs into older two-prong receptacles that are wired with ground wires. A ground wire is attached from the adapter to the screw on the faceplate. After the receptacle is wired, the wires are pushed back into the outlet box and the receptacle fastened to the box with screws. A faceplate covers the outlet.

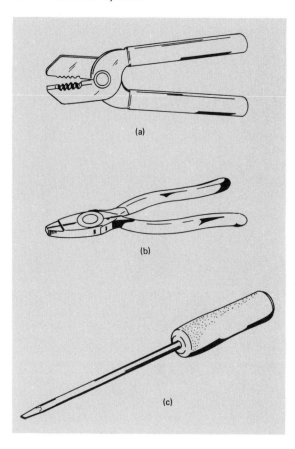

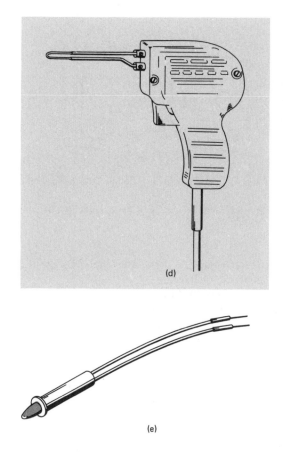

Fig. 9–14 Electrician's tools: a) wire strippers, b) linesman's pliers, c) electrician's screwdriver, d) soldering gun, e) test lamp.

TOOLS

As pointed out in the chapter on tools, very few specialized tools are required for electrical repairs or installations. Most of the work can be done with everyday tools such as pliers, screwdrivers, saws, a hammer, a brace and bit, and chisels. However, a few specialized tools (Fig. 9–14) will make the work easier and faster. Purchase those that will be most useful. Insulation can be removed much faster with a wire stripper than with a knife. Linesman's pliers are handy for bending and cutting heavy electric wires. An electrician's screwdriver with its straight thin blade is required to reach recessed screws. And a test light rated at 240 volts is useful to check a circuit for current without risking electrical shock.

SAFETY

Electrical wiring is potentially dangerous as a cause of electrical shock and fire. To contain the current, wires and fixtures are heavily insulated. Since insulation sometimes fails due to fray, cracking or abrasion, appliances, electrical boxes, wiring, and the service entrance panel are grounded.

Insulation (Fig. 9–15) prevents current from traveling from hot wires to other wires or uninsulated metal components. If the insulation fails or is inadequate, there may be a short circuit and fire, or the ungrounded metal, such as a refrigerator casing, may become electrically hot ("live"). Touching a hot refrigerator casing and a sink or waterpipe at the same time could cause a fatal shock.

Appliance cords are likely to fray where the cord enters the body of an appliance. If enough insulation rubs off a hot wire, the wire may form a live circuit through the casing of the appliance. Where wires are jointed in electrical boxes, the insulation should be stripped only from the part of the wire encased in the connecting wire nut (Fig. 9–16). Electrical tape should be used to wrap any questionable section of wire in a box and to secure the wire nuts in place. Frayed wires should be removed and replaced. When working near electrical wiring, care should be taken not to damage the insulation with nails or other instruments.

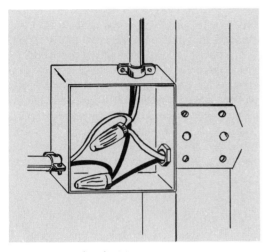

Fig. 9–15 Insulated wiring.

Fig. 9–16 Connection with wire nut.

Fig. 9–17 Ground clamp for cold-water pipe.

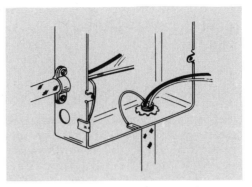

Fig. 9–18 Ground wire fastened to box.

Fig. 9–19 Two-prong grounding adapter.

Grounding the metal components in a circuit provides a safe path for current to follow to ground if there is a short circuit. The neutral wire (white insulation) in the circuit is continuous and is connected to the neutral block at the service panel and to a grounded cold-water pipe when the circuit is operating normally (Fig. 9–17). However, additional grounding is required for times when a hot wire may touch the neutral wire or another metal component. Electrical boxes, receptacles, fixtures, and appliances are connected through a ground wire or armored cable to a ground at the service entrance. This permits current to flow, for example, from a short-circuited refrigerator casing through a ground wire to a grounded cold-water pipe, and blows out the fuse or trips the breaker to prevent electrical shock to anyone touching the refrigerator.

The bare ground wire in a two- or three-wire cable should be connected to the electrical boxes (Fig. 9–18) and to the green grounding terminals on receptacles or switches. This will automatically ground appliances using three-prong plugs. Appliances without three-prong plugs can also be grounded with heavy No. 12 grounding wires connected directly to cold-water pipes. Connect the wire under a screw on the appliance casing so that it makes good contact with bare metal and run it to a grounding clamp on a convenient cold-water pipe. Some electrical tools use double insulation rather than a three-prong plug, to protect the user from shock. With older, two-prong receptacles connected to a ground wire, three-prong plugs can be grounded by attaching a two-prong adapter (Fig. 9–19) to the screw on the wall plate.

Avoid touching hot wires. Trip circuit breakers or remove fuses before working on any part of a circuit. When working on an appliance, simply unplug it. To ensure that the circuit breaker has been tripped in the right circuit, use a test light lamp in a receptacle or across the hot (black) and neutral (white) wires. If the circuit is still hot, the lamp will light. When working at the service entrance, stand on some insulating material, such as rubber or wood, rather than on the cellar floor and avoid touching any metal parts. Fuses and circuit breakers should be replaced with fuses and circuit breakers with the same ratings to avoid overloading the wiring in the circuit. As a general safety practice, avoid touching plumbing when using or working on anything electrical.

ELECTRICAL REPAIRS AND REPLACEMENT

FUSES AND CIRCUIT BREAKERS

Fuses or circuit breakers are installed at the service panel between the service entrance cables and the hot wires (black) carrying current to the individual circuits. If the maximum current-carrying capacity of the fuse or circuit breaker is exceeded, the fuse will blow or the circuit breaker will trip and cut off power to the circuit. This avoids the dangers of the wiring overheating from a short circuit or overload and starting a fire.

Types of Fuses and Circuit Breakers

There are several modifications of the standard electrical fuse. The standard plug fuse (Fig. 9–20(a)) blows out immediately when the amount of current exceeds the capacity of the fuse. A *time-delay fuse,* such as a Fusetron (a tradename), permits a momentary current overload without blowing out. Such fuses are often used in circuits with motor-driven appliances, since a motor may draw twice as much current when starting as when in continuous operation. Non-tamper, type-S (Fig. 9–20(b)) have bases of different sizes for different current capacities. This prevents a fuse of the wrong capacity from being used. To use these fuses an adapter (Fig. 9–20(c)) must be screwed into a standard fuse holder. A *pushbutton-type fuse* with a reset button is halfway between a fuse and a circuit breaker. Instead of replacing the fuse, the reset button is pushed to restore the circuit.

Circuit-breaker type panels use both single-pole and double-pole circuit breakers. Single-pole circuit breakers (Fig. 9–20(d)) control the current in single 120-V circuits; double-pole circuit breakers control the current in 240-V circuits. Circuit breakers, like fuses, are rated by their maximum current-carrying capacities. If these capacities are exceeded, the breaker trips and cuts off current to the circuit. A time-delay mechanism allows momentary overloads.

Current from the main service-entrance cables may be cut off in several ways. Circuit-breaker-type service panels use a main circuit breaker. The breaker is tripped to cut off the current. Fuse-type panels use cartridge-type fuses (Fig. 9–20(e)) in a disconnect. The main disconnects are pulled to turn off the power. Some installations use knife-type disconnects operated by pulling a lever on the side of the fuse box.

Finding the Cause of a Blown Fuse

When an overload or short circuit exceeds the capacity of a fuse or circuit breaker, the fuse will blow or the breaker will trip. Too many appliances on the same circuit is a common cause of overload. For example, appliances with a total capacity of 2000 watts will overload 15-amp circuits since they can carry a maximum of 1800 watts (15 amps X 120 V equals 1800). A motor with a longer than usual startup overload may also blow a fuse. If an insulated section of a hot wire (black or red) touches a neutral wire (white), ground wire, electrical box, or any metal part on an appliance, it will cause a short circuit and blow a fuse.

An overload can be distinguished from a short circuit by the appearance of the window on the blown fuse. A blackish smudge on the window indicates that the fuse blew because of a short circuit. A clear window with a broken metal strip indicates that there was an overload.

The source of the overload or short circuit must be found and corrected before the circuit can be used again. If the fuse blew as a particular appliance or light was being turned on, the cause should not be hard to find. For example, if a toaster, electric frying pan, and another appliance were being used on the same kitchen circuit, the circuit was probably overloaded. The individual ratings of the appliances can be added and compared with the circuit's capac-

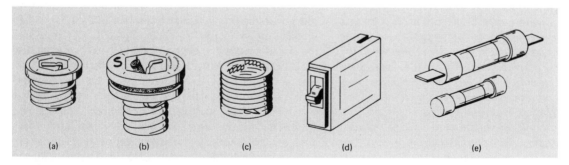

(a)   (b)   (c)   (d)   (e)

Fig. 9–20 Fuses and circuit breakers: a) plug fuse, b) type-S, non-tamper fuse, c) adapter for type-S fuse, d) single-pole circuit breaker, e) cartridge-type fuses.

ity (1650 watts for 15-amp circuit and 2200 watts for a 20-amp circuit).

If it appears that the circuit was not overloaded and the window on a blown fuse is smudged black, each appliance and light fixture should be checked for a short circuit. Start with all of the appliances and fixtures turned off and a new fuse in place. Turn on the appliances one at a time until the fuse blows again. The short circuit will be in the appliance that was being turned on as the fuse blew. Unplug the appliance and check it for frayed and loose wires.

If the fuse blows with all of the appliances turned off, there may be a short circuit in the circuit wiring. Again, consider any recent change that has taken place. If a new receptacle or fixture was installed recently, remove the face-place on the box and look for a short between an uninsulated section of a hot wire (black or red) and the ground or a neutral wire (white). If a pet has been chewing on extension cords, check them.

Conceivably, the main circuit breaker has been tripped or the cartridge fuses have been blown. An open circuit breaker will be in the tripped or Off position. When a cartridge fuse blows, there is no indication except that the power to all of the circuits has been cut off. The cartridge should be pulled with a fuse puller and replaced. If there is a problem with the service entrance wires from outside the house, an electrician or the electric company should be called.

FLEXIBLE CORDS AND PLUGS

Flexible cords and plugs are used to carry current from receptacles to lamps and appliances. Light-duty cords are used for lamps, radios, and other small appliances and heavier cords and plugs for larger appliances.

Types of Cords

Light-duty flat cords insulated with plastic (Type SPT) or rubber (Type SP) are sometimes called "zip cords." Their separately insulated wires can easily be pulled apart to connect them to the appliance terminals. The current-carrying capacity of these cords depends on the size of the conductors. For example, a common light-duty cord with No. 18 stranded wire has a rating of 7 amp, while a cord made of heavier No. 16 wire can carry a maximum of 10 amp. If more than two small appliances are used on a light-duty cord the load may exceed the cord's capacity and cause it to overheat. Safety also requires that zip cords be limited to 6 ft lengths for most uses.

Heavy-duty, round cords are insulated with either plastic (Type ST) or rubber (Types S or SJ). The separately insulated wires are encased together in a second, single layer of insulation. These cords are used where there are heavier

wear or current-carrying requirements, such as with refrigerators, vacuum cleaners, power drills, and other medium-size appliances.

Heater cord (Type HPD) is insulated with asbestos wool or neoprene rubber. This is the type of cord used for irons, frying pans, and toasters.

Three-wire cords contain a grounding wire and are used with a three-prong plug for appliances that must be grounded such as uninsulated tools and some outdoor appliances.

Using Cords

When replacing appliance cords, use the same type and size of cord as was previously used. The cord should also be of the same length (generally a maximum of 6 ft) as the original cord, though a longer cord can be used for lamps and light appliances where it will eliminate a short extension cord. The voltage will drop over an unusually long cord (for example, a No. 18 cord greater than 25 ft long). This can be injurious to an appliance or motor that requires higher minimum voltage and also may overheat the cord and cause a fire.

Plugs

Most lamps and appliances use either flat or round plugs to match their cords, though there are many other types of plugs.

Light-duty cords generally use plugs (Fig. 9–21(a)) designed with rectangular openings for flat cords. The unstripped end of a cord is inserted in the opening where it is clamped to make contact with the prongs. Teeth in the plug bite through the insulation to the bare wires. Many extension cords are manufactured so that the molded plugs are integral with the cords.

Plugs for heavy-duty cords may be either round (Fig. 9–21(b)) or flat. The cord enters the plug through an opening in the back and the insulated wires are tied in an Underwriter's knot (see below) to transfer strain on the cord to the plug rather than to the terminals. A half inch of insulation is stripped from the wires and the strands twisted together to make them easier to work with. Each wire is wound clockwise around one of the terminal screws and the screw is tightened down onto the wire. The wire will stay under the screw since the wire is wrapped in the same direction as the screw is being turned. The excess wire is trimmed off and the insulating disc is slipped over the prongs and pushed flat against the plug.

Special plugs are made for many types of installations. Cords that carry different combinations of voltage and current, such as 30 amp/240 V or 20 amp/240 V, require plugs with specially shaped prongs (Fig. 9–21(c)) located to connect to outlets designed for these currents and voltages. Cords for 120 V containing a ground wire require a plug (Fig.

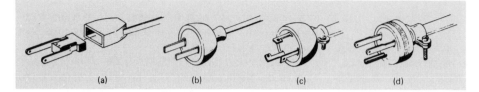

Fig. 9–21 Types of electrical plugs: a) self-connecting, for flat cords, b) round heavy-duty, c) 240-V, d) three-prong, heavy duty.

Fig. 9–22 Tying an underwriter's knot.

9–21(d)) with a round, third prong for the ground connection.

(To tie an Underwriter's knot (Fig. 9–22), make a loop in the white wire, run the black wire through the loop and around the extended end of the white wire. Finally, run the black wire through the looped white wire again in the same direction, and tighten the knot.)

LAMPS

Look for the following defects when repairing a lamp (Fig. 9–23). The plug may have bent prongs, a bad connection to the cord, a short circuit between wires, or a cracked case. The cord may be frayed, with the bare wires touching each other or the lamp. The wires may be loose at the socket terminals, or they may be touching each other where strands stick out from the terminals. The socket switch or contacts for the bulb may be faulty. The bulb itself may be burned out.

There may be more than one problem in a faulty lamp. If the plug, cord, and bulb appear to be all right, inspect the wiring at the socket terminals. After unplugging the lamp and removing the shade and bulb, remove the socket shell by pressing inward at its base just above the switch. Some shells have a small notch where they can be pried up with a thin screwdriver. Shells without this notch may be bent and damaged if a screwdriver is used. When the shell is loose, slip it off over the socket together with the insulating liner. The wires from the cord should be tied in an Underwriter's knot in the cap at the base of the socket, and connected to the socket's terminal screws. If the plug and wiring are all right, the socket switch or contacts are probably defective. The

Fig. 9–23 Lamp socket and components.

simplest solution is to replace the socket with a new one. Use a brass or aluminum shell to match the lamp.

To replace a socket, detach the wires from the terminals on the old socket and unscrew the socket cap from the body of the lamp. Disassemble the new socket and run the wires through the cap before connecting them to the new socket. The cap should be screwed onto the threads at the top of the lamp and a knot tied in the insulated wires. Loop the ends of the wires clockwise around the terminal screws on the socket and tighten the screws. Cut off the excess wire. Slide the insulating liner and shell over the socket and snap the shell into place in the cap. The wire should be pulled taut at the bottom of the lamp and the bulb and shade replaced. All the lamp's components should now be in good condition.

WALL SWITCHES

Wall switches are used to control current to fixtures and receptacles. They may be single-pole, on-off switches (Fig. 9–24(a)), dimmer control (Fig. 9–24(b)), or three-way or

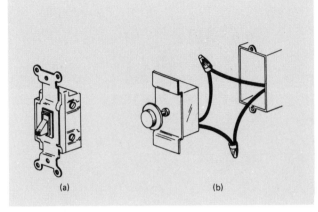

Fig. 9–24 Wall switches: a) single-pole switch, b) dimmer control.

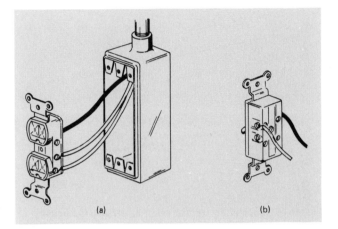

Fig. 9–25 Three-wire receptacle: a) wiring hookup at receptacle, b) push-in openings on back of receptacle.

four-way switches. Though the quiet toggle switch is probably most widely used, there are also pressure-type, pushbutton switches, silent mercury switches, and a flush lever-type switch.

To *replace a switch,* buy the same type of switch, with the same current and voltage rating, and connect it to the wiring exactly as the old switch was connected. A single-pole switch can be replaced with a dimmer control, since they both have the same wiring connections. With three- or four-way switches, record the colors of the wires and where they are connected before removing them from the old switch. This will minimize confusion in making the new connections.

Cut off the current to the circuit by tripping the circuit breaker or removing the fuse. Double-check by trying to turn on the lamp and by testing the hot wire in the switch box with a test lamp. Remove the cover plate by unscrewing the two short screws at the top and bottom. The switch is fastened to the box by two long screws, one at the bottom and one at the top. Remove these and pull the switch and connecting wires a few inches out of the box. A single-pole switch will have a hot (black) wire fastened to each of its terminals. The hot wires may be either fastened under screws at the terminals or inserted in grip-type holes in the back of the switch. The neutral (white wires) are connected together with a wire nut in the box in back of the switch. With ground-wire type cables, the ground wires will be connected to each other at a grounding screw at the back of the box.

Disconnect the hot (black) wires from the switch and loop them clockwise under the screws at the terminals on the new fixture (or insert them in the holes in the back of the switch). Tighten the screws down, push the device back into the box, and fasten it with the two long screws. The switch should be plumb, and the On designation should be at the top, before the screws are tightened. Finally, replace the cover plate.

Three- and four-way switches are connected to each other by three-wire cables so that each one can bypass the others. Wiring a new switch will be confusing if the old switch is completely disconnected first. The safest way to avoid confusion is to record the color of each wire and where it is connected. The wires can then be disconnected, one at a time, from the old switch and attached to identical terminals on the new switch.

OUTLETS

Modern receptacles for three-prong plugs are fitted with ground terminals that are connected to the ground wire and outlet box. Older receptacles lack ground terminals and can be used only with two-prong plugs. These receptacles can be replaced with three-wire grounded receptacles (Fig. 9–25(a)) in circuits that use a groundwire type cable. The bare or green wire from the cable should be connected to both the ground terminal on the receptacle and a grounding screw on the back of the outlet box.

To remove a standard duplex receptacle, turn off the current and unscrew the small center screw that holds the cover plate. The two long screws that hold each end of the receptacle to the outlet box should be removed next. The receptacle can now be pulled out a few inches from the box. The hot (black) wires are always connected to the darker-colored brass fitting on one side while the neutral (white) wires are connected to the lighter-colored, chrome plated fittings on the other side of the receptacle. If the receptacle has push-in openings, the wires can be fastened on the back (Fig. 9–25(b)). Multiple receptacles in the same box, or receptacles connected to more distant receptacles, will have

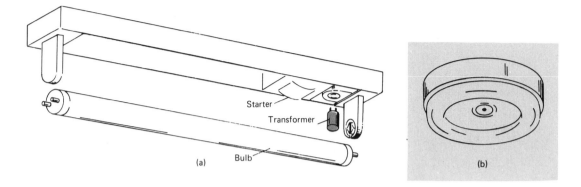

Fig. 9–26 Types of fluorescent lights: a) straight, b) circular.

wires attached at both the top and bottom. Those at the top supply current and those at the bottom carry the current to the next receptacle. The ground wire, either a bare wire or a wire with green insulation, will be connected to the green-marked ground terminal. Note the colors of these wires and where they are connected in order to connect the new receptacle in the same manner. Disconnect the wires, either by loosening terminal screws or by inserting the end of a screwdriver to release the wires in a grip-type fitting.

Connect the wires to the new receptacle in the same order as they were connected to the old receptacle. If a three-wire grounded receptacle is used to replace an ungrounded receptacle, fasten the bare or green-insulated wire to the ground terminal (marked with green) and connect the terminal to a grounding screw on the outlet box as prescribed by the local code. After it is wired, the receptacle should be pushed back into the outlet box by folding the stiff cable wires behind it. Fasten the receptacle to the box and replace the cover plate before turning on the current.

FLUORESCENT LIGHTS

Fluorescent lights (Fig. 9–26) operate on different principles from incandescent lights and require different components. A current passing through the vapor in the tubes causes the fluorescent coating on the tube walls to glow and give off light. The life of the tubes and starters depends on the number of hours the light is on. In standard preheat fluorescent fixtures, starters establish the current flow. Starters may be operated either by a single-pole switch, such as a wall switch or pull chain, or by push buttons, as on a desk lamp. Rapid-start fixtures don't require starters. A ballast is installed in the fixture to control the level of current flow. The ballast, tubes, and starters must be matched in ratings or they will be damaged.

Installing Fluorescent Fixtures

A fluorescent fixture can be installed by connecting it to a 120-V circuit at an electrical box. The hot (black) and neutral (white) wires from the cable should be attached to wires with similar-colored insulation that extend from the fixture. Different types of straight and circular fluorescent lights are wired differently internally, but only one hot and one neutral wire are connected to the house circuit (in addition to a ground wire). A diagram on the ballast shows the circuit wiring and lists the electrical specifications for the fixture.

To install new tubes in straight-tube fixtures, line up the pins with the slot openings in the sockets, slide the pins sideways into the slots, and twist the tubes a quarter-turn to lock them in place. Tubes are installed in circular fixtures by pushing the tube pins into the socket holes.

Each preheat tube requires a separate starter, a cylindrical-shaped component that fastens into a socket under one end of the tube. The ballast is attached inside the fixture, where it is wired to the other components.

Repairing Fluorescent Fixtures

Repairing fluorescent fixtures is usually a matter of replacing components or tightening electrical connections. The tubes wear out first. They may start to become dim or blink. The ends may turn black after they have been used for a long time. Eventually, they will fail to light. To protect the other components, the tubes should be replaced as soon as there is any hint that they are wearing out. Old or defective tubes place a greater load on the starters and ballast.

Starters should be replaced when the tubes are replaced a second or third time. Some indications that starters are wearing out are blinking in a new tube, or a new tube that won't light.

The ballast is least likely to fail. If the light blinks, swirls, or won't turn on after the tubes and starters have been

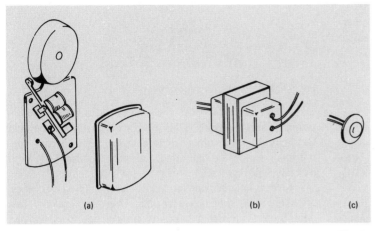

Fig. 9–27 Doorbell system: a) bell, b) transformer, c) push button.

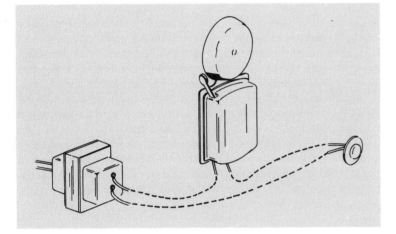

Fig. 9–28 Doorbell circuit.

replaced and the electrical connections checked, the ballast is probably defective. Replace it with an identical unit that matches the specifications of the tubes being used. The wires will have to be disconnected or cut and rejoined with wire nuts where necessary.

DOORBELLS AND CHIMES

Doorbells (Fig. 9–27(a)) and chimes are connected to a transformer (Fig. 9–27(b)) and pushbuttons (Fig. 9–27(c)) in a low-voltage circuit. The transformer lowers the house-circuit voltage to 10 to 24 volts. One or more pushbuttons are used as switches to close the circuit and ring the bell.

Installing Doorbells and Chimes

To install doorbells or chimes, the transformer should be attached to an accessible electrical box convenient to either the pushbuttons or the bell. Choose a doorbell transformer with the voltages required by the particular bell or chimes. Most transformers are mounted on the side of the box over a knockout. With the current in the circuit shut off, use wire nuts to fasten the neutral (white) and hot (black) wires from the transformer to the same-colored wires in the electrical box. Light bell wire is run from the low-voltage terminals on the side of the transformer to the pushbuttons and bell. If there is more than one terminal on the transformer, the voltages will be marked.

In a system (Fig. 9–28) with only one pushbutton, bell wire is connected between the transformer and bell with the pushbutton wired into the circuit. The pushbutton is connected by a third wire to the bell. Without the pushbutton in the circuit to act as an open switch, the doorbell would ring continuously. Run the bell wire along the joists in the cellar or in some other accessible space. The wire can be stapled in place and run through holes in the walls to connect to the pushbuttons and doorbell. Locate the doorbell or chimes where they can be heard throughout the house.

Systems with several pushbuttons can be installed by following the wiring diagrams accompanying the bell or chimes. Each pushbutton is wired so that it can bypass the other pushbuttons and close the circuit.

Repairs

Doorbells and chimes that won't stop ringing have a short circuit. Check the pushbutton at the door and follow the wiring until you find where the two wires are touching. The ringing can be stopped, temporarily, by disconnecting the wires at the bell or transformer.

When a doorbell system that has been operating normally stops working, the wiring or any of the components may be at fault. Check the pushbutton to see if corroded contacts or loose wires have broken the circuit. Unscrew the housing and pull the wires out far enough to inspect their condition. If the bell rings when the wires touch each other, the pushbutton isn't closing the circuit. Use sandpaper to clean the contacts and the ends of the wires. If the pushbutton is clearly at fault and can't be made to operate correctly, it should be replaced.

If the bell doesn't ring when the wires are touched together at the pushbutton, the problem is probably somewhere else in the circuit. Either inspect the wires by tracing them from the pushbutton to the other components, or go directly to the doorbell, chimes, or transformer. When inspecting the wires, look for a broken wire. At the doorbell, chimes, or transformer look for a loose connection. To see if the transformer is delivering current, jump a wire across the terminals. If the transformer is operating normally, there will be a spark when a wire is touched to the two terminals at the same time. If there is no spark, shut off the current to the house circuit, and open the electrical box to inspect the wiring to the transformer. A wire may have come loose or the transformer may have burned out.

When the transformer, pushbutton, and wiring seem to be all right, the problem is likely to be in the doorbell or chimes themselves. They should be inspected for obvious poor connections, damage, or tampering. A bell of the same voltage requirements can be substituted in the circuit to determine whether the original doorbell or chimes are faulty.

Motors

Instructions are usually provided for the simple maintenance of electric motors in small appliances and power tools. For most appliances, nothing more than a periodic lubrication is required. Different types of motors, however, are noted for certain difficulties.

Small appliances such as light-duty fans and blowers and electric can openers use *shaded-pole motors*. When these fail to start, or when they stop unexpectedly, check the

Fig. 9–29 Brush for universal motor.

switches and terminals. Dirty or corroded switches should be cleaned with a solvent or sandpaper. Loose wires at the terminals should be tightened. Lubricate the bearings periodically with light oil.

Motors in larger appliances, such as washing machines, are likely to be *split-phase motors*. These motors contain a centrifugal switch that needs to be cleaned occasionally. Dirt and grease on the contacts can be removed with a cloth and solvent. Corrosion should be rubbed away with fine sandpaper. These motors may have a reset device.

Power tools, such as saws and drills, and many household appliances use *universal motors* that can be operated on either alternating or direct current. In these motors, the carbon brushes (Fig. 9–29) and the commutators cause most of the problems. As the brushes wear down, they no longer maintain good electrical contact with the commutator. Access caps are often provided through which the brushes can be removed and replaced.

To clean the commutator, a section of the casing must be removed so that the motor is accessible. Hold a sheet of fine sandpaper lightly against the commutator as it rotates, to clean the surface of the commutator for better electrical contact with the brushes.

INSTALLING NEW CIRCUITS AND FIXTURES

Additional circuits may be needed if the existing circuits are overloaded or if an addition to a house is being built. If the fuses blow or circuit breakers trip when several appliances or lights are operated simultaneously, it's evident that the circuits are overloaded. Older installations with one outlet in each room are clearly insufficient for the electrical equipment in a modern home. Even modern installations may be overloaded if electrical appliances have been added without installing additional kitchen and special circuits. The local electrical code or inspector should be consulted about requirements for installing new circuits.

PLANNING

The minimum number and types of circuits in a modern installation can be determined by the criteria recommended by the National Electrical Code.

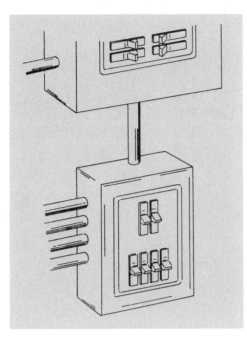

Fig. 9–30 Service panel with add-on installation.

In terms of *outlets,* there should be outlets for general-purpose circuits every 12 ft along the wall, with a minimum of one on each wall narrower than 12 ft in a living area or bedroom. Kitchen-type circuits should have outlets every 4 ft along the back of the kitchen counter. Appliances operated by motors with heavy power requirements, such as dishwashers, dryers, washing machines, and garbage disposers, should have their own separate circuits.

In terms of *floor space,* there should be a minimum of one 15-amp general-purpose circuit for every 375 sq. ft, or one 20-amp circuit for every 500 sq. ft. A 2000-sq.-ft house, for example, should have a minimum of four 20-amp, or six 15-amp, general-purpose circuits. The average kitchen should have a minimum of two 20-amp circuits for appliances.

In terms of *power requirements,* more general-purpose and kitchen-type circuits are usually needed than the minimum called for by the National Code. Determine the actual power requirements by adding up the ratings of the lights and appliances that are likely to be used simultaneously on the same circuit, and compare this with the circuit's capacity. A 15-amp, general-purpose circuit has a practical capacity of 1650 watts (110 V X 15 amp equals 1650 watts). A 20-amp circuit has a practical capacity of 2200 watts (110 V X 20 amp equals 2200 watts). If the total power requirements of appliances being used simultaneously on a circuit is 2000 watts, for example, a 20-amp circuit, instead of a 15-amp circuit, should be installed. Separate circuits for motor-operated appliances with heavy start-up loads should

have capacities 25 percent greater than the rating of the motor, to allow for overloading during startup.

The *number of circuits* in a modern installation (without electric heat or central air conditioning) in a typical 2000-sq.-ft house might include: six 15-amp, general-purpose circuits; two 20-amp, kitchen-type circuits; four separate 120-V circuits for motor-operated appliances; four separate 240-V circuits for heavy appliances. There should be at least two general-purpose circuits for lighting on each floor, so that the entire floor will not be blacked out if one circuit fails. Six general-purpose circuits allow the lights to be kept on different circuits from the appliances.

Service entrance panels may have an unused space position for a new circuit. Otherwise, an add-on panel will have to be installed (Fig. 9–30). If there is an unused knock-out on the side of the box and a vacant position for a new circuit breaker or fuse, the new cable can be connected to the existing service panel. Stand on an insulating surface while working on the wiring at the service entrance. Open the main disconnect or circuit breaker and remove the panel cover. Stay away from the terminals and wires connected to the hot service cables. Remove the knockout, strip several inches of insulation from the cable, and insert it through a connector in the knockout. A new, single-pole circuit breaker or fuse unit should be installed in the vacant position in the panel and the hot (black) wires from the new cable attached to the terminal. The neutral (white wire) should be attached directly to a screw on the neutral central strip. Fasten the ground wire directly to the grounding terminal on the panel.

An *add-on panel* will have to be installed if there is no room for additional cables in the main panel. The add-on panel is connected by cables to the power take-off terminals at the bottom of the main service panel. Circuit breakers and fuses should be installed in the add-on panel just as they were in the main panel. Cables for the new circuits enter through connectors clamped in the knockouts on the sides.

INSTALLING WIRES

When new circuits are installed or old circuits extended, cables must be run between the new outlets or fixtures and a source of power, such as the service panel. The size of the wires depends on the capacity of the circuit: 15-amp circuits require No. 14 copper or No. 12 aluminum wire; 20-amp circuits require No. 12 copper or No. 10 aluminum wire. Even heavier wires are required by heavy-current appliances, such as electric clothes-driers and ranges. Where there are long runs of cable in any circuit, a heavier wire should be used to reduce the voltage drop in the circuit.

An *old circuit* may be extended by connecting a new cable to a box. An unused knockout is removed and the cable is run through a connector into the box. Electrical codes prescribe the number of wires that can be used in

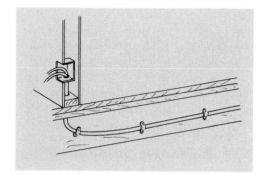

Fig. 9–31 Cable stapled to joist.

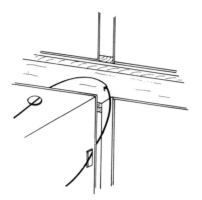

Fig. 9–33 Fishing a cable.

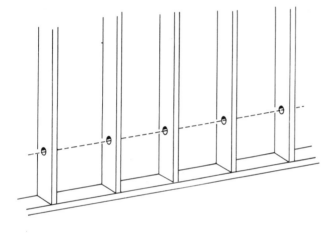

Fig. 9–32 Studs with cable holes in new construction.

each type and size of box. A 4-in., octagonal junction box might hold no more than eight wires, while a switch box or outlet box could hold even fewer. A circuit can generally be extended from the last box in the circuit, since it has fewer wires than the other boxes.

New construction is wired by running the cables along joists (Fig. 9–31) and through holes bored in the center of the studs (Fig. 9–32). The cables should be supported at least every 4½ ft and within 1 ft of boxes and fittings. Cables can be run along the lengths of joists and on narrow "running boards" perpendicular to the joists. Large staples are used to hold the cables to the boards.

New circuits can be installed under existing walls and ceilings by fishing cable through the interior spaces or they can be installed by using surface wiring. Fishing (Fig. 9–33) refers to using an electrician's fish tape to pull cables through the spaces between the walls and above the ceiling. Holes are cut for the switches, outlets, or fixtures and the fish tapes worked through the holes and between the studs or joists until their ends hook together. A cable can be attached to

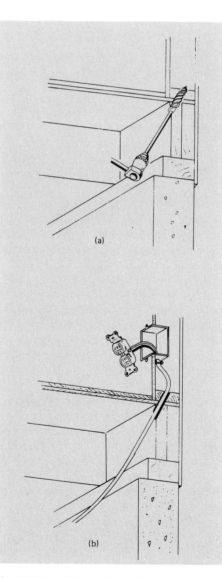

Fig. 9–34 Installing outlets: a) boring cable hole, b) installing cable receptacle.

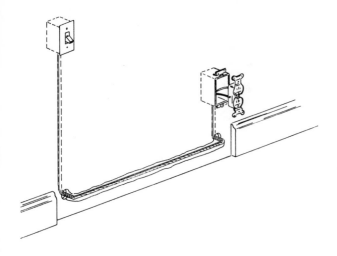

Fig. 9–35 Cable installation behind baseboard.

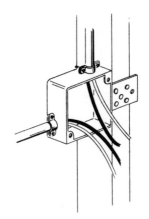

Fig. 9–37 Box installed on stud in new work.

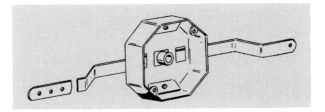

Fig. 9–38 Box and hanger.

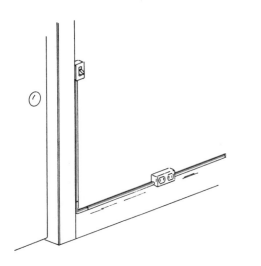

Fig. 9–36 Metal raceway and wiring.

one end of a tape and pulled through the walls and above the ceiling until it emerges from the next hole. Auger power bits are used to drill holes diagonally through joists and headers for cables (Fig. 9–34). Cables can also be installed under the trim by removing baseboards (Fig. 9–35) and door casings.

Cables can be run along the surface of a wall by using some form of surface wiring, such as metal raceways (Fig. 9–36). These metal conduit strips are fastened along the baseboard or between a power source and outlets, switches, or fixtures. For safety, the metal raceway is grounded. Cable can also be recessed into a channel gouged out of the plaster along the baseboard. The gouged channel

is replastered after the cable is in place. Local codes specify whether this is permitted and, if so, what type of cable is required.

INSTALLING ELECTRICAL BOXES

Switch boxes are generally located 48 in. above the floor. Outlet boxes may be installed above the baseboard about 12 in. above the floor, or higher, if they are more convenient to use. Kitchen outlets are placed at counter or table level.

In new construction, boxes can be nailed to the studs (Fig. 9–37) or to crosspieces (Fig. 9–38) between studs. Where there are existing walls, holes must be cut through the plaster and lath or gypsum board (Fig. 9–39). After the location for the box is selected, find the studs by tapping along the wall and making test drills. Cut a hole for the box between the studs. Mark a position between the studs and trace an outline of the box on the wall as a guide in cutting. Allow space for the mounting ears and leeway to slide the box into place. Bore two holes in diagonally opposite corners of the outline, as starting points for a keyhole saw.

With *plaster and lath walls,* try to position the box so that it is centered on a lath. In this way, the middle lath will be cut completely through, while the upper and lower laths will be cut only halfway through. The box can be fastened

Fig. 9–39 Installing box in plaster and lath wall: a) outlining box pattern on wall, b) fishing wire through hole, c) installing box.

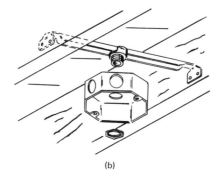

Fig. 9–40 Ceiling boxes and hangers: a) shallow, for old work, b) deep, for new work.

Ceiling boxes are supported by hangers (Fig. 9–40). A hole slightly larger than the box is cut through the plaster or gypsum board. With a lath ceiling, the box is centered on a lath, which is cut through. After the cable is fished to the hole, a metal hanger is pushed through and laid flat on top of the lath or gypsum board. The ceiling box, usually a shallow box, is attached to the hanger and the cable is run through a connector in the top of the box. Recessed fixtures are installed in much the same way, except that the holes are larger. They are held up by different types of supports, or by crosspieces between joists.

Cables are fished to the holes before the boxes are installed and run through connectors into the boxes. Knock-outs are removed and the cable run through connectors clamped to the box. When the boxes are fastened down, the wires from the switches, receptacles, and fixtures are connected to the cable wires with wire nuts. Hot (black or red) wires are connected only to hot wires, neutral (white) wires only to neutral wires, and ground wires to ground terminals on the boxes and grounded receptacles. Switches are connected only to wires in the hot (black) circuit. The new cable can be connected to the service panel either before or after the switches and receptacles are installed. If it is connected before the units are connected, the current must be kept off until the installation is complete and the connections safely insulated.

to the upper and lower laths with screws. With *gypsum-board walls,* the box can be a self-supporting or flange-type box. One type of self-supporting box uses sheet metal supports inserted in the wall and bent around the front edge of the box to support it. Flange-supported boxes are nailed to the front of a stud where a patch of gypsum board has been chiseled away. After the box is installed, the hole is repaired with plaster of Paris.

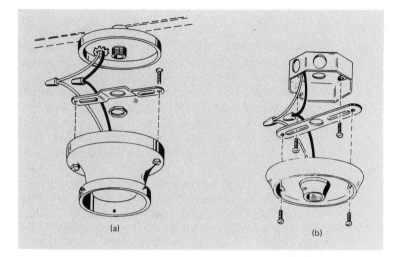

Fig. 9–41 Mounting devices for ceiling fixtures: a) stud and bracket fitting in shallow box, b) bracket fitting in deep box.

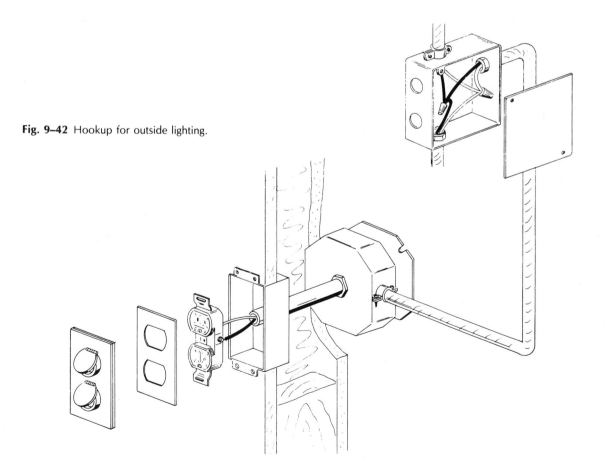

Fig. 9–42 Hookup for outside lighting.

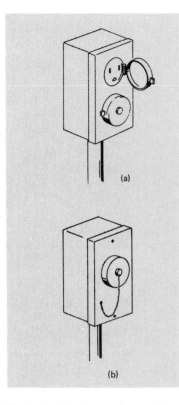

(a)

(b)

Fig. 9–43 Weatherproof outside boxes with: a) hinged, spring-loaded covers, b) screw-on type cover.

CEILING FIXTURES

Ceiling fixtures are made with different devices for mounting on ceiling boxes. Some fasten to a threaded stud extending down from the center of the box (Fig. 9–41(a)). Others are attached with a metal bar that fastens both to the box and to the light fixture (Fig. 9–41(b)). The fixture has to be held in position while it is being connected to the wires from the box. When the connections are complete, the fixture is mounted on the box.

OUTDOOR LIGHTING

Outdoor lights may be operated on either standard 120-V circuits or special 12-V (low voltage) circuits (Fig. 9–42). Power for 120-V circuits is carried by weatherproof, type-UF cable from the house to special outdoor electrical boxes, outlets, switches, and fixtures (Fig. 9–43). Lawn and garden power tools require 120-V circuits. Low-voltage circuits are used for low-key, decorative landscape lighting. Flexible low-voltage cable can be run over the ground, along fences, and overhead in trees, without the danger of shock inherent in 120-V wiring.

120-Volt Lighting

An outdoor circuit may be connected into the electrical system either at the service panel or at a convenient junction box (Fig. 9–44). In either case, rigid metal conduit and type-UF cable must be run from an inside box through the outside wall to a special weatherproof, outdoor box. The same conduit and cable are used to extend the circuit to connect other outlets or switches. Fixtures or outlets installed away from the house are connected to the box at the house by type-UF cable buried at least 18 in. in the ground (Fig. 9–45). The cable is protected by conduit where it enters the ground at the house and where it emerges at the outlet or fixture. Although No. 14 wire can be used for lighting, No. 12 wire should be used where power tools are to be used. The circuit must be grounded with a ground wire and ground-fault interrupter, for protection against accidental short circuits.

A homeowner who can install a new indoor circuit will be able to install an outdoor circuit if allowed to by the local electrical code. Determine where the cable is to go through the wall and bore a hole large enough for ½-in. rigid conduit. The conduit will be threaded onto a junction box on the inside and an outdoor, weatherproof box on the outside.

Install the outlet or switch boxes on the outside of the house and connect them with conduit and fittings. Recessed boxes should be caulked around the edges to prevent water from entering the outside walls. Type-UF cable with a grounding wire should be worked through the conduit and connected to the receptacles and switches. The section of cable that runs through the wall conduit to the inside box is connected with wire nuts to type-NM cable or armored cable at the inside box.

To carry current to a box or fixture away from the house, dig an 18-in. deep trench between the house and the distant outlet. Thread a length of conduit into the outside box at the house and extend it to the bottom of the trench. Another length of conduit should be run from the fixture to the bottom of the trench at the other end. Enough type-UF cable is cut to run from the house to the fixture. The cable is laid loosely in the trench and worked through the conduit at the fixture. The other end of the cable is worked through the conduit at the house and connected to the wires in the outside box. Sand (4 in. deep) on boards that will protect the cable from accidental cutting can be placed over the cable and the trench filled in (Fig. 9–46). When the wiring connections are complete, the circuit can be safely turned on.

Special precautions should be taken to avoid electrical shock when using outdoor 120-V circuits. Power tools should either be grounded with three-prong plugs or have double insulation. Tools, wiring, and fixtures should be kept away from water. A short-circuit in a tool or fixture in contact with a pond or pool could electrocute anyone touching the water.

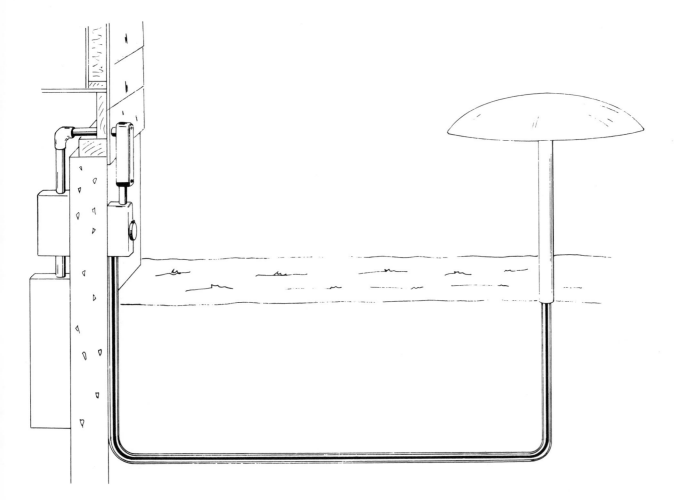

Fig. 9–44 Wiring for outdoor lighting.

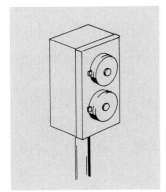

Fig. 9–45 Free-standing electrical box.

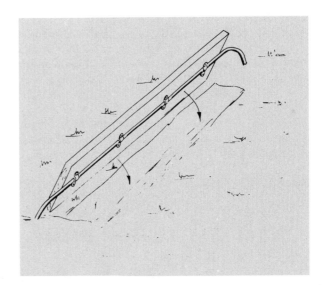

Fig. 9–46 Protecting cable with a board.

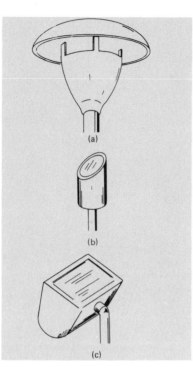

Fig. 9–47 Types of low-voltage fixtures: a) mushroom, b) shrub-illuminating, c) adjustable.

Low-Voltage Lighting

Installing low-voltage fixtures is similar to working with flexible cords and lights indoors. A 100-watt, step-down transformer plugged into an outside outlet will supply current to several 15-watt outdoor lights. A special weatherproof, two-wire cable for 12-V circuits is run from the transformer to the light fixtures. Several lights can be connected to one cable as long as the length doesn't exceed 100 ft, because of the low voltage. The cable doesn't have to be buried or protected by conduit but can be strung over the ground or overhead. If the cable is accidentally cut or the wires short-circuited at a fixture, the low voltage will not injure anyone.

Low-voltage fixtures (Fig. 9–47) are available individually and in kits. Bushes and trees may be silhouetted or illuminated with spotter lights or uprights. Mushroom-type lamps are used to light walks and driveways. Sealed-beam floodlights provide illumination for patios, entrances, and decks. Low-voltage lighting is primarily a decorative type of lighting.

ALARM SYSTEMS FOR HOME PROTECTION

Alarm systems can be installed to signal when a detector or sensor is activated by fire, an intruder, or other source of danger. Heat sensors and smoke detectors are used in fire-alarm systems. Burglar-alarm systems employ magnetic switches, pressure buttons, metal foil, and other detectors, to indicate the opening of doors and windows, the breaking of glass, or the presence of intruders. Special detectors may be used to signal other dangers, such as freezing temperatures and flooding. The sensors and detectors are connected to a control panel, and some form of alarm, such as a siren or bell. In addition to alarm systems, individual, self-contained detectors and alarms can be installed separately where only one or two detectors are required.

Alarm systems for home protection may have either perimeter or interior sensors. The perimeter system guards doors and windows, sounding an alarm before an intruder has gained entrance. Such a system may have relatively complex wiring or may be wireless. An interior system utilizes any of several means of detecting intruders who have already entered the building; ultrasonic transmitters and receivers, photoelectric cells, and microwave or passive infrared sensors are the common types. The infrared sensor, one of these more sophisticated types, reacts to the body heat of a person entering a protected area. Less liable to give false alarms than motion-detectors such as photoelectric devices, the infrared type can be "aimed" at the top half of a room so that pets will not set them off.

Perimeter and interior sensors can be combined in a single system. For example, infrared sensors can guard rooms and halls while magnetic contact switches protect all entry doors.

Several types of *switches* are used to detect intrusion (Fig. 9–52). Magnetic, button-type, and leaf-contact switches are used on windows. Plunger switches and bypass switches are used on doors. Metal foil is glued to windows to detect the breaking of glass. Pressure switches can be used under mats and carpets to signal the presence of an intruder. Tamper switches are mounted in control boxes to sound the alarm if someone tries to open the box. A push-button is used as a panic button to set off the alarm if the homeowner needs help.

TYPES OF ALARM SYSTEM CIRCUITS

Components may be wired in one of two ways in an alarm-system. Wires are run, in both cases, from the control panel to the detectors and switches in the circuit. In an *open-circuit system* (Fig. 9–48(a)), the detectors and switches are connected between two wires (in parallel). If a detector is activated, it closes the circuit and the alarm sounds. In a *closed-circuit system* (Fig. 9–48(b)), only one wire is connected to the detectors and switches (in series). A low-voltage current in the circuit flows continually through each detector. If the detector is activated, it opens the system and the current stops, causing a relay to close and sound the

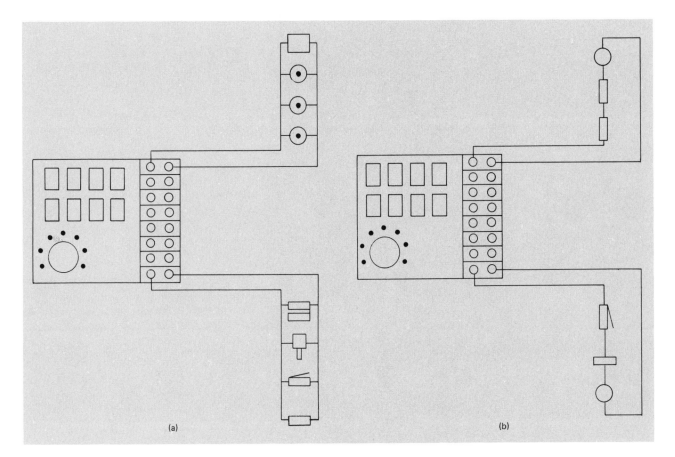

Fig. 9–48 Alarm system circuits: a) open, b) closed.

Fig. 9–49 Alarm bell.

Fig. 9–50 Alarm siren.

alarm. The open-circuit system is considered to be the simpler of the two. False alarms are more common with a closed circuit where cutting the wire causes the alarm to sound. (Cutting the wires in an open-circuit system makes the circuit inoperative.)

MAJOR COMPONENTS

Alarm systems include various types of detectors, a control panel, an alarm bell (Fig. 9–49) or siren (Fig. 9–50), a power source, and various accessory devices wired in one or more circuits. Separate circuits may be used in a zone system so that detectors in different parts of the house can be energized while others remain inoperative. Fire-alarm circuits are always wired separately from burglar-alarm circuits. Accessory devices include remote-control switches for deactivating the alarm, bypass switches to allow doors to be opened without sounding the alarm, and a constant ringing drop (CRD) to keep the alarm sounding even though the detector switch is turned off by an intruder.

Fire-alarm *heat sensors* (Fig. 9–51(a)) used in living areas are activated at 135 degrees. Those used in hotter

Fig. 9–51 Fire and smoke detectors: a) heat sensor, b) smoke detector.

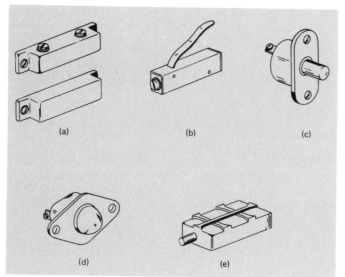

Fig. 9–52 Types of burglar-alarm switches: a) magnetic, b) leaf, c) button, d) pressure, e) tamper.

spaces like attics are designed for 190 or 210 degrees. *Smoke detectors* (Fig. 9–51(b)) operate on either optical or ionization principles. The standard optical-type detector reacts to the presence of a few particles of smoke that pass through a light beam. An ionization-type of detector reacts to the ions in smoke and other gases.

Several types of *switches* are used to detect intrusion (Fig. 9–52). Magnetic, button-type, and leaf-contact switches are used on windows. Plunger switches and bypass switches are used on doors. Metal foil is glued to windows to detect the breaking of glass. Pressure switches can be used under mats and carpets to signal the presence of an intruder. Tamper switches are mounted in control boxes to sound the alarm if someone tries to open the box. A pushbutton is used as a panic button to set off the alarm if the homeowner needs help. Sophisticated alarm systems may employ other detectors, such as ultrasonic transmitters and receivers, photoelectric cells, and infrared light detectors.

The *control panel* unites all of the detector circuits, the power source, and alarm wiring. Circuits may be deac-

tivated at the control panel or by a remote-control device. Simple panels may have terminals for only one detector circuit, while more complicated panels can handle a number of separate circuits. The alarm may be built into the control panel, but it is mounted separately in most systems. Sirens and bells are often used for fire alarms, while bells, horns, and flashing lights are used in burglar-alarm systems. The alarm is powered by either a battery or a transformer connected to the 120-V house circuit. Some systems automatically switch from the house circuit to a battery in the event of power failure in the house system. These components are connected with light, No. 18 to No. 22 wire.

INSTALLING AN ALARM SYSTEM

The control panel should be located in a protected place, such as a closet or attic entrance. If 120-V current is required, the panel should be close to an electrical outlet or junction box. Instructions accompanying alarm-system kits

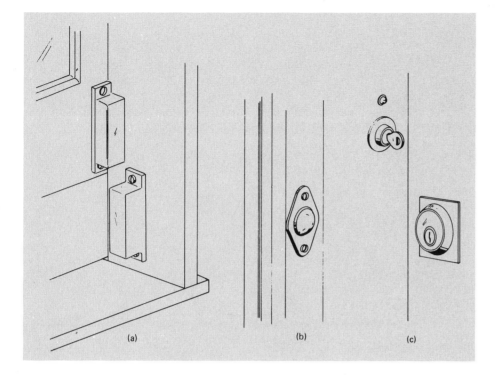

Fig. 9–53 Installing switches: a) magnetic switch on window sash and frame, b) pressure switch on door frame, c) shunt lock and light on door.

provide detailed information on general installation and options such as wiring circuits in zones.

Open- and closed-circuit systems use different types of detectors and switches. Those used in an open-circuit installation are called "normally closed" (NC) detectors and switches. Those used in closed circuits are called "normally open" (NO) detectors and switches. A detector designed for one system will not work in the other. Some systems, however, may be combined NO and NC.

Double-hung windows use magnetic switches, button-type switches, or leaf contact switches. Attach the two parts of the magnetic switch to the frame and adjacent sash (Fig. 9–53(a)). Pushbutton switches are installed in the sill beneath the lower rail of the bottom sash. Leaf-type switches and plunger switches can be used on *casement windows* to activate an alarm when the window is opened.

Doors use a simple pressure button switch mounted in the frame on the hinged side of the doorway (Fig. 9–53(b)). Bypass switches are mounted beside exterior doors to allow the circuit to be turned off at that point so the door can be opened.

Heat detector *sensors* should be mounted on the ceiling in the middle of the room for greatest coverage. Sensors

that are too close to a wall may be protected from the heat of a fire by cooler updrafts. *Smoke detectors* should be mounted where smoke is likely to rise, such as at the head of a stairway or on the ceiling in a hallway outside bedrooms.

An *entrance shunt lock* should be installed at entrances so that the system can be deactivated by a key before the door is opened (Fig. 9–53(c)). *Panic buttons* can be placed where they are likely to be needed in an emergency, such as inside an entrance or in a bedroom.

The various detectors and switches are connected to the control panel by bell wire. In a closed circuit, the single wire is cut to insert the director. In an open circuit, one wire is attached to one of the terminals of the detector and another wire is attached to the other terminal. Heavier, flexible cord may be used to connect the alarm and battery to the control panel. House current is connected by a standard flexible cord or an electrical cable.

Test buttons allow alarm circuits to be tested without sounding the alarm. Open circuits, in particular, should be tested frequently to be certain that the wires and connections are intact, since there is no other indication of a broken wire or loose connection.

When the exterior of the house needs to be repaired, it has to be mended promptly or rain, wind, and snow will soon gain the upper hand. Damaged shingles, for instance, will be followed by a leaking attic unless the shingles are replaced. This chapter provides the homeowner with information about the different types of materials, construction, periodic maintenance, and repair of the major sections of the house's exterior.

ROOF COVERINGS

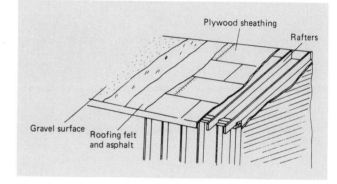

Fig. 10–1 Layers of material on flat or builtup roofs.

TYPES OF ROOFING

Several types of materials are used to protect roof sheathing from the weather. The type of roofing used depends on the roofing styles in the locality, whether the construction is expensive, and whether the roof is sloped or flat. Tile roofs are more common in western and southern sections of the United States, for example, than in northern areas. Slate, wooden shingles, and shakes are more likely to be found on expensive homes.

Some of the most common types of roofing materials used for sloped roofs are: asphalt shingles, wood shingles and shakes, slate shingles, and ceramic tiles. Other roofing materials, such as asbestos-cement shingles, terne, and copper or galvanized steel, are also used for qualities such as greater resistance to fire, an attractive appearance, and durability. *Asphalt shingles* are generally made in 12 × 36-in. sections with tabs cut in the lower part to give the appearance of several units. The shingle is made of felt that is saturated with waterproof asphalt and coated with mineral particles for durability. *Wood shingles* and *shakes* are made in 16-in., 18-in., and longer lengths. The shingles are thin and uniform, while hand-split shakes are thick and irregular.

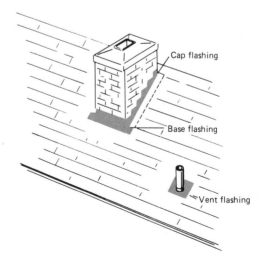

Fig. 10–2 Flashing used around chimneys and vents.

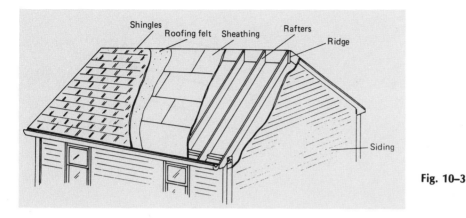

Shingles
Roofing felt   Sheathing   Rafters
Ridge
Siding

Fig. 10–3

Slate shingles are cut in rectangular shapes from thin sheets of slate. *Roofing tiles* are made in two forms: Curved tiles are manufactured to be used in concave and convex rows; flat tiles are made to overlap like other flat shingles.

Flat or *builtup* roofs (Fig. 10–1) are usually covered with several layers of asphalt-saturated felt bonded with hot asphalt. Gravel or sand is spread over the top layer and embedded in the asphalt to protect the roof from abrasion and drying.

Flashing is used to supplement roof coverings where the roof meets a chimney, soil pipe, wall, or other protruding object (Fig. 10–2). Either a noncorroding metal or plastic must be used, to withstand the weather. One edge of a strip of flashing usually extends under the adjacent shingles while the exposed edges are sealed with asphalt cement or caulking.

REPAIRING ROOFING

A homeowner can take care of minor roofing repairs with a can of asphalt cement, a cartridge of exterior caulking compound, and a few shingles and roofing nails. One should inspect the roof periodically from both the inside and outside. Inspection of the sheathing from the attic may reveal water stains from leaks that the homeowner can repair. Inspection from the outside may reveal areas of damaged or missing shingles or faulty flashing. The general condition of the roof can be observed from the ground without running the risk of damaging shingles by walking on them. Asphalt and wooden-shingle roofs and builtup flat roofs can be expected to last for 15 to 25 years if good materials were used in their construction. Slate and tile roofs, however, will last indefinitely. With age, asphalt shingles lose their protective coating of minerals, dry out, and curl. Wooden shingles and shakes also dry out and warp or split with age. Slate and tile roofs will remain intact unless they are mechanically damaged by wind or heavy objects. When roofing must be complete-

ly replaced, a second layer of shingles can usually be installed over the first layer as long as the structure can bear the weight. *Both* layers will have to be removed when the second layer eventually wears out. Installing a completely new roof on a house is a substantial undertaking that requires extensive experience in roofing. The homeowner can gain useful experience by installing roofing on smaller shed and garage roofs.

The watertight integrity of a roof (Fig. 10–3) will be lost if water backs up under the shingles or if the shingles or flashing are damaged. An ice dam at the edge of the roof or a leaf-filled roof valley, for example, may cause water to back up under the overlapped shingles and leak through the roofing. Shingles that are lifted by the wind, cracked, torn, or worn out will also create leaks.

The *source of the leak* is more difficult to find on sloped roofs than on flat roofs. Water leaking through a sloped roof follows rafters and sheathing and may drip to the attic floor several feet away from where it entered. If the inside of the roof rafters and sheathing are uncovered, the dripping water can be traced backward to where it entered by inspecting the sheathing and joists while it is raining or while water from a hose is played on the roof. Holes and cracks may also be visible during the daylight as bright openings that contrast with the dark attic interior. On flat roofs, water usually drips straight down from where it leaks through the roofing. When insulation or ceilings in finished attics hide the source of the leak, they must be removed to trace the leak. When the source of the leak is found, it can be marked inside the attic to make it visible from the outside by pushing a thin wire or nail through the roofing. Leaks through flashing that has come unsealed can be located by inspecting the flashing on the roof.

Working on a roof is potentially dangerous and can also damage the roofing. Wear soft-soled shoes with a good grip to protect the roofing and provide a firm footing. The base of a ladder that extends to the roof should be placed one quarter the length of the ladder away from

Fig. 10–4 Proper angle for ladder to roof.

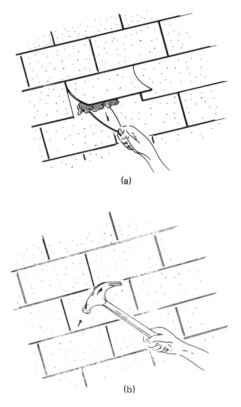

(a)

(b)

Fig. 10–5 Repairing loose shingles. (a) Apply asphalt cement under shingle. (b) Nail corners with roofing nails.

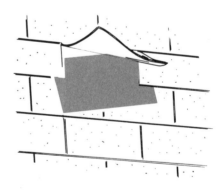

Fig. 10–6 Covering small crack with noncorroding aluminum.

the building for stability (Fig. 10–4). Use a ladder long enough to extend beyond the edge of the roof so you can step off it onto the roof. For steep roofs or easily damaged roofing materials, such as slate, mount a ladder flush against the roof and fasten it securely over the ridge. The ladder provides something to hang onto and spreads the user's weight over a large area.

Small holes and cracks in roofing materials and sheathing can often be repaired by sealing them with asphalt cement. When shingles are curled or split, asphalt cement and nails are used to hold them down. If the shingles are severely damaged, however, they must be removed and replaced.

Asphalt Shingles

Shingle roofs are awkward to repair because of the way the shingles must be overlapped to shed water. Shingles are laid in rows starting from the lower edge of the roof and moving upward. Each shingle is nailed through its upper section and overlapped by the next row of shingles.

Asphalt shingles are easiest to repair when they are warm and flexible. Shingles on a roof sloped toward the south may be warm enough to work with even on a cold day. If a leak cannot be pinpointed from inside the attic, the condition of the shingles will often provide a clue. Badly abraded, curled, or cracked asphalt shingles are likely to let water pass under the roofing.

Shingles that are loose from being blown by the wind or that are slightly curled can be repaired by fastening them down with asphalt cement and roofing nails. Coat the bottom of the shingle with asphalt cement (Fig. 10–5(a)) and press it against the shingle beneath. Nail the corners of the tabs with roofing nails (Fig. 10–5(b)) and cover the nailheads with asphalt cement. Shingles that are split only in the lower exposed section can be repaired in a similar way. Coat the underside of the shingle with asphalt cement, press it down, and nail both parts of the split section to the sheathing. Cover the nailheads with asphalt cement.

A *small hole or crack* under a good shingle can be repaired by removing the shingle and sealing the opening with asphalt cement or by covering it with a sheet of noncorroding aluminum or copper (Fig. 10–6). Cut the sheet metal large enough to fit under the shingle, and coat the underside with asphalt cement. Work the patch

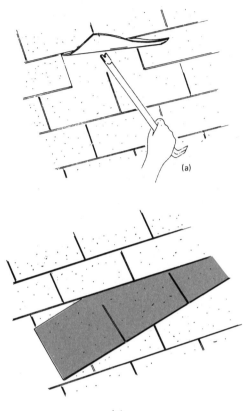

(a)

(b)

(c)

Fig. 10–7 Three steps in replacing damaged shingles.

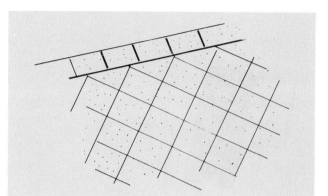

Fig. 10–8 Replacing shingles on a roof hip.

holding the shingle are too far under the next shingle or if the shingles are too brittle to bend, the nails can be cut with a hacksaw slipped under the shingle or they can be removed with a flat spade. This tool is designed to slip under the shingles to pry up the nails. After the damaged shingle and nails have been removed, asphalt cement should be used to seal any openings in the roofing paper or sheathing. A new shingle is then slipped into place so that it aligns with the other shingles (Fig. 10–7(b)). Lift the lower section of the next row of shingles so that the new shingle can be nailed in place several inches under the overlapping shingles (Fig. 10–7(c)). Use the existing nailholes where possible. Cover the nailheads with asphalt cement.

Shingles on roof hips are cut in a rectangular shape. When hip shingles are replaced, asphalt cement is used to cover the bottom of the new shingle and *all four corners* are nailed down (Fig. 10–8). Each shingle overlaps the next one, covering the nailheads, by three or

up under the shingle that covers the opening until it extends several inches above the hole. It may be necessary to remove the nails holding the shingle in order to slide the sheet into place.

To *replace a shingle,* the old shingle and its nails must be removed. Since the nails are covered by the lower section of the next row of shingles, the shingle above the one to be removed must be bent back far enough to expose the nailheads (Fig. 10–7(a)). If the nails

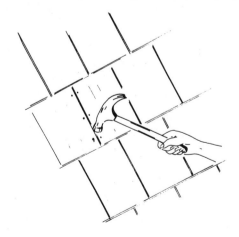

Fig. 10–9 Refastening loose wood shingles.

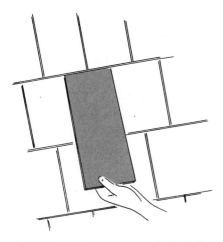

Fig. 10–10 Fitting a new wood shingle into place.

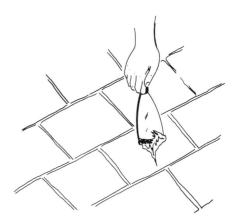

Fig. 10–11 Sealing cracks in slate shingles.

four inches. (Follow the pattern of the roof being repaired.) Before they are covered, the nailheads are coated with asphalt cement. As with other replacement shingles, study the placement and pattern of the shingles on a hip and try to nail new shingles in the old nailholes to minimize holes in the sheathing.

Wooden Shingles and Shakes

Loose wooden shingles and shakes can be fastened down with roofing nails and asphalt cement (Fig. 10–9). Where asphalt cement is sufficient to hold the shingle, apply it under the bottom edge, and press the shingle down. When a wooden shingle is nailed, the nailheads must be coated with asphalt cement to prevent water from entering through the nailholes. Shingles that are only slightly warped can be split vertically with a chisel, flattened out, and nailed down. The crack should be sealed with asphalt cement. As in repairing other shingles, a metal patch made of a piece of noncorroding sheet metal can be slipped beneath a wooden shingle to cover a small hole or crack.

Damaged wooden shingles can be removed by splitting them and working the pieces loose. Cut nails covered by other shingles with a hacksaw. A new shingle should be cut to fit the opening and worked up under the overlapping shingles (Fig. 10–10). Nail down the four corners of the exposed section of the shingle and cover the nailheads with asphalt cement.

Slate Shingles

Cracks in slate shingles can sometimes be sealed with a heavy coat of asphalt cement (Fig. 10–11). Work the cement into the crack and to either side of the opening. A special tool is used to cut through nails holding a damaged shingle. A long, flat, metal strap that is notched

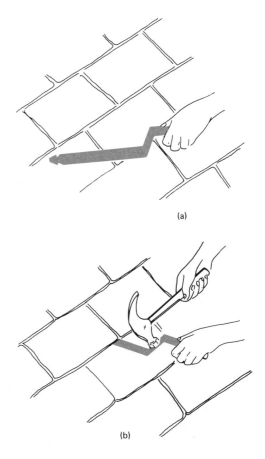

(a)

(b)

Fig. 10–12 Long flat metal tool in use to search out and cut nails under slate shingles.

near the end is shaped to reach under slate shingles and pull or cut the hidden nails (Fig. 10–12). A new slate shingle can be cut to fit by scoring it with a cold chisel and breaking it over a sharp edge. Place the shingle in position to measure and mark two points just below the top edge for nailholes. Remove the shingle, and use an electric drill or a nailset to make the holes. Slide the slate into position and nail it through the precut holes. The nailheads should be covered with asphalt cement.

Fig. 10–13 Overlap of curved tiles.

Tiles

Tiles crack and must be replaced, occasionally. Curved tiles overlap both vertically and horizontally (Fig. 10–13). Tiles in the convex column are easy to remove since they are held in place either by gravity or by wires. Concave tiles can be replaced after the overlapping convex tiles and the nails holding them in place are removed. Flat tiles are removed by lifting them until the ridge on the back of the tile is free from the horizontal furring strip on which it is mounted.

Flat Roofs

Flat roofs are repaired by patching them with asphalt-saturated felt and asphalt cement. Surface blisters should be cut with a utility knife and repaired in the same way as other small cracks and holes. Asphalt cement is worked under the edges of the cracks and the material is

Fig. 10–14 Asphalt-saturated felt used to patch flat roof.

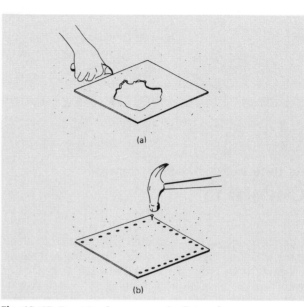

Fig. 10–15 Repairing large areas of a flat roof.

pressed down. Over the opening apply a layer of asphalt cement that extends on either side of the crack. Next press a patch of suitable size down onto the cement (Fig. 10–14). Nail the edges of the patch down with roofing nails and cover both the patch and nailheads with asphalt cement. If desired, a second and larger patch can be applied over the first patch in the same manner.

To repair larger areas, the roofing material around the damaged section should be cut away (Fig. 10–15(a)). Cut a rectangular pattern around the area and remove a layer or two of roofing. Coat the exposed surface with asphalt cement and cut a felt patch to fit into the opening. Press the patch in place so that it is flush with the surrounding roofing, and nail down the edges (Fig. 10–15(b)). Apply asphalt cement over the patch so that it extends a few inches beyond the nailed edges. Cut a larger patch and press this into the cement. Nail the edges again and cover the entire patch with asphalt cement. Sand or gravel can be spread on top of the cement to protect the surface.

Flashing

Flashing surrounding a chimney or vent pipe or abutting a wall should be sealed with asphalt cement or caulking compound. Nailheads should be covered also. If the flashing has become torn or corroded, especially where it is overlapped by shingles, it should be removed and replaced. Replacing and repairing flashing in valleys is a complicated task that requires the assistance of someone with extensive experience in roofing work. Replacing chimney flashing is more likely to be within the capabilities of a homeowner.

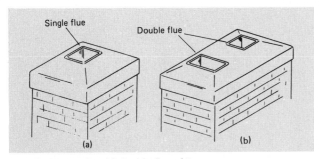

Fig. 10–16 Single and double-flue chimneys.

Fig. 10–17 Removing old mortar with a chisel.

CHIMNEYS

Chimneys should be inspected periodically to determine whether they need to be cleaned or repaired. Cleaning is in order if the inside of the flue is caked with soot or creosote from burning softwood. Repairs will be required if there are cracks that let water enter between the bricks or along the chimney flashing.

A masonry chimney may enclose several separate flues (Fig. 10–16). A chimney serving both a furnace and a fireplace should have at least two flues, to prevent interference between the two updrafts. If a chimney does not extend high enough above the peak (ridge) of the roof, or if it is shielded by a nearby wall or trees, the heated air may be unable to flow up the chimney as required for a good fire. Instead of extending the height of the chimney, a chimney cap or rotating ventilator may be added to remedy the situation.

CLEANING CHIMNEYS

The inside of a flue can be inspected from the roof, or from a fireplace, with the aid of a strong flashlight. Soot or hardened creosote that has built up on the sides of the flue should be removed to avoid the danger of a chimney fire. If the top of the chimney is accessible, the homeowner can employ the traditional method of dragging a weighted object through the chimney to scour the sides of the flue. Close the fireplace damper and, for further protection against dust and ashes, cover the fireplace opening with a sheet of polyethylene. Attach a rope to a weighted bag made of rough material, to a doubled-up length of chain, or to a burlap-wrapped brick and work the scouring device up and down inside the flue to strip the sides clean. Be prepared to clean the ashes and soot out of the fireplace when the damper is opened.

REPAIRING CRACKS AND LEAKS

Cracked or crumbled mortar and defective chimney flashing should be repaired before leaking water causes further damage.

Defective Mortar

Remove old mortar with a cold chisel and mallet or hammer to a depth of ½ to 1 inch (Fig. 10–17). Mix fresh mortar from masonry cement (one part) and fine sand (three parts) and wet the inside surfaces of the opening. Apply the fresh mortar with a trowel and point the joints by compacting the mortar with a small tool. After the mortar has cured, it should be sealed with a masonry sealer to protect it from the weather.

Cracks in Concrete Caps

Cracks between a flue and the surrounding concrete cap should be repaired before water leaks between them. Clean out the face of the crack and seal it with exterior caulking, asphalt cement, or fresh mortar (Fig. 10–18).

Fig. 10–18 Sealing face of a crack in a concrete cap.

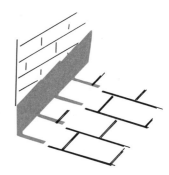

Fig. 10–19 Two separate layers of chimney flashing.

Leaking Flashing

Loose flashing can be reattached and sealed, but flashing worn through by corrosion must be removed and replaced. Chimney flashing consists of two separate layers (Fig. 10–19). The base section fits under the shingles, wraps around the chimney corners, and extends several inches upward over the bricks. The cap section is cut in narrow segments to fit over the base and the bricks and cover them in a step-wise pattern. The base of the flashing is covered with shingles, while the upper edge of the cap is attached to the chimney with mortar or asphalt cement.

If the flashing is loose at the side of the chimney, repair it by reattaching it as it was originally. Inspect the flashing to determine whether it was embedded in the mortar between the bricks or cemented to the side of the chimney. If it was embedded in the mortar, clean out the crumbled mortar and wedge the flashing between the bricks. Mix a batch of fresh mortar and fill the joint surrounding the flashing. If the flashing was cemented to the side of the chimney, coat the inside edge with asphalt cement and press or brace it tightly against the chimney until the cement sets. Seal the joint by applying a wide strip of asphalt cement along the edge of the flashing.

Flashing that is perforated with corrosion should be removed and replaced. Shingles overlapping the flashing will have to be removed to free the base section. Use the old sections as patterns for cutting the new flashing. Since the flashing on the upslope face of the chimney must overlap the lower sections, install the flashing on the lower face and the two sides of the chimney first. Finally, place the base or cap flashing on the upslope face of the chimney and wrap it around the corners to overlap the lower sections. Use roofing nails and asphalt cement to fasten the flashing to the roof and to seal nailheads and joints. The upper edges of the flashing should be embedded in mortar between the bricks or cemented to the sides of the chimney. All joints and cracks should be thoroughly sealed with asphalt cement to prevent leaks (Fig. 10–20).

GUTTERS AND DOWNSPOUTS

Gutters and downspouts are used to control roof drainage (Fig. 10–21). From where they are attached at the edge of the roof, the gutters catch and carry water to the downspouts. At the bottom of the downspout, drainage pipes or splash blocks are used to divert the water away from the foundation.

Where gutters are missing or fail to function properly, water may damage the exterior and interior walls

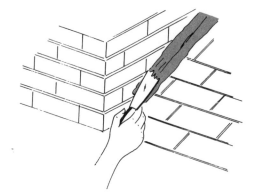

Fig. 10–20 Sealing joints and cracks with asphalt cement.

Fig. 10–21 Gutters and downspouts.

and the foundation of the house. Water running down the side of a frame house will enter cracks in the paint and between the boards and cause the paint to blister and peel. As the wood becomes wet, it starts to rot. Water may also leak through the siding and into the insulation and interior walls. If water from the roof saturates the soil next to the foundation, the basement walls and floor may become very damp. Water may even rise to flood the basement floor. During freezing weather, a faulty gutter may become blocked with ice and force melt water back up under the shingles, where it can leak into the attic.

TYPES OF MATERIALS USED FOR GUTTERS AND DOWNSPOUTS

Gutters and other parts of roof drainage systems may be made of metal, vinyl, or wood. Wooden gutters are still found on some older houses, but aluminum, galvanized steel, copper, and vinyl are used almost exclusively today. (Different types of metals should not be used to-

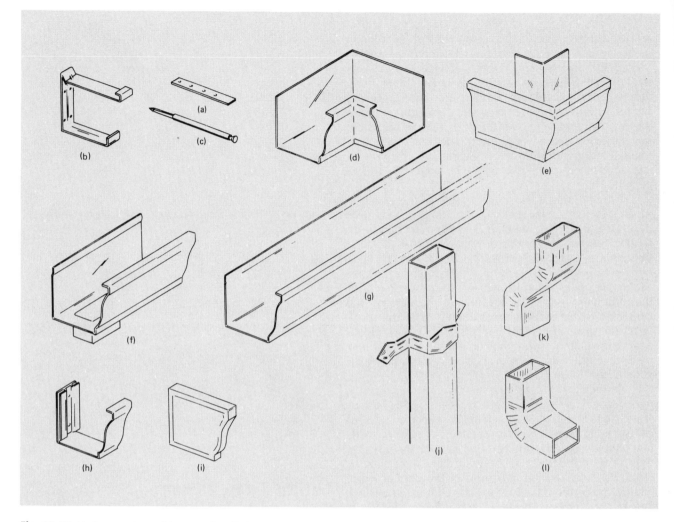

Fig. 10–22 Various parts used in gutter installation.

gether because there is likely to be an undesirable corrosive reaction where they meet.)

Aluminum doesn't corrode and is convenient to work with because of its light weight. Since it isn't as strong as other metals, however, aluminum is easily damaged by heavy objects. Aluminum may be used unfinished or with a baked-on, white-enamel finish. *Steel* is stronger than aluminum, but it corrodes when the galvanized surface wears through. Galvanized steel gutters may be purchased unfinished or finished with baked-on white enamel. *Copper* makes a strong, high-quality, but expensive drainage system. After the sections are soldered together, copper gutters need little maintenance since copper doesn't corrode and doesn't require paint. (The greenish color of old exterior copper is not corrosion. It is a natural weathering process and an "added attraction" in itself.) *Vinyl* systems also require little

maintenance, but they are much cheaper than copper. *Wood* gutters must be coated periodically to prevent them from rotting. (No matter what the material of the gutters, it is important to keep them clear of leaves which may clog the opening to the downspout.)

STRUCTURE

Gutters are installed just below the edge of the roof, slightly higher near the middle of the run, so that the gentle slope allows the water to flow toward the downspouts. The gutters are fastened, in 10-ft. sections, every few feet with strap hangers, bracket hangers, or spikes and ferrules. *Strap hangers* (Fig. 10–22(a)) fasten around the gutter and are nailed to the roofing boards under the shingles. *Bracket hangers* (Fig. 10–22(b)) also wrap around the gutter but are fastened to the fascia board just

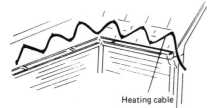

Fig. 10–23 Splash block to carry water away from house.

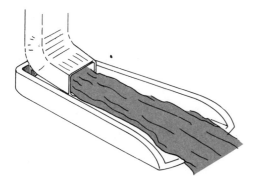

Heating cable

Fig. 10–24 Heating cable to prevent ice buildup.

Fig. 10–25 Removing leaves and sticks from gutter.

Fig. 10–26 Screening placed over gutter to keep out foreign objects.

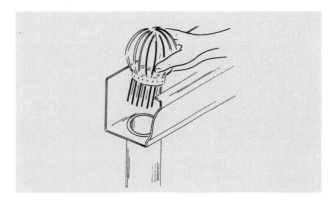

Fig. 10–27 Drainspout strainer.

below the edge of the roof. Spikes and ferrules (Fig. 10–22(c)) penetrate the upper edge of the gutter and are driven into the fascia. *Inside* and *outside corners* (Fig. 10–22(d),(e)), *drop outlets*—outlets to downspouts—(Fig. 10–22(f))—and sections of gutter (Fig. 10–22(g)) are fastened together by connectors (Fig. 10–22(h)). *End caps* (Fig. 10–22(i)) close the ends of terminal sections of gutter. Joints between these components are sealed with exterior caulking compound to prevent leaks. *Down-spouts* (Fig. 10–22(j)) are connected to the drop outlets in the gutter system by *elbows* (Fig. 10–22(k)) that permit the downspout to be placed flush against the side of the house. A *side elbow* (Fig. 10–22(l)) at the base of the downspout can be used to pipe the water to a *splash block* (Fig. 10–23) or other means of carrying the water away from the foundation. Along the edge of the roof adjacent to the gutter, *heating cables* (Fig. 10–24) may be installed to supplement the drainage system by preventing ice dams from forming during freezing weather.

Maintenance

Periodic inspection and maintenance of gutters and downspouts will prevent unexpected clogging, leaks, or collapse. Accumulated leaves and sticks should be removed from the gutters (Fig. 10–25) two or three times

a year. Blocked downspouts should be cleared with a cable or auger. Leaves can be kept out of gutters by covering the tops with open, wire-mesh screening (Fig.

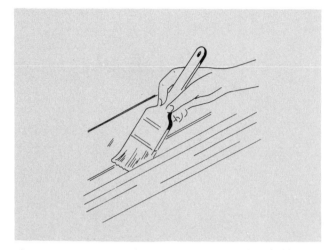

Fig. 10–28 Paint the inside of wooden gutters with boiled linseed oil and asphalt paint.

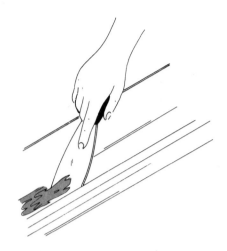

Fig. 10–29 Applying asbestos cement over a gutter patch.

10–26). Special strainers are made to fit into the mouth of the drop outlets to the downspouts (Fig. 10–27). If wet leaves accumulate in a gutter, not only will they block the drainage, but their weight may pull the hangers loose and cause the gutters to sag or collapse. Sagging gutters collect water in valleys rather than carrying it to the downspouts. Correct this condition by adjusting the hangers. Bend or raise them until the gutters are at the correct slope.

Aluminum, copper, and vinyl gutters and downspouts can be left unpainted, but galvanized steel and wood gutters must be protected. The inside of wooden gutters should be cleaned, dried, and treated with boiled linseed oil to revive the wood. The inside surface should then be covered with a coat or two of asphalt paint (Fig. 10–28). The outside should be painted with two coats of exterior paint.

Galvanized steel gutters will corrode once the galvanized surface wears off, if they aren't protected. Paint the inside of the gutter with asphalt paint. The outside should be painted with a special primer for galvanized steel and finished with two compatible top coats. Before painting, rust must be removed from old gutters; and new gutters should be allowed to weather at least six months so the paint will adhere.

Aluminum and copper are sometimes painted for aesthetic reasons. Unfinished aluminum will weather. To paint aluminum gutters, use metal primer and two coats of exterior paint. Copper can be cleaned and coated with a clear exterior varnish, or it can be painted with a metal primer and exterior paint. Either alternative will avoid stains on the siding from water discolored by the greenish film on weathered copper. Copper, like aluminum, can also be left unfinished.

Repairing Holes and Cracks

Holes and cracks in gutters and other parts of the system can be repaired with patches, asbestos cement, epoxy sealants, vinyl sealants, caulking, or solder. Before being patched, rusted metal should be cleaned with a wire brush and ragged edges need to be cut away. If the hole or crack is small, it can be sealed with a thick coat of asbestos cement spread several inches on all sides of the opening. Epoxy sealants can be used to seal small openings in aluminum, galvanized steel, and copper. Leaks between joints in copper gutters, however, should be resoldered. Solder can also be used to close small openings in steel gutters. Small leaks in vinyl gutters can be repaired with special vinyl sealants.

Large openings must be patched. Patches can be cut from sheet metals (such as aluminum), fiberglass, asphalt-saturated roofing paper, heavy canvas, or similar materials. The patch is fitted snugly over the crack or hole and asbestos cement applied over the entire area (Fig. 10–29). Fiberglass repair kits use a special resin instead of asphalt cement.

DOWNSPOUT DRAINAGE

Water can be carried away from the downspout in several ways. A simple channel-shaped *splash block* can be placed on the ground under the downspout to divert the water. Concrete and heavy plastic blocks are made especially for this purpose. Water can also be carried by a large fabric hose attached to the bottom of a downspout. However the water is diverted, it should be discharged into a drainage area several feet from the foundation (Fig. 10–30). The drainage area can be nothing more than an

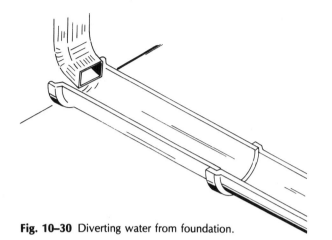

Fig. 10–30 Diverting water from foundation.

absorbent area downslope from the foundation, or it can be a storm drain or dry well. Downspouts can also be connected by underground drainage pipes to dry wells constructed of loose stones and gravel to facilitate underground drainage. In some regions, downspouts are attached to cisterns to collect and preserve rainwater for domestic use.

EXTERIOR WALLS

Siding is used on exterior walls to protect the house from the weather. To remain watertight, there must be no unprotected openings in these walls. Joints at door and window frames must be sealed with caulking, and damaged boards or crumbled mortar must be replaced. Since exterior walls are accessible and materials for repairs easy to work with, most homeowners will be able to repair or replace damaged siding themselves.

TYPES OF SIDING

Most siding is made of wood or masonry in some form. Although wood siding is cut and milled in many shapes and sizes, individual styles generally fall into one of the following groups: clapboards (beveled siding), shingles or shakes, tongue-and-groove or shiplap boards, board-and-batten, or plywood. Masonry siding is usually made of brick, stone, stucco, or concrete block. Stucco is applied either over masonry or to wire lath on a wood-frame structure. Among the other types of siding used, asbestos shingles and vinyl and aluminum siding are the most common.

MAINTENANCE AND REPAIR OF SIDING

All types of siding are affected to some degree by the sun, expansion and contraction from moisture and temperature, wind, and rain. Wooden siding must be protected from these elements by paint, stain, wood preservative, or some other type of protective coating. Masonry will last longer if it is sealed against moisture with a waterproofing solution. Regardless of whether the siding is made of wood or masonry, all open joints must be sealed at junctures with porches, roof structures, and window and door frames. Damaged siding should be either repaired or replaced as soon as possible to keep the walls watertight.

Clapboards

Clapboards are overlapped vertically to prevent water from entering between them (Fig. 10–31). The nails along the lower edge also penetrate the next row of

Fig. 10–31 Diagram of overlapping clapboards.

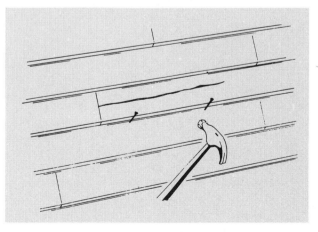

Fig. 10–32 Repairing cracked clapboard.

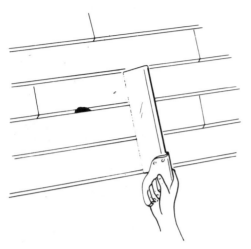

Fig. 10–33 Removing a damaged section of clapboard.

Fig. 10–34 Overlapping of shingles.

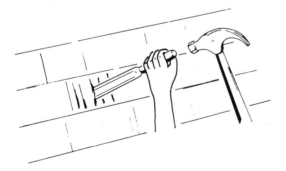

Fig. 10–35 Using a chisel to split a shingle.

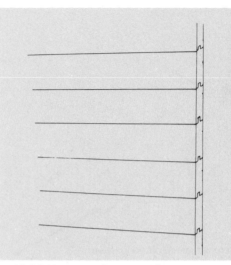

Fig. 10–36 Tongue-and-groove siding.

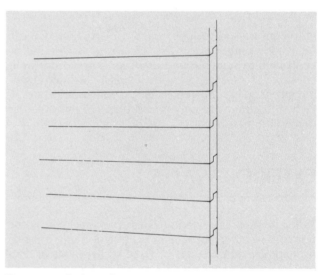

Fig. 10–37 Shiplap siding.

clapboards. Split clapboards can either be fastened down and sealed or replaced. To repair a split clapboard, pry the section below the split away from the wall and coat the edge with a waterproof adhesive. While the adhesive sets, clamp the split edges together by tacking a few nails in the siding below the clapboard. Force the nails against the edge of the clapboard so that the lower section is pushed upward (Fig. 10–32). When the joint is tight, remove the temporary nails, and nail the clapboard to the sheathing.

The most difficult step in replacing clapboards is removing the nails from the overlapping clapboards. If an overlapping clapboard can be pried up slightly without damaging it, the nailheads can be raised so that the nails can be pulled out with a claw hammer. Otherwise, wedges and a hacksaw blade can be worked up under the clapboard to cut the nails. After the nails are removed or cut, the entire clapboard can be removed. If only a section of a clapboard is to be removed, use a backsaw or keyhole saw to make vertical cuts (Fig. 10–33) in the damaged section. The clapboard can then be split with a chisel and removed. Before a new clapboard is installed, the building paper beneath should be patched and sealed, if necessary, to make it watertight. Cut the replacement clapboard to the correct size and slide it under the overlapping clapboard. Nail the lower edge every six inches or so and fill the nailholes and the joints at the ends with caulking.

Wooden Shingles and Shakes

Wooden shingles and shakes overlap like clapboards (Fig. 10–34). They are also tapered so that they can be laid in even rows. Split shingles can be repaired by gluing and nailing them down, if they are otherwise in good condition. Work adhesive into the crack, push the parts together, and nail them to the sheathing. Shingles that are cracked in several places or more severely damaged should be removed and replaced. Use a chisel to split the shingle and work the pieces free (Fig. 10–35). Nails can be removed with a claw hammer or by cutting with a hacksaw under the shingle. Repair any tears in the building paper and nail the new shingles in place.

Tongue-and-Groove and Shiplap Boards

Tongue-and-groove (Fig. 10–36) and shiplap (Fig. 10–37) siding are difficult to remove because of the interlocking joints. They should be cut through with a circular power saw set slightly shallower than the depth of the boards. By cutting next to the tongue or bevel, the damaged boards can be split and pried loose. Repair any damage to the building paper beneath and cut new boards to fit the openings. The bevel or the inner lip of tongue-and-groove siding should be trimmed off to allow the board to be fitted into place. The boards can be face-nailed or fastened with screws. Openings at the ends of the boards should be caulked, and countersunk screws covered with a filler.

Board-and-Batten Siding

Cracks and other small openings in board-and-batten siding (Fig. 10–38) are easy to get at and should be sealed with caulking. When damaged boards have to be replaced, the battens can be pried off to uncover the edges of the boards beneath. Use a small pry bar to pry the sides of the boards loose so that they can be removed. After new boards are cut to size and nailed in place, the battens can be replaced.

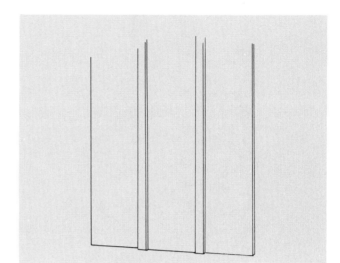

Fig. 10–38 Board and batten siding.

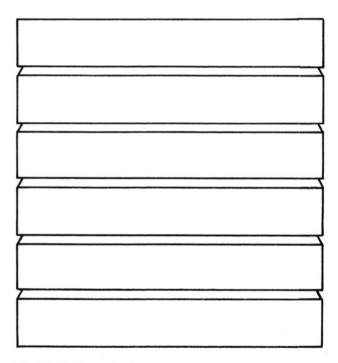

Fig. 10–39 Plywood siding.

Plywood Sheets

Damaged sections of plywood siding (Fig. 10–39) can be nailed to the sheathing and caulked, or they can be removed and replaced. If the nails can be raised and

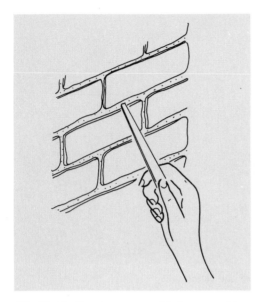

Fig. 10–40 Cleaning out crumbled mortar with a cold chisel.

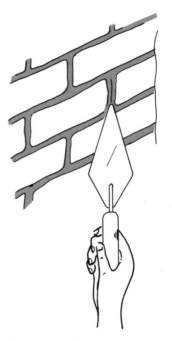

Fig. 10–42 Pointing mortared joints.

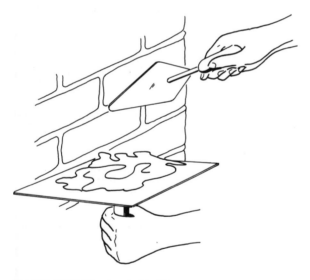

Fig. 10–41 Putting in new mortar.

pulled out, the interlocked joints can be pulled free. Otherwise, the sheet should be cut with a circular power saw inside the rows of nails at the edges. The damaged section can then be pried out and replaced with a new piece of plywood siding cut to size. Caulk the joints between the patched area and the rest of the siding, and apply a matching protective finish.

Brick Walls

Cracked or crumbled mortar can be repaired by cleaning out the joints and filling them with fresh mortar. Use a

cold chisel to remove the mortar to a depth of one-half to one inch (Fig. 10–40). Mix a new batch of mortar from masonry cement and sand or from premixed mortar. Then wet the openings between the bricks with water and work the mortar into the joints with a trowel (Fig. 10–41). Remove the excess and finish off by pointing to compact the mortar and spread it evenly across the face of the joints (Fig. 10–42).

Damaged bricks should be replaced. Use a cold chisel to remove the mortar and the brick. Clean the old mortar from the adjacent surfaces. A coat of fresh mortar should be applied to the surface of the brick below the opening. Slide a new brick into the opening, and fill the joints with fresh mortar. Remove excess mortar, and point the joint while the mortar is still workable.

Cracks in mortar next to door and window frames should be sealed with caulking instead of mortar. Caulking will expand and contract as the width of a crack varies, while mortar would crack again.

A white, powdery coating called *efflorescence* sometimes appears on masonry walls that contain excess water. Soluble salts in the masonry are called to the surface where they crystallize as the water evaporates. These salts can be removed by wirebrushing the masonry or by treating it with a neutralizing solution of muriatic acid and water. Follow the directions accompanying the acid for mixing the solution, protecting your skin and eyes with rubber gloves and goggles. The source of the excess water must be found and eliminated in old masonry walls, but new walls will usually take care of themselves. Excess water used in constructing new walls will eventually evaporate and eliminate the problem. In an old wall, efflorescence indicates that water is leaking into the wall, and the condition will continue until the leak is sealed.

Stone Walls

Cracked or crumbling mortar between stones (Fig. 10–43) should be removed and replaced in the same way as in brick walls. If stones have been damaged in some way, they should be removed and replaced, also. Follow the same procedure as for replacing bricks. Use a cold chisel

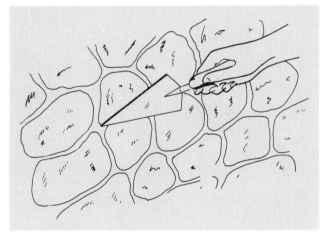

Fig. 10–43 Removing cracked mortar from between stones.

or heavier bricklayer's chisel to remove the mortar and stones, wet the area with water, and work mortar around the new stones. Scrape off the excess mortar and point the joints.

Stucco Walls

Stucco may be used to cover a wood frame or a masonry surface. Cracks should be cleaned out with a cold chisel (Fig. 10–44(a)) and dampened before being filled with mortar (Fig. 10–44(b)). Use one part masonry cement and three parts sand in mixing the patching mortar. A more fluid grout can be made by adding more water so that the mixture will flow into cracks. If the surrounding stucco has been colored with pigment, mix pigment into the patching mortar to the same shade. Work the mortar into the crack and level it flush with the sides. Keep the patch moist for a few days while it cures.

Stucco should be removed down to the supporting structure where it needs to be replaced (except in very small cracks). Chip the edges back to solid stucco with a hammer and chisel. If the wire lath on a wooden frame has been damaged, patch it with another section of wire lath or mesh. Masonry surfaces, such as concrete block, should be thoroughly cleaned of old stucco before new layers are applied.

New stucco should be applied in three layers, and each cured for at least two days before the next layer is added. Wet the area to be patched with water. Work the first, or "scratch," layer of mortar into the wire lath or mesh, or into the irregularities in a masonry wall, to ensure a firm grip (Fig. 10–45(a)). Build this layer up to

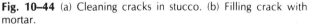

(a)

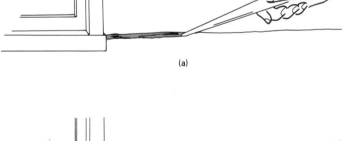

(b)

Fig. 10–44 (a) Cleaning cracks in stucco. (b) Filling crack with mortar.

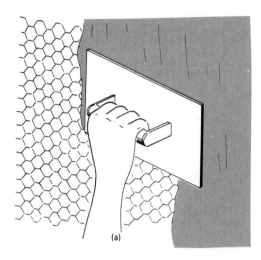

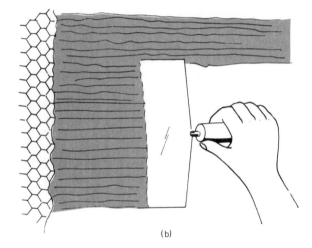

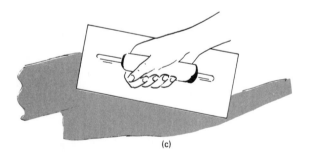

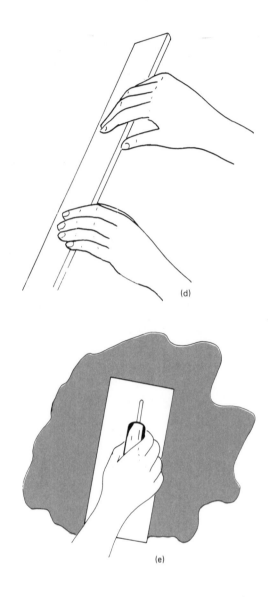

Fig. 10–45 New stucco being applied in three layers.

10–45(d)), and kept moist. This layer should be built up to within 1/8 in. of the surface. After the second layer has cured for at least two days and dried for several more days, it can be covered with the finish coat. The finish coat is made up of the same mixture as the earlier layers. Dampen the second layer, trowel on the finish coat flush with the surrounding stucco, and finish it to match the rest of the wall (Fig. 10–45(e)). The finish coat should not be moistened too heavily. Let it cure for a few days.

Other Types of Siding

Vinyl and aluminum siding are subject to different kinds of damage. A blow from a falling branch or other heavy

within 1/4 to 1/2 in. of the surface. As the mortar begins to set, use a nail to scratch grooves across the surface (Fig. 10–45(b)) to hold the second layer. Keep the first layer of mortar damp for at least two days before applying the second layer. The second layer should be applied over a damp surface (Fig. 10–45(c)), smoothed off (Fig.

object will crack vinyl and dent aluminum. Both types of siding may buckle from the forces of expansion and contraction if they are not cut and installed properly. Since special tools are used to install vinyl and aluminum siding, repairs or replacements may require the assistance of a siding contractor.

Asbestos shingles may eventually slip loose, split, or become damaged in some other way. A cold chisel can be used to split a damaged shingle before removing it. Lift the nails in the lower section of the shingle or saw them off with a hacksaw. Slip the new shingle under the overlapping edge of the shingle above, and nail it with galvanized nails through the holes in the lower section. These nails should clear the top of the shingle underneath and drive into the sheathing.

FOUNDATION WALLS

Water penetrates foundation walls by leaking through cracks in joints or around pipes, and by passing through the pores of the masonry itself. This can be remedied by taking steps to drain water away from the foundation, by patching cracks, and by waterproofing the walls.

DRAINAGE AROUND FOUNDATIONS

Water that leaks through foundation walls may come from the roof, from surface runoff, or from water in the ground below the water table. Roof drainage can be controlled by installing or repairing gutters and downspouts. If the downspouts are discharging water next to the foundation, some means should be found to carry the water away. One method is to attach drain tiles or drain pipes to downspouts to carry the water to an acceptable area. Surface runoff can be diverted from a foundation wall by changing the slope of the surface next to the house. The surface should slope away from the wall for at least eight to ten feet. If the house is built into the side of a hill, it will be necessary to cut back the slope and build a retaining wall. It may also be necessary to install drainage pipes in a trench at the foot of the foundation. When part of the foundation wall is below the water table, hydrostatic pressure tends to force ground water through openings in the walls. Water is also forced through porous masonry, such as concrete. Drainage pipes along the foundation footing and waterproofing may be combined to stop dampness or leaking. These pipes are installed by digging a trench to just below the foundation footing, and laying the pipes so that they slope to carry the water away from the house. Connect the drainage pipes to drainage outlets and fill the trench with gravel and sand to maximize drainage.

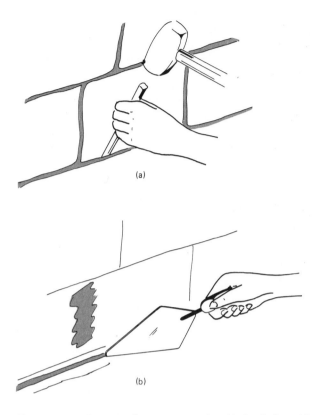

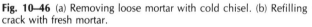

Fig. 10–46 (a) Removing loose mortar with cold chisel. (b) Refilling crack with fresh mortar.

PATCHING CRACKS IN FOUNDATION WALLS

Cracks in foundation walls may be caused by the settling of the house or by local stresses. If a house is relatively new, a growing crack in the foundation may indicate a serious structural problem that should be brought to the attention of someone experienced in construction. Cracks in mortar between blocks or stones and cracks in concrete walls caused by local stresses should be repaired before leaking water and expansion from freezing makes the cracks larger. If a crack is on the exterior, the soil should be cleared away and the area around the crack cleaned off. Use a cold chisel and hammer or mallet to remove loose masonry and mortar (Fig. 10–46(a)). Undercut the edges of the crack in a wedge shape so that the patching material will be held in the wider cross-section at the bottom of the crack. Either mortar or some type of waterproof patching compound can be used to fill the crack. If mortar is used, wait until a dry period so that leaking water will not spoil the patch before it cures. Dampen the masonry inside the crack and fill it with mortar (Fig. 10–46(b)). Remove the excess mortar and keep the patch damp for a few days while it cures. Other types of patching materials can be used to repair cracks that are too wet for ordinary mortar.

Cracks around water pipes, sewer pipes, and other pipes that enter through the foundation walls can be sealed with mortar, patching compounds, or caulking. Large cracks should be sealed with mortar, asphalt cement, or a similar patching material. Caulking should be used in smaller cracks, where the sealant must remain flexible as the crack expands or contracts.

Fig. 10–47 Covering patched wall with sealer.

WATERPROOFING

New foundation walls should be waterproofed before the sides are filled in. They can be coated with sealing compounds that fill the pores and bond to the surface or covered with sheets of polyethylene or asphalt-saturated felt coated with a sealing compound. Gravel and sand should be used as fill next to the walls to increase the rate of drainage.

If roof water and surface water have been diverted from the foundation and the walls continue to be damp or to leak, all cracks should be repaired and the walls made waterproof. Although the inside wall is the easiest to waterproof, sealing the outside wall is the most effective way to keep water out. Paint, whitewash, and dirt must be removed from the inside wall so that the sealing compound can fill the pores and adhere to the surface. Cement-base, asphalt-base or another type of waterproof sealing compound should be used. Work the sealer into the crevices and pores with a stiff brush;

more than one coat may be needed. The outside wall is waterproofed in the same manner as the inside wall. Dig a trench along the wall and thoroughly clean the dirt from the surface. If polyethylene or asphalt-saturated felt has been used to seal the wall, patch breaks with pieces of similar material and bond them with asphalt cement or a waterproof mastic. Clean out cracks and fill them with mortar or another patching compound. Cover the entire wall with at least two coats of sealer to create a durable waterproof barrier (Fig. 10–47). When the last coat is dry, fill the ditch with gravel and sand to help carry the water away from the wall.

Commercial firms employ several methods to waterproof foundation walls below the ground line. The dirt may be dug out and the wall sealed using professional equipment, or the dirt may be left in place and a sealant forced over the surface of the wall below the ground line to bond to the outer surface. Commercial firms use specialized equipment and special sealing compounds to make their work more efficient.

MILDEW

The fungus that causes mildew requires moisture and shade. These conditions can be minimized by moving bushes that shade the siding away from the exterior walls of the house. Mildew can be washed off the walls with a strong solution of trisodium phosphate (⅔ cup), water (3 qts.), bleach (1 qt.), and detergent (⅓ cup). Wear rubber gloves and goggles to protect your skin and eyes and avoid breathing in the solution's noxious fumes. If the siding is to be painted, rinse off the cleaning solution and use an exterior paint containing a mildewcide.

DAMAGE FROM ROT AND TERMITES

Wood rot and termites both destroy timbers by consuming the cellulose fibers in wood. Rot-causing fungi establish themselves on moist wood and spread quickly over the surface. Termites tunnel within the wood, leaving no evidence of their presence on the surface.

Rot

Rot attacks moist wood. Wood buried in soil, such as fence posts and tree stumps, and wood in moist spaces, such as crawl spaces, beneath porches, basements, and under wooden stairs, will decay rapidly if it hasn't been treated with a preservative. Boards and timbers likely to be used in moist locations should be treated with some type of preservative, such as pentachlorophenol, before construction begins. Wooden materials that have had preservative forced into them under pressure are available from suppliers. The homeowners can treat wood themselves by soaking it in a preservative for a day or so.

If rot is suspected, the wood should be tested to determine whether it must be replaced. Push an awl or other sharp-pointed instrument into the wood. If it penetrates a half inch or more rather easily, rot is present. The surface wood may also crumble or become powdery. Decayed boards should be removed and replaced, especially if they are in a load-bearing part of the structure. To prevent decay from continuing, moisture must be eliminated from the area by ventilation, drainage, or in some other way. The surface can also be soaked with a preservative.

Termites

Although termites build their nests in the soil, they will enter a house in search of wood as food. Termites require a dark, moist environment, and they build tunnels through the soil and wood to protect themselves from light and dryness. Where there is no wood or soil, they build a mud tunnel (Fig. 10–49). Such mud tunnels may be found on the face of the foundation or along pipes entering the house. Worker termites consume cellulose fibers in wood as they tunnel in the process of making food for the colony. This causes timbers to become weak as the inside is riddled.

The termites themselves may never be seen except during spring, when the reproductive members of the colony fly away to establish other colonies. Mud tunnels along foundation walls, discarded wings, and

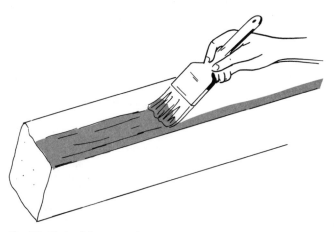

Fig. 10–48 Applying creosote.

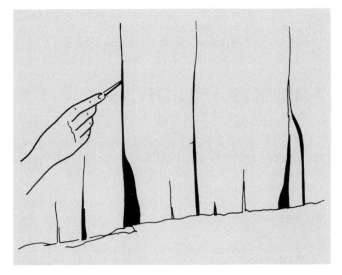

Fig. 10–49 Mud tunnels built by termites.

Follow the directions for the particular preservative being used and wear rubber gloves for protection. Creosote is one of the least expensive preservatives for treating wood to be buried in dirt, such as fenceposts (Fig. 10–48). Where untreated wood has been used in construction, paint the exposed surfaces liberally with a clear preservative. If a conventional paint has been used on untreated wood, it must be either removed or thoroughly scratched so that the preservative can penetrate the surface. Moist areas should be ventilated, as well, to eliminate the dampness necessary for the growth of the fungus.

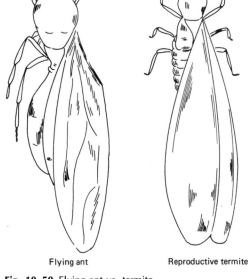

Flying ant   Reproductive termite

Fig. 10–50 Flying ant vs. termite.

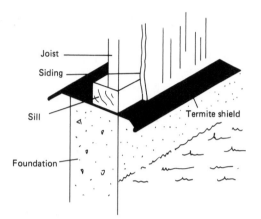

Fig. 10–51 Position for installation of termite shield.

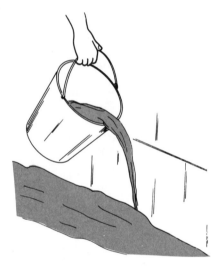

Fig. 10–52 Solution of chlordane and water being poured into trench around foundation.

spongy wood are good indications that termites have been in the vicinity. As with wood decayed by rot, a sharp-pointed instrument will easily penetrate a half-inch or more into wood tunneled by termites. Reproductive termites may be seen when they leave the nest in the spring. Although they may look like flying ants at first, they can be distinguished by the shape of their bodies and the length of their wings (Fig. 10–50). A termite's body is almost uniform in width from front to rear, while ants have narrow, constricted waists. Termites' wings are equal in length while ants' rear wings are shorter than their forewings. Both reproductive termites and flying ants are dark-colored. Look for tunnels and termite damage in the vicinity of the house wherever there is wood close to the ground. Wooden treads and stringers, sills, basement window frames,

siding, basement beams, crawl spaces, porches, and all supporting posts should be inspected.

Preventive measures can be taken to keep termites away. To reduce the termite's food supply, wood scraps buried near the house, old stumps, and other wood should be dug up and removed. Dirt should be shoveled away from wooden posts and the lower edges of the siding. When a new house is built, a termite shield can be installed between the foundation and sill to protect the sill and wooden siding (Fig. 10–51).

Termites can be exterminated by poisoning them. One type of poison frequently used by homeowners is chlordane. A solution of the chlordane and water is poured in a two-foot deep trench dug around the foundation (Fig. 10–52). As dirt is shoveled back into the trench, the solution should be mixed with the dirt every few inches of depth. Since chlordane is toxic to humans and animals and remains in the soil for several years, it should be used judiciously and handled with care. Exterminators use chlordane in addition to other poisonous substances to kill termites. Animals and children should be kept away from the treated areas until several days after the substances have been applied. After using poisons such as chlordane, all exposed parts of the body should be washed with soap and water.

PORCHES AND DECKS

Since porches and decks are continuously exposed to the weather and to wear, they frequently require repair. Floors should be stained or painted with deck or porch enamel every year or two to keep them watertight. The supporting structures are particularly subject to decay because they are close to the ground and remain moist

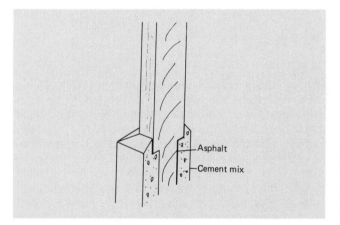

Fig. 10–53 Correct method of putting in supporting post.

Fig. 10–54 Jacking up sagging timbers.

and shaded. Inspect the supporting posts or piers for decaying wood or crumbling and cracked masonry. Look for rot along the joint where the porch is connected to the house and where the stairs meet the ground.

Supporting posts or *piers* must be kept in good condition to ensure the safety of the entire porch or deck. Wooden posts may rot where they rest on footings or in concrete. If only the outer surface of the base of the post has decayed, the defective area can be sawed away leaving the sound section of the post beneath. Soak the exposed wood with a preservative, coat it with asphalt cement, and build a wooden form an inch or two wider than the post around the cut-away section. Fill the form with concrete and slope the top edge sharply downward away from the post to shed water (Fig. 10–53). After the concrete has cured, fill any cracks between the post and concrete with caulking. Wooden posts set in concrete footings will rot if water gets between the wood and the concrete. The porch should be propped up by 4 × 4's or larger timbers, and the decayed post and footing removed. A new post protected by pressure-induced preservatives should be used to replace the old post. Coat the base of the post with asphalt cement and pour concrete around it to above the soil line. When the concrete has cured, seal any cracks between it and the post with asphalt cement or caulking.

Cracks or crumbling mortar in masonry piers can be repaired like any other masonry. If the entire pier has become too weak to support the porch or deck, however, it should be replaced. Place a house jack on a broad, sturdy base and use a wide timber on top of the jack to raise the porch slightly above the old pier (Figure 10–54). If the old footing is defective, remove the pier and prepare a new footing that extends below the frost line. Use blocks, brick, or reinforced concrete to construct the new pier. If blocks are used, set them on a mortar base and fill the cores with mortar for additional strength. Cap the top with mortar to keep water from entering the blocks. The outside surfaces can be coated with cement or sealed with a masonry sealer to make the pier waterproof. Use either mortar or wooden wedges treated with preservative between the pier and the beam; shim the porch to the proper slope to allow for rain runoff.

Railings may weaken or decay where the supporting posts are attached to porch joists. If the joint between the post and joist or beam isn't sealed, water will enter and the wood will decay. Inspect these joints and replace the posts if necessary. Loose horizontal rails should be nailed down, peeling paint scraped, and a fresh coat of stain or paint applied to keep railings in good condition.

Stairs leading from the porch or deck to the ground should be inspected where they join the porch and where they rest on the ground. (The base of the stairs should rest on a concrete slab that can form the bottom step.) Wood in both areas is likely to retain moisture and suffer from rot. Termites may also tunnel into the lower end of the stringers. Joints can be caulked if the wood is sound, but decayed boards should be removed and replaced with boards pressure-treated with a preservative.

Flooring may be spaced or butted side-by-side. Spaced boards drain more easily, but the joists should be inspected for decay along the upper edges. Floor boards that are butted side-by-side may decay along the edges

Fig. 10–55 Hinged garage door.

from moisture that collects between them. Pry up decayed or split floor boards and replace them with preservative-treated boards. An exterior stain or porch and deck enamel will protect them from future decay.

GARAGES

Garages require the same kinds of repairs as the exterior of the house. Roofing must be kept watertight; siding should be repaired and painted; cracks in foundations have to be filled; joints must be sealed to keep out water. Garage doors usually need more attention than the rest of the garage because their weight is likely to cause hinges to loosen or overhead tracks to be forced out of adjustment.

Hinged doors should be checked periodically for sagging (Fig. 10–55). Sagging caused by loose hinges can sometimes be corrected by tightening the screws. If the holes have become too large, longer screws can be used. The hinges should be moved a few inches upward or downward if the wood around the screws has become too decayed to hold them. Although its hinges are tight, the garage door may sag if joints in the frame become loose. This usually can be remedied by fastening a reinforcing brace, tightened by a turnbuckle, diagonally from the top of the hinged side of the door to the lower, outside corner (Fig. 10–56).

Overhead doors become difficult to operate when they work their way out of alignment (Fig. 10–57). A

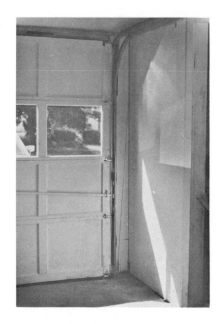

Fig. 10–57 Overhead garage door.

carpenter's level will reveal whether the tracks are parallel and square. Loosen the mounting screws and tap the track with a mallet to realign it. Once the tracks are square, tighten all of the hold-down screws and bolts. Clean old grease from the tracks and use a light coat of fresh grease to lubricate the track surface. Hinges, wheels, rollers, and bearings should be lubricated with a light oil or graphite. Use powdered graphite to lubricate the latch and lock mechanisms.

Both hinged and overhead doors should be weatherstripped to seal out water and cold air. The lower section of the doors should be treated with a preservative and painted as soon as the old paint starts to peel because of the door's susceptibility to decay.

MORTAR AND CONCRETE FOR MASONRY REPAIRS

Mortar and concrete differ in that mortar contains lime to keep it pliable but no gravel or crushed stone. Concrete, on the other hand, contains gravel or crushed stone (aggregate) for strength, but no lime. Portland cement, sand, lime or aggregate, and water are mixed in different proportions for various degrees of strength. In general, a lower ratio of sand and aggregate to Portland cement is used in both mortar and concrete where the conditions are more severe.

Mortar can be prepared in different ways, depend-

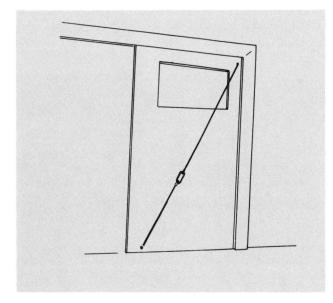

Fig. 10–56 Reinforcing brace with turnbuckle.

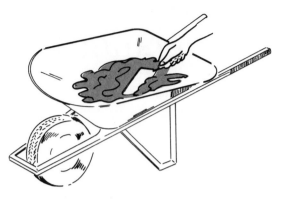

Fig. 10–58 Mixing concrete in a wheelbarrow.

Fig. 10–59 Mixing concrete in hole to be filled.

ing on the desired economy and the size of the job. The easiest but most expensive way is to purchase dry-mixed mortar and add water. The dry mixture contains Portland cement, lime, and sand in the proper proportions. For a moderate-sized repair, masonry cement (one part), which already contains lime, can be mixed with sand (three parts) and water to produce mortar. The cheapest method is to mix Portland cement (one part), with sand (four to five parts), and then mix in lime (one-half part) and add water. Mortar should hold its shape but remain plastic enough to slide off a trowel when used for repairing masonry joints, stucco, and cracks in concrete. Sometimes it's easier to repair a deep, narrow crack if more water is added to the mortar. This makes a grout that can be poured into the crack.

Concrete, like mortar, can be prepared in several ways. Ready-mixed concrete contains Portland cement, sand, and aggregate, and requires only water before it is ready to use. The mixture can be made less expensively by mixing Portland cement (one part), sand (two parts), and gravel or crushed stone (three parts), and adding water until the concrete holds its shape.

Mortar and concrete can be hand-mixed in small quantities in a wheelbarrow (Fig. 10–58) or small wooden frame. Concrete can also be hand-mixed by mixing the dry elements together in a mound and pouring water into a depression in the top (Fig. 10–59). Shovel the dry mixture into the water and mix them together. For making large quantities of concrete, use a mixer, or purchase the concrete commercially mixed and delivered by truck ready to use.

11 *Remodeling: General Considerations*

The information in the following chapters is intended to assist the homeowner in planning remodeling projects. Cross references are given wherever descriptions of repairs or improvements in earlier chapters are applicable. Professional sources of assistance for projects that are beyond the scope of this book are given.

This chapter presents an overview of the remodeling process, from evaluating the financial aspects to analyzing the homeowner's responsibilities in working with an architect or contractor. The following chapters focus on the types of rooms and spaces that are remodeled most frequently. Since storage facilities are notoriously inadequate in most homes, a separate chapter is devoted to guidelines for better storage. The last chapter describes some of the unique problems in remodeling apartments, subdivision houses, and old houses and offers suggestions for appropriate solutions.

DETERMINING NEEDS AND FINANCIAL EFFECTS

Before one becomes too involved in the excitement of remodeling, it is important to take a hard look at what improvements are really needed and how they will affect the resale value of the house. Improvements that make a significant difference in the value and use of the house should be distinguished from repairs and from redecorating. Homeowner who is concerned with his investment should budget remodeling costs so as not to overprice his house for the local market.

DETERMINING NEEDS

By living in a house before you remodel it, you will have a better idea of what needs to be done and what can be ignored. The family members will eventually develop a list of features that they would like to see changed and suggestions about how to proceed (Fig. 11–1). As a list of needs is developed, relationships and priorities will emerge. When planning plumbing for a remodeled kitchen, for example, it may be well to have plumbing roughed in for a half-bath to be installed in the future. If the kitchen facilities are badly outdated, you will probably assign kitchen remodeling priority over less critical improvements.

If a family plans to live in a house for several years, the remodeling can be done over a period of time, as money becomes available for the work. The initial list of needs will evolve and can be used as a basis for a preliminary masterplan.

> **Kitchen improvements**
>
> New Counters
> Range and Hood
> More Storage Space
> Better Lighting
> Vinyl Floor
> Replace Old Windows

Fig. 11–1 Typical list of necessary improvements

FINANCIAL EFFECTS

Financially, remodeling makes sense if it is a better investment than buying a new house or a house that has already been remodeled (Fig. 11–2). Psychologically, remodeling can give you the satisfaction of creating your living space as you want it to be. However, living in the house through a drawn-out remodeling process can be quite a strain, depending on the nature of the remodeling.

If remodeling is to be worthwhile, the project should be sound in respect to the following: The house should be well constructed (to be worth improving in the first place); the cost of the remodeling project should be consistent with the

Remodeling Costs	
Kitchen	$6,000
Bath	3,500
West Addition	10,000
Contingencies	2,000
Total	$21,500

Fig. 11–2 Rough cost estimates for improvements

value of the rest of the house; the particular improvement: that are anticipated should be sufficiently valuable in the eyes of others to increase the resale value by an amoun comparable with the cost of the improvement; and the in creased resale value of the house should be in line with the market value of other houses in the neighborhood.

If the remodeling cost is out of line with the value o the house, the situation can sometimes be salvaged by pre serving the basics and cutting out the nonessentials. An elaborate and expensive kitchen, for example, can be transformed into a more modest but equally efficient kitchen by using a simpler layout and less cabinet and counter space.

Not all improvements are equal in their influence on the resale value of a house. Buyers are likely to be willing to pay more for a house with additional bedrooms or other essen tial living spaces than for less spacious houses. The best remodeling investment generally lies in such projects as building additions, converting attics into bedrooms, and building family rooms in basements.

The remodeling of out-of-date kitchens and bathrooms ranks close to space additions as a reliable investment. If the costs are kept under control, the resale value of the house can be increased by almost the full amount of the invest ment. A kitchen with modern cabinets, laminated-plastic countertops, and modern appliances naturally will have great sales appeal, especially to the housewife.

If remodeling raises the amount of the investment in the house beyond the market value of most of the other houses in the neighborhood of about the same age, you probably won't get your money back. New houses at comparable asking prices will also have an edge over a remodeled older house. This situation can be avoided by budgeting the re modeling to keep the resale price of the house at the desired level. If this is impossible and finances are limited, you might consider buying another house where investment conditions for remodeling are more favorable.

ROUGH SKETCHES AND WORKING DRAWINGS

Rough sketches, however unskilled, are useful to record and convey ideas visually (Figs. 11–3, 11–4). In remodeling

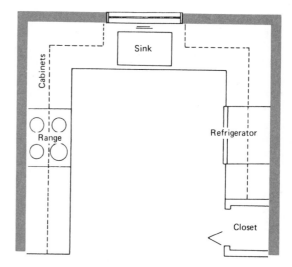

Fig. 11–3 Rough sketch of U-shape kitchen layout

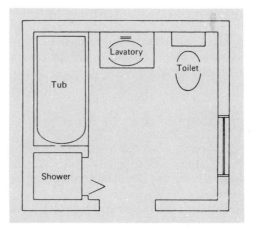

Fig. 11–4 Rough sketch of bathroom layout

kitchens, for example, draw several sketches to show the effect of placing sinks, ranges, and refrigerators in different locations. Vary the arrangements to include U-shape and L-shape layouts, where they are practical alternatives.

The homeowner who wants to prepare his own *working plans* should gather detailed information about the types and costs of materials he plans to use, check the building codes, and measure the spaces to be remodeled. A plan of the area that is to be remodeled should be drawn indicating the locations of doors, windows, stairs, and utility connec tions. Use graph paper with a 1/4-in. grid for a scale of 1/4 in. to 1 ft. This plan will be helpful in experimenting with different types of layouts. (Planning kits with proportionally sized cutouts and graph paper are also available from many fixture and appliance dealers and remodeling centers.) Where vertical spacing and proportions are important, as in kitchens, a vertical section should be drawn also. A detailed plan will satisfy building code requirements and serve as a working drawing for construction. Where building codes require that plans be drawn to certain technical specifications, the plans can be redrawn by a draftsman. Some building codes require that all plans be approved by an architect. An architect may be willing to approve and sign plans if he is consulted for before the plans are drawn.

PROFESSIONAL ASSISTANCE

Professional assistance is available for all phases of remodeling and may be employed for all or part of a project. If the construction is not too complicated, and you are willing to spend the time to study materials and prepare rough sketches, you may be able to hire a carpenter or other workman and instruct him as to what you want done. You may even do the work yourself. At the other extreme, if the finished product is your main concern, an architect, design specialist, or contractor will take the job completely off your hands. Usually, it is a matter of deciding what type of assistance is needed and at what stage.

TYPES OF ASSISTANCE AVAILABLE

The remodeling process can be divided, for this purpose, into the following stages:
• Evaluating the needs and determining what improvements are required.
• Developing designs for the improvements, and preparing preliminary plans, working drawings, and specifications.
• Seeking bids, getting approvals from local agencies, arranging insurance and financing.
• Carrying out the remodeling work. (The work must be inspected by a homeowner or agent and payments made to the contractor or workmen.)

The architect and contractor may come immediately to mind as the types of professionals to call. They are, in fact, the principal professionals in many kinds of construction and remodeling. Architects are most valuable where structural changes are required or where there is extensive remodeling to be done. If a bearing wall is to be removed, doors or windows altered, or the exterior of the house changed, an architect is the best source of advice on design. He will also be able to help develop an overall plan when an entire house is to be remodeled. The contractor's primary responsibility is to see that the remodeling work is performed as planned and stays within the budget and time limitations. In

addition, he can usually provide standard remodeling plans, such as plans for conventional kitchens. Whether such a plan is appropriate for the circumstances has to be decided by the homeowner.

There are also a variety of specialists who are available to advise on particular aspects of remodeling. *Kitchen designers* for a fee, will suggest designs, types of appliances, and decoration. They may also undertake the responsibility of engaging and supervising contractors. *Kitchen planners,* who have different credentials than kitchen designers, are often employed by utility companies, remodeling centers, and department stores. Where an old house is being purchased for remodeling, a professional building-inspection service can be employed to inspect the house and to provide a list of repairs that are required.

ARCHITECTS

There are some people who feel that an architect is an unnecessary luxury for everyday remodeling. Others feel not only that an architect will improve the design but that his presence will help to ensure a high-quality job. In general, the more important the design features are in remodeling, the more extensive the project, and the more money being spent—the more valuable an architect can be. Some or all of these conditions will apply when remodeling an entire house, when designing exterior additions to fit in with the style and proportions of a house, and when creating custom-designed living spaces.

Services

Although an architect is frequently thought of primarily as a designer, his services in taking care of the financial and legal requirements, inspecting construction and workmanship, and generally supervising the entire project may be as important as his design work. Select an architect whose previous work in remodeling is compatible with your plans.

Once an architect is engaged, he will begin his task by discussing needs, problems, and ideas for the project. He will look at the spaces to be changed and gather data on their dimensions, the location of utilities, and the relationships of other rooms. From this background, he will create preliminary schematic designs that illustrate alternative solutions for satisfying family preferences. When the homeowner agrees on an alternative to pursue, the architect will prepare a series of increasingly more-detailed drawings until a final set of working drawings and specifications is ready to be approved.

In the course of preparing these designs, cost estimates are made to keep the plans within the planned budget. Upon approval of the final drawings, copies of the plans and specifications are sent out for bids to the contractors who have been selected by the homeowner with the advice of the architect. Since he usually knows the work of local contractors, the architect is in a position to recommend which bid should be accepted.

The actual remodeling work must be inspected to ensure that it conforms to the drawings and specifications. An architect will do this and take the responsibility for authorizing payments to the contractor as the work progresses. When the project is complete, an architect will make a final inspection and certify that the provisions of the contract have been carried out.

An architect can, of course, be employed for only certain tasks, such as creating a design and providing working drawings. His fee will depend on the extent of his services and on the contractual arrangement with the homeowner.

Architects' Fees

Fees may be charged according to any of several customary bases. Some architects use only one basis; others may be more flexible. The most common method is to charge an agreed-upon *percentage of the costs* of labor and material in remodeling. This method would apply when the architect provides his full range of services, from initial design through inspection of construction. Percentages charged may vary between 12 and 20 percent of the total costs depending on the particular services, the reputation of the firm, and the locality. A *flat fee* may be charged for services where it is important to determine the exact costs of the project in advance. The homeowner would also be charged for additional expenses, as agreed upon, for travel, reproducing plans and documents, and other related activities. Where an architect is hired as a consultant, he may charge *by the hour or day.* If you have merely requested some rough ideas on design, for example, he may charge you on an hourly basis for visiting your home and offering suggestions for layouts or design. Travel expenses and other minor expenses incurred in providing architectural services are usually charged to the client, in addition to the basic fee.

The best time to ask about fees is on the first visit to an architect's office. He will be able to suggest a method of payment appropriate for the type of services that you require. Provisions for payment are contained in a contract that is signed before the work begins. Payments are generally made to the architect on signing the contract and at subsequent stages in the design and construction process. If the project is simple and is completed quickly, the payments may be made in one or two installments.

CONTRACTORS

A general contractor, once he is employed, is responsible for the entire remodeling project. He hires carpenters, electricians, and other subcontractors, schedules their work, and pays them. He buys materials and fixtures from suppliers. The contractor also assumes liability for personal injuries and carries Workmen's Compensation and other types of liability insurance.

Selecting a Contractor

A contractor is eventually selected for the job from a group of several bidders on the basis of reputation and the amount of the bid. Choose the contractors carefully before asking for their bids. If an architect has been engaged, he will be able to offer advice regarding the work and the reputations of contractors who do business in the local area. Because of his experience in the trade, an architect can easily investigate a contractor's recent work and his financial reliability. A homeowner can do this, too, but it will probably take him longer.

If an architect is not engaged, begin the search for a general contractor with recommendations from friends, trade associations, the Yellow Pages, and other sources in the building trade. To save time, narrow the list to contractors who specialize in remodeling work. Try to find three or four contractors who you feel would be acceptable. Inquire about their reputations for good workmanship, length of time in business, financial responsibility, promptness, and good business practices. This type of information can be gathered from subcontractors, credit-rating institutions, and people for whom they have worked. Ask the contractors for recommendations from clients and look at other remodeling jobs that they have done. Finally, talk with the contractors themselves to see how they react to your ideas and plans. Good rapport with the contractor will make it easier for everyone to work together during the remodeling process.

Bids

Except under unusual circumstances, it is customary to request bids from three or four contractors. This will give the homeowner some alternatives among bids and also among contractors. Each of the contractors who is bidding should receive copies of the same working drawings and detailed specifications; otherwise, the bids won't be on a comparable basis. If this is a small job, a rough sketch may be sufficient as long as all of the details involving costs are included. More complicated remodeling jobs will require plans prepared by a draftsman or architect or a standard plan adapted to the space to be remodeled. Ask the contractors to provide written and signed bids by a certain date and to return the working plans and other documents that they have received. Be sure you allow plenty of advance time to get your bids and make your decision. Good contractors may have obligations far in advance especially for major work.

When the bids are reviewed, all of the background information about the contractor should be considered together with the amount of his bid. The lowest bid, of course, is not necessarily the best bid to accept, though it will be in some cases. Be sure that the contractor has based his bid on the same requirements for performance as the other bidders, and that he can carry out the work within the specified time period. Again, because of his professional experience, an architect can be of considerable help in choosing the best combination of bid and contractor.

Contracts

Standard contractual forms are available from architects, contractors, and their professional associations. Contracts differ in emphasizing those aspects that are most important to the people who prepared them. An attorney should review any contract prepared by architects or contractors, or he can prepare his own contract. Regardless of the source, the contract should cover the following general categories:

• Detailed description of the work to be performed and the materials to be supplied by the contractor.

• Time of starting and completing the work.

• Total payment to be made by the homeowner to the contractor, schedule of payments, and basis for final approval and payment.

• The general conditions of agreement between the parties.

On major projects in some localities, the contractor can be asked to provide a bond to protect the homeowner against liability if the contractor defaults on payments to the subcontractors or suppliers or if the work isn't completed.

HOMEOWNER'S RESPONSIBILITIES

No matter what course is taken, the homeowner will have certain responsibilities in remodeling. He can minimize these by turning over the project to a combination of professionals. In these instances, his most important responsibility is to select reliable people and to pay them. At the other extreme the homeowner can become heavily involved in planning and selecting materials, subcontracting, or actually doing the construction himself.

FINANCIAL RESPONSIBILITIES

In remodeling, the principal financial responsibilities are to make payments for services and materials and to purchase adequate insurance coverage. The homeowner should be prepared to pay a retainer to the architect when the contract is signed and to pay for other services in accordance with an agreed-upon schedule. To avoid liability for mechanics'

and suppliers' liens, the contractor or other builder should agree in the contract to indemnify the homeowner or to provide bonds for protection. Upon completion of the work, the contractor should provide a waiver of claims signed by his subcontractors and suppliers. If the contractor or builder agrees to provide liability insurance and Workman's Compensation Insurance, the homeowner only has to provide insurance that covers fire and other damage to the structure that is being remodeled.

There is a joint responsibility among the several parties involved to keep the project within an agreed-upon budget. The homeowner must avoid adding features that the budget can't support, unless the agreement is revised. Budget control begins with the initial rough sketches and compilation of rough costs. As the work progresses, some features may have to be altered or discarded to keep the project within the budget.

The homeowner who employs carpenters or other workmen under contract will have greater financial responsibilities and should carry liability insurance for personal injury and property damage during the course of remodeling, in addition to general insurance protection for the structure and materials. An insurance agent is a good source of information about the need for coverage in this situation. The remodeled property will be subject to mechanics' liens and liens from suppliers if their services and materials aren't paid for. Since the homeowner is acting as the general contractor in this case, he must pay the subcontractors and collect releases from liability.

SUPERVISION

The extent to which the homeowner accepts responsibility for supervising and inspecting remodeling work depends on whether he has chosen an architect, contractor, or subcontractor and how he plans to work with him. He undertakes the greatest responsibilities in this respect when he employs workmen. This alternative is practical only when remodeling work doesn't require closely coordinated installation work. A homeowner who is doing the carpentry work, for example, can hire a plumber or electrician as needed. Where electrical, plumbing, and carpentry work have to be performed in close, consecutive sequence, they must be reliably coordinated so that none of the workmen are delayed by others. A carpenter, for example, can't cover wall studs and floor joists until the plumbing is roughed in or wiring installed. In any case, if workmen are engaged, it should be on a contractual basis in which the homeowner inspects and approves the work before paying for it.

When a general contractor coordinates a remodeling project, the homeowner will have little supervisory responsibility. The plumber and flooring men work for the contractor, not for the homeowner. Advice, requests for changes, complaints, and other comments on the work should be addressed to the contractor. When the project is complete, the homeowner or architect is responsible for inspecting the work to see that it conforms to the plans and specifications as agreed upon in the contract.

RECORDS OF EXPENDITURES

For tax purposes, records should be kept of all remodeling expenses. Keep a list of what was done and how much was spent. Record the date and retain cancelled checks and other receipts. If the situation is complicated, discuss it with an accountant before filing tax returns.

TYPES OF FINANCING

A lending source, such as a savings bank, may offer several types of financing for home improvements. Some of these will have lower interest rates than others, some will require securities or cash as collateral, and some will be insured by the federal government. The homeowner should become familiar with the various types of loans, as well as with the lending institutions that offer them.

The most common sources of home-improvement loans are savings and commercial banks, savings and loan associations, credit unions, mutual savings banks, and life insurance companies. Some contractors and private individuals also make arrangements for remodeling loans. Interest rates, the term of the loan, collateral, maximum amounts, and other conditions can vary considerably. After the homeowner has looked into the practices and reputations of several sources, he will be better prepared to discuss terms with those lenders with whom he prefers to do business. The homeowner should allow plenty of time for this process of selection.

Federal and state *truth-in-lending laws* protect the person who borrows money for home improvements, as well as for other purposes. The lender must state the true annual rate of interest and the total interest in dollars, as well as reveal any added costs. These laws apply to the transaction regardless of whether the loan is received from a bank or from a private individual.

Lending institutions usually require extensive information about the borrower. They will require a statement of financial condition: income, debts, savings and investments, and life insurance. Credit references will be requested to determine whether the borrower pays his bills on time. The lender will study the plans and cost estimates to see if they are sound and reasonable.

Some of the more common types of financing for home improvements are described below.

HOME-IMPROVEMENT LOAN

This is the standard type of home-improvement loan made by banks, savings and loan associations, and other lenders. The rates of interest are usually in line with current rates for other types of unsecured loans. Terms of 5 to 8 years for amounts of up to $7500 are customary.

FHA TITLE I, HOME-IMPROVEMENT LOAN

The Federal Housing Authority will insure loans for home improvements made by accredited lending institutions. As with other types of loans, the borrower must find a bank or other source that is willing to make a loan under FHA conditions. An FHA loan also protects the homeowner from hidden costs and below-standard construction. It has the advantage of a comparatively low rate of interest. Amounts of up to $7500 can be borrowed for terms up to 8 years.

PERSONAL BANK LOAN

This type of bank loan may be secured by cash, securities, or other collateral owned by the borrower. Although the value of the collateral must be substantially more than the amount of the loan in some cases, the rate of interest is likely to be lower than that for many other types of loans. Monthly payments will be high, however, because personal loans have shorter terms than traditional home-improvement loans.

OPEN-END MORTGAGE LOAN

If the original mortgage is an open-end mortgage, money can be borrowed for remodeling and repaid as part of the mortgage payments. Open-end mortgages allow the borrower to borrow a sum up to the amount of the principal that has been paid off at the time of the loan. The bank that holds the mortgage may charge a higher rate of interest for the loan for home improvements than for the original mortgage. The cost of the loan should be calculated in total dollars (including the ultimate interest costs) and compared with the costs of other types of loans.

REFINANCING A MORTGAGE

Mortgages can be refinanced to cover the costs of remodeling, but the interest rates on such new mortgages are likely to be much higher today than on mortgages that are several years old. Additional costs for closing are also incurred in refinancing. If a mortgage can be paid off without a penalty and a homeowner wishes to pursue this alternative, the total costs of refinancing should be compared with the costs of retaining the original mortgage and the costs of other types of loans.

LIFE-INSURANCE LOANS

Loans against life insurance policies offer some of the lowest rates of interest available. The policy holder may borrow amounts up to a level just less than the accrued value of the policy at the time of the loan.

LOANS FROM CONTRACTORS AND OTHER PRIVATE INDIVIDUALS

Some contractors include arrangements for loans as one of their services. These loans may originate with banks, private individuals, or other organizations. Although this may be a good alternative in some cases, it should be kept in mind that the contractor's fee for arranging the loan is included in the rate of interest or in other costs paid by the borrower.

Private individuals also lend money for home improvements. Like traditional lending institutions, they want to be certain that their loans are safe. Financial statements, credit references, and collateral are usually required. Rates of interest and terms of repayment, of course, will vary with the individuals and the circumstances. As when borrowing from other sources, the borrower should inquire into the reputation and business practices of the lender.

APPRAISAL INSTRUCTIONS: ....

APPLICATION FOR A MORTGAGE LOAN
1 - 4 FAMILY DWELLING

I (WE) hereby apply to THE FAMILY MUTUAL SAVINGS BANK for a loan of $............................ to be secured by a mortgage on the property described below.

INSTRUCTIONS TO ATTORNEY
Type ....
Valuation ....
% ....
Property Class ....
Reval. Code ....
Tax Required ....
Lgl. Descr. ....
Ser. Chg. ....
FHA Ins. Prem. ....
Occ. Date ....
Funds
Well ....
Septic Tank ....
Land ....
Other ....
Disclosure ....
Rescission ....
Chap. 184, Sec. 17B ....
RESPA ....
Remarks ....

Title To Be Taken Joint, Individual

FULL NAME OF BORROWER (S):

....

Soc. Sec. No. ....

....

Soc. Sec. No. ....

1. Purpose: Purchase $................ Construction $................ Reloan $................

Repairs ....

2. Location of Property
Street and Number ....
City or Town ....
Directions ....
Remarks ....

3. Property Description
Lot size .... x .... Improvements; Water, Gas, Sewer, Septic, Electricity, Sidewalk, Street **Paved.**
Year Built .... Exterior .... No. Units .... No. Stories .... No. Rooms ....
No. Baths .... Heat .... Annual Cost $ .... Garage .... Rents ....

4. Liens, Title Taxes
Present Owner .... Address ....
First Mortgage Amount. .... Holder .... Price Paid ....
Outstanding Balance .... Annual Real Estate Taxes .... Assessment ....

5. Personal Information
Present Address .... Tel. No. ....
Previous Address (if at above less than 5 years) ....
Birthdate .... No. & Age of Dep. ....
Present Employer .... Address .... Tel. No. ....

Estimated Payment
Position .... Years Employed .... Type of Work ....
....
Former Employer (if at above less than 5 years) .... Wages ....
Present Wages $............... Other Income $............... Co-Borrows Income $...............

12 *Kitchen Remodeling*

As a guide in developing remodeling plans, the homeowner should consider the following questions: (1) Why is the kitchen being remodeled? (2) How will the kitchen be used after it has been remodeled? (3) What kitchen layouts and materials best suit the family's lifestyle?

The reasons for remodeling may be obvious, but it will be helpful to list them. For example, old countertops or cabinets may be worn out. There may be insufficient storage space. The arrangement of appliances and counters may be awkward. More electrical outlets, better lighting, or ventilation may be necessary. At the extreme, the entire kitchen may be completely out-of-date. This list of problems will help to determine the extent of the work that is required. Some improvements, such as better lighting or ventilation, can be made with a minimum of cost and interruption. However, major improvements, such as installing new cabinets, will require more time and money.

How will the kitchen be used after it has been remodeled? Consider how the family has used it in the past. Note the kitchen's shortcomings. Decide whether it will be used mainly for snacks and light meals or for gourmet or organic cooking, baking, or dinner parties. Decide whether you want to use the kitchen as a social center for guests or children. Also look at the kitchen in relation to the rest of the house. Design the layout so that the kitchen does not become a major passageway between rooms. If the eating area is part of or adjacent to the kitchen, food can be served directly to the table. For a more distant dining room, however, some provision should be made for a serving area in the kitchen where food can be assembled for transfer to the table.

In planning the remodeling, the homeowner has an opportunity to apply personal preferences. For example, either a formal or informal kitchen may be chosen. Where open shelves are preferred instead of closed cabinets, the kitchen can be designed for open storage. If cooking is a minor activity in the household, the kitchen can be made compact to save space for other activities. Where natural light is important, windows can be enlarged or added, and if the roof is accessible, skylights can be installed.

Once problems, needs, and personal preferences have been identified, the homeowner will be prepared to assemble ideas and information on remodeling from sources such as magazines and books, kitchen planners, designers, cabinet dealers, architects, contractors, and friends, without losing sight of his own particular goals. Cabinet dealers and contractors will generally suggest fairly routine solutions using standardized counter and cabinet units. Kitchen designers and architects on the other hand, are more likely to go a step further, and suggest layouts and designs that are more unique and imaginative. The following sections include an outline of principles that are basic to good kitchen design and descriptions of popular types of improvements and materials.

KITCHEN DESIGN

There are several basic features that must be taken into account in designing any kitchen.

• **Countertop working space.** The amount and type of working space depends on how the kitchen is to be used. A kitchen in an average-sized three-bedroom house should have 5 to 8 feet of available counter surface, in addition to the space occupied by the range or sink. Kitchens that are used for preparing elaborate meals or for frequent baking may require several more feet of counter space.

• **Cabinet storage.** Even a small kitchen should have at least 6 feet of base cabinets for storage. In an average-size house, 10 feet of base-cabinet storage and 10 feet or more of wall-cabinet storage will provide sufficient space. In addition to "wall and base cabinets, utility cabinets can be used for large-sized equipment and for pantry-type storage.

• **Arrangement of Work Centers and Appliances.** The countertop work areas, cabinet storage, appliances, and the sink must be placed so that they form an efficient working arrangement in the particular space that is available.

• **Lighting and ventilation.** Natural and artificial lighting should be planned to provide both general illumination in the kitchen and individual illumination at work centers. Windows and skylights should be designed to cast light on these areas. There should also be some provision, like an exhaust fan, for removing odors, moisture, smoke, and other cooking byproducts.

WORK CENTERS

Work centers are areas where everything that is required for a specific kitchen activity is brought together. Each work center should have storage space for utensils, foodstuffs and other supplies, and adequate counter space for working. Preparing food, cooking on a range or in an oven, and washing dishes each require different equipment and types of work areas. The preparation area, the range, and the sink and dishwasher should be located close enough to each other to help the process move smoothly. There are also passive centers in a kitchen, such as refrigerator storage, storage for canned and loose foods, utensil storage, and eating areas.

Food-Preparation Center

The areas where foods are prepared for cooking or for serving require considerable counter space (Fig. 12–1). A three- or four-foot working space is ideal. This should include a wooden chopping block for cutting and, if frequent baking is planned, a surface such as marble for working with pastries. Cabinet or shelf storage will be required for the various ingredients that are used at the preparation center. Several electrical outlets will be required for small appliances. Generally it is advisable to have the center located between the sink and the range, so that it is convenient to both of them.

Fig. 12–1 Food preparation center

Fig. 12–2 Cooking center

Cooking Center

There should be at least two feet of counter space next to the range for cooking equipment (Fig. 12–2). This can include heat-proof insert, such as tile or ceramic glass, for setting down hot containers. If the food-preparation area is adjacent to the range, hot pans can be placed on a wooden chopping block or marble insert without injuring the counter surface. A range shouldn't be placed in front of a window (where curtains might catch on fire) or next to a passageway (where passersby might be accidently burned). If a range hood is to be used, place the range where the hood can be ventilated through an outside wall, if possible.

Sink-and-Cleaning Center

The sink and food-preparation centers should be close together so that foods can be washed if necessary, as they are prepared (Fig. 12–3). At a minimum, the sink-and-cleaning center should include a single- or double-basin sink, a storage area, and at least two feet of countertop on each side of the sink for stacking and draining dishes and utensils. The space under the sink is well suited for general storage, but poisonous cleaning supplies should be kept somewhere else where they are inaccessible to children. If a dishwasher is installed, it should be placed where it can be connected to the same hot-water line and drain that serve the sink.

A garbage disposer will increase the versatility of a sink. by allowing food remnants to be disposed without moving away from the sink area.

Storage

Foods, kitchen utensils, and other equipment should be stored where they are easily accessible (Fig. 12–4). Place refrigerators where groceries can be placed on a counter surface next to the handle side of the door. A counter width of 18 inches will generally be sufficient. Use the limited storage space in the food preparation area for ingredients and equipment that are used most frequently.

Other Kitchen Areas

Kitchens may be designed to include accommodations for other functions such as eating, play areas for children, or

Fig. 12–4 Storage pantry

Fig. 12–3 Sink and cleaning center

Fig. 12–5 Snack counter

Fig. 12–6 Dining area

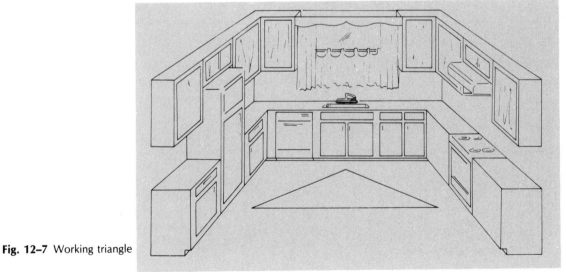

Fig. 12–7 Working triangle

entertaining. These spaces should be located so that they won't interfere with the preparation of food. Play areas, in particular, should be well separated from the cooking center. For informal meals, either a snack counter (Fig. 12–5) or a table (Fig. 12–6) can be included. Allow at least two feet of elbow room at each seat.

KITCHEN LAYOUT

Work centers, appliances, storage areas, and counter space must be arranged properly if the kitchen is to fulfill its functions efficiently. This arrangement depends on the size and shape of the kitchen. Work centers should be far enough

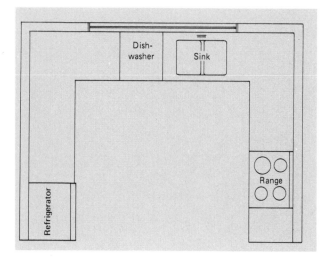

Fig. 12–8 U-Shape layout

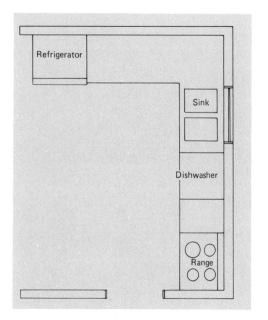

Fig. 12–9 L-Shape layout

distance. Distances greater than eight feet require more walking than is desirable (or efficient). If the distance around the triangle is too small (less than twelve feet) or too large (more than twenty-four feet), the arrangement will not work efficiently.

Of the several traditional kitchen layouts, the best layout for a particular kitchen depends on the size of the room and the number and location of walls available for counters, cabinets, and appliances. By starting with the location of the sink, a basic design can be modified to fit the physical limitations of a particular kitchen. U-shape and L-shape layouts work well in medium- and large-size kitchens, but small or narrow kitchens require more limited one- or two-wall layouts.

U-Shape Layout

In typical U-shape layouts, counters and appliances are placed against three adjoining walls (Fig. 12–8), though one leg of the U may be free standing. This arrangement offers flexibility in locating the appliances and work centers. The sink, range, and refrigerator can be placed against separate walls with ample counter space between them and still be close enough together to use conveniently. In the U-shape layout, the sink is often placed at the base of the U and the refrigerator at one end of the counter to create continuous stretches of working surfaces. The extensive wall areas above the counters provide more wall storage than any other layout. This arrangement will allow ample space for storing necessary food stuffs and equipment at each work center.

If a kitchen is too narrow, the passageway between the opposite counters will be quite restricted. At least four feet of space is desirable between the counters; distances greater than ten feet are too wide for efficient work.

L-Shape Layout

Counters and appliances are placed against two adjoining walls in L-shape layouts (Fig. 12–9). This is a good arrangement where the kitchen is also to be used for a related activity, such as dining. The corner area between the two unoccupied walls is open and is a convenient location for a table. Food and dishes can be easily moved back and forth between the counters and table.

Since appliances compete with the counter surfaces for space along the two walls, at least 14 feet of wall space are required for an L-shape design. A sink, range, and refrigerator will take up a total of about eight feet of wall space. Each leg of the counter should be eight feet or more long in order to provide sufficient working surface and cabinet storage in addition to room for the sink and range. Where a peninsula is used to form one leg of the layout, hanging cabinets can be used for overhead storage. Counter surfaces in corners

from each other to allow sufficient space between them for storage and counter areas, but they should be close enough to eliminate unnecessary walking.

A standard measure of the efficiency of the layout is the distance between the sink, range, and refrigerator. A triangular arrangement of these facilities is referred to as a *working triangle* (Fig. 12–7). Such an arrangement is effective in keeping the units within easy reach of each other while providing adequate work surfaces between them. Four- to six-feet spacing between each pair of units is an efficient

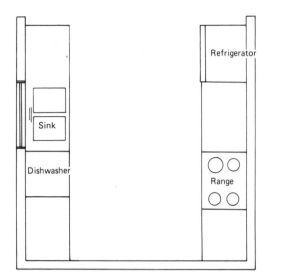

Fig. 12–10 Opposite-wall layout

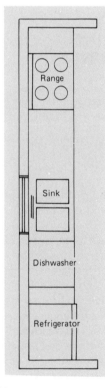

Fig. 12–11 One-wall layout

should not be made inaccesible by placing a range or sink too close to a corner.

Two-Wall Layout

A layout along two opposite walls is an effective arrangement for narrow kitchens (Fig. 12–10). The appliances may

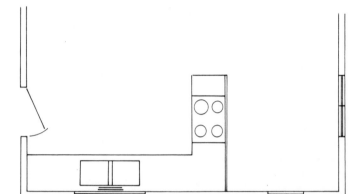

Fig. 12–12 Use of penninsular to form L-shape

be placed against one or both walls within convenient reach of each other. If they are all on one wall, the distances between them must be kept short to avoid constant walking from one end of the kitchen to the other. The refrigerator is usually placed at one end of the counter to keep from breaking the continuity of the working surface. With wall and base cabinets on both walls, extensive storage space is available.

The narrow width between the counters makes two-wall kitchens poor passageways. Ideally, there should be only one doorway into the kitchen to prevent it from becoming a passageway. In order to have at least four feet between the counters, the room must be at least eight feet wide. If it is narrower, another layout should be used.

One-Wall Layout

In a one-wall layout, the sink, range, and refrigerator are placed against one wall with only enough counter space for preparing food and stacking dishes. (Fig. 12–11). Since there is little cabinet storage space, a nearby closet may have to be fitted with shelves for supplementary storage. If a kitchen of this type is part of a larger room, it is often closed off with folding doors when the meal is over.

Peninsulas and Islands

Peninsulas and islands can be used to create more efficient work triangles and to provide additional countertop and cabinet space.

A *peninsula* built out from a wall will transform a one-wall kitchen into an L-shape kitchen (Fig. 12–12). Similarly, a peninsula can be used as one leg of a U-shape kitchen. The countertop on the peninsula can be used just as if it were flush against a wall except that a backsplash will be needed behind a sink or range to prevent splattering beyond the peninsula. Since a peninsula is likely to extend out into a traffic area, the countertop's sharp corners should be

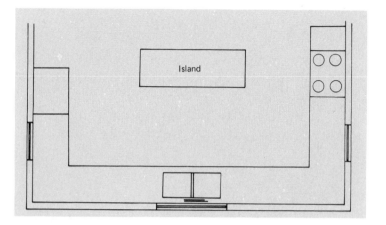

Fig. 12–13 U-Shape kitchen with island

rounded to prevent injuries. For additional storage space, wall cabinets with reinforced tops can be hung over the peninsula. This will also set the kitchen off from the nearby areas.

The side of a peninsula away from the kitchen is a popular location for a snack bar. The countertop can be extended at the standard 36-in. height for use with stools, or a narrow counter can be attached to the peninsula at a 30-in. height for use with chairs. There should be one or two feet of knee room under the counter and two feet of elbow room for each stool or chair.

Islands require plenty of space. They can be incorporated in working triangles to create different layouts or to provide additional working surfaces. An island placed parallel to a counter area along one wall, for example, can be used to create a two-wall kitchen. In a large U-shape kitchen, an island that is centered can be used to supplement the counters around the perimeter of the room (Fig. 12–13). Islands can be used for work centers and appliances as well as for additional working space. Provisions must be made, however, for connecting sinks and ranges to the necessary utility outlets.

Like a peninsula, an island offers a convenient location for a snack bar. A snack counter can be built either along the side away from the kitchen area or wrapped around two or three sides of an island. Separate the eating area from the rest of the island by lowering the eating surface to 30 inches or by building a barrier along the countertop.

SIMPLE IMPROVEMENTS

Kitchen remodeling can involve anything from a few relatively simple improvements to extensive structural changes. Improvements, such as recovering hard-to-clean floor and wall surfaces, adding electrical outlets, and increasing stor-

age space can be made inexpensively without rearranging cabinets or work centers. All of the following improvements can be made to stand independently or as part of more extensive renovations.

NEW FLOORING AND WALLCOVERINGS

Kitchen floors and walls that are subject to wear and abuse from heavy traffic and moisture and grease particles from cooking can be recovered with durable easily cared for materials.

Flooring

Resilient flooring (Fig. 12–14) and carpeting (Fig. 12–15) are the most practical and comfortable types of materials for kitchen floors when they are used appropriately. Other types of materials, such as masonry and wooden floors, may be preferable as part of a particular design or decorative style, however. Flooring materials should be selected to fit in with the overall house and kitchen designs and the manner in which the space is to be used. If the kitchen is heavily used, and food spills are frequent, select a resilient flooring that doesn't show wear and cleans easily. Vinyl, vinyl asbestos, and linoleum have the best wearing and maintenance characteristics of the several types of resilient flooring.

Vinyl flooring not only withstands abrasion and heavy traffic, but it requires little maintenance. Since the color and pattern are continuous throughout the thickness of the vinyl, the surface appearance doesn't change with wear. Many types of vinyl require no waxing. For comfort, cushioned vinyls are made with foam laminated between the layers. Vinyl tiles and sheets are also available in one of the largest arrays of colors and patterns of any flooring materials.

Vinyl asbestos flooring is cheaper than pure vinyl, yet it is also highly resistant to wear, stains, and abrasion, and

Fig. 12–14 Resilient flooring

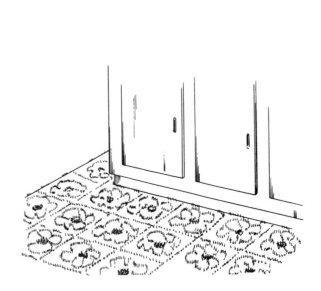

Fig. 12–15 Kitchen carpeting

Fig. 12–16 Quarry-tile flooring

is available in almost as many colors and designs. Like vinyl, vinyl asbestos can be installed as tiles or sheet flooring.

Linoleum is less expensive than either vinyl or vinyl asbestos, but it requires more frequent maintenance. With periodic washing and waxing, linoleum will hold up without showing wear for many years.

Where spills are infrequent and traffic relatively light, other types of flooring may be used. *Kitchen carpeting* is made in many attractive colors and patterns and is quiet and comfortable. It can be vacuumed and washed to remove dirt and stains. *Vinyl-coated cork tiles* are used for their soft, warm tones and quiet resiliency. Uncoated cork tiles, however, stain easily and wear along traffic patterns. *Wooden floors* that are protected by varnish or urethane will withstand moderate use and add an appearance of warmth to a kitchen. *Ceramic tiles, slate,* and *brick* make impressive floor surfaces (Fig. 12–16), but they are hard to clean and less comfortable to walk on than resilient flooring.

Wallcoverings

When deciding on how the walls are to be treated, consider how the kitchen is to be used and whether it is to be ventilated. Where there is little moisture or grease from cooking, natural-finished wood paneling and some of the more fragile wallpapers may be used. Where children frequent a kitchen or where cooking vapors are plentiful, vinyl wallcoverings, semigloss or gloss enamels, or plastic-coated plywood or hardboard paneling are more practical selections.

The individual boards in *wood paneling* will be spoiled by moisture and grease unless they are coated with a protective finish such as wax, stain, or urethane (Fig. 12–17). With a resistant finish, they will be no harder to clean than wooden cabinets. *Wallpaper* is very susceptible to the effects of moisture from cooking and scrubbing. Uncoated wallpapers will soften and rub thin. Even coated wallpapers may start to peel if there is enough moisture to soften the paste. *Vinyl-coated* wallcoverings stand up well to all of these abuses and are made in a large variety of bright colors and patterns. *Painted plaster* and *gypsum board* walls can be washed without fading. Their colors can also be changed easily with a new coat of paint. *Prefinished plywood* and *hardboard* can be purchased with laminated plastic surfaces that are moisture resistant. Hardboard panels are available in colors and patterns rivaling those of wallpaper and paint. *Brick* (Fig. 12–18) and *brick veneer* are often used along one wall of a kitchen for their color and texture. If the cooking vapors are removed from the air with an exhaust fan, brick can be kept in good condition with periodic cleaning.

Fig. 12–17 Wood paneling

Fig. 12–18 Brick wall

LIGHTING, ELECTRICAL OUTLETS, AND VENTILATION

Lighting

The kitchen requires good general illumination as well as individual lighting at the work centers. Ceiling lights should be located where they will eliminate shadows in passageways and the interiors of wall cabinets. Individual area fixtures should be placed so that there are no shadows on the work surfaces.

A typical 10- X 12-ft kitchen should have anywhere from 140 to 180 watts of fluorescent lighting, or 300 to 400 watts of incandescent lighting. This includes individual pairs of 30-watt fluorescent or a 100-watt incandescent light at work centers. More lights may have to be used in irregularly shaped kitchens and in dining areas.

Light fixtures may be installed in the ceiling for direct illumination and behind wall brackets or above wall cabinets for indirect lighting. Units may be recessed in the ceiling (Fig. 12–19) or fixtures hung down into the room (Fig. 12–20). Spotlights may be attached to the ceiling or walls. If there

Fig. 12–19 Recessed fixtures

Fig. 12–21 Light fixture over sink

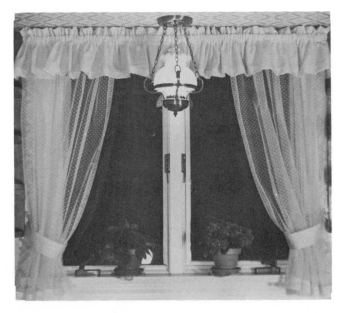

Fig. 12–20 Hanging fixtures

Fig. 12–22 Electrical outlets in mixing and baking center

Fig. 12–23 Range hood

are several entrances to the kitchen, three- or four-way switches should be provided for controlling these lights. Work centers can be illuminated by fixtures installed under cabinets, over the sink (Fig. 12–21), or in a range hood. The type of fixture selected will depend mainly on the style of the kitchen. Hanging fixtures, for example, might be used in a colonial kitchen, while spotlights would fit better into a contemporary design.

Electrical Outlets

The usefulness of work areas can often be increased by installing additional electrical outlets. Food-preparation and baking centers, for example, should have enough outlets for three or four small appliances to be used at the same time (Fig. 12–22). The most convenient location for outlets is usually on the wall behind the counter surface. Duplex outlets can be installed by themselves or in groups of four or six, but where several appliances are to be used at the same point, a strip with several receptacles is preferable.

Outlets can be added either by extending an existing circuit or by running a new cable to the service panel. Since many kitchen circuits are already loaded to capacity, new circuits will have to be installed in most cases. Modern kitchens require two 20-amp circuits for small appliances, a separate 15- or 20-amp circuit for lights, and individual

heavy-duty circuits for range and motor-operated appliances. Where there is only one kitchen-type circuit for small appliances, adding a second will eliminate the danger of overloads and increase the overall working efficiency of the kitchen.

Ventilation

The kitchen will look and smell better if cooking odors, grease, and moisture are removed. Either a range hood (Fig. 12–23) or a ventilator with an exhaust fan (Fig. 12–24) can be used to clear the air. Range hoods are the more effective of the two (if they are ducted to the outside), since they trap the air over the range before it can circulate.

A *ducted range hood* (Fig. 12–25) uses a fan to exhaust the air through duct piping to the outside of the house. Choose this type of hood to remove moisture, odors, smoke, grease, and hot air. A *ductless range hood* (Fig. 12–26), on the other hand, is less effective since it relies on a charcoal filter to absorb odors and a metal filter to collect grease. Neither water nor heat are removed. Use a ductless hood only where a range is lightly used or where ducting a hood to the outside is impossible.

Range hoods require careful selection because ducted and ductless models look very similar. They are generally installed beneath a wall cabinet over the range. To match

Fig. 12–24 Ventilator

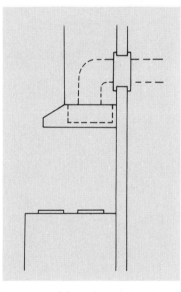

Fig. 12–25 Operation of ducted range hood

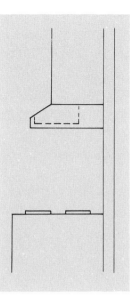

Fig. 12–26 Operation of ductless range hood

the size of the range, hoods are made in standard widths from 30 to 42 inches. The capacity of exhaust fans for removing air is rated in cubic feet per minute (CFM). Fans in ducted range hoods handle about 180 to 275 CFM, while those in ductless hoods may handle only 100 to 175 CFM. In selecting a range hood be sure to check the noise factor of the exhaust fan.

Ventilators can be mounted in either a wall or ceiling. Since it is easier in most kitchens to duct an exhaust fan through the wall to the outside, the ventilator is usually mounted in the wall instead of the ceiling. The unit should

be installed immediately over the range to remove the wastes from the air before they circulate. The capacity of the ventilator depends on the size of the kitchen and the volume of cooking. A 10-inch fan with a capacity of 270 to 300 CFM would be sufficient for a 12- by 12-ft kitchen with an 8-ft ceiling. Like other fans, some ventilator fans are noisier than others. Listen to several before selecting one.

STORAGE

Inadequate storage space is a problem in most kitchens. However, storage capacity usually can be increased without installing additional cabinets by making more efficient use of existing space.

• **Cup hooks.** More shelf space can be made available for large items by removing cups and hanging them on special cup hooks under cabinets or shelves (Fig. 12–27).

• **Dividers.** Large, flat pans, such as trays and cookie sheets, will take up less room if they are stored vertically (Fig. 12–28). Plywood or hardboard dividers can be installed with strips of quarter-round (moulding) for vertical storage in base cabinets that are otherwise poorly used. For example, there is often adequate space under the sink for a number of flat items.

• **Pegboard.** Items that can be hung from hooks can be grouped on a sheet of pegboard mounted on an unused wall (Fig. 12–29). Pegboard is available in 4- by 4-ft squares with bright, baked-on enamel surfaces or the homeowner can buy unfinished pegboard cut to size and paint it with an enamel. Mount pegboard a quarter of an inch or so away

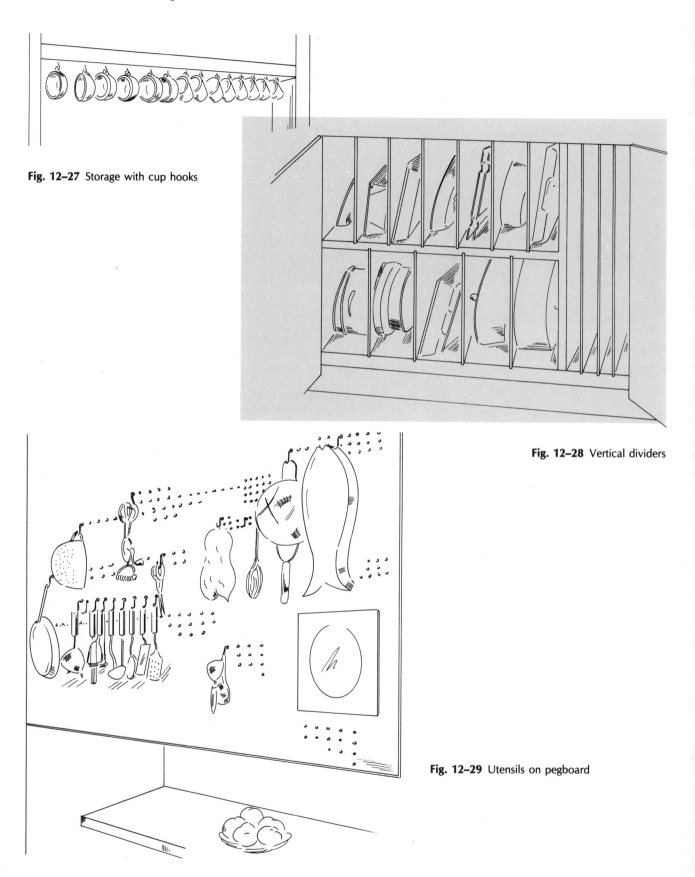

Fig. 12–27 Storage with cup hooks

Fig. 12–28 Vertical dividers

Fig. 12–29 Utensils on pegboard

Fig. 12–30 Spice rack

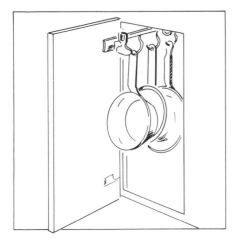

Fig. 12–31 Pull-out rack for utensils

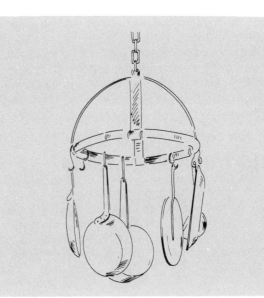

Fig. 12–32 Ceiling rack for utensils

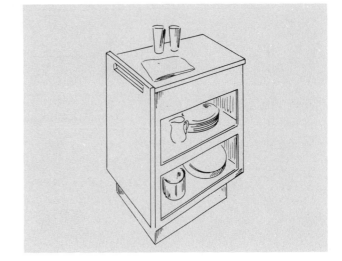

Fig. 12–33 Serving and storage cart

from the wall to leave room for the mounting hooks to be inserted. Special mounting sleeves are available.

• **Narrow shelves and racks.** Spices and other dry foods in small containers can be stored on narrow shelves installed on the inside of cabinet doors, or on the walls behind the counters (Fig. 12–30). If a shelf is to be mounted inside a door, allow sufficient clearance between the inside shelves and the new shelf.

• **Pull-Out Racks.** Deep cabinets beneath a counter can be made more functional by installing pull-out racks for hanging utensils (Fig. 12–31).

• **Wall and ceiling hangers.** Strips of wall hangers or decorative ceiling racks can be installed adjacent to work centers for hanging utensils (Fig. 12–32). This frees cabinet and shelf space for other materials and adds to the decorative appearance of the kitchen.

• **Kitchen organizers.** Hardware stores carry a variety of plastic and metal devices for mounting on cabinets, doors, and walls for storing items such as brooms, mops, lids.

• **Carts.** A cart can be used for storage as well as for serving (Fig. 12–33).

MAJOR IMPROVEMENTS

Remodeling may call for changes in a range of projects, anywhere from building new storage spaces to completely rebuilding the interior of a kitchen. In major projects, walls may be moved, entryways changed, and new windows in-stalled. More commonly, however, the kitchen layout is merely rearranged to make it more functional, by installing new cabinets, counters, and appliances. Work centers are planned to improve working surfaces, storage, and work center locations in relation to each other and to major appliances. Ceilings, walls, and floors are refinished with improved materials to make the kitchen attractive, comfortable, and easy to maintain. It is advisable to lay out your new plan on graph paper (Fig. 12–34).

CABINETS

Kitchen cabinets can be purchased as prefabricated units ready for installation, or they can be custom built. *Prefabricated* or *stock cabinets* are produced in standard sizes that meet the requirements of most kitchens. Units can be

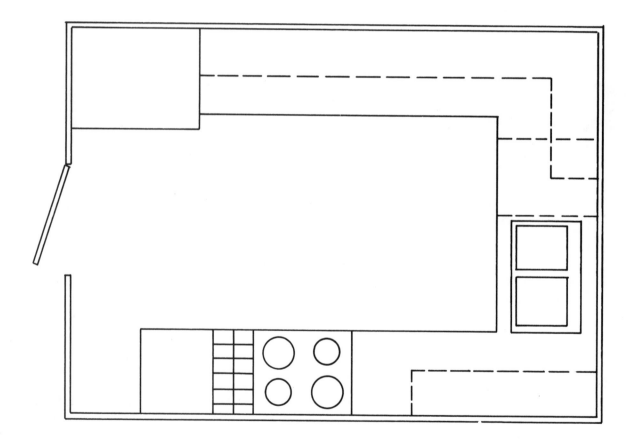

Fig. 12–34 Rough plan for a kitchen layout

Fig. 12–35 Base cabinets

Fig. 12–37 Wall cabinet mounted above a cooking area

Fig. 12–36 Wall cabinets

ordered in various widths to fill allotted spaces. *Custom-built cabinets* are built to whatever sizes are required. Cabinet doors and drawers are usually constructed in the shop beforehand, though the cabinet body may be built on the spot.

Most kitchen cabinets are made of wood, panels covered with plastic laminate, or metal. The best quality cabinets are made of solid wood and finished with stains. Cabinets with plastic-laminate surfaces are widely used in remodeling, however, because they are durable, economical, and similar in appearance to wood. The cabinets are made of wood, chipboard, or other rigid material and covered with a veneer of plastic laminate that is finished in solid colors, patterns, or realistic-looking wood grains. Steel cabinets are also made for kitchen storage, but they are not widely used in good quality remodeling.

Base cabinets (Fig. 12–35) are produced in a standard height of 34½ in. and a depth of 24 in. They can also be purchased slightly higher or lower in height for such purposes as pastry or candy making. Units are available from different manufacturers in widths that range from about 1 ft to 5 ft, in 3-in. increments. Cabinets are available with shelves, drawers, and special types of interiors; they may be faced with doors or false fronts for sinks and ranges. There is an indented 4-in. toe space, where the base may be leveled to adjust for any slope of the floor. To hold the cabinet in place, the back is fastened to the wall with screws or nails.

Wall cabinets are produced in a standard depth of 12 to 13 inches and in various widths similar to base cabinets (Fig. 12–36). They are generally mounted on the wall 15 to 18 in. above a counter and 1½ to 2 ft above a range or cooktop (Fig. 12–37). Wall cabinets are available in heights from 1 ft to over 3 ft in increments of 3 in. They should be mounted so that supplies stored on the top shelves are within reach. Cabinet tops at a standard 84-in. height will be a foot or so below many ceilings unless a soffit is built above them. If not so covered, this space can be used for indirect lighting or for displaying kitchenwares. Hanging cabinets (Fig. 12–38), similar in dimensions to wall cabinets, are hung free over peninsulas or other counters that do not back up against a wall.

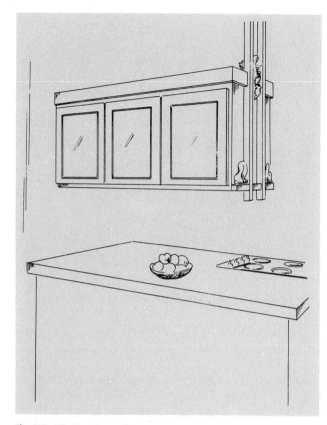

Fig. 12–38 Hanging cabinets

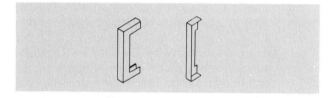

Fig. 12–39 Filler strips

Utility cabinets are built to a height of 84 in. to align with the tops of the wall cabinets. These tall cabinets provide storage space for items that won't fit into base or wall cabinets. Utility cabinets are made in standard 24-in. depths to match the line of base cabinets, as well as in 12-in. depths for shallower storage. Widths vary in 3-in. increments from 12 in. to over 40 in.

Special cabinet units and accessories are also available. Filler strips (Fig. 12–39), for example, are used to fill in odd-width spaces left between cabinets and walls or between cabinets in corners. Extra spacing is often necessary to allow drawers or doors to open. To avoid losing storage space in corner cabinets, revolving turntables (Fig. 12–41), blank corner cabinets, and other special accessories are used. Refrigerator, wall-oven, and sink-base units, as well as various cabinet fronts, are used for built-in appliances and sinks.

COUNTERTOPS

Countertops are prefabricated or custom-built to fit over the base cabinets. A rigid material, such as chipboard or plywood, is fastened over the cabinets and finished with a thin working surface. The thickness of the counter (1½ to 2 in.) is designed to bring the overall height to a standard 36 in. (Fig. 12–42). The countertop overhangs the edge by an inch or less and may be either rounded and integral with the top, or square and self-edged with a strip of the same material. At the back wall, the counter may butt the wall stop or it may curve upward into an integral backsplash. Backsplashes, whether integral with the counter or separate, extend anywhere from 4 in. to the entire 15 to 18 in. to the bottom of the wall cabinets.

Various types of counter surfaces are needed for chopping and cutting, for holding hot pans, for rolling dough or making candy, and for general food preparation and serving. Most areas are covered with a general-purpose material, while special inserts are placed where they are needed at work centers. Some of the more widely used materials are described below.

• **Plastic laminate.** This is one of the most popular materials for kitchen counters because it is easy to clean, withstands stains and chipping, lasts indefinitely, and is available in many colors, designs, and patterns. Plastic laminate, however, can be injured by excessive heat and by cutting instruments.

Fig. 12–40 Full-length storage cabinet

Fig. 12–41 Revolving turntable

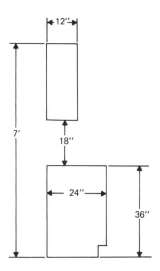

Fig. 12–42 Counter and cabinet measurements

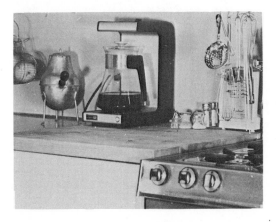

Fig. 12–43 Butcher-block countertop

Fig. 12–44 Marble insert at baking center

Fig. 12–45 Countertop of ceramic tile

• **Butcher-block wood.** A laminated, wooden surface is ideal for cutting and chopping in preparing foods (Fig. 12–43). A 1½ or 2 ft section should be located either next to a sink or food-preparation area. When laminated wood is used for an entire length of counter, it creates a warm, functional appearance. However, because stains and food spots are difficult to remove, butcher-block surfaces require substantially more maintenance than plastic laminate.

• **Marble.** This is one of the best surfaces for making pastry and candy (Fig. 12–44). It must be well cared for, however, because it can be cracked, chipped, stained, and scratched. On the other hand, it will not be injured by moisture or heat.

• **Ceramic tile.** The hard, impervious surface of ceramic tile is durable and easy to clean and maintain (Fig. 12–45). When used on a counter, its colors and patterns can be one of focal points of the kitchen. Tile isn't injured by heat, moisture, or cutting, but it can be cracked. One of the main

Fig. 12–46 Storage at food preparation center

Fig. 12–48 Drawers in base cabinet

Fig. 12–47 Pantry-type storage cabinet

Fig. 12–49 Storing appliances on the counter

problems with tile is that when dishes or glasses are dropped on the counter they almost always crack or break.

Other types of materials, such as resilient coverings and stainless steel, are also occasionally used to cover counters. Sheets of vinyl and linoleum give an effect similar to plastic laminate, but they are not at all comparable in durability. They can be easily cut, burned, and stained, and require frequent cleaning. Stainless steel provides a hard, moisture- and heat-proof surface that must be cleaned and polished frequently to remain attractive.

STORAGE

Major renovations provide an opportunity to increase the amount of kitchen storage. Refer to earlier sections under Cabinets and under Minor Improvements for suggestions on storage (Figs. 12–46 to 12–49).

SINKS AND BASIC APPLIANCES

Except in unusual cases, a remodeled kitchen will require at least a refrigerator, range or cooktop and oven, and a sink. Beyond this, other appliances, such as dishwashers and garbage disposers, may be installed either as a necessity or as a convenience in a particular kitchen. To assist the remodeler in deciding what he should use, several of these basic appliances are described below.

DISHWASHERS

A 24-in.-wide section should be left under the counter next to the sink for installing a dishwasher, even if the present homeowner doesn't plan on having one. The empty space can either be left uncovered, or it can be covered with a temporary cabinet front. As long as there is sufficient space, the dishwasher can be located on either side of the sink, though the left side is the traditional location.

Types of Dishwashers

Dishwashers are made either to be installed under the counter or to be used as portable units. Undercounter, front-loading models (Fig. 12–50) are used almost universally in remodeling because they don't take up working space. Where there is no room for an undercounter model, or where there are other reasons for wanting the dishwasher to be mobile, a portable model (Fig. 12–51) can be used. Portable dishwashers may be purchased either as front- or top-loaders. Some can be converted to undercounter models.

Fig. 12–50 Undercounter, front-loading dishwasher

Fig. 12–51 Portable, front-loading dishwasher

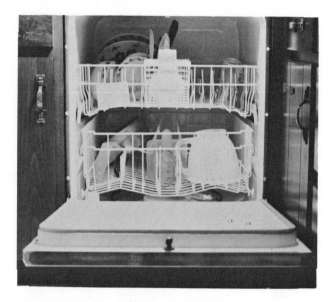

Fig. 12–52 Typical arrangement of dishwasher racks

Front-loading portables are usually equipped with a top such as a maple chopping block, that can be used as a work surface.

Installation

An undercounter dishwasher requires hot water, a drain, and electricity. It should be installed next to the sink where it can then be connected by tubing or a hose to the hot-water pipe and drain. Dishwasher drains can also be attached to a special connection on garbage disposers. A dishwasher will use 12 to 16 gal of water in its complete cycle. The water should be 140 to 160° for thorough washing and rinsing. A separate 15- or 20-amp, 120-volt circuit is required to ensure that the dishwasher's motor will have sufficient current regardless of what other appliances are being operated at the same time.

REFRIGERATORS AND FREEZERS

Type of Units and Storage Capacity

The most commonly found refrigeration units include refrigerators with freezer compartments, combined refrigerator-freezers, separate freezers, and compact refrigerators. Of these, the storage needs for perishable foods in modern kitchens are best fulfilled by a combined refrigerator-freezer. The refrigerator and freezer compartments are available arranged in three different ways. Top- and bottom-freezer models (Fig. 12–53(a)(b)) employ compartments that extend the full width of the units. In side-by-side models (Fig. 12–53(c)), the freezer and refrigerator compartments extend vertically from the top to the bottom of the units.

The side-by-side units contain substantially more freezer space than the other models. They are also more convenient to use since they have a number of easily accessible shelves for storing frozen foods. Side-by-side models, however, are more expensive to purchase and to operate than the other models. Bottom-freezer models are awkward to use when storing or removing frozen foods. Children, however, find it easier to retrieve ice cubes from a bottom-freezer than from a top-freezer.

A refrigerator's storage capacity is rated by the number of cubic feet (cu ft) of storage space. Combined refrigerator-freezers with an advertised total of 16 to 20 cu ft will be large enough to provide sufficient storage space in most kitchens. The freezer units in medium-size, top- and bottom-freezer models usually have storage capacities of 4 to 6 cu ft. In a side-by-side model, the freezer unit will usually contain 6 or more cu ft, but the refrigerator unit will usually have less space than in other designs. The actual cubic-foot volume in all models is generally less than the advertised volume.

Temperature and Electricity

A refrigerator should be capable of holding a temperature of 37°F in the center of the compartment when the air around the unit is at room temperature. Freezers should provide a reliable temperature of 0°F, though there may be slightly warmer spots around the door. Temperature controls permit these values to be varied by a few degrees. Since these temperatures usually can't be observed in the showroom, you will have to inquire into the experience of someone who owns a similar model.

Refrigerator-freezers are also rated by the amount of electricity they use. The manufacturer generally indicates the number of kilowatt hours (KWH) used per month. Side-by-side units, in addition to costing more to purchase, also use more electricity than comparable top- or bottom-freezer models. Typical side-by-side refrigerator-freezer units may use from 140 to more than 200 KWH per month. Top- and bottom-freezer models may use 100 to 170 KWH or so, depending on the size and model. The amount of electricity required can be reduced in some models by turning off the frostless systems.

Location

Because of its large size, a refrigerator-freezer is usually placed at the end of a length of counter. The counter top adjacent to the handle side of the door is convenient for loading and unloading groceries. Models with either right- or left-hand opening doors are available to fit into any layout. In a small kitchen, ample space should be left in front of the

(a)

(b)

(c)

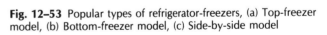

Fig. 12–53 Popular types of refrigerator-freezers, (a) Top-freezer model, (b) Bottom-freezer model, (c) Side-by-side model

refrigerator for opening the door. In a one-wall kitchen, the distance between the refrigerator at one end of the working area and the range or other appliance at the other end should be kept reasonably short. In a two-wall or U-shape kitchen, the refrigerator can be placed opposite the range or sink. Most medium-size refrigerator-freezers require no more than a 33-in. width along the wall and a vertical clearance of less than 6 ft. Where space is limited, as in very small apartments or vacation homes, a compact refrigerator can be installed under a counter.

Refrigerator-freezers can be installed as free-standing uprights by themselves or placed adjacent to cabinets. They can also be built in by using a refrigerator cabinet and a wooden door.

RANGES, COOKTOPS, AND OVENS

Cooking units are made in various combinations and sizes to satisfy almost any kitchen design. Ranges are built to stand independently or to fit between base cabinets, to contain single or double ovens, and to operate on gas, electricity, coal, or wood. If the layout calls for a separate baking area, a cooktop unit can be built into the counter and the oven or ovens located separately at the baking center.

Types of Units

• **Free-Standing Range.** This type of range (Fig. 12–54) is styled to stand independently, though it can be used equally well installed between base cabinets. It usually has a back panel to house an automatic timer, clock, and light. Burner and oven controls are on the back panel on electric ranges and on the front on gas ranges. Side rims extend above the cooking surface to match the height of the adjacent counters for situations that call for the range to be used between base cabinets. The base of the range may contain either a single or double oven. In some models, a second oven is placed at eye level, well above the burners. The number of burners varies, from four heat units on utility ranges, to six or more supplemented by a griddle on large, deluxe ranges. Electric ranges often use three 6-in.-diameter, low-heat elements and one 8-in.-diameter, high-heat element. Gas ranges use both medium- and high-heat units.

When a free-standing range is to be installed between base cabinets, the cabinets must be spaced for the width of the particular model selected. A 30-in. space will be sufficient for standard-size models, but others may require 36 or 40 in. So you must decide on your range size to complete your planning. With a free-standing range, crumbs and spilled food are likely to collect between the side rims and the counters.

• **Slide-In Range.** The side rims and rear panel found on a free-standing range are eliminated on the slide-in range to allow it to fit flush with the counter and backsplash (Fig.

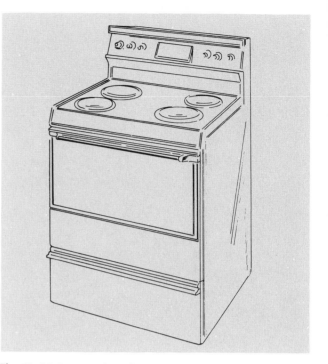

Fig. 12–54 Free-standing electric range

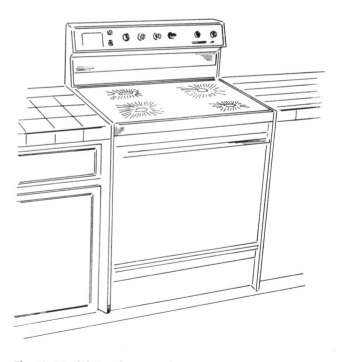

Fig. 12–55 Slide-in, glass-ceramic range

12–55). The protective rim that bridges the narrow spaces between the countertop and the surface of the range makes the unit appear as a built-in part of the counter and base cabinets. Since there is no rear panel, the controls are usu-

Fig. 12–56 Drop-in gas range

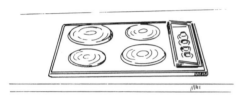

Fig. 12–57 Built-in electric cooktop

Fig. 12–58 Smooth-top range

ally mounted along the front edge of the range. Like the free-standing range, the slide-in range rests on the floor and is available in several widths.

• **Drop-In Range.** Flanges resting on the edge of the adjacent countertops support the drop-in type range (Fig. 12–56). The space beneath the oven is filled in with a low panel connecting the cabinets on both sides. The continuity of the base cabinets along the floor gives a drop-in range an even more built-in appearance than a slide-in range.

• **Built-In Cooktop.** A built-in electric or gas cooktop (Fig. 12–57) contains the same burners, griddle, and controls (except for oven and broiler controls) as the surface units on a range. However, a cooktop takes up less space than a range and is used where the layout provides for a separate oven or ovens. Since a cooktop extends only a few inches below the countertop, the cabinet space beneath can be used for drawers or shelves. Cooktops vary from approximately 28 to 36 in. in width but have a standard 21-in. depth to fit over a 24-in. base cabinet.

• **Smooth-Top Units.** A smooth-top range (Fig. 12–58) uses a sheet of glass-ceramic material mounted over specially-designed electrical burners. On slide-in, drop-in or cooktop units, the smooth white tops look more like counter inserts than cooking surfaces. In fact, when a smooth-top unit is not being used for cooking, it can be used as a working surface. Some models use a single sheet to cover all of the burners; others use several ceramic sheets, separated by metal strips, to cover each burner individually. Because of their unique characteristics, the ceramic sheets pass heat vertically from the electric burner to the cooking utensil but do not transmit heat horizontally. As a result, the surface of the sheet outside the burner area remains unheated.

A ceramic surface is much simpler to clean than burners on a conventional electric or gas range. Debris can be wiped away as easily as if the smooth-top were part of the countertop. The ceramic material is also strong enough to withstand heavy blows. Heavy utensils can be dropped on a glass-ceramic surface without cracking it. However, the material does heat more slowly than do standard burners, uses more electricity, and is therefore more expensive to use. Efficiency can be increased by using utensils with flat bottoms designed to match the cooking surface. As with electric and gas units, smooth-tops are available in freestanding, slide in, and drop-in ranges and in separate cooktops.

• **Range Ovens.** The conventional standard-size range has a single oven in its base. However, ovens may also be mounted at eye level, a foot or so above the cooking surface. Large models may contain double ovens, one standard size and one small oven, for simultaneous baking or broiling (Fig. 12–59). Where space is limited and a second oven is required, a range with upper and lower ovens can be used instead of wider models (Fig. 12–60). Although the double-oven design saves counter space, the upper oven may be awkward to reach.

Fig. 12–59 Range with double oven

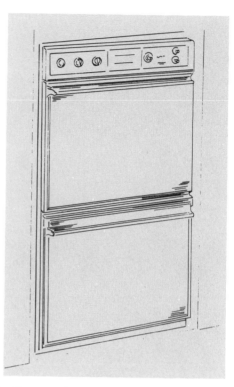

Fig. 12–61 Built-in wall ovens

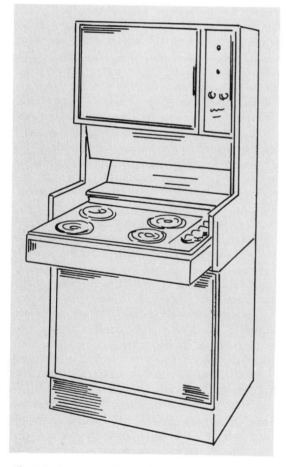

Fig. 12–60 Range with eye-level oven

Fig. 12–62 Microwave oven

• **Built-in Wall Ovens.** Specially designed cabinets are used to house single and double wall ovens (Fig. 12–61). Like range ovens, these ovens are made with automatic controls and other convenience features. Some double-oven combinations consist of a microwave oven and a conventionally heated oven.

• **Microwave Ovens.** Microwave ovens (Fig. 12–62) cook food in a fraction of the time required by conventional ovens. Food is cooked by heat given off from vibrating molecules of moisture that are part of the food itself. These molecules receive their energy from electromagnetic waves disbursed throughout the oven. Unlike a conventional oven, neither the air nor the food containers are heated in a microwave oven.

Since metal reflects microwaves, the usual steel, aluminum, and copper cooking utensils can't be used. They would prevent the microwaves from heating the food. Instead, food is placed in ceramic, glass, plastic, or paper containers that can be handled without hot pads. Special ceramic cooking dishes are also made specifically for use in microwave ovens.

Because of the way they heat food internally, microwaves do not brown foods as in ordinary baking and roasting. To make up for this, many models have supplementary browning units to give steaks and pies their usual browned appearance. The length of cooking time in a microwave oven and not the temperature determines when the food is cooked, since there is no temperature setting.

Microwave ovens are available as built-in, freestanding, portable, and combined double-oven units (one conventional oven, one microwave). Portable countertop units are also popular as second ovens for thawing frozen foods, heating leftovers, and rapid cooking.

• **Self-Cleaning Ovens.** Many ovens are designed to use heat to burn off food spills and grease. Two different systems are employed: self-cleaning and continuous-cleaning. *Self-cleaning ovens* use very high temperatures (900° to 1000°F) to clean the inner surfaces. The process must be carried out separately from cooking because of the high temperatures. Interlocks prevent the oven doors from being inadvertently opened during the self-cleaning process, thus preventing any danger of fire. The cleaning cycle requires 2 to 4 hours and leaves a fine ash that can be easily wiped off. In this type of oven, the walls must be heavily insulated to contain the extreme heat. *Continuous-cleaning ovens* are coated with a catalyst that causes grease and spills to partially oxidize during the cooking process at temperatures between 350° and 450°F. Thick spills, however, should be cleaned up as much as possible by hand because they won't oxidize. Spills won't burn away as completely in these ovens as they do in self-cleaning ovens. The buildup of debris in many continuous-cleaning models is often harder to clean off by hand than spills in conventional ovens.

GARBAGE DISPOSERS

There are two basic types of disposers: continuous-feed and batch-feed. Continuous-feed disposers are the most popular because they can be fed continuously as garbage is ground into fine particles and washed away. Batch-feed disposers can be loaded only when they are not operating. Garbage is loaded into the chamber and the cover locked into place to start the motor. When the chamber is empty, the disposer can be reloaded.

Modern disposer (Fig. 12–63) will grind up bones, corn cobs, paper products, and all kinds of soft foods without jamming. A continuous flow of cold water is used to flush away the particles during the grinding process. In a number

Fig. 12–63 Garbage disposer

of communities, garbage disposers are required in newly constructed houses and apartments to reduce the amount of garbage that must be processed by municipal facilities.

SINKS

The placement of the sink in remodeling is usually determined by the location of the water-supply lines and drain. Because it is expensive to move plumbing lines, the kitchen layout is generally designed so that the sink can be connected directly to existing plumbing. The sink is usually placed in a central location, such as in the middle of a U-shape kitchen or in the middle of a length of counter. Such a location makes the sink conveniently close to work centers on either side. A second sink may be installed in another part of the kitchen for special purposes, such as cleaning vegetables or serving a kitchen bar.

In selecting a sink, a decision has to be made on the number of basins, the type of material, and the color. Single- and double-basin sinks are the most popular, but there are designs with three basins, pie-shaped basins for corners, special shallow basins, and other variations. There are also numerous accessories, such as sprayers and soap dispensers. The *single-basin sink* (Fig. 12–64(a)) is generally recommended for use with a dishwasher. It will provide a larger basin width for washing large platters and pans than is allowed by double-basin models. Although specially-designed, single-basin sinks vary in size, the standard is 25-in. wide and 22-in. from front to back. Depths usually range from 7 to 7½ in. *Double-basin sinks* (Fig. 12–64(b)) are recommended for use either with or without a dishwasher. Without a dishwasher, one basin can be used for washing and the other for rinsing or preparing vegetables. Standard-size double-basin models are 33-in. wide and 22-in. from front to back. The insides of the basins will be 15 to 16 in. from front to back. *Triple-basin sinks* (Fig. 12–64(c)) supplement their two larger basins with a shallow middle basin that contains a garbage disposer. This smaller basin is usually used to prepare vegetables.

(a)   (b)

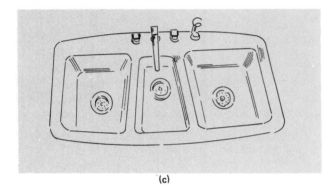

(c)

Fig. 12–64 Kitchen sinks. (a) Single-basin, stainless-steel, (b) Double-basin, stainless-steel, (c) Triple-basin, porcelain-coated, cast-iron

There is also a choice between stainless-steel and a porcelain-coated sink. *Stainless-steel sinks,* the most popular and most expensive, are finished in nickel and chrome to make their polished surfaces durable and easy to clean. Good-quality, stainless-steel sinks will not warp, chip, or tarnish. Also, dishes will not break as easily when dropped in a stainless-steel sink. A porcelain coating is used on both steel and cast-iron sinks. Coated cast-iron sinks are expensive and are not often used in routine remodeling. *Porcelain-coated steel sinks,* on the other hand, are cheaper than stainless-steel sinks and are popular because of their bright colors. The porcelain-coating must be treated carefully to avoid chipping.

Most types of sinks are available with openings for either a single-control faucet or dual faucets. Sinks and faucets are usually selected separately, though some sinks are sold with their own faucets.

COMFORT, CONVENIENCE, AND MAINTENANCE

With forethought, a kitchen can be designed to be comfortable, convenient to use, and easy to maintain. These features depend primarily on how the kitchen is laid out and what types of materials are used.

A good layout of the work centers and appliances can save many steps. A work triangle of 12 to 22 feet will allow meals to be prepared with a minimum of moving to and fro. Well-planned storage will place baking ingredients and tools at the baking center, cooking utensils within arm's reach of the range or cooktop, and food stuffs handy to the food-preparation area.

Appliances should be selected that will reduce the drudgery of cooking and cleaning. A dishwasher, self-cleaning range, easy-to-clean sink, self-defrosting refrigerator, and garbage disposer will lighten the basic chores. The dishwasher is not essential where the workload is light, but it is invaluable when dirty dishes are plentiful. A range with a self-cleaning oven will stay cleaner than a less expensive, continuous-cleaning oven. The choice between a stainless-steel sink and a porcelain-coated sink is not as critical as the size of the basins. Although stainless steel is easier to keep clean, porcelain cleans up well also. The basins should be large enough for large platters and broiler pans. Modern refrigerators require little care. Choose a model with sufficient refrigerator and freezer storage space for your needs. A garbage disposer in the sink will simplify disposing of food scraps from plates before loading them into the dishwasher.

A kitchen must be well lighted, ventilated, and heated to be comfortable. Light fixtures should be installed both for general illumination and at individual work centers. The layout of counters and appliances should also take into account the availability and direction of natural light. Either a range hood or ventilator is necessary to keep the air free of cooking byproducts. Ventilation will also reduce the amount of scrubbing and repainting required. The shortage of wall space and lack of baseboard areas make it more difficult to install a heating system in the kitchen than in other rooms. Heating units can be built into recesses in the base cabinets or installed in the wall above the counters or wall cabinets if a lower wall area is unavailable. Radiant heating can be installed in the usual manner in the ceiling or floor.

A resilient floor covering or kitchen carpeting will be much more comfortable to walk on than wood, brick, or tile. Vinyl and vinyl asbestos require the least maintenance. Choose a covering that is appropriate for the type of activities in your kitchen.

Counters, walls, ceilings, and other surfaces in a kitchen should be covered with materials that clean up easily and do not stain. Plastic laminate and ceramic-tile countertops are durable and easy to clean. Stainless steel, laminated wood, marble, and other surfaces require more work in varying degrees. Vinyl wallcoverings and enamel paint stand up well to moisture and stay in better condition than uncoated wallpaper or flat paint. Backsplashes should be used behind counters, sinks, and the range, where foods and liquids may be spilled or splashed.

Closed cabinets and covered shelves will collect less dust than open storage areas. Even with cabinets, there will be unprotected horizontal surfaces, such as window casings, baseboard trim, and cabinet tops, that require periodic dusting and washing. Wooden cabinets, board and plywood paneling, and other wooden surfaces can be coated with urethane or other resistant finishes to reduce cleaning and polishing.

The convenience of an outside entrance into a kitchen may be offset by the extra cleaning that is required. In designing the kitchen layout, reduce maintenance by limiting the traffice to the people involved in kitchen activities.

The kitchen should be decorated in a way that makes it more comfortable without increasing the workload. Use high-quality paints, fabrics, wallcoverings, and other materials that are durable. An attractive color scheme is easy to keep looking fresh if good materials are used. Light-colored paints will make a small kitchen appear larger and lighter. On the other hand, a dark paint or wallpaper on one wall will provide color and make the room smaller, visually.

Small touches may contribute to an individual's sense of comfort. If the telephone is used frequently, an extension should be installed in the kitchen. A radio can be included to provide music and conversation during the long hours of preparing meals. Television may be a mixed blessing; it may or may not divert the viewers from their tasks. A small desk (Fig. 12–65) may be included in the kitchen layout (if there is room) for taking care of household-related paperwork. Stools or a table and chairs in a corner will give the weary worker a place to rest. A bulletin board, if there is well space, is convenient for reminders and other items that need open display.

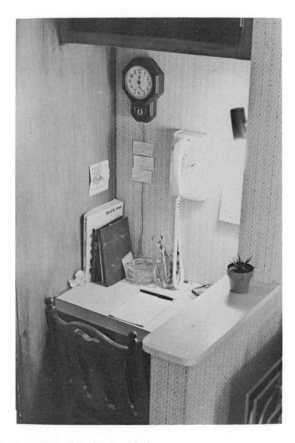

Fig. 12–65 Built-in kitchen desk

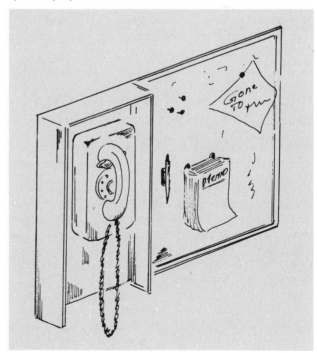

13 *Bathroom Remodeling*

Bathroom remodeling ranges from replacing fixtures and fittings to enlarging an existing bath, or—in the larger sense of home remodeling—to adding an entirely new bathroom. Homeowners who are adept at household repairs will be able to replace wall and floor coverings, electrical units, and fixtures such as lavatories and toilets by themselves. By contrast, professional know-how and specialized tools are usually required to install new plumbing lines, move bearing walls, and make other major alterations.

This chapter contains advice on bathroom layouts and guidelines for choosing locations for new bathrooms. As a background for selecting new materials and fixtures, different types of bathtubs, shower units, lavatories, toilets, and other bathroom furnishings are described also. Finally, suggestions are offered for both minor and major alterations. The emphasis in these sections is on thorough planning. Reference is made to earlier chapters on repairs and installation for more applied information where it is applicable to remodeling.

nearby rooms. Early morning showers or toilets flushed during the night may also awaken others who are sleeping in adjacent bedrooms unless the walls are specially constructed to reduce the sound.

The costs of long connections to water lines, drains, and vents may equal all the rest of the remodeling costs combined. These costs can be kept at a minimum by building a bath in a space that backs up to an existing bathroom (Fig. 13–1) or kitchen, or by using a space that is either over or under a bathroom or kitchen.

Whether the location of a bath is convenient or not depends mainly on which members of the family use it.
• **Family Bathroom.** If there is only one bathroom, it should be located where guests, children, and other members of the family can reach it easily when preparing for bed and when arising in the morning. Customarily, this means that the family bathroom (Fig. 13–2) should be located off a hallway near the bedrooms. A small bathroom that is already in this location can be enlarged into a more spacious bath for the entire family by moving a wall and expanding

BATHROOM LOCATION

The location of a new bath is usually determined by the availability of space, the proximity of the bath to the living areas, and the cost of connecting the fixtures to existing plumbing lines. The space that is most conveniently located and closest to existing plumbing is often the best compromise, if other aspects of the location are satisfactory. A few, common sense precautions should be taken in choosing the location. Bathrooms should be located where they can be reached without having to walk through private rooms. If possible, they should not open directly into rooms where visitors are likely to be sitting; take into consideration how the noise from showers, lavatories, and toilets will sound in

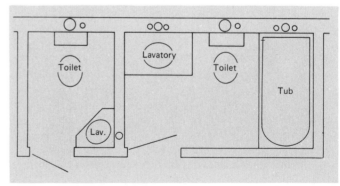

Fig. 13–1 Back-to-back baths

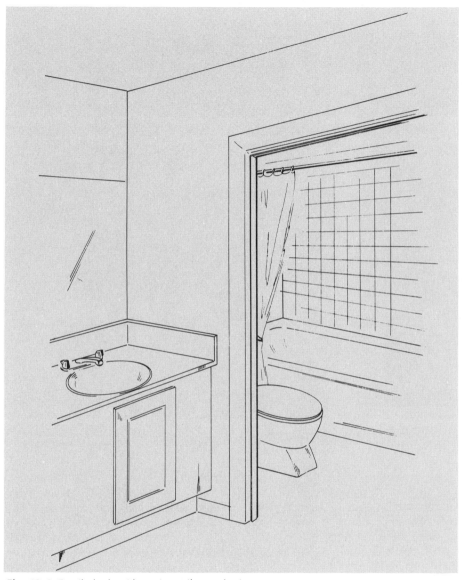

Fig. 13–2 Family bath with vanity, toilet, and tub

into an adjacent room. On the other hand, if a new bathroom is being built for family use, consider converting a bedroom that backs up to an existing bathroom or one that is located over a kitchen.

• **Second Bathroom for Children or Guests.** A second bath should be convenient to the children's or guests' bedrooms. This bath will require less space than a family bathroom. Since the bath will probably include a tub, the *minimal* dimensions will be approximately 4 X 5 ft. However, if several children are to use the bathroom, select a space that is large enough for two lavatories or a double vanity.

• **Half-Bath.** A small bathroom with a lavatory and toilet can be a great asset by easing the load on the main bathroom at rush times (Fig. 13–3). Since a half-bath can be installed in a space as small as 4 X 4 ft., there are likely to be several places in the house where it can be built, such as under a stairway, next to a back entrance where children can wash up as they come in, adjacent to the kitchen, or in a basement family room.

• **Bath for Master Bedroom.** A separate bath for a master bedroom can be made large enough to include (or be built around) storage space for clothing and bed linens, a dressing area, and separate lavatories for washing. The bathroom should, of course, open into the master bedroom rather than into the hall. Space may have to be borrowed from a neighboring room. Closet space in either the master bedroom or an adjacent room can be sacrificed and the common wall

Fig. 13–3 Half-bath

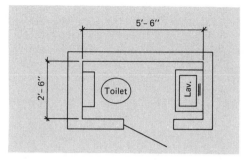

Fig. 13–4 Small, oblong half-bath

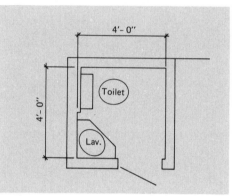

Fig. 13–5 Small, square half-bath

moved a few feet. Another alternative, although expensive, is to build an addition onto the exterior of the house.

• **Other Types of Bathrooms.** Bathrooms designed for special purposes generally require special locations. Some baths include sunbathing facilities, others open into outdoor gardens. Bathrooms for the elderly or the infirm should be close to their bedrooms or on the ground level.

BATHROOM LAYOUT

In a large bathroom, the fixtures can be placed almost anywhere, as long as they can be connected to the plumbing lines. But where space is at a minimum, the placement of the fixtures generally depends on the shape of the bathroom. Often there is little choice. In a small bath, the tub is usually run along the longest wall and the lavatory and toilet placed next to it. An even smaller half-bath may have just enough room for a corner lavatory and a toilet.

There are a few general rules that should be observed in designing bathrooms. Since people, at one time or an-

other, may be ill when using the bathroom, there should be enough room for them to lie on the floor or to faint without having to fall against a fixture or the wall. This is possible only in a larger bathroom. Neither a tub nor a lavatory should be placed under a standard-height window. A window over a tub will be a safety hazard, and its wooden sashes and frames will deteriorate rapidly from the abundance of moisture. A window over the lavatory makes it awkward to install a mirror to use when washing, shaving, or otherwise using the basin. Most designers place the toilet where it cannot be seen from the door. A view of a tub or lavatory is generally preferred. As for plumbing, it is most economical to locate fixtures where they can be readily connected to existing lines.

SMALL BATHS

Although bathrooms can be built in very small spaces, most adults will feel cramped in baths that are only minimum size. The addition of a few feet to the minimum dimensions will make a substantial difference in the space. A *half-bath* can

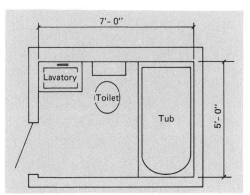

Fig. 13–6 Minimal, oblong full bath

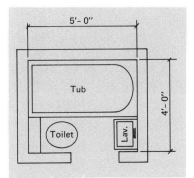

Fig. 13–7 Minimal, square full bath

be squeezed into a space under a stairway as small as 2½ X 5½ ft. (Fig. 13–4) or into a 4 X 4 ft. corner (Fig. 13–5) next to a back entry. If the space is oblong, the toilet would have to be placed at one end of the bath and the lavatory at the other end. Where the bath is square, the toilet could be placed against one wall and the lavatory placed in a corner or on an adjacent wall.

In a small *bathroom with a tub or shower stall,* the layout is limited by the size of the tub or stall. A standard 5 ft. tub, a lavatory, and a toilet will require a minimum-size space of 4 X 5 ft. In a 4 X 5 ft. space, the tub can be installed across the longer dimension and the toilet and lavatory squeezed in opposite each other (Fig. 13–6) in a very cramped layout. In a larger oblong 5 X 7 ft. space, (Fig. 13–7), the tub can be placed across the end of the room, and the lavatory and toilet can be installed side-by-side against one wall. This will provide more elbow room and leave a narrow passageway to the door. To further conserve space, remodelers can use a 4½ ft. tub, replace the tub with a smaller shower stall, or use a small corner lavatory.

LARGE BATHS

There are few limitations to design in a large bathroom. The homeowner may choose to include a sunken tub, exercise area, sauna, or washing machine and dryer. Where several people must use the bathroom simultaneously, the space can be separated into compartments. Compartmenting is especially useful in a master bathroom or a bathroom to be shared by several children. If the toilet is separated by a divider or door from the lavatories, shower, or tub, at least two people can use different facilities at the same time. A dual vanity is useful for storage and allows both basins to be used simultaneously. For maximum use of the bath, every fixture should be separated from the others by a screen, divider, or door. This requires considerable space, but it may be preferable to building another bathroom to handle the crowd.

FIXTURES

Bathroom fixtures are available in an ever increasing variety. Since fixtures are likely to outlast several changes of wallpaper, paint, and other decorative materials, they should be chosen with the future use and the resale value of the house in mind. In addition to the standard lavatory, tub or shower (or both), and toilet, other fixtures, such as a bidet, a soaking tub, a second lavatory, or a special shampooing basin, may be added as space allows.

The *style and size of the fixtures* depend heavily on the overall design of the bathroom and the amount of space that is available, as well as on personal taste. Bathtubs, for example, may be square or rectangular, sunken or conventional, short or long, high or low-edged, wide or narrow, white or colored. In prefabricated bathrooms made of fiberglass-reinforced plastics, all of the fixtures (except for the toilet) are integral parts of the prefabricated unit.

Most fixtures are available in a *choice of materials.* Vitreous china is used in the best-quality lavatories and in almost all toilets. Enamel-coated cast iron and enamel-coated steel are used for both bathtubs and lavatories. Fiberglass and fiberglass-reinforced plastic are now being used for fixtures such as molded tubs, showers, and lavatories. In some prefabricated units, the walls and the fixtures, except for the toilet, are all made of fiberglass.

Naturally, cost is directly related to quality and design characteristics. For example, vitreous china lavatories are more expensive than those made of enameled cast iron or fiberglass. The most expensive tubs, however, are made of enameled cast iron. Fixtures made from enameled steel or fiberglass are the least expensive. Design and color also effect cost. A sunken tub will be more expensive than a conventional tub of similar size, and one-piece toilets are much more expensive than the standard two-piece toilets. Color also adds to the cost.

Fittings such as faucets, spouts, and shower heads are made in an even greater range of designs than are fixtures

(Fig. 13–8(a) (b)). Some effort is made by designers to keep abreast of contemporary styles. Nevertheless, most fittings are constructed from sturdy, chrome-plated brass. Choose fittings with care. A low-price fitting could perform badly and lead to costly repairs. More expensive, better-designed fittings may be better in the long run.

LAVATORIES

Lavatories range from the old-fashioned, free-standing washstands made of marble or enameled cast-iron, to modern fiberglass basins. The most popular types for use in remodeling are the wall-hung and the countertop models. Wall-hung lavatories are attached to the studs with hangers

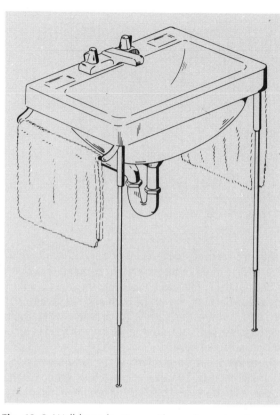

Fig. 13–9 Wall-hung lavatory with supplementary legs

(a)

(b)

Fig. 13–8 Faucets. (a) dual control, (b) single control

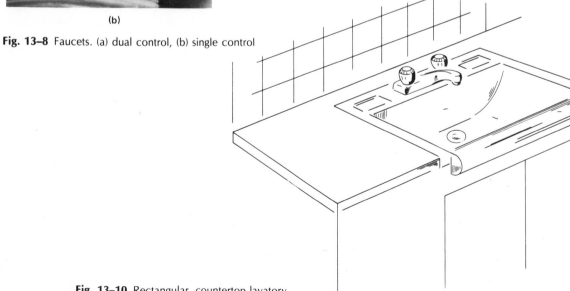

Fig. 13–10 Rectangular, countertop lavatory

Fig. 13–12 Recess-type bathtub

Fig. 13–11 Oval, countertop lavatory

so that they will be able to support the downward force of someone leaning on the fixture. Countertop lavatories, on the other hand, are installed in the top of vanities and base cabinets that stand on the floor.

Wall-hung lavatories are generally rectangular (Fig. 13–9). Some models have a ledge at the rear to hold soap and other articles, others have a tapered backsplash. Some models also have chromed legs for additional support.

Countertop lavatories come in an abundance of shapes and sizes. The most common shapes are oval, circular, rectangular, and triangular. The shapes of the inner basins may differ from the exterior shapes. They vary from rectangular to oval, while the basin sides may be rounded, straight, or a combination of the two. A lavatory may be positioned at any one of several spots on top of a vanity. Some models are designed to completely cover the top of the vanity. Others reach from the backsplash to the front of the counter where they project over the edge (Fig. 13–10). Most lavatories, however, rest in the center of the vanity top (Fig. 13–11), where they are surrounded by a plastic laminate or tile.

More storage space can be made available under a wide cabinet by placing the lavatory at one end. Although the area directly under the lavatory is crowded with plumbing lines, the remaining space can be used for shelves or drawers. With a long vanity used with dual lavatories, the large space in the center is often used for drawers and shelves.

The standard distance from the front to the back of a countertop lavatory is usually between 18 and 20 inches. This distance allows a lavatory to be installed in a vanity top of 22 to 24 inches. Heights are less standardized since they are determined by the needs of the users. Most people find a height somewhere between 30 and 36 in. to be convenient. If the bathroom is designed for small children, the lavatory should be lower.

High-quality lavatories are made from a number of different materials. As mentioned earlier, lavatories made of vitreous china are most expensive. Enameled cast iron, stainless steel, and simulated marble lavatories are cheaper but often of excellent quality. Frequently, the cost varies more with the design of the fixture than with the material of which it is made.

BATHTUBS AND SHOWERS

Bathtubs and shower units may be installed either separately or as combined units. Separate units are preferable where there is space for them, since each has to serve only one purpose. For example, a receptor in a shower stall is easier and safer to stand in than a bathtub that is used as a combined shower and tub.

There are several distinct types of bathtubs. The conventional, *recess-type tub* (Fig. 13–12) is rectangular and usually enclosed on three sides. Although the standard length is 5 ft., shorter (4 ft. 6 in.) tubs and longer (5 ft. 6 in.) tubs are often used. Tubs are usually 30 to 32 in. wide, with

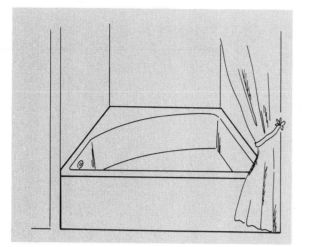

Fig. 13–13 Square bathtub

sides, 14, 15, or 16 in. high. The lower height is more convenient for washing small children, but water does splash over the side more easily than in a higher tub. *Square tubs* (Fig. 13–13) range from approximately 39 to 48 in. square. The sides are likely to be lower than those on recess-type tubs and the inside is difficult to reach for cleaning. One corner of a square tub usually is shaped into a small, diagonal seat. *Corner tubs* (Fig. 13–14) are similar to recess-type tubs except that the outside foot of the tub is finished, since the tub is designed to be enclosed on only one side and at the head. *Sunken tubs* (Fig. 13–15) are usually deeper and larger than conventional tubs and extend just above the surface of the floor. Special precautions should be taken to make a sunken tub and the area around it safe. A barrier, nonslip footing, stairs, and grab bars should all be used.

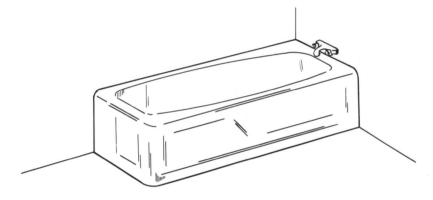

Fig. 13–14 Corner bathtub

Fig. 13–15 Sunken bathtub

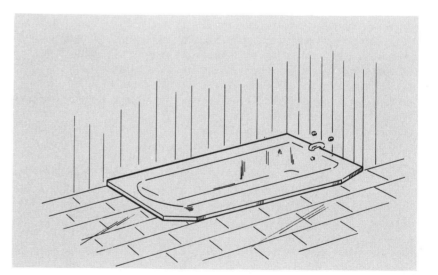

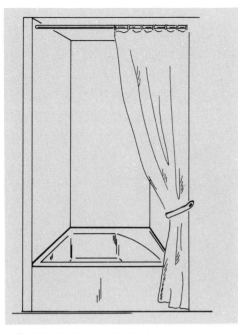

Fig. 13–16 Receptor bathtub

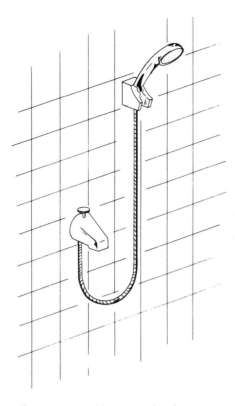

Fig. 13–18 Flexible shower head

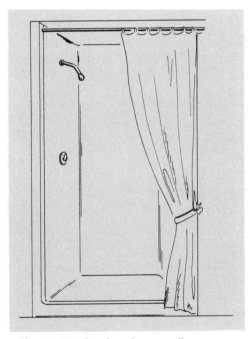

Fig. 13–17 Fiberglass shower stall

Receptor-tubs (Fig. 13–16) are designed to be used both as small tubs and as shower bases. Consequently, they are smaller than most tubs, typically 38 by 39 in., and have low, 12 in. sides.

Bathtubs are made of *enameled cast iron, enamel-coated steel,* and *fiberglass.* Enameled cast-iron tubs are the heaviest and most expensive of the group. Fiberglass tubs are unique in that they may be molded individually or as an integral part of a combined tub-shower unit (Fig. 13–17). In a custom-built installation, ceramic tile can also be used to line a tub. Whatever material is used, the surface must be acid resistant to avoid permanent stains on the finish.

Shower facilities may be built separately or combined with a bathtub. Separate shower stalls may be custom-built of ceramic tile or plastic panels, or they may be purchased in prefabricated form. Prefabricated fiberglass or metal stalls can be boxed in after they are installed to create a built-in look.

Where a shower and bathtub are combined, a receptor-tub, conventional tub, or a single, integrally molded shower-tub can be used. Ceramic tile and plastic panels are usually used to cover the wall areas around combined shower-tub units. Plastic panels are available in three-piece enclosure kits for standard-size bathtubs. Integral fiberglass units, of course, are molded to provide a continuous waterproof sheet of fiberglass from the bottom to the top of the shower.

The minimal size for comfort in a shower unit is 36 X 36 in. If there is enough room, a 42 X 42-in. or larger stall shower should be considered.

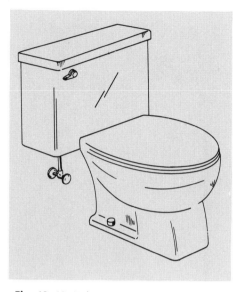

Fig. 13–19 Siphon-jet toilet

Fig. 13–20 Wall-hung toilet

Two particularly useful fittings that can be used in a shower unit are an *automatic temperature-control valve* and a *flexible shower head.* An automatic temperature-control valve will ensure that the hot and cold water are mixed so as to maintain the set temperature. For the young and the elderly, this is an important safety feature. A shower head attached to a flexible hose (Fig. 13–18) can be placed in a fixed position on the wall of the shower or moved around for shampooing and to direct the spray at different levels. This type of fitting is common in modern bathrooms in Europe. Shower heads that provide a massage spray are also available.

TOILETS

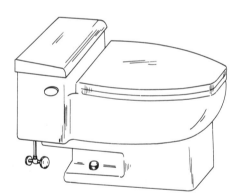

Fig. 13–21 One-piece toilet

Toilets differ more from each other than might be imagined. Besides different colors and makes, there are different types of flushing mechanisms, different methods of installation, and different ways of combining the tank and bowl.

The *siphon-jet toilet* (Fig. 13–19) has virtually replaced the old, round, *washdown toilet,* especially in remodeling. (*Reverse-trap toilets* are similar to siphon-jet toilets, but they are smaller.) In addition to having a more effective design for flushing, the siphon-jet has a larger water area and a larger trap than the washdown toilet. The larger water area keeps the bowl cleaner, and the larger trap minimizes clogging and overflowing. A siphon-jet is also quieter. Washdown toilets that are still found in older and less expensive installations should be replaced with the more sanitary siphon-jet when these baths are remodeled. There are also

other types of flush mechanisms. Some operate almost silently, some create a whirling vortex, and others use less water than conventional toilets.

The remodeler has a choice of a *floor-mounted* or *wall-hung toilet* (Fig. 13–20). A floor-mounted model will be cheaper to install if the plumbing is already roughed in under the floor, or if the previous toilet was mounted on the floor. Since wall-hung toilets are attached to wall studs, the floor under the toilet is easier to clean. For this convenience and for its design features, the homeowner will have to pay more for a wall-hung toilet than for a comparable floor-mounted model.

Although *two-piece toilets* are much more widely used, *one-piece toilets* (Fig. 13–21) are also available. In a one-piece toilet, the low tank at the rear of the toilet merges with the bowl in low-silhouetted but expensive design. Since the tank is at the same level as the bowl, the one-piece toilet is unlikely to overflow.

Almost all toilets used today are made of vitreous china, although fiberglass-reinforced plastic has been used in a few designs. Vitreous china is acid resistant and does not stain easily, but it can be cracked by a blow from a wrench or other heavy object.

MINOR ALTERATIONS

The appearance and comfort of an old bathroom can be greatly improved in a number of relatively inexpensive ways. The least expensive method is to redecorate with new materials and colors. Bright vinyl wallcoverings or subdued wood paneling can be used to improve old plaster walls. Carpeting or resilient flooring will be more comfortable underfoot and easier to clean than most older materials. New fittings and accessories, such as faucet handles, drawer pulls, towel bars, and grab bars, can also be installed. A large mirror can be used imaginatively to make the bath seem larger. Where there is room, a vanity will also provide more storage space than a wall-hung lavatory. Safety features can be built in as part of the remodeling project. If ventilation has been poor, a combined ventilating unit and ceiling light or heat lamp can also be installed. Most homeowners will be able to redecorate and make many of these minor alterations themselves.

REDECORATING

Redecorating is one of the simplest ways to improve the appearance of a bathroom. Colors and textures can be changed, decorative fittings installed, and new accessories added. Color can be used to liven up an antiseptic-looking bath or to make a small bath seem larger. Where greater elegance is desired, ornate handles and other decorative fittings (Fig. 13–22) can be used, and the walls can be covered with more formal (or dramatic) patterns. Accessories such as mirrors, racks, and holders can be used to bolster almost any style. Choose colors to create atmosphere. A color picked up from the hall or other adjoining room can be used as a background color or as an accent. Bathrooms lend themselves to using a background color for the walls or floor, either white or colored fixtures, and accent colors on accessories. (A color wheel will help you to select colors that look well together.) Light-colored walls will make a bath seem more spacious. White or neutral-colored fixtures will be less conspicuous and may be a good choice where the resale value of the house is important. Towels, carpeting or rugs, shower curtains, lids on toilet seats, and other easily replaceable items can be used to provide strong accent colors.

RECOVERING FLOORS AND WALLS

Installing flooring is a more difficult project than painting walls or hanging wallpaper. However, many types of flooring materials, as well as wallcoverings, are specially designed for easy installations.

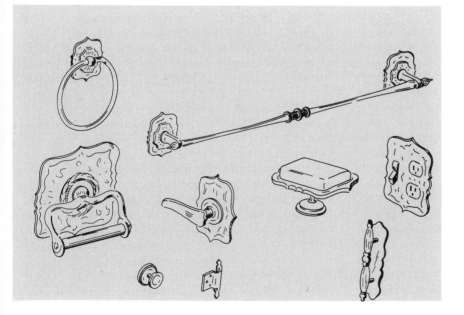

Fig. 13–22 Decorative hardware

Floors

Most bathrooms require flooring that can withstand repeated minor flooding from the shower or bathtub. A few baths can get along nicely with less sturdy materials, such as carpeting. Ceramic tiles and some types of resilient flooring (vinyl, vinyl-asbestos, and linoleum) are impervious to water and also wear well. *Ceramic floor tiles* are available in small mosaics and in larger tiles that mesh into various patterns. Most types of resilient flooring are available in tiles as well as in sheets. Many homeowners will be able to install both kinds of tiles themselves but will need professional help with sheet materials. (See Chapter 6.)

Modern *bathroom carpeting* can withstand a moderate amount of moisture and abuse and still look attractive. Furthermore, this type of carpeting is washable. The homeowner has a choice of carpeting in tile or roll form. Self-stick tiles are easier for the inexperienced person to install, but roll carpeting can be installed if there aren't too many obstructions. Cut newspapers or kraft paper to the proper pattern and cut the carpet to match. Whatever materials are used, they should be capable of withstanding the degree of moisture present in your particular bath. (See Chapter 4.)

Walls

Bathroom wallcoverings, like floor coverings, must be able to withstand heavy moisture and frequent cleaning. Paint, coated wallpaper, vinyl wallcoverings, plastic-coated hardboard, fiberglass, plywood and wooden paneling, laminated plastics, ceramic tile, and other moisture-resistant materials may be used in various combinations.

Semigloss and *gloss enamels* are much more durable than flat paints. Dirt will be less likely to stick to them and they will not rub through with frequent cleaning. Paper or fabric-backed wallcoverings must be coated or they will soon disintegrate if the shower or bath emit heavy moisture. *Vinyl wallcoverings* with fabric backings are probably the best choice. Use a mildew retardant in the paste to prevent mildew from flowing under (or on top of) the wallcovering. The walls may also be covered with *plastic-coated panels* or *fiberglass panels*. (Each manufacturer has his own system of mounting and joining these panels.) *Plywood* or *board paneling* can be used if it is protected with a moisture-proof finish. A coat of wax will be sufficient in some baths, while others will require an inpenetrable coat of polyurethane. Ceramic tile is an old but attractive standby for wall areas around the tub and shower and around the lavatory. It is seldom used alone but usually in combination with other wallcoverings. In a combined shower-bathtub installation, the tile (though expensive) should extend all the way to the ceiling. This not only protects the walls, but it unifies the appearance of the bath. (See Chapter 3.)

LIGHTING, ELECTRICAL OUTLETS, AND VENTILATION

Older bathrooms can be modernized by replacing lighting fixtures with new units, adding more electrical outlets, and installing ventilating fans. (See Chapter 9.) *Local electrical codes* are very specific about bathroom installations because of the proximity of water and electricity. Switches for the main lights, for example, may have to be placed outside the bathroom door. Codes and common sense also require that light fixtures over shower stalls or bathtubs be sealed and moisture proof.

Lighting and Electrical Outlets

A bathroom needs good, general illumination throughout the room as well as individual lighting at mirrors. Natural light will take care of *general illumination* during the daytime if the room is fortunate enough to have large clear (rather than opaque) windows or a skylight. Ceiling fixtures are necessary for general illumination at night and also to supplement natural light during the day, especially in baths with small windows. A single ceiling fixture with several incandescent bulbs (60 to 100 watts each) or two fluorescent lamps (50 watts each) will be sufficient for moderate-size bathrooms. Large bathrooms will require several ceiling fixtures, especially if the rooms are compartmented. Contemporary-styled baths often employ soffit lighting or a luminous ceiling rather than ceiling fixtures. (Fig. 13–23.) Both types of lighting create softer diffused light.

Mirror lights should be placed where they will light the face without creating shadows. Side lighting does this best. Fixtures with one or more bulbs should be installed on both sides of a mirror (Fig. 13–24(a) (b) (c)). If these fixtures are a standard 30-in. apart, single, 60-watt incandescent bulbs or a pair of 15- to 20-watt fluorescent bulbs will be bright enough. The farther apart the fixtures, the more light will be needed. Strips of incandescent bulbs give off the most flattering light. If fluorescent fixtures are used, it is best to install warm-toned bulbs. Where side lighting is not practical, a fixture placed over a mirror is second-best. Although these bulbs throw an even light over the upper parts of the face, they will create shadows under the eyebrows, nose, and chin.

Other types of lights may be required for special purposes. *Night lights* are important safety devices. A plug-in unit can be inserted in any handy outlet in the bathroom. *Heat lamps* and *sunlamps* may be installed as permanent fixtures or used as portable units. (Local codes may limit their use, however, unless they are permanently installed.)

Electrical outlets are necessary for portable hairdryers, electric shavers, and the many other electrical accessories used in the bathroom. Place the outlets where the danger of electrical shock from the plugged-in accessories will be min-

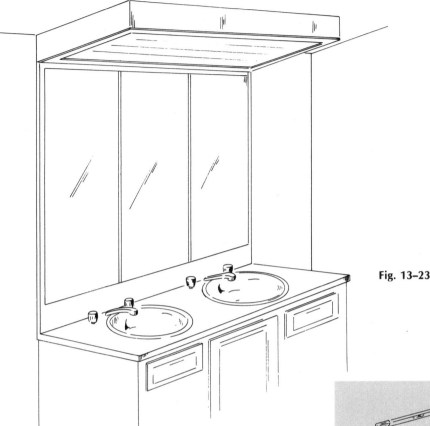

Fig. 13–23 Soffit lighting

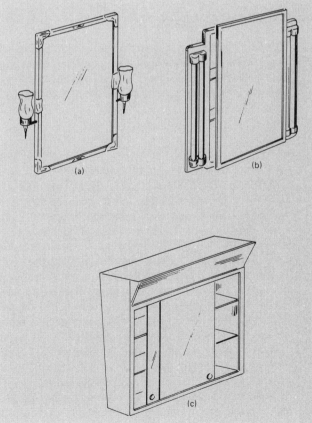

Fig. 13–24 Mirror lighting. (a) Incadescent side lighting, (b) Fluorescent side lighting, (c) Front lighting.

imal. Generally, electrical codes will require that outlets be located where appliances cannot be accidentally dropped into a tub or lavatory. (This may cause a fatal electrical shock.) Where there is room, install a mirror and outlets at a distance from the lavatory. Since some devices, such as electric toothbrushes, must be used at a lavatory, an outlet will have to be located there also.

Ventilation

A combination of windows for natural circulation and a ventilating unit for forced circulation will effectively remove odors and water vapor from the bathroom. (Windows alone are usually not enough to remove the intense vapor given off by a shower, especially in the winter.) A *ceiling* or *wall-mounted ventilating unit* (Fig. 13–25(a) (b)), in a moderate-size, 8 X 10 ft. bathroom should be capable of removing water vapor at a rate of 80 to 90 CFM (cubic feet per minute). Larger baths will require ventilators with greater capacities. Ventilating units are also made in combination with lighting fixtures and heat lamps. (Fig. 13–26). Ceiling units are generally ducted to the outside, though they may be discharged into the attic in some cases. Wall units are installed so that they discharge directly through an outside wall.

SAFETY FEATURES

The potential hazards in the bathroom of slipping and falling, receiving an electrical shock, being scalded, being cut by broken glass, being poisoned with toxic drugs, or otherwise being injured can almost be eliminated by careful attention to built-in safety features.

Standard Features

At the outset, the bathroom should be located where it is *safely accessible.* Children, the elderly, and members of the family who are sick should be able to reach the bath without having to walk through areas where they might fall. (A bathroom directly at the top of a stairway would be a disaster on several counts.) Bathrooms should have *nonslip floors.* Most standard flooring materials are safe when they are dry unless they are coated with wax or some other slippery substance. Only rugs that stay firmly in place should be used. The *bottoms of bathtubs and showers* should be surfaced with nonslip materials. In this respect, a separate shower stall is safer to use than a combined shower-bathtub. Where a combined unit is used, a *receptor-type tub* will provide safer footing than a curved-bottom bathtub. Falls can be avoided and bathing made easier by installing *grab bars* both inside and outside a shower stall or bathtub. Vertical or L-shaped bars should be attached to studs a foot or

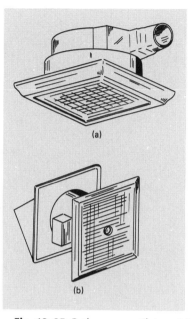

Fig. 13–25 Bathroom ventilators. (a) ceiling unit, (b) wall unit.

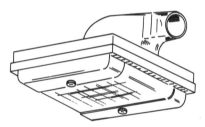

Fig. 13–26 Combined ventilator and heat lamp

so outside the shower or tub. The bather can grip the bar when entering or leaving the bath. A grab bar inside the shower or over the tub willl give the bather something secure to hold onto when he needs it. Avoid *protruding holders* of sharp-edged plastic, metal, or glass. Avoid using fixtures, shower doors, towel racks, ornamental handles, or other accessories that are made of *glass.* Windows over bathtubs are another potential danger to anyone who slips and falls.

Electrical fixtures, outlets, and appliances that are installed and used as prescribed by the local electrical code will be reasonably safe. None of these should be placed within reach of the shower or bathtub. A *night light* will give off just enough light for the bathroom to be used safely at night. To control flooding at the lavatory, tub, or toilet, *shutoff valves* must be installed where the fixtures are connected to water lines. Members of the family should also be

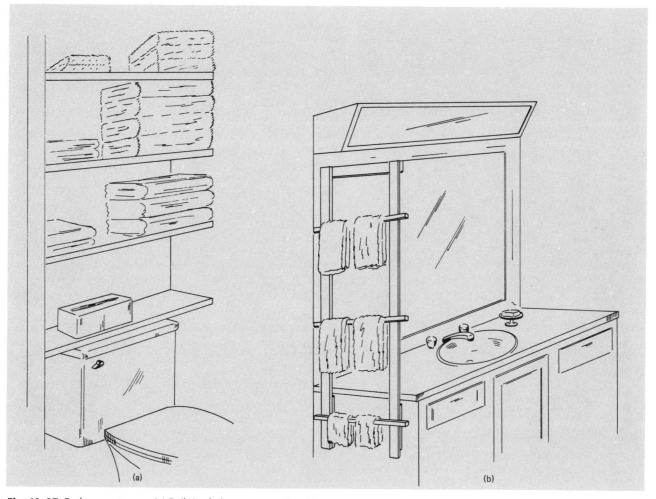

(a)

(b)

Fig. 13–27 Bathroom storage. (a) Built-in shelves over a toilet, (b) Towel ladder.

instructed how to stop the flow of water from an overflowing toilet. Finally, vanities, shower stalls, storage cabinets, and other bathroom structures should be built without *sharp edges* or *corners.*

Special Precautions

Where a bathroom is used primarily by the elderly, children, or those who are sick or otherwise infirm, special precautions must be taken to make the room safe. *Adequate space* is important. An elderly or a sick person could faint or fall down in the bathroom. A bath with a clear 8-ft. space, grab bars, no sharp corners or protusions, and reasonably soft flooring will be less dangerous in this situation. For summoning help, a button or switch for an *alarm bell* will be useful, especially if the bathroom is isolated or soundproofed.

Children can be protected from dangerous drugs by storing medications in a *locked cabinet,* either in the bathroom or in some other room. Confine an accessible medi-

cine cabinet to storage for fingernail clippers, cotton, soap, shaving gear, and what-have-you. *Dangerous cleaning supplies,* such as drain cleaners, must be stored safely away from children also.

As described in the material on bathtubs and showers, an *automatic temperature-control valve* will prevent the unwary from being scalded. The valve will keep the water at the faucet or shower head at a constant, preset temperature. This is especially important where the temperature of the hot water is close to 180 degrees and where the system is subject to sudden losses of water pressure.

STORAGE

There are a number of obvious ways to increase the storage facilities in the bathroom without major alterations to the room. *Shelves* can be built on the wall over the toilet (Fig. 13–27(a)) or in a little-used corner. *Pole-type racks* can be

Fig. 13–28 Fiberglass tub and panels

installed where they are not in the way. *Towel bars* and *ladder-type racks* (Fig. 13–27(b)) can be installed to hold towels and washcloths. *Holders* can be added for toothbrushes, soap, and magazines. *Spaces under lavatories,* if they are boxed in, will provide deep storage for cleaning supplies and surplus towels. *Old medicine cabinets* can be replaced with larger units that are recessed between the wall studs. Where there is space, vanities can be replaced or enlarged to provide additional drawer and shelf space. In large bathrooms, a utility storage cabinet with 12-in. deep shelves can be built in to hold linens, cleaning supplies, hair dryers, and other bulky items. (See Chapter 16.)

MAJOR REMODELING

Improvements that involve major changes in plumbing, relocating or replacing fixtures, moving walls, or converting other rooms into bathrooms would be considered major remodeling. Plans and budgets should be worked out carefully since the costs of labor and materials will be substantial.

PLUMBING AND FIXTURES

Homeowners who plan only to replace bathroom fixtures may find that sections of the soil pipe or water pipes have to be replaced also. In older installations, cast-iron soil pipes may have cracked, or the water pipes may be made of lead. All of these pipes must be replaced before new fixtures are installed.

Replacing Fixtures

If the existing plumbing is in good condition, an old lavatory or toilet can be replaced with a new fixture without much difficulty. Once the old lavatory is removed, a stock-type vanity or a new wall-hung lavatory can be installed. Drain and water lines can be hooked up to the old connections in a short time. Only the wall area around the new lavatory may have to be refinished to cover the exposed plaster. A new toilet can be mounted on the same floor flange as the old toilet, as long as the flange and closet bend leading to the soil pipe are in good conditions. (See Chapter 8.)

Replacing a bathtub or shower stall is difficult because of the weight of some tubs and the awkward sizes of both tubs and showers. Large, cast-iron tubs are especially heavy and should be braced against a bearing wall, if possible, to help support their weight. Fiberglass units, on the other hand, are light-weight and often come with interlocking panels to cover the walls (Fig. 13–28). If the new units are a different size or shape than the old ones, the original space for the fixture may have to be altered. The tile or plastic panels that surround the old tub will have to be modified so that the space between the edge of the tub and the walls can be sealed. Drain and water lines can usually be connected to the existing plumbing with a few extensions and adapters. (See Chapter 8.)

Changing the Layout

If the bathroom layout is to be changed, new pipes must be installed to connect the fixtures to the old lines. Lavatories, tubs, and showers will require new drain and water pipes. When a toilet is moved, a new closet bend to connect the bowl to the soil stack must be installed, also. A cold-water pipe has to be run to the wall behind the toilet tank to supply water for the tank.

When fixtures are moved, parts of the floor and walls will have to be torn out to install the new plumbing lines. Chances are, however, that the interior walls and floor are being refinished in a major remodeling job, anyway.

Plumbing in a New Bathroom

When a bedroom, closet, or other space is being converted into a bathroom, there is no choice but to have new plumbing lines run. The labor and materials will be less expensive if the new bath is on the other side of the wall from the original bath (or a kitchen). The water pipes and drains can be run through the wall and connected to the existing pipes. Venting is more complicated. Codes are generally quite strict about the permissible distance of a new fixture from an existing vent. New vents will probably have to be run, but the local code should be consulted or a plumber asked about the requirements. (Some plumbing codes require that every fixture be vented.)

EXPANDING A BATHROOM

Where more space is needed, expanding a bathroom is usually cheaper than building a completely new one. An expanded family bath can be designed so that more than one person can use it at the same time by separating the toilet and tub or shower from heavily used lavatories. (Fig. 13–29). Drawer storage in the lavatory section will also allow that part of the bath to be used as a dressing room. A bath off the master bedroom can be expanded into a more flexible compartmented bath complete with a double vanity and additional storage.

Expansion usually means moving a wall and preempting space from an adjoining room. If the adjoining room is not critically needed, or if it is large enough to give up 5 ft. or so along one wall, a new partition can be built. (Nonbearing walls are easier to move than bearing walls.) Where the opposite side of the common wall is used for closet space, the loss will be less noticeable. To make up for the loss, a smaller closet can be built in another part of the room. (In measuring space for the enlarged bathroom, remember that the plumbing wall must be much thicker than a regular wall.)

Another possibility for creating additional space is to *extend or add a wing* to a house. If a family bathroom or a master bedroom and bath are already located in a wing, ample space can be gained for a larger bath by extending an outside wall by several feet. The cost of plumbing will be kept to a minimum since the lines will have to be extended only a short distance. The outside of the house will change little in appearance if the addition is covered with the same

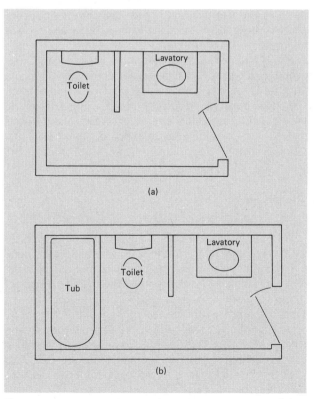

Fig. 13–29 Compartmented baths. (a) Lavatory separated from toilet, (b) Bathtub and toilet separated from lavatory

siding and roofing as the original wing. Although additions are expensive alternatives, they may be good investments if there is no other way to gain the needed space.

Installing a dormer off the bath on the second floor will be cheaper than building an addition. A dormer may provide several more feet of useable space. This will be sufficient to change a 5 X 8 ft. bathroom into a more spacious 8 X 10 ft. room. The fixtures can be relocated, and dividers and doors installed to create more flexible compartments.

INSTALLING A NEW BATHROOM

As described in the section on bathroom location, new bathrooms should be located where they are convenient to use and as close as possible to existing plumbing. For planning the types and placement of fixtures, refer to the earlier sections in this chapter that describe bathroom fixtures and layouts. When a large bath is to be added, it should be designed for multiple use. One person should be able to use a lavatory while another is using the tub or toilet. Sliding doors of wood or opaque plastic and folding doors can be used to conserve space. Sometimes, just a simple partition is required to separate the lavatory, tub-shower, and toilet areas.

Prefabricated, packaged bathroom units that provide an entire bathroom enclosure and all of the fixtures except the toilet are also available. These units are designed for relatively small baths. Since the fixtures, walls, and floor of the lower section of the bath are molded in one piece, this section is fastened in place before the upper section is attached. Fixtures must then be connected to water lines and drains and electrical cables hooked up. Once the entire unit is in place, it can be enclosed with studs. The sides of the unit are then fastened to the studs for stability and the walls covered with paneling or gypsum board.

OTHER CONSIDERATIONS

Cleaning

Bathroom remodeling should be planned so that the new fixtures and surfaces are easy to clean. Use modern, high-quality wall and floor coverings. Vinyl wallcoverings and enamel paints clean well and stand up to moisture and rubbing. Vinyl and vinyl-asbestos flooring require little maintenance. If carpeting is used, it should be designed for the moist bathroom environment and it should be washable. Good lighting and storage space for bathroom supplies and accessories will make it easier to keep the room picked up and clean. Use fixtures that clean easily and are difficult to stain. A siphon-jet toilet is an obvious choice over a washdown toilet.

Buy a lavatory of good-quality material that cleans well and is stain resistant. A conventional oblong bathtub is easier to clean than a square tub or receptor. (The interior dimensions make the sides of a square tub difficult to reach without standing inside the tub.) The problem of stained grout in a tile wall can be circumvented by using fiberglass tub and shower units or plastic-type panels on the walls. Painted surfaces will last longer and there will be fewer problems with mildew if a ventilating unit is included in the plans. A window will also contribute to better air circulation during warm weather.

Noise

Bathroom noise can be reduced by better construction. Ordinarily, the sound passes through a bathroom wall as if it were a sounding board. If an old bath has been gutted or a new bath is being installed, a double row of offset studs can be used in constructing the walls between the bath and other rooms, to reduce the transfer of sound. Wind blanket insulation between the rows of studs to absorb the sound further. (See Chapter 17.)

Other steps can be taken to reduce noise. Almost any model toilet can be purchased with a silent-flush valve, but installing a quieter type of ball-cock assembly is cheaper. If water hammer is bothersome, air chambers should be installed to absorb the force of the moving water when the water is turned off at the faucets (See Chapter 8.) Ceilings can be covered with acoustical tiles. This may be especially helpful where a bedroom is located over a first-floor bathroom that is used late at night or early in the morning. (See Chapters 2, 3.)

Heating

Bathrooms are generally easy to heat because of their small size. Locating the heating units may be a problem because so much of the wall area is occupied. There is usually space for small baseboard units to be installed along the floor either against a wall or recessed under the edge of a cabinet. Radiant heating can be installed in the ceiling, just as in any other room. (See Chapter 6.) For quick response, heating lamps can be installed in ceiling fixtures. These lamps will make a bath much more comfortable on a cool day when the central heating system is not in operation.

Laundry Facilities

Laundry facilities may be installed in a bathroom (if there is enough space) to reduce the cost of running separate plumbing lines to another part of the house. To maintain a traditional bathroom decor, sliding or hinged doors can be used to hide the washer and dryer.

14 Remodeling Attics

One of the least expensive ways of creating more living space is to remodel an unfinished attic. Attics in some types of houses, such as traditionally designed capes, are often left unfinished intentionally by the builder so that they can be turned into bedrooms or other living spaces as more room is needed. In an expansion attic, plumbing may already be roughed in from the bathroom on the floor below, while gable windows and dormers are usually built as part of the original construction.

Before the advent of effective insulation, the air space in the attic served as a buffer between the heated rooms below and the outside air above. Since fiberglass and other types of insulation do the job much better, the attic can be put to more valuable uses. Because of its location, the attic lends itself to conversion to bedrooms, a den, a playroom, rooms for hobbies, and even a small apartment, if the space is large enough. A moderate-size attic will hold two 8 X 10 ft bedrooms and a 5 X 5 ft bath (Fig. 14–1). An attic also offers the kind of isolation from the rest of the house that is usually preferred for a den or playroom. Insulation under the attic floor, and perhaps in the ceilings below, will help soundproof the rooms.

A small apartment with a living area, bedroom, kitchenette, and bathroom may require more space than is originally available. One method of increasing the amount of space is to build a shed-type dormer along the back of the house. This will increase the head-room and allow the entire floor area to be used, out to the outer rear wall.

Besides serving as a buffer, attics traditionally are ideal storage places. Old furniture, books, clothes, toys, and out-of-season sporting equipment can be more or less dumped on the floor along the eaves and ignored, until someone gets the urge to clean the attic. Although this storage may be extremely convenient, it isn't a very economical use of valuable space. In remodeling, storage areas should be built in to hold this paraphernalia. The empty spaces behind the knee walls are especially suitable for boxes and long awkward things like skis and bed slats.

Building codes, in most localities, have sections that govern the methods of construction, types of finishing materials, electrical wiring, plumbing, and the means of access and escape in remodeling attics. Actually, the code is a valuable guide for safe and reliable construction. If the attic is being converted into a small apartment, consult the local zoning ordinances to see if the apartment can be rented. Though members of the family may plan to use the apartment at present, the situation may change in the future. If the zoning ordinances permit two-family dwellings, a small apartment will undoubtedly increase the resale value of the house, also.

The cost of converting an attic into more useful living space depends on who does the job and how complicated the plans are. If the homeowner does all but the more complicated or technical work, the costs will be minimal. The most expensive phases will be the installation of plumbing, electricity, and heat. Beyond that, the remaining costs are for framing materials, plywood, insulation, and interior finishing materials. The cost of remodeling will jump considerably if a dormer has to be installed, the roof raised, or new roofing put on by a professional. Carrying out these more complicated alterations usually requires previous experience, though a particularly capable homeowner might be able to construct a satisfactory gable-type dormer on his first attempt. Compared with buying a larger house or building an addition, however, the cost of remodeling an attic into living space that can be used day-in and day-out can be a bargain.

This chapter summarizes the steps necessary in converting attics into living spaces: evaluating the suitability of an attic for conversion; planning the layout; carrying out the construction in a definite sequence.

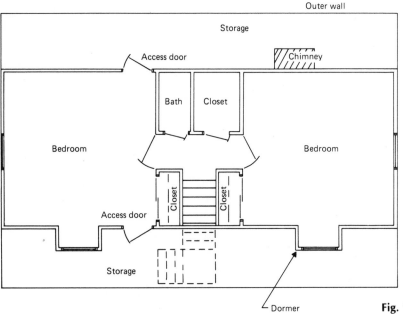

Fig. 14–1 Floor plan for two bedrooms and bath

EVALUATING THE ATTIC SPACE

One of the first steps is to evaluate the attic to see if it is suitable for its intended use. There must be sufficient floor area and head-room for the living spaces. These depend mainly on the size of the house and type of roof. There should be a standard-size stairway or, at least, room for one to be built. The structural members of the floor and roof should be of adequate size for a living space and the roof should be in good condition. Undersized joists and beams can be reinforced, if necessary. If utilities are to be installed, connections must be accessible. Access to heat and plumbing may be a problem in some attics. For light and natural ventilation, the attic should be adaptable to medium-size gable windows and, if necessary, gable or shed dormers.

FLOOR SPACE AND HEAD-ROOM

The rooms in a finished attic will be bounded by knee walls that extend from the sloping roof to the floor several feet inward from the eaves. These walls are usually built at a point where the roof is at least 4 ft above the floor. The ceiling may follow the slope of the rafters for a distance and then level off (Fig. 14–2). The ceiling height should be about 7 ft 6 in. where there is full head-room, though much of the sloped ceiling may be lower.

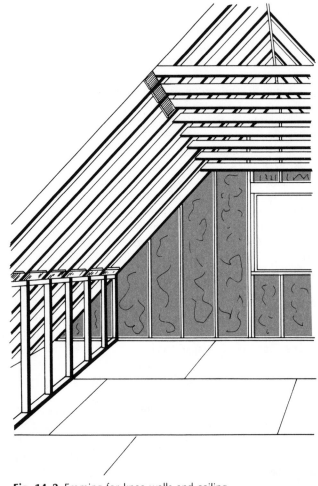

Fig. 14–2 Framing for knee walls and ceiling

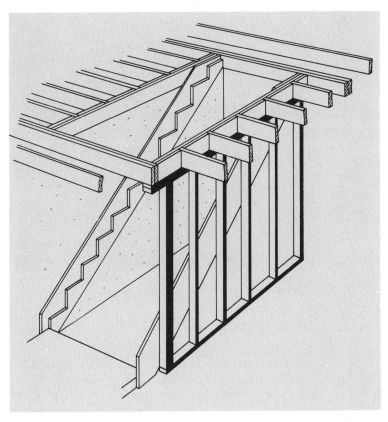

Fig. 14–3 Structure of attic stairway

With the standard heights for knee walls and ceilings in mind, measure the perimeter of the usable floor space. Transfer these dimensions to a sheet of paper (graph paper is best) and draw in boundaries for the rooms. Allow space for the entrance to the stairway. If there is not enough space for the rooms because of the lack of head-room, consider building a shed dormer along the width of the attic. This will provide full head-room from the ridge to the rear wall of the house. Another alternative to consider is raising the roof. The raised roof will have a shallow slope from the ridge to the front or rear wall, where large windows can be installed for light and ventilation.

STAIRWAYS

The stairway to the attic should be of comparable quality with the finished rooms (Fig. 14–3). A full-width stairway will allow bulky furniture and building materials to be moved without undue difficulty. (The attic rooms should be directly accessible from the stairs, since there is seldom room for a hallway in the attic.) This is more easily arranged with a central stairway that allows rooms to be built on both sides. A stairway at the end of an attic will pose problems in planning the layout. Local building codes may require more than one means of escape from a finished attic, such as a second, narrower stairway or an outside fire escape.

STRUCTURAL SOUNDNESS

Inspect the floor joists, rafters, collar beams, and the roof. For spaces used as living areas, the floor joists should be at least 2 X 8 in. in size. If they are smaller, they can be reinforced with bracing installed every 16 in. Rafters and reinforcing horizontal collar beams should be in good condition. Neither should be cut or removed in the process of finishing the attic, except when a dormer is installed. To avoid damage to finished ceilings, both the wooden sheathing and the roofing itself must also be in good condition. If water seeps through the roof after the attic is finished, the leaks will be difficult to trace.

ADAPTABILITY FOR UTILITIES, WINDOWS, AND DORMERS

In evaluating an attic, review the requirements for utilities, light, and ventilation. Electrical cables can be run to the attic without difficulty, if they aren't already present. There should be at least two general-purpose circuits, in addition to special circuits needed for air conditioners or kitchen appliances. Plumbing may already be roughed in. If not, pipes can be extended upward from a lower bathroom or kitchen. The bath or kitchen facilities in the attic should be placed where they can be tied into the soil stack. For heat,

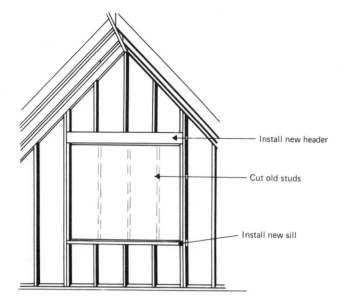

Fig. 14–4 Enlarging opening for attic window

Install new header

Cut old studs

Install new sill

Fig. 14–6 Shed dormer

Fig. 14–5 Gable dormer

consider both the present central heating system and the possibility of a separate system. If the present system lacks the necessary capacity, or if distribution to the attic is a problem, a separate unit such as an electrical baseboard heater can be installed.

For light and ventilation, plan on installing large windows (Fig. 14–4). These can be used to replace the typical, small attic windows at the gable ends of the attic. Where more light or a broader distribution of light is required, consider the feasibility of installing gable dormers (Fig. 14–5). These will let in light and fresh air but they won't affect the head-room. If a higher ceiling is required, a shed dormer (Fig. 14–6) or raised roof should be considered.

PLANNING AND CONSTRUCTION

There are decisions and plans to be made before construction actually begins. Different types of materials should be looked over and selected, sketches and working plans drawn, and costs calculated. The actual construction may be carried out by a contractor or by the homeowner with the assistance of professionals to install plumbing, heat, and electricity.

PLANNING

The feasibility of bedrooms, a small apartment, or other spaces depends on the family's immediate and future needs for space, the size and condition of the attic, and the cost of the alternatives that are being considered. If there are children in the family, consider how their needs for play space, bedrooms, and privacy will change during the next five to ten years. If an evaluation of the attic indicates that a shed dormer is necessary in order to provide the space required, the cost of building the dormer and recovering part of the roof must be taken into account. As a long-term improvement, installing a shed dormer or raising the rooof may be a good investment.

Use the measurements of the floor space and headroom to prepare sketches of the proposed rooms. Floor plans drawn on graph paper should show the knee walls, partitions, windows, dormers, doors, and utility outlets. Graph paper with ¼-in. squares will allow the plans to be drawn on a scale of ¼ in. to 1 ft. (A 16 X 32-ft floor space, for example, would be drawn as a 4 X 8-in. rectangle.) Also, draw elevations to show vertical cross sections of the space. These will indicate the heights of the windows, doors, and knee walls. As plans for the work are developed, construction details can be added to the drawings. When the drawings are complete, they can be used as working drawings for purchasing the materials and for construction.

CONSTRUCTION

In finishing an attic, construction generally takes the following sequence: installing subflooring; building knee walls and partitions; framing in windows and doors; installing louvers in the tops of the gables; installing ceiling joists if necessary; roughing in electrical cables, plumbing, and heat ducts or pipes; putting up insulation, furring out studs and ceiling joists or collar beams; installing wall and ceiling materials; constructing built-ins; installing bathroom fixtures, electrical outlets and fixtures, and kitchen appliances; painting; putting down carpeting or a finished floor.

Subflooring

Before subflooring is installed, plumbing and other utilities must be roughed in and insulation placed between the joists. Either use loose insulation or staple blanket insulation to the joists. The vapor barrier should face the rooms below. (See Ch. 6.)

Floor joists that are smaller than 2 X 8 in. should be reinforced with bracing to provide a sturdy floor for the new living space. Use 2 X 4-in., 2 X 6-in. or 2 X 8-in. braces placed 16 in. on center between the joists. Cover the joists and bracing with panels of ¾-in. plywood staggered so that the ends of adjacent panels will not butt at the same seam (Fig. 14–7). Butt the edges of the panels over joists and nail them in place with 8d box nails. Extending the subflooring to the outer walls allows the floor space around the edge of the attic to be used for storage. (See Ch. 4.)

Knee Walls

To establish the location of the knee walls, mark rafters at both ends of the attic at the desired height above the subfloor. Drop a plumb bob from the marked points to the subfloor to establish a line for a base plate or sole (Fig. 14–8). Snap a chalk line between these two points. With the chalk line as a guide, nail the base plate through the subfloor to the joists with 16d box nails.

The studs can be nailed either directly to the rafters or to a top plate attached horizontally across the rafters (Fig. 14–9). If the rafters are not spaced at the desired 16 in. on center, a top plate is preferable since it will allow the proper spacing. Each stud must be cut exactly to length so as to be plumb. Toenail the bottom of the studs to the base plate and nail the top to the rafters or top plate. Allow space for framing in access doors to storage areas behind the knee walls.

Partitions

Partitions between rooms or between finished and unfinished sections of the attic consist of a base plate nailed to the floor, studs, and a top plate (Fig. 14–10). Attach the top plate to the rafters, ceiling joists, or collar beams as required by the location of the partition. Studs should be placed every 16 in. on center.

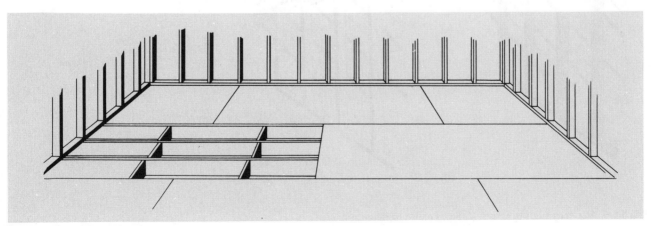

Fig. 14–7 Plywood subflooring

Fig. 14–8 Locating the knee walls

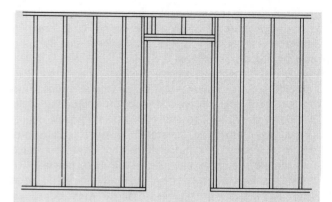

Fig. 14–10 Framework for partition

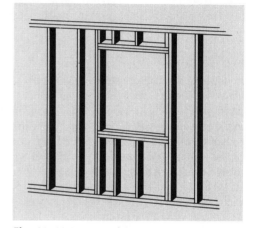

Fig. 14–11 Window framing

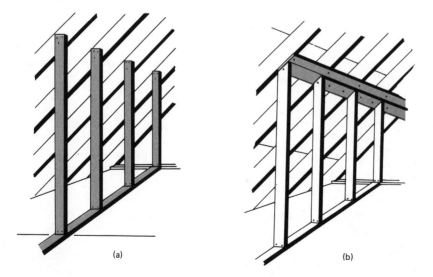

Fig. 14–9 Attaching studs to rafters. (a) Studs nailed to rafters, (b) Studs nailed to top plate.

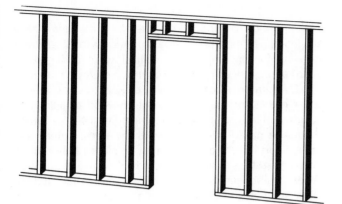

Fig. 14–12 Doorway framing

Framing Windows, Doors, and Louvers

Windows at the gable ends of the attic should be removed and the studs cut to frame in new windows.(See Ch. 7.) With the new frame as a guide, install a double header, double studs on both sides, and a double 2 X 4 sill below the frame (Fig. 14–11). Doorways in partitions should also be framed in. Install double studs on both sides, and a double header at the top, and remove the section of base plate nailed to the subfloor (Fig. 14–12). Space for louvers should also be framed in at each end of the attic. The louvers can then be fastened in place to ventilate the space above the ceilings (Fig. 14–13). Ventilation to the outside is necessary wherever there is moisture in the air to avoid condensation and consequent rotting of rafters and sheathing.

Ceiling Joists and Collar Beams

If the collar beams are already at the desired height, they can be used as supports for the ceiling. Otherwise, ceiling joists should be nailed to the rafters at the proper height.

Roughing in Utilities

Before the walls or ceiling are covered, electrical cables, water pipes and drains, vents, and heating ducts or pipes must be connected to the utilities previously roughed in at floor level. Outlet and switch boxes, ceiling boxes, and other electrical units should also be installed. Plumbing lines must be accessible between the studs for hooking up fixtures when the walls are finished. (See Ch. 6, 8, 9.)

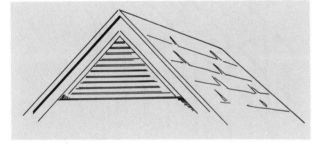

Fig. 14–13 Attic louver

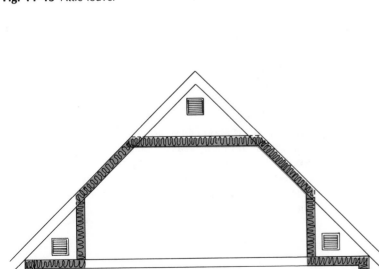

Fig. 14–14 Cross section of insulated attic

Insulation

The walls and ceiling areas exposed to unheated spaces must be insulated (Fig. 14–14). Staple blanket or batt-type insulation between the ceiling joists or collar beams, and between the wall studs. (The space between the floor joists should have been insulated before the subflooring was installed.) Turn the aluminum or asphalt-impregnated vapor barrier toward the heated area; moisture will then be contained within the attic. If insulation is placed between the rafters, space should be left between the sheathing and the surface of the insulation for the air to circulate. Otherwise, the insulation and sheathing will become damp. Insulation faced with aluminum foil should also be spaced a half-inch or so from the interior wall so that the foil can reflect heat back into the room. Fit loose bits of insulation around the pipes, cables, and fixtures to make the seal as uniform as possible. (See Ch. 6.)

ceal, and there is considerable waste of paneling in cutting and fitting. The most practical compromise is to use grooved paneling for uncomplicated, vertical walls and gypsum board or ungrooved plywood for angled or sloped surfaces.

Gypsum board can be nailed directly to studs, rafters, collar beams, or ceiling joists; but plywood paneling and acoustical tiles usually require furring (Fig. 14–15). Furring should be nailed perpendicular to the studs, rafters, and joists. Short lengths of furring must be placed between the long furring strips to support the ends of the panels and tiles. Where wall materials are attached directly to the studs or joists, short lengths of 2 X 4 should also be nailed between these members to support the ends of the panels (Fig. 14–16). Suspended ceilings can be attached to the walls by using beveled moldings to make the angles at the walls plumb. (See Ch. 3.)

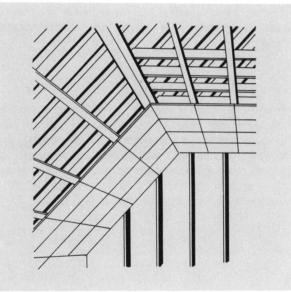

Fig. 14–15 Ceiling tiles mounted on furring

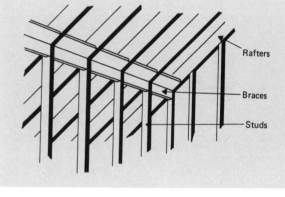

Fig. 14–16 Bracing between studs

Ceilings and Walls

How ceilings and walls are installed depends on the type of materials that are used. Gypsum board is preferable to grooved plywood paneling in many cases. Plywood paneling is difficult to fit to angled walls and sloped ceilings. Panel grooves run in different directions, edges are hard to con-

Finishing the Interior

Once the walls and ceilings are in place, the interior of the attic can be finished. Walls should be painted or papered (except where paneling is used), bathroom fixtures and kitchen appliances installed, doors hung, molding installed, heating units hooked up, and carpeting or other finish flooring placed over the subflooring.

15 *Remodeling Basements*

Basement spaces are often wasted. They are generally used only for plumbing lines, heating systems, rough storage, and, occasionally, for workshops. Since the amount of floor space in a basement is approximately the same as that above it on the first floor, there is ample room for converting the space to more useful purposes. This chapter describes how to plan the conversion, common problems to look for and how to solve them, and the sequence of work that should be followed.

PLANNING

Plans for remodeling basements must take into account not only the types of rooms or facilities that are to be built but also questions about who will do the work, what the costs will be, how much time will be involved, what specific steps will be required, and whether a remodeled basement will be more useful than one that is left unfinished.

TYPES OF ROOMS AND FACILITIES

Basements lend themselves to conversion to certain types of spaces better than to others. (Fig. 15–1). There is plenty of space for a large family room or game room. The walls and floors are sturdy and can take the abuse of active games. A den or TV room will be away from the active hustle and bustle of the rest of the house, and rooms for hobbies such as sewing, photography, or collecting will have the necessary privacy. Doors can be locked to keep children from

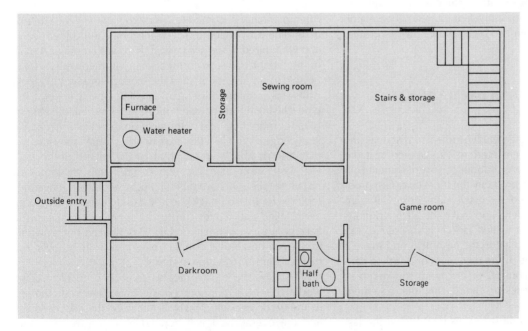

Fig. 15–1 Floor plan for remodeled basement

handling equipment that is easily damaged or that might be dangerous to them. Sawdust, the noise of power tools, and the customary stacks of boards are at home in a basement workshop. More ambitiously, a basement can be converted into a small apartment if the problems of access and natural light can be solved. Such an apartment would be useful for an extended family or for rental income. (Before planning the conversion as a *specific* source of income, however, investigate local zoning laws!)

Another possibility is to remodel only part of the basement. This will reduce the time and cost and leave an unfinished section of the basement for storage. If space for expansion is needed later, the remainder of the basement can be finished.

Regardless of how the basement is finished, it should provide adequate storage. Outdoor equipment such as lawnmowers, stepladders, hoses, and the like, can be kept in built-in storage lockers. Shelves and drawers should also be built in, to house the innumerable small items found in most basements. Further storage spaces can be incorporated within the partitions that are built around the furnace area, under the stairway, and overhead between the joists.

The layout of the rooms and storage spaces must take into account the locations of supporting posts, beams, and utilities. Some posts can be enclosed within partitions; others can be boxed in. Try to plan the layout so that posts do not interfere with open spaces required for table tennis or other space-consuming games. If kitchen facilities or a bath are to be installed, plan to place them next to the water lines and drains; this will reduce the cost of plumbing. The stairs from the floor above should open into a public area, such as a family room or hallway, rather than into one of several, smaller rooms set aside for individual interests. These individual rooms should open into a common hallway or other public area.

RECOGNIZING AND SOLVING PROBLEMS

The basement should be carefully studied to discover any physical problems that might interfere with converting it into finished rooms. Dampness or flooding, a low basement ceiling, and poor lighting are probably the most common problems that are encountered. Excessive dampness will warp paneling, encourage mildew, and make the air uncomfortable in both summer and winter. Flooding, of course, can damage just about everything in the basement and make it completely uninhabitable. If the dampness or flooding cannot be brought under control, or if it costs too much to control them, then plans for remodeling the basement should be dropped.

Basement ceilings in most houses built within the last fifty years are about seven feet high. Ceiling joists in older

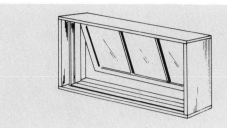

Fig. 15–2 Standard-size basement window

houses, however, may be so low that it is impossible to walk around the basement without stooping. If the joists are much below seven feet, it may not be practical to remodel the basement at all. Pipes and ducts will hang down even lower and a finished room will feel cramped. Although the ceiling height can be increased by lowering the basement floor, the amount of floor space is reduced by the offset at the foundation walls. Excavating is expensive, however.

Standard-size basement windows (Fig. 15–2) are usually too small to provide sufficient light. In most cases, these windows can be replaced with larger windows by enlarging the openings in the masonry. If the windows can't be enlarged, or if the process is too time-consuming or expensive, the use of the basement will be limited.

Similarly, other problems that may interfere with the use of the basement should be confronted at the planning stage and resolved.

TIME AND MONEY

After planning is complete, homeowners will be able to determine how much of the work they can do themselves and what hired labor will cost. If there are no major repairs or alterations to be performed, many homeowners should be able to do just about all of the work themselves. Building walls and partitions, putting up a ceiling, boxing in posts and pipes, laying floors, hanging doors, and finishing the interior requires more time and determination than skill or technical knowledge. With a little experience, some homeowners may also be able to install some of the utilities. If they can use plastic or copper pipe, they can run lines for lavatories. Installing toilets is more difficult because of the connections required for the soil stack. Electrical outlets and switches can be installed and cables run to the service entrance in the basement for additional circuits. Experienced homeowners may even be able to connect basement heating units into their present distribution systems.

Usually, the most practical solution is to hire skilled workmen for the more complicated tasks and to do the rest of the work yourself. This will minimize the cost of labor, and the overall cost will depend more on the type and quantity of materials that are used.

FINAL PREPARATIONS

If the layout is satisfactory, if there are no major obstacles to converting the basement, and if the budget is acceptable, the homeowner can prepare to start construction. The basement should be cleaned out and minor repairs made to the walls and floor, where necessary. Working drawings should be prepared as a guide to ordering materials and to the actual construction. The building inspector may want to look at these before issuing a building permit. He may suggest changes that would reduce costs or improve the plans.

The sequence of work should be established. Tasks that are to be performed by plumbers and electricians should be scheduled for completion before the walls and ceiling are covered. Lumber, paneling, gypsum board, electrical supplies, and other materials that are to be used can be purchased and stored in the basement so that they will be available when they are needed. Plywood paneling must adjust to the temperature and humidity of the basement before it is installed. When the basement is clear and the plans have been approved by the building inspector, the work can begin.

COMMON BASEMENT PROBLEMS

If serious problems turn up during the planning phase, they should be resolved before going any farther. Several typical problems and their possible solutions are described below.

DAMPNESS AND FLOODING

Dampness may be caused by internal moisture in the basement or by moisture entering from the outside. Internal moisture can readily be brought under control, but moisture seeping in from the outside is usually more difficult to stop.

Condensation on cold masonry walls and cold-water pipes can be prevented by drying the air and insulating the pipes. A dehumidifier or air conditioner will remove moisture from the air during the warm summer months. As an additional precaution, wrap fiberglass or another type of insulation around the cold-water pipes to prevent the warm air from condensing on the cold surfaces. During the winter, moisture and condensation can be reduced by a good heating system. The present system may be extended, or a small, independent unit can be used to heat only the basement. (See Ch. 6.)

The control of *moisture that enters from the outside* depends on the source of the moisture. Water that leaks in from gutters and downspouts can be channeled away from

the house to a downslope catch-basin or drainage area. Water that comes from a high water table or an underground stream in the vicinity of the basement has the help of gravity to push its way through cracks and pores in the basement walls and floor. To seal out this type of water, the walls and floor must be made water-tight. If the soil around the outside of the foundation walls drains poorly, trenches should be dug next to the foundation and drains placed around the footings. Cracks in the walls should be repaired and the exterior of the foundation waterproofed. This is generally a job that requires professional equipment and skills. A reputable company will guarantee the water-tight integrity of the wall once they have waterproofed it. Although waterproofing materials and sealers can be applied to the inside walls, they are not as effective as external waterproofing. Cracks in the floor and in inside walls should be cleaned out and repaired with hydraulic cement. If water continues to rise through the floor, a two-inch layer of concrete can be poured over the entire basement floor after it has been coated with waterproofing. (See Ch. 10.)

Periodic flooding in the basement may be eliminated by the same measures used to keep out water that is under hydrostatic pressure. Installing drains around the foundation footings, waterproofing the outside walls, filling the trench with gravel and sand, and repairing cracks with hydraulic cement will create a water-tight barrier. If a small amount of water continues to rise through the floor, a sump pump may be used to keep it under control.

LOW CEILINGS

If the joists are less than seven feet above the floor, the ceiling will be too low for the basement to be remodeled in a normal manner. The only practical way of increasing the height is to excavate part or all of the basement floor. In this case, a one-foot wide strip next to the foundation wall must be left intact to ensure the stability of the walls.

If the joists are high enough but the pipes and ducts hang below the joists so that they interfere with the headroom, the problem is easier to solve. Pipes and ducts that run in the same direction as the joists can be moved so that they run between the joists. Notches can be cut for those pipes that run perpendicular to the joists, so that the pipes can be raised. Pipes can also be rerouted and placed next to the walls and partitions. The most practical way to handle a soil pipe, because of its size and slope, is to box it in or enclose it in a storage area.

WINDOWS

Small basement windows are designed to ventilate an unfinished basement but not to illuminate the area. Without more

Fig. 15–3 Enlarged window in light well

natural light during the day, the basement rooms are likely to convey a feeling of being hemmed in. If the windows are well above the ground level, the openings should be enlarged and larger windows installed. Where the basement walls are almost completely below grade, light wells can be dug and oversize windows mounted in the walls (Fig. 15–3). Light wells must be well drained and lined with materials such as brick or concrete. If a house is on a slope, large windows or sliding glass doors can be installed on the downslope side of the basement. A downslope exposure is also an ideal location for a patio or garden. Where large sections of masonry are removed for windows, beams or girders will have to be installed over the openings for additional support.

STORAGE

It is important not to underestimate the need for storage space. Perhaps the best way to determine the amount and type of storage that will be needed is to take a rough inventory of the things that are already in the basement. Some things can be stored elsewhere or thrown out. For most of the things stored there, however, the basement is probably the best place. It will be an even better storage area for such items as clothing and books after it is remodeled. If the basement is to be only partially remodeled, shelves and hangers can be built in the unfinished section. Large equipment, such as lawnmowers, gardening tools, and wheelbarrows can be stored in this section, also. Lumber can be stacked on hangers between joists or on shelves projecting out from the walls. Within the remodeled area, built-ins, such as floor-to-ceiling and wall-to-wall cabinets, can be used to increase storage space. Use the enclosed space beneath stairways for large items as well as clothing (Fig. 15–4).

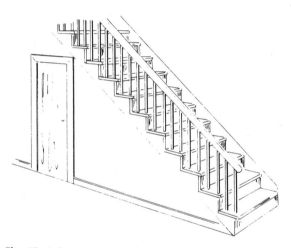

Fig. 15–4 Storage area under stairway

ACCESS

Building codes often require two means of exit from an inhabited basement—usually a stairway and an outside entry. The stairway from the main level of the house should be wide and attractive, especially if basement rooms are to be used by guests or relatives. An old, utilitarian stairway should be widened and replaced with a stock staircase. To be safe and functional, the new stairway should be at least three feet wide, well-lighted, carpeted, protected by handrails and not too steep. If the stairs are steep or narrow, they will limit the use of the basement rooms. The location of the entrance to the stairs can also cause difficulty. The stairs should be easily accessible from the first floor.

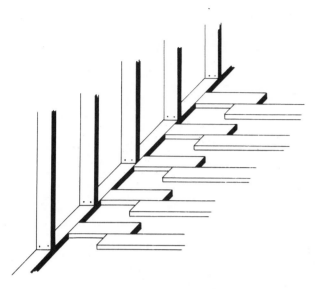

Fig. 15–5 Covering a basement floor

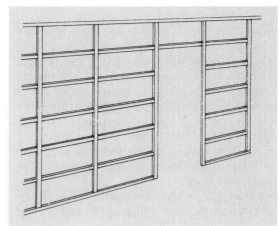

Fig. 15–6 Furring a basement wall

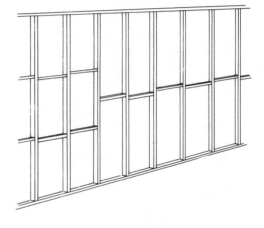

Fig. 15–7 Frame work for a partition

SEQUENCE OF WORK

Once the homeowner decides that remodeling the basement is feasible and that the inherent problems can be solved, the sequence of work can be established.

Problems that require *major repairs* or *structural changes* should be tackled first. Basement walls should be repainted and waterproofed, if necessary. Floors should be sealed and sump pumps installed where required. Outside entryways should be built and larger windows installed. The structural strength of the foundation walls can be preserved by mounting beams over the new openings. Stairways should be widened or rebuilt. If pipes, ducts, or other utilities intrude on the space to be remodeled, these must be relocated before construction begins.

Utilities should be roughed in at an early stage. Run pipes from the main system to the areas where the lavatories, sinks, and toilets are to be installed. Heating ducts or pipes should be connected to the heating units located in the basement. Electrical cables do not have to be roughed in until studs and furring are installed.

Basement floors can be painted, finished with tiles, covered with indoor-outdoor carpeting, or built up with 2 X 4's and plywood to make the surface drier and warmer. If the floor is to be covered with plywood, it should be prepared before the walls and partitions are constructed. Seal the concrete with a waterproof substance (such as a mastic), cover it with sheets of polyethylene, and lay a network of wooden screeds (Fig. 15–5). Exterior-grade plywood should be nailed over the screeds so that the panels are staggered. Butt their edges along the screeds. (See Ch. 4.)

Basement *walls* should be waterproofed with a waterproof paint and sheets of polyethylene, if necessary. Furring can be attached with masonry nails, adhesive, or other types of masonry fasteners (Fig. 15–6). Attach a horizontal furring strip an inch or so above the floor and another at the level of the ceiling. Other horizontal strips must be mounted in between at 16-in. intervals. Vertical strips should be attached wherever panel edges need support. If the dampness problem has been solved, gypsum board, plywood paneling, or hardboard can be installed safely. Space the lower edge of the panel an inch above the floor to protect it from water that may spill on the floor. (See Ch. 3.)

Partitions can be constructed and nailed to joists or beams (Fig. 15–7). Use 2 X 4's for the base and top plates. The base plate can be nailed to the concrete floor with masonry nails. Studs should be placed 16 in. on center with double studs and a double header used to frame doors. Partitions can be covered with the same paneling as the furred walls, after the electrical cables and boxes have been installed.

Ceilings can be installed after all of the electrical fixtures and pipes are in position. Tiles (Fig. 15–8) and plywood paneling require furring, but gypsum board can be attached directly to the joists. Suspended ceilings are probably the easiest to install. The angles are nailed to the walls at the desired height and wire hangers attached to the joists to support the framework of runners and cross tees. Pipes and cables above the ceiling can be reached easily by removing the ceiling panels.

Built-in storage areas should be constructed before the walls are painted or the floor is finished. Shelves, closets, drawers, access doors, and utility cabinets may take considerable time to build. Finally, *doors* must be hung, *molding* cut and put up, the *walls* and *woodwork painted,* and *carpeting* laid.

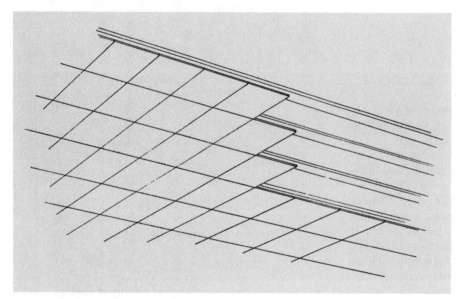

Fig. 15–8 Tile ceiling

16 Storage

The problem of storage is usually two-fold. First, storage facilities are often insufficient to hold the many things that have to be stored. Secondly, even where there is a reasonable amount of storage space, belongings tend to accumulate until they overwhelm whatever facilities there are.

The most practical solution to this problem is to provide several types of storage in at least minimal amounts, as well as to develop some method of organizing and setting priorities for storage so that these facilities will not become overcrowded. This chapter lists several guidelines that can be followed in planning storage facilities and describes some basic types of units that can be used.

GENERAL GUIDELINES

To be workable, a storage plan must make adequate provisions for storing things according to how often they are used. Storage should be provided for those things that are to be *actively used,* those that are to be *used only seasonally,* and those that are to be kept in *dead storage.* Things that are actively and frequently used, obviously, should be kept where they will be accessible. Also, they are more likely to be used if they are kept in the open where they are visible. Shelves and drawers in children's rooms, for example, should not be cluttered with toys that have been outgrown, but should be used for possessions that are currently in favor (Fig. 16–1). Further, children are more likely to use toys that are kept where they can be seen.

To supplement wall storage in a children's room you might consider adding drawer space under a bed. Ideal for either toys that have been outgrown or clothing, under-the-bed drawers are simple plywood cases, usually

with two large drawers mounted on full extension ball-bearing slides. Each drawer has two removable trays for organizing the storage space for smaller items. The drawers add both order and convenience under a standard twin-size bed.

In finishing your under-the-bed storage drawers, you might take a little extra time to sand off any splinters that could stab small fingers. The drawer fronts, which show under the edge of the bed when the drawer is pushed in, can be finished to match the bed. You may want to finish the case side of the drawer at the foot-end of the bed—if it also shows.

Fig. 16–1 Shelf and cabinet storage in children's room

Fig. 16–2 Adjustable, wall-hung shelves

Sports equipment, clothing, and other things that are used seasonally may require two storage areas: one for off-season storage and the other for periods of active use. Some storage spaces will serve both purposes. Basement and garage storage are often used for active as well as for out-of-the-way, off-season storage. Anything that isn't used at least once a year should either be thrown out, given away, or consigned to dead storage. Use the less-accessible corners of basements and attics, as well as awkwardly high shelves, for these things. Periodically, the contents of dead-storage areas should be sorted through, to prevent the spaces from becoming stagnant and therefore useless for new storage.

The design and size of the storage units should be determined by the *sizes* and *shapes* of the things that are to be stored. Shelves, for example, might be spaced at different heights for reference books, nails and screws and paint cans (Fig. 16–2). To hold this variety of sizes, the shelves should be built 8 to 12 in. deep and spaced vertically from 8 to 14 in.

Whether storage units should be *open* or *closed* depends on what is being stored. Clothing and other items that must be protected from dust should be stored in closed containers. In the kitchen, use closed cabinets rather than open shelves, to keep dishes and glassware clean. Open storage is often best for equipment that is used daily or where dust is not a problem.

Storage units may be either *built-in* or constructed so that they are *movable*. Built-in units (Fig. 16–3) are attached to the interior walls or floors and become part of the house, while movable units remain mobile and flexible. Built-ins are more appropriate for homeowners who expect to remain in

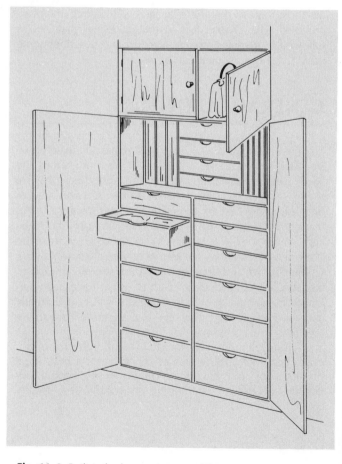

Fig. 16–3 Built-in bedroom storage cabinet

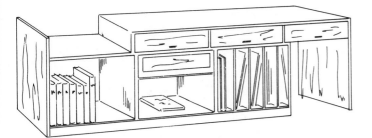

Fig. 16–4 Sectional stereo cabinet

the same house for several years. Often, such units can be built into an unused corner or wall so that they don't intrude onto crowded floor areas or they can be used as room dividers. Attractive built-ins can also enhance the interior design of a room. Where flexibility is important, sectional furniture (Fig. 16–4), variable shelving systems, chests, and cabinets can be used. Units such as these can also be moved along with other furniture when a house is sold.

Locate storage units in *spaces that would otherwise be wasted.* Use, whenever it is possible, areas under stairs and windows, alcoves, and recesses in attics and basements. By converting these areas into functional storage spaces, other parts of the house can be freed to be used as living spaces.

In determining the *amount of storage space* that is needed, allow for future growth and needs. Children will develop new interests as they grow older and will require more space for storing clothing, tools and materials for hobbies, sporting equipment, and other newly acquired possessions. Space should also be provided in newly built houses for growing collections of equipment and tools for house, lawn, and garden maintenance.

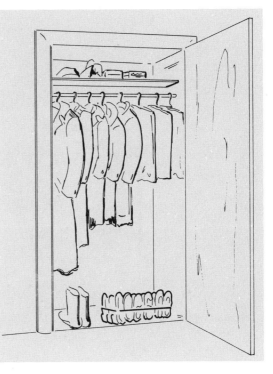

Fig. 16–5 Ordinary coat closet

TYPES OF STORAGE

The following descriptions are intended to suggest general types of storage that the remodeler can use, rather than to serve as an inclusive list of storage devices. Typical storage units are illustrated as examples of each major type of storage.

CLOSETS

The amount of closet space in a house tends to vary with the age of the house. Older houses are likely to have only a few shallow closets while newer houses often have large walk-in closets in the bedrooms but little closet space elsewhere. When a house is being remodeled, closets should be added or expanded wherever they were previously insufficient.

Fig. 16–6 Coat hooks mounted on a wooden strip

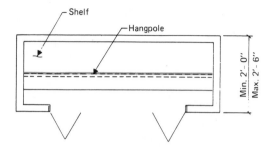

Fig. 16–7 Layout of typical bedroom closet

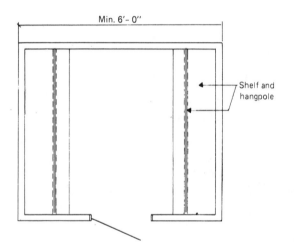

Fig. 16–8 Layout of typical walk-in closet

Both the front and back doors should have closets nearby for coats, hats, and footwear (Fig. 16–5). The back closet should be specially designed to hold work and play clothes, boots, and similar apparel. Coat hooks or pegs made from dowels will be particularly useful here (Fig. 16–6).

Bedroom closets differ somewhat from coat closets since they must be built to hold a different selection of clothing and accessories. They are likely to be larger. Also, ceiling-high doors are often used in order to make high shelves accessible.

Walk-in closets must be large enough for a central passageway and rows of clothing on either side.

There are certain minimal dimensions that should be observed in building closets. The standard minimal depth is 24 in., but depths up to 30 in. may be used, especially if coat hooks are mounted at the back of the closet (Fig. 16–7).

Closets deeper than 30 in. waste space since the area in the back is too deep to reach for ordinary storage. Closets should be at least 3 ft. wide. Narrower closets will hold a few things but they are inefficient for the space that they use. A coat closet (27 to 30 in. deep) should be large enough to hold two or three coats for each member of the family.

Bedroom closets are usually larger than coat closets since they must hold entire collections of clothing, shoes, hats, and accessories. Typical bedroom closets range from 4 to 8 ft in width. Wooden or adjustable metal clothes rods should be fastened at least 2 in. below the lowest closet shelf. This should provide a space of at least 5 ft above the floor in which clothing can be hung. To make closet shelves fully accessible, doors should be installed that extend almost to the ceiling. If this is impossible, use half-shelves rather than full shelves above the clothes rod. If more than one shelf is used, the shelves should be at least 8 in. apart. Wider spacing will make it easier to reach in between the higher shelves. Walk-in closets (Fig. 16–8), of course, are much larger than standard bedroom closets. Typical widths range from 6 to 8 ft. Depths depend on the amount of storage desired and the space available.

Closet doors may be selected from several different types. Hinged, bi-fold, and folding doors are usually the most practical. *Hinged doors* can be used for closets that have doorways 30 to 36 in. wide where there is room for the door to swing back against the wall. The inside of the door can be used for accessories such as shoe racks or full-length mirrors. *Bi-fold* doors (Fig. 16–9) consist of hinged panels that ride on an overhead track and fold back against themselves on one or both sides of the doorway. Several panels can be hinged together for unusually wide closets. *Folding doors* (Fig. 16–10) are made up of narrow vertical sections that also fold up on themselves and hang from a track at the top of the doorway. Since they are available in almost any useful width, they can be used for closets that are too wide for either hinged or bi-fold doors. Sliding and pivot doors are also used occasionally. Sliding doors, however, have the disadvantage of blocking half of the closet entrance, unless they have been built to slide into the wall. Pivot doors are installed so that they rotate, allowing the back of the door to be used for shallow storage racks.

Closets that are damp or poorly lit by outside light can be improved by installing an incandescent light bulb. A 75- or 100-watt bulb will light the closet and, in a few hours a day, dry out the air sufficiently to prevent mildew from growing. Where the air is excessively damp, a wall or ceiling ventilating unit can be installed. Louvered doors will also help to decrease the dampness by increasing the circulation of air. Closets that are next to outside walls or immediately under a roof should be insulated. Variations in temperature can be reduced by installing batt or blanket-type fiberglass insulation between the walls and over the closet ceiling.

Fig. 16–9 Louvered bi-fold doors

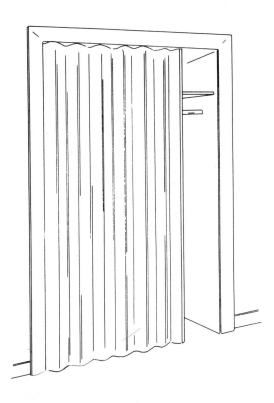

Fig. 16–10 Folding doors

Fig. 16–11 Floor-to-ceiling linen closet

Fig. 16–12 Utility closet

Linen Closets

Locate linen closets (Fig. 16–11) in areas that are too dry for mildew to grow. For maximum use of the space, build the shelves so that they extend from the floor to the ceiling. This will require an equally high door. The shelves should be shallow, no more than 12 to 14 in. deep, so that all of the linens are accessible.

Cedar Closets

Cedar closets, which protect woolens against moths, must be built tightly. Tongue-and-groove cedar boards are used either to line an existing wall or to cover a framework of studs. The floor, ceiling, and the inside of the door should also be covered with cedar boards to ensure the effectiveness of the closet. Use weatherstripping to seal any cracks between the door and the frame. In damp areas, such as basements, build the closet on sleepers a few inches off the basement floor. Air that circulates under the closet will help keep the floor dry.

Utility Closets

Utility closets (Fig. 16–12) may be built with shallow or deep shelves depending on how they are to be used. Shallow closets (12-in. deep) are more practical for storing things such as cleaning supplies. Adjustable shelves should be installed in the upper section of such a closet, while the lower area should be left empty for storing brooms, mops, and vacuum cleaners. Large objects such as folding chairs, card tables, and equipment for games will require deeper closets.

SHELVES

Shelves are one of the most basic types of storage structures. They may be combined with other types of storage or used independently. Cabinets, for example, often combine shelves and drawers in one unit. Shelves that are built to be used independently can be fastened to a wall, hung from the ceiling, or built as freestanding units.

Wall-hung shelves (Fig. 16–13) are probably the simplest shelves to erect because of the hardware that is available. A supporting structure of brackets and vertical standards (Fig. 16–14) can be easily attached to a wall. The cheapest supports are made of metal and are available in several finishes. More expensive shelving systems can be purchased in attractive hardwood finishes. In a basement or attic, where the appearance is less important, L-shaped brackets can be screwed into the studs to support shelves.

Freestanding shelves require some type of vertical support between the shelves. One of the simplest types of support is a *block* of some sort (Fig. 16–15). Cinder blocks, bricks, plastic blocks, or blocks made of any other kind of sturdy material will do. The height of the shelving is limited, however, because the shelves become unstable as they become higher. *Wooden sides* probably make the best supports. Actually, particle board, or any other rigid wood substitute, can be used. The shelves can be permanently fastened to the sides with nails or screws or by cutting dados or mounting wooden cleats (Fig. 16–16 (a) and (b)). Adjustable shelves can be mounted on any of several types of metal clips, brackets, pegs, or on ordinary wooden dowels (Fig. 16–17 (a), (b), (c), and (d)). Other types of materials are also used as supports. Heavy *steel standards* and shelves are made for basement-type storage (Fig. 16–18). Finished *metal rods* and *shelves* are also available to use in living areas (Fig. 16–19). Even *plastic pipe* can be used with cross-sectional supports to make an attractive shelf framework.

Built-in shelves, unlike wall-hung shelves, are generally designed to look like an integral part of a wall (Fig. 16–20). They may be recessed into a wall or built out into the living area. Often, they are built to extend from the ceiling to just above the base cabinets. Shelves in more formal built-ins are likely to be permanently installed with dado joints.

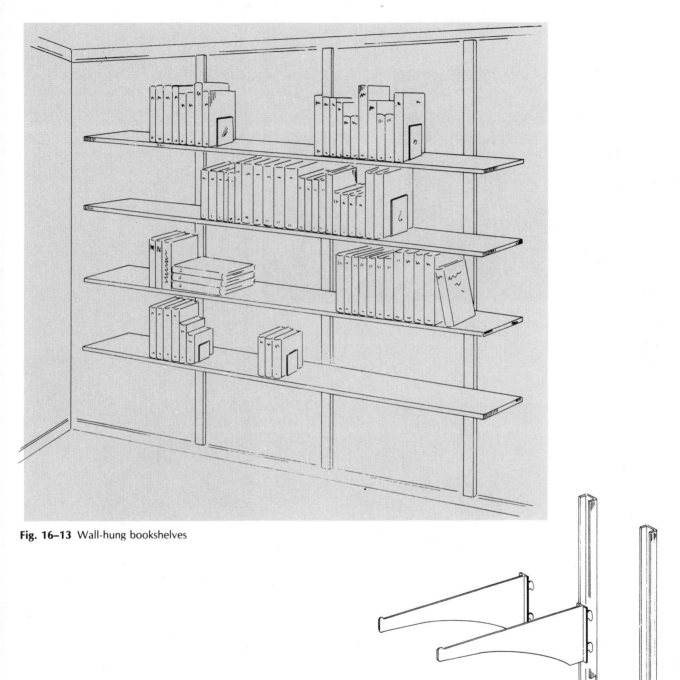

Fig. 16–13 Wall-hung bookshelves

Fig. 16–14 Brackets and standards

Fig. 16–15 Shelves supported by cinder blocks

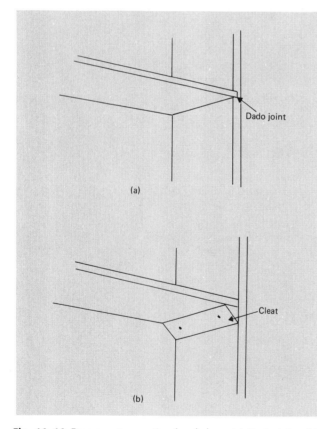

Fig. 16–16 Permanent mounting for shelves. (a) Dado joint, (b) Wooden cleat

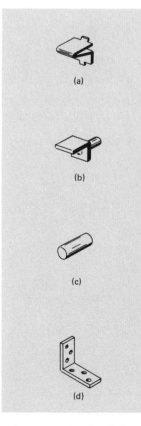

Fig. 16–17 Adjustable mountings for shelves. (a) Metal clip, (b) Peg, (c) Wooden dowel, (d) L-bracket.

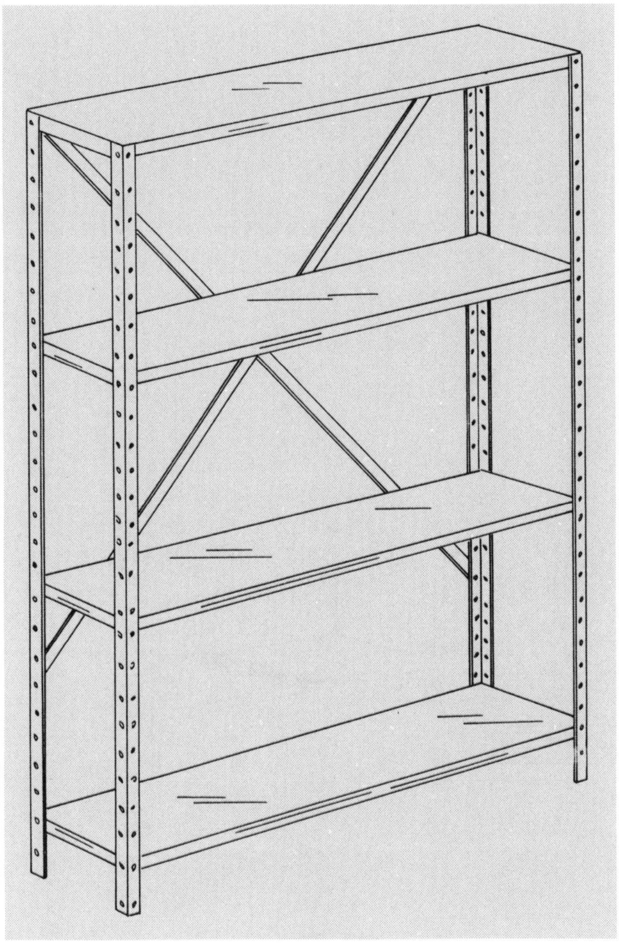

Fig. 16–18 Heavy steel shelving

Fig. 16–19 Decorative metal shelving

Fig. 16–20 Built-in shelving

Cabinet shelves can be fastened in many of the same ways as freestanding or built-in shelves (nails, screws, cleats, dados, clips, brackets, and pegs). Multiple shelves in kitchen cabinets and in utility closets should be mounted on adjustable supports so that they can be varied in height. Single shelves in smaller cabinets, such as stereo enclosures, can be permanently fastened in place, if desired, since they are less likely to be moved. To be useful, cabinet shelves must not be too deep. Shelves that are deeper than 12 to 16 in. are awkward to use, since articles toward the rear are difficult to reach.

There are also many types of special-purpose shelves. *Magazine racks* are specially built at an angle to hold and display magazines. *Pop-up* or *lift-up* shelves and *sliding shelves* are useful for equipment that is to be stored in cabinets and for retractable working surfaces.

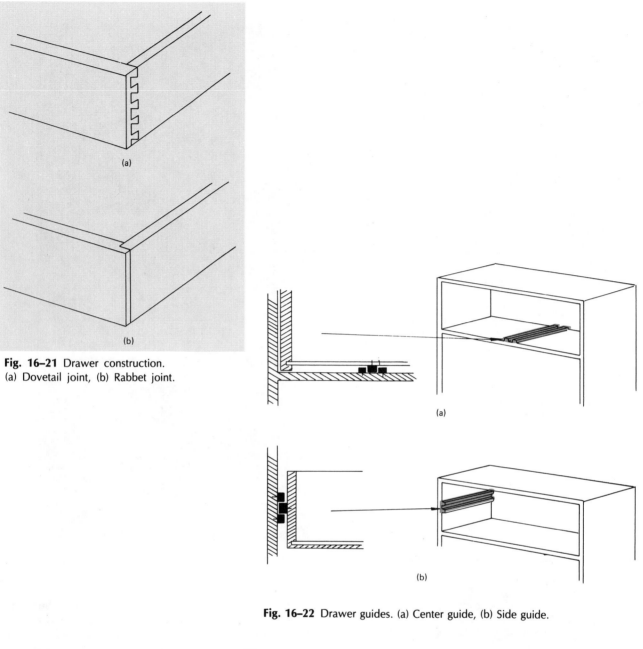

Fig. 16–21 Drawer construction.
(a) Dovetail joint, (b) Rabbet joint.

(a)

(b)

Fig. 16–22 Drawer guides. (a) Center guide, (b) Side guide.

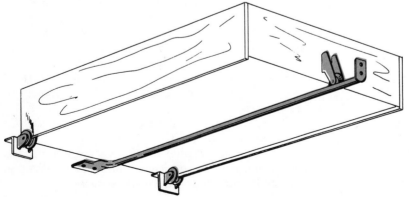

Fig. 16–23 Roller and track system

Fig. 16–24 Section-type storage wall

DRAWERS

Since drawers are somewhat difficult to build, most home-owners will prefer to buy finished chests or cabinets. Stacks of drawers can also be purchased in open frames to be used as built-ins or for finishing as freestanding units. Before buying drawers in any form, look to see how they are constructed. Dovetail or rabbet joints (Fig. 16–21, (a) and (b)) are used to fasten the front to the sides on the best-made drawers. There should also be some type of center or side guide on which the drawer can ride as it is opened and closed (Fig. 16–22, (a) and (b)). Either runners and grooves or more elaborate rollers and tracks can be used (Fig. 16–23). Large, wide drawers should have a center guide, as well as a stop to prevent them from pulling completely out of the frame.

Drawers are also available in materials other than wood. Steel drawers are frequently used for storing file folders and tools. Molded plastic, tray-type drawers are made to fit into specially designed, tubular frameworks. Drawers of corrugated cardboard are available for light-weight storage in modular units.

CABINETS

Cabinets can be used either as built-ins or as freestanding units, wherever closed storage is needed. Large built-in cabinets are particularly useful in attics and basements for dead storage. Smaller cabinets can be built or purchased for special uses such as storing china ware or installing stereo equipment. The use of cabinets for kitchen and bathroom storage has been described at length in the chapters on remodeling kitchens and baths.

STORAGE WALLS

Storage walls usually consist of a combination of shelves, drawers, and cabinets. They may be built-in or made up of sectional units that are fastened together. Drawers of various sizes can be combined with vertical compartments and half-shelves to hold everything from clothing to decorative knickknacks (Fig. 16–24). Adjustable shelves are often used to vary the sizes of the compartments as needs change.

Like built-in shelves, storage walls may be built so that they become an integral part of a wall. Room-length storage walls will generally provide all of the storage space required in a family room or bedroom.

OTHER TYPES OF STORAGE

Hooks and hangers are among the handiest types of storage devices. Either clothes hooks or pegs made from dowels can be used to hang clothing and hats. Hangers of different kinds can be attached to walls or to pegboard to hold a diversity of things such as utensils, shelves, tools, clothing, and plants. *Bins* and *boxes* serve primarily to hold unorganized collections of small items. A series of medium-sized boxes can be used in children's rooms to store toys, art supplies, and miscellaneous playthings. Childrens' toys can also be stored in large drawers built on rollers to slide under beds. Some beds designed for children already have such built-in drawers at floor level. Built-in bins, such as tip-out bins, are useful for storing bulk ingredients in kitchen cabinets. *Storage chests,* such as cedar chests, are convenient for storing things that are used seasonally or infrequently. In a bedroom, a chest might be used to store blankets, linens, pillows, or clothing. In a children's room, it might be used to hold toys that have been picked up from the floor.

17 Special Remodeling Problems: Apartments, Subdivision Houses, and Old Houses

Standard remodeling methods are not always applicable. Tenants in apartments are usually restricted in the types of change that they can make. In order to remodel, they often have to devise temporary improvements that can be removed later. Owners of houses in subdivisions have different kinds of problems. They are likely to give a high priority to making their houses distinctive and to creating some measure of privacy. Houses that are noted for their historical architectural style or for their valuable structural details are generally renovated in such a way as to preserve these features. At the same time, these houses must also be made livable and comfortable for their occupants according to modern standards. Other older houses, though lacking in historical or architectural significance, offer generous amounts of space and sound construction at bargain prices. To make them livable, these houses usually require extensive renovations. The following sections offer suggestions for handling many of these special remodeling problems.

APARTMENTS

The alternatives in apartment remodeling depend primarily on who is remodeling and why. Tenants are often severely limited in the changes that they can make. Structural changes are almost always prohibited. In some cases, even the color of the paint cannot be changed. Tenants in this situation must usually resort to using materials that are removable.

Landlords are concerned with costs as well as with attracting tenants. They generally prefer low-maintenance materials and modern interiors. Old-fashioned, ornate moldings and fixtures are likely to be torn out and replaced with mass-produced modern equivalents.

Occupants who own their own apartments or condominiums are relatively free to remodel in any way they like. They may be limited to some extent by the proximity of other apartments or by restrictive clauses in condominium ownership.

In spite of these various limitations, there are still many ways in which apartments can be attractively remodeled, as described in the following sections. Readers who plan to do the work themselves should refer to earlier chapters for practical details on how to perform these alterations. Many of the ideas in the chapters on remodeling kitchens and bathrooms are applicable to apartments as well as to houses.

TREATMENTS FOR WALLS AND CEILINGS

Walls, because of their size, play a major role in remodeling and decorating. They can be painted in light hues to visually enlarge rooms. Texture and colored patterns can be added by covering walls with wallpaper or other wallcoverings. *Paneling* and *vinyl-coated wallcoverings* are favorite types of low-maintenance materials. Prefinished plywood and hardboard paneling are available in many colors, textures, and wood finishes, to harmonize with different interior styles. The appeal of paneling lies in its ease of installation and upkeep as well as in its appearance. Paneling can be fastened directly to walls that are in good condition by using either adhesive or nails. Furring is necessary for uneven or damaged walls. Vinyl-coated, fabric-backed wall-coverings are easy to maintain because they withstand moisture and most stains. Additionally, vinyl colors are very stable and do not fade in sunlight.

Where wall coverings cannot be altered, *paint* and various kinds of *hangings* can be combined to improve the appearance of a room. If painting is permitted, striking effects can be achieved by painting one or more of the walls with different colors. Paint can also be used to create special effects, such as the visual lowering of a ceiling by painting it darker than the walls. Large mirrors or mirror tiles can be placed where they will add depth to a room or cover sections of objectionable walls. Shelves can also be used to hide walls. Where shelves cannot be fastened to walls, they can be installed with floor-to-ceiling tension rods. Freestanding bookcases and storage walls can also be used to hide walls in the same way. Large wall areas can be covered with decorative rugs, oversize draperies, or wall screens. Anything that can be hung from the walls or ceiling or that can be placed freestanding against a wall will serve the same purpose.

In refinishing ceilings, tiles are easier to use than most other materials. *Ceiling tiles* are available in various shapes, sizes, and finishes. Interlocking tiles with tongue-and-groove edges are available in several sizes (12 × 12 in., 12 × 24 in. and 24 × 24 in.). This type of tile can be either cemented or stapled to the ceiling or to furring strips. Tiles for suspended ceilings are made in several sizes, also. Rectangular 24 × 48 in. tiles and square 24 × 24 in. tiles are used in most installations. Tile surfaces may be vinyl coated, textured, embossed, perforated, or smooth. Where noise is a problem, acoustical tiles should be used. They are available in the same sizes and shapes as other tiles.

Suspended ceilings because of their grid framework, have special advantages. In addition to standard ceiling tiles, radiant-heat panels or recessed light fixtures can also be installed in the grids. Using electric energy, one or two radiant-heat panels will provide enough heat for a moderate-sized room. Another advantage of suspended ceilings is that fiberglass insulation can be installed above the framework to reduce noise transmission from the rooms above, as well as to lower the heat loss.

COVERING FLOORS

If floors are in poor condition, the simplest solution is to cover them. *Vinyl* and *vinyl-asbestos flooring* is widely used for kitchen and bathroom floors because it requires little maintenance and is long wearing. In tile form, vinyl-asbestos flooring can be installed without professional assistance. Wooden floors in poor condition can be covered with thin (5/16-in.) *strips or blocks of wood* to recreate a finished, hardwood surface. *Carpeting,* whether wall-to-wall, loose-laid, or tile, can be used to cover almost any floor. Loose-laid carpeting and carpet tiles are designed so that they can be installed without professional help. Other flooring coverings can be used, of course, but vinyl, vinyl asbestos, thin wooden strips and blocks, and carpeting are particularly popular for apartment remodeling.

RENEWING CABINET AND DOOR SURFACES

Where occupants are allowed to replace kitchen and bathroom cabinets, the information in the chapters on remodeling kitchens and bathrooms will apply. However, if worn cabinets must stay where they are, there are several ways to improve their appearance. Stained wooden cabinets that have not already been sealed can often be cleaned and restained; and painted cabinets can be sanded and repainted. Metal cabinets, cabinets covered with plastic laminate, and wooden cabinets that cannot be stained or painted can be made to look like new by covering them with strippable, *vinyl-coated papers*. These papers are available in various colors and patterns as well as in wood grains. Since they are strippable, they can be removed from most surfaces when the occupants move out.

USING DIVIDERS

Many kinds of dividers can be used to divide rooms into more functional spaces. *Screens* can be used to separate dining areas from living rooms or kitchens. *Waist-or head-high storage cabinets* can be constructed to hold materials such as glassware and linens, as well as to separate activity areas. *Bookcases* can be used in a similar manner for decorative and functional separation.

Dividers can either be freestanding or they can be anchored to supports, such as tension poles, walls, or ceilings. Hinged screens and cabinets will stand on their own.

Divider panels and screens are usually made from materials such as hardboard, Plexiglas, and decorative fabrics. Specially cut decorative *hardboard panels* are available with pregrooved moldings. Thin (⅛- or ¼-in.) panels of opaque or translucent *Plexiglas* in various finishes and colors can be used to add texture and color. *Louvered panels* are useful to create an open feeling and allow air to circulate through the dividers or screens.

ADDING STORAGE SPACE

Where there is sufficient floor space and occupants are allowed to make structural changes, closets can be expanded or added and storage cabinets can be fastened to the walls. Suggestions for this type of storage are contained in the chapter on storage. However, many apartment dwellers will have to be satisfied with temporary storage devices. Where they can be fastened to the walls, stock cabinets and shelving can be used. Wall-hung shelving systems and storage walls are available with enclosed cabinets, drawers, shelves, cubicles, and other storage features for almost every room. Bedroom storage walls, for example, have closet spaces for hanging clothes, drawers, and compartments for shoes and other accessories.

Where units cannot be fastened to walls or ceilings, freestanding units and tension devices can be used. Storage walls are also made in freestanding forms and can be used as decorative walls as well as for storage. Tension rods may be used either horizontally or vertically to support shelves, clothing, or other storage units. Horizontal rods can be installed in alcoves to serve as clothes rods. Vertical rods will support elaborate storage systems almost as well as permanent supports.

Many of the minor storage devices described in the chapters on remodeling kitchens and bathrooms will be as useful in apartments as anywhere else. Pegboard-mounted hangers can be used to hold everything from kitchen utensils to shelves and radios. Shelf units designed for mounting over toilets or in corners will provide additional storage for towels, washcloths, and other supplies in bathrooms.

REDUCING OUTSIDE NOISE

Few apartment occupants will be able to (or want to) make the structural changes necessary to virtually eliminate outside noise. Interior walls would have to be rebuilt or new walls erected with staggered studs separated by insulation. Fortunately, there are a number of less-complicated methods to minimize both outside and inside noise.

Windows are prime sources of noise from the outside. If they can be kept closed, they can be sealed or covered in a number of ways. A second layer of glass installed a few inches from the original glass will have an insulating effect. An ordinary *outside storm window* will do the job, but the thicker the glass the better. Where an outside window cannot be installed, an *aluminum-framed auxiliary window* can be mounted inside the original window. Windows should also be *weather-stripped* to seal cracks.

Heavy draperies will further reduce noise entering through windows. Porous fabrics and tightly woven fiberglass materials are the most effective. Use enough material so that the draperies can be fully gathered and lined. Draperies are most effective in reducing noise when they are mounted several inches out from the wall.

Noise that enters through large wall areas can be reduced by covering the walls with sound-absorbing materials. (The most effective treatment, however, is a layer of insulation *within* the wall.) Window draperies can be extended to cover the full length of a wall. Draperies may also be used on other walls as well. Walls can also be covered with carpeting, acoustical tiles, cork tiles or sheets, hanging rugs, or any other sound-absorbent material.

Wall-to-wall carpeting is the one of the best materials for absorbing noise that travels through the floor. Carpeting is most effective when used with a *foam pad* beneath.

Ceilings lend themselves to using *acoustical tiles* to reduce noise. *Suspended ceilings* can be further insulated by installing fiberglass above the tiles. Tiles that are cemented or stapled should be attached to furring strips instead of directly to the ceiling. This will create a sound-absorbing, dead-air space above the layer of tiles to reduce noise even further.

Noise also enters through and around exterior doors. Thick, *solid-core doors* will transmit less sound than those with hollow cores. Exterior doors can also be weatherstripped and the inside surface covered with carpeting or other absorbent materials to reduce outside noise.

SUBDIVISION HOUSES

Remodeling a subdivision house provides an opportunity to add a touch of individuality that reflects the owner's tastes. Alterations should be planned in such a way that they create greater privacy and improve the resale value, as well as making the house more distinctive. The following sections describe a number of approaches that can be taken.

MAKING A HOUSE MORE DISTINCTIVE

Individuality does not mean that a house should stick out from its neighbors like a sore thumb. Houses should fit in with their environment in terms of architectural style, materials, and proportions. Their individuality can be reflected in structural variations and details, color, and textures. Since most subdivision houses are already similar in architectural style, these variations are usually made in windows, doors, trim, and landscaping—in addition to using different colors and textures. Additions, in particular, should fit in with the lines and proportions of the house. The roof lines should be unified and similar materials used for the siding.

Additions

The general appearance of a house may be significantly altered by building an addition. Additions may range from simple open decks to two-story wings. Decks are relatively straightforward to build and are within the capacity of many homeowners to construct themselves. Additions, such as enclosed porches, are more complicated to build and will probably require the services of carpenters. Even small additions (like entryways) will set a house apart from its neighbors. The course or construction of a sidewalk from the street to a front entry can also be modified. Introduce a curved, brick sidewalk, for example, to replace a straight, concrete walk. Where there is access from indoor living areas to the outside, an enclosed patio will add to the owner's enjoyment as well as make the house slightly different. Larger additions, such as one- or two-story wings may be used to change the shape of a house. A long, rectangular house, for example, can be changed into an L-shaped house by adding a perpendicular wing. As described in the following section, a house of this shape will have a sizable private area.

Dormers

The addition of front dormers will also set apart similarly constructed houses. Dormers are frequently used to increase the usable floor space in converted attics. The remodeling plans should be carefully drawn to ensure that the dormers fit in with the size and proportions of the house.

Windows and Doors

When windows or doors are changed in any way, it is important to maintain a consistent width-to-height relationship. Otherwise, they will look completely unrelated. Larger windows can be substituted for smaller windows and vice versa, as long as the proportions are consistent. Except in unusual circumstances, all of the windows should be of the same style. Double-hung windows should not be mixed with casement windows. Different types of windows and doors, such as picture windows or sliding glass doors, can be installed without disrupting the overall design of a house if these principles are adhered to.

Siding

Wooden siding can be covered with materials such as wooden shingles, asbestos shingles, and vinyl and aluminum siding without the original clapboards being removed. In changing the type of siding, homeowners should be selective in choosing new materials. Asbestos shingles are seldom as attractive as well-kept wooden or masonry siding. Vinyl and aluminum siding tends to change the lines and proportions of the exterior surfaces because of the different spacing of their clapboards. Vertical corner boards made of vinyl or aluminum also lack the width and visual strength of wooden corner boards. However, vinyl and aluminum siding are relatively maintenance free and, if properly applied, can provide an additional layer of insulation. Brick and stone siding are too valuable to cover with inferior materials. Old masonry should be cleaned with chemicals and repointed if necessary. Although brick siding *can* be painted, it must be repainted every few years after the first coat has been applied.

Interior Remodeling

Almost any interior structural change will make a subdivision house more individual. Expanding or adding closets, building additional baths, altering kitchen layouts, converting attics or basements, building dividers, and making other similar structural and nonstructural changes will usually make a house more convenient to live in and increase its market value if the improvements are well designed.

CREATING MORE PRIVACY

Subdivision houses have as much potential for privacy as other houses. Even where houses are built wall-to-wall, as in Europe, they are able to achieve a high degree of privacy by the use of walls, gardens, and courts. In this country, landscape planting, fences and screens, and structural modifications, such as additions, are more commonly used. There is considerable variation in different sections of the country. Methods that are popular in some areas are looked on as unfriendly in others. Screens and solid fences that are found throughout communities on the West Coast, for example, are regarded as unusual in the southeastern section of the country. Most homeowners will have little trouble in selecting types of fencing, screening, and plantings that are appropriate for their localities. Local ordinances frequently provide specifications for the height and setback of most structures.

Fences and short lengths of screening should be strategically placed to provide privacy for windows and outside activity areas. Solid fencing can be used in critical areas and open fencing or plantings elsewhere. This variation will help avoid a penned-in feeling. A large variety of materials are available for screens and fences. Wooden boards, slats, and pickets, opaque or translucent plastic panels, canvas, bamboo, and wire are probably the most frequently used. Homeowners also have a wide choice among the types of construction that can be used. Wooden barriers include such attractively designed structures as basket-weave, picket, slat, board-on-board, bamboo, stockade, louver, and solid board fences and screens. Each of these can be designed in several different ways to harmonize with its surroundings. They can be built to emphasize either the horizontal or vertical lines of a house. Long horizontal stretches of fencing are often used to unify landscaping around a house. To soften the lines of the boards, consider placing trees, bushes, and smaller plants along sections of fence to visually tie the barrier to the lawn or garden areas.

Additions should be oriented to provide their own privacy. A wing attached to a house at right angles will provide a sheltered area for windows and doors. Carports, garages, decks, and other lesser additions can sometimes be positioned to create private areas in a similar manner.

Major remodeling offers an opportunity to create greater privacy in a different way by altering and rearranging windows. In some instances, skylights can be installed to bathe rooms in daylight with complete privacy. A row of awning-type windows placed high along a wall will also let in light without exposing the interior of a house to outside view. Other types of windows and sliding glass doors can be built wherever they are protected. Walls toward a street may be built with no windows at all, if desired. Existing windows can, of course, be treated in various ways to shield the inside of a house. Besides the conventional use of inside shutters, curtains, and translucent glass or plastic, windows can be treated with sunscreening to produce a mirror-like appearance from the outside. The light that passes through the window is slightly diminished, but the occupant's view is unaffected.

RESALE VALUE

Resale values of subdivision houses are more limited by the nature of their neighborhoods than those of most houses because of the similarity of style and construction. However, within the range of market values in the area, homeowners can take definite steps to increase the resale values of their homes. In addition to alterations that set them apart from other houses, subdivision houses will also benefit from the standard types of remodeling.

A good coat of paint or stain is one of the least expensive ways of improving the appearance of a house with wooden siding. The new finish will not only make a house look better but it will also create the impression that the house is well cared for. In the same way, houses with masonry siding can be cleaned to renew the original surfaces.

Tasteful exterior landscaping will also give a subdivision house greater appeal. Properly placed plantings and fences will set a house apart and increase privacy, as described in the previous section.

Interior remodeling will have a great influence on the value of a house. A third or fourth bedroom added to a small house will increase its living capacity and also its resale value. An investment in a second bath for a house with several bedrooms will also be likely to bring a good return. Where kitchens are small or poorly laid out, it will be worthwhile to expand and modernize them. Contemporary, low-maintenance materials and new appliances should be used for the owner's present enjoyment and future investment. Small additions, such as decks and porches, may contribute to the resale value beyond the amount invested in them, simply by making a house more distinctive and improving its design.

OLD HOUSES

Special problems arise in restoring houses of historic value and also in renovating older homes that have been neglected. Both types of houses may be well constructed, spacious, and offer good investments, but they should be selected with care if they are to be renovated. This section briefly points out where standard remodeling techniques can be used and where other techniques are necessary.

RENOVATING TO PRESERVE HISTORICAL FEATURES

Old houses with valuable features, such as a fine architectural style or handcrafted interior woodwork, are often partially restored to their original condition and partially renovated. Windows, doors, chimneys, and other exterior features that are representative of the architectural period are usually restored or duplicated. Interior features, such as old fireplaces and mantels, wide pine or attractive hardwood floors, and hand-carved balustrades are also worth restoring.

In many cases, it is necessary to tear out walls and other structures built during later periods in order to expose the original features of a house. Before starting to restore or renovate such a house, buyers should consult old records—often available at local historical societies—and publications on preserving antique houses, to determine what structural details are representative of the period.

Interior living spaces that are designed in a more modern vein should be carefully integrated with the original features to avoid a discordant contrast. Conventional methods can be followed in remodeling kitchens and baths and in installing modern plumbing, lighting, and central heating. New materials should be selected that harmonize with the style, texture, and colors of the restored features.

REMODELING NEGLECTED BUT SOUND HOUSES

Neglected old houses that are available cheaply can be excellent investments for knowledgeable buyers. Such houses are often soundly built and well located. Because of the architectural styles at the time they were built, they generally have spacious rooms, large windows, woodwork of oak or other fine hardwoods, and similar luxurious features more common in earlier times.

Although conventional remodeling techniques can be used in most of these houses, evaluating the scope, costs, and time that are required for renovation is more complicated than in ordinary situations. The most reliable approach is to hire an architect, building contractor, or building inspection service to evaluate the condition of a house and to make recommendations for repairs and renovations. An expert will quickly discover the positive features of an old house, as well as its shortcomings.

WHAT TO LOOK FOR

Buyers with previous experience in renovating old houses will frequently be able to judge conditions for themselves. The following conditions should be checked in a preliminary inspection.

From the outside, consider the general appearance of the structure. Crooked or leaning walls, as well as windows and doors that are out of plumb, indicate uneven settling of the foundation. Large cracks in foundation walls or in masonry walls are further evidence of uneven settling. Loose chimney bricks and worn or loose shingles on sloping roofs can be seen at a distance with the help of field glasses. The condition of the siding, gutters, and downspouts will also be apparent from the outside. Chimneys, roofs, and drainage systems can be repaired at a reasonable cost, but faulty foundations or uneven settling are very expensive to correct.

In the *basement,* check for dampness, signs of past flooding, termites, and dry rot. Evidence of leaks, rot, and dampness will usually be found in the sill that separates the outside walls from the foundation, in columns and beams, and in floor joists. Also inspect the furnace, heating ducts or pipes, water pipes, drains, and soil pipes, and the electrical service entrance and wiring. The utilities in houses such as these are usually out of date and have to be replaced. If sills, beams, or joists have been damaged, however, the cost of repairing or replacing them (unlike replacing utilities) will usually be prohibitive.

Dampness is also the first problem to look for in *attics.* Look for signs of leaks and dry rot in the rafters and sheathing and around chimneys and vents where flashing may have failed. A new roof can always be put on but replacing both the rafters and the roof is very expensive.

Cracks in walls and ceilings in *interior rooms* and warped window and door frames are also an indication of uneven settling. Walls, ceilings, and floors that are in poor condition can be repaired or replaced without excessive costs, especially if the owner does some of the work.

A PLAN FOR REMODELING

If a house is in good enough condition to be renovated, plans should be prepared for the project. Owners who plan to do some of the work themselves should selectively assign major jobs to professionals and retain jobs that call for less skill. Homeowners with previous experience in renovating may be able to perform many of the following tasks by themselves: tear out walls and ceilings, install gypsum board and paneling, refinish floors, install electrical boxes and fixtures, hang doors and build simple cabinets, and paint and refinish interiors.

Estimating costs is difficult at this stage, but some form of rough costs is necessary to determine whether the house is a good investment. A potential buyer can use the same methods for gathering expert advice and cost information as are used in standard remodeling projects.

Index

Note: Page numbers in italics indicate illustrations.